LOVE AND INTIMATE RELATIONSHIPS

LOVE AND INTIMATE RELATIONSHIPS
Journeys of the Heart

Norman M. Brown
Ellen S. Amatea

BRUNNER/MAZEL
Taylor & Francis Group

USA	Publishing Office:	BRUNNER/MAZEL
		A member of the Taylor & Francis Group
		325 Chestnut Street
		Philadelphia, PA 19106
		Tel: (215) 625-8900
		Fax: (215) 625-2940
	Distribution Center:	BRUNNER/MAZEL
		A member of the Taylor & Francis Group
		47 Runway Road, Suite G
		Levittown, PA 19057-4700
		Tel: (215) 269-0400
		Fax: (215) 269-0363
UK		BRUNNER/MAZEL
		A member of the Taylor & Francis Group
		27 Church Road
		Hove
		E. Sussex, BN3 2FA
		Tel: +44 (0) 1273 207411
		Fax: +44 (0) 1273 205612

LOVE AND INTIMATE RELATIONSHIPS: Journeys of the Heart

1 2 3 4 5 6 7 8 9 0

Printed by Edwards Brothers, Lillington, NC, 2000.
Cover design by Tina Serenshock.

A CIP catalog record for this book is available from the British Library.
∞ The paper in this publication meets the requirements of the ANSI Standard Z39.48-1984 (Permanence of Paper).

Library of Congress Cataloging-in-Publication Data
Brown, Norman M., 1942–
    Love and intimate relationships : journeys of the heart / by Norman M. Brown, Ellen S. Amatea.
      p. cm.
    Include bibliographical references and index.
    ISBN 0-87630-979-1 (alk. paper)
    1. Love. 2. Intimacy (Psychology) I. Amatea, Ellen S., 1944– II. Title.

BF575.L8 B75 2000
306.7—dc21

                                                   99-053202

ISBN 0-87630-979-1 (paper)

Norman Brown: *To my wife, Pamela, and my daughter, Hannah. To the hundreds of relationship class students over 10 years who have lent their stories, their curiosity, and their hopes to the creation of this text.*

Ellen Amatea: *To my husband, Frank, my sons, Christian and John, and my mother and father, Vivian and John Sherlock.*

Contents

Contributors

Dana DeHart, Ph.D., College of Social Work, University of South Carolina, Columbia, South Carolina

Paul Edson, Ph.D., Department of Humanities and Social Sciences, Embry-Riddle Aeronautical University, Daytona Beach, Florida

Diana Estrada, Ph.D., (collaborator on Chapter 12), Department of Counselor Education, University of Colorado at Denver, Denver, Colorado

Nina Silver, Ph.D., private practice, Worthington, Massachusetts

Acknowledgments

We could not write a book of this magnitude without many contributions and kindnesses from people in both of our universities and around the country. We have been blessed with many friends, colleagues, students, and family members who helped us, either by inspiring and discussing ideas, critiquing early drafts, or assisting in research and development of the manuscript.

Paul Edson, Ph.D., contributed writing and ideas to both the content and the structure of the book. Dana DeHart, Ph.D., and Nina Silver, Ph.D., contributed both content and numerous first-person interviews. Diane Estrada, Ph.D., collaborated on the communication chapter. Donald Nathanson, M.D., mentored the sophisticated affect theory that runs through the entire chapter on emotions. Critical reading, inspiration, and support have been offered by Patricia Hurff, Ph.D., Larry Kurdek, Ph.D., Nancy Parker, Ed.D., Janice Presser, Ph.D., Peter A. D. Sherrard, Ed.D., Lori Secouler, Ph. D., and Paul Yelsma, Ph.D.

Student assistance has been essential to our scholarship and the production of manuscripts. The most notable helpers have been Christian Amatea and Laura Pelletier Amatea in Gainesville and David Conz, Heriberto Cruz, Elizabeth Kilday, Leonard Ruppert, and Nadirah Saleem in Daytona Beach. Our departments have given us great understanding and support for the seven years this book has needed to develop. The library personnel of Embry-Riddle Aeronautical University have devoted countless hours to obtaining the hundreds of research sources we have needed. We also thank Toby Wahl, Lansing Hayes, Stephanie Weidel, and the staff at Brunner-Mazel for their patience and perseverance in producing this book.

In addition to all these helping hands, many researchers from around the country have given generously of their time and expert knowledge. They include Arthur Aron, Ph.D., Thomas Insel, M.D., Victor Johnston, Ph.D., Luis Monti-Bloch, M.D., and Peter Nardi, Ph.D., to name only a few. So many researchers in the International Network on Personal Relationships and the International Society for the Study of Personal Relationships have contributed ideas and unpublished papers that the book has literally grown up in their far-flung neighborhood.

Finally, we thank our students and clients. We are grateful to them for allowing us to witness their triumphs and agonies, and for honoring us through sharing their most intimate lives. They have far more to teach about resilience and the quest for growth and goodness than could ever fit into one book. We give them special thanks for allowing us to tell some of their stories in this book.

Ellen: Without my husband's belief in equity and his earthy sense of humor, I would certainly have not had the time or interest to create and complete this book. Without his personal strength and integrity, I would never have learned about the importance of respect in and commitment to a long-term intimate relationship. My two sons, Christian and John, have taught me more about how people develop in relationships than they will ever know. My parents have done the same: their commitment to sustaining a marriage and continuing their personal development have taught me about what is essential for men and women to be happy in intimate relationships.

Norman: My wife, Pamela, is a psychotherapist and contemplative, yet she shouldered most of the domestic burden for me for all these years. She kept me close to the reality I tried to capture by asking, "How can people use this information?" To balance all my preoccupation with romantic love, my daughter, Hannah, has spent over 11 years training me to be a father.

Preface

Unlike most other academic subjects, students approach intimate relationships with varied personal experience, combined with little or no conscious or disciplined training. They bring knowledge, concerns, and sometimes passions or wounds that inspire teachers everywhere with unusual enthusiasm, compassion, and responsibility. They want to know what love and intimacy are, what the research means, and how they can apply it to their own lives. Therefore we have brought together **theory**, **research**, **experience**, and **skills** in this book. Both theories and research are drawn from a wide spectrum of disciplines. Describing the actual experience of intimacy, with mental and emotional details, connects with the readers' own experience and enables them to pinpoint where the knowledge applies to their lives. And instruction in relationship skills enables them to achieve more of what they want in this arena that is so central to our happiness and well-being.

Our approach to the experience of relationships stems from many perspectives and respects the variety of forms of contemporary partnerships rather than advocating for some presumably "right" way of making relationships work. Three decades of rapidly expanding research into love, intimacy, and family relations have brought the best scientists to the humbling realization that the possibilities of human relations are complex beyond imagining, and that scientific certainty and predictability may be ultimately impossible. But our decades of listening to relationship stories from students and counseling clients shows us that if the research results are considered as part of individual story lines, both research and personal experience are more comprehensible and more useful.

Organization of the text

Though they all make use of research, the four parts of this book approach our subject from four different perspectives: **descriptive**, **situational**, **theoretical**, and **process/skills**. Part I **describes** experiences in the life cycle of relationships; Part II explores the **situations** of people in relationships—their gender, sexual orientation, and natural (biological and evolutionary) and cultural (sociological) condition. Part III delves into **theories** of love and relationship changes from history and both individual and family psychology. Part IV explores key relating **processes** and related skills for practical relational enhancement.

In the seven years of developing this book, the challenges of diversity, multidisciplinary complexity, and comprehensibility have led to new insights into men and women, love, and relationships not present in the research of any one discipline. These new ideas, explanations, and applications are presented as an invitation to readers to join the growing scientific inquiry into intimacy. For example, Chapter 6 and the accompanying Teacher's Manual invites young adult children of divorce to test patterns and profiles from current research on themselves and to join in the search for the currently under-studied positive effects of parental divorce. Chapters 4 and 14 describe John Gottman's pioneering approaches to marital decay and conflictual communication. Chapters 9 and 13 explore developmental and affective roots of typical gender differences in conflict, and Chapters 8 and 13 cover expanded emotional explanations of homophobia and of shyness and jealousy, respectively.

Features of the text

Here are some features of this text that are either unique or significantly more extensive than in other texts:

Teaching and learning aids

- FIRST-PERSON STORIES. There are hundreds of examples from students, clients, friends, and our own relationships.
- AROUND 100 CARTOONS done especially for this text by Don Edwing, senior artist at *MAD Magazine* that aim to make the information more comprehensible and light-hearted.
- CHAPTER SUMMARIES focus readers toward central issues and help in preparing for exams.
- EXERCISES. Activities in the reading (and the Teacher's Manual) invite self-reflection, application and critique of ideas and strategies. Role-plays enable students to discover the relationship between situations and reactions and to personalize their knowledge.
- RESEARCH CHALLENGES in the Teacher's Manual invite students to consider both results and methods of research and devise their own approaches to develop the field. Critical thinking is fostered for both laypersons and future specialists.
- THE TEACHER'S MANUAL also offers teaching strategies, discussion topics, research assignments, books and movies for enhancement, and test questions.

Content features

- DIVORCE. Broad and deep examination of both research and experience of divorce, including the children of divorce and a special focus on their relationship issues.
- GENDER AND RELATING. Physiological, cognitive, and developmental aspects, gender role socialization, marriage types, and biosocial theories provide background for understanding similarities and differences.
- DEVELOPMENTAL approaches to individuals and relationship stages highlight significant processes that change over time.
- THE RELATIONSHIP LIFE CYCLES OF HOMOSEXUAL AND BISEXUAL PEOPLE are explored in stages and first-hand stories in the same way as heterosexual romances. We discuss the psychology of homophobia and the experience of people of these alternative sexual orientations in today's society.
- THE CENTRALITY OF EMOTIONS in relationships is honored by presenting a psychobiological theory of emotions and coping strategies and by applying it to relationships.
- ANGER, CONFLICT, AND SEXUAL AGGRESSION receive extensive theoretical, research, experimental, and practical coverage. This includes approaches to managing and changing anger, conflict, couple violence, and sexual aggression in college.

About the authors and our illustrator

Norman Brown: My personal history and educational background have led me to seek a holistic picture of intimacy. My young adult search for the truths of the heart took me through many humanistic and artistic disciplines and into psychoanalytic theories on the way to my first doctorate in Humanities and German. As a new professor I began exploring and sharing myself through men's growth groups and experiencing and then learning psychotherapy, which has been my second profession for 25 years. I have done empirical research into intimacy since 1989 and completed my second doctorate, in research psychology, in 1999. My most effective teachers have been the women I have loved in several long-term relationships and in my present 15-year marriage. Much of this text material has been tested on my own experiences, with individual and marital therapy clients, and with hundreds of students over the 10 years I have taught my course.

Ellen Amatea: For much of my life I have been concerned with what makes intimate relationships work and what causes them to fail. As a partner in a 30-year marriage, and as a couples counselor and a professor of counseling, I have sought new answers to the perennial questions about long-term intimacy. Because I married in an era when the old stories of how life was to be when one fell in love were changing, my husband and I found ourselves trying to find new ways to be. Rather than assume that we would marry and have children who I would care for at home while he supported us out in the work world, we wanted something different. How would we transform the old model of husband as leader and wife as emotional barometer of the home with which we had each grown up? We both expected that I would have a professional life outside the home. But we also expected that we would still have a family where both of us would have a say both in the home and outside of it. We have had much to learn in our marriage to cope with these issues. Our growth as partners has not been smooth, but we have always been convinced that our relationship is worth fighting for and that we will work things out—though the outcome may not always be perfect.

Don Edwing, MAD Magazine: What a ball I had illustrating a book about a creature whose knuckles used to drag on the ground! I think it's hilarious that this silly-looking primate has so many problems with reproduction. What was more fun than a barrel full of monkeys gets the depth treatment in this revealing and powerful study. I envy the journey you are about to take into this epic, which digs into the nitty-gritty of humankind's existence. Enjoy yourself, it's quite a ride.

Norman M. Brown, Embry-Riddle University
Ellen S. Amatea, University of Florida

Introduction

What does this book offer you?

Unlike most other academic subjects, love relationships are a vital part of your life that you start learning about long before you ever enroll in a class on the subject. However, you still may wonder why some of your relationships started and ended the ways they did, or why things happened in the relationships of people you know.

How can you learn more about love relationships? There has always been an abundance of popular magazine articles and self-help books filled with well-intentioned advice and information, such as how people can "keep love alive" or get over a break up. But these guides often present conflicting advice because they are based more on the writer's personal and professional experience than on any scientific study of love relationships (though both are valuable). The last three decades have seen an unparalleled burst of scientific research on relationships, as well as greater cross-fertilization between research and relationship counseling approaches. This book seeks to make sense of this evolving body of ideas and scientific knowledge. We will present the current theories and research on love relationships, coupled with a picture of the actual experience—the mental and emotional details—reported by a few hundred persons.

Critical thinking about relationship knowledge

This text aims at a middle ground between two kinds of texts about close relationships. One kind is designed for advanced undergraduate and graduate courses that prepare social science majors for research careers in this exciting area. These texts review current social scientific research, emphasizing scientific methodology, contrasting results and the limitations on conclusions. They make little use of writings on couples counseling and give students little advice about love relationships, but they pinpoint tantalizing questions that have not been resolved by research. Their scientific neutrality and curiosity is a great strength as they seek to separate research findings on how people *actually* behave from popular and therapeutic counsel on how people *should* behave. The other, more common kind of text focuses on relationship issues and emphasizes useful information, whether it comes from research or clinical practice. Like practical self-help books, they tend to avoid research controversies and focus on how one *should* behave to optimize success, rather than what actually occurs in interaction.

This book is quite a bit of both types. Though based on a thorough reading of current research wherever possible, it does not deal with scientific controversies over results or methodology. And it also goes beyond social sciences to biological and crosscultural research. It examines evolutionary theories, participating in the new integrative **biopsychosocial perspective**. We have also relied on clinical sources and even our own teaching and counseling experience to fill in gaps that have not been addressed by empirical research. We give many practical suggestions (often in tables) and lay the groundwork for relationship skills training. But we also critique widespread ideas and prescriptions for behavior which are not confirmed by current research (such as "always talk things out"). We present multiple perspectives for the diversity of people and their different relationships.

Since we offer a wide variety of insights and possible strategies for coping with issues, it is important that you think critically about the knowledge base relied upon for these descriptions and suggestions. Is an explanation based on empirical data? Could an idea or recommendation be tested by systematic methods? This material will need to be revised in the future, as even many of the most strongly supported research findings will be revised when new research methods are used and new generations of relationships are studied. You can begin the revision of existing knowledge now by joining the worldwide research team that pursues the answers to relationship questions. Describing and criticizing the knowledge base for each point would clutter the text too much; so we invite you to distinguish what we *really* know from what we *think* we know and what we *don't* know. The teacher's manual notes many areas tht merit such critical attention. We hope you will explore practical knowledge and practice scientific inquiry at the same time.

Learning objectives

You can expect specific learning in at least several areas. You can:

1. Analyze your own beliefs about intimacy and their impact on partners.
2. Enhance relating skills dealing with emotions, listening, communicating, problem solving, and managing differences and conflicts.
3. Weigh the influence of the social context, as well as the gender, life stage, family background, and personal relationship history of each partner on a relationship.
4. Understand the processes of uniting and separating, thinking, feeling, communication, affection, and managing power and conflict as they develop through the life cycle of relationships.

Limitations

This book does not try to explain all sorts of relationships. We focus extensively on romantic relationships in young adulthood, but not on non-romantic friendship or "purely" sexual encounters and buddyships. Our chapters on marriage, divorce, and homosexual and bisexual relating are comprehensive but less detailed. We explore the impact of the family of origin and of child and adolescent development on relationships, but parenting and issues specific to the middle and older adult years receive little attention. Gender and sexual orientation are considered, but ethnic, racial, and national diversity are simply too vast and under-researched for us to do them justice here. If you are middle-aged, divorced, or do not identify with mainstream American culture, please pay special attention to the ways your experience is *different* from what the text describes.

Journeys of the heart

The early twentieth century philosopher and scientist Otto Neurath saw scientists as

> sailors who on the open sea must reconstruct their ship [by making] use of some drifting timbers of the old structure. But they cannot put the ship in dock to start from scratch. During their work they stay on the old structure and deal with heavy gales and thundering waves (Neurath, 1987).

This is a wonderful analogy for the challenge we face on relationship journeys in a changing world. We must rebuild the boats of our love relationships even while we are living in the midst of our current ways of acting and feeling. Hilary Putnam extended the analogy to include the community.

> [There is] a fleet of boats. The people in each boat are trying to reconstruct their own boat without modifying it so much at any one time that it sinks. People are passing supplies and tools from one boat to another and shouting advice and encouragement. People sometimes decide they do not like the boat they are in and move to a different boat altogether. It is all a bit chaotic; but since it is a fleet, no one is ever totally out of signaling distance from all the other boats. We are not trapped in individual hells, but invited to engage in a truly human dialogue, one that combines collectivity with individual responsibility.

Thus we and our partner are not just building our "love stories" alone, but others in the larger culture have had a hand in designing them with us—as they shape our thinking about what we want and can do in a love relationship.

This book presents navigation charts drawn from studying love relationships in contemporary America. They can foster understanding about journeys you have taken in the past and relationships you see around you. If you are in a relationship now, perhaps these charts can help you consider your attitudes and feelings, your interpersonal processes and your relating skills, and your options and their consequences. There may be maps of relationship stages, scenarios, or issues that are beyond your present experience—indeed, the greater your experience, the more you will find here to ponder. But you can also keep this manual and use it again whenever a future relationship takes you into unfamiliar territory.

The life cycles of relationships

Young adult relationships 1

The interdisciplinary scientific study of couple relationships

Half a century ago scientific study of love and marriage was rare. But today many social and biological disciplines have turned their attention to couples and produced a rich variety of description, theory, and research. The varieties of relationships across time and space are studied by Anthropologists and Historians, as well as Cross-Cultural Psychologists living all around the world. The biological bases of relationships have been explored by biological psychologists and through comparative research on animals, or Ethology. In the recent past, the largest body of research and writing focused primarily on couples originated in the disciplines of Sociology, Family Therapy, and Psychology (Berscheid & Peplau, 1983).

Sociology has focused on social interaction and on the social institutions of marriage and the family. Family Therapy grew out of psychologists' and psychiatrists' efforts to improve the treatment of distressed marriages and families by directly observing what goes on and by devising new theories that go beyond individual psychology. Psychology contributed indirectly at first, through studying human nature, the dysfunctions of indi-

viduals, and the motivations of people in relationships. Now these three social sciences have spread out into more disciplines, including Social Psychology of Close Relationships, Family Studies, and Communications, all of which study couples as well. Still beyond this interdisciplinary field now known as Personal Relationships, cognitive neuroscience is beginning to add new knowledge about the brains of women and men that will cast light on some of the perplexing problems that occur when they interact. And finally, a new superdiscipline called Sociobiology has arisen that seeks to combine the findings of all biological and social sciences with the upgraded theories of evolution, especially in the areas of gender relating, mating, parenting, and emotions (see Chapters 9 and 13). Psychologists' contribution is called Evolutionary Psychology (Buss, 1994). We have a rich and growing source of knowledge in the emerging science of personal relationships.

A developmental perspective

Stage models

If you are walking across campus and a person of the opposite sex you hardly know catches your eye, what does it mean? Does he or she have some romantic interest in you, or think you are weird? Or was it an accident that meant nothing? If you were already casually dating, the glance might be flirtatious; if you were already a committed couple, it might be a "look of love" or signal a need to talk. The meaning depends very much on the history the two of you have with each other.

In order to better understand what goes on in premarital couple relationships, we will divide their life cycle into stages and focus on specific processes which develop and change in the stages. Viewing relationships in this way can help us understand why we experience a glance one way at one point and another way later on. And it helps us focus on what attitudes and skills might be appropriate at different points in our relationships.

This developmental stage organization has its limitations. For the concepts of processes and stages overlap, and there are few clear cut boundaries between stages. If we generalize about the sequence of events in a "typical" relationship, there will be many exceptions to the rules. But if we distinguish several different paths of relationship development, we may exhaust the reader's tolerance for complexity without getting much closer to an individual relationship as it is actually lived. Therefore we will describe a model of relationship development which is an extension of what has been used before.

At first American writers divided relationships into four stages: dating, courtship, engagement, and marriage. **Dating** was viewed as "casual," with little intention to proceed towards marriage. **Courtship**, or more recently **serious dating**, began as soon as love was declared or intentions toward the future were hatched. The sequencing of **engagement** and **marriage** was clear. But the sexual revolution in the sixties led to a decline in the rituals of courtship and the replacement of many engagements and marriages by the alternative of living together. Meanwhile social scientists were devising other criteria for making sense out of what happens between romantic partners.

Social psychologists developed the Stimulus-Value-Role (SVR) theory to cover three main aspects of choosing a future mate, and then theorized that these considerations would play major roles in three successive stages of premarital relationship (reviewed in Murstein, 1986). In the **stimulus** stage, prospective partners would be drawn to each other on the basis of perceived attractiveness and other initial impressions. After "checking each other out" in initial contacts, dating couples would proceed to express and compare their **values**, attitudes, interests, and beliefs to see if they were compatible. The final stage would involve experimenting to find out if the variety of **roles** each person could play as a member of the couple were satisfying to the other's needs and expectations.

Communications specialists developed a different way of dividing the life cycle of relationships into parts (Knapp, 1984). The verbal interaction in a relationship was categorized either as facilitating coming together or coming apart. Coming together was subdivided into five stages: **initiating**; **experimenting**, or finding common interests; **intensifying**, or expressing feelings; **integrating**, or identifying with each other; and **bonding**, or making formal future oriented commitments such as marriage. Coming apart was also subdivided into five stages: **differentiating**, which means pinpointing personal differences; **circumscribing**, or separating out individual activities and privacy; **stagnating**, or expressing boredom with the partner; **avoiding**, or arranging to stay apart; and **terminating** the relationship. Except for the terminating stage, the coming apart stages are not considered "declining" aspects, because both uniting and separating are vital to a continuing relationship, as we shall see in what follows.

For our own account of relationship development we have chosen to expand the traditional stages, because they provide more global categories easily recognizable by everyone. We divide premarital relationships into

TABLE 1.1. Stages of premarital relationships (Rows indicate roughly equivalent stages.)

Traditional stages	Interactional stages[1]	Our stages
	Initiating	Initiating
Dating	Experimenting	Casual dating
Courtship (Serious dating)	Intensifying	Being in love
	Integrating	Deepening
Engagement	Bonding	
Marriage	Differentiating	
	Circumscribing	Decay
	Stagnating	
	Avoiding	
	Terminating	Terminating

[1]From Knapp, 1984: These stages are not strictly sequential, but may reoccur at any time.

the following stages: **initiating, casual dating, being in love, deepening, decay**, and **terminating**. This sequence eliminates the previous distinction between dating and courtship and focuses more on developmental processes than on the culturally prescribed outcomes of engagement and marriage.

Each stage of an evolving relationship contains a different mix of some basic processes, which grow and change in their prevalence, intensity, and meaning for the partners as the relationship develops. These processes include (a) **communicating** with one another, (b) developing and changing **relationship roles**, (c) coping with **thoughts** and **emotions** in the relationship, (d) being **sexual** and **affectionate**, (e) **uniting and separating** in dynamic interplay with each other, and (f) coping with needs for power and **control** and dealing with **conflict**.

The research we will describe in the next three chapters has been gathered among college students. Since our readers are also college students, the empirical basis for our conclusions is appropriate. However, the students sampled in almost all empirical studies have represented only white American culture. Therefore students whose cultures are significantly different from this mainstream should consider what is said here critically. In fact, you should keep the limitations of empirical research in mind no matter who you are, and ask: Do these statistically based generalizations fit for me? And if they do not, why not?

The initiating stage

I was introduced to Rick by my friend Ron. Rick is attractive and smart, and I really liked his eyes. The first time Rick called me, we talked on the phone for an hour. On our first date, he took me to dinner and a movie. By the time he brought me home, I had laughed so hard that my stomach hurt. I just knew I would see him again, because we got along so well.

The initiating stage begins when one person first becomes aware of and interested in meeting the other. Therefore, whether you see someone you would like to meet or just hear about him, the initiating stage of your relationship has already begun. You may spend minutes, hours, days, or weeks thinking about meeting the person before you actually take the plunge. Some people act immediately, while others prefer to dwell in the realm of possibility, gathering information and playing out fantasy scenarios in their minds.

This stage ends when the first agreed upon one-to-one meeting, or first date, ends. But often prospective partners will prolong the initiating stage by meeting numerous times as parts of a group of friends who are not "paired off," thus avoiding any overt demonstration that they have a "dating interest" in each other. Therefore, for many young people today, the key distinction is between "dating" and "just friends" meetings.

I had known Carole from classes since my Freshman year. She was attractive and fun to be around. We had gone out lots of times with our mutual friends. I was looking for a relationship that would last awhile, because I was tired of being single. We enjoyed doing things together, so I asked her if we could start seeing each other.

Attraction

How do potential partners meet? About a third of college students report meeting dating partners through a friend (Knox & Wilson, 1981; replicated by first author in 1993). The next most frequently mentioned initial meeting occurs at parties or other special events, such as concerts, dances, vacation spots, and conferences (19% in Knox & Wilson, 1981; 22% in author's replication). Another significant portion of future dating connections are made through shared classes or work (17% in Knox & Wilson, 1981) or through peer groups and other shared activities (31%). Since over half (and 55% in Murstein, 1986) of dating partners meet through friends or at special events and a lesser number rub elbows at work, in class, or in friendship groups, perhaps the context in which people meet makes a difference.

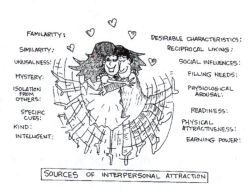

SOURCES OF INTERPERSONAL ATTRACTION

The numbers indicate that a sudden approach with a comparative stranger seems to be attractive to slightly more young adults than a gradual acquaintance with a person already familiar. Perhaps people who meet in class, at work, or in peer groups are more influenced by hearing group gossip about each other and by seeing each other behave in a socially normal and "friendly" manner, and hence are more likely to feel comfortable and expect to be "just friends." By contrast, being introduced by a friend can surround the new person with mystery and evoke some anxiety. The friend can turn this into anticipatory excitement by offering only positive and enticing information. Unusual events provide a novel or exciting atmosphere and opportunities for intense one-to-one encounters and flirtatious behavior. The initial high of a sudden approach with uncertainty and high expectations retains its appeal, because research indicates that the greater emotional arousal may contribute to stronger feelings of attraction (Dutton & Aron, 1974; Allen et al., 1989).

How do people attract each other?   Attraction has been studied quite a bit, perhaps because attraction feels so good that it is fun to study. Some of the ways that romantic attraction can come about are listed in Table 1.2.

Though many **desirable characteristics** have been studied, physical appearance has the most non-rational impact on the most people, so it has received the most research attention. We will consider physical appearance in the context of overall attraction.

If men had more up top, we'd need less up front. (Jaci Stephen)

Physical attractiveness.   At first glance, more attractive people are more likely to be viewed as sexy, warm, sensitive, kind, modest, and competent (Dion et al., 1972). A cross-cultural study of thirty-three cultures indicates that all over the world, physical appearance is more likely to be mentioned as an attracting factor by men, while women are more likely to notice a man's financial prospects and ambition or industriousness (Buss, 1989, 1994). Does that mean that the stereotypes many now consider sexist are actually inborn human tendencies with evolutionary survival value? Do sex objects mate with success objects?

It is not that simple. In all thirty-seven samples in Buss' crosscultural study (1989), both men and women ranked the personality characteristics "kind-understanding" and "intelligent" higher than either "earning power" or "attractiveness." Research differs on whether men's earning power and women's attractiveness is considered *before* (Hassebrauck, 1998; Townsend & Wasserman, 1998) or *after* (Desrochers, 1995) other personality factors have been verified. Little research has been done on the perceptions of "kind-understanding" and "intelligent." But "personality" may be more important than looks in mate choice (Cunningham et al., 1997), and "agreeableness" or prosocial attitudes may be sometimes more desirable in a man than social dominance (Graziano et al., 1997). When interviewed, American college men typically say that women have to reach a certain level of

TABLE 1.2. Sources of interpersonal attraction

General and dyadic factors

1. **Familiarity**: Having spent time together, living near the other, exposure to the other, thinking about the other, or anticipating interaction with the other.
2. **Desirable characteristics of the other**: Appearance, physical attributes, and personal characteristics, such as kindness, intelligence, sense of humor, etc.
3. **Similarity**: Similar attitudes, some similar personality traits, customs, ways of thinking.
4. **Reciprocal liking**: Finding out that the other likes us.
5. **Social influences**: Norms of social desirability, such as status and socially approved goals and lifestyle, and approval of others in our social network.
6. **Filling needs**: Particularly needs experienced as stable personality traits, such as affection, companionship, self-esteem, security, and emotional support and help in areas of personal vulnerability, such as mental or social skill deficits and anxieties.

Situational factors

7. **Unusualness of the situation**: Unfamiliar or special places, novel experiences, non-routine activities, such as vacations, conventions, or travel.
8. **Mystery** in the situation or about the other person, or **uncertainty** about the person or the future of the relationship.
9. **Physiological arousal** through emotions or physical activity: Sources include excitement, anxiety, conflict, laughter, muscular exertion, and more.
10. **Isolation from others**: Being alone with the other person, or sharing exclusive attention.

Individual factors

11. **Specific cues**: Some characteristic of the other, such as voice, eyes, posture, or mannerisms, which for a particular person triggers an automatic strong attraction, perhaps explaining the phenomenon of "love at first sight."
12. **Readiness** for entering a relationship, related to the condition of prior attachments, social norms about the timing for becoming a couple, and other personal psychological factors.

Source: Expanded from Aron, Dutton, Aron, & Iverson, 1989.

attractiveness to evoke interest (Snyder et al., 1985). However, that level may depend on the available competition (Gladue & Delaney, 1990). And despite what they say about their ideals of attractiveness, both sexes may actually choose partners whom they perceive as similar to themselves in attractiveness (Critelli & Waid, 1980).

The popular stereotype that "what is beautiful is good" works to the advantage of good-looking people in schools, jobs, and courtrooms (Hatfield & Sprecher, 1986). Attractiveness is important for awakening desire both in the individual and in others—desire in one sex and admiration or envy in the other. One attitude study in fraternities and sororities found the most important factors in popularity as a potential date for both sexes were attractiveness and being a trend-setter (Speed & Gangestad, 1997). Being with an attractive partner contributes to social status. But social status, that is, how people are viewed by their peers, is more important for some people than for others. Men with a high concern for how others view them are more interested in appearance in a partner, while those less concerned with social status value personality factors more and looks less (Snyder et al., 1985).

Unusual physical attractiveness can be a handicap as well as a benefit. Extremely attractive people are besieged by sexual advances that press against social norms, and societal attitudes toward the very handsome and beautiful are influenced by discomfort, irritation, and competiveness. Men admit being afraid to court a strikingly beautiful woman because they assume that every other man would desire her too. Therefore, women in the top echelon of attractiveness may have to initiate relationships with less attractive partners and frequently prove their loyalty.

> Even though I somehow got the guts up to ask her out, I was still pretty scared as to how to act with her. She was extremely attractive, and I figured that any girl who was that good looking would expect certain behavior at predetermined times, and I never got the memo on how to do that. I asked her out after the first date because she kept on talking to me and telling me she had a good time.

Height and weight: Research confirms that being overweight has a negative effect on both perceived and self-perceived attractiveness for women, much more so than for men (Stake & Lauer, 1987). There is also an attractiveness bias associated with height, with tall men and short women having more frequent dates than short men and tall women (Shepperd & Strathman, 1989). Both sexes normally prefer that a man be taller than his date (Pierce, 1996). Nevertheless, research indicates that good looks probably do not lead to more marital satisfaction or a happier life (Berscheid et al., 1972).

Once they find him personally attractive, American women look for success potential in a man (Desrochers, 1995), typically seeking "a strong personality who is going places." This attitude continues even though women are now free to seek success through their own careers and develop more ego strength of their own rather than just seeking success and strength in their partner. In addition, women may look for physical attractiveness as a desire factor and social status symbol in ways very similar to men, even if they prefer not to mention it (Sprecher, 1989; Hadjistavropoulos & Genest, 1994):

> Bill's body was to die for, and he looked like a replica of Tom Cruise. My last boyfriend wasn't exactly a ten on the good-looks scale, and Bill was pushing a nine plus. But I knew I could never marry him, because his sense of responsibility was close to nil, and he didn't care about getting good grades.

The quotation shows a young woman in high school who is attracted to masculine beauty and the status it would confer, but realistically holds out for character traits with success potential as well.

Similarity and liking. Numerous research projects have demonstrated that students consider similarity (factor 3 in Table 1.2) of characteristics and attitudes important when they have no contact with a prospective romantic interest (Feingold, 1990). But when people do meet, projecting liking (factor 4) through smiling, eye contact, leaning forward, and appearing interested, can completely overshadow the negative effect that concrete dissimilarities normally have (McClanahan et al., 1990). Furthermore, in a study of students' accounts of falling in love, being liked by the other person appeared in 90% of the stories, far more frequently than any of the other 11 factors listed in Table 1.2, and 2 to 5 times as frequently as similarity (Aron et al., 1989). Perhaps similarity is comparatively un-

important in partners' accounts of their attraction because locating similar attitudes serves as an initial way of determining the field of eligibles in a melting-pot of ethnic, cultural, and attitudinal diversity. As important as similarities and attractiveness can be, some research on attraction suggests that timing and situations conducive to falling in love (factors 7 to 10 and factor 12) have actually been more influential in choosing a mate (Lykken & Tellegen, 1993).

Unusualness, mystery, and arousal. Both unusualness (factor 7) and mystery (factor 8) are conducive to hyperalertness, which is an altered state of consciousness. Research has found that novel events and vacations stand out more in our consciousness, are remembered as lasting longer, and may produce more dreaming (reported in Ornstein & Carstensen, 1991). Both the news and novels make use of the power of novelty to take priority in our consciousness. If we meet someone we are attracted to in a novel situation, our altered state increases the meaning that attraction has for us.

Hyperalertness is one of several types of physiological arousal that have been linked to attraction by research for over two decades. Others include anxiety (Dutton & Aron, 1974; Hoon et al., 1977; Riordan & Tedeschi, 1983), humor, horror, anger (Dutton & Aron, 1989), and even bodily arousal through physical exercise (White et al., 1981). In all of the experiments, attractive persons were perceived as significantly more attractive after the arousal than without it. In one experiment (White et al., 1981) noticeably unattractive persons were perceived as significantly more unattractive. In another (Dutton & Aron, 1989) a less attractive person in a movie (compared to another movie subject) was perceived as somewhat more attractive, but not as much more attractive as the more attractive person with whom he or she was being compared. So emotional arousal does not create attraction feelings, but seems to **amplify** those that are already present. A limitation of these studies is that only one (Dutton & Aron, 1989) tested the arousal effects on attractions of women as well as of men. In that test (viewing an angry encounter between two men and then rating them on attractiveness) the women did perceive the men as more attractive after the anger arousal, even though they didn't **like** them any more. They were also much more likely to label their own arousal as anxiety than as anger, as the men did when viewing a similar movie of two women.

Specific cues and readiness for a relationship will be discussed in Chapter 9, while **isolation** from others requires no elaboration.

Nonverbal attracting behavior.   An anthropologist observed people in bars and categorized three kinds of behavior that serve to attract sexual attention among humans, just as they do in the animal kingdom (Givens, 1983). These behaviors announce one's **presence** ("I am here"), advertise one's **gender identity** ("I am female/male"), and declare one's **receptivity** ("I am harmless and hospitable").

Movement serves to announce one's presence, since the eye is hypersensitive to motion. People will move in ways that show off their gender identity. College men will swagger, subtly flex their muscles, or playfully display strength and agility, such as punching or arm-wrestling during greetings, or tossing a frisbee. Women can groom themselves, toss their hair, and allow their hips to sway to show they enjoy being in their bodies. Both sexes may laugh or make exclamations that broadcast the ring of their voices and their capacity for enjoyment and pleasure.

In addition to attracting attention and advertising gender, one's behavior must also assure onlookers that one is harmless and hospitable to approach (Givens, 1983). Lifting or shrugging shoulders, tilting the head to one side, toeing in slightly, leaning forward slightly, and relaxed positions or uncrossed limbs are all subliminal postural signals inviting others to approach. Shrugging, tilting, and pigeon-toeing are all remnants of the protective startle reflex which can be easily seen in young children confronting a stranger. With these actions our brain unconsciously communicates that we are "struck" or startled by the other and therefore closer to fright than aggression. By broadcasting that we are reacting more like a child than a predator, we may stimulate caring and protective reactions in the onlooker, or invite him or her to approach and capitalize on his or her superiority. Women and subordinates shrug, tilt, and toe in more than men and bosses, and are frequently seen tilting or gazing down or away in magazine ads. But both sexes do it in attraction scenes.

For those of us who complain that we wouldn't recognize a come-on until it hits us in the face, college students have listed the following nonverbal cues employed by women, in order from the strongest to the weakest indication that she would be willing to accept a date. They are

1. touching while not laughing,
2. touching while laughing,
3. smiling,
4. standing close (eighteen inches),
5. leaning sideways toward the man of her interest,

6. speaking with unusual animation,
7. catching his eye during sexual humor,
8. leaning forward, and
9. catching his eye during nonsexual humor (Muehlenhard, 1986).

Two other cues reflecting women's attentiveness and involvement were nonoccurrences of distraction: avoiding public grooming during conversation, and not looking at other men who happen to come by.

Rainville and Gallagher's (1990) findings on the role of dominance and vulnerability in attraction lend further support to Givens' observations on harmlessness. Men were more attracted to more vulnerable rather than dominant women, such as those who expressed some self-doubt rather than complete confidence before making a shot at a pool table. This fits with the traditional "damsel in distress" behavior pattern as a way that women can invite men in.

Rainville and Gallagher (1990) found that women were more attracted to more dominant rather than vulnerable men, such as those who win, relish competition, and express self-confidence and courage. But women were most attracted to dominant men who showed *some* vulnerability, rather than uninterrupted self-confidence or cockiness. Men were enticed by vulnerable women who showed some confidence, competitive spirit, or feistiness as well.

Another class of unconscious attraction cues that has been widely observed (Givens, 1978; Perper, 1985) and also videotaped (Cappella & Palmer, 1990; Crown, 1991) is **behavioral synchrony**, that is, doing the same thing at the same time. People unconsciously telegraph their involvement with each other by mirroring each other's movements, such as crossing their legs or arms and changing their directions of leaning. They unconsciously tune in to each other's style and pace of movement and begin a nonverbal dance to the same imperceptible beat. The establishment of synchronized positions and movements may be the best indicator that both neutral cues, such as leg crossing, and potentially attractive cues, such as forward leaning, are actually communicating attraction.

Eye contact. Length of gaze, rate of blinking, and dilation of pupils all have effects on attraction between people. In America, a gaze lasting slightly longer than the cultural norm of two seconds communicates modest interest, while a longer stare takes on a predatory boldness. In some cultures, staring curiously at strangers is allowed, while in others, anything more than a fleeting glance is considered rude.

Since proper eye contact is strictly limited by cultural norms, how does one give out adequate visual signals without violating cultural norms? The answer lies in "gaze-crossing" (Givens, 1983) or "catching his eye" (Muehlenhard et al., 1986). Both men and women can signal the intention to gaze by sweeping their eyes across another person's viewfield, apparently in the course of shifting their attention between two other targets of interest.

Several times during the class she would turn from the instructor to look out the window, but sort of trip over my eyes in the process. When I figured out that I was supposed to catch her catching my eye like that, I started to really have fun with her. It was a lot more fun playing eye-tag than listening to the lecture.

If gazing rights are culturally determined, increased blinking is a normal involuntary response to the emotional arousal which mutual gazing causes (Williams & Kleinke, 1993). Some women wear mascara or artificial lashes to accentuate the blink. Since people blink faster when they are anxious, women who blink or "bat" their eyes are telegraphing that another person is arousing them. But men are not expected to blink faster when attracted, and many of them experience the anxiety associated with emotional arousal as a stumbling block in initiating relationships.

Expanded pupils are also an involuntary response, and they both induce and respond to attraction in powerful ways that are not yet fully understood. In the middle ages women took the drug belladonna ("pretty woman" in Italian) to enlarge their pupils and make themselves more attractive (Cook & McHenry, 1978). Dilated pupils still have the same effect. In a modern study, men compared two nearly identical photos and rated the one with artificially enlarged pupils as more attractive, though they couldn't say why (Hess, 1965). Research has linked dilated pupils with increased alpha brain waves in a pleasant "altered state" of relaxed attention. Dilated pupils seem to be gazing intently, but in a relaxed, not anxious, state and they invite one to gaze back and match their state. Perhaps humans welcome the chance to shed their anxiety and join one another in the rapture of a shared altered consciousness (also known as "goo-goo eyes").

As I got to meet her face to face, I looked into the most beautiful eyes I had ever seen. She was very beautiful, she was also quite interested in me, and when I looked into her eyes I could see all her feelings shining through. I felt that I could look into her eyes forever.

Communicating interest in another. Who starts it? It is generally assumed that males usually take the initiative to start the courtship dance, while females play the receptive role. But the truth is more complicated than that.

In contemporary colleges, male students prefer that women deliver hints about their approachability. Both sexes declare that men and women can be equally free to initiate courtship contact (Kleinke et al., 1986). In many situations, deciding who really initiates a courtship approach may be as difficult as sorting out the proverbial chicken and egg. Males may resolve their anxiety over making the first direct overtures by approaching only women who have already signaled their interest nonverbally (Perper, 1985; Grammer, 1990). Researchers have coined the term "proceptivity" (Perper, 1985; Perper & Weiss, 1987) to describe actions that women take that indicate that they are receptive to a man's advances. In contrast to verbal approaches, nonverbal proceptive behavior (such as gestures, facial expressions, postures, etc.) can mean what the viewer thinks it means, or something different, or nothing. The vagueness of inexplicit signals of liking allows the signaler to plausibly deny having given them. Thus the signaler can avoid the loss of self-esteem or embarrassment that often come with overt self-exposure or rejection (Symons, 1972).

> If I'm interested in a guy, I'd rather just catch his eye a few times than get somebody to tell him I like him. Catching his eye just makes him think about me. I figure if he approaches me without knowing for sure how I feel, it's more likely that he really likes me.

The disadvantage of such plausible deniability is that the signals may be missed or misunderstood. Both men and women can overlook plausibly deniable attraction cues, and the receiver's lack of response can be misunderstood by the signaler to mean "Don't approach me that way. I don't want that." On the other extreme, men are more likely than women to misinterpret female attraction signals as a sexual "come on" (Grammer, 1990). They may then orient themselves mentally for a quick sexual conquest, while discrediting the woman's moral character: "If she's that blatant about wanting me, perhaps she does this all the time."

How do people communicate verbally when they are attracted to one another?   In approaching or being approached by a stranger, both men and women prefer opening lines that are either direct (e.g., "I'd like to meet you,") or innocent (e.g., "Could you tell me what time it is?" or "Did you understand the lecture?"). Women, more than men, dislike lines that are cute or flippant, such as "Is that really your hair?" or "I'm easy. Are you?" (Kleinke et al., 1986). Women prefer to use innocent lines themselves, choosing indirectness to allow **plausible deniability** of their intention to attract. Many men still claim they like cute or flippant "pickup" lines despite women's general disapproval. Cute and flippant pickup success stories may be popular because they can cover up and deny men's fears of rejection and serve as a humorous release of their social anxiety.

Blatant conversation starters:
   "I spent a lot of time in prison dreaming of a woman like you."
   "I'm looking for a husband to be a good role model for my six children."

Once people are on speaking terms, the possibilities are endless. Yet research suggests some behaviors that we commonly experience.

Table 1.3 lists 22 verbal cues female students give to convey interest in dating (Muehlenhard et al., 1986). All but two clearly belong to the two most socially appropriate categories of strategies for **testing a potential partner's liking** found by another study (Douglas, 1987). These categories are **sustaining contact** and **offering favorable conditions for approach** or dating.

Two other attraction cues mentioned by participating students were not investigated because they were considered demeaning to women: giggling and agreeing with everything the man says. Giggling is a childlike behavior, and a glance at cross-cultural research (Eibl-Eibesfeldt, 1989, in Grammer, 1990) suggests that in the anxiety-provoking ambivalence between attraction and caution, childlike feelings and behaviors are quite normal. On the other hand, agreeing with everything the man says might not be so much an abdication of intelligence as it is a way of drawing him out.

> *Woman serves as a looking glass possessing the magic powers of reflecting the figure of man at twice its natural size.* (British author Virginia Woolf)

The effects of self-esteem and personal power

Different levels of self-esteem can effect the ways people interact to produce attraction in initial meetings. Hatfield (Walster, 1965) showed that a male conversation partner's projection of liking and acceptance is more attractive when a young woman's self-esteem has just been lowered than when it has just been raised. These findings could fit the general situation for adolescents in high school. Adolescents' self-esteem is normally on shaky new legs, and their need for group acceptance is great. Under peer pressure to date, high school kids often accept anyone of the appropriate looks and social status who likes them.

> Example 1. *I liked her because of her looks and her popularity around school. I was very excited to have a good looking girl interested in me, and I wasn't about to blow that opportunity.*

> Example 2. *My desire to have a boyfriend for the sake of fitting in at my new high school pushed me to start dating Robert. I jumped at the chance to go out with the first good-looking guy who asked me out.*

An intuitive understanding of the effectiveness of lowered self-esteem (or shame) for catalyzing attraction may be behind some of the cute-flippant "putdown" approaches that people love to hate.

> *I'd tell a pretty girl at the beach that she was fat and ugly, and she'd get so mad! She'd come after me just to tell me what a jerk I was. Then I'd keep joking and putting her down and start buying her drinks to make up for it. I tell you, if the girl doesn't ignore me right away I'll wind up taking her out.*

TABLE 1.3. Potential verbal attraction cues and their affinity-testing categories

Affinity testing category	Potential verbal attraction cues
Sustaining contact	1. She compliments him.
	2. She is helpful.
Sustaining contact	3. She keeps talking rather than ending the conversation quickly.
Desiring contact[1]	4. She gives a specific reason to end the conversation (a class in 10 minutes) rather than a vague reason ("Well, I guess I should get going.")
Offering favorable approach conditions	5. If he asks her out and she refuses because she is busy, she adds something like, "Could we put it off until some other time?"
Offering favorable conditions	6. She does not talk as if she is so busy she has no time to date.
Sustaining contact	7. She asks him questions about himself.
Offering favorable conditions	8. If he asks for her phone number, she gives it to him.
Sustaining contact	9. If there is a short or medium pause (3 or 10 seconds) where she spoke last, she speaks rather than waiting for him to speak.
Offering favorable conditions	10. She mentions an activity that they could do together, such as stating what she heard about a movie she'd like to see. She did not specifically mention their doing the activity together. She did not say there was a movie she would like to see and then stare at him expectantly.
Sustaining contact	11. While he is talking she backchannels—i.e., says a few words to show she is listening ("Umm hmm" or "Yeah").
Sustaining contact	12. She asks him questions that provide her with information of no direct use to her, rather than information she could use. It will appear her motive is to talk to him rather than to gain information.
Sustaining contact	13. She does not interrupt him.
Sustaining contact	14. She engages in small talk after, rather than before, she asks for a favor. If she talks to him and then asks for the favor, it appears her motive was to ask for the favor; if he has already agreed to do the favor, it appears her motive was to talk to him.
Desiring contact[1]	15. If he mentions where he will be at a future time, she says she might see him there.
Desiring contact[1]	16. She makes it clear she has noticed him in the past (e.g., she noticed he was absent from class or what books he typically carries).
Sustaining contact	17. If he asks a question, she gives more than the shortest possible answer.
Sustaining contact	18. She is responsive to what he says (comments & laughs at his jokes).
Sustaining contact	19. She empathizes—comments on how he might feel ("I bet that hurt").
Sustaining contact	20. She, rather than he, starts the conversation.
Sustaining contact	21. She starts a conversation with him rather than remaining silent.
Offering favorable conditions	22. She mentions that she has no plans for the weekend.

Adapted from Muehlenhard, 1986, with affinity-testing categories from Douglas, 1987.
Sustaining contact: the category of affinity-testing strategies judged most socially appropriate.
Offering favorable approach conditions: for the partner's approach or dating.
1. Desiring contact: Strategies for signaling past interest in contact or desire to resume contact in the future, a hypothetical addition to Douglas' Sustaining Contact category.

What about playing hard to get?   People can attempt to gain control in initial encounters by appearing less available, less interested in relationship, or more popular than their potential partners. This has been called the principle of least interest: "That person is able to dictate the conditions of association whose interest in the continuation of the affair is least." (Waller & Hill, 1951). But the accent is on continuation. Playing "hard to get" doesn't seem to work very well until a relationship is already established. Studies of a "hard-to-get effect" in pre-relationship behavior only showed that people like prospective partners who are selective, but not too selective (Wright & Contrada, 1986), or liked people who liked the research subject, but lacked interest in anybody else (Walster et al., 1973). In the initial encounters, prospective partners may already establish some control over the process by being less available or more assertive. But they must first appear to have enough interest in the other person that a desirable relationship appears to be possible. Without the hope and experience of satisfying times together, few people will submit for long to the intermittent reinforcement of: "I really like you—but I won't be available for awhile, because I'm too busy with other things."

One-night stands and the pick-up game.   The process that occurs in first-encounter sex is fairly simple, at least as culturally defined in a bar. By showing up alone or with only woman friends, a woman signals that she may be open to new contacts, and these might possibly include sex. Normally, enough alcohol is consumed so that stranger-anxiety is anaesthetized away and conversation is more playful than intimate. The "right moves" are blatant, to avoid embarrassing or potentially dangerous misinterpretation. If both people keep saying yes, they may end up in bed together.

   Why choose this kind of sexual encounter? Some people, such as those in the military and workaholics, may be starved for contact, affection, and sex because they lack time, and few potential partners are available. Others may be unwilling to get more involved than one-night affairs because of the pain of a recent relationship breakup, fear of intimacy, or fear of the type of men or women to whom they are attracted. Or they may want to revive their belief in themselves as an attractive person. Sometimes the motive of enhancing self-esteem with the peer group outweighs all the others. For some men daring the pick-up game with friends and beer, masculine history seems to be at stake:

> *For thousands of years, men have had to make quick decisions based on signals received during situations that require us to take a stand and fight or to run. He has to first build up enough courage to go over to her and try to make conversation with a total stranger and act very strong, yet gentle at heart. And that's not even the worst part. You know that nobody goes to a bar alone, so all your friends are watching you, so you're about to get the embarrassment of your life. So you finally get enough beers in you that you feel comfortable enough to ask her to dance. Then WHAMMO, the turn-down happens; you*

can hear your friends laughing at you in the background, as you sit there not knowing whether or not to pick up your shattered ego and go get drunk with the boys or to take another shot (only if you're really drunk).

If this is **his**tory, what must **her**story be like? Several verbal accounts have been collected and excerpted, because the double moral standard deters women from writing about their experiences with "one-night stands." These three women relay their experiences with the "pick-up game":

I go to bars to have fun. I get approached and it's okay. If he's honest and nice then I'll be kind, but if he starts b.s. I get unkind and blow him off.

*I go to bars to see **who** will notice me. I check out the other girls to see who's the prettiest. If I'm the prettiest, then I'll act bitchy with the guys, because they'll keep coming back anyway. It doesn't matter what a guy says or does, he has to be confident for me to choose him.*

I went once to pick someone up and lost my nerve. I met one guy who was really sweet. I saw him as he was, because he wasn't trying to get me. I told him that was the secret to meeting a girl and the last thing most guys will try. We are still friends (not lovers).

The casual dating stage

For the purposes of our discussion we define the casual dating period as beginning with the second planned meeting or date and ending when both partners experience themselves as being "serious" or in love. There are two different kinds of casual dating, which are most likely to be distinguished by the time period in which they occur. First, during adolescent exploration, young people experiment with romantic involvements. They may "spend time" or "mess around," but they often end relationships suddenly because they feel awkward or just get tired of being in a relationship and want to try something or someone else. Adolescent couples are beginning to learn about love, and the main way of distinguishing between casual and serious dating is the length of the relationship. On the other hand, in college casual dating, cultural norms encourage both sexes to put off seeking a marriage partner until they have finished their studies and gotten established in their careers. Many students also have not recovered enough emotionally from the breakup of a long-term relationship during and after high school to be comfortable with a serious involvement during the early years of college. Though they may not hold back from sex, and they may allow themselves to explore and experiment with passion and intimacy, they believe in avoiding commitments (Roscoe et al., 1987). Adolescent exploration occurs widely in Europe and many other places, but casual dating or "going out as friends" in college is prevalent only in North America. We shall consider below whether relationship development really does stop at this casual stage, or perhaps continues to deepen, even if the partners do not consider themselves ever to be in love or overtly make any other commitments other than to "play it by ear."

Expectations, involvement-restricting styles, and duration

What if you don't even date?   Many young people in America and in much of the world go out together in mixed groups, which allows potential partners to interact for weeks or months without ever having to commit themselves through word or deed to pairing off (Murstein, 1986). This allows people to explore their compatibility while being "just friends," thus creating another preliminary relationship stage which is even less committed and exclusive than casual dating. Among today's college students some "good friends" may be similar to casual daters, since in one study 20% or more of such friends reported having had intercourse (Rauter & Gibson, 1995). In another way, the "good friends" label can be used to keep prospective partners in the "on-deck circle" (like baseball batters not yet up to bat) while one explores other romantic interests.

> There was a guy I was really attracted to, and he went out of his way to make sure I came to a party he was having. Then, the second time we were together, we were dancing at my apartment, and the music stopped. He bent down, and I thought "here it comes." And he said, "I gotta tell you something. I can't get involved with you, because I have a girlfriend back home. But I really like you a lot, and I want us to be friends." I hate that word 'friends'! A week or so later he introduced me to another girl from a nearby college and called her his "good friend." I could see her take an instant dislike for me, and I didn't like the way she hung around him. I thought he liked me more, and I think she wanted me to think he liked her more.

Are casual dating relationships stable or transitory?   When students were asked what influenced them to enter the most significant romantic involvement of their lives to date, the most frequently mentioned factor was the "social clock," that is, their reactions to getting older combined with expectations of those around them that it was time to find a mate (Jacobs, 1989). Until then, however, some choose to hold off commitment:

> I am afraid of actually falling in love with someone at a time that is inconvenient to me and the scheme of events I have planned. So serious relationships are out of the question.

If a decision to seek (or not seek) intimate involvement can make the difference between casual and serious dating, can casual dating relationships be stable in themselves? A medieval treatise on courtly love tells us

> It is well known that love is always either increasing or decreasing.
> If love diminishes, it quickly fails and rarely revives. (Capellanus, 1184/ 1941)

If this is true about human nature, then once the increase of love is thwarted by words or actions designed to keep the relationship casual, it is on its way to extinction.

But couldn't two casual lovers counteract this instability by agreeing to keep their feelings dampened in order to mutually avoid either having to commit to "love" or terminate? To answer this, we should find out how long casual dating relationships usually last. When long-term collegiate couples described their casual dating, the average lengths of the casual relationships varied between 7.72 weeks for the group whose sexual involvement was most rapid and 9.56 weeks when the involvement was most gradual (Christopher & Cate, 1985). Loyer-Carlson (1989) studied 48 casual dating relationships that dissolved, and found the median length to be 3.25 months, with the most frequently mentioned length being 4 months.

The commitment dance.   The first author (unpublished data) found support for these results by asking students to report weekly on the state of their relationships. The preliminary data suggests a typical commitment dance going on in half the young adult couples between weeks six and twelve. Eighty percent of women moved from signaling their love to gently seeking more commitment, while 50% of men kept dancing away from the issue while suggesting, "Let's just go with the flow." This drama has been around for awhile.

> *The hardest task in a girl's life is to prove to a man that his intentions are serious.* (Helen Rowland, 1903)

We can speculate about why casual romantic relationships normally don't last longer than two to four months. Long-term friendships are more emotionally stable than marriages (Davis & Todd, 1982), because friends don't usually try to meet as many personal needs with each other as lovers. Casual daters may think they are managing a friendship, but once they start meeting important emotional needs, they start to become more emotionally volatile, like people in love or in marriages. A female student described the development of her "friendship" this way:

> *We agreed at the beginning of last semester that we could never be anything different than good friends. Then we got to seeing each other every day and sometimes calling each other three times a day. We don't hold hands like other couples, but our friends all said we acted like a married couple. We've kept it platonic, except for a couple of times when we were drinking. We were seeing too much of each other, so we backed off because he said he really just cared for me as his best friend. We tried to do less and start seeing other people, but then he kept coming over, and now we're just as thick as we ever were. We're stuck. We don't want to lose the best friendship we've ever had, but we keep feeling too much and getting all confused.*

Is casual dating (or "going out as friends") a good way to shop around and experiment with romance without hurting anyone too much, as its advocates declare? Or is it an attempt to stifle the psychodynamics of the mating process, as some detractors (e.g., Cobliner, 1988) insist? It is probably both of these.

Communication do's and don'ts

How do casual partners communicate? It is very important for most casual dating partners to be able to talk comfortably with each other. In one study of problems college students experienced on dates, 35% of men and 20% of women listed communication, while 20% of men also mentioned shyness (Knox & Wilson, 1983). This is how one man views the problem of making clever casual conversation:

> *I'm more of a shy guy, so if men are supposed to take control of conversation, I'm going to need some serious help. I find it hard sometimes to create small talk due to the fact that I don't want to say anything offending yet not too boring. That narrows it down to very little to talk about. Women seem to take insult easier to men's comments. With that, I believe women should take charge of the encounter.*

Casual dating conversation is supposed to be fun, and yet some important information is being gained about both the partners and the process of relating to each other. Conversation is likely to focus directly on activities and attitudes the two people have in common, mapping out new territory the two might explore in their time together (Knapp, 1984). Or, conversely, one may strive to identify herself in an area as a distinctive individual. Most people do some of both—of seeking inclusion by fitting in, and of differentiating oneself by standing out.

As students compare attitudes and interests, they usually come out in favor of honesty and directness. Yet, in order to avoid committing themselves prematurely to any potentially risky attitude or a statement that might offend the partner, they are likely to speak indirectly about such matters. One way that casual daters explore their potential for a relationship is to discuss highlights of their own past relationships and those of other couples that they know. By exchanging opinions about carefully selected and edited incidents and aspects of these other relationships (to avoid any self-incrimination), people can drop hints about how they want to act and be treated this time around. Prior relationships are far more likely to be discussed by casual daters or cross-sex friends than by those in a romantic involvement (Afifi & Burgoon, 1998; Baxter & Wilmot, 1985). When asked by the first author, both casual and committed daters explained it this way:

> *Prior relationships are not taboo topics for me. There is much too much information to gain from discussing past attractions and the reasons for them.*

Indeed, the most consistently taboo topic in casual dating and cross-sex friends conversations may be the state of the relationship itself (Afifi & Burgoon, 1998: Baxter & Wilmot, 1985). This topic is far more universally avoided by those less romantically involved (88% of Baxter's romantic potential and 72% of the first author's casual dating sample) than by those more involved (the topic was avoided by 58% of Baxter's romantic type and 21% of the author's sample of serious relationships). The most common reasons given for not talking about the relationship (Baxter & Wilmot, 1985) were that unequal commitments to the relationship might be revealed (41%) and that feelings might get hurt (19%) or were better left to wordless understanding (17%).

> I am scared of leading a person to believe I am interested in a long-term relationship when I have no such intentions. To avoid doing this I would shy away from commitment or conversation of the future together. I knew I was moving on, and I wanted my partner to be aware of that fact so he would be hesitant to get too close to me.

Several other topics are also avoided, including rules for the relationship, negative personal behavior, negative life experiences, romantic relationships or friendships with others, and sexual experiences (Guerrero & Afifi, 1995). Of these topics, only relationship rules and negative personal behavior were avoided more often in casual than in serious dating relationships.

What are the right moves on casual dates?   If conversation ranges widely, yet avoids certain topics, proper behavior is a mixture of adhering to slightly shaky codes of behavior and providing excitement through spontaneity and the unusual.

In the traditional gender behavior code, the male opens doors and pays for everything and is in charge of "showing her a good time." He defers to her desires. But her first priority is to please him. Even after twenty-five years of liberation, young men worry about their assumed responsibility for the "success" of the date, but women may be as frequently concerned about the right places to go and significantly concerned about money and who pays (Knox & Wilson, 1983).

The penalty for not doing the right thing can be not getting a second chance. Both partners normally avoid any corrective feedback and act as if everything is going fine all during the date, in order to convince each other that they are "fun to be with." The critical evaluation is made afterwards, often in a report to one's friends, and it contributes to each person's reputation for gender-appropriate behavior. One coed experienced the first few dates as an audition:

> I felt very awkward and dumb, not quite knowing exactly what I should do or say. I felt I was being put on display for that one moment and had to do everything perfect or else the guy would never call again. To me, it sometimes

feels like an audition. If I pass the first one, then there'll be a next; if not, it's back to the beginning.

Anxiety, alcohol, and the right moves.   All this social emphasis on being humorous, an interesting conversationalist, fun, impressive, and gender-appropriate in actions is anxiety-provoking for both sexes, but perhaps more so for more men than women (Knox & Wilson, 1983). The pressure caused by anxiety is only worsened by the normal dating expectation that one will *not* be "uptight," and that one will be condemned and avoided later if one is. Instead, one is expected to be relaxed and relaxing for the other person to be around. One way both sexes (but especially men) respond to this pressure is to drink for anaesthesia.

> *When I'm drinking, I can say and do things with women that I'd never even think of when I'm sober.*

Women can also experience alcohol as a "permission giver." In the bar scene, they can use their altered state as permission to be more sexual than their normal moral attitudes allow. They can still disavow what they did later, saying it was a mistake they made after drinking too much. Some men also express the desire to escape from restrictive behavior codes on dates through spontaneity and risk:

> *I want a woman to be open to things on the spur of the moment and to try new things that are risky.*

Of course the woman might feel uncomfortable departing from a planned date, because she wouldn't know what to expect. The man could transform his own social anxiety into coping with risk and feel more in control, because it is *his* choice of risk.

Humor is another way to cope with anxiety, by laughing it off. Laughter and fun are among the most frequently desired aspects of a dating partner, both in newspaper personal ads and in casual dating surveys.

Changing sexual customs.   In the fifties and sixties before the sexual revolution, norms of sexual behavior on a date were often quite explicit. Men learned how far to go with a "nice girl" (as opposed to a woman with reputedly loose morals) and kept track of each other's sexual progress in bull sessions. A middle-aged man recalls:

> *In my college dorm in the early sixties, I learned that you were supposed to kiss the girl on the third date. I found that out when one girl I had taken out three times let it be known through her friend and mine that she was worried that I didn't like her very much, because I hadn't kissed her. Another time I had a sudden impulse and kissed a girl good night on the second date, but not on the third. She got all confused and fell in love with me.*

The sexual revolution brought a new ethic: If it feels good, do it. It was said that women could be just as sexually motivated as men. The old double standard—namely, that men who want sex or are good at it are more manly, but women who want sex or are good at it are sluts—was wrong and needed to die out. Researchers have differing views on what has happened to these attitudes more recently. For some, the double standard may only have softened somewhat (e.g., Roche, 1986), for males are still considerably more permissive than females toward casual sex (Oliver & Hyde, 1993).

Most recently, young adults express at least three attitudes about progressing toward sex:

1. "Anything goes; just play it by ear and do what feels right in the moment."
2. "Don't be too eager; be respectful of your partner and feel out what he or she wants."
3. "Wait till you get to know the person a little. You should be concerned about AIDS. You don't want to spoil things by talking about it, but you can wait to see if the person might be a risk."

Another traditional attitude seems no less potent for being less publicly expressed: "Men always want sex, while women want a durable relationship." To the extent that both men and women believe in this attitude as a norm, the culturally typical dating game continues: Men press for sex, and women put them off while they are assessing the prospects for a satisfying and durable relationship (Roche, 1986; Knox & Wilson, 1981; Christopher & Cate, 1985).

> **A male student says:** *I don't push for sex when I'm getting to know a girl. I want to go with the flow and be responsive to what she wants. But I've had girls turn me down after the first date, and then I hear later that they thought I was a wimp because I didn't make a move on them.*

> **A female student says:** *There was this one guy who really put the moves on me on our second date. I was really mad. If that's all he wants, I don't want anything to do with him. He called back several times for another date, but I always turned him down. I lost respect for that relationship (or lack of it).*

What do men really think about sex on dates? According to research (Snyder et al., 1985, 1986), the men who expressed the most interest in casual sex also valued attractiveness in a partner more than character and were likely to be high self-monitors. That means they were very concerned with their approval rating in their peer groups, as in the male student's description of the pick-up scene on p. 18. They were good at social conversation, at dramatizing themselves, and at gaining attention. It makes sense that such an extraverted character type is fostered by American culture, in which selling oneself is a major avenue to success (see Riesman et al., 1950, "other-directedness"). Male peer groups typically reflect the attitudes of these more persuasive and entertaining members. The more introverted (or low self-monitoring) men who also have less interest in casual sex and more interest in closeness might not support the split in sexual attitudes, but would be unlikely to debate the issue in their peer groups.

Among men, being older and adhering less to traditional sex role expectations (Glick, 1985), strong religious connections (Roche, 1986), as well as being sexually inexperienced (Christopher & Cate, 1985) are all correlated with greater caution and respect when approaching sexuality. Experienced or not, many men are simply not ready to engage in intercourse until they feel physically and emotionally comfortable with the woman, which could take anywhere from a few days to many months. Unless under the influences of alcohol and peer pressure, most men do not become sexually aroused enough to ignore emotional discomfort or anxiety about rejection unless the woman is affectionate or sexually provocative herself (Grammer, 1990; Perper, 1985). On research questionnaires, men appear to want more sex sooner than women, but they indicate that sexual intimacy should come in stages, rather than all at once on the first date (Roche, 1986). In a recent study of Penn State students, males expected to have an average of 9 to 11 dates before their first sexual intercourse within a relationship, while females expected 15 to 18 dates before sex (Cohen & Shotland, 1996). Both men and women thought they were more cautious and conservative about sex than the average student. The women's expectations for their timing matched their experience, while the men's did not. Though both sexes agreed that it is best to get sexual when both people feel good about it, women may still need to put the brakes on men's desires for the timing of first intercourse.

> Men say that women "control" relationships by deciding **when** they will have sex. But men want sex sooner and more often than we do. Holding out for what we want is not "control," but wanting to feel right about the guy and where things are going. Sometimes I don't want to rush in too deep too fast. And I want to be able to say "I don't feel like having sex," without always being in control of what's happening.

A split in men's sexual attitudes.   Many college men seem to have a split in their sexual attitudes of the same sort as the traditional "Victorian split." In the nineteenth and early twentieth centuries in Western Europe and urban America, men weren't very sexually aggressive with the women they respected and married, but they could be quite abandoned with women of inferior status who were not considered "mate material." This parallels male student attitudes in a recent study (Kenrick et al, 1990). Males had about the same high standards for a mate as females, but they would settle for a lot less in a casual sex partner than females would. Compared to women, men also gave significantly lower average minimum requirements for **a partner for sex relations** than for an **exclusive dating partner** in nearly all areas except attractiveness. Male standards for a **casual sex partner** were even lower than for a **first date** in the following areas (from most, to least significantly lower): intelligent(!), easygoing, college graduate, popular, high social status. This does not imply that all college men have especially low standards for casual sex partners, but rather that a significant number say they do. Since intelligence is an important world-wide standard for mate selection (Buss, 1989), its appearance with social status in this survey suggests that some men typically put casual sex partners in a separate category for those who are not "mate material." For men with this "neo-Victorian" split in attitudes, there are two ways to approach women, as illustrated below.

> Debora was still a virgin. This slowed me down in pressing for sex. If we had sex, I wanted it to be when she was ready because it would be her first, which I believe is a special time for everyone when it happens. Since it would be her first, I felt if we did have sex that it would be an explicit statement of our commitment to each other.

> I pressed for sex rather than feelings from Sandra from the start. I believe girls usually get turned off by that. But I pushed more towards passion because I didn't fear losing her, so if I got it, good, and if I didn't, tough luck. I had gone out with Cathy for a year without ever having sex, but after two weeks with Sandra we were already in the sack.

What about women's attitudes?   Women have traditionally taken the lead in defining sex as a milestone of relationship progress. In Kenrick's survey (Kenrick et al., 1990), women indicated only slightly lower overall requirements for having sexual relations than for serious dating. This is consistent with the popular notion that most, but not all, college women consider having sex to be indicative of a serious relationship, and they will follow this guideline most, though not all of the time. If women once gave sex to get the security of love, they may still give in to their date's pressure for increasing sexual activity in order to keep them interested and to increase the possibility of a serious relationship (Knox & Wilson, 1983).

A recent study found that both college women and men were more likely to endorse casual sex when they thought it would make them more popular with other men (Levinson et al., 1995). After trying this approach to popularity, some young women have returned to a clear-cut sexual rule: No sex without love:

> If involved in a casual relationship I won't have sex. I used to, but I can't do that any more. I want to be loved exclusively by the person I sleep with and I can't get that in a casual relationship.

Other women may have a neo-Victorian split of their own. Kenrick's (1990) study indicates they may go to bed with some men they are unusually attracted to, despite those men being poor prospects for a serious partnership.

Casual sex is not something I practice, but I cannot say it's never happened. There was one guy I was attracted to the moment I saw him. It took a while before anything occurred, but it was still casual. I could have fun with him, but I didn't want to be with him all the time and didn't think of him often either.

Sexual aggression and date rape

Sexual aggression has been defined as engaging in a sexual activity against one's partner's will (Stets & Pirog-Good, 1989a). It ranges from mild (necking and fondling) to severe (genital sex acts under threat or use of force). Estimates of sexual aggression during dates vary from 15% to 78%, with both sexes inflicting it (men more) and receiving it (women more) (Stets & Pirog-Good, 1989a). Like sexual harassment, sexual aggression must be defined by the recipient, for it is only pressure or aggression if one doesn't like it. It is therefore likely that sexual aggression is under-reported by both recipients and perpetrators. It is estimated that mild male-inflicted sexual pressure may occur on about 15% of dates and female-inflicted pressure on 12%, with severe male pressure on about 10% and female on 4%. However, female pressure is more likely to occur in serious than in casual relationships, while male pressure begins in casual dating (Stets & Pirog-Good, 1989b). Over 95% of women reported being pressured into unwanted sexual behavior at least once (Christopher, 1988). Since sexual aggression is normally threatening, such incidents are likely to be long remembered and to have an effect on the recipient's subsequent attitudes and behavior. It is likely that a person who has once experienced very unpleasant sexual pressure will also experience subsequent incidents as more threatening.

One coed became very cautious with men:

This semester I have been thrown in with a group of "singles" and I don't like the way I've reacted. I'm much more inhibited and making a conscious effort not to be too friendly. I know exactly why I've reacted this way. It's because of a past experience when all hints and diplomatic acts of disinterest failed me and I was forced to be direct in fending off somebody's advances. I don't want to place myself in that position where I must sacrifice someone else's feelings to preserve my freedom. [Note that part of her distress derives from feeling bad about hurting the man's feelings when he ignored her indirect refusals, so there was no way for her to come away feeling good about her experience.]

Why do some men and women pressure others for sex, and sometimes unmercifully? Is the number of male initiators higher mainly because the male sex drive is more insistent, especially in adolescence? The presence of half to two-thirds as much sexual pressure initiated by women argues against such a simple biological explanation. We have suggested above (p. 24) that taking initiative to be in control over a situation is a common way for dealing with anxiety. A survey of most commonly experienced problems on dates (Knox & Wilson, 1983) found that the most significant differences between the sexes in reported problems were that 36% of women and no men mentioned potential or actual sexual aggression, while 43% more men than women were worried about communication or shyness. Perhaps some men turn their social anxiety on early dates into sexual pressure. Correlations have been found between a desire for interpersonal control and sexual aggression in both men and women (Stets & Pirog-Good, 1989b) and between social anxiety and severe sexual aggression in young men (Gwartney-Gibbs et al., 1987; Rapaport & Burkhart, 1984).

Of a nationwide random sample of over 3,000 women in 32 representative colleges, 15.3% had experienced sexual aggression that met the legal definition of rape. Of these victims, 10.6% had been raped by strangers, 9% by spouses or family members, 25% by non-romantic acquaintances, 21% by casual dates, and 30% by steady dates (Koss et al., 1988). Over half of the rape victims had been using intoxicants, as had two thirds of the aggressors. Only 5% of these rapes were ever reported to the police. A recent study of college men found 26% admitted having committed some form of sexual aggression, including 14% who had verbally coerced sexual intercourse and 10% who had attempted or completed rape (Abbey et al., 1998). Since over half of these rapes occurred in dating relationships, let us construct two generic stories of what most typically happens, based on descriptions derived from research data (Muehlenhard & Linton, 1987; Koss, 1988; Koss et al., 1988; Wilson et al., 1983; Muehlenhard & McCoy, 1991).

Her story: *It happened a couple of years ago, when I was 18. I went to a party with this guy I had dated a few times. We both had a bit to drink, though he had more than I did. We drove to my place, because it was closer. We were making out on the couch, and he was fondling my breasts, as he had done before. But I wasn't much into it, and when he started to go below the waist I pushed his hand away. He didn't stop, and he didn't pay any attention to me when I said no, that I didn't want to have sex. At first I tried to reason with him, but that didn't do any good. He pushed me down on the couch, and I started to get scared. I argued, pleaded, and finally tried to fight him off, but he only got more insistent and forceful. He was much stronger and just overpowered me. He seemed pretty drunk, and I was scared he'd hurt me. I should have screamed, but I didn't know what would happen if I did, and I knew it was partly my fault for getting into this spot. After a while I just gave up.*

Afterwards I was really mad at him, but I was mad at myself, too, and depressed, because I guess maybe I led him on and then changed my mind too late. I don't know if I'd really call it rape, because maybe I should have known better. Maybe every guy would do the same thing in that situation. I don't know. I finally told my girlfriend, but I didn't want anyone else to know (certainly not any authorities!). Things can get really nasty, and your reputation can be ruined for life if you press charges.

Most of the relationships in which the rape occurred (87%) eventually broke up. But 42% of the women had sex again with the offender, and 41%

said they expected similar incidents to happen again (Koss, 1988). Early experiences of sexual abuse may affect women's behavior so that they are more vulnerable to college-age date rape (Belcastro, 1982; White & Humphrey, 1992). But the men involved are likely to have experienced the event differently.

> **His story:** *This happened a couple of years ago, when I was 19. I took this chick I was dating to a party, and she really looked good. We had been getting hotter and hotter on each date, like we had already gone beyond heavy petting. When I saw she was wearing this cool sexy dress, I figured, "Tonight's the night." We both got pretty buzzed at the party, and then she said we'd better go to her house. About as soon as we got in the door, we were making out madly on the couch. About the time I went for her pants, she pushed my hand away. Now I'm not dense; I figured she'd been brought up prudish like all the rest, so she had to put up some resistance to prove she was a decent girl. They're all taught to put up a bit of a fight, so you'll want them more. She said no, but to this day I don't know if she meant "Don't! Stop!" or "Don't stop!" First she was into it, and then all of a sudden she was saying no and struggling. But at a certain point you lose the right to say no, and we were way past that point.*
>
> *Anyway, things got a little wild. She really didn't resist very much. She acted like she didn't like it. But when we went out again after that, we had sex again too. So she must have liked it, but she wouldn't say so, because it would spoil her good girl image. I've never told anybody about it, but I haven't got anything to hide. It was definitely not rape, not even close. If I ever get into the same situation again, I might do the same thing again. I can't help it if some women can't make up their minds whether they want to have sex or not.*

What kinds of people commit sexual aggression?   The man depicted above is far more hostile toward women than the vast majority of young men, who don't ever commit rape. According to research, men like him tend to be socially irresponsible, have more hostile attitudes toward their mothers and women in general, expect adversarial relations between the sexes, and accept traditional sex roles, rape myths (e.g., "women instinctively want to be raped"), and violence toward women (Bernard et al., 1985; Check & Malamuth, 1983; McCollaum & Lester, 1997; Rapaport & Burkhart, 1984; Wilson et al., 1983). They may also have reduced capacity for empathy and intimacy which may be linked to distressful childhood experience (Lisak & Ivan, 1995). On the other side, women who reported sexual aggression toward men (i.e., verbal pressure, sexual abuse, physical threats, or violence) also were likely to believe in adversarial relations between the sexes and to have experienced sexual abuse in the past (Anderson, 1997).

Sometimes the young man's confusion may be authentic (Marx & Gross, 1995), and his blaming of the woman may be understandable. In two studies (Muehlenhard & Hollabaugh, 1988; Muehlenhard & McCoy, 1991), 37% and 39% of college women admitted engaging in "token" or "scripted" refusal of sex in one or more first sexual encounters with men, that is, they said "no" when they meant "yes" to sex. The most common internal reasons given were fear of appearing promiscuous (which derives from the sexual double standard) and a desire to be the one in control. After 36% of these refusals sex did occur (Muehlenhard & McCoy, 1991). After 20% of the refusals the woman had indicated verbally or physically that she had changed her mind about refusing. But in the other 16% she either submitted silently and passively or continued to refuse—despite her admission on the subsequent questionnaire that she did want sex. These figures could translate to 6.2% of college women reporting they had willingly had sex without ever explicitly consenting, compared to 10.1% who have been raped by either a date or an acquaintance. Since two thirds of these token refusers had done it from a few to numerous times, the actual incidence of sexual intercourse involving insincere reluctance *might* be comparable to that of date rape (Muehlenhard & Hollabaugh, 1988). It doesn't follow, however, that men might have been exposed to pretended reluctance as often as to clear-cut refusal. Even if many college women say no sometimes when they are willing or unsure (Muehlenhard & Hollabaugh, 1988), it only shows that women sometimes have mixed feelings about having sex. On the other hand, college men's tendency to assume that a woman wants more sexual intimacy than she actually wants is strongly related to how much alcohol they regularly consume and less strongly to the number of their sexual experiences and to rape-supportive beliefs (Abbey et al., 1998).

What can women do about sexual aggression? Early research indicated that the single most effective thing which the woman in our scenario could have done was to scream (Bart & O'Brien, 1985; Levine-MacCombie & Koss, 1986). What else do college women say or do to resist sexual advances, and when do men understand that a "no" means no? In addition to a scream, another indicator of a "true" refusal may be the woman's physical resistance, which most men accept as a sign of their sincerity (Nurius et al., 1996). Judging from women's reports, the longer the resistance lasts, the more sincere it is; and there were no token refusal incidents reported in which physical resistance was continued all the way until intercourse (Muehlenhard & McCoy, 1991). Furthermore, another study found that college men are not confused about a direct verbal refusal, such as "I don't want to do this" (Motley & Reeder, 1995). But men in that study interpreted indirect refusals as significantly less resistant to sex than women did. The indirect refusals studied included "We can do other things, but not that," "I'm not sure we're ready for this yet," "It's against my religion," "It's getting late," "I'm seeing someone else," and more. Women were more reluctant to use direct than indirect refusals of sex because they expected their partners to be angry, hurt, and reactive and they feared negative effects on the relationship. But men's responses were significantly less negative than the women expected. They expected only to be "disappointed," whether the refusal was direct or indirect, and would not stop dating. So apparently women can afford to be direct when they don't want sex without worrying about the future of their relationship.

The painful wrestling match which the woman in our example has with blame illustrates a bind inherent in traditional sex role behavior. A man could push hard for sex without censure from his own gender, and it has been the woman's job to put on the brakes at the right time. If she were unable to stop him, then the woman could be censured for failing her own task and also for leading him on too much. Assertiveness training is needed to help young women learn how to communicate clearly when they don't want more sexual activity. The "plausible deniability" of indirect signals is too easily misinterpreted by men who see what they want to see in sexually suggestive situations. Too much alcohol or other intoxicants at a party may put a woman at risk, both because her own abilities are impaired (Harrington & Leitenberg, 1994), and because her date's self-control may be down, while his sexual expectations are up (Abbey et al., 1998).

Women who have suffered from date rape and other forms of sexual aggression need to talk about what happened (Koss, 1988), for two reasons. First, they are likely to be significantly more anxious and depressed than the average college woman, because they have endured a trauma (Koss et al., 1988). Talking about what happened is the single most effective strategy for their psychological healing. Second, the more the victims talk, the more the others in their environment will talk about such sexual aggression.

What can men do? College men often cite male peer pressure to get sex as a justification for their own aggression (Abbey et al., 1998). Therefore, widespread social disapproval of this behavior is needed, especially from other young men, as well as training to change the beliefs legitimizing sexual violence which are still held by some men (Muehlenhard & McCoy, 1991; Schewe & O'Donohue, 1996). Since male anti-feminist attitudes are closely associated with other attitudes conducive to sexual aggression (Truman et al., 1996), education toward equal rights and respect for women may be the best path available to reduce sexual aggression (Hall & Barongan, 1997).

Emotional management

How are emotions handled during casual dating? The first guideline that casual daters seem to follow with regard to emotions is "don't show any feeling that your partner isn't feeling too." After repeatedly exchanging plausibly deniable nonverbal indications of feeling (e.g., physical affection) couples may proceed to riskier verbal expressions. The possibility of dismissal without any possibility for discussion makes expressing strong positive or negative feelings very risky. Research confirms that in early relationships each person "manages" both positive and negative emotions by suppressing them more than later (Aune et al., 1996).

A male student says: *When feelings bubble up about the sex or the person, ignore them.*

A woman says: *Don't ever let a man know you want to see him again soon. It's the kiss of death to ask a man when he is going to call.*

Denial of emotions serves to protect this coed from anxieties and disappointments: *In a casual relationship, I'm not insecure or jealous as in a serious relationship. My attitude is simply that if he wants to go out with someone else, let him, because it's no great loss to me. This is mere fact.* [said with no apparent feeling.] *Where there is one, another can usually be found. Many times this is the best attitude to have because it shields you from undeserved pain; and in many cases the partner will be very grateful because you aren't putting any pressure on him to have feelings he might not have.*

This quotation shows how the casual dating culture has taught some people that they will be more desirable if they avoid expressing emotions and expectations for each other. What this woman is denying by making herself so "cool" is an emotional process the she mentions later: "I am a person who can sometimes fall in love too easily."

Many people seem to fall in love "too easily" to be able to keep moving comfortably into and out of potential mating situations for five, ten, or more years after they reach sexual maturity. So they overcome their budding love feelings and redefine them out of existence as a crush, infatuation, just lust, or even as an outright psychological defect. Staying out of love allows people control over their time, willpower, and choices in life.

> *After having a serious relationship, I have realized that I don't have the time to fulfill the obligations that are required. Having casual relations allows me to set the sex aside and finish . . . work obligations. Also, a casual relationship allows me to be in control, be able to say no to allowing the relationship to get serious.*

What are the effects of denying emotions? Some counselors believe "setting the sex aside" and limiting emotional involvement by denying one's own feelings and discouraging their expression in others runs contrary to human nature and gives rise to psychological problems. Cobliner (1988) suggests that avoiding emotional intimacy by staying "casual" even when sleeping together "clash[es] with the fundamental urge to form human attachments, . . . diminish[es] and often shut[s] out the experience of passion, rapture, and voluptuousness in sexual intercourse, and . . . bring[s] inner turmoil that weakens self-confidence" (p. 112). Specifically, denying emotions of attachment may contribute to depersonalization, a state of feeling adrift and out of touch with reality. One's feelings can also become flat and lifeless. A sex life of easy gratification without spontaneous emotions or much courtship, obstacles, and delays to make the heart grow fonder can become barren and meaningless (Cobliner, 1988; Crosby, 1991). Some young people state that after some years of experience, sexual relationships without love are unsatisfying and certain to be short-lived. But little research has been carried out on this issue (for an exception, see Hendin, 1975).

On the other hand, denial and the anti-anxiety effects of alcohol can also be viewed as valuable defense mechanisms for adolescents and young adults. They enable young adults to enjoy the fruits of sexual relationships in an exploratory way without the anxieties such intense experience could trigger. In a period when the young person is increasing his separation from parents and testing out paths of individuation, it may be useful for some to avoid dependency needs and other emotions that would compromise one's psychological freedom (Ehrlich, 1986). This approach does not appeal to people who believe sex belongs only in a committed relationship.

Attachment theory (Chapter 10) suggests that feelings can grow when personal needs are being consistently met, even when one denies that "love" is present. Often, all it takes is a reversal in the relationship for strong feelings to emerge. It is a common motif in movies and real life for the threat of loss to evoke passion, which shocks us out of the "casual" or "just friends" denial.

> Sharon and I were doing great, talking about everything, doing lots of things together. We were important to each other, but it was cool to see other people. But then her ex-fiancé called and wanted her back. He was far away, but she told me she wasn't going to let anything more happen between us that could lead me on romantically. Everything else was still cool. Now I can't figure out how to live with that, and I can't get her out of my mind. I can't sleep. I'm jealous, but I shouldn't be. It's driving me crazy.

How casual relationships end

A casual dating relationship can end either by becoming serious or through disengagement. Since we will discuss more serious relationships later, only disengagements concern us here. In one study of 48 breakups of casual dating relationships (Loyer-Carlson, 1989) 54% pointed to a desire for independence, with almost always (92% of the 54%) one person wanting more from the relationship than the other. The rest of those breaking up either cited disagreeable characteristics of their partner as their main reason, or relationship problems that couldn't be resolved (22% each). Since the unresolvable relationship problems may have been negotiated and worked on for some time before the breakup occurred, this type of breakup will be dealt with in our deepening stage rather than casual dating. After all, many deepening or serious relationships may be defined as casual in conformity with contemporary customs.

> Finally, at some point in all my casual relationships it comes to a head, the other person wanting a commitment. This always happens but sometimes can be resolved with a simple "I'm not ready to get involved," but not always, and it ends.

Some students don't consciously draw the line at falling in love, but they do still find themselves discouraging and dissolving relationships in which the other person starts "wanting too much" or acting "clingy" or possessive because of love. Those who don't want their casual relationships to get too serious often assign low priority to their dating relationship (Loyer-Carlson, 1989), or refuse to commit to any sort of exclusivity (Baxter & Bullis, 1986; Lloyd & Cate, 1985) or to make any changes in their friendships, time schedule, or other commitments in life. Therefore, these issues are important in the deepening stage to be discussed in the next chapter.

Resistance to being in love. Many casual relationships end because one or both partners is too frightened or unwilling to be in love. Caught between the associations of love and marriage and current norms about keeping things casual during our college years, many students struggle with a mental definition of love that welds feelings to an overwhelming commitment (Fehr, 1988). The impact which this attitude can have on a relationship is spelled out in the following account by a career-minded coed:

> *I was one of those people who believed that love had to equal commitment and marriage. I would say, "How do you know when you're 'in love'—how do you know when you're ready to spend the rest of your life with someone?"*
>
> *My last relationship lasted almost six months. We were so afraid of our feelings, and I think we both had to fight getting too close to each other.*
>
> *We couldn't just enjoy the relationship because things were so good between us that we were drawn closer. I told myself that I couldn't let myself fall in love. I think I would do things to distance myself from him because I had to prove that I couldn't love him. He wouldn't like me pulling away, so he would move closer, and then he would feel just as scared as I did and back away.*
>
> *Finally, neither of us could deal with it any more. We turned our confused feelings into anger and argued about something trivial (but blew it out of proportion) and decided to stop seeing each other. Of course we did this over the phone. It was like we both knew that if we tried to break up in person we'd never be able to do it!*
>
> *I couldn't understand why I couldn't get him out of my mind, because I told myself that I wasn't in love with him . . . [Finally] I realized that I did love him. I still have a fear of admitting it. However, it does feel good to be able to admit that I do have those feelings and to know that I don't have to worry about having them or feel guilty about it.*

This account may be typical for long-lived casual dating relationships. Disowned emotional involvement may be felt as fear and confusion, and acted out in approach/avoidance behavior and anger. Then love feelings are finally felt as obsessive longing only after termination brings the paradox of safety and loss. Resistance to love can also become acute in conflicts about initiating sexual relations.

> *Fred had a reputation of being with a lot of women and I was wary of him. We had been going out for a long time before we finally made love. I never felt like I had to do anything and when we made love I felt so free and giving. I was not nervous at all; it seemed so natural to be with him. Fred, on the other hand,*

was nervous, almost like it was his first time instead of mine. In a way it was, because before me he only conquered women, he never made love with any- one.

A week after we were together he told me that he picked up a woman in a bar and that he never wanted to see me again. I was shattered; I just couldn't believe that it was happening. Since that time we have both moved away from home. He calls and writes to tell me how sorry he is for doing what he did to me. He says that he was so afraid of what he felt that he didn't know what to do so he ran. It's so weird because at first I talked and wrote to him, at the time when I hated him the most. But now I just don't do anything and don't feel anything toward him.

Again we see how love can turn into anger when it is feared and avoided. Perhaps these same emotional dynamics are present in many of the casual relationships that end due to unequal involvement (Loyer-Carlson, 1989). The less involved partner may be fearing while the more involved is fuming. The reversal of denied love into hate might also contribute to some of the other kinds of casual dating breakups by fueling one person's dislike for the other's character traits or by intensifying differences and problems into a break up. It is difficult to establish empirically just how much the failure to cope with love feelings contributes to relationship decay in these early stages. For when one asks people to account for their terminations, one doesn't get raw feelings, but rather thoughts and thinking about feel- ing. Pure feelings do not come clothed in words, and "the heart has its reasons which reason knows nothing of" (Pascal, 1670/1966). Certainly love is a powerful force, so fending it off may disrupt our emotional equilibrium as much as falling into it.

Chapter summary

- Concepts of love relationships evolve from assuming they are mi- raculous and permanent to experiencing a journey of development in which perspectives will change.
- Relationship knowledge is pursued through the disciplines of An- thropology; Biological, Clinical, Social, and Evolutionary Psychol- ogy; Cognitive Neuroscience; Communications; Family Studies; Fam- ily Therapy; History; Sociology; and Sociobiology.
- Dividing young adult romantic relationships into 6 stages—initiat- ing, casual dating, being in love, deepening, decay, and termina- tion—helps us focus on how key processes change.
- Meeting a stranger launches slightly more relationships than gradual development with someone familiar. This may reflect arousal, un- usualness, and mystery versus familiarity.
- Despite perceptions that "what is beautiful is good," physical attrac- tion may be only a threshold for romantic interest. But short men

and tall or fat women are often considered unattractive.

- Apparent similarity may be another threshold in attraction. But expressions of liking are more attractive than similarity. Unusualness, mystery, and physiological arousal are situational factors.
- Attracting behaviors include signaling one's presence, gender, and harmlessness, matching body rhythms and movements, and gazing, blinking, and dilated pupils (possible altered consciousness).
- Men feel anxious about making the first moves. Women signal their receptivity with plausible deniability and may draw men out, but not like the resulting information and attraction.
- Vulnerable self-esteem leads young adults to like anyone who approaches them. Playing hard to get only works when the pursuer has hope for success.
- One-night stands may involve low self-esteem as often as loneliness, and men know the choice for sex rests with the woman, while women's agendas vary.
- Casual dating, group socializing, and being "just friends" allow exploring commonalities while avoiding romantic commitments. Casual relationships normally last two to four months before ending or changing.
- The double standard for sexual behavior has not completely disappeared. But both men and women may have split attitudes toward casual and courtship sex.
- Sexual aggression and date rape usually involve drinking and some prior sex play. Female victims react with anger, distress, and self-blame, while male offenders self-justify with gender-war and rape-myth beliefs. The double standard leads some women to say "no" to sex when they mean "maybe" or "yes," and men to misread these signals of ambivalence.
- Casual daters typically avoid some intimate topics and feelings, so romance flourishes more in long-distance relationships. They break up because of unequal involvement or when a partner cannot cope with intimate feelings which their closeness engenders.

Love and relationship development 2

- **The In-Love Stage**
  What is Romantic Love?
  The Breakthrough in Communication
  Union and Separation
  Thinking and Feeling
  Anger, Power, and Control
- **The Deepening Stage**
  What Do We mean by Deepening?
  Social Penetration Theory
  From In Love to In Doubt
  Loss of Independence and Balance
  Possessiveness
  The Dynamic of Union and Separation

The in-love stage

What is romantic love?

There are many different approaches to defining and understanding love, which we will explore in Chapter 10. In order to begin discussing what *romantic* love is, we will divide it here into three main components—**passion, intimacy, and commitment** (Sternberg 1987, 1988). The **passion** component refers to the **motivations** that lead to romance, including attraction and sex, but also other needs, such as self-esteem, closeness, and self-actualization. For example, a person who had an insecure childhood in a chaotic family might be strongly drawn to a partner with a warm, accepting family. Passion includes the many **emotions** we feel toward our partner, such as yearning, shyness, vulnerabili-

FALLING IN LOVE!

ty, admiration, and excitement. Thus passion is the **emotional** and **motivational** component of love.

The **intimacy** or **behavioral** component refers to actions and behaviors done together that promote closeness, including mutual support and understanding, communication, and sharing ourselves, our activities, and our possessions. Chapter 10 lists 13 kinds of intimacy.

The **commitment** component refers to the short-term decision to label our attitude toward another as love and also the long-term decision to try to maintain that love into the foreseeable future. Thus commitment involves cognitive acts, rather than emotions, and may include conscious intention and willpower. So commitment is a cognitive component of love.

If complete love consists of passion, intimacy, and commitment we can define **being in love** as a feeling state most closely associated with the passion factor. The **"instant intimacy"** of highly emotional encounters can lead us to fall in love. We can also feel the passion and euphoria of love after minimal or misleading contact with a stranger. Since we don't have any scientifically neutral criteria for distinguishing **being in love** from the mildly negative term **infatuation**, we consider them equivalent. Table 2.1 outlines many features of the in love state.

The in-love state may be associated with several neurochemicals, as we will see in Chapter 9. However, the recognition that love exists is influenced by our culture. Because of the strong association between love and commitment to marriage in America (Fehr, 1988), admitting that one is in love typically plays a part in the transition from casual to serious dating. For many, "love at first sight," the first few weeks of sexual intimacy, or the first period of separation and reunion can be the most intense and passionate (Table 2.1, #2, #3, #4, #6, and #9). Others may deepen their relationships without ever noticeably being in love. But a period of highly emotional attraction and love, with or without sexual passion, often forms a major watershed in the life of a relationship. Though sexual relations may lead people to feel in love, new lovers typically value the emotional closeness more than the sex (Fisher, 1998), as in these two disclosures:

> I fell in love in four out of six of my relationships. I passed the limit of casual dating when I would say "I love you" before the other person was able to say it back. My partner would shy away from me for a while and then come back when she found me truthful. All four became serious.
>
> There was no commitment to begin with, but after Fran began spending two or

TABLE 2.1. Psychophysical properties of being in love

1. The beloved has **special meaning**, and one is unable to feel romantic passion for more than one person at a time.
2. **Intrusive thinking** about the beloved, obsession.
3. **Idealization**, accentuating positive and overlooking or misperceiving native qualities.
4. **Unstable psychophysiological responses:** exhilaration, euphoria, shyness, increased energy, sleeplessness, anxiety, etc.
5. Longing for **emotional reciprocity and union**.
6. **Emotional dependency**: hope, hypersensitivity to cues, jealousy, fear of rejection, mood swings with relationship.
7. **Empathy, responsibility** toward the beloved, willingness to **sacrifice** for the beloved.
8. **Reordering daily priorities** to be available and desire to **make an impression** on **beloved** by changing habits or values.
9. **Adversity intensifies passion** in the relationship.
10. **Sexual desire** coupled with desire for **sexual exclusivity**.
11. **Precedence of craving for emotional union** over desire for sexual union.
12. Experience of romantic passion as **involuntary and** uncontrollable.

Source: Abridged from Fisher, 1998.

three nights a week at my apartment (without sex), I was willing to not date anyone else. I was completely engulfed in the relationship we were forming, not wanting or needing anyone else. I am very certain that she felt the same, but neither of us expressed how we felt.

Is there a fast and a slow form of falling in love? Emotions come and go quickly, while thinking about love can take much longer. Love at first sight is considered rare. But there is no hard and fast standard for assessing the feelings involved in love. Strong initial feelings may be discounted as infatuation or lust, rather than called love. Over 2,300 years since Plato, we are still not sure whether love is divine or insane.

Many love researchers subscribe to the "thinking comes first" hypothesis. They believe that love feelings develop gradually from two people thinking about relationship experiences and developing a common interpretation of what they mean to each other, which includes a desirable future together (Duck, May, 1991). On the other hand, those who study emotions, physiological arousal, or sociobiology (and most adventure movies) usually portray love as arriving suddenly or by fits and starts. Perhaps a key factor in the experience of **rapid falling in love** is **feeling out of control**. This could account for the formerly reluctant heroine in many adventure movies falling in love with the hero after he saves her from imminent death. It also applies to "falling for" someone who intention-

ally or unintentionally controls the relationship, and thus passionately loving someone who may turn out to be bad for our well-being. Passion may arise from circumstances beyond our control, such as when Romeo and Juliet's parents prohibited them from seeing each other, and when military furloughs allow for only the briefest romances.

Love probably comes both ways, quickly and slowly, with steps forward and backward which are both emotional and cognitive in nature, whether acknowledged or not. If you are used to falling in love quickly, a slower growth of feelings may convince you that this partner is a mediocre fit. On the other hand, if you usually develop your feelings slowly, a partner's early declaration of love may seem calculated or unstable. Depending on your habits and history, a feeling rush of your own could mean "something's not right," or "this could be the start of something really big." Most of us got very little explicit education about what love feels like on the inside. Teenage girls typically read and talk quite a bit about love, while boys' discussions are centered on lust. Yet in one study college men reported falling in love earlier in a relationship than women (Rubin et al., 1986).

In addition to being out of control, **jealousy** and **longing** are among the feelings men most readily identify as part of love. For they are not lust, yet they are potent enough to force themselves into awareness without being invented or dominated by thinking.

> When she went away for the holidays I missed her terribly. I hated it and called her almost every day. I've never felt this way with anyone else. It was scary and amazing. Looking back now, I guess it was love.

Yet jealousy and longing can be devalued as "insecurities," just as euphoria is discounted as "infatuation." Thus, love feelings may well occur in most long-lasting couple relationships, even if they are never recognized as such and never allowed to develop.

The breakthrough in communication

Where the casual stage was characterized by reticence and self-control of feeling expression, the first mutual expressions of love can act like bursting a dam. Suddenly it is acceptable to express all the positive feelings that one held back in order not to "lead the partner on" or commit oneself beyond the safety of plausible deniability. As soon as both partners have agreed to define their feelings as love, they are likely to reveal that their casual dating period was seething with romantic desires.

Expressing love feelings creates a euphoria that is contagious. If one partner does not feel like joining in the feelings, he or she will get very uncomfortable and try to squelch the other or withdraw. If both partners are in love, they are likely to share many attitudes, including strong emotional and physical attraction to and idealization of each other, and generosity and concern for the other's well-being, along with an increased willingness to sacrifice one's own priorities for the partner's benefit (Hendrick & Hendrick, 1988). Since common experience and preliminary evidence (Hendrick & Hendrick, 1988) indicates that most people feel the same things when they are in love, it makes sense that new lovers would experience being "on the same wavelength" (Duck, May, 1991) and find it natural to respond with complete understanding and acceptance. Often experiences that seem like mind-reading occur to further this euphoric sense of union and harmony: "I was just going to say that!"

The new lovers' experience of unconditional acceptance can transform the way they live. This experience motivates them to trust each other and to assume that they can always return to this idyllic state in the future. The belief that they are completely and unconditionally accepting of each other is a powerful double-edged sword for the lovers, for they will be all the more outraged later when inevitable differences reduce the scope of their acceptance. But they may still be able to recover the **feelings** of acceptance and harmony they once had by working out, compromising on, or shelving their differences and reenacting their feelings of union. The idealization of their acceptance and trust at this time provides an anchor and a hope during all the adjustments to come (Wallerstein, 1995).

Union and separation

New lovers normally "wish above all things the embraces of the other and . . . to carry out all of love's precepts in the other's embrace" (Capellanus, 1184/1941). Time spent together can intensify the in-love experience, if the pair spontaneously agree on everything they do and say. However, new lovers who move in together immediately often find their passion quickly fades or turns into bickering over privacy and autonomy. In a study of easy sexual intimacy in college (Hendin, 1975), men were more inclined than women to be romantic, but the romance was felt toward the "far-off, unavailable woman," rather than those who were present and available.

Thus alternation between separation and togetherness is vital to the new lovers' experience. The temporary obstacles of being separated by the constraints of real conditions allow the partners to alternately dwell on their love states alone and then bring those feelings to what they do together. Euphoric anticipation makes the experience of the couple together more intense. Love poems, love songs, and love letters are composed (or chosen from popular sources) when the lovers are apart. The meanings in these love documents are likely to be enshrined as monuments to the couple's love that will have the power to renew their early faith and euphoria for decades.

Just being together and dwelling on feelings can contribute more to love than having sex. This may come as a surprise to some people who have grown up since the sexual revolution.

> *Within a week of dating we had some pretty intense "lovemaking" sessions without having gone all the way. When we finally did it was the most incredible experience, because as we were getting off physically it seemed as though we were fused spiritually. It was the first time that I had ever experienced love-making on something more than a physical level.*

New lovers are fond of going to great lengths and sacrifices for each other, which reinforces the specialness of their relationship and bears witness to the new persons they have become. Like love documents, specific and dramatic romantic (gallant, generous, surprising, beautiful, loving, risky, funny) acts done at this time are recorded as milestones in the budding love, to be recalled or repeated later when the love feelings need refreshing (Cate, May, 1991). Being in love has long been reputed to bring about great changes in people.

> *It can endow a man even of the humblest birth with nobility of character; it blesses the proud with humility; and the man in love becomes accustomed to performing many services gracefully for everyone. . . . It adorns a man . . . with the virtue of chastity, because he who shines with the light of love can hardly think of embracing another woman, even a beautiful one.* (Capellanus, 1184/ 1941)

Preliminary research (Hendrick & Hendrick, 1988) concurs with much of what Capellanus says. New lovers are much less inclined to play around with love (ludic style in Chapter 10). They feel better about themselves and delight in generous service, at least to their beloved (agapic style). They also have increased self-esteem and sense of competence (Aron, Paris, & Aron, 1995) and are less concerned with the approval of others. And they are less inclined to feel bored and seek excitement or sensations (Hendrick & Hendrick, 1988), perhaps because their love is such a renewable source of emotional arousal.

The combination of experiences of union with the joys of anticipation often leads new lovers to construct fantasies of a future together and even of marriage; disclosing such fantasies may be embarrassing because they are premature by rational standards. Yet it is exciting to confess these fantasies, because the thrilling embarrassment is usually reinforced by the partner's response that he or she has felt the same way.

Thinking and feeling

New lovers definitely see each other through rose-colored glasses, admiring and idealizing each other (Hendrick & Hendrick, 1988). New lovers are pervasively present in each other's thoughts (Alapack, 1984), thus prolonging the state of union by recreating it in revery. Medieval authority Capellanus (1184/1941) stated that love was *caused* by "excessive meditation on the beauty" of the other, and *resulted* in "every act . . . end[ing] in the thought of his beloved . . . " Modern theorists agree that dwelling on ideas of union with the beloved, along with the resulting euphoria, are fundamental to being in love (Brehm, 1988; Person, 1988).

" ...NEW LOVERS JOIN EACH OTHER EMOTIONALLY... "

New lovers are likely to experience some emotions more intensely than ever before, especially if they are young adults in their first great love (Alapack, 1984). It is not the intensity of sexual pleasure but the ongoing state of being in love that exposes young people to the overwhelming attachment feelings that set the stage for an emotional education that can't be turned off. Even when we have already experienced similar feelings in previous romances, we are likely to experience our new feelings as unique.

Anger, power, and control

Two areas of feeling and thinking are usually underrepresented during the in-love state: anger and power/control. As new lovers we often choose not to pursue petty irritations or express any anger we might feel. We experience anger, irritation, and differences as painful disturbances to our inner state of euphoria, safety, and belonging together. Therefore we enjoy letting go of them, and we forget them as soon as possible. We may also react to shorter experiences of anger, differences, or distress by accentuating the positive harmony to which we yearn to return. Thus both denial of negative feelings and their heightening of emotional arousal contribute to the compelling nature of roller-coaster romances.

Incidents do occur in which one partner controls what the couple will do. Sometimes one partner actually controls almost every aspect of the relationship. But new lovers often welcome such experiences. Being out of control supports the euphoria of union, and surrendering ourselves to our partner's wishes feels good and underlines the specialness of our altered state of love. We do not usually start evaluating the balance of power in the relationship until the euphoria fades a bit and our rose-colored glasses start to turn clear.

As an exception, new lovers are often irritated when obstacles prevent them from individually enjoying the blissful feeling of harmonious union inside. Thus they can be quite hostile when confronted with some "sobering" (that is, disturbing) details about their partner.

Conclusion

Being in love is unquestionably a peak experience, and it can come and go over a period of several years. (We will discuss how long passionate love normally lasts in Chapter 9.) But it is not the beginning of an endless plateau of euphoric union. Love begins a far-reaching transformation of our personalities, our lives, and every other close relationship we have. We will survey this transformation and its issues below.

The deepening stage

The paths that relationships take after casual dating are so varied that it is difficult to sketch a general development. Empirical studies of newlyweds have found three (Cate, Huston, & Nesselroade, 1986) or four (Christopher & Cate, 1985; Surra, 1985a) general types of relationship trajectories. These types were categorized by the overall length of the premarital period and types of changes in the couples' own estimated probability of marriage as they recounted what happened in their relationships. The four trajectories were

1. rapid,
2. gradual,
3. mixed slow and rapid rise in commitment, and
4. more frequent downturns later in the development.

We don't know if these types of paths are also present in other relationships that result in alternatives to marriage or that eventually terminate. Since we cannot explore all these paths, we will focus on the issues and processes found in people's descriptions and reflected in the most common relationship turning points found in the research. The turning point types in Table 2.2 reflect some of the most significant **processes** that propel or impede relationship development. By understanding these issues and processes, we may be able to achieve more of what we want in each relationship, whether it be progression, stability, or disengagement. We will focus on the same processes we studied in Chapter 1, relating to fundamental issues of intimacy, autonomy, and interdependence, and highlighting emotions, self-awareness, communication, and power.

What do we mean by deepening?

Our term "deepening phase" corresponds with "serious dating" or "considering and being a couple" (Christopher & Cate, 1985). But with the increase in cohabitation and high commitment noncohabiting relationships in today's society, it is no longer appropriate to assume that relationship growth is always directed from lesser toward greater estimated chance of marriage (as in Lloyd & Cate, 1985, and Surra, 1985b). Nor should we continue to assume that greater emotional involvement, greater intimacy, and estimated commitments more closely resembling marriage are all the same, or always develop together at the same rate (Duck et al., 1991). By empha-

TABLE 2.2. Main types of turning points in relationship commitment, according to retrospective accounts

Turning point type	Mean % change in commitment*	Standard deviation	Occur in stage	Our issues discussion
Get-to-know time	+21.13	17.59	Casual	
Quality time	+15.18	13.07	In love, deep.	Time priorities
Passion	+20.35	17.56	In love, deep. Decay, term.	Passion-affairs, sex, Getting back together
Exclusivity	+19.21	21.91	Deepening	Possessiveness
External competition	−13.44	23.83	Deepening	Competing relationships
Disengagement[1]	−23.28	26.74	Deep., decay	Backing off, withdraw
Making up[2]	+21.60	28.85	Deep., decay	Communication, getting back together
Physical separation	−0.30	22.69	Deepening	Long distance
Reunion	+10.72	21.28	Deep., decay	Long distance, Getting back together
Positive psychic change[3]	+18.98	20.00	Not tied to	Too individual to discuss,
Negative Psychic Change	−9.00	13.96	couple life	Long distance
Sacrifice[4]	+17.61	14.70	In love, deep.	Supporting relations
Serious commitment[5]	+23.26	24.78	Deepening	Communication, long distance

* Percentage commitment means percentage of commitment to a serious and exclusive relationship projected to continue into the forseeable future, but need not lead to marriage.
1. Disengagement means relationship deescalation, including a breakup.
2. Making up means repairing a relationship after disengagement or breakup.
3. Positive & Negative Psychic Changes are the respondent's attitude changes not catalyzed by relationship events.
4. Sacrifice means providing crisis help to a partner with a problem or giving or receiving gifts or favors.
5. Serious Comitment refers to couple decisions to move in together or make marital plans.
Source: Baxter & Bullis, 1986

sizing deepening, we shall focus our attention on processes leading to greater emotional involvement and intimacy, instead of to engagement and marriage. Much of what we will discuss cannot be based on existing empirical research, because the details of emotional involvement and relevant processes are only partially conscious and may be different from the partners' reconstructions of what went on.

Our preference for examining emotional processes over formal commitments reflects a recent shift in cultural norms toward expecting greater intimacy. Many middle-aged couples have made explicit commitments and kept them, without facing many of the issues involved in today's definition of intimacy. For example, a recent study of marital conflict found most of the older couples in the sample (average age 39) were "pseudointimate," while the "intimates'" average age was 30 (Prager, 1991). Intimacy also is a higher value for college students, who are likely to rate concepts related to intimacy as most central to the meaning of love (Aron & Aron, 1994). Some couples now deal openly with issues of communication, autonomy, priorities, and interdependence which would not have occurred to their parents' generation. Yet they may conclude that they do not want to stay together for a lifetime. Thus, deepening is a different process from growth in commitment. It doesn't go **up**, toward a 100% chance of marital commitment, but rather **in**, to involve increasing layers of a person's psychological being. Deepening may not proceed gradually, either, for resolving tensions or opposing attitudes may suddenly change thoughts, feelings, and behavior and usher in new forms for the relationship (Duck & Montgomery, 1991).

Social penetration theory

Psychologists Altman and Taylor developed a theory about deepening and communication in social relationships (1973). They described the process of relationship development among any two people as **social penetration**, or increasing self disclosure.

The progressive deepening of social communication can be divided into four stages. The first two, **orienting** and **exploratory affective exchange**, would roughly correspond to our initiating and casual dating stages. The third, **affective exchange**, would begin with declarations of love and expand in our deepening stage. The fourth, **stable exchange**, occurs in trusting, committed partnerships, friendships, and close family relationships. Along with the deepening of self-disclosure and sharing of emotions, other aspects of communication also increase as one progresses through the stages. There are more shared in-jokes, mutually understood gestures or glances, and private references to past experiences, and more nonverbal communication, such as touching and teasing. Communication becomes more accurate and efficient, since partners are more tuned into each other, know what verbal and nonverbal cues mean, and can predict what their partner means or will do or say with a higher degree of accuracy.

However, research shows that relationship development does not just proceed in a straight line toward deeper and broader communication. Changing needs for personal privacy act as a counter force against the drive for openness, since we continue to need both closeness and separateness (Altman et al., 1981). In addition, decaying relationships don't experience a reversal of social penetration stages, as was expected at first. Instead, research finds an increase in avoidance of disclosure **and** an increase in sharing both negative and positive disclosures and feelings (Baxter, 1983). Thus, deepening of communication involves contradictory tendencies throughout relationships, which can continue right up to termination.

Deepening begins with the dramatic transformation of being in love, which songs have likened to a rebirth. At its most fundamental level, **the deepening phase takes up the task of integrating the new selves and new couple experience of the new lovers with the worlds in which they each lived before they met**. The ideal harmony of being in love is only a temporary vacation from everyday reality. Then the couple's first challenges begin with issues of self-in-couple and couple-in-world which will recur throughout their relationship.

From in love to in doubt

According to American tradition, after the honeymoon comes a great **disillusionment**. As they settle in to everyday life together, the newly married couple begins to lose their romantic idealization of each other.

> Most of us marry while we are in love. . . . The sexual excitement, the uncertainties and novelties of the new relationship, actually lift us out of ourselves for a time. With the best will in the world we cannot during the falling-in-love stage show ourselves to our beloved as we really are, nor see our beloved's everyday personality. We are quite genuinely not our everyday selves at this period. We are more intense, more vital than usual. (Levy & Munroe, 1938)

Now that regular sexual relations prior to marriage and long nonmarital relationships and cohabitation are quite common, we are likely to experience some of this disillusionment well before the traditional honeymoon. Popular wisdom suggests that "what goes up must come down." This implies that the higher our euphoric idealization is while in love, the more painful the disappointment will be. Research has not explored this area yet, but personal accounts indicate that disappointment can damage or destroy a budding relationship.

Many different incidents can trigger disappointment, including even the proverbial hair in the sink or toilet seat left up. Unknown to the offender, trivial incidents may be interpreted as sloppy, inconsiderate, and indicative of serious character flaws. Anger that has been hidden while in love can surface at the first unmistakable disappointment to intensify our reaction. When not expressed, these feelings may percolate into our overall evaluation of our partner and the relationship (Canary & Cupach, 1988), lending negativity to several minor differences or complaints. **Thus, the first "realistic" reevaluation may not be realistic at all, but a negative backlash driven by disappointment and anger.** If we don't discuss the negative reevaluation with someone (not necessarily our partner) who can help separate real issues from their emotional charge, we may suddenly back away from the relationship. Or we may retaliate against our unsuspecting partner in ways that lead to escalating hurts and revenge acts in an atmosphere of distrust. Then we may each blame the other for a breakup. A student traces his gradual devaluation of his new love:

> As Ellen was allowing herself to fall deeper and deeper into the relationship (she was really very happy and so was I for the most part), I was beginning to notice little incompatibilities between us, and to dwell upon them in my internal thoughts. I was having a great time with her, and was happy to be in a relationship because it seemed to cure my loneliness, so I overlooked and ignored my negative thoughts for then. . . . One of the things which I had noticed that bothered me about Ellen was her insecurity. With the combination of my doubts and her insecurity, the stage was set for a breakup.

This man's label of "insecurity" diminishes his respect for his partner. If he had interpreted her behavior as "highly responsive to my presence and absence," or as "totally into me," he might have preserved his respect. When he distanced himself in response to her desire for reliable access to him, he was increasing her uncertainty. Thus, they could have discovered that her **pursuing** and his **distancing** were both part of the same couple dance. Here is another reevaluation with a different outcome:

> Ever since Prince Charles and Princess Diana had the royal wedding, I have been waiting for a prince to sweep me off my feet. Then I met Frank, who was born in England and was as princely as my heart and soul desired. However, this began to get on my nerves rather quickly. He was too proper, too generous, and too much like a gentleman. Was this what I wanted in life? I think not.
>
> Well, for once in my life I am happy that one of my ideals has collapsed. Frank has a genuine temper, tells people off, and dresses in torn blue jeans. . . <u>I find that romance is what you make of it, not what is given to you</u> [emphasis added]. By having the chance to experience a princely gentleman, I discovered that ideals are much less fulfilling than reality. Thank God that behind my Prince Charles was a good old country boy.

Loss of independence and balance

After a period of joyously bending many priorities to be together, new lovers may gradually begin to fear their loss of independence. The intensity of this fear is related to family background, previous relationships, and gender socialization. Men are socialized to experience themselves as independent individuals in control of their time. Today's college women also may feel a great need to preserve their independence as a support for pursuing their own careers.

These background factors are conducive to different responses to rising interdependence in each gender. Men are likely to start fearing union with their partners sooner than women, as the man's account of the woman's "insecurity" above may reflect. But they may remain unconscious of their anxiety, because they may automatically extend their approach to self-control to include making all the major choices for the couple. The man may experience his new couple identity as **the woman joining him on his life path,** as in the Biblical Ruth's statement "whither thou goest, I will go." Thus he may pursue a male-dominant relating style and remain unaware of his motivation as long as the woman fits in by being submissive. But if the woman does not "put her life on hold" in order to surrender, then a struggle for power may ensue that brings both discomfort and greater awareness.

Some young women may appear compliant and submissive because they learned to read people's needs and desires and adjust to them without being asked. But if their partner is not as responsive as their mothers once were, they are likely to complain about this lack of support and closeness. This complaint can trigger their men to fear losing their balance through too much emotional intimacy. On the other hand, if a young woman is building a separate self on her way to her own career, she may identify her new love relationship as a hypnotic temptation to give up her developing self to fit in with her man's path. In that case, she is likely to be consciously afraid of "losing herself" in the relationship. And she may respond by pulling back or by attempting to control attitudes and events, just as the man might. Thus, men are socialized to expect to be in control, so are less likely to be aware of their controlling actions. But women may be more consciously pulled both ways, toward self-surrender and automatic adaptation, as well as toward control of themselves and of the relationship.

What was experienced as glorious self-surrender in the early days of new love begins to feel like powerlessness when other life priorities prevent the couple from responding gladly to each other's every desire. When faced with conflicting demands of everyday reality, partners may be unable to respond to each other's feelings much of the time. That is when they start to notice how powerless they are to control the emotions their love has aroused. In a culture oriented toward individualism and self-control, this helplessness is often regarded as a weakness, as dependence or codependence. The earliest known wisdom about love's power over people is found in the Chinese Book of Changes, the "I Ching" (1950), developed between 2200 and 1150 B.C., and worked on by both Confucius and Lao Tzu. Section 61, "Inner Truth," suggests that sharing the center of our being with another **is** destabilizing, but not blameworthy. It is a fact of life.

> *Here the source of a man's strength lies not in himself but in his relation to other people. No matter how close to them he may be, if his center of gravity depends on them, he is inevitably tossed to and fro between joy and sorrow. Rejoicing to high heaven, then sad unto death—this is the fate of those who depend upon an inner accord with other persons whom they love. Here we have only the statement of the law that this is so. Whether this condition is felt to be an affliction or the supreme happiness of love, is left to the subjective verdict of the person concerned.* (p. 238)

Anyone feeling helpless may attempt to regain self-control. One way to do this is by controlling the relationship and the partner (**possessiveness**).

Possessiveness

> *Never be possessive. If a female friend lets on that she is going out with another man, be kind and understanding. Tell her 'Kath, you must go right ahead and do what you feel is right.' Unless you actually care for her, in which case you must see to it that she has no male contact whatsoever.* (Friedman, 1977)

When approached from our inner experience of being unable to control our feelings in love, possessiveness appears to be an attempt to insure reliable access to our beloved and to guarantee that he or she will remain constant in affection. Since our experience of harmonious union is conducive to fantasies of "forever after," we often want reassurance that we can be united whenever we wish. In order to reduce our anxiety over feelings we cannot eliminate, we may try to control our partner's behavior.

> **A woman says:** *Whenever Jerry would be gone for a few days I would be so jealous wondering what he was doing and who he was with. It used to drive me crazy not knowing what to think . . . I would use anything I could to have some kind of control over him. I'd do all kinds of things for him just so he'd feel somewhat in my debt.*

> **Another woman says:** *Jay's friends would say they liked him when he was by himself, but if he was around me with them he wanted my attention and would get upset if he did not get it. I felt like I was trapped inside of Jay's box, and he would not let me out. He questioned me about people, who I was with and what I was doing. He was obsessed with me.*

Conflicts over possessiveness and autonomy in student romances are intensified by opposing psychological tendencies. College students identify as threatening to their relationship not only their partner's extra-relationship flirting and sexual behavior, but also his or her friendships and group socialization with the opposite sex (Yarab et al., 1998). And yet in post adolescence both sexes are likely to be avidly exploring the opposite sex as study collaborators, friends, and party companions. In addition, young adult development includes striving for increased autonomy and a moratorium on binding relationship ties. In one study (Baxter, 1986), restricted autonomy was the most frequent reason given for college relationship breakups, by 44% of women and 27% of men.

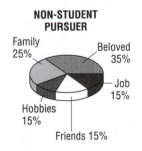

The painful circle of possessive feelings, complaints, and arguments is one of the paths by which unequal involvement intensifies into a breakup. The person who devotes more time and emotional energy may be more passionate and act more possessive. But this *pursuer* may feel not only frustrated, unappreciated, led-on, and angry, but also one-down, overly needy, and insecure. The person devoting less time and energy, the *distancer*, is likely to feel happy about being sought after, but also smothered, cautious, guilty, and threatened with loss of autonomy. It can be next to impossible to remember the love and excitement that once existed when this repetitious *pursuer–distancer* dance is going on.

Two aspects of this dance are most important to note: 1. This is a two-person relating pattern that can be ignited by either the *pursuer* "coming on too strong" or the *distancer* becoming comparatively unavailable; 2. Each partner can be in either role at different times or in different aspects of the relationship. (This pattern will show up many times in this text.)

Disrupted habits.　New lovers can also lose their balance because so many of their prior habits, priorities, and schedules are disrupted. At first they may be so excited by their new lives together that they are blissfully unaware of what they are leaving behind. But after fitting themselves into some of their partners' habits and schedules, they may realize that they are

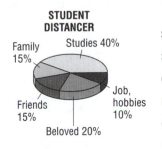

FIG. 2.1.
Pie-graphs of energy allotment in a couple pursuer–distancer dance.

not "themselves" anymore. When new lovers feel powerless, lost, or unbalanced, they may take some steps to restore a sense of continuity with their previous life.

Backing off is retreating from involvement temporarily in order to revive former habits, schedules, and relationships. The feeling of being lost or unbalanced is often not conscious, and the lover may be unaware of his or her first steps of retreat as well. A college man reports:

> One night when I came up to her room she was talking to her girlfriend, and she hardly noticed me. She just went right on gabbing as if I didn't exist. Was I fried! Then she finally interrupts herself to tell me that they're going shopping in a few minutes, and could I please make sure the door's locked when I'm done studying. Like I come up there to study and not to see her! I couldn't believe it.

The person who backs off from the new couple's routine may only be aware of needing to do something familiar from his old life, or of a particular friend or social event suddenly being his highest priority. He is usually unaware that this urge may be driven by fear of losing that life and his old identity with it. But the other partner is usually surprised by such a breach of the couple's habits, and is feeling scared, shocked, or outraged because her trust in the relationship is threatened. Thus, by suddenly backing off, one person's fear of losing identity can lead the other person to fear for the relationship. Though adults can suppress their feelings, their basic reaction to backing off is similar to a child's response to the threat of losing an attachment figure: anxiety, alarm, protest, clinging, or seeking to recover the lost person (Shaver, Hazan, & Bradshaw, 1988). This ignites the *pursuer–distancer dance*, and the person who feels "left" seeks to recover his or her sense of control by turning the tables: "I'll go out with somebody else." Both pursuit/distancing and this revenge cycle may lead to escalating manipulations that could bury our enthusiasm for a developing romance.

The dynamic of union and separation

Backing off is a signal that the normal dynamic tension between needs for union and for separation is reemerging after the extraordinary early period of being in love. For a while, external time constraints such as work, obligations, and exhaustion may have provided sufficient interruption of the union for new lovers. But now the partners need to recognize that they don't always *want* to be together.

> Men want a woman whom they can turn on and off like a light switch. (Ian Fleming, author of the James Bond novels)

When the desire for separation gets stronger than the desire to be together, we may think that our love is dying, saying "Things have changed between us." Our crisis in faith can pass when we back off for a while and discover that our desire to reunite is strong again. The issue will keep coming up, for differences in need, timing, and tolerance for separation threaten relationship stability. Partners who cannot find a way to cope with their opposing needs for autonomy and closeness may decide they are fundamentally incompatible and break up.

The psychological dynamics of separation and reunion are usually obscured by the specific issues of time and activity priorities in which they show up. The need for separation may emerge most clearly in the extravert's craving for other people and the introvert's urge to be alone, when these are not connected to a normal obligation, such as social events or studying.

When we become fully aware of our need for separation, we may fear that something irretrievable will be lost. We worry about separating for too long, or at the wrong time, or in the wrong way. Indeed, something irretrievable **is** lost. When we realize that being separate is sometimes more satisfying than being together, we lose the belief that **this** union is potentially a never-ending state of bliss and antidote for all of life's struggles. The need for a rhythm of time apart and time together signals the triumph of time and the transitoriness of happiness over the hope of an eternal paradise for a couple in love.

Passion.   Passion is brought about by a combination of attraction, emotional arousal, hope for an idealized union, and obstacles to the realization of that hope. Passion grows through intermittent closeness and motivates us to overcome any obstacles to a durable union. Passionate lovers from Tristan and Isolde on have embraced an entire lifetime of ecstasy, thrills, and despair by allowing obstacles and other people to come between them without ever ceasing to love, fantasize, and hope for each other.

Distance and time conflicts are common external obstacles. Opposition from family (the "Romeo and Juliet effect"), culture, peer groups, or rivals enhances passion. Passion is high in a typical extra-relationship affair because the coupled person may have more control over getting together and separating, but may be emotionally aroused by the danger of being caught. The other partner's high arousal derives from the lack of control over what happens and the possibility of losing the beloved "forever" at any moment. Here is a female student's "illicit" experience:

> I thought it could never become serious with him because he was friends with my ex-boyfriend and he had also dated one of my friends. It seemed perfect at the time because everything was so exciting and confusing. . . . The problem is that we got so involved in the sneaking around and always assumed that we'd never be together, so we forgot to keep a check on our feelings. To our surprise, we had fallen in love and it was becoming more and more difficult to keep everything a secret.

The *pursuer–distancer* dance, too, can heighten passion in the pursuer because of the distancer's reluctance to commit. If one partner is an addict or mentally unstable, she or he can also trigger a roller-coaster of passion by being only intermittently available in a sane or sober state.

Love addiction. People can also become psychologically addicted to being in love (Peele, 1975). One type of love addiction involves an unwillingness to "come down" from the euphoria of being in love and integrate the couple relationship into one's former life. Some people feel unable to bring about change in their normal life, such as in their family and significant relations, in work and financial condition, or in their sense of competence and respect. They therefore glory in the "rebirth" that comes through being in love, but avoid returning to deal with their normal lives.

This love addiction is a type of sensation seeking (Zuckerman, 1979) maintained by a constant search for passion, excitement, danger, and emotional intensity. Some lovers are able to stay in a "whirlwind romance" right up to and including their wedding. Others leave their partner as soon as their passion "goes flat," only to fall in love again with someone new. There are also people who don't resist their opportunities for thrilling eye contact and flirtation, no matter how committed they are to a partnership.

Communication: from indirect to direct. Topics that were avoided during casual dating start to come up when things get serious. The state of the relationship, the ways the partners want to be treated, and conflict-inducing differences may be discussed in around four fifths of serious relationships, which is 25–50% more often than in casual relationships (Brown, 1993, unpublished data). Nevertheless, 30% of serious couples may still hold back on damaging self-disclosure and a third will not talk about previous loves.

Emotional reactivity greatly increases through being in love, making serious daters more likely to express their emotions. Some people don't feel comfortable controlling their emotions for social desirability, so they cannot cope with casual dating.

> *I've always been too intense for casual dating. I get impatient with all that game playing. I know right away if I really like somebody or not, and I don't want to hide it. Some people are scared off, but there are others who feel like I do.*

In addition to needing to communicate some emotions, serious daters usually have to start building some explicit commitments. Relationships develop implicit rules about how often to meet, how much time to spend and what to do together, timing and types of emotional, affectionate, and sexual communication. Neither partner is normally conscious of these routines as "rules" (discussed in Chapter 11), because they are only patterns that have been repeated enough times to become unspoken expectations. But when one person does something that breaks the routine, the other may react as if betrayed. Then what was just a habit must be discussed and may become an explicit agreement or rule for the relationship (Planalp et al., 1988).

> *I remember the big fight we had when he stood me up on a Friday night. I know he doesn't see it that way, but he'd always just come over or call me to*

*meet him somewhere. Then one Friday there's no Tony and no call. I finally
called his place, and his roommates didn't know where he was. I was furious.*

*When he finally called me the next day, about noon, he was mad, too. He
said I had no right to expect him. I said if he felt that way, we didn't have a
relationship, so he shouldn't expect anything either. We said some pretty nasty
things before we decided we'd better talk it over in person.*

*We worked it out pretty well. He told me he'd just gone out with his co-
workers after work. (I didn't ask. He volunteered the information.) He said I
shouldn't have waited for him. (But I know he was glad I did.) He didn't want
to be obligated to see me every Friday night. But he'd call. We suggested either
one of us should call by Thursday if we were going to do something else on
Friday. He didn't like the idea (and neither did I). We'll see who tries that idea
first.*

As the incident above illustrates, people often resist making explicit
commitments, if only because they don't want to lose their spontaneity
and freedom of action. But once the issue of spending Friday nights together has been discussed, it is likely to remain in both people's minds as a
matter to be negotiated. Thus, even though Friday nights are not defini-
tively resolved, other messages have been conveyed which have more
far-reaching consequences than the couple could realize at the time. The
uncertainty which this disruption stirred up has motivated them to seek
more information about each other's personalities, how they affect each
other, and why they behaved the way they did (Surra & Bohman, 1991).
Research indicates that people who didn't talk the way this couple did about
issues that disrupted their sense of trust and reli-
ability are likely to wish later that they had
(Planalp et al., 1988).

But isn't something essential lost from a
relationship when our spontaneity is reduced by
a network of expectations which have to be
negotiated each time one is violated? Issues of
freedom and accountability will arise repeatedly.
But consistent behavior is a foundation of basic
trust. Though talking everything out is not always the best way, one study (Parks & Adelman,
1983) found that the less a couple communicated
overall, the more likely the relationship was to
have broken up three months later. Spontaneity
and reliability have to coexist in relationships,
and explicit communication helps to ease the
shocks.

Expressions of love and concern are typically spontaneous at first, but later are expected
as a routine. "Why don't you tell me that you
love me?" "Did you miss me?" "How do I look?""
These are likely requests for reassurance from

some women. Men may tell stories and expect rapt attention and praise. These reassurances help maintain the relationship. We don't like to request them: "It doesn't mean anything if I have to ask!" Intimate relationships often lead the partners to conceptualize their identities in relationship to each other. An older student discovers these dual selves:

> It is very interesting to us how different our personalities are, yet are very the same. It is also interesting how we seem to come to the same conclusions in entirely different fashions. We really don't disagree on anything besides trivial things.

Communicating about self, partner, and relationship to other people also supports the co-construction of meaning: **co-construction,** because both the **speaker's expectations** about what the listener is likely to understand and the **listener's actual responses** have an influence on how the speaker describes people, events, and reactions (Baxter, May, 1991; Duck et al., May, 1991). For example, a woman may speak about her relationship in one way to her parents, who want her to get through school and launch her career, and in another way to her fellow students, from whom she expects normal collegiate attitudes. Each of these different public descriptions helps shape the speaker's own definition of what she is experiencing (Duck & Pond, 1989).

Who we talk to about our relationships can affect relationship stability. The more we communicate with **our partner's family and friends,** the more stable the relationship is likely to be. This may be partly because we develop more common bonds and community and partly because we match our versions of what is going on by speaking with the same outside people (Parks & Adelman, 1983).

Shifting priorities. In order to integrate their couple relationship into both of their individual lives, the partners need to readjust their time and energy priorities. Though college men do not want their friends to call them "whipped," serious daters want to keep their partners happy too. To resolve this dilemma, many partners present any priorities that could offend their partners as "unfortunate but necessary." But denying decision-making power to the partner signals a low priority for the relationship, as in this story:

> As our relationship progressed, I noted a sense of jealousy she had toward my Air Force ROTC and engineering. There was one night in particular that she wanted to come over and stay with me. I told her I was sorry but I had to go to an AFROTC function that night. She tried to convince me that I should stay with her instead, but I told her I had to go. I also realized that I was spending a lot more time on AFROTC and engineering work than usual.
>
> She called me one night and told me she was tired of playing "second fiddle" to AFROTC and engineering. I told her that was unfortunate, but right now in my life, any girl will play "second fiddle" to those two. And that was that.

In this example, the man's emotional reactions are hidden behind his priorities. In the face of his partner's escalating reaction, their breakup may have come as a relief.

The Tug-of-war of Relationship Loyalty

Competing relationships: *Friends.* Conflicting priorities can be even more difficult to cope with when they concern other relationships. We can conflict not only over time spent with other people, but also what we do with them and what we tell our partner about them. The most significant competitors are family members, friends, and past or potential romantic partners. Romantic relationships frequently become strained when partners and friends engage in a tug-of-war for time and affection.

> *I worry about giving all my attention to one person. I always feel like I am being unfair to my friends. I have a hard time making both sides happy. Sometimes it gets to be too much of a struggle, at which point the boyfriend usually goes. Either I'd rather be with friends, or he gets tired of sharing me.*

This tug-of-war leads to an unequal balance of power when the partner in the middle either puts the friends first or insists on being the sole decision maker in each conflict. Such struggles can lead to the breakups of many of those people whose reasons Baxter (1986) labeled "threatened autonomy" and Loyer-Carlson (1989) called "independence" or "partner disposition." Shifting priorities away from friends and toward our partner is likely to lead to more rapid progression toward marriage, while courtships with less withdrawal from other relationships develop less interdependence and proceed more slowly (Surra, 1985a).

> *The number one priority at first was the relationship itself. Unfortunately we sort of let our friends slide for a while and this caused problems too. I couldn't believe how jealous my friends were. They would razz me every chance they got about how whipped I was. This really annoyed me because Beth would feel like she was holding me back. It did sort of settle down in the later months. Guys can be pretty tough on each other sometimes.*

Ex-partners. The issues are usually pretty clear where ex-partners are concerned, and their effects on the new relationship are strong (Baxter & Bullis, 1986). The person who is maintaining contact with an ex-partner typically insists that they are now just good friends, that their friendship goes way back, and that any interference from the new partner would prove a lack of trust. The new partner typically feels threatened and has to rely on intuition and proofs of loyalty. The person with the "ex" is therefore called upon to prove, in word and deed, (a) that he is "completely over" the previous romance, (b) that his new partner is definitely his first priority, and (c) that there are no secrets or secret contacts with the "ex."

But often, past relationships are not "completely over." People avoid many of their feelings at the end of a relationship, or break up due to external conditions, such as moving away to college. Therefore, some of these ex-partners are uncompleted romances, with both painful and pleasurable feelings waiting to flame up and be either revitalized or resolved. In the absence of research, it seems that in the affairs of the heart the first priority may be to encounter the former partner "just this once." For when our past feelings are rekindled, we want to savor and reflect on them, and sometimes share them as well. Then we are ready to move on, whether to a revitalized old love or to the new lover. In addition, a brief encounter with a past partner, even via letter or telephone, can stimulate communication with the new partner about his or her priorities and where their relationship is going.

Family. Though less visible and intense than with ex-partners, many complex issues of loyalty involve the partners' families. The couple's loyalty struggle between family and partner may become obvious on traditional family holidays, such as Thanksgiving or Christmas, when both families want them to come home, and the partners want to be together.

Parental relationships reach so deeply into us, that the deepening process is bound to interact with them sooner or later (Blanck & Blanck, 1968; see our Chapter 11). Even when the parents make no obvious efforts to keep their grown children close, such as financial "strings," regular calls, or needing emotional support, they arouse intense feelings—of joy or anticipation or of concern, worry, or hostility. Loyalty conflicts between our family and partner can arise, even though our family may be thousands of miles away, as this woman reports:

I realize that by coming to college I have distanced myself from my family and their discipline, but I am not emotionally strong enough to separate from the parent–child bond. The agony of my mom's face when I leave home and the choked back tears of my father are something I cannot handle. Rich constantly tells me that I must not live for my parents and that I have my own life. I may not need to live with my parents, but I need them "close" by. Sometimes I feel half-human and half-beast when anything comes between myself and my parents. I get scared of my own loyalty towards them and it makes me question: Will this loyalty destroy the precious relationship with Rich? Will he feel that he is number two in my life? Nothing seems capable of breaking this parental bond, and I'm not sure that I want it broken.

Sex.   Sex is one aspect of intimacy that provides "special" occasions, because we go into an altered state of consciousness and focus on mutual pleasure. In both sex and affection we put our partner first, and yet experience our partner centering on us, too. But the regularity of these "special" occasions has some consequences.

First, we are more likely to **expect** regular sex as a part of our relationship. Men initiate and press for sex more frequently than women, but women may increase their initiation (Cupach & Metts, 1991) and even pressure for sex as well (Stets & Pirog-Good, 1989a). Second, a study of motives for sex in a serious relationship (Sprague & Quadagno, 1989) found young men more likely than young women to seek sex for physical pleasure, but after the age of 45 women were more physically motivated than men. For women younger than 35, love feelings and commitment were a more important motive for sex than they were for young men, but after 35 the love motivations of both sexes were equal. Thus, there is statistical support for the cliché that "men give love to get sex, while women give sex to get love"— but only for lovers under the age of 35. Two male students question these conflicting cultural requirements:

> *Does sex have to always be a love feeling when you are with someone you love? Can it be something for just pleasure once in a while, or is there something wrong with that?*

> *What does it mean when thoughts of other women pop in your head while making love? If you have thoughts about an old flame, does it mean that you don't really love your girlfriend that much?*

The majority of both men (60%) and women (57%) report having fantasies during intercourse (DeMunck, 1998). But it does not matter how many sex authorities insist that purely pleasurable, "adulterous," or even "perverted" thoughts are both decidedly **normal** (Hariton & Singer, 1974; Campagna, 1985–1986; Chick & Gold, 1987–1988) and also **not deeds** and therefore not morally wrong (Crosby, 1991). Many of us are still uncomfortable, because we attribute **meanings** to our imagination, and we want these meanings to fit with our thoughts about ourselves and our relationship.

If sex becomes a habitual high point for the relationship, partners can try to release their emotions via sex. Many couples endorse the traditional magnification and stereotype of the male sex drive ("always ready") as a positive attribute (Snell et al., 1988; Zilbergeld, 1978). Both partners may give in to this mythical power of sex that is presumed greater than both of them. Sex can provide a pleasurable experience to make up and obliterate an argument. But it can also merely cover up conflicts and destructive emotional patterns that are developing in the relationship. When closeness is achieved via sex to the exclusion of other intimate relating, the bond may lose its energy without either partner understanding what happened. A young man reports:

> In the past week, five nights in a row my partner came up with a different excuse on why she didn't want to have sex. She wasn't in the mood, she was tired, she had to leave in half an hour, and we didn't have time. I heard it all this week. I don't see a promising future between me and my girlfriend.

For this student, intimacy means sex, and his girlfriend may not know how to tell him anything different. The suppressed need to back off from the relationship, which the woman in the story may have, can certainly dampen sexual arousal. But once a partner does retreat, the disruption of certainty can bring out some intimate communication and enhance sexual passion as the lovers reunite and rededicate themselves to strengthening their threatened bond.

Sexual differences. Differences in sexual frequency, duration, arousal, style, and goals are normally suppressed during early encounters and in the heights of being in love. Now these differences begin to arise as issues for direct or indirect communication. Both partners may bring ingrained sexual habits and fantasies into their union, so when the newness wears off, they may begin pushing for sexual expansion and accommodation. The initiative can come from either sex.

> I'm reasonably experienced in sexual matters, but I'm perplexed about what to do now. My girlfriend likes to mess around in public places, and I can't get into that very much. I'm not saying it's right or wrong, but I'm just not turned on to it. I've never been called a prude before. But I don't know how to change, and I'm not sure I would if I could.

People are often reluctant to deal openly with sexual differences, for fear of implied negative moral or psychological judgments and threats to self-esteem. Therefore they may broach the subject indirectly through books such as *The Joy of Sex* (Comfort, 1972). Books or friends can provide mind-expanding tips and vouch for new standards of normality which one partner wants the other to embrace. A middle aged woman had this advice on sexual communication:

> Don't **ever** tell a guy you didn't like something he did in bed! That's the quickest way to ruin a relationship. Some guys say they can take it, but it's not worth the risk. Just let him know what you like and don't like by the way you act. If you want him to stop doing something, slow down your breathing and get quiet. If you want him to do more, pant harder. He'll get the picture eventually and think it's all his own idea.

In order to get a relationship going, a woman may give in to male sexual initiatives and sometimes initiate sexual behavior and embrace whatever sexual frequency her partner desires. But later she may need to find a way to get the man to alter his pace and activity to fit with her needs for arousal and orgasm. Though communication about sex is associated with more satisfaction with both sex and relationships (Cupach & Metts, 1991), verbal communication is *not* the first tactic employed, as the example above illustrates. Nonverbal signals have the advantages of vagueness and plausible deniability. Explicit discussion concretizes the commitment to mutual sexual satisfaction, so discussions are more likely to begin when other relationship commitments are stable.

One important step in deepening may be establishing the right to say no to sex without jeopardizing the relationship, as this coed hopes:

> *Do you think that the point at which a relationship could be considered "stable" is when either partner can say no to sex and the other partner doesn't feel fearful or insulted? When you can be with someone and not have sex every time, then that is when you are secure with each other.*

Even when couples believe in the mythical inevitability of the male sex drive, the men are likely to signal their interest in sex indirectly, through sexual touching, and women are likely to signal their readiness to accept an initiative as well (Cupach & Metts, 1991). Both sexes are likely to comply with sexual initiatives even if they are not in the mood, or to resist in indirect ways (Snell et al., 1988). But in marriage and cohabiting relationships, direct verbal refusals are more effective and not as threatening as couples in undeveloped relationships expect (Byers & Heinlein, 1989). Men and women are actually equally unlikely to say no, though perhaps for different reasons. If men identify with masculine potency, then having sex is self-affirming and sets a precedent for future entitlement.

> *Say no to sex? Are you kidding? I don't **ever** have a headache! If I'm not interested to start with, I'll **get** interested. Besides, I don't want her withholding it, so I'd better not set a bad example myself.*

In an effort to retain the title of his partner's "best lover" a man may attempt to lead his partner into better orgasms or multiple orgasms. Paradoxically, his intentions can easily become a pressure on her to "perform spontaneously." For she may assume he's rating his quality as her lover and their compatibility as sex partners on how well she loses control and has orgasms. On her part, a woman may feel too guilty to ask for any changes in sexual behavior. Or she may expect all men to reach sexual release quickly and pretend to reach a peak when he does, in order to protect herself from performance expectations on his part. No amount of authoritative pronouncements about normalcy, freedom, and honesty in sex can change the fact that sex carries multiple meanings about the relationship and both partners' sexual self-esteem. With so much symbolism involved, sexual communication could not be simple for long.

Affection. Affectionate communication often has an ambiguous connection to sex. On dates affectionate gestures are often perceived as signals of sexual desire, so affection gets associated with foreplay. But affection is also often sought and given independently of sex, especially when we are in love or have been brought up with lots of affection. The conditions are ripe for mixed messages, because exactly the same affectionate gestures can carry both meanings. The accusations are well known:

> "All you want is sex!"
> "You get me all interested, and then you don't want to. Stop torturing me!"

In order to minimize the frustrations and arguments, partners typically develop consistent nonverbal signals or scripts for both sex and affection (DeLamater, 1991). For example, cuddling or neck rubs may be acknowledged signals for nonsexual affection.

Changes in power and control. Young people come to a relationship with expectations about who will play dominant and submissive roles and who will put the most effort into making things work (Berg & McQuinn, 1986). At the beginning and as a relationship develops, power dynamics are also affected by the relative competence, successfulness, popularity, and dependence of the partners.

As the relationship deepens, the distribution of power may have to be renegotiated. If they agree to an exclusive dating relationship, both partners relinquish some of their alternatives for meeting their needs. Therefore each becomes more powerful in the ability to give or take away what the other wants. To some extent, most everyone in a love relationship tries to influence each other to guarantee accessibility and loyalty and to make each other fit expectations deriving from gender roles, ideal partner fantasies, and past relationships (Weiner, 1980). Young adults may reject the notion of any control, **in principle**, because they are embarked on the process of gaining psychological freedom from their families. They also normally think in more absolutistic categories than when they get older ("either you're free or you're not"). But experts argue for **control mutuality**, or an equal ability to exert or resist control over matters of importance (Stafford & Canary, 1991).

In order to gain influence, each person uses a variety of tactics. These can be direct or indirect, as in asking versus just showing positive or negative emotions. They can be mutual or one-sided, as in bargaining, or persistence versus just withdrawing or doing what we want without communicating. They can also be conscious, as in arguing, or unconscious, as in giving in but inadvertently sabotaging an agreement by getting sick or depressed. By asking partners in both heterosexual and homosexual couples to describe the ways they would influence their partners, Falbo and Peplau (1980) found that significant gender differences occurred only in heterosexual couples. In heterosexual couples, men reported more use of direct and mutual power strategies, such as talking or bargaining for what they wanted. Women in those couples were more likely to use indirect and one-sided strategies, such as manipulations and withdrawal; but so, too, were people of both sexes in both heterosexual and homosexual relationships who considered themselves to have less power than their partners (Howard et al., 1986). Thus, mutual, open, explicit, and flexible influence strategies are more likely to be used by people who feel they have equal or more power in their relationships, and these people are more likely to be men. Also, people who value their autonomy over interdependence are likely to prefer one-sided strategies, such as just doing their own thing without negotiation. Using direct strategies is associated with greater satisfaction with the relationship (Howard et al., 1986). Thus, people who believe they have more power in relationship are more likely to come right out and negotiate for what they want because they expect they will be successful, and they may also feel better about their tactics. Those who are less powerful use less socially approved strategies and end up less satisfied with both the relationship and themselves.

Developing a style of conflict. Since nearly all couples will eventually have conflict, it is vital to develop a style of dealing with disagreement that is tolerable for both partners. They may minimize or dramatize, or emphasize reasonableness, passion, or silence. But until partners arrive at compatible styles, they may continue to have smoldering resentments about the differences in the ways they behave during conflicts (Braiker & Kelley, 1979), that can lower their satisfaction with the relationship (Lloyd, 1987, 1990).

The paths couples actually follow in developing workable styles of conflict are not well known (Rusbult et al., 1991). Retrospective studies of relationships that led to both marriage (Braiker & Kelley, 1979) and termination (Lloyd & Cate, 1985) indicate that conflict during serious dating does not necessarily lower a couple's love, as long as their expectations for the future are good. But a high level of premarital conflict may be followed by lowered satisfaction in marriage (Kelly et al., 1985). Therefore the lack of a statistically significant effect of conflict on relationship love may reflect two opposing underlying trends: Some people accept conflict, whether they find satisfactory ways of dealing with it or not, while others don't adapt to conflict and become dissatisfied with their relationship. Thus, the way partners **react** to their conflicts is a key determinant of whether or not a relationship lasts (Rusbult et al., 1986).

Couples have much to gain from facing and airing their differences. Airing and successfully resolving the conflict with our partner makes us more confident about the future. Giving in to or compromising with our partner's interests increases our personal investment in our partner and strengthens our image of ourselves as generous and as part of a couple with interests and goals of its own. Paradoxically, even if the conflicts are not well resolved, gains can be made for the relationship. As we saw in the "Friday night fight" on pages 56–57, mutual caring is evoked, commitments are implied or expressed, and specific rules of behavior in the couple are devised, all with the goal of containing future conflicts over the same issues. In the heat of open conflict, couples may reveal not only criticisms and negative feelings, but also love, dependency needs, possessiveness, and protectiveness to an extent which they had not yet recognized in themselves. If the partners in an uncontrolled outburst are inclined to interpret positively the intensity of hurt and emotional involvement that has been so roughly expressed, they can enrich the emotional dimension of their relationship.

> *I had never seen her that upset before. But I had never nit-picked at her for days either. She was embarrassed about some of the outright lies she said just to hurt me. But I wasn't too proud of what I said either. Understanding where we're both coming from really means a lot more to us since that fight.*

Most young adults start out their romantic arguing careers suppressing or falling into the styles they experienced with their parents, or what they did themselves in their families. Most young people are not pleased with how they appear to themselves when they lose control, and many are shocked by how much they remind themselves of their parents.

> *I am proud to be like my mother in many ways. However, I unfortunately learned her suppressive way of dealing with conflict. She and I have concluded that we hate to fight because it is extremely difficult to make your case when your face is streaked with tears, your nose is running, and you are gasping for air. I think the explanation for our behavior is simply that there is no way for us to win. If I care about the person, I value their opinion of me, so anything they say in anger hurts, especially if they have some truth to their argument. If I engage in the dispute, feelings of guilt and regret begin to haunt me before I've finished my first sentence. Another aspect which makes fighting such an awful experience is how defensive and irrational I become. I'm astonished and ashamed at how unreasonable I'm capable of being. Fighting is so frustrating and humiliating, that I put all my effort into avoiding conflict, rather than facing it.*

In the early months (and even years) of a relationship, the threat of breaking up can make reconciliations vital to our sense of security. We may be so threatened that we rush to resolve, forgive, and forget. Premarital couples usually leave their conflicts unresolved. In one study, only 22% of reported conflicts reached mutual resolution, compared to 32% ending with agreement to just drop the subject, 29% with apology, and 16% with one-sided avoidance of the subject (Lloyd, 1987). Despite the apparently peaceful outcomes in 84% of these conflicts, Lloyd found the women were dissatisfied with the lack of resolution and more likely to bring up the issue again. By contrast, overall, the men preferred to avoid the conflicts and were more dissatisfied when the women kept bringing them up. We shall examine conflict more extensively in Chapters 4 and 14.

Long-distance relationships: Can they last?

Countless people in long-distance partnerships have tried to keep the flames of their love burning brightly, even if they were convinced that time and human nature were working against them. A current study found 38% of a sample of University of Minnesota students had such relationships (USA Today, March, 1994).

Can they last? One two-year study of students found long-distance relationships had a higher survival rate than close-up relationships (Stephen, 1984). But this may be because long-distance daters are likely to be somewhat older and more stable in their lives (Johnson, 1983), in older relationships, and more uniformly serious in their intentions. They are likely to make commitments to marry in the future in an attempt to guarantee their own and their partner's loyalty. Research suggests that banking on future marriage does promote stability somewhat (Lloyd et al., 1984). In fact, males in long distance relationships are especially likely to emphasize exclusivity, loyalty, and devotion (Stephen, 1986), which stands out in contrast to the nonchalance that such men normally express. Being long on loyalty and short on talk may actually fit some men's personalities quite well (Stephen, 1986). Even so, compared to other college student relationships, long distance partners reported equal closeness but less satisfaction (Van Horn et al., 1997) and more depressive symptoms (Guldner, 1996).

> *Every September and January I find myself saying good-bye over and over again to the one I love. It has now become a perpetual motion . . . for the past three years. I suffer from a long distance relationship.*

Frequent visits are the most important factor in keeping these relationships alive (Holt & Stone, 1988). The emotional pattern of the passionate affair, with its waiting, obstacles, and idealization of limited time together, can be invoked for a long time. Stories suggest that a reunion frequency of once a month might be best for facilitating a "recurrent honeymoon effect" (Attridge, personal communication, 1994).

One Year Later. Julia Roberts & Lyle Lovett. They live in separate houses and two different time zones. No matter. Says Lyle: "We're still on that same honeymoon." (Cover headline in *People Weekly*, Aug. 8, 1994)

It probably boosted the romantic feelings of this movie star and country star couple to jet off to new places to meet every month. Yet a year after this article was published the stars split up: Apparently, major marital conflicts were not being addressed. In their case the issue was the timing of having children. Living apart may have provided too many good alternatives to engaging in a conflict with no ready solution. So **unexpressed conflicts** may well be a major unacknowledged (and unresearched) threat.

Usually more love and serious relationship talk is expressed in letters and telephone calls over distance than in close-up relationships (Stephen, 1986). But distant communication provides much less everyday information than is available face-to-face (Van Horn et al., 1997). So "partners must fill in missing or ambiguous information with their own interpretations and inferences," into which they can "project their own preferences" (O'Sullivan et al., June, 1993, p. 12). That means long-distance partners are freer to construct idealized partners and relationships in their own minds, without the tangle of daily face-to-face interaction to trip them up. **Idealization** may be one of the most important factors in romantic love (Brehm, 1988), and it plays a big role in long-distance relationships (Stafford & Reske, 1990).

Another strength and potential downfall of distant relationships is the greater **emotional autonomy** of each partner (O'Sullivan et al., June, 1993). Secure in the connection feelings and idealization in our minds, we can organize our time and energy to build a full life without each other. Having our main relationships with each other's family and friends can cement our relationships (Felmlee et al., 1990), but this is not always possible. New experiences of importance or intensity may have no relevance to our absent partner. To alleviate separation distress and depression each of us develops aspects of life and connections that supplement our interest in each other, but could replace it. In less committed relationships, the ax can fall:

> *About two weeks after she returned to school, she called me and wanted to break off the relationship. She claimed that she was so unhappy when she was not with me and that it was interfering with her school and sorority life. Her friends were mad because she never wanted to go out and party.*

What sorts of collegiate long-distance relationships are more likely to break up? A study of college freshmen found that women were more likely to end their relationships if they had experienced a high degree of "consensus identity" with their partners, that is, identified themselves with their boyfriend's ideas, attitudes, and values (Schwebel et al., 1992). Young women are more likely than young men to identify themselves with their most significant others (Gilligan, 1982). The woman in our example can not continue to live her former couple identity with her new peers, who want her to take on a new role as sorority sister. In contrast, first year college men were more likely to break from their girlfriends back home, the more they had valued recreational or intellectual intimacy before (Schwebel et al., 1992). Recreation and sharing ideas would be among the easiest aspects of relationship to replace in a college setting.

To preserve a long-distance relationship, the conventional wisdom is not to date other people, for "new love puts an old love to flight" (Capellanus, 1184/1941). We may guard against being "swept away" by a new interest by dating only people who don't "measure up" to our old partner, by our own standards. We may also use our distant involvement as a reason to keep new dates on a "friendly" basis and back out as soon as feelings get too strong. This "half-in, half-out" approach gives us more power in these relationships than new dates who don't have alternative commitments.

What might happen, then, when we reunite with our old lover? Despite our commitments, we may have transferred our emotional energy to other things. If we expect to be as passionate as we were in our idealized fantasies, we may feel deflated, because our daily lives have become unrelated. Amid their disillusionment, many long-distance partners need to spend time getting to know each other all over again. If one partner insists that things be like they were before, their growing autonomy can be threatened. Not being accepted "just as we are" can be perceived as further proof that the comfortable harmony that we once counted on is gone. No wonder Christmas and summer vacation are often such rocky times for college romances, and a significant increase in breakups occurs then and shortly thereafter (Hill et al., 1976).

On the other hand, long-distance relationships can thrive when both partners are as committed and stable in their careers as they are toward each other. Such long-distance partners report being just as satisfied with their relationship when separated as they stated when they were together (O'Sullivan et al., June, 1993). It would seem that constructing the meaning and security of romantic relationships in our heads with limited partner interaction can lead us to be as satisfied as dealing with the ups and downs of day-to-day events. Shifting the balance of closeness and autonomy toward autonomy can be desirable for those who devote most of their energy to career or personal projects. Men in such relationships are likely to accord women equal decision-making and worldly rights, since they are accepting that their partners are as oriented toward something other than the traditional nurturer-caretaker role as they are themselves (Attridge, personal communication, 1994).

As good career positions and advancement for both sexes become more precious and highly competitive, the frequency of long-distance relationships and "commuter marriages" should increase as well. Human nature is flexible enough that in some ways it can work **for**, as well as **against**, the satisfaction and preservation of separated relationships. With more experience as both distant and close-up partners, we may learn more about balancing the roles of committed mates and single people, as well as more about each experience in comparison to the other.

Conclusion

Among the main issues in the early deepening stage are dealing with disappointments, with managing closeness and disconnecting, and with shifting priorities for time, companionship, and loyalty. Integrating our couple life with the rest of our existence is a major challenge. In contrast, in long-distance relationships autonomy and connection develop along separate tracks without colliding as much. And idealization, serious commitments, and respect for partners' independence all bolster the relationship. Unexpressed disappointments, differences, and fears can lead to backing off that is misunderstood. But conflict, expressed or unexpressed, is the issue most likely to lead to relationship decay, which we will explore further in Chapter 3.

Chapter summary

- Communication deepens as a relationship develops. Though sometimes out of control, new lovers experience identical feelings and increased self-esteem, as well as mutual idealization and generosity.
- Emotional sharing and alternating separation and reunion may be more central to being in love than sexual behavior.
- Integrating the new partnership with the partners' previous lives presents challenges. Differences or complaints may lead to romantic disillusionment, which makes interest wane.
- Fearing loss of independence, men may assume they are in control. More comfortable with interdependence, young women may expect intimacy like that with their mothers and be frustrated. Self-surrender may turn into powerlessness, and yearning for stable closeness become possessive control.
- New love disrupts so many habits that partners may back off to "refind" themselves. This can trigger separation anxiety, and emotional pursuit or retaliation can escalate. Needs for disconnecting and reconnecting can test the relationship.
- In passionate affairs, obstacles such as distance, family, culture, unwillingness to commit, affairs, and addiction prevent a reliable union, and anxiety heightens passion.
- Communication turns interaction habits into commitments, as partners co-construct meanings for self, partner, and relationship. Joining social networks furthers stability. But partners have struggles over time and loyalty with friends and family.

- Sex may symbolize love, but undiscussed differences in sexual desire and style may lead to performance pressure, and affection may get confused with foreplay.
- In conflict, mutual and direct negotiating styles are likely for people who feel more powerful, while some others do what they want without negotiating. Most premarital conflicts are left unresolved, which can either strengthen or erode commitment, depending on expectations for the future.
- Long-distance relationship stability depends on stable careers and lifestyles and on social networks. Idealization and autonomous daily lives can make reunions disappointing and erode commitment.

The decay and termination of premarital relationships 3

Premarital relationship decay

Relationship decay begins when one partner comes to a realization of fundamental dissatisfaction which makes the future of the couple uncertain for her or him (Lloyd & Cate, 1985). The process of decay and termination may last from 1 to 8 months (Lee, 1984). By contrast, marital decay can easily last 3 to 5 years or longer (see Chapter 5). Decay need not be irreversible. It might lead only to a de-escalation to casual dating or low time commitments, rather than to a complete breakup (Rusbult, 1987). This reduced relationship can be stable if either the

TABLE 3.1. Attractive qualities later mentioned as reasons for dissatisfaction

Attractive quality	Reasons for dissatisfaction
Opposite	Too different
Age difference (older)	Same age
Offbeat, very unique	Too hippie-like, no real common interests
Mysterious	Addictive, evil
Sense of humor, funny	Played too many jokes, embarrassed me in public
Spontaneous, fun	Irresponsible, childish, avoided serious issues
On the wild side	Drank too much
Very outgoing and social	Too social
Strongwilled, persistent	Domineering, inflexible, never lets up, stubborn
Intense interest in me	Jealous, possessive, devouring
Successful and focused	Driven, workaholic, relationship always came second
Confident	Arrogant, egotistical
Quiet and shy	Insecure, no self-confidence, restricting my activity in public
Relaxed, easy-going	Constantly late, procrastinator, didn't care about anything
Sincere, friendly	Too nice, no sparks
Nurturing, caring, helpful	Smothering, mothers everybody
Spunky	Argumentative
Very sarcastic	Judgmental
Likes to have sex	Couldn't say no, was always hounding me

Adapted from Felmlee, 1995, 1998.

partners' commitment to each other remains strong, or the costs of breaking up are high, taking into account emotional losses, social stigma, shared possessions, and disruption of the partners' lives and of their networks of family and friends.

Why do premarital relationships decay? The most common explanations are distance, competitors, growing apart (Davis, 1973), and unresolved or escalating conflicts (Kelly et al., 1985; Lloyd & Cate, 1985). Drigotas and Rusbult (1992) found that decaying collegiate relationships were more likely to end if the terminator had good alternative people to fill his or her needs for emotional involvement, intimate sharing, and companionship. A breakup was most likely if all three needs were filled by one alternative companion. In addition, relationships with lower involvement, commitment, communication, rewards, support from family and friends, and less hours spent together are also more likely to end (reviewed in Cate & Lloyd, 1992). Sometimes an initially intriguing or outstanding quality in a partner can eventually become a major source of dissatisfaction. Felmlee (1995) found over 29% of those who recently terminated a college relationship pointed to at least one such "fatal attraction" to their ex-partner. These attractive characteristics were most likely to be perceived as fatal in hindsight if they were striking, extraordinary, extremely, or significantly **different** from the respondent (Felmlee, 1998; see Table 3.1). Thus, perceived differences and abnormalities often become sources of friction and explanations for a breakup.

Conflict and decay

Conflict arises when differences in personalities or interests clash with desires to do things together. (She likes to stay home; he likes to go out. Their tastes clash in music, movies, sports, food, clothing, financial management, or friends.) Tensions rise as well, when only one partner is pursuing the deepening issues, such as dealing with competing priorities or coping with emotional reactivity and desire for more closeness with the partner. Avoiding, smoothing over, or acting one-sidedly ensures that such conflicts will remain unresolved (Schaap, July, 1992), resulting in more dissatisfaction (Pistole, 1989).

> *She wanted me to spend most of my time with her, which kind of cramped my style. So when I had a week break, I went camping with my friends. When I came back, she was pretty cold to me, and she broke it off a few weeks later.*

When conflicts go unresolved, the participants are likely to make a *fundamental attribution error*: believing, in effect, *my* behavior is understandably caused by the situation I'm in, and will change once things get better, but *your* behavior is the result of unchanging personality traits (Jones & Nisbett, 1972). As humanly normal as it is, this error in thinking can be very destructive in relationships. Negative portraits of the partner's character and intent are prevalent in decaying relationships (Lloyd & Cate, 1985) and among reasons for breaking up (Loyer-Carlson, 1989; Baxter, 1986):

> *The first disappointments came with Ted when his **selfishness** became too much for me to handle [Viewed as a stable personality trait—author]. I could go on for days about the problems we had, but his selfishness was the reason for most of our problems. I finally told him how selfish he was and he really didn't like that, but I had to let him know how much he was hurting my feelings by not respecting them.*

The pursuer–distancer dance. Attempts at discussing differences can easily backfire. The roles of pursuer and distancer can be created by either initiating discussion of a difficult topic or going a separate way without consulting the other person. This pattern is also called "demand/withdraw" (Christensen & Noller, July, 1992), because it can be ignited by a withdrawal as well as by a demand. Some typical relationship issues, such as separating after a period of union, prioritizing another person above our partner, and reallocating our energies to nonrelational pursuits, are all likely to be experienced as withdrawals, which stimulate our part-

ner to approach with a demand. Men are as notorious for dodging conflict as women are for pursuing it (Lloyd, 1987, 1990). One study (Christensen, July, 1992) found 60% of withdrawals carried out by men and 30% by women, with 10% undeterminable. The withdraw/demand sequence is worsened by the pursuer's fears of loss and anger at the distancer for refusing to deal adequately with the issue, as well as by the implied discounting of his or her feelings (as in the story above). The pursuer often considers the relationship inequitable: "I'm not getting back as much as I put in" (see equity theory in Chapter 7). The distancer may feel trapped, angrily reject the charges against him or her, and denigrate the pursuer as "clingy," "controlling," or "insecure." Thus, the pursuer–distancer dance helps escalate unresolved problems into an intolerable situation for both partners.

Communication during decay

Communication cycles between openness and restriction during decay periods. There are unpredictable shifts between conflictual openness, positive feelings expressed during attempts to make up, and periods of withdrawal or superficial contact. Despite growing doubts about the relationship, the ability to predict or intuit the other's thoughts does not shut down (Baxter, 1988). Intimate knowledge may actually **increase**, especially through our recognition of unpleasant emotions and characteristics.

Differentiation of self (Knapp, 1984) is one communication strategy that has been observed to increase in deteriorating relationships. Couples may focus more on their differences and disagreements, rather than similarities and may increase the use of "I" and "mine," rather than "we" and "ours," especially when talking about their relationship (Surra et al., July, 1992).

How can decay last so long?   Outside observers often wonder how struggling lovers in deteriorating relationships can stay together so long when the pain and frustration they complain about is so great. There are several factors that serve to prolong the period of decay.

First, people want to avoid experiencing grief and loss. So they may postpone and deny a definitive break up as long as possible. Second, backing off and restricting involvement may give one more decision-making power than one's partner (Vaughan, 1986), by **the principle of least interest** (Waller & Hill, 1951): Whoever is least interested in continuing a relationship has more control. Though this is gratifying at first, watching a partner give in repeatedly may not restore love, but foster disrespect instead.

Getting back together

Clinical experience points to another psychological process during decay. Hurt, anger, and resentment may seem to have extinguished the love that was once there. But if the negative feelings are expressed and responded to with "we can work it out," hope may spring up again. Some of the most passionate love scenes in romances occur during these reunions that temporarily reverse a period of decay. The basic ingredients for passion are all there: **arousal** (through anger, anxiety, longing, and sadness), **obstacles** (from unresolved differences and likely distance), **hope** (for a loving paradise that the lovers once shared), **lack of control** (both of our own feelings and of what our partner will do next), and the **restoration of union** against the **threat of permanent loss**. Once hope is rekindled, we may give up the delicate and drawn-out process of negotiating and tinkering with solutions to our problems. We would rather be swept away by our passionate emotions, as this lover reports:

> We were on the verge of breaking up for about a year. We fought so much that we were miserable most of the time. But the good times were really good. Sometimes Fran would say, "Let's have a moratorium on discussing anything for a day, so we can just love each other." Those "time out for love" days were great. I felt like we were both tied to the tracks in front of an onrushing train, but we could turn off the heat in our fights, and the train would slow down to a snail's pace.

But the sidetracked issues have a way of coming back to plague us. In many cases the sweeping changes and grand compromises which were conceived in the heat of passionate reunions turn out to be unworkable. We may still stay on the roller-coaster of decay and revitalization for months, because our desperate reunions are providing us with euphoric vacations from ordinary reality that are unrivaled by anything except our first days of love.

Third parties as helpers. Confidantes can give us comfort, help us understand ourselves, our partners, and what is happening, and act as a go-between to help work things out. They help us tell our stories of what is wrong several times, so that we find out what makes sense to others and also shores up our own self-esteem as a good person in a bad situation (Duck & Pond, 1989).

Bothered by the guilt of spoiling our partner's public image with negative stories and by the possible failure stigma of a breakup, we are likely to seek support and agreement very intensely, particularly from someone who knows our partner well. A few failed attempts to negotiate, change, or compromise qualify our confidante to verify for us that there is no way to resolve the problems, so termination is an honorable way to proceed.

In the midst of all this confiding, comforting, and counseling, a third person may also emerge as a potential replacement for our estranged partner. This is especially likely if most of the help comes from one person of the appropriate sex, who spends long hours alone with the sufferer and gives good support. Such helpers are usually more understanding, more supportive, and much less self-centered than the polarized partner. Even if the helper scrupulously avoids "taking advantage" of the situation, an emotionally distraught partner may be in great need of a safe third person to restore his or her disrupted security. Though these relationships are mostly platonic, focusing our needs for support, understanding, intimacy, self-esteem, and affection onto a third party can lead to emotional closeness that is precious to both people.

The termination stage

When, why, and how young adults break up

For college students, breakups are about twice as likely to occur around the beginning and end of the summer (June and September) and around Christmas vacation as in any other month (Hill et al., 1976), so it appears that moving around seems to make it easier to formally break up. Thus distance and a new relationship or alternate sources of personal support, such as close friends and family, facilitate the disengagement. Three fourths of the breakups in one study were attributed to cumulative dissatisfaction, and one fourth were precipitated by a critical incident, such as deception or infidelity (Baxter, 1984).

> The first real conflict came when I cheated on Cora at about the year-and-a-half point. It was a one-night thing, and I didn't have sex. I guess I cheated because I was getting scared, being a senior in high school talking about marriage already, and maybe I thought the other girl might be a way out. After this little incident the relationship never got back on the right track, and a few months later we broke up, for the first time.

Table 3.2 categorizes the ways that young people break up. In Baxter's (1984) study, 81% of college students chose to break up without any direct discussion of issues. Students avoided discussion in the hope of causing, witnessing, or feeling less of the unpleasant emotions involved in breakups. The disadvantage of avoiding direct discussion is that 75% of indirect breakups were resisted by the other person. So breaking-up strategies had to be repeated, often many times, before the relationship was finally laid to rest. Baxter's subjects' most frequent regret was that they had not been more direct with their partners about their reasons for wanting to break up.

Breaking up via "withdrawal" means one person eliminates contact and also avoids discussing it. In "onesided pseudo de-escalation," one per-

TABLE 3.2. Types of premarital breakups with percentages of those reporting each type

Baxter's breakup categories	Percent	Lee's negotiation categories	Percent
Onesided & indirect	52% total	No negotiation on issues	27%
Onesided withdrawal	34%		
Onesided pseudo de-escalation	11%		
Onesided cost escalation	6%		
Mutual & indirect	17% total		
Fading away	14%		
Mutual pseudo de-escalation	3%		
Unilateral & direct	16% total		
Accomplished fact	12%		
State of the relationship talk	4%	Some negotiation on issues	17%
Bilateral & direct	15% total		
Negotiated farewell	7.5%	Extended negotiation	25%
Attributional conflict	7.5%	Ext. negot. & repeated decisions	31%

Sources: Baxter, 1984; Lee, 1984.

son expresses desire to reduce the level of closeness, when what he or she really means is that it is over. An example of this would be: "Let's see each other less frequently and be open to seeing other people."A method Baxter called "cost escalation" involves making the relationship unpleasant for the partner in indirect ways. These could include being disrespectful, breaking dates, preferring one's friends, or blatantly flirting with other people. By making the relationship unpleasant, the rejector calculates that both his partner's pain and his guilt for breaking up will be less, if his partner thinks *she* is initiating the separation herself.

> I knew that if I told her that I did not want to continue the relationship it would really hurt her, so I thought I would be an 'asshole' for a while to make her like me less and then I would tell her.

The "accomplished fact" style involves one person directly telling the other that the relationship is over, with no discussion allowed. By contrast, a "state of the relationship talk" is initiated by one person, who listens to her partner's response, but still ends it.

> The way I handled the breakup was by going over to his apartment and telling him face-to-face. I tried to explain how I felt, although I knew it was a shock for him. We talked calmly about the situation and I ended it instantly. I did not think it was good to drag it out once I knew it was over. We both felt extreme sadness and were both fighting back tears. As I left he also got very angry, which is how he usually handles things when he is hurt.

"Fading away" involves a mutual understanding without any direct mention that the relationship is over, as in "saying it by not saying it." "Mutual pseudo de-escalation" involves both partners asking for a reduction when they really want an ending. Only 15% of Baxter's sample engaged in extensive direct negotiations, with half of them bickering over who was to blame for the breakup ("attributional conflict") and half parting more amicably.

Baxter's termination reports must have come from predominantly casual relationships, since they lasted an average of 6.2 months. The second study of reported breakups in Table 3.2 (Lee, 1984) covered older students (21.5 compared to 19.4 years old) with longer relationships (14.7 months) which were more serious—95% had been going steady, considering marriage, or living together. Most of these breakups (73%) involved negotiation. They took an average of **7 months** from the first awareness of serious dissatisfaction to the final breakup, and the longer the relationship, the longer the period of deterioration and breakup was likely to take (see also Cate & Lloyd, 1992). Around 30% of breakups in both studies included attempts to repair and start over again. In 36% of the more serious relationships, de-escalation had been tried, such as dating other people. But rather than disguising an intended withdrawal, these partners had been reluctant to make a complete break and many wished to leave open the door to restoring the former relationship at a later time. The key factor in these longer decay periods might be **attachment**, since around two years may be the normal time it takes for young adults' romantic relationships to become attachments (Hazan, July, 1992).

Attachment in the termination process

Bowlby's (1969) concept of attachment (in Chapter 10) is very useful for understanding what goes on during termination. We will distinguish two types of attachment, which we will call personal and generic.

Personal attachment is very specific, and the capacity for it derives from early infant–caregiver interaction (Bowlby, 1969). It is the magnetism

"PERSONAL ATTACHMENT IS THE MAGNETISM BETWEEN TWO PEOPLE..."

SEPARATION IS OFTEN PAINFUL!

between two unique people, triggered by the sight, sound, habits, conversation, and personality of our partner. Our response to this type of attachment is to want to be near only this one person out of everyone in the world. This creates an acute longing, which for some people may be the most convincing experience of "true love" in their lives. We may yearn for our "special person" and feel contentment in his or her presence without consciously choosing these feelings and sometimes in spite of our conscious efforts to extinguish them. Such apparent "imprinting" of the beloved's characteristics leads people to seek reunions frantically and offer anything, including marriage, demeaning compromises, or "just friends" status, just to keep the beloved in sight. We are normally unaware of our "imprinting" of specific aspects of lost partners, but may find ourselves attracted to those aspects when we encounter them in someone else.

It is important for us to recognize the personal attachment in our love relationships for what it is, and not to add other meanings to it. Being attached to specific aspects of my beloved, and feeling abandonment when he is gone **does** mean I truly love him. My heart, or emotional nature, is acting normally. But it **does not** guarantee that this is the right or best relationship for me. Though my feelings may lead me to believe that such a "soul mate" only comes along once in a lifetime, there is no empirical evidence for this. If I have "imprinted" my partner's characteristics, it may be hard to get over my attachments to these characteristics.

> Now it is another year later, and Charlene and I are still trying to get each other back. We haven't been together in such a long time, and yet I still feel that she is the one I'm supposed to marry. . . . We were made for each other.

Such intuitive certainty may have little or nothing to do with partners' goals, compatibility, and mutual resources for making a long-term relationship satisfying. If my previous experience has convinced me that this relationship will not work, then my specific attachment only shows that it will be harder to get over this person than I would like, and that I may have some residual attachments that will color my attractions and perhaps impede my becoming equally attached to a new love.

Generic attachment has to do with fulfilling our own needs, and is easier to replace. Our response to losing these generic needs can be overwhelming. But the three main aspects of attachment outlined by Bowlby (Collins & Read, 1990; Hazan, July, 1992) can often be fulfilled temporarily by alternative people. When we are suffering acute separation distress, we may transfer our companionship need (which Bowlby called "proximity") to someone else who is comfortable to be with. We can find another "safe haven" by seeking comfort and support with someone else, and we may still have an alternative "secure base" (of unconditional acceptance) in our family to which we can return, either in our minds or in reality. Separation distress is usually greater when we have fewer alternatives to meet these needs (Sprecher et al., 1998). Some other specific but still replaceable needs our partner may have met for us are pleasure and playfulness, lowering of inhibitions, touch, sex, cuddling, sleeping together, self-esteem, and security. During a relationship most of these needs are filled without our noticing them, so we are likely to be quite surprised at how much we hurt when they are all disrupted (Stephen, 1984).

If unfilled, our generic relationship needs can combine with our specific attachment to our lover to create an aching void. Then our excitement and relief from pain during reunions can be so great that we will keep getting back together to try again, convinced that our feelings are telling us it is "not right" for us to be apart. If our reasons for breaking up remain unchanged, however, we will soon need to break up again. If this painful roller-coaster is long or intense, we may become afraid of ever getting that deeply involved again.

Sex and affection

Lee (1984) found that 43% of former partners considered themselves friends and one fifth were still occasional lovers as well. Sex is usually not part of what has been going wrong, so it can be used as a painkiller and as a nonverbal way to experience (and plausibly deny) the love we can no longer continue. As in reunions, most of the ingredients for high passion are present:

> The one thing that never got bad between us was sex. During all the messy fighting we had, it seemed like the sex never slowed down, and even got better. Toward the end, we had to avoid being in either one of our apartments alone, because we couldn't keep our hands off of each other.

Power and the need for self-control

When relationships come to an end, both partners need to readjust their priorities to put their power of self-centered choice above keeping the relationship stable. The partner who is most willing to leave the bond can be more uncompromising and still get her way. The partner who wants to keep the relationship is likely to feel one-down, devalued, and helpless (Hill et al., 1976). Since most of us don't like feeling helpless, both partners may maneuver to put themselves in charge of what is going to happen. For this reason, if we are being rejected, we may try to get our partner to agree to give the relationship a "second chance" and then take more initiative in the final breakup at a later time.

> When Laura told me she needed more space in our relationship so she could think things over, it really hurt. I told her we could work it out. But I connected with a girl in my apartment complex who I knew was interested in me. So when Laura said maybe we should be open to seeing other people, I dropped the bomb. She really flipped out. But I was only agreeing with her!

Rejecters and rejectees experience the breakup differently

Over 85% of the breakups Hill and colleagues (1976) studied were initiated more by one partner than the other, with an estimated 51% by women and 42% by men. But both partners in a break up preferred to view themselves as the initiator, whether this was true or not. This study found a general tendency for some post-breakup feelings in partners to be inversely related, that is the freer, happier, and less depressed and lonely the rejector felt, the less free and happy and more depressed and lonely the rejectee was likely to feel.

If we are the rejectors, we are likely to feel guilty for the pain we have caused our partners (Hill et al., 1976). But since we can anticipate this guilt before the breakup, we can put some effort into developing an "ironclad" justification for our actions to protect ourselves against possible criticisms. If our justifications are too thin, we are more likely to cut ourselves off from our partner and her friends and family in order to avoid any questions. Building up a thoroughly negative portrait of the rejectee, as crazy, destructive, hostile, deceitful, or weak, can serve to render him or her less worthy of compassionate concern and thus reduce our guilt. Rejected partners are likely to lose control and show emotions in immature or socially unacceptable ways, such as breaking out with rage or sadness in public, harassing the rejector, or destroying things. Rejectors can use these acts as proof of the rejectee's character defects, which further justify breaking up.

As rejectors, we are likely to use our anger, our justification, and sometimes a new attraction to quickly "get over" and suppress our own grief reactions. Finding alternative companionship reduces reported post-breakup pain. But believing the partner has more alternative companionship is associated with more pain for the one who does not have it (Sprecher et al., 1998).

Not wanting a breakup but being unable to prevent it from happening is likely to leave a rejectee feeling helpless and out of control, which makes the experience more devastating (Peterson et al., 1985; Sprecher et al., 1998). While the rejector's reasons for the breakup help to ward off guilt and grief, the rejectee needs an explanation to restore some sense of meaning and control to his life. He needs to discover some plausible explanation for why his relationship came apart, or pinpoint some qualities in his partner or himself that caused irreparable damage. Then he can watch out for the danger signs, and try to change destructive aspects of himself or avoid them in future partners. In one study two thirds of rejectees and only half of rejectors mentioned something they learned about themselves (Druen et al., June, 1993). Here are two lessons learned:

> **A woman rejector says:** *The minute I hear a guy wants to know where I am 24 hours a day, I'm heading in the other direction.*

> **A rejected man says:** *I realize I didn't communicate my feelings enough, so now I always try to do a better job of that.*

It is debatable whether these changes in guidelines we may make for the next relationships will actually fit the new circumstances. But *believing* that we can do something to increase our acceptability and safety in the future makes us feel less helpless. Since both shame and sorrow are natural emotional responses to loss (see Chapter 13), we may also feel personally worthless and suspect there was something about us (usually in appearance or character) that led to our rejection. If we can find out what it was, we can either try to change it or disqualify our former partner for singling it out. In these ways we can save our self-esteem from the stigma of being defective.

My girlfriend used to say that I was too skinny, and she was turned on to men who were buffed out. I hated that. After we broke up for the last time, I started working out in a gym. I gained ten pounds . . . probably all muscle. Nobody but me ever noticed the change—certainly not my next couple of girlfriends. But five years later I dated a woman who did notice my muscles, and she said she liked them. I ended up marrying her, but not because of that.

Research into the effects of understanding on post-breakup adjustment has focused on divorce and is inconclusive (reported in Brehm, 1992). It suggests that pinpointing our own contribution to the breakup may have some short-term benefits, while blaming the partner may actually do harm, if the blame lingers on as a hostile attitude.

Grief reactions

Hazan (July, 1992) found that young adults needed about two years in a love relationship to become fully attached, that is, to shift their "secure base" (emotional home) from parents to partner. Grief reactions to a breakup may be briefer and less intense when such a "secure base" attachment has not been formed (Weiss, 1988), perhaps because the relationship did not last long enough, or because we were not fully committed. A survey of the typical stages of grief (Kübler-Ross, 1969) can help us understand some of the experiences which lovers have after a breakup.

Denial.   At first the mourner is so shocked that she feels numb and may carry on as if nothing had changed. When someone dies, denial may typically last as long as a week (Bowlby, 1980). Relationship breakups are so subject to misinterpretation, that the denial phase can frequently last quite a bit longer than that. Both the de-escalation of "scale-down" breakups (36% of Lee's sample) and the "pseudo de-escalations" (14% of Baxter's sample; both in Table 3.2) serve to deny that a breakup is actually taking place. One-sided withdrawal without any clarification (34% of Baxter's sample) is also conducive to denial on the rejectee's part, since it requires some trial and error to discover that a complete break is actually what the rejector desires.

Of course, denial can be a useful defense mechanism, since it allows us to carry on with our lives and postpone dealing with overwhelming emotions until they are less immediate. Since many students put social timing and their career goals first, they may deny emotions throughout their relationships, from extending casual dating to minimizing their losses. But grief may eventually escape this defense, as this student reports:

When my girlfriend in high school broke up with me, it was quite a shock. At first I couldn't believe it. My immediate reaction was to try to rectify whatever pissed her off so we could get back together. She said we should just stop seeing each other because we would be going to college soon and would prob-

ably meet other people there. I still didn't believe her and I continued to try to get back together with her. She continued to resist so finally I gave up.

By this time I was full of emotions. I was angry because I felt like I had given my all into this relationship and then she just shit on me. I also felt lonely because she was like my confidant and I could tell her anything and now I lost that. I was also afraid. I was afraid because my self-image was at an all time low and I figured, "Who would ever want to go out with a loser like me?" I basically felt worthless.

Emotional chaos.   **Anger** comes up in several ways, not just as rage at being dumped, as in the cry of indignation: "How dare you do this to me!" Anger is often a defense against other feelings, such as helplessness, sadness, and shame, especially among men. Sadness, guilt, relief, and love can also erupt during this phase, along with great confusion and fear. Thoughts of suicide are common during the period of emotional chaos, for we have lost a part of ourselves (Kast, 1987). We can experience **fear** of helplessness, fear of the overwhelming emotions that come unpredictably and make us feel insane, and fear that absolutely **anything** unexpected could happen in our world, since a major focus for our sense of belonging and continuity is gone. The last fear could be most intense, if our partner had become our only **secure base** in life, that is, if our family of origin were no longer available or had not functioned as that secure base in the past.

If the terminated relationship had functioned as a secure base, one or both partners may go on trusting subconsciously in each other's unqualified support, even though they may be consciously quite content with breaking up. Though they may never ask for anything, their symbolic reliance on each other may be a core meaning of their remaining "friends for life," as this college woman puts it:

> *I still love him to this day, and we still stay in touch. He is working for a company in Maryland. We write each other and I plan to see him this spring when he visits for his sister's graduation. He is someone I think I will be friends with for the rest of my life.*

The persistence of **secure base attachment** can contribute to emotional confusion, because of our conviction that unconditional love must still be present underneath all of the negative feelings and actions of the breakup. This conviction can manifest itself as an unshakable faith that the partner "still loves" us and lead us to repeatedly test this faith by intruding into the other's post-termination life. If partners are still attached, their ambivalent emotional expressions may cycle between "I will always love you" and "Please get out of my life." Both of these feelings can be sincere and present simultaneously. This coed expresses her ambivalence about a meeting with her high school sweetheart a year after breaking up:

> *I saw Jim for two days before I left for my sophomore year of college. There was something bittersweet about the whole thing. I hadn't seen him in so long and it felt so comfortable to be back with him even if it was for a short time. . . . I was proud that I didn't need him anymore. I felt more grown up. Even though I didn't need him I still wanted him back with me too. I was flooded with memories of the past, some good, some not so good, and I basically just wanted the opportunity to ask him questions, yell at him, cry my heart out, and at the same time reassure myself that he always did and always will love me.*

Revivifying our love experiences prolongs the helplessness which forms the basis for depression (Peterson et al., 1985). The more vivid the memories of past loves are, the greater the depression is (Harvey et al., 1986). But we are not completely helpless during this time. For we can choose to stop ourselves from dwelling on our past positive experiences, and clarifying our past relationship's "fatal flaws" should aid in separating (Kingma, 1987). We are in the process of letting go of the internal image of our partner as a significant orientation symbol in our life. For this reason many former partners cling to pictures and symbols of each other, then relinquish them much later as a ritual completion of letting go.

> *I have lost myself—the most important years of my life, when I came to be myself, when I began to really live. I have to discard these years like a burnt page!—if I can.* (German poet Novalis in a letter after his fiancée's death in 1797, in Ritter-Schaumburg, 1986, translated by the first author)

Search, bargaining, and separation. Like mourners after a death, ex-partners have a powerful urge to search out their former mates, and they see the person in dreams and spontaneous hallucinations. They may also awaken two or more hours early in the morning with their minds preoccupied with restoring the broken relationship. Many stalk their separating partners, as portrayed in the movie "Fatal Attraction" and the Police song "Every Breath You Take." They are obsessively concerned with catching up with their partners and initiating a "bargaining" session aimed at winning them back.

Though our initial motivation for seeking out and bargaining with our ex-partner is to revivify the relationship and not to let go, repeated encounters eventually show us why revivification will not work. If we share our feelings honestly, without chasing each other away with too much reactivity, we may discover that our feelings are not so incomprehensible to each other, and that our previous images of each other are not so radically contradicted as we thought. We may also help each other understand why we need to let our heads rule over our hearts. Thus, the result of bargaining with our ex-partner can be that we begin to let go of each other more willingly than before.

Depression, acceptance, and returning to worldly life. The general public normally labels its sadness "depression" and considers depression unhealthy. But the American Psychiatric Association, in its definition of bereavement from the *Diagnostic and Statistical Manual of Mental Disorders* (DSM-IV), recognizes depression as a normal reaction to loss:

> **Bereavement** [includes] symptoms characteristic of a Major Depressive Episode . . . such as insomnia, poor appetite, and weight loss. . . The diagnosis of Major Depressive Disorder is generally not given unless the symptoms are still present 2 months after the loss. [Normal grief could include] 1. guilt about actions taken or not taken . . . 2. the survivor thinking that he or she would be better off dead . . . 3. hallucinatory experiences [of] hear[ing] the voice of, or . . . see[ing] the image of the [lost] person. [It would not include] 1. morbid preoccupation with worthlessness, 2. marked psychomotor retardation [slowness of movements], 3. prolonged and marked . . . impairment [of daily functioning]. (American Psychiatric Association, 1994)

Other manifestations of post-breakup depression include apathy, fatigue, and lack of interest or pleasure in almost all activities most of the time. We are in the process of accepting that our beloved is really lost to us. In contrast to uncomplicated bereavement after a death, the frequency of post-breakup information about and encounters with an expartner who is out and about can cause us to cycle between emotional chaos and depression many times. Depressive symptoms may also be our most common experience of grief if we are masking and minimizing other reactions to avoid social embarrassment, as in this man's story:

> *I had a very difficult time sleeping those first couple of weeks after the breakup. I would just pick at my meals. I was also very depressed and my friends could notice this. We would go out, yet I wouldn't appear to be having any fun because I would constantly be thinking about her. It was very difficult for me to talk to any of my friends about her because I didn't want to appear weak. I had to try to maintain my "macho" image as best I could. I also never talk to my family about how I feel, so I had to keep most of how I felt inside. I have learned that these feelings and behaviors are still the same for me when I get hosed, because I reacted in exactly the same way after my last girlfriend broke up with me.*

Perhaps our most dignified and typical manifestations of the breakup blues are work obsession, heavy drinking (more prevalent in men, Stephen, 1987), overeating, and listening to music. Many students measure their recovery of psychological health by **how soon** they return to worldly life, which for some means going out on dates again. But grief reactions for deeply attached partnerships are normally intermittent processes which may take months or years to be completed, as in this student's story:

> It has been about two and a half years since I broke up with Sarah, and I can finally say that I am over her. When we broke up a month after I got to school in September, I was a wreck, and it took me about a month to get my life back in order. As I began putting the pieces back together, I built a wall around myself and refused to let anyone in. . . . The day after I got home for Christmas, the wall was shattered. Memories of her were everywhere. Emotions came flooding out of me. I felt about as helpless as I did that first month after we broke up.
>
> When I came back to school I heard my first Andrew Dice Clay tape and discovered I could really hate women! . . . and that kept them away for a year and a half. Then the next summer I had a best friend come down and also shared the apartment with my roommate's girlfriend. I still was filled with hate, but living with Kate forced me to deal with a girl for the first time. We fought a lot and didn't get along at all, but she gave me a woman to vent anger at, and it did me a world of good.
>
> Finally, this semester I've started to have some dates. I've been able to be with another girl without thinking of Sarah even once. I just let myself have fun. . . I feel confident that I am over Sarah. I even think I could handle having a talk with her. People have been hinting that she wants to get back together. I've been politely telling them that it will never happen, but they don't stop. I think it's time I had a talk with her.

Post-termination commication: Can't we be friends?

The American cultural norm of being friends with everyone extends to the expectation that ex-lovers will remain friends. But the presence of unexpressed and unresolved romantic or breakup feelings could make such friendships very uncomfortable in person, as this student testifies:

> Often you see your ex in the same clubs or restaurants that you met in. If you have the same class together in school, you are a captive audience in her presence. You **have** to be with her. You try to show your ex, your friends, and even yourself that you are over her first, and you feel compelled to act cool around her, so that you can show everyone you are over her. The problem is that, in the midst of all of the different emotions you **are** feeling and trying to show you **are not** feeling, you have to **really** want to be just friends to have the friendship endure this difficult time. How do you separate the feeling that you want to be with that person again dating from wanting to be around each other as friends?

Perhaps the answer to this man's question is that most of these post-breakup friendships involve much less contact and need fulfillment than a typical active friendship, and function more as symbolic reassurances that some affection still exists. The deep emotional intimacy lovers once shared may lead them to spontaneously confide in each other at similar levels and exchange unselfishly loving advice. This makes such contacts precious and unique, whether they occur regularly or rarely. Existing research (Lee, 1984; Metts et al., 1989) suggests that post-termination friendships are more likely to work if the partners were good friends before their romance and if the breakup was handled with direct communication and a positive emotional tone. More qualitative research is needed to sketch out what post-romantic friendships are actually like.

Rebounding and rebonding

It can be argued that our recovery from a breakup is not truly complete until we are ready and able to form a new relationship of **equal** passion, intimacy, and commitment. It is impossible to either prove or disprove this definition of complete recovery, however. Playing the field or focusing our primary energy on career development or family can certainly help us to "compartmentalize" our grief (Weiss, 1988) or protect a broken heart.

Rebound relationships can be described theoretically by referring to our distinction between personal and generic aspects of attachment on page 80. The first one or two relationships after a major breakup are likely to fulfill the most personally important of the recovering person's generic needs, such as companionship and sex. They also fill in for aspects of the previous relationship that may have been lacking or painful, such as being listened to or being appreciated for some quality that was ignored or devalued before. The likelihood of being attracted to someone who responds positively to specific aspects of our wounded self image allows us to give rebounds the more charitable name "healing relationships."

If we were rejected, we may choose someone who is noticeably more attracted to us than we are to him or her. Thus, without being aware of it, we try to heal the wound of being loved less than we loved before by being loved more than we are loving this time. This type of rebound becomes shaky, however, once we become convinced that we are lovable enough to be safe from rejection. The tendency for healing attractions to fade once our self-esteem wound is better may be intensified, if remnants of our attachment to specific aspects of our past partner begin to resurface in contrast to our new partner. Then we may begin to feel more embarrassment and guilt than joy. We are likely to back out in indirect ways, in order to avoid having to confess feelings that are unflattering to both ourselves and our new partners.

> Very shortly after I began dating this new girl, I found out we could not have a long term relationship. The girl was crazy about me as I found out, but I was not that excited about her. We were real good friends and I would do nothing to hurt her. We had several good times together and most of all she really helped me get through the past relationship. She was a real good friend and was very understanding. I feel real bad sometimes for ending the relationship, as she became closer to me than I was to her. I did not want to hurt her, but this was not right for me.

If our theory is correct, the two key internal factors that can doom healing relationships are the impact of our past wounds on our new attractions and our attachment to aspects of our former partner. We may be relatively unaware of both influences. Here a college man reports a tenacious attachment to the experience of sex with his past beloved, which is particularly confusing because he doesn't know what to call it:

> After about 8 months I told myself that this was the one and I was never going to let her go . . . I had never been so open with my feelings and thoughts as I was with her. I was sure that if this was what love was like then I would never find it this good anywhere.
>
> As I look back now on the relationship it could very easily have been lust instead of love. We had great sex, but it seemed we had much more than this. I can say that I do miss the sex the most, though. Does this mean that it was lust? No one had ever turned me on sexually more than she did. I couldn't see how anyone could fulfill that sexual pleasure more than she did . . . I hope someday to find the right girl and be sure that it is love and not another sexual encounter. . . . The older I become, the more I realize it's important to communicate with your partner. But there also must be great sex.

This man's efforts to match the sexual experience of his first love have disappointed him every time, because the sex hasn't been the same, *and* because it has been "just" sex, without the feelings which made his love experience so special. Placing such a high value on sex may make it hard for him to find satisfaction, because women are less likely to share that value than men (Frazier & Esterly, 1990).

But healing relationships seem to help people loosen and let go of previous attachments, if they are capable of replacing one romantic attachment with another. Both research and common experience assures us that parental attachments can be replaced by romantic partnerships (Hazan, July, 1992), and our society currently affirms that partnerships are fully replaceable as well.

Learning from our relationship histories

One way to explore the long-term effects of partnerships is to examine one's entire relationship history to see if any patterns emerge. People report that they have learned how to love again (Krantzler, 1987), and certainly many second great loves and second marriages are more durable than the first. Studying our own and others' relationship histories can teach us a lot about what happens as we love and lose.

The graph (Figure 3.1) represents 85% of the histories the first author collected in a pilot study of college students. Each person's first most significant relationship is mapped onto the middle, with relationships before it to the left and those afterwards to the right. All of the relationship histo-

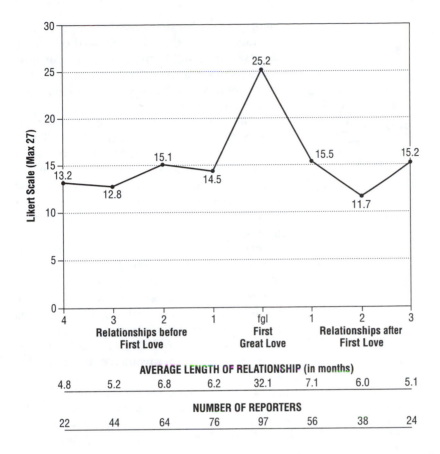

Relationships before First Love				**First Great Love**	**Relationships after First Love**		
4	3	2	1	fgl	1	2	3

AVERAGE LENGTH OF RELATIONSHIP (in months)

4.8	5.2	6.8	6.2	32.1	7.1	6.0	5.1

NUMBER OF REPORTERS

22	44	64	76	97	56	38	24

FIG. 3.1. Student means of Likert Scale totals for passion, intimacy, and commitment combined in their first great love, compared to their previous and subsequent involvements.

ries analyzed showed an increase in intensity of passion, intimacy, and commitment (on a 1–9 Likert scale) up to a peak, which we have called a "first great love." These great loves were most likely to have occurred between the first and fifth relationship recorded, with 23% reporting it as their fifth, 23% as their fourth, 20% as their third, 12% as their second, and 22% as their first relationship. Forty-three percent of those responding were either still in their first great love or had not dated anyone since, while 18% had one subsequent liaison, 14% two, and 25% three or more. Most (78%) first great loves lasted at least 2 years, which may be the amount of time it takes to become securely attached. Despite eliminating short casual relationships of one month or less, both prior and subsequent liaisons were much shorter and less passionate, intimate, and committed. Thus, we could characterize prior couplings as "learning to love" and those afterwards as "healing relationships." The 7% of this sample who had found their second great love to be of equal intensity did so after 2 or 3 lighter relationships and after 2 to 5 years. The 15% of young people not depicted in the graph had not bonded to a first great love, and were having either shorter or multiple relationships. The actual proportion of college students who have

"...COLLEGE STUDENTS HAVE ONLY ONE "GREAT LOVE" FROM WHICH THEY HAVE NOT YET RECOVERED BY 2 TO 4 YEARS LATER."

not experienced a first great love must be considerably higher, though, because this nonrandom sample came from an elective course on relationships, and even there, an additional 10% chose not to write a history, usually because they "didn't have enough to write about."

Nevertheless, the fact that so many students showed this pattern of a first great love followed by a period of low involvement for some years thereafter suggests that there may be some fundamental forces in young human nature and culture at work. There were no significant differences between men (average age 22) and women (average 21). The lack of deep involvements in college has previously been explained as a customary moratorium on commitment. But it may also stem from the students' lingering attachments to their first great loves, which may have rendered them temporarily unable as well as unwilling to form full-fledged new attachments. Here is a young man whose 14-month relationship still puts all other women in the shade:

> *Another thing is that even though I know I will never date Sal again, I compare her with every girl I meet. I also think I will never like a girl as much as I like Sal, or find a girl as perfect as Sal. I had a few dates after that summer with a few girls, but I never had enough interest to get anything started.*

This young woman's story is typical of many, in that she experienced an unexpected and frightening submerging of herself into her first love which she is unwilling to risk again:

> *When I fell in love, I was no longer my center. He took my place, the second and third also. I got weak every time I saw him. I constantly needed him to reassure me of his love. If he had a problem, it was my problem. His pain was mine, as was his love. I had no life if I could not see or hear him. It was like death. Constantly I would ask myself: What is happening to me?*
>
> *It was the "loss of ego boundaries" stage. The problem is I never got out of that stage. Up to the very last day together, I was still living for him. This is one of the reasons why I find it so hard to fall in love again. After this relationship, I seem to have put up a defense mechanism in order to keep from getting involved with anyone deeply. The recovery was very difficult.*

Such loss of a self-center has been called **codependency** by some counselors. Many popular books, aimed primarily at women, have been written about this (e.g., Beattie, 1987).

Imprinting

In addition to making people slow to commit to a second love, it is possible that our first long-term love (or even a long-cherished fantasy love) may have an "imprinting" effect, filling in an unconscious **template** (Perper, 1985) or **archetype** of "romantic partner." This partner-image might then exert an influence over subsequent love feelings that could be as important or more important than the opposite sex parent or other early attachment figures, as suggested in Freudian theory (Chapter 10). We can also speculate that a "first great love" partner who was disturbed, attached to someone else, not ready, or otherwise unable to love fully could get imprinted as a *"flawed first love."* This might lead us to unconsciously embrace more flawed loves. Or we might expect all love to be damaging—as many people do who grew up with especially toxic parents. On the other hand, a flawed first love might be easier to replace with a much more fulfilling love later in life. Research on this aspect of past loves has not been carried out, but it would make a fascinating study.

What do students learn from their early relationships?

Druen and her colleagues (June, 1993) asked undergraduates to list their **significant** relationships and then write about how each one had influenced their approach to subsequent liaisons. Forty-seven percent of all responses focused on what students had learned about themselves, while 19% focused on ideas about what makes partners good or bad, 16% focused on relationship factors, and 18% reported their relationships had no influence at all. Those most experienced in long-term relationships chose to write most often about **themselves** (65% of their writings, compared to about 50% for all others). Those who had had only a few very long relationships mentioned **relationship** factors more often than others did, but still in only 16% of their comments. Apparently college students are likely to learn about **themselves** in relationship, but few are considering the factors involved in the relationships. Here are some sample learnings:

> **About oneself:** *I learned that I couldn't share myself with anyone else until I learned to like and be confident myself. I learned to be a better partner (a friend).*

> **About partners:** *I'm still hoping for a better complementation of personalities. C.M. is a little on the shy, crafty side. Also too anal-retentive for my taste.*

> **About relationship:** *The relationship with her made me realize that two people can love each other no matter how difficult the odds are.* (Druen et al., June, 1993)

Learning by leapfrogging

From counseling and classroom experience, we will sketch some of what students learn from relationships. As students move through their first relationships, they typically progress towards more intimate sexual activities, which may strain or break through their previous moral codes. If they perceive one relationship as having crashed over a specific problem, such as possessive jealousy, they are likely to tackle it in their next liaison. This desire to be successful at love can prompt young people (and those not so young as well) to rush through the acquaintanceship process of casual dating in order to arrive at the issue that bothered them before. By *leapfrogging* over stages, people are choosing the *issue* more than the full personality of their new partner. But research has yet to explore what effects such a "healing relationship" approach could have on the relationships in which it occurs. Perhaps mastering a devastating previous problem, such as being assertive or mixing autonomy and commitment, would allow a healing relationship to break through to a deeper level. Such a breakthrough could motivate us to adjust to our new partner's uniqueness and to overcome our previous attachment.

Young people are more passive in their earliest relationships, typically latching on to the first person with appropriate attributes who offers to fill the peer-defined position of boyfriend or girlfriend. Then they learn from experience to choose partners more carefully and decide what to do and not do. College women may learn from experience to be more discriminating in their choice of partners than college men and they may be naturally predisposed to such learning (Chapter 9). One study indicates that women's attitudes toward love and mate choice become more practical as they get more experience in their twenties, while men's attitudes are less likely to move away from being idealistically romantic (Frazier & Esterly, 1990). Some gender differences in the process of learning from experience show up in these college students' writings:

A young man says: *Looking at my relationship resume, it seems that a lot of the time we moved from one stage to the next unintentionally, or unplanned. The factors that push me from one stage to the next have usually centered around trust, and just whether or not I thought the girl was a nice person. I pretty much feel that if I can trust a person and this girl can turn me on, I'm more than willing to try a relationship with her.*

A young woman says: *I always felt that for me, it was easier to find one guy and stick with him. I am somewhat of a shy person who often has trouble getting to know new people. So, once I found someone, I got to know a lot about that person, because once I began to feel comfortable with the person, I just continued the relationship from there.*

I can usually spot who will make a serious partner and who will not, so I guess by those means I somewhat pick and choose. I wonder if I don't make things happen sometimes that maybe shouldn't. Not that I have regretted any serious relationships I have had, but I wonder sometimes if maybe I didn't push the relationship farther than it should have gone.

In both accounts, trust and comfort (and for the man, sexual excitement) are enough to motivate further involvement, with no clear criteria for evaluating the partner's character or compatibility. Perhaps such a broad focus is appropriate for exploration in the absence of strong prior learning about relationships. But the young woman is questioning her previous involvement choices, perhaps in search of criteria for greater power of choice in the future, while the man is not. One study of premarital breakups (Stephen, 1987) showed that women were more likely than men to change their explanation of what happened as time passed. It is likely that young women would be more able to discuss such relationship issues among themselves. But young men may not know how, because their peer groups don't compare relationship lives with much frankness or sophistication.

However, men can also learn quite a bit from romantic relationships, especially about the nuts and bolts of intimate relating, as this man clearly sees:

> *We would sometimes fight over the stupidest things, just because I wasn't expressing my emotions the way I should be able to. She would sometimes express her emotions too much, and this would cause me to feel guilty and I would start to open up to her through my words and actions. I had never really cried until I saw her cry. Then my emotions overwhelmed me and I was unable to hold back the tears. It seemed that whenever she would cry over something I would start to cry because she was crying. It sounds kind of stupid, but I didn't feel free to express my emotions unless I was with her.*
>
> *My lack of ability to express my emotions has led to quite a few breakups and has not helped in family matters either. Since then I feel that I have come a long way in realizing my emotional needs and expressing them in a way which is easy for another to understand. I will even allow others to see me in emotional states in an effort to let them know that I am upset or angry with them over something.*

Many students conclude from their experiences that they want more freedom and less commitment than they did when they were younger. But these people may also be striving for more freedom from their families and may be loosening their lingering attachments to their first great loves as well. Not every lesson learned from early relationships survives further evaluation some years later, as noted by this young man:

> *When I started college I had pretty well formed the opinion that really good looking girls could never stay faithful and would cheat on you sooner or later. I felt caught in a bind because I still felt the need to go out with and be seen with a girl that my friends and father would look at and say "Good work Jack!!" Yet I had no trust for them any more. As my defense against this I decided not to give any more attention to the best looking girls, and at that*

time I really didn't feel the need to date anyone below those standards. So I just did not date.

After a year of no dating I had reevaluated what was important to me in a partner and decided even though physical attractiveness was important to me, I had better look for a girl with high goals, friendly personality, and more stable in terms of commitment. I had shifted looks toward the middle of my list of what I wanted.

Some of what we learn from our relationships is valuable and some is misleading. We can learn strategies for defending against involvement, or for taking care of ourselves within an involvement. Frazier and Esterly (1990) found that the price of **not** learning from the past may be that men are less likely than women to increase their satisfaction when they have had more experience with relationships.

Learning from our past relationships requires three things: a vocabulary for expressing our experience in words, a systematic exploration of the relevant aspects of past relationships, and a fruitful dialogue to produce new insights. This text provides the vocabulary of concepts and stages for exploration. It is up to you to develop the dialogue you need to learn from your experience.

Chapter summary

- Unresolved conflicts cause decay when partners avoid intimacy and develop negative attitudes, exacerbated by a pursuer/distancer dynamic.
- Decay of long-term relationships averages 7–8 months. Backing off gives a power advantage: the other keeps giving in. Reunions after separation or breakup create passionate love feelings.
- People terminate when they do because of changes in time and energy investment and alternative relationships. Only one fourth are triggered by critical incidents, such as deception or infidelity.
- Less serious relationships break up through one-sided withdrawal or accomplished fact or mutual fading away. But extended negotiation and repeated decisions are likely factors in serious relationships.
- Personal attachment to the partner's personality makes us want only that person. We may "imprint" our beloved and be attracted to others with similar specific aspects.
- Generic attachment is to our couple needs—intimacy, involvement, sex, security, and self-worth. But replacements may falter against personal attachment, leading to confusion, longing, and guilt.
- Reunions are likely, until being together hurts more than being apart. Sex and affection may continue to be attractive.
- Each partner may try to be in control of the breakup process, and

may maneuver to reject the other first.
- Rejectors may feel anger, guilt, relief, self-righteousness, or sometimes new attraction, which blots out grief reactions. Rejectees may feel helpless, intensifying anger, grief, and loneliness.
- Denial of loss can be extended when expartners try to continue as friends. America devalues grief and downplays adolescent loss of love.
- Emotional chaos brings confusion and helplessness. Internalizing an ex-partner as a secure base leads to supportive symbolic mutual love. But frequent remembrance and contacts can catalyze more depression.
- Post-termination friendships are more likely to continue if ex-partners were good friends before and their breakup had a positive tone. They may be more for support than sharing time together.
- Rebounds help heal wounds. But rebounders may avoid passion toward new partners and leapfrog over stages into passionate wounds and issues instead. Their unpassionate attraction can subside into guilt and embarrassment.
- Many college students have had only one "great love," from which they have not fully recovered 2 to 4 years later. Perhaps the college years offer a moratorium on love/commitment, and perhaps young adults increase their ability to love to a peak and then take time to recover.
- Students try to learn most about themselves from their relationships. Women may learn more from past relationships, because they talk more, and more intelligently, about them.
- Men may learn about feelings. Women learn about not living for their mate (codependency). People may overreact to hurt by generalizing about what hurt them and trying to avoid it.

Becoming partners: Developing marital relationships 4

- **Trends in Marriage**
- **Understanding the Process of Partnering**
- **Building Trust**
- **Balancing Needs for Connectedness and Autonomy**
- **Cycles of Closeness and Separateness**
  Reconciling Differences
- **Tolerating Change**
  The Impact of Children
  Reconnecting in the Empty Nest

Trends in marriage

There has been much cynicism about marriage over the last two decades. Many people feel that persons who stay married are either conservative or insecure. Many feel that living together is better than marriage. Yet current statistics reveal that 58% of the couples who marry stay together more than fifteen years (Cherlin, 1992). In this chapter we will consider some of what develops during a long-term marriage and what distinguishes people who are satisfied with their marriages from those who are not.

Despite the high divorce rates, the bad name that marriage may have in some quarters, and the greater acceptability of alternative ways of coupling, statistics show that most American men and women continue to believe in marriage as the ultimate expression of their love for one another (Ahrons, 1994). More than two million couples marry in America each year, so that close to 90 percent of adults marry at some point in their lives (Cherlin, 1992). According to the National Center for Health Statistics (1994), the marriage rate during the early 1990s was slightly lower than during the 1980s, but has generally remained stable over the past few decades. But while the "institution" of marriage is still quite popular, when people marry, what they want and how they are structuring married life has been changing dramatically.

Most of today's young adults marry significantly later than did their parents (Cherlin, 1992). The proportion of men aged 20–24 who had not yet wed in 1988 was 78%—23% higher than it was in 1970. For women in this age group, the proportion of those who had never married increased from 36% in 1970 to 61% in 1988 (U.S. Bureau of the Census, 1989). By the end of the 1980s, the average age for women entering a first marriage is at a twentieth century high (See Figure 4.1). Blacks postpone marriage even more than whites. In 1988 the median marrying age for black women was 3 years older than for white women. The proportion of never-married black women in their early 20s was 75% compared to 59% for white women. For black men as compared to white men, the figures were 87% and 76% respectively (Cherlin, 1992; Saluter, 1988).

Not only are men and women choosing to marry at a later age, they are more often marrying people who are similar to them in age. In 1988 the median age at marriage was 23.6 for women, compared to 25.9 years for men (U.S. Bureau of the Census, 1989). This is the smallest age difference on record. This similarity in age between partners may be reflected in expectations for greater equality in both roles and decision-making power.

Understanding the process of partnering

Because married life has been considered a private matter, it is only recently that we have been able to study how participants experience mar-

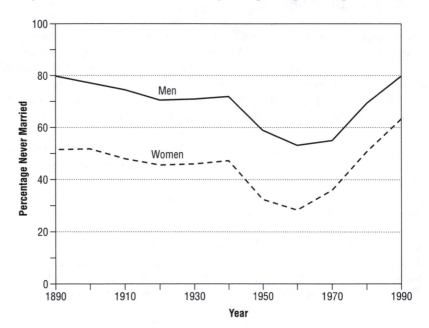

FIG. 4.1.
Percentage of never-married men and women age 20 to 24.
Source: Cherlin, 1992, p. 9.

riage. Now we have reports of clinicians (Dym & Glenn, 1993; Kovacs, 1992; Malone & Malone, 1987; Schnarch, 1991; Whitaker, Greenberg & Greenberg, 1981) working with couples experiencing relationship problems as well as research conducted on "normal" couples who have been together for a long time (Amato & Rogers, 1997; Gottman, 1994c; Gottman et al., 1998; Veroff et al., 1993; Wallerstein & Blakeslee, 1995). They show that an intimate partnership is not a stable, unchanging arrangement but rather a changing, growing entity. Thus, it is more realistic to think of a long-term committed relationship as a **process of partnering**, "of changing and accepting change, of settling differences and living with differences that will never be settled, of drawing close and pulling apart and drawing close again" (Klagburn, 1992, p. 16).

Many clinicians have depicted the process of partnering as developing through a series of challenges to our ways of thinking about ourselves, our partner, and our relationship. They suggest that these challenges, even more than the individual personalities of each partner, shape the partnership—that is, the way the couple responds to each other and to the outside world (Dym & Glenn, 1993; Kovacs, 1992). These challenges can be organized into four basic interrelated issues:

1. building trust,
2. balancing needs for connectedness and autonomy,
3. reconciling differences, and
4. tolerating change.

In this chapter we will look at each of these issues more closely.

Building trust

What is trust? And how is it built and maintained over a lifetime together? According to a noted psychiatrist, Thomas Malone, "trust means sharing one's true self with one's partner, knowing that one will not be ridiculed or violated, but will be nurtured and protected" (Malone & Malone, 1987, p. 18). Reflected in this definition are some of the elements of intimacy described by Erik Erikson, a renowned psychoanalyst who defined intimacy as the "capacity to commit oneself to concrete affiliations and partnerships and to develop the ethical strength to abide by such commitments, even though they may call for significant sacrifices and compromises" (Erikson, 1963, p. 82).

Does this mean that long-term relationships require that one sacrifice or "give up" on oneself to be with another? Erikson seems to emphasize that rather than losing oneself, loving another requires one to stretch one-self and develop one's abilities to nurture another—feeling what our lover feels, knowing what he or she needs and wants, and putting oneself out, when necessary, to satisfy the other person's feelings and needs. This will-ingness to put oneself out, to give to one another without resentment, and then in turn receive from another, is how trust develops in satisfying rela-tionships. One man, married thirty years, epitomizes the state of trust that can develop:

> *You want to know what it means to be married? It means I got someone I'm pretty dammed close to, closer to than to anyone else. She's there to listen to my good times and my bad times. She's in there pulling along with me. Be-cause of her, I'm not lonely—at least not most of the time.* (Cited in Klagburn, 1992, p. 24).

Another element contributing to the development of acceptance and trust is the sense of specialness and exclusivity of the relationship. Couples who report they are close seem to have a special bond —a kind of secret club that excludes all others from its innermost core. A young wife ex-presses this expectation:

> *Although it may seem like a silly complaint, I have asked my husband if there could be a type of en-dearment that is just ours. He is a very warm, af-fectionate person who treats all his friends and rela-tives as if they are very special. But when I hear him say "I love you" to his sisters, or call his mom or sisters "Honey," I feel that there isn't much spe-cial between us.*

Trust cannot endure, however, unless we feel safe—that is, that our partner will not betray or violate our trust. Our sense of safety is strengthened by the development of secrets that just the two of us share. The sense that each part-ner can be trusted with the really damning se-cret parts of the other, that these will not be thrown up in one another's face during some particularly heated battle, is a central element in the glue that cements a partnership together.

But this sense of trust and acceptance does not develop over night. It takes a long time to uncover ourselves, to share our innermost pains and doubts, to reveal those powerful emotional needs that wash over us at times. Many couples report that while they "fell in love" with each other quickly, the bonds of trust and acceptance were welded much more slowly as they lived with each other and built a life together, chapter by chapter. As one mother who endured the death of her baby daughter from a lingering disease said:

> Who else could ever feel what it was like when my daughter died? He (her husband) knew what it was like, he was grieving too!

Sharing the pain of their child's illness and death brought these two people closer, and wrote a chapter in their history which no one else could ever duplicate (Borg & Lasker, 1981). Developing a sense of trust is not a straight, unchanging, uphill climb in long-term love relationships, however. Most couples report that the closeness comes and goes.

> There are times when you are both so involved with your work or your family that you have little energy for each other. You go through days, sometimes weeks, of anger, of hatred, in which you wonder how you will ever get connected again. You go through periods of such distancing that you question what you are doing together in the first place, no matter how long you have been married. (Cited in Klagburn, 1992, p. 30)

How do couples achieve this sense of trust in each other and this belief that if they do grow distant from one another, time is on their side and somehow they will get close again? Researchers have found that trust derives from our perception that our partner is not just caring for us because we meet his/her needs, or even because of our attractive looks, abilities, status, or qualities, but for intrinsic reasons that cannot be explained logically (Rempel et. al., 1985; Holmes & Rempel, 1989). Thus, the trusting couple has the secure feelings of **object constancy** we learned as small children (Mahler et al., 1975). That does not mean that trustworthy adult love is **really** unconditional, since we know rationally that intentional betrayal, maltreatment, and neglect might destroy it. But we prefer to believe that there are no ways we could **unintentionally** lose the love we rely on.

Another source of trust derives from the substantial knowledge and understanding partners develop with each other (Burleson & Denton, 1997; Wallerstein & Blakeslee, 1995). Heller and Wood (1998), for example, reported that men and women reporting a high level of satisfaction and intimacy with their marriage are very accurate in predicting their partners' feelings and beliefs, and hold similar values and beliefs about the amount of closeness or intimacy they prefer in their relationship. In another study, Fields (1983) reported that partners in long satisfying marriages (averaging twenty-four years) could very accurately describe their spouse's personality, interests, feelings and social needs. They described their mates in the same way that the mates described themselves in appearance, feelings, strengths, and weaknesses. These couples reported that they got to know each other so well through spending time together, talking to each other, and hearing about each other's sensitivities. Swapping everyday information about what happened, what the baby said, or what one's coworker said, were the small events which built connection and trust.

In contrast, in dissatisfying marriages, partners reported little intimate sharing with each other, primarily because they had little interest in their mate's daily life (Amato & Rogers, 1997; Gottman, 1994b; Kitson & Holmes, 1992). For example, Mirra Komarovsky (1962) reported that one out of three working-class marriages which she studied seemed to be barren of a sense of connection and self-revelation. She quoted one twenty-two year old man, married three years, who spoke of his boredom with his wife: "What does she have to talk about? Dirty diaper stuff. I don't care about that." Yet it is just this kind of "dirty diaper stuff" that couples who feel close talk about. Knowing there is a receptive ear to listen, they talk about the little things that are on their mind rather than weighing topics for their worthiness or significance to their partner. One young husband stated:

> We always find time to sit down and discuss any feelings we have. When we see how other parents discipline their children, we discuss our feelings on it and how we would like to discipline ours. We both have our opinions, and I know a couple of times she's done things that I didn't feel were right. And I've done some things that she didn't feel were right. But whenever it happens, we just tell the other person we didn't think it was right and we talk about it. (Cited in Blumstein and Schwartz, 1983, p.339)

The ways couples communicate may vary greatly. Some may be calm and guarded in their disclosure, while others may be intense—saying whatever comes to mind. Both ways may be quite satisfying. What seems necessary is that partners learn how to accommodate to each other's styles and needs.

Balancing needs for connectedness and autonomy

Carl Whitaker (1976), a renowned family therapist, said: "Marriage is our emotional finishing school. For it is in marriage that we continue to work on and hopefully to 'finish' learning the lessons that we began in our own families of origin of how to give love and be loved, yet also to be separate selves" (p. 211). Embracing Whitaker's perspective, we assume that **in order for an intimate relationship to endure, partners must learn how to resolve the challenge of balancing their own needs and those of their part-**

ner for closeness, nurturance, and emotional acceptance with their needs for separateness, autonomy, and independence.

Many people in our society put such a value on independence that we are reluctant to admit that, no matter how self-reliant we are, there are still areas in our lives where we need and want emotional support and connection with others. Long-term intimate relationships such as marriage are one way in which we find the enduring emotional support we are searching for. But there is a hitch. For being in a partnership is always a seesaw between dependence and independence.

THE EXPANSION STAGE

" AT THIS STAGE, WE DEMONSTRATE OUR DESIRE TO CONNECT WITH ANOTHER PERSON"

Cycles of Closeness and Separateness

How do we balance our needs for closeness with our own and our partner's needs for independence and autonomy? Many clinicians (Dym & Glenn, 1993; Wallerstein & Blakeslee, 1995; Whitaker, 1976) believe that we balance our needs for closeness and separateness by regularly moving through cycles of moving close, then moving apart, then moving close again. According to Dym and Glenn (1993) this dance of closeness and distance forms a **repeating three-stage cycle** composed of: (a) an **expansion** stage when we reach out for connection and support from each other, (b) a **contraction** stage when we pull in and withdraw from our partner, and (c) a **resolution** stage when we struggle to move past our disillusionment with our partner and gain a sense of perspective and calm that allows us to reengage with them. Let us look at how partners think and feel about each other as they move through each stage of this recurring cycle.

The expansion stage. At this stage, we demonstrate our desire to be concerned about someone other than ourselves, to feel alive with the feelings of love and romance. The young couple in their mid-twenties interviewed in Box 4.1 are about to be married.

The couple reflects many of the expectations, hopes, and blind spots of partners in the expansion stage. There is a sense of emotional expansiveness and promise, a feeling that they have created a common vision or purpose for their lives—of building a life together, having common goals, enjoying each other, supporting each other's dreams. Every moment together is to be savored and enjoyed. They have eyes (and ears) only for

BOX 4.1. A couple at the expansion stage

"Why are you getting married?" I asked them.

Chuck answered immediately. "Why not? I have never found anyone I want to be with more. I'm ready to let the whole world know how much I love her."

"For me it's a little different," Dianne said. She looked at him as she spoke. "I know Chuck is the one for me. He is the one I want to spend my life with, marriage or not. But I was not in a hurry to marry. Not because I don't love him, but because I wanted to get finished with college first and get us launched job-wise."

"That's true," Chuck went on. "I looked at it differently. I had decided that I wanted Dianne by my side. And while I know we've still got a lot to do to get our careers where we want them, I wanted to make our relationship permanent. Also, I think we are ready now, too, to take this step—to be a part of the adult world. I have a job, she's almost finished school. We are entering the grown-up world now. And getting married is a grown-up thing to do."

"Are you planning to have children?" I asked them.

"Yes, but it's a long way off." Dianne said. "At least five or six years." "I'm not ready to think about it happening now."

"Why?" I asked.

"Yeah, why?" asked Chuck

"I have seen a lot of my friends marry and immediately have a baby. I don't want to be saddled with a child right away. I don't want to take on that responsibility right away."

"But I have a big responsibility too. I believe that the male has to be the breadwinner (at least the main breadwinner), I have a responsibility too, you know!"

"But it's different for you. I will have to take off three years of my life to have a baby! You can at least leave it and go to work."

"But Dianne, I am not going to saddle you with this. I am going to be involved with our child from the beginning, feeding it and changing diapers, and . . ."

"You talk that way," countered Dianne, "but would you really get up at 2 a.m. to feed it, or stay up with it all night if it is sick? It seems like mothers get stuck with all of that!"

"It won't be like that, I promise you," Chuck said with conviction. "If I have to take time off from work, I'll take time off. I don't mind taking a few years off from my career to care for my child."

Dianne looked pleased and surprised. Apparently, this was the first she had heard of Chuck's convictions. "Would you really do that? I didn't know you would be willing."

. . . "In what ways would you like to see each other change?" I asked.

continued

Chuck answered "It's not worth even going there. We're as different as two people can be and both of us are too stubborn to change."

"Yeah," said Dianne, with a smile on her face. "He's extroverted and ambitious."

"And she's serious and hard-working," Chuck said mischievously. "She likes us to work and get things done. I think we need to work and then play. But it's okay, we respect the differences between us."

"Do you believe in marital fidelity?"

"Oh, yes," They spoke almost in unison. "What's the point of getting married, if not?"

"I trust Chuck," Dianne said "I think he's really good-looking and women find him attractive, but I know that when he makes a promise he keeps it."

"I feel the same about Dianne," Chuck said. "She is an absolutely trustworthy person. When she gives her word, it's unshakable."

We ended the interview and they escorted me out the door. Chuck turned around, "You wanted to know why we are getting married?" he said. "Because now we're making a public statement. This is forever."

each other, and often act as if all their wants and needs as individuals can readily be met in this relationship. They want to show to the whole world their commitment to each other.

It is in the expansion stage that we frequently tell our "whole story" to our partners, who hear of our fears and vulnerabilities and share their own, thus signalling their acceptance and affirmation of us "warts and all." Much of our time together is spent communicating, and as we weave our individual stories together, we form a joint story of "how we are" or "how we do things as a couple." Research confirms that the more newlywed couples report a joint story of courtship as a joyful series of accelerating events (versus a fitful path of stops and starts), the more likely they are to report satisfaction and stability even four years later (Stephen, 1984; Surra et al., 1988; Veroff et al. , 1993).

In their common life story couples have a sense of being able to speak about each other (as when Chuck and Dianne insisted they were so different from one another) as well as about the relationship. They have both a common identity as a couple and a separate one as individuals. Partners at this stage of the cycle are able to be eagerly available to each other, emotionally speaking. They not only invite the other to share their feelings and perspective, but listen with rapt attention. This is not a phony "trying to do the right thing," but a genuine responsiveness to the other that comes from being appreciated so unconditionally (Kovacs, 1992; Whitaker et al., 1981).

Fed by this sense of expansiveness and responsiveness to the other, sex in this stage of connecting—both the thought of it and the actual experience—often has a heightened charge of electricity. As Dym & Glenn (1993) report:

> Each touch, glance, or gesture is loaded with significance. Of course there may be fears and anxieties about how one will perform that can make the anticipation of sex incredibly troubling. But even such anxieties are soothed somewhat by the appreciation one feels from one's partner. (p. 27)

At this stage, couples often seem to operate from a sense of plentifulness—that there will be enough of everything to go around, that both partners can have what they want, and that they will be treated fairly by the other. Thus both partners are often willing to accomodate to each other's wishes. If they have not been living together already, they have had little experience with the constricting patterns of each other's role expectations for themselves or the other—*expectations that will become more pronounced as the relationship unfolds* (Larson et al., 1998). Thus, they encourage a kind of spacious, generous thinking, encouraging both exploration and experimentation in the structuring of roles and handling of differences.

> There is often a loosening of gender role expectations. Men are typically more talkative, more emotionally vulnerable. They seek connection and do not run from it. Women, in turn, often proceed more cautiously, feel more open to spirit and adventure, and to being seen as separate independent persons. As in courtship, in this early stage they are still the pursued; the man the pursuer. (Dym & Glenn, p. 27)

Partners often take delight in taking turns being the nurturer, the protector, or the imaginative one. Without realizing it consciously, they develop unspoken emotional contracts as to "how I promise I will be with you and how you promise to be with me," with each genuinely trying to be what the other wants them to be (Sager, 1976). Because these contracts are hidden, it is easy for them to become a source of trouble later when parts of them go unfulfilled.

While this **expansion** stage provides partners with most of the key patterns for how they will enjoy each other and be happy together in later times, the blissfulness of this stage does not last forever. Partners begin to discover (often one partner before the other) that they do not always see things the same way or want the same things. The original terms of the contract for "how I will be for you and you for me" start to chafe. There is often so much closeness and connection with the other that it is hard to live up to the terms of the contract one has unconsciously shaped. Inevitably one will slip, not behave as expected, and trigger hurt and disappointment in one's partner. Although these difficulties surface during this period, they are often like summer storms, quickly brewing and then resolving themselves. But these everyday disagreements give way to major quarrels and accumulated hurts and disappointments as the pressures of everyday life insinuate their way into the life of the couple, moving them into a stage characterized by conflict and defensive withdrawal (Larson et al., 1998).

The contraction stage. As partners live together, differences in expectations and needs emerge that cannot be overlooked or integrated. These cover a wide range of aspects of daily life such as: differences in when one sleeps (one partner may be a "night person"; the other comes alive at 6:00 a.m.), differences in how people deal with money and how much importance they give to material acquisitions, differences in how social each is (one partner may like to stay home and relax while another may like to socialize and party), and differences in the relative importance of career recognition and status and the amount of time committed to career achievement. The list goes on and on. Trying to build a life together when two people have differing needs and expectations and each want things their way results in a sense of disillusionment that one's partner is "not the way he/she was supposed to be."

As partners disagree more with each other and view the other as inflexible, the intense closeness and reliance on the other for support and affirmation that they experienced during the expansion stage gives way to feelings of resentment and betrayal. Gone are the times when partners had a sense that "I can be generous. I will get mine." There is now a full-fledged power struggle to get the other to be the way he or she is "supposed to be." Partners begin to argue more, angry at one another that they are not more amenable to change, and inwardly feeling that they have been deceived. As one's sense of betrayal and resentment grows and one tries harder to change the other, partners see each other's behavior in more rigid terms. This only makes each partner feel less accepted and more defensive. As one partner pushes to get his or her way, the other reacts to being controlled, and becomes more entrenched in opposition (Burleson & Denton, 1992; Markman et al., 1993). These negative feedback cycles begin to replace the positive cycles present before.

> Over time we come to believe that our partners have violated the most basic terms of our original contract. Instead of getting what we thought we had bargained for, we fear that we have gotten something else. (Dym & Glenn, 1993, p. 82)

Research indicates that couples in the contraction stage change their interpretations of each other's actions from positive to negative self-fulfilling processes. Happy couples view positive actions by the spouse (a) as generally likely and not restricted to any specific situations, (b) as resulting from the spouse's as well as their own wishes, and (c) as eliciting positive reactions from themselves. Negative actions, on the other hand, were discounted as rare and involuntary. In contrast, unhappy couples provided a mirror image: (a) they viewed their mate's negative behaviors as commonplace, extensive, deliberate, and provoking, and (b) they discounted their mate's positive actions (Burleson & Denton, 1992; Fincham & O'Leary, 1983; Noller & Fitzpatrick, 1990). Other studies also seem to indicate that the degree of conflict and reactivity in a relationship may act as a filter for our perceptions of our partner's behavior (Acitelli et al., 1993; Jacobson & Addis, 1993).

Reinforced by such negative interpretations of many interactions, partners become more disappointed and react by criticizing or distancing, or both, which reinforces the other to do the same. Researchers have documented that different couples express this power struggle in different ways (Christensen & Shenk, 1991; Heavey et al., 1993; Klinetob & Smith, 1996). Some partners become quite confrontational by openly arguing to get their way. Others distance themselves from their mate, hoping to avoid conflict by creating "separate turfs" where each can have his or her way. Still others adopt a rigid "top dog/bottom dog" role in which conflict is denied by agreeing that one person is always right and the other always wrong. Box 4.2 shows how Tom and Sara, a couple in their late thirties, married eight years, struggle with these issues.

BOX 4.2. Struggling with power issues

Married eight years with one child, Tom and Sara were hard-working professionals—he a lawyer and she a physician. As they spoke they revealed how tense they were, seated on opposite ends of a long sofa.

"So how was it that you picked each other out of every one else on earth to marry?" I asked.

After a long pause Sara spoke up. "I met Tom when we were in med school and law school. He and I hit it off right away. He was such a hard-working, bright person, and did so much for other people. I really admired him."

Tom broke in, saying "I really admired Sara. She was such a caring person and so intelligent, and she was so alive and full of fun! I don't know what happened to that. I don't see any of that fun and aliveness now!"

"You've beat it out of me with your selfishness!" Sara retorted with a grim look on her face. "There's no possibility for any fun with the kind of critical, cruel remarks you make to me constantly!"

"So it feels like the strong connection you had at the beginning has been buried over by a lot of hurts," I said, looking at them both.

"Yes," Tom retorted. "We used to tell each other everything. I felt that Sara was the one person who knew me better than anyone. But that's all changed now. We have nothing to say to each other except biting remarks like the one you just heard."

continued

BOX 4.2. *continued*

"You're the one who has changed, Tom," insisted Sara. "We used to have fun together because you would be open to what I suggested we do. But it hasn't been that way for a long time. If you don't want to do something that I suggest, that's the end of it. If I keep at it, you say I'm nagging you. It's lopsided. If you want to do something, of course I'm supposed to go along with it. I'm tired of always doing things your way."

Tom got very quiet. Sara kept on talking: "And you just tune me out when I talk to you about something. You don't listen to me at all anymore. I'm fed up with it. I've tried for eight years, but it's no use. You can be by yourself and do whatever you damm please!"

"What are you feeling as you hear that, Tom? You seem real quiet," I asked.

"It's always the same old battle," Tom said, letting out a long sigh. "According to Sara I never give enough. But she tugs at me all the time. I don't think she will ever be satisfied. No matter what I do, it's not enough." He looked dejected.

"How long has it felt this way to both of you?" I asked.

"We never really argued like this when we were courting," Sara spoke with conviction. "But it's gotten more and more this way."

Tom shook his head. "I don't know if we can make it, if we keep on like this."

I thought to myself: What had gone wrong in this marriage? Why do they feel so alienated from one another? As we talked on, their unspoken relationship contract became clearer to me. Tom originally saw Sara as a sensual, happy, exciting woman who would draw him out, make him feel special, and be responsive to his needs. He admired her enthusiasm and independence. This was a strong, challenging woman who was a real equal to him. Sara initially viewed Tom as a man who both respected and supported her drive for independence, yet was very open and available to her emotionally, signaling his vulnerability and need for her. Out of these initial interactions, Tom and Sara seemed to have built a series of unspoken agreements. He would be more outgoing, loving and communicative. He would extend himself, would not compete or try to overpower her, if she would draw him out, make him feel loved, be responsive to his needs and give him an intense loving relationship. She, in turn, would be an easygoing, fun loving, sensual, challenging partner for him, if only he would pursue her, be loving, tell her what he thinks and feels, and make her feel like a real equal.

But over time, the original behaviors drawn out by the other's admiration lessened and in their place defensive behaviors increased. Now Tom withdraws when threatened by Sara's anger. Sara interprets Tom's withdrawal as disinterest. Feeling wronged, she criticizes him. Tom withdraws more, telling her less of what's on his mind for fear of her reaction.

In the constricting mindset depicted in Box 4.2, the partners grow more and more pessimistic about their relationship, worrying that they cannot reach each other as they once could, wondering if they should stay committed to what seems their worst nightmare of a relationship. In such a mental state, sex becomes less and less appealing. It is often one more area in which the more one partner feels criticized and cut-off from the other, the more he or she retaliates by being less available sexually. Partners escape into individual pursuits. He may become more consumed by his job, staying later at work and being more involved by work than home matters. She may become submerged in caring for children, cultivating old friendships, or being with her family.

Although this is a very dangerous time in the life of a relationship, when many splinter apart and die, this is also considered a very necessary phase in the development of a relationship. This period of contraction provides the primary arena in which partners develop a true sense of their own separateness and autonomy. Many clinicians (Dym & Glenn, 1993; Whitaker et al., 1981; Wallerstein & Blakeslee, 1995) consider this withdrawal into individualism a vital balancing action which serves as a natural response to the intense, all encompassing closeness of the expansion stage.

> Partners sense a need (often one partner first before the other) for more autonomy, and distance from their partner as a move toward greater differentiation as to who we are and what we need. But this move is always disturbing to our partner who feels the pain of angry disagreement as a rejection of our original terms for how we would be together. The result is a sense of angry, intense struggles in which we create distance, shut down much of our close communication, and build emotional defenses to protect ourselves. (Whitaker et al., 1981, p. 194)

Researchers (Cochran & Peplau, 1985; Rankin-Esquer et al., 1997) have documented the needs that partners have for autonomy and relatedness, and conceptualized these as two *coexisting* aspects of a love relationship which contribute to relationship satisfaction.

To establish this distance, partners often emphasize how **different** they are from one another. Thus we hear Tom and Sara making statements like: "Why do I have to do things your way all the time? Why can't you see things my way for once? You don't even try to understand my point of view! I sometimes wonder if you ever have!" But partners cannot stay this way forever and survive as a couple. How do partners do this without losing their own voice (knowing and honoring their own perspective and feelings), yet responding to their partner less defensively?

The resolution stage.   The way out of the emotional distancing is not quick and easy. Let us follow the story of Tom and Sara (first depicted in Box 4.2) again in Box 4.3, a year down the road.

What happened here? As the couple depicts, getting past the power struggles of the contraction stage is no easy matter. How did each person

BOX 4.3. Moving from contraction to resolution

Our initial counseling sessions had not produced dramatic results. Both Sara and Tom were entrenched in their positions, wanting the other to change back to the person they first knew; neither willing to appreciate the differences each stood for. Cynical and worn out by their perception of the other's stubbornness, they cycled back and forth between feeling totally hopeless and making half-hearted efforts to "negotiate" on the "big" decisions (like the opportunity Sara had to take a job that she really wanted in another city) and hoping the other would "come through for me" and be "the person I had thought I had married." After a year, Sara reported that when she asked Tom to move for her, he resisted. She became furious. After all, this was the job she had always wanted. Finally, in the face of her anger, Tom relented. They moved and he found a position with a local law firm. But he was not happy with it, did not perform well, and was fired. Sara interpreted this as evidence that he was "getting back at me." She withdrew and would not make up. Although he soon got another position, he told her that he felt that it did not have the excitement of the one he had given up in order to move for Sara's new job.

Sara felt that they were working harder than ever. She was engrossed in the demands of her new position. Tom spent a great deal of time with their son, Sean, taking him places and playing with him. They had sex infrequently, and it felt perfunctory rather than exciting. Then Sara became pregnant again, went through a difficult pregnancy, and delivered the baby prematurely. As they watched their child struggle to survive in the prenatal care unit and then die, they pulled closer, consoling each other, and experiencing a sense of support that they had not felt for some time. Sara blamed herself for not carrying the baby to term. Tom comforted her, letting her cry in his arms. For a few days each let go of the hardness and anger they felt for each other.

Over the next few weeks, as Sara recuperated from the delivery, Tom was attentive in small ways. He would call her at home to see how she was doing, and cook dinner for her and Sean. As Sara began to consider how out of touch they had grown from each other, and how much Tom had really seemed to be more considerate in very small ways, she called me. She felt that she had a lot to think about. On the one hand, she felt that Tom really was good with Sean. He was not critical or aloof with Sean as he seemed with her. For the first time she wondered if it was she who was the one making such a mess of things. She had wanted so much to do well in her work and she had, but what had it cost her? She felt out of touch with herself and what she wanted. Perhaps she had been too hard on Tom . . . what was all her fighting for anyway?

They both came in to counseling to talk about their relationship.

continued

BOX 4.3. *continued*

Tom talked about the changes he had had to make over the past year. It was obvious that Tom enjoyed being with Sean and playing with him. "Sean knows I love him and he loves me back," Tom said. "Because of him I guess I've learned to relax more." He seemed to be less critical of himself and less critical of Sara. "I know she works hard. I've made efforts to pick up the slack with Sean." Sara admitted that this was a side of him she had never seen. "I do appreciate the ways he plays with Sean and gets dinner for him," Sara admitted looking at me. "He really does not seem so selfish and self-absorbed." Then she looked at Tom: "I guess you aren't the same person you were earlier. I don't feel that you are always signaling that I do everything wrong like before. I feel less pressure to do things your way." I thought to myself, not only had Tom seemed more responsive, but he stopped making demands of her. Sara was now on her own.

Sara's anger and distrust softened. She told me: "Maybe he has made mistakes, maybe he has hurt me, but haven't I made mistakes too?" As she let go of some of the resentment she felt, her feelings of appreciation grew. She began to evaluate what she was doing at work and consider that it was not the all important thing, it did not make her completely happy. She began to let her guard down, relaxed with Tom, and nothing bad happened. As a matter of fact, no one seemed to notice. She started to act kindly to Tom, and he responded with kindness to her. The sense of being hurt and neglected, and of blaming the other fell away. Pushing oneself and one's partner to do everything right seemed less important. Things would get done. They felt calmer with each other. They could live with this person.

develop a greater willingness to accomodate to the other, valuing partnership over being right?

According to Dym & Glenn (1993), the resolution stage ushers in not only a new contract or agreement between partners, but a new perspective on oneself and one's partner:

> Whereas the contract of the expansive stage represents the promise of the relationship, and contraction represents our defensive fortress, the contract of the resolution stage focuses on working things out. . . . we now measure our relationship by the arrangements we work out—the compromises and accomodations we negotiate with ourselves and each other. (p. 45)

What might trigger the beginning of resolution out of a long-lasting period of contraction? Several possibilities come to mind. Sara and Tom had a family tragedy which they faced together. Many other impactful events in a family's life cycle could have a similar effect: a parent gets sick; a partner gets or loses a job or has a health scare; a child leaves home. Many an impactful event in the outside world can evoke a supportive response from both partners, as they discover that the commonality of their fate and their teamwork is more important than the differences and disappointments which plagued them before. We will review some of these events in the couple and family life cycles later in Table 4.3.

One of the most compelling features of this stage of the cycle is the way we learn to loosen the grip of our own emotions as we respond to situations with our mate. We learn how to "stand apart" and analyze our conflicting feelings—wanting to move close to one's mate, yet feeling hurt and insisting on needing to "be right" and stand apart. Hand in hand with greater acceptance of our own feelings, we sharpen our ability to "put ourselves in our partner's shoes," take our partner's perspective, and identify how *he or she* might be feeling and thinking. We learn that there may be several different ways in which our partner's behavior might be interpreted. For example, rather than continuing to see Tom as distant and withholding, Sara began to consider how he might not know whether she cared for him any more.

This ability we develop to "stand apart," to examine and analyze our own thoughts and feelings, facilitates our being able to compromise and negotiate. While all of us want things to go our way, and *that doesn't change*, in this stage we can see compromise as more than a process of "giving in or giving up." We are more able to see that our partner does have a point of view different from our own, without getting triggered into deciding who is "more right." Unlike the phases of the cycle in which our feelings were characterized by intense excitement and love, or of anger and withdrawal, successfully weathering the resolution stage depends upon our ability to calm ourselves and to **think through** a more practical way to handle our wants and needs. This leads to the paradox of feeling closer by recognizing our partner as a person separate from ourself, which Kahlil Gibran spoke of so well in his poem *The Prophet* (emphasis added):

> And what of Marriage? . . .
> Let there be spaces in your togetherness. And let the winds of the heavens dance between you.
> Love one another, **but make not a bond of love**; Let it rather be a moving sea between the shores of your souls.
> Fill each other's cup, but drink not from one cup. Give one another of your bread; but eat not from the same loaf.
> Sing and dance together and be joyous, but let each one of you be alone, Even as the strings of a lute are alone though they quiver with the same music.
> Give your hearts, **but not into each other's keeping**. For only the hand of Life can contain your hearts.
> And stand together, yet not too near together; for the pillars of the temple stand apart, and the oak tree and the cypress grow not in each other's shadow. (Gibran, 1923/1982, pp. 16–17)

It is striking that these suggestions, the opposite of how most people live their lives, are coupled with the outcome they crave:

> You were born together, and together you will be forevermore. You shall be together when the white wings of death scatter your days. And you shall be together even in the silent memory of God. (Gibran, 1923/1982, p. 16)

Reconciling differences

When a couple says they are living together we picture two people sharing the responsibilities of running a home as well as the emotional needs of a partnership. But with that picture come a thousand and one decisions. Who will make the money? Who will decide how it is spent? Who will decide if there will be children? If yes, how are they to be raised? The decisions of who will do what (or get to do what) is not just a rational one of deciding who is most able to do a job or most willing, but an emotional one of who gets to *say* who does what (i.e., who has the power to decide). Thus, intimate relationships have often been characterized as power struggles to see whose version of intimate relating will win out.

Every culture promotes distinctive ideas as to how partners should structure their responsibilities and allocate power and influence. Fifty years ago, American men were expected to earn a living, and be the formal power or "head of the household" even though they might contribute minimally to the actual day-to-day operation of the home. Wives were to stay home, care for the children, and maintain the house. Because men made the money they controlled the couple's finances and all the choices that went with them (unless the woman had independent wealth). The "good" marriage was one in which people were calm and agreeable; people did not fight or openly disagree. A low level of disagreement was equated with happiness. We believed that the claim "we never fight" was a sign of marital health. But the rules, images, and expectations that shaped the relationships of fifty years ago (e.g., our parents' marriages) do not necessarily fit couples today. We see profound changes in men and women's expectations as to the way roles should be structured, and how influence should be exercised.

Nowhere is this more evident than in the question of whether to have children. If we look back to the 1950s, having children was assumed to be a common purpose of a couple's getting married. Now many couples are choosing to postpone having children or questioning whether to have them at all. Conversely, many unmarried couples are choosing to have children outside of wedlock. These attitudes are reflected in researchers' data on married women's fertility patterns (i.e., the number of children a married woman is predicted to bear over the course of her life). For those women born around the 1930s (who came of age in the 1950s), their lifetime fertility level was 3.12 for white women and 3.86 for nonwhite women. The fertility level of women born in subsequent decades has fallen so that white women currently of childbearing age are predicted to have 1.967 children and non-white women 2.19 children (Cherlin, 1992). Thus, if women choose to have children at all, they are bearing them later than did their mothers and grandmothers, resulting in smaller families and proportionally less of their lifetime devoted to childrearing.

Coupled with these changing attitudes about childbearing, are the profound shifts in men's and women's attitudes about how roles should be structured in marriage. Many of us have moved from the belief that the male should be head of the household (and often the primary if not the sole breadwinner) to the ideology that egalitarian arrangements are best. Nationwide surveys show that "Americans today are more likely to believe that marriages in which the partners share the tasks of breadwinner and homemaker are a more satisfying way of life than they are to prefer the traditional marriage in which the husband is exclusively a provider and the wife exclusively a homemaker and mother" (Weitzman, 1985). This shift in the nature of married life can be traced to the changing attitudes regarding married women's employment outside the home. Over the past thirty years there has been a rapid increase in the proportion of married women who are employed outside the home. This proportion has risen from 20% in 1947 to 60%, or three out of every five married women, in the nineties. Nowadays, more and more women expect to work outside the home when their children are young and to pursue careers which are just as demanding and financially rewarding as their husbands'. In turn, many men expect to be more engaged in child care and domestic chores than were their fathers or grandfathers before them. Thus, ours is an age where neither partner is assumed automatically to be "in charge." But there are no time-tested models of how to live as an egalitarian couple. Instead, the old traditional images of how to "run" a relationship live right next door to the new images of equality that partners invent or learn from the media (Larson et al., 1998). We have to ask many more questions, and there is much opportunity for conflict and difference of opinion. Questions as to who should care for the children, take on the chores, earn money, make decisions, or even how to make love can become mammoth battles.

So how do people decide who will do what and how it will be done? Given that each partner may have a different "set of rules" developed from his or her own needs and family experiences (see Chapter 11), each hopes to convince the other one of the rightness of his or her position. With no strong tradition to dictate the answer or third person to cast the tie-breaking vote, how do they decide how they will handle their differences?

While conventional wisdom assumes that people who are deeply **compatible** (i.e., who agree on the important things—such as sex, money, religion, and children—and honestly and calmly compromise on everything else) have the most satisfying marriages, researchers are reporting a much more complex picture. Certainly, people who share many of the same ideas about life together may report being satisfied with their relationship (Houts et al., 1996; Olson et al., 1993). But as we saw in the last section on balancing needs—many satisfied couples who stay together describe periods of significant unhappiness with their partner. Furthermore, many partners who seem quite dissimilar in goals and preferences stay together for a lifetime and report their partnership to be quite satisfying. What researchers (such as Gottman et al., 1998; Gottman & Krokoff, 1989) who have tracked large numbers of married couples over a long period of time and studied how partners interact are discovering, is that satisfied couples can have very different **styles** of handling their differences and solving problems. Rather than discovering that partners had to be free of conflict to be happy with one another and stay married, these researchers found that conflict was an inevitable part of life for most partners. There also were several different ways to handle conflicts, each potentially effective.

What makes conflict styles work? As a result of analyzing the interactions of partners in over 2,000 marriages that they followed over many years, Gottman and his colleagues (Gottman, 1994a, 1994b) discovered that there were three different styles of problem solving into which satisfying marriages tended to settle:

1. a validating or reasonable style in which couples compromise often and calmly work out their problems as they arise to the mutual satisfaction of both partners,
2. a passionate or volatile style in which conflicts between partners erupt often, resulting in passionate disputes, and
3. a minimizing or conflict-avoiding style in which couples agree to disagree, rarely confronting their differences head on.

What made these three different styles of problem-solving equally capable of satisfying was that in each style, marriage partners maintained a balance between their positive interactions (i.e., "good" moments, which include touching, smiling, compliments) and their negative ones (i.e., "bad" moments, such as fights, broken promises)which kept the overall climate of the marriage satisfying.

Gottman (1994a) reported further that what made these marriages, which differed radically in terms of how partners handled conflict and disagreement, were **equally stable and satisfying was a five-to-one ratio of positive to negative interactions.** Whether couples fought a lot or not at all, whether they seemed intensely engaged with each other or somewhat distant, whether or not they were compatible socially, financially, or sexually, were not as powerful factors in predicting couple satisfaction and stability over time as the overall balance of positive to negative interactions. These new findings are scrambling much of our previous thinking about what makes long-term relationships last. Many marriage counselors along with the general public have assumed that the only style of conflict resolution that leads to a satisfying marriage is the validating or reasonable one where partners acknowledge their differences openly and address them honestly and calmly before they degenerate into shouting matches. This kind of marriage—what Gottman and his associates call a validating style of marriage—can work well. But the other two styles of marital conflict resolution, Gottman and his colleagues discovered, the volatile and the minimizing style, can be just as satisfying to those who use them.

Validating style. Validating partners tend to follow a particular pattern during their conflicts—of first listening to what each has to say, then trying to persuade each other about the rightness of their own position, and then negotiating a compromise both like or at least can live with. This sequence of *validation/persuasion/compromise* is demonstrated in the following conversation.

> Husband: You've never been to church with me. I wish you'd come some time.
>
> Wife: You know I don't believe in organized religion.
>
> Husband: I'm not asking you to believe.
>
> Wife: What then?
>
> Husband: I get lonely without you.
>
> Wife: You're saying you miss me?
>
> Husband: Yeah, I am.
>
> Wife: You're not trying to convert me?
>
> Husband: Maybe a little, but no. I just wish we'd be together as a family.
>
> Wife: I kind of miss you too on Sunday morning.
>
> Husband: I also think it's good for the kids.
>
> Wife: I agree.
>
> Husband: What about coming some time?
>
> Wife: No pressure?
>
> Husband: No pressure.
>
> Wife: I'll think about it.
>
> Husband: Fair enough. (Cited in Gottman, 1994c, pp. 47–48)

You can see that this couple follows the validation/persuasion/compromise pattern we talked about. Each not only presented an individual opinion, but listened to that of his or her mate before attempting to persuade one another of a particular option. Gottman and his colleagues (1994a, 1994b, 1994c; Gottman et al., 1998) reported other interesting features of couples demonstrating this style. One is that there seems to be a fair amount of stereotypical sex-role behavior in which each spouse has a separate sphere of influence. For example, the wife is in charge of the home and children,

"THE TRADITIONALS"

and the husband is usually the final decision maker. "While he tends to see himself as analytical, dominant, and assertive, she views herself as nurturing, warm, and expressive" (Gottman, l994c, p. 38).

This style is similar to "traditional" married couples described by Fitzpatrick and her colleagues (Fitzpatrick, 1984; Noller & Fitzpatrick, 1988, 1990). According to Fitzpatrick, "traditional" couples demonstrate a high value for "we-ness" (i.e., cohesion) over individual goals and values. They also highly value verbal openness, shared time and shared activities, and being in love. Thus, you would rarely find couples who demonstrate a validating style voicing a great need for privacy or having "off-limit" zones in their homes. One of the pitfalls of this style of relating is that the balance between personal development and togetherness may get too skewed toward togetherness. But, on the whole, a validating-style marriage seems to be a pretty solid one.

Volatile style. In stark contrast to the ease and calm of the validating style, volatile-style couples jump right in and advocate their position instead of listening to their partner's opinion. With their epic brawls and take-no-prisoners attacks on each other, these couples certainly do not seem to care if they hear their partner's point of view or "fight fairly." Instead, they go for the jugular, rarely listen to or empathize with their partner during the course of a battle, and often attempt to steamroll the other into accepting their point of view. This doesn't mean, however, that they do not have satisfying marriages. According to Gottman (1994b):

> In a successful marriage of this type, for every nasty swipe, there are five caresses, so to speak. Indeed far more than other marriages, however solid and satisfying, volatile marriages are inclined to be deeply romantic and frequently dramatic. And because the spouses tend, as one would expect, to be passionate and intense people, their relationship—when it is satisfying—can be much more exciting and deeply intimate than the marriages of less emotionally engaged people. (p. 44)

Now, here's how that "church" conversation might sound if a volatile couple were having it:

> Husband: You've never been to church with me. I wish you'd come some time.
>
> Wife: You know I don't believe in organized religion.

Husband: I want to get Jason baptized.

Wife: (*Raising her voice*) Why? So he doesn't go to purgatory for original sin if he dies?

Husband: Because I feel it says that he has a spiritual life, that he's part of a religious community.

Wife: You got that from the priest.

Husband: Well, he said it quite well.

Wife: (*Sarcastically*) You're a lawyer and you can't put it in your own words?

Husband: God's got too good a case.

Wife: (*Laughs*) Yeah, we don't want to fight God.

Husband: (*Laughs*) Since you don't believe in any of it, why not go along with what I want? (Cited in Gottman, 1994c, pp. 48–49)

The discussion above is littered with examples of speaking for the other, interpreting the intent with "Yes, you do" and "No you don't." While it might seem like these arguments are a sure route to disaster, Gottman's research (1994a, 1994b) confirmed that often these arguments are part of a warm and loving marriage in which the passion with which they fight seemed to fuel their positive interactions with each other. Partners who demonstrate this volatile marriage style parallel a group of married couples Fitzpatrick (1990) called "independents." Unlike "traditionals," the "independents" seem to value autonomy, and are much more likely to support a nontraditional sex-role arrangement (such as both partners following careers and sharing childcare), and do not pay much attention to schedules or traditional values. "Independents" also tend not to avoid conflict but, instead, to do considerable negotiation and sharing of opinions.

Of course there are pitfalls with this style of interaction. Because they have a "no holds barred" way of interacting, when they fly at each other without thinking (as they are often prone to do), they can inflict irreparable harm. Furthermore, their constant quarreling and bickering may consume their marriage, overwhelming the balance of their happy times during times of stress (such as the birth of a baby or loss of a job) such that they may have a hard time keeping their ratio of positives to negatives in balance.

The avoidant style.   At the opposite end of the spectrum are the couples who don't fight at all. These couples—whom Gottman termed **conflict avoiders** or **minimizers**—tend to step around conflict, to smooth over or ignore differences rather than confront them head on, and to resolve differences by "agreeing to disagree" (Gottman, 1994c). Surprisingly, these couples can also have very stable and satisfying marriages. This group parallels the group that Fitzpatrick (1990) called the "separates." These couples tend to value harmony and predictability in their lives, and personal privacy. Let us look at how one such couple might deal with the religion issue:

> Husband: You've never been to church with me.
>
> Wife: Um-humm, that's true.
>
> Husband: I wish you'd come some time.
>
> Wife: I prefer the time alone.
>
> Husband: Well, okay. It's not real important to me actually.
>
> Wife: We have a lot else going for us, you know.
>
> Husband: Oh I think ours is a great marriage. Yeah, my sister and Jeff go all the time and they fight like cats and dogs. Religion doesn't do much for them. I just thought I'd ask.
>
> Wife: I'm glad you brought it up. But you know I could put in the time on our remodeling. We're so close to getting started with the plans.
>
> Husband: That'd be more important, really, than your going with me to church. Go ahead.
>
> Wife: You don't mind?
>
> Husband: No. It's no big deal. It's not an issue.
>
> Wife: I'll come to the picnics.
>
> Husband: Fine. That'd be fine.
>
> Wife: You don't mind?
>
> Husband: Not really.
>
> Wife: Good. (Cited in Gottman, 1994c, p. 49)

Although it is obvious that this husband and wife disagree on the issue of her attending church with him, neither attempts to persuade the other to follow his or her position. Nor do they really reach a conclusion about this issue. Instead, they minimize it, concurring that it is just not that big of a deal. Each person states his or her case, they do not push one another to accept their point of view, and that is the end of it. According to Gottman:

> In these relationships, solving a problem usually means ignoring the difference, one partner agreeing to act more like the other, or most often just letting time take its course. And yet, if you ask these couples whether they ever argue, many will readily say they do. In a sense they do air their conflicts, but they follow up with only minimal attempts to convince each other of their point. They resolve their issues by avoiding or minimizing them. . . . Thus these marriages look like calm lakes. (1994b, p. 45)

This way of settling differences may fly in the face of our ideas about how married people should "talk things out." However, these marriages are often quite satisfying for several reasons. First, avoidant-style partners often do hold very similar beliefs about finances, childrearing, and sex so that there are often not as many areas on which to disagree. Secondly, they look upon their marriage as "a secure bastion, a solid fortress of 'us,' so strong that we can afford to overlook disagreements" (Gottman, 1994b, p. 45). Of course, these marriages have vulnerabilities too. Because conflict is not usually handled directly, partners may have real difficulty dealing with differences resulting from changed life circumstances which cannot be avoided. For example, if the husband loses his job and the wife must work, resolving that issue may be monumental for them. However, according to Gottman these marriages can be quite stable and satisfying to their participants if the five-to-one ratio of positive to negative is honored.

How does the five-to-one ratio work? What are the positive and negative behaviors that make up this vital balance? Gottman and his associates recorded stable ratios of positive to negative interactions by using two different coding systems to analyze the videotapes of marital conflict resolution (see Table 4.2.). The first is the Rapid Couples Interaction Scoring System (RCISS) which records behaviors known to impact problem-solving in positive and negative ways. The second is the Specific Affect coding system (SPAFF), which focuses only on evidence of emotions.

The ratio of positive to negative interactions for distressed couples was approximately one-to-one on both the RCISS and the SPAFF coding systems. In contrast, even when other coding systems were used, the ratio

TABLE 4.2. Positive and negative behavior and feeling codes

Positive behaviors coded	Negative behaviors coded
Rapid Couples Interaction Scoring System (RCISS)	Complain, criticize
Neutral or positive problem description	Defensive
Task-oriented relationship information	Negative relationship issue problem talk
Assent	Yes-but
Humor-Laugh	Put down
Other positive	Escalate negative affect
	Other negative
Specific Affect Coding System (SPAFF)	
Affection/Caring	Anger
Humor	Disgust/Contempt
Interest/Curiosity	Sadness
	Fear
Joy/Enthusiasm	Whining

Source: Gottman, 1994a.

POSITIVE BEHAVIORS VS. NEGATIVE BEHAVIORS

of positive to negative interactions for stable (that is, the relationship endured rather than ended in divorce) and satisfied couples was at least five times as many positive as negatives. This ratio is five times as high as the ratio for distressed couples who were on their way to divorce a few years later.

Surprisingly, this research rarely found any couples whose count of positive to negative feelings fell in between the five-to-one and the one-to-one ratios. What could be happening? Apparently, all the positive-to-negative ratios in between are unstable, so they do not show up in a filmed interaction. Gottman's explanation for this may provide insight into the processes through which couples become distressed, and thus illustrate the mental and emotional transition between the expansion and contraction stages we discussed earlier.

How do couples change from holding a positive to a negative estimation of each other? According to Gottman (1994a), negative emotions affect us much more strongly than positive emotions. When anger, disgust, or sadness occur too frequently in a relationship even to be counterbalanced by five times as many positive emotions, we are flooded with unpleasant emotional arousal and can only try to fight or flee. If we enter this fight-or-flight mode often enough, we become arousal-prone and can no longer hold on to our positive interpretations of our partner and our relationship. Instead, we develop a stable negative evaluation of our partner, assuming he or she is selfish, mean-spirited, pathological, threatening, or undesirable. We dismiss anything positive our partner does. These negative judgments about our partner solidify to defend us against feeling again the acute hurt and disappointment that have occurred in our frustrated attempts to get what we needed from each other.

In addition to the five-to-one balance of positive to negative interactions, Gottman and his associates discovered that, for marriages to survive, it may be necessary that the partners **prefer the same style** of resolving their differences. If a validator (someone who is disposed to calmly and rationally working problems out) or a conflict-minimizer (someone content to let problems remain unresolved) marries a volatile type (someone who loves passionate battles), serious problems are likely. The volatile-style partner expects that the mate will go "nose to nose." If their partner avoids engaging or continues to push for reasonableness, the volatile partner may grow angrier, feeling he or she is being ignored or patronized. If partners cannot change to the same style, conflicts may spiral out of control and destabilize the relationship.

Gottman's studies support those of other researchers (e.g., Fowers et al., 1996; Matthews et al., 1996; Raush et al., 1974) who report that couples appear to develop a style of dealing with their conflicts very early in the life of their relationship (i.e., in courtship and the first few years of marriage). And while these styles of conflict resolution may change somewhat around the birth of the first child, the change is not major. These findings suggest that couples unconsciously set their own "emotional thermostat"—that partners know how cold or hot they want their relationship to be, how close or distant—a point on which many clinicians agree (Dym & Glenn, 1993; Whitaker, 1976). Because one's style of conflict resolution is inextricably tied to one's temperament, accommodating to a different style sometimes may be just too big of a jump. Thus, it appears that couples who sustain their love relationship over time are compatible but in a way far different from what we might expect. **Rather than seeing eye to eye on what to fight about, partners whose marriages survive seem to come to an implicit agreement as to how they will fight and handle their differences.**

But what happens when life somehow manages to change that thermostat, to heat it up or pull it down? What are the events which partners experience together in the relationship or which happen to one of them outside the relationship which affect the balance they have set and cause them to need to adjust? Let us take a look at how couples tolerate change.

Tolerating change

Every relationship is going to go through changes. We are all familiar with the predictable crises of having children and rearing them, trying to balance this with work, career advancement, and dealing with in-laws. But what are the unexpected events that can stir up controversy and pain in a marriage and shift the vital balance of positives to negatives that make up its fragile emotional balance? Let us look first at how social scientists have thought about the predictable events in the life of married couples.

It has become fashionable in recent years to organize changes in adult life in clear-cut stages, in much the same way that children's development has been described as occurring in an organized sequence. Two psychiatrists, Ellen Berman and Harold Lief (1975), have, for example, mapped out a marital life cycle in which they created a parallel between the stages of marriage and the stages of individual adult development. As charted by Berman and Lief, in Stage 1 (which occurs during the late teens and early twenties), an individual begins to leave the family of origin and go out into the world. If partners marry during these times, Berman and Lief contend that most conflicts will center on tensions between emotional ties to each partner's original family and the partner's ties to each other. Stage 2 is characterized by the birth of children and the need to share attention and affection three-ways rather than just two. By Stage 3, when the average age of partners is between 29 and 31 years old, most are employed and struggling with balancing commitments to marriage and family life and to their work. Marital partners at this age struggle with restlessness and doubts about their own abilities and their commitment to one another, especially if they are still caught up in parental expectations. By Stages 5 and 6, however, when individuals are in their forties and fifties, partners are beginning to reorder their priorities in life. At this stage, marital conflicts may be churned up over attitudes toward success and concerns about the passing of youth. The last stage, Stage 7, spans from 60 years onward. According to Berman and Lief, now partners must deal with older age, and marital conflicts center around fears of desertion, loneliness, and sexual failures.

Other descriptions by clinicians and researchers (Carter & McGoldrick, 1989; Haley, 1972) offer similar schemes organizing the marital life cycle in terms of events going on in the family life of the couple. Carter and Goldrich (1989), for example, identified the general issues faced by couples in adapting to the demands of having a family, and the specific tasks couples must successfully address in becoming a family and adjusting to changes in family life (see Table 4.3). Lee Combrick-Graham (1985) has broadened the lens to describe how couple life is shaped by events in the larger extended families of each partner. She suggests that all extended families (and the couples who build them) move back and forth between periods characterized by a strong **centrifugal** pull on their members (i.e., when the emphasis is upon increased distance or separation, and upon independent action and autonomy among family members) and periods characterized by a strong **centripetal** pull (i.e., when the emphasis is upon a high degree of connection and cooperation among members, responsiveness to each other, and commitment to shared activities). During centripetal periods of the life cycle (such as with the birth of a baby or the death of a grandparent) there are clearer boundaries around the family system in relationship to its context. In contrast, as the family moves toward a centrifugal period (such as when the children start school, or older children leave home), the boundaries between the family and the outside world must be able to open up and facilitate increased emotional distance between family members and increased involvement with their surroundings. In effect, the family must be able to modify its original structure and free family members to separate and become more autonomous. According to Combrick-Graham (1985), each cycle of development within the extended family as well as the immediate couple sends shock waves through the family pulling on partners to loosen their ties with each other or pull closer. Figure 4.2 depicts the family life cycle of these changing connections.

How do couples handle these pulls for greater closeness or greater distance? We would guess that their response to these life changes would be greatly influenced by the particular way that couples have "set their thermostat" for closeness and distance and the amount of "stretch" built

TABLE 4.3. The stages of the family life cycle

Family life cycle stage	Emotional process of transition: Key principles	Second-order changes in family status required to proceed developmentally
1. Leaving home: Single young adults	Accepting emotional and financial responsibility for self	a. Differentiation of self in relation to family of origin b. Development of intimate peer relationships c: Establishment of self re work and financial independence
2. The joining of families through marriage: The new couple	Commitment to new system	a. Formation of marital system b: Realignment of relationships with extended families and friends to include spouse
3. Families with young children	Accepting new members into the system	a: Adjusting marital system to make space for child(ren) b. Joining in childrearing, financial, and household tasks c. Realignment of relationships with extended family to include parenting and grandparenting roles
4. Families with adolescents	Increasing flexibility of family boundaries to include children's independence and grandparents' frailties	a. Shifting of parent child relationships to permit adolescent to move in and out of system b: Refocus on midlife marital and career issues c. Beginning to shift toward joint caring for older generation
5. Launching children and moving on	Accepting a multitude of exits from and entries into the family system	a. Renegotiation of marital system as a dyad b. Development of adult to adult relationships between grown children and their parents c. Realignment of relationships to include in-laws and grandchildren d. Dealing with disabilities and death of parents (grandparents)
6. Families in later life	Accepting the shifting of generational roles	a. Maintaining own and/or couple functioning and interests in face of physiological decline; exploration of new familial and social role options b. Support for a more central role of middle generation c. Making room in the system for the wisdom and experience of the elderly, supporting the older generation without overfunctioning for them d. Dealing with loss of spouse, siblings, and other peers and preparation for own death. Life review and integration

Source: Carter, B., & McGoldrick, M. (1989). *The Changing Family Life Cycle*. Boston: Allyn & Bacon.

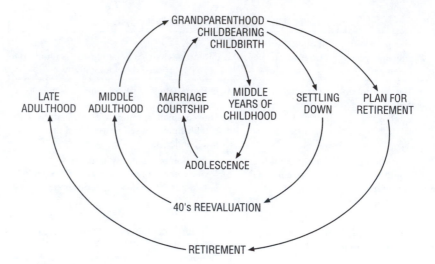

GRANDPARENTHOOD
CHILDBEARING
CHILDBIRTH

LATE   MIDDLE   MARRIAGE   MIDDLE   SETTLING   PLAN FOR
ADULTHOOD ADULTHOOD COURTSHIP   YEARS OF   DOWN   RETIREMENT
                                       CHILDHOOD

ADOLESCENCE

40's REEVALUATION

RETIREMENT

FIG. 4.2.
The Family Life Spiral.
Source: Combrinck-
Graham.

into these thermostats. We have just seen in the stages of marital closeness section that both positive crises (such as a great success of a family member's marriage) and negative crises (such as the death of a child or parent) can trigger a resolution stage in a marriage. But we know that these crises can lead to divorce as well. What makes the difference? How do couples handle these changed circumstances which pull them toward greater closeness or greater distance?

Wallerstein and Blakeslee (1995) interviewed fifty happily married couples and found four processes that helped them weather changes and crises.

1. The couples thought and planned as realistically as they could for the duration and consequences of the crisis/change;
2. They didn't blame each other, and they even tried to protect each other from inappropriate self-blame;
3. They took steps to keep some pleasure and humor in their lives to balance the tragedy; and
4. While accepting their feelings and anxieties, they watched out for each other to prevent inappropriate, hurtful, and self-destructive responses from taking over. (p. 122–123)

The second and fourth processes above reflect the ability to take the partner's perspective, which we found in the case of Tom and Sara earlier in this chapter. Happily married spouses apparently also cared about the course which their partner's responses could take. The key elements in these processes are the urge to nurture one's partner, which joins with problem-solving and emotional coping skills to guide the couple to greater calm and clarity after their crisis. Effective marital partners develop and use these crisis-coping processes throughout their relationship. They adjust and readjust their ways of relating—or "stretch" their thermostat as a result of the demands they face. This is nowhere more evident than when children enter into a couple's life.

The impact of children. For some couples childbearing brings greater closeness, while for others it breeds distance (Crohan, 1996; Hackel & Ruble, 1992; Mitchell & Gee, 1996). For example, some couples approach the task of childbearing with a strong sense of "we-ness:"

> *I never felt closer to my wife than at the moment when John was born. I had been there with her through the whole thing—helping her breathe, rubbing her back between contractions, and wiping her forehead. I really felt a part of the birth process. When our baby was finally delivered, my wife and I cried and laughed and cried again. It was such a powerful moment we shared together.*

In contrast, other partners who felt more comfortable with the calmness of couple life may see the baby as an assault on life as they knew it:

> *If I had it to do over again, I would have waited at least three years before having children. We were barely married a year before our twins came and we had to learn to deal with them as well as learn how to live with each other. It was a really rocky time for us. I dealt with it by trying to put my nose to the grindstone and crank out a living, but I really missed the closeness that my wife and I had had before.*

The impact of children on marital satisfaction has been a subject of much controversy. Prior to 1980 at least a dozen studies (summarized in Ade-Ridder & Brubaker, 1983) reported a curvilinear relationship between family stage and marital satisfaction. That is, satisfaction was high initially, then fell off during the middle childrearing years, and then rose again late in the marriage. Researchers hypothesized that the stresses and strains of family responsibilities and work contributed to this period of low marital satisfaction. During later years, when careers were well established and children were launched in their own independent lives, the role demands on marital partners decreased. Thus researchers concluded that the pressures of rearing children shaped the changing levels of marital satisfaction. Recent research (Johnson & Booth, 1998; Kurdek, 1998b) has thrown these findings into question however. When these researchers gathered data on couples longitudinally (over 12 years and 6 years respectively), they found that both parents and nonparents reported a decline in marital satisfaction and feelings of love for one another. Although the parents in another sample

(Huston et al., 1986) did report experiencing a change in companionship and the way they had structured their roles, they did not differ from nonparents in the level of satisfaction or love reported. Thus, researchers are revising their ideas about the impact of children on a marriage, and are now considering that the dip in satisfaction during the middle years may be a function of the length of the marriage rather than the impact of children.

Recent research provides a new view of the changes in marital satisfaction. Fincham and Linfield (1997) found that marital satisfaction scales need to measure two separate factors: aspects of the marriage that are rewarding or satisfying; and aspects that are frustrating or unpleasant. Since satisfactions and dissatisfactions may be remembered as separate piles, a spouse might ignore or minimize the negatives when feeling good in the present—or he or she might amplify the negatives and ignore the positives when feeling bad about the partnership. Such a process of selective attention has been suggested in our three-stage model of marital closeness and separateness.

But children do have a dramatic impact on married life. In her humorous but serious novel *Heartburn*, Nora Ephron (1983) describes the effects of having a child this way:

> After Sam was born I realized something no one ever tells you: that a child is a grenade. When you have a baby you set off an explosion in your marriage, and when the dust settles, your marriage is different from what it was. . . . The baby wakes up in the middle of the night, and instead of jumping out of bed, you lie there thinking: whose turn is it: If it's your turn, you have to get up; if it's his turn, then why is he still lying there asleep while you're awake wondering whose turn it is?" (p. 192)

MATERNITY WARD

"AFTER MY CHILD WAS BORN, I REALIZED SOMETHING NO ONE EVER TELLS YOU. A CHILD IS A GRENADE!"

Children are the focus of many disagreements in a marriage. A wife's involvement with a baby may make her husband feel left out. Or having a baby can trigger career tensions that partners thought they had resolved. For example, many couples who think they are going to have a child and have two careers, hit real difficulties in making this reality work. Good childcare is not only difficult to find, it is often prohibitively expensive. Partners often have to juggle the job of childcare and work, trading off the responsibilities of caring for the baby when the other goes to work. Then there are the unexpected complications of hidden role expectations. Some women find that while their husband may have been very accepting of their work or career before children, once they have a child, they want their wives home, if not full time, then most of the time. In such struggles, the baby can trigger a deeper struggle not just over who cares for the child, but whose preferences for how roles are to be structured win out.

Reconnecting in the empty nest.   Just as having children may trigger one set of changes in a couple, the freedom from having children in the house begins to stir up a totally different set of issues. Able to catch their breath from the constant demands of making a living and caring for children, some couples find that they almost need to get acquainted again. The couple depicted in Box 4.4 discuss their adaptation.

As this couple depicts, most couples go through a series of different times in their marriage, some characterized by closeness and comfort, others by distance and struggle. And as Leslie and Eric admitted, most partners in long-term relationships, at one time or another, experience times that seemed so painful that they wondered if they should get out of the marriage or stay in it. But among partners who stay together, the thought of separation or divorce seems to be a fleeting one, followed by a decision to recommit. Most satisfied couples report that for them divorce is not a viable alternative, that they must somehow see their way clear to try and jump start things. They tend to demonstrate a commitment to each other and to the marriage. While they might not know what to do to get the good feelings back, they believe that they can somehow get things on the right course again.

One of the apparent contradictions of marriage is that one must be committed to a way of life that doesn't stay the same. Although at the start of marriage, partners often make public commitments to each other in their marriage vows to spend their life together, the ways they are thinking and feeling when they begin their marriage cannot and will not last. It is not that the statements are meaningless—they may be felt as the absolute truth at the moment—but as people live with each other in a marriage they discover that it is not what they expected. But parents usually go on loving their children as they grow from babies to teenagers and independent adults. So it is not surprising that marital love can survive an equally large set of changes. What appears necessary is that people are willing to commit themselves to a process of personal development which is often painful and perplexing. As Jung (1925/1971) said: "Seldom, or perhaps never, does a marriage develop into an individual relationship smoothly and without crises; there is no coming to consciousness without pain."

Furthermore, as the different partners we interviewed reveal, this commitment comes and goes. Each partner will in all likelihood consciously reevaluate and redecide whether the relationship is important enough to fight for and, if so, how he or she will commit renewed effort and energy to do that. Thus, partners are more likely actively *committing and recommitting themselves over time* than merely committing themselves once and for all time. Accepting this contradiction of being committed to a changing rela-

BOX 4.4. Adapting to an emptying nest

Busy professionals in their early fifties, Leslie and Eric had married in their twenties and had a child in the first year. Twenty-five years later, with two children, they spoke about the mid-course changes they had made in their marriage.

Leslie began: "I think that in many ways we are much richer versions of the people we married twenty-five years ago. I've seen a number of different sides of him and I know he feels like he has been married to at least four different versions of me!"

Eric responded: "We've never had a very standard or conventional marriage. It's always been different from what I expected it would be like when we married. Both of us have been so fiercely independent. We each felt so strongly that we had to prove ourselves and become somebody. That took a lot of energy in the early years. And of course we expected that the other one would approve, would support our dedication, would not pull us away or ask too much of us."

Leslie laughed, and said: "It's been hard being married to a superman. It's even harder being one myself. It has taken years of working ourselves to death to realize that this is not what we wanted."

"How did these ideas play themselves out in your marriage?" I asked.

Eric responded: "The first few years of marriage were a rude awakening for both of us. We had our first child while we were still in grad school, and I was holding down several part-time jobs. I think both of us assumed a 'work harder' attitude as we juggled rearing a baby, going to school, and working our jobs."

"We each had our ideas of what the 'job' of wife and husband was supposed to be and needless to say they were miles apart!" Leslie quipped. "Eric seemed less and less like the person I married. He didn't want to have sex very often and often didn't even want to talk. I felt that I must be doing something wrong and pressed harder to be a good wife and mother and to be more competent in my work, but I did not talk with him about how I felt. Of course my efforts to "communicate" were more often talking to him about what was not working—complaining about not having sex or him not doing his "fair share" at home—than anything else."

"How did you get through these rough times?" I asked.

"Our disagreements just went underground," Eric explained. "Neither Leslie or I knew how to fight. So we just tried to avoid the painful areas."

"Our good times were overrun by a load of responsibilities—babies, house, bills—'the whole catastrophe' as Zorba says," Leslie joined in.

"What happened to change things?" I asked.

"As the kids got older and we got older I think both Eric and I began to question the rat race we were in. I began to wonder if I hadn't
continued

BOX 4.4. *continued*

devoted myself to our children and my job too much. I seemed to have had no time for Eric and me."

"I think that one event that made us both want to change things was a marital encounter weekend sponsored by our church," Eric answered. Each of the couples leading the encounter talked about the small hurts and misunderstandings that had divided them, and about their efforts to rebuild their sense of partnership. I came away realizing how much deciding to love someone took a really conscious effort to try to be loving."

"Yeah," Leslie nodded her head. "By that time, I think we each wondered if the other person really did love us. In that weekend I realized that Eric's long-term actions spoke louder than his short-term ones. He really had been choosing to live with me for thirteen years, even though on a daily basis it didn't always live up to my definition of loving."

Eric chimed in, "I began to see how hard it was for each of us to show our feelings—good or bad. We were each very private people. It was scary to show how much we felt for the other person and how much we wanted their love and understanding. We were very self-conscious and clumsy at talking to each other."

"One of the rituals of the weekend involved making a commitment to build a more 'married couple' versus 'married singles' life together," Leslie said. "I decided to commit myself to working with Eric in some way in Boy Scouts. Our youngest was just getting the right age to start, and I decided that could be an activity we would do together."

"You surprised me with that, " Eric said. "But it told me how much you were willing to devote to working for us. It made a big impression on me, and over the past ten years we've spent a lot of time in Boy Scouts and other activities in our church. We've built a lot of memories of fun and hard work."

"This didn't happen over night, mind you," Leslie said. "I think we have each learned and changed ever so slowly. Where before I experienced Eric as abrupt and quick to cut me short, now he is willing to stop and listen. He asks my opinion and listens to my response. He respects me and what I have tried to accomplish in my life. I think we have both tried to live up to our commitments to ourselves and to each other."

As I ended with this couple, I felt optimistic. These two people obviously really cared for each other. Their marriage was alive and well.

tionship, yet having to live with its imperfections, often results in a more compassionate and philosophical view of life as described by some of the poets. For example, Osbon (1991) writes:

If you go into marriage with a program
you will find that it won't work.

Successful marriage
is leading innovative lives together,
being open, non-programmed.
It's a free fall: how you handle
each new thing as it comes along.

As a drop of oil on the sea,
you must float,
using intellect and compassion
to ride the waves. (p. 47)

There is still much to learn about the experience of living in a long-term love relationship such as marriage. While poets, married people, and clinicians wax eloquent about the paradoxes of living in tandem with another, we still have a very limited social scientific knowledge on the subject. Perhaps you will be the future social scientists who help us understand more about what loving long-term is like.

Chapter summary

- Ninety percent of adults in the United States marry at some point in their lives.
- People today tend to delay marriage until they are in their mid-twenties—thus marrying significantly later than did their parents—and to marry someone usually only two or three years different in age.
- Marriage is a process of dealing with challenges to one's ways of thinking and feeling about oneself and one's partner around four issues: building trust, balancing needs for connectedness and autonomy, reconciling differences, and tolerating change.
- Marital trust develops through getting to know one's partner's feelings and beliefs, and holding similar beliefs about preferred amounts of closeness and intimacy.
- Clinicians believe that couples balance their needs for connectedness and autonomy by repeatedly moving close, moving apart, then moving close again in a three-stage cycle of: expansion, contraction, and resolution.
- Researchers have discovered that satisfied couples reconcile differences in three distinctly different styles. All three styles—validating, volatile, and minimizing—can be satisfying if couples share a similar style and have a balance of five positive interactions to every negative one.
- Too many negative compared to positive moments can set off an

emotional cascade in which partners are negatively aroused, develop a negative evaluation of their partner, and avoid interaction because they expect it to be negative.

- Couples often experience predictable life events (crises) such as the birth of children, which pull them to change how they structure their relationship. Satisfied couples tend to adapt to these events by planning realistically, not blaming the other, taking steps to keep a positive balance in relationship, and protecting each other from destructive responses.

Divorce, adjustment, and remarriage 5

- **Why study divorce?**
  The rising rate of divorce
  Reduced barriers against divorce
  Couples' reasons for divorcing
  Psychological and sociocultural bases of divorce
- **A multiple process model of marital dissolution**
  Bohannon's six transition tasks
  Steefel's four stages
- **Post-separation adjustment: General characteristics**
  Trajectories of former spouses' divorce adjustment
  Gender differences
  Child support
  Issues in emotional recovery
  Long-term attachment
  Gains after divorce
- **Post-divorce dating**
  Stages of dating
- **Staying single: Lonely or self-fulfilled?**
- **Remarriage: It's not the same**

Why study divorce?

It can be depressing to study divorce. One uncovers so much inhumanity, so many private wars, innocent victims and petty atrocities. But studying the processes of divorce has helped us understand what people go through when marriages come apart, so some suffering can be lightened. It might give us early warnings of impending decay, so we can intervene sooner to repair relationships in trouble. Studying what happens when a love relationship breaks down might also yield new insights into the nature of love itself. Perhaps then we can take better care of it.

Divorced: Previously married. Despite their bad press, people who have recently escaped from the institution of marriage are really no more disturbed or dangerous than anyone else who has recently escaped from an institution.

The rising rate of divorce

The rate of divorce has been rising in the United States since the mid-nineteenth century, but it peaked in 1979 and has leveled off and dropped slightly since then (see Figure 5.1). Before the statistics from the 1980s became well established, it was normal to extrapolate from the dramatic rise in divorce rates since the mid-sixties and predict continuous rises in the eighties and nineties (see Figure 5.2). Prior predictions of doom typically contrasted the low rate in the 1950s with the rapidly rising rate in the 1970s (Price & McKenry, 1988). But now the 1950s are viewed as atypical, a period of stability and prosperity following depression and war, which saw the creation of the suburban wage-earner/homemaker family (Cherlin, 1992). Leading sociologists now predict that the divorce rate will stabilize at a relatively high level, with couples who married in 1985 having a 51% chance of their marriages ending in divorce (Cherlin, 1992; Weed, 1988). *Thus, it may be that the forces of biology, economics, and psychological and cultural attitudes have reached equilibrium.*

The most basic reason for rising divorce rates and falling birth rates is industrialization and resulting urbanization (Cherlin, 1992; Price & McKenry, 1988). Specialized education of workers and separation of the workplace from the family leads to mutually reinforcing social changes:

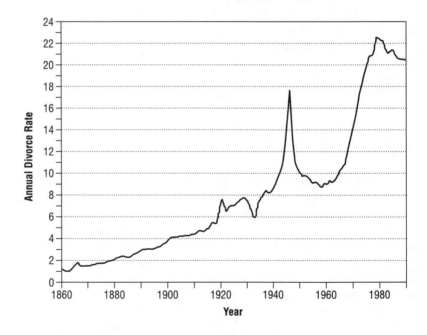

FIG. 5.1.
Annual number of divorces in the United States, per thousand marriages. Source: Cherlin, 1992.

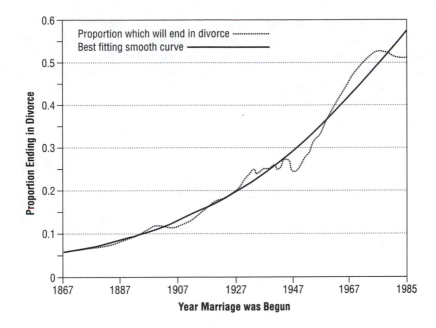

FIG. 5.2.
Proportion of marriages begun each year that will end in divorce, 1867 to 1985. Source: Cherlin, 1992.

1. A spiraling breakdown of communal living and relating combines with an increase in spending for material goods and services to commute, take care of domestic work, and pursue happiness, along with increasing taxes and inflation. This leads to a greater need to work for more money.
2. Farm children helped produce food and income, but urban children take longer and cost more to raise and train, so birth rates have declined.
3. The basic reason for marriage all over the world may be to stabilize the traditional division of labor by gender: women care for children while men provide materially for the family (Murdock & White, 1969). But post-industrial society is creating a more complex organization of labor which parcels out material provisions and childcare to more than two people, making the marital couple with children a less necessary structure in society.

One result of these developments is the dual-career couple who pays for childcare and does not divide up its tasks on a traditional gender basis. But couples without children can succeed as well or better in the workplace, and same-sex couples are just as functional as male–female couples. Group living and single living are as functional too, if exclusive pair-bond attachments are not as vital to human well-being as was traditionally assumed. Thus, today's social organization has drawn into question our cultural meanings of both sex roles and couple intimacy.

Is divorce therefore both a result and a cause of social change? Yes, if we connect it in interactive loops to industrialization, urbanization, splintering of community, relative impoverishment, separation and alienation of children from adults, and adolescent anger and emotional trauma. But even if divorce has been part of a spiraling process of social disintegration, it has not increased in frequency in over a decade, so we could assume that the escalation of divorce has stopped, and some other factors are affecting the present and future rates.

Scanzoni (1979) has argued that the rise in divorce has been due to *working women increasing their bargaining power against male attempts to hang on to control. Two thirds of divorces are initiated by women* (Buckle et al., 1996). Women are divorcing because they don't need or want to put up with male privilege and control anymore (Scanzoni, 1979). Perhaps the more that men accept women's equal power, the more couples will learn to negotiate priorities and issues through to **both** partners' satisfaction. Emerging egalitarian, negotiating marriages could be more satisfying and stable than what we have experienced during this transition in the distribution of power between the sexes. Then divorces might occur predominantly in those situations where life or career paths diverge too much to be harmonized, or where one or both of the partners are too damaged or dysfunctional to negotiate and harmonize.

At this point we don't know which way divorce rates will move in the future. We can take our pick between a negative projection based on continuing individualizing effects of the industrial revolution, and a positive projection based on constructive effects of the sexual revolution. In time, other explanations will probably be developed as well.

REASONS
FOR
DIVORCE

Reduced barriers against divorce

The last four decades have seen a reduction in the **barriers** to divorce, a variety of factors including religion, divorce laws, community attitudes, traditional marital obligations, and family influences. The improvement of **alternatives** to marriage includes increased economic support (from government and spousal child support) and employment opportunities for women, as well as greater economic and social viability of a single lifestyle for divorced adults. However, barriers and alternatives are extrinsic factors, shared by couples who stay together and those who divorce. We will first survey and then interpret the reasons that couples themselves give for divorcing.

Couples' reasons for divorcing

Divorced persons normally develop reasons for their breakups during many conversations in which they try to "make sense" out of "what went wrong" (Weiss, 1975). We will survey what people say about their divorces and then weigh these in relation to other unexpressed psychological or relational dynamics that may have generated the reasons they express.

The basic reasons given for divorce in recent research studies are lack of communication, role conflict, infidelity, family life differences, and

TABLE 5.1. Percentage of divorcees mentioning complaints and ranking for the Cleveland Marital Complaint Code by gender: 203 upper middle class, middle class, and working class suburbanites selected at random (Source: Kitson, 1992)

Cleveland marital complaint categories category	Pychosocial basis[a] (in this chapter)	Mention of the complaint by gender	
		Female % (Rank)	Male % (Rank)
Lack of communication or understanding	5. (Coping skills)	31.8 (1)	26.5 (1)
Untrustworthy; immature	3. (Individual psychology)	21.5 (2)**	9.8 (14)
Alcohol	3.	21.5 (2)***	7.8 (16)
Extramarital sex	2. (Love issues) & 3.	20.6 (4)*	10.8 (12)
Out with the boys/girls	2. & 3.	19.6 (5)**	7.8 (16)
Change in interests or values	2. & 3.	18.7 (6)	16.7 (5)
Joint conflict over roles	4. (Role issues)	16.8 (7)	20.6 (2)
Different backgrounds; incompatible	2. & 3.	16.8 (7)	17.6 (3)
No sense of family	1. (Network)	15.0 (9)	12.7 (8)
Financial and employment problems	4.	15.0 (9)*	6.9 (20)
Not enough social life together	1.	12.1 (11)	12.7 (8)
Too young at time of marriage	2. & 3.	12.1 (11)	12.7 (8)
Arguing all the time	5.	12.1 (11)	7.8 (16)
Inflexible; stubborn	3, 4, &/or 5.	12.1 (14)	6.9 (20)
Emotional/personality problems	3.	12.1 (14)*	4.9 (22)
Internal gender role conflict	4.	9.3 (16)	13.7 (6)
Other, personality	3.	8.4 (17)	8.8 (15)
Problems with in-laws and relatives	1.	7.5 (18)	13.7 (6)
Jealousy	2. & 3.	7.5 (18)	10.8 (12)
Disagreements over money	4. & 5.	7.5 (18)	7.8 (16)
General neglect of household duties	4.	5.6 (21)	3.9 (24)
Physical and psychological abuse	3.	5.6 (21)	3.9 (24)
Threatened physical abuse	3.	5.6 (21)	2.0 (29)
Overcommitment to work	1. & 4.	3.7(24)**	12.7 (8)
Desertion	3.	3.7 (25)	3.9 (24)
Self-centered	2. & 3.	2.8 (26)	3.9 (24)
Not sure what happened (attempted explanation)	?	1.9(27)***	17.6 (3)
Conflicts over the children	3, 4, &/or 5.	1.9 (28)	2.9 (28)
External events	? 1, 3, &/or 5.	0.9 (29)*	4.9 (22)
Premarital pregnancy	? 1, 2, &/or 3.	0.9 (29)	2.0 (29)

[a]Psychological bases: 1.Social network; 2. Love issues; 3. Individual psychology; 4. Role issues; 5. Coping skills

* Probability of percentage difference between genders arising by chance less than 5%, p<.05
** Probability of gender difference less than 1%, p < .01
*** Probability of gender difference less than 0.1%, p < .001

personality conflicts. A more complete listing of male and female reasons for divorce ranked by frequency can be found in the table below.

The table shows us that lack of communication or understanding is by far the most common complaint mentioned. Furthermore, of six main spousal roles, "someone to talk things over with" was by far the least satisfied desire for the same sample of people, with 64.4% mentioning that this dissatisfaction influenced their decision to divorce (Kitson & Holmes, 1992). Dissatisfied couples are quite aware of their lack of communication, and it is both a cause and a result of their failing rapport.

There are several significant gender differences in complaints that bear mention. The importance to women of immaturity and alcohol as marriage-wreckers (both second ranked) seems lost to men. When interviewed an average of 5 months after their separation over a sixth of the men weren't sure what caused their divorces. Perhaps this is because women normally express more complaints than men in studies of divorce (twice as many in Cupach & Metts, 1986). The gaps in the men's awareness could have various sources: (a) People are likely to deny problems with alcohol, immaturity, and personality, (b) Many men didn't want to divorce, so didn't have reasons of their own, and (c) They also normally tell their story fewer times than women do (Harvey, May, 1991), so many of them had not yet developed plausible reasons for what went wrong,

Twenty percent of women and 10% of men mentioned a partner's extramarital sex as a complaint, which is probably around half the actual incidence of their affairs (since respondents reported more than twice as many affairs for their spouses as for themselves). However, these affairs are just as likely to be a *result* as a *cause* of marital distress, since two thirds of those reporting an affair said the marriage was already bad at the time. In another study (Spanier & Thompson, 1984), the same percentage of divorcing women as men (38%) admitted extramarital affairs. Sexual infidelity was widely experienced as very painful, for it was the only marital complaint that was still likely to be associated with psychological distress for the partner four years later (Kitson & Holmes, 1992).

Changing divorce complaints. We can understand current divorce dynamics better by reviewing three types of change in complaints over time:

1. changes in recent decades,
2. differences between complaints based on the divorcees' ages or on the length of their marriages, and
3. changes in the reported reasons as time passed after separation.

Changes over recent decades. A comparison between a 1948 sample (Goode, 1956) and a 1975 sample (Kitson & Holmes, 1992) of divorcing mothers reveals a shift from more serious complaints against husbands, including "nonsupport," authoritarianism, and running around (out with the boys/girls, infidelity, drinking), to more emotional aspects of marriage, including personality, home life, and values. But male authoritarianism was still a significant complaint. In 1948 wives had to show their husbands to be at fault to get their marriages dissolved, and the situation had to be more desperate for women to brave the social attitudes and economic hardships facing divorcees. By the 1970s women could divorce over home life and personality differences, instead of staying until things were much worse.

The issue of male authoritarianism may have declined since the 1970s. A comparison of divorcing women in Cleveland in 1975 and 1985 (Kitson & Holmes, 1992) showed mentions of "joint conflict over roles" declining from 16.8% to 6.4%. Of course role conflict could include reasons other than male dominance, such as feminine role changes, domestic work issues, and greater task flexibility. The women (in 1975) who complained most about needing to get more out of life may have married with more traditional expectations of the wife role, but wanted to take advantage of the expanded opportunities in the seventies. The 10% decline by 1985 could be a signal that more couples have come to expect more equal distribution of power and flexible roles and are coping with it successfully.

Differences according to partners' age and length of marriage. People who are under the age of 20 when they marry are two to three times more likely to divorce than those who marry in their twenties, and divorce becomes progressively more unlikely the older one is when one marries, even after 30 (Norton & Moorman, 1987). Where young people complained about immaturity and spouse's time with friends, for older divorcees this issue boils down to *alcohol*. Perhaps it takes many years for social alcohol use to lead to personality impairment and even more time for an affected spouse to become frustrated enough to leave.

Changes in complaints as time passed after separation. Ex-spouses tend to revise their view of the causes of their divorce as time goes on. Several complaints declined in frequency between six months and four years after separation in the 1975 sample. These include "arguing all the time," "inflexible," "out with the boys/girls," "overcommitment to work," "not enough social life together," and "joint conflict over roles" (Kitson & Holmes, 1992) Later on, these complaints may have been regarded more as results or manifestations of the disintegrating marriage than as underlying causes for the breakdown.

A different set of explanations for the divorce increased in frequency at the later time, including "incompatibility," "change in interests or values," "emotional/personality problems," and women's need to get more out of life. These revised complaints imply "a greater realization of just how different the partners were or had become during the marriage" (Kitson & Holmes, 1992, p. 145). At a deeper level, they may represent divorcees' revisions of self-image and partner-image away from the previously shared beliefs about similarity, shared characteristics, and trust. Married couples often develop ideas of "soul-matedness" to include each other in a "we-ness" or couple identity. Divorcees replace this with ideas of irreconcilably clashing or defective personalities, to justify rejecting their former couple-identity and excluding the ex-partner from their concept of self.

Reasons for divorce in preindustrial cultures. As Table 5.2 shows, some of the most common causes of divorce in preindustrial cultures are also common in America today, including adultery, childlessness, and inadequate support. On the other hand, the prominent American themes of authoritarianism, gender role conflict, and lack of communication/understanding are quite the opposite of their nearest equivalents in preindustrial times: husbands complained of disobedience and talkativeness (by wives!).

This difference in marital complaints reflects a male-centered point of view in the preindustrial cultures. The gender role and communication themes in contemporary America reflect both the gender equality and the intimacy function of marriage that have grown with industrialization.

Psychological and sociocultural bases of divorce: A multilayered model

How can we interpret all these shifting explanations and complaints? What social and psychological factors support staying married, and what factors are conducive to divorce? Figure 5.3 synthesizes research and clinical experience into a multilayered model with 7 interactive factors.

Here is our overview of these 7 factors:

1. Outside the marriage, alternative living and partnering can be more or less attractive than staying married.

TABLE 5.2. Principal causes of divorce in 160 preindustrial cultures compared to leading causes in America

Cause	Cultures Reporting	Related?	American Causes Prevalent 6–48 months after divorce	Rank 1975
Adultery	88	Same	Extramarital sex	6
Childlessness	75	No mention	Childless couples divorce more than parents	
Cruelty or maltreatment	54	Related	Alcohol	9
Displeasingness	51	Unclear	Change in interests/values	2
Displeasingness	51	Unclear	Incompatible	3
Laziness	32	Related	Untrustworthy/immature	5
Inadequate support	21	Related	Economic/employment problems	8
Disobedience or disrespect	14	Related/ Contrast	Gender role conflicts	4
Quarrelsome or talkative	10	Contrast	Communication/understanding	1
Bad temper	10	Related	Arguing all the time	7

Sources: Betzig, 1989; Kitson, 1992.

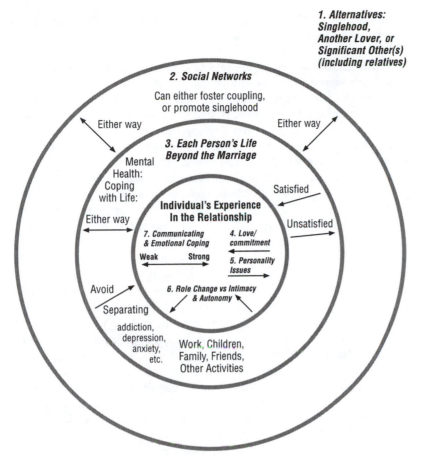

FIG.5.3.
Multilayered model of personal and interpersonal factors fostering a trend to divorce, or stay married.

Arrows toward center: Support continuing marriage
Arrows *away* from center: Support separating from marriage

2. Social networks can foster separating or staying together. Industrialization has fostered disintegration of family, community, and social network which may pull the couple apart.

3. Each partner may be satisfied or dissatisfied with life outside of the marriage and may be functioning adequately or inadequately in that life.

4. Romantic love has an expanded function in our spiritual and communal lives and may be central in decisions about commitment to marriage.

5. Individual personality psychology may undermine our ability to love, contribute, and commit to each other.

6. The fluctuating balance of intimacy and autonomy is impacted by the challenge of work and marital role change.

7. Communication or emotional coping skills may be inadequate for dealing with all the other marital stresses and issues.

These possible psychosocial bases are related to the categories of expressed reasons for divorce in column 2 of Table 5.1.

Alternatives to marriage. Being single may offer advantages over marriage, such as more time to devote to career and career-enhancing relationships, greater variety in relationships, and freedom to structure one's own life. An extramarital affair could provide a pleasant "parachute" for bailing out of one's marriage and even develop into a new and better marriage. One might prefer the tranquility of living alone or with another family member or a gang of buddies. The ease and attractiveness of such alternatives can make divorcing more comfortable to contemplate. But even if the grass does look greener outside the fence of marriage, satisfied partners are not likely to pay much attention to it (Miller & Simpson, May, 1991). So we need to look further inside the model for other factors as well.

Industrialization and the dis-integration of social networks. In a preindustrial society the integrated social network of family, village, and workplace relationships helps to keep a couple relationship together. But in today's society, if the extended family is dispersed and the two partners have different networks of work and friendship relationships, the resulting loyalties and satisfactions may act to pull the couple apart.

It was the separation of work life and home life due to industrialization that began eroding the web of community relations and has resulted in concentrating many of our emotional needs in our couple relationships (Gadlin, 1977). The demands of the workplace and material security now take precedence over home life and community connections. In a typical preindustrial culture couples didn't have to struggle to meet most companionship, recreational, emotional, and communication needs with each other, because they were, in effect, "married" to their entire clan, tribe, or neighborhood. Industrialization also began the liberation of sexuality from family and community control, so that sex could develop into a dominant facet of relating and compete with communal motivations as a more temporary reason for coupling (Lindholm, 1998).

Satisfaction and competence in life beyond the marriage. Marriage is not the only important aspect of life. If our life is satisfying through our involvement in work, children, family, friends, activities, and/or passionate pursuits such as art, music, or collecting, then an unsatisfying marriage need not spell the end of our world. We saw in Chapter 4 that a couple could stay together in a contraction stage for years, and Kitson's (Kitson & Holmes, 1992) divorcees stayed an average of 3 to 5 years in their unsatisfying marriages.

A life that is working well except for the marriage could make it comfortable *either* to stay married *or* to divorce. But divorcing brings so many physical and emotional disruptions of many lives, that one normally prefers to not "rock the boat" of the partnership as long as life is tolerable. If we *don't* have significant outside sources of satisfaction, however, or if our marital problems are undermining other areas of our lives (as with physical, emotional, or financial abuse), then we cannot buffer our marital dissatisfaction, and divorce is a necessary remedy. On the other hand, even if one's life is miserable and one's marriage is the worst part, one may not feel capable of taking the steps necessary to obtain a divorce. Thus, people who are psychologically unable to cope with the complexities of adult life, due to anxiety or depression or to personality disorders, may fear abandonment and the challenges of change more than they dislike their marriages. Preferring the devil they know to the one they don't know, some people choose not to act but to stay in the dysfunctional marriage that contributes to their instability and distress.

The social and spiritual function of love. Love in America is more than just the normal reason for being committed and getting married. It is also the aspect of humanity most sanctified in popular culture, from the schools and pulpits to the movies and the soap operas. Love is idealized as a superhuman, invincible force. Even much of popular religion asserts that "God is love." Why do we praise love so much?

Since the post-industrialization human condition is extraordinarily individualistic, competitive, and isolated, love has taken on an expanded cultural function as the antidote to human isolation and alienation. *We experience love as the counterbalancing force that reunites us with our world, whether through romance, familial closeness, or universal compassion.* Love's connecting force is all the more precious, and perhaps endangered, the more we are separated by individualism and materialism. Thus we may *need* love to provide us with more life structure and psychological buffering against alienation than it can reliably provide.

We may also *idealize* romantic love as paranormal because it provides both *peak experiences* and *altered states of consciousness* (Chapter 9). But this romantic altered state may be closely associated with *sex* (Lindholm, 1998), and it reinforces *having* a beloved, but not *keeping* that beloved once the high has worn off. If we expect marital love to provide us with recurring peak experiences, we may become disappointed and then find that extramarital sex provides new highs that outshine our home life. Since Americans identify love with commitment to marriage (Fehr, 1988), we are challenged to find ways to define what we are feeling as love when it no longer resembles our early years of romance—and even when it shifts into negative feelings for extended periods of time. Thus our cultural idealiza-

tion of love may contribute to divorce by magnifying our disappointment when passion dies down. When we haven't felt love for our partner for a long time, we may conclude that our love is "dead," so our marriage is unsatisfactory and *should* probably be dissolved. "I'm just not in love with him/her anymore," are words often heard in divorce counseling. If one partner believes that love *should* be felt often and that some problems are unresolvable, these dual disappointments may convince her/him that the marriage isn't worth struggling for.

Individual psychological factors. A great many personality and psychological factors can eventually undermine one's ability to love, contribute, and commit to our marital partner. Such factors may be involved in as many as 18 out of the 30 reasons for divorce in Table 5.1.

For example, as a facilitator of pleasure and altered states, *alcohol* is a potent competitor with love. When young adults do not have romance, their "partying" closeness with buddies is a well-practiced substitute. Many marriages decay with alcohol abuse because drinking provides a semblance of the altered state once experienced in love. For some people who work all week, drinking facilitates a vacation from ordinary reality long after love's rose-colored glasses have faded. After learning the hard way, millions of Alcoholics Anonymous members have come to believe that alcohol and drugs were only "short-cuts" to experiencing the spiritual connection they didn't know they were missing.

A wide variety of personality features can either undermine one's partner's loveableness or one's own ability to love, or both. For example, one could be so bothered or frustrated by the partner's anxiety, depression, abuse, self-centeredness, or avoidance of intimacy that one's love would gradually wither. But one could also be so anxious about hurt or abandonment or so intolerant of anything less than an idealized image of the other that any of the partner's personality frailties are magnified into a negative, dismissing indictment and love is smothered by fear or contempt.

Intimacy, autonomy and the challenge of gender role change. Balancing a couple's we-ness with the partners' separate careers and social networks is another key issue for today's marriages. For partners to cope with their differences and often conflicting priorities and stay a "we," they must balance commitments to self and career with loyalties and sacrifices to spouse and family. As long as roles are neatly divided into provider–careerist–leader and homemaker–nurturer in a traditional marriage, the partners' personality and priority differences seem to be due to their complementary roles. Therefore their belief in essential similarity can remain intact along with their "made for each other" roles. However, when both partners have meaningful work outside the home, they become more separate and individualistic, which takes them away from their expectations for how their marriage should feel. A vital support role, the unconditionally loving cook-maid-lover and all-around helpmate, is reduced and fragmented at this stage of our gender role revolution. As one woman put it:

> What my husband wants is a good old-fashioned wife to do everything he needs done and give him sex and support whenever he needs it. But I need that too, I need a good wife too. He complains that I'm too busy to be a good wife, but I don't see him being a very good wife to me either.

Working couples are doing the best they can to make their relationships fulfilling without one person taking the traditional nurturing helper role. Some can hire cooks and maids, while others resort to microwave ovens, fast foods, and reduced living space. But now the nurturer and helpmate roles are subject to limited schedules and repeated negotiation. So the soothing expectation of inexhaustible unconditional love is likely to be frustrated. These unmet unconscious needs might lead to depression, fears, and resentments that could smother the feelings of love.

Many husbands cannot cope with the loss of nurturing and react angrily, which leads to divorce. It is hard to tell from the trends in expressed reasons for divorce just how potent the hidden issue of nurturing is. At present, women seem to be more capable of fulfilling both gender roles than men and hence they are freer to take marriage or leave it.

Job change. We saw earlier that the shift from patriarchal marital roles is becoming a less significant cause of divorce as greater numbers of men are accepting the need for women to seek fulfillment beyond the home. But rapid changes in technology and economic conditions are forcing both men and women to change jobs and even careers more frequently than ever before. When a man loses his job, he ceases fulfilling the provider role, thus effectively breaking the traditional marital role-contract just as decisively as when women break out of the homemaker role. A man and a woman react to such a loss:

> **A man says:** *My business failed about six months ago, and my wife went to work as a waitress. She's gone long hours, and she's talking about a divorce. I'm afraid she's seeing somebody else. If I could just get a good job, I think we could put our marriage back together again.*

> **A single woman says:** *I've worked very hard to get where I am financially, and I don't want a man taking that away from me. I meet plenty of men who want to marry me, but they can't pull their own weight financially. I'm not picking up the tab for anybody else's unsuccessful career or a batch of ex-kids.*

In the near future, changing careers may continue to force marital partners to let go of stable marital expectations and renegotiate their roles. The decades of adjustment as women have diversified their roles may turn out to be practice for coping with career endings and beginnings by both sexes.

Communicating and emotional coping skills. We noted that the single most frequently mentioned divorce complaint in America is "lack of communication or understanding." Yet lack of communication or understanding is not among the major causes of divorce in preindustrial societies. On the whole, no such high degree of communicational intimacy among spouses is expected or needed.

It is fashionable to insist that couples need better communication, especially when their satisfaction is low. Marital therapists have built much of their practice around facilitating empathic communication between distressed spouses and then teaching them to do it for themselves. But the most experienced marital therapy researchers admit that communication and conflict resolution training does not work very well to restore a distressed marriage (Jacobsen, July, 1996). Couples don't use their validating and supporting skills when their emotions are triggered (Gottman, July, 1996). In fact, an old and still growing tradition of research emphasizes **emotional reactivity** and the resulting tendencies to increased conflict as a key interpersonal process in the trajectory of divorce, rather than communication itself (Kelly & Conley, 1987; Davies & Cummings, 1994). Thus, in addition to communication (Chapter 12) and conflict resolution training (Chapter 14) we need to understand more about our emotions and how to cope with them (Chapter 13) if we want to equip ourselves for surviving marital difficulties.

Many of the roots we have discussed are likely to be intertwined, as they are here in Diane Vaughan's account of her own divorce in her book on dissolving marriages, *Uncoupling*:

> I could retrospectively pick out turning points—moments when the relationship changed, times when the distance . . . increased. These turning points did not hinge around **arguments** or the typical **emotional catastrophes [7]** that beset any relationship. Instead, they appeared to be related to **changes in each of our social worlds [2]**. For example, I started college because I realized I was never going to have the **steady companionship of my partner [4/5]** and **needed something of my own [3]** to do. (Vaughan, 1986, p. 3; emphasis and divorce cause numbers added.)

A multiple process model of marital dissolution

Bohannon (1970) divided the divorce into six transition tasks, and each transition can be divided into four stages (Steefel, 1992). These six tasks

TABLE 5.3. Process and stage model of divorce

Process	Stages			
	Shock & denial	Depression & anger	Testing behavior	Establishing new ways
Emotional divorce				
Legal divorce				
Economic divorce				
Community divorce				
Coparental divorce				
Psychic divorce				

Based on Bohannon, 1970; Steefel, 1992.

and four stages are shown in Table 5.3 and are described in some detail below.

Bohannon's six transition tasks

1. The **Emotional Divorce** involves separating from the habits of the relationship. It can lead to total disengagement in all areas of living or, especially when children are present, only partial disengagement. The losses of intimacy, of physical access to the partner, and of one's own identity as a marital partner can each set off strong feelings (Hagemeyer, 1986; Kast, 1987).

2. The **Legal Divorce** consists of dates for termination of marriage and agreements about property, finances, and child custody.

3. The **Economic Divorce** includes practical arrangements for housing and managing financial resources, and often also changes in employment and financial support of dependent children. Two households cost more than one, so both partners normally lose some disposable income, property, and status and feel cheated. Though well-employed men normally recover from these setbacks to be wealthier than their ex-wives (Wallerstein & Kelly, 1980), they often resent losing control of a sizeable portion of their income.

4. The **Community Divorce** involves changes in friendship and community connections and relationships with extended families. Many friends and relatives seem to choose sides, and married friends often drift away. Relationships that were rock-solid may suddenly become unreliable, contributing to the divorcees' experience that everything is falling apart.

5. The **Coparental Divorce** involves agreements about child care and upbringing, dealing with the children's reactions to the divorce, and changing expectations of oneself and one's partner in parenting roles.

6. The **Psychic Divorce** involves developing autonomy and new attitudes as a single person or single parent and reducing attachment to the partner which can persist despite the absence of love. In-

THE UNCOUPLING

deed, the ex-spouse's image may persist in the mind and appear in dreams for a lifetime, prompting some experts to say that we are never "entirely through" with an ex-mate (Price, 1992, personal communication).

Steefel's four stages

Each of these six transitions can manifest itself in four stages, which are a blending of grief reactions to losing the familiar and a transition to embracing the new. The first stage, **shock and denial**, begins when a person recognizes that some aspect of the marriage is no longer tolerable. The reaction can vary from a small startle of recognition to a psychological breakdown or months of denial.

In the second stage partners cycle back and forth between **anger and depression**. They may fight for the old reality or bargain and negotiate for some compromise so that all is not lost. Old habits of thought and behavior are broken up, and often destructive outbursts occur that create physical damage and long-lasting psychological wounds to both people. Since one partner's depression and self-destructive acts (e.g., a suicide attempt) often weigh heavily on the other, the emotional connection between ex-partners can remain very intense, despite efforts to sever it.

When **testing new behaviors and interpretations**, the third stage, people's emotions can fluctuate from excitement and soaring self-esteem with new discoveries, to discouragement with what does not work, and anger, confusion, and exhaustion from disrupted living patterns and the effort to keep making changes.

The final stage, **establishment of new actions and attitudes**, involves practicing and incorporating new ways of being and thinking and marks the completion of a transition.

The multiple process model helps us cope with divorce. This model of six separate transitions of four stages each can help make sense out of some chaos that occurs during a divorce. Though many situations occur in most divorces, they do not follow each other in a consistent and linear fashion, because the timing for the partners entering the transitions and their styles of progressing through them are different. Though much of the legal and economic divorce processes affect both partners simultaneously, the other four transitions are quite likely to proceed differently for each partner.

When a person is overwhelmed during a divorce and unable to proceed, we can guess that one or more of these four processes might be occurring:

1. The partner or external conditions may make progress impossible

in the particular divorce process which the person wants to move forward (e.g., parental, economic, legal).

2. The emotions involved with a divorce process are temporarily overwhelming and need additional attention.

3. Aspects of the emotional or psychic divorce processes have been catalyzed by the current legal, economic, parental or communal process, and they need attention.

4. There are too many divorce transitions occurring at once, and it is humanly impossible to cope with all that often contradictory thinking and feeling, so confusion and psychological crisis is the natural result.

What can we do? In case 1, the person can restore a sense of progress by shifting attention from the blocked divorce process to another one where movement is possible (such as shifting from the legal issues to restructuring community relationships). In cases 2 and 3 one needs to give some attention to the feelings involved. And in case 4 one needs to back off, recover, and then take on fewer transitions and choose the ones in which progress can occur without too much mutual interference.

The road to emotional divorce prior to the decision.   In most marital dissolutions, the emotional divorce is not mutual, but may be a solo process for months or years before the other partner understands what is happening. In *Uncoupling,* (1986) Diane Vaughan relied on interviews to develop a description of this early stage.

According to Vaughan, most divorces do not develop in a linear way out of escalating arguments around clear-cut differences. They begin as a secret dissatisfaction growing in the mind of one partner, which leads him or her to evaluate events in a different way than the spouse does. Part of the "we-ness" of a couple lies in interpreting life events similarly by adjusting over the years to thinking in the same ways. When one person is secretly dissatisfied, the partners' thinking is no longer similar, though the other person doesn't know it. The dissatisfied person often can't communicate the true nature of his discontent because it is too vague and undefined. He or she doesn't want to take a chance on hurting the spouse or losing control of the marital situation through the partner's overreaction. So the subject is avoided, or discontent may be revealed tangentially through chronic criticisms and minor complaints. Then the other partner may think that these are only minor complaints and nothing to get worried about. The couple is in a **contraction** stage, as described in Chapter 4, but the partners' private thoughts may differ greatly.

> *Well, what happened, I just was afraid to talk about it. I just didn't want to open it up then . . . She would prod me but I was afraid if I really said to her, "I don't love you. You know, you're a wonderful person, I can't fault you anything, but I have no sexual attraction for you, and sexual intercourse is*

unfulfilling for me. I'm not intellectually stimulated by you, I don't feel a sense of home and companionship that I really feel like I need . . . and I want out." That's what I was feeling, and I was afraid . . . that would really, really crush her. (quoted in Vaughan, p. 67)

Sometimes partners try to change to meet the minor complaints, and often the initiator tries to solve the big, but vague problem by embarking on a major structural change, such as having a baby or an "open relationship" with freedom to have other partners. More often, however, the partner who has been discontented gives up on conflict and change and withdraws, engaging in activities that keep the couple apart. Vaughan's interviews are corroborated by statistical indications that withdrawal from marital conflict, particularly by the wife, is the best indicator that initiation of a divorce is likely within a year (Gottman & Krokoff, 1989).

I finally came to the point where I realized I was never going to have the kind of relationship I had hoped for. I didn't want to end it, because of the children, but I wasn't going to let it hurt me anymore. The children and I were going to be the main unit, and if he occasionally wanted to participate, fine—and if not, we would go ahead without him. I was no longer willing to let being with him be the determining factor as to whether I was happy or not. I ceased planning our lives around his presence or absence and began looking out for myself. (Vaughan, p. 19)

The initiating partner begins to redefine herself or himself as an individual instead of as part of a couple, thus beginning the psychic divorce process. This redefinition of self is not discussed with the partner. Thus, what began as a secret and often vague dissatisfaction often leads to increasing estrangement from the spouse, including avoidance of issues and of intimate sharing and redefinition of the partner and the relationship in negative terms.

Let us summarize this section into an "early warning checklist":

1. One person has a pervasive but unclear dissatisfaction with the relationship.
2. The global dissatisfaction is not shared, but numerous complaints or recurrent criticism may leak discontent. A pattern of comments indicates a negative definition of the partner and the relationship.
3. The noninitiating partner's efforts at insuring similar thinking about everyday events meet with perfunctory assent or contradictory arguments which accentuate the opposition instead of mutuality.
4. Intimate sharing is avoided, and outside priorities are chosen without discussion. There is less "we-ness" and a sense of knowing less and less about the partner.

If we recognize these signs, perhaps we can intervene in this early stage before the "alienation of affection" has gone too far to be repaired.

We need to seek feelings, rather than facts or explanations. We cannot expect to find out everything in one discussion. For there are probably very good reasons—in both partners' characters and in the situation itself—that the secrets could not be shared before. We may need to contain our reaction to new aspects of a partner's life that may surprise us. We cannot be sure that interrupting the comparative comfort of silence and separate trajectories won't make matters quite a bit worse without leading to a reconciliation. But we can increase the synchronization of our relationships, whether divorce or renewal is the eventual outcome.

Post-separation adjustment: General characteristics

Around two thirds of divorces are initiated by women (Buckle et al., 1996; Kitson & Holmes, 1992). The initiators of divorce usually feel more distress during the period *before* the decision to divorce is made (Crosby et al., 1987), while noninitiators feel more distress afterwards. The initiators go through the strong emotions of the first two transition stages in the emotional divorce process and perhaps begin to build some social support and plan for economic changes while they are privately coming to their decision to end the marriage. But, if they are caught by surprise, the noninitiators begin to cope with the loss of their married identity, intimacy, and other factors, at the same time as they are expected to deal with economic, legal, and coparental divorce processes in a rational and responsible manner (Grebe,1986).

Once a couple has separated and initiated divorce proceedings, the initiator's head start on coping with the emotional, communal, and psychic divorce processes begins to evaporate, and other factors more related to the gender, psychological makeup, and life situation of each partner affect the process of adjustment. Crowded with stressful changes in financial condition, emotions, friendships, parenting and family relationships, dwellings, and even jobs, the period between separation and legal divorce is usually chaotic and overwhelming. Yet the severity of this initial reaction is often unrelated to how divorcees adjust in the longer term (Chiriboga et al., 1991).

Research into post-separation adjustment indicates that older people with longer marriages do not necessarily have more difficulties than younger people, as might be expected (Kitson & Holmes, 1992). Having had more time to get used to failing marriages, older people may have the same or less psychological distress than younger people, but they usually take more time to rebuild their lives.

In a study by Rank and Davis (1996), African Americans expected less negative effects from divorce than did whites. Blacks specifically reported less residual attachment, less distress, and less illness complaints at all times from six months to four years after being separated (Kitson & Holmes, 1992). With a divorce and single parenting rate estimated at 60–66%

'ATTA BOY! DIVORCE COURT WELCOME BACK TO THE FOLD! 35

AFRO AMERICANS RECOVER FROM THE EMOTIONAL EFFECTS OF DIVORCE MORE EASILY THAN WHITES.
COMMUNITY ACCEPTANCE AND SUPPORT ARE A BIG FACTOR.

(Dickson, 1993), Blacks' greater resilience may be due to more community support and acceptance of divorce. Black women tend to have a stronger sense of power, survivorship, and responsibility than white women, since so many have grown up with divorce and generations of strong or single-parent mothers. With marriageable males in short supply, divorce, extended family collaboration, and single parenting may be a better deal than marriage for a high percentage of black women (Dickson, 1993).

Trajectories of former spouses' divorce adjustment

What constitutes a desirable adjustment to divorce? For divorced parents, Ahrons and Rodgers (1987) posit successful divorce adjustment to be a mutual commitment to an ongoing coparenting relationship. A more individual approach could prioritize complete psychic disengagement or distant respect. Following the first standard, Graham (1997) conducted interviews of single and remarried parents an average of 8 years after their divorces and found 11 types of turning points and typical trajectories of adjustment toward (or away from) committed coparenting. Table 5.4 shows the turning points, with means and standard deviations of changes in commitment to the post-divorce spousal relationship.

The majority of parents interviewed reported adjusting gradually *toward* stable committed relating with the former spouse, though a third of these reported substantial disturbing emotional events over the years. These would constitute the first two of Ahrons and Rodgers' coparenting relationship types which, together, make up about half of all coparenting ex-spouses (Ahrons & Rodgers, 1987):

> **PERFECT PALS**, who become best friends when they are no longer lovers, cooperate well and highly respect each other as parents. They are not common in our society.
>
> **COOPERATIVE COLLEAGUES** have had a rough road since divorcing and continue to face differences over childrearing, but they manage to put their responsibility as parents ahead of personal goals and reactions enough to prevent escalations and make durable compromises.

The rest of Graham's (1997) interviewees had either an erratic cycle of ups and downs that left the future of ex-spousal commitment in doubt or a gradual deterioration that led to disengagement. These would correspond roughly to the other half of Ahrons and Rodgers' coparenting types:

TABLE 5.4. Turning points in post-divorce events which affect the commitment of former spouses to an ongoing coparental relationship (Source: Graham, 1997)

Turning point type	Affect on commitment
1. Well-functioning binuclear family	Positive 2.31
Settled routine, realizes children will be OK	
Nice visits, moves closer to kids	Stan.Dev. 2.81
Children's sicknesses, special events	
New roles defined, successful coparenting	
2. Dysfunctional ex-spousal relationship	Negative 1.91
Court battles, custody & parenting disagreements	
Noncompliance with divorce agreements	SD 3.42
Painful disclosure, decline in relationship	
3. Life-improving events	Positive 2.39
Hope, laughter returns, self-affirming moments	
Financial stability, career success, buys a home	SD 3.82
Looks good, appreciates freedom, goes to school	
Children growing up, kindness of others	
4. Respondent remarries	Positive 1.56
	SD 3.42
5. Former spouse remarries	Negative 0.25
	SD 3.77
6. Parent-child problems	Negative 1.71
Parent (or stepparent) & child conflicts	
Children out of control, drinking & sex problems	SD 3.86
Ex-spouse hits child, lets child down	
7. Emotional divorce	Negative 4.10
"In your face" moment, property division	
Realizing there is no future in relationship	SD 4.41
Ex-spouse starts dating, letting go	
8. Relocation	Negative 0.94
Ex-spouse moves away, threatens to move	
Respondent & child move, new job move	SD 3.69
9. Personal hardships	Negative 1.31
Financial troubles, health problems	
Feelings of personal failure	SD 2.49
10. Respondent's 2nd marriage ends	Negative 5.0*
	SD 2.83
11. Ex-spouse's 2nd marriage ends	Neutral 0.0*
	SD 4.24

High SDs indicate many types had both + and – impacts.
* Number of events too small for drawing conclusions.

ANGRY ASSOCIATES cooperate grudgingly as parents and don't speak much because their bitterness toward each other will not go away. These couples are less likely to have shared custody, but yo-yo back and forth for years over incomplete support payments and shifting visitation habits.

FIERY FOES fight at every occasion, often involving the children and forcing them to take sides. Legal battles are often renewed years later, and most family ceremonies are marred by struggles for control or exclusion of one parent. Joint custody doesn't work for these couples.

Gender differences

Women have somewhat different typical patterns of adjustment from men. Though residual attachment to ex-spouse and damage to self-esteem is about equal for both sexes during the first year and a half, women report significantly more psychological distress and illness complaints. But this difference is tied to gender differences in self-expression, since the gender difference in reported distress and illness complaints between *married* women and men was just as big as the gap between the male and female divorcees (Kitson & Holmes, 1992). By the fourth year after separation, reported self-esteem and illness rates for both sexes had returned to the same level as the married control group. But divorced men continued to report about as much distress as women, and much more than married men. Since even remarried men continued to report more distress than first-married men, either divorced men have permanently raised their levels of distress, or they have gained greater awareness of their negative feelings.

In the first year following separation, studies show women's incomes declining by an average of 33% (Hoffman & Duncan, 1988) to 37% (Kitson, 1992). Most men suffered little or no decrease in income except for paying child support, which they had been doing while married anyway. Of 19.2 million ever-divorced or currently separated women, less than 15% were awarded alimony, and only 73.3% of those owed alimony in 1985 received some of it (Kitson, 1992). Since women are normally less prepared for earning income than men, most can only get low-paying jobs. In 1984, 60% of all female-headed families lived in poverty (Sidel, 1986).

Women adjusting to divorce. Since most women lose a great deal of income through divorce, it is not surprising that having a good job and a positive work identity after divorce is conducive to high self-esteem and lower distress. Work is a source of social interaction and support as well as meaning, especially if it provides the satisfaction of helping others and feeling productive (Bisagni et al., 1995). However, having a job leads women with children to face more numerous stresses than divorced men. Since they struggle to perform up to their own expectations both on the job and at home, and they may face continued conflict with their ex-husbands, divorced mothers' psychological distress apparently does not gradually subside after divorce. Instead it may continue to be directly related to the frequency of these and other daily stresses (Oppenheimer, 1987).

Since the initial changes demand so much of women's time, receiving help from others, working toward financial security, and sense of competence are very beneficial in the early months after separation. Eighteen months later their dating and close personal attachments are more significant for their well-being (Stewart et al., 1997; Sansom & Farnill, 1997). Conversely, women's likelihood of depression 5 to 20 years after divorce has been correlated with abuse and infidelity during the marriage, poor legal representation and lack of close personal support during the divorce, and low income and social activity and lack of a romantic partner afterwards (Thabes, 1997).

Men adjusting to divorce.   Initially men are more likely to be behind in making the emotional transition, for two interlocking reasons:

1. Men are generally less aware of their feelings than women and more likely to act them out without understanding them as well. Therefore they don't take marital distress as seriously as women.
2. Men are more likely to be heavily invested in their work away from home, so they can avoid marital discomfort by getting more meaning and social needs met through work. Kitson (1992) found divorcing men were dissatisfied in their marriages for an average of 5.2 years, compared to 3.1 years for women, and men are twice as likely to distance themselves from marital problems as women (Christensen & Noller, July, 1992).

Though male noninitiators may get a late start in coping with the divorce, most seem to catch up during the post-divorce recovery phase. Hetherington (1987) found that 6 years after divorce, men were likely to be more satisfied with life than women. There are several reasons for this:

1. Men usually have more money to help with adjusting to a new lifestyle, so their economic transition is not as devastating as it can be for newly impoverished women. Men can try more new things, because they have more money and more social permission to experiment.
2. Men are less likely to endorse expressing their feelings and more likely to take action to get away from post-separation distress (Berman & Turk, 1981). Therefore men will usually not admit to as much distress as women, and their repeated actions are more likely to help them out of the "learned helplessness" aspect of depression. Thus, one psychological key to men's adjustment may be a sense of taking action and control over one's life. Bursik (1991) found that women with more traditionally masculine characteris-

tics, such as assertiveness, independence, and initiative, were better able to adjust to divorce than their more passive counterparts.

3. Men are less likely to have to change their employment, and they can rely on the identity and self-esteem of their careers. Work distracted them from marital distress before, so they can use it again. This contrasts with women's more confusing struggles to balance work and home demands.

4. Men date and remarry more often (Cherlin, 1992) and sooner than women. Men who are strongly relationship oriented are aware of more adjustment problems than those who are not (Stewart et al., 1997). But they are less able to benefit from friends and children than women (Stewart et al., 1997), so they are more likely to seek a new partner. Kitson and Holmes (1992) found that within 18 months of separation, 30% of men were deeply involved, that is, remarried, cohabiting, or engaged, compared to 11% of women. On the other hand, men may suffer some long-term effects as much as 10 years after divorcing (Diedrick, 1991). They may be less able to relinquish their attachment to an ex-spouse and less likely to provide an adequate social support network for themselves, unless they remarry and the new wife provides one.

Child support

Studies in the 1970s and 1980s found around half of divorced mothers received their court-ordered child support, a quarter got less than ordered, and a quarter got no payments at all (Price & McKenry, 1988; Arditti, 1991). Why do "dead-beat dads" run away and refuse to pay child support? Income plays a role, since higher income fathers are more compliant. But the amount of the child support may not be directly related to fathers' willingness to pay until it exceeds 35% of the father's wages (Meyer & Bartfeld, 1996).

Many men may be unable to cope with the combined shocks of losing their marriages, reducing their connection to their children, and losing control over a portion of their income all at the same time. Noncustodial fathers complain about unfair divorce proceedings and custody, visitation, and child support arrangements, and about continuing conflict with their ex-wives (Dudley, 1996).

Hostility toward ex-wives may be the key factor. A study of remarried upper middle-class fathers an average of over 6.5 years after their first divorce revealed astonishingly negative attitudes toward their former wives (Schuldberg & Guisinger, 1990). These men devalued their former wives by comparison with their new wives in several specific areas: expressiveness, control of hostile impulses, and interpersonal power—which included dominance, self-abasement, deference, autonomy, and masculine attributes. Apparently many men interpret their ex-wives' struggling with them for control as *being controlled by their ex-wives* (Coleman & Ganong, 1992) and view the courts as allied against them (Mandell, 1995). Therefore they often try to "shut the door" emotionally and financially on their first family and just "start over."

Issues in emotional recovery

The disturbing events catalogued in Table 5.4 can stall divorce adjustment for years. After interviewing 150 participants in divorce adjustment seminars, Robert Weiss (1975, 1979b) asserts that the keynote of divorcees' emotional relationships is **ambivalence**. Intense yearning and warm feelings exist side by side with anger and dislike. As one woman put it:

> It is like the battered child syndrome. You never find a battered child that does not want to be back with its parents, because they are the only parents it has. I just have very much this feeling. (Weiss, 1979b)

The intense positive and negative feelings give rise to contradictory moods and statements. Initially separating spouses may be uncomfortable making any boundaries between them, even though they may need to stay apart to avoid pain or conflict. They often continue to carry out some marital roles, such as finding and fixing things, cooking, or paying bills. The initiating woman may feel too guilty to shut her ex-spouse out of the house.

> The first six months were a nightmare. There was no keeping him out of the house. . . . He was there all the time. He was lost. Talk about guilt! I went around one whole year feeling so guilty; it was like I had deserted one of my children. (Weiss, 1975)

In order to rationalize away their guilt many divorcees develop a negative portrait of their ex-partner. Ex-spouses may also keep track of each other's lives, partly for caring and partly for comparing. They may compare successes and failures in prestige, economics, profession, parenting, friendships, and romance. Though they may want their ex to do well, they often look for evidence that they have fared better and complain of unfairness when they fare worse:

> He always did know how to make money. That was one thing he was good at. But most of the friends we used to have don't like him anymore. Except the ones he spends money on.

In comparing subsequent romantic relationships, ex-mates struggle to define themselves as the *more lovable* person, or, more accurately, *not the unlovable one*, compared to a partner who now loves someone new.

Though getting angry at the ex-spouse may help with separation and recovery (Kalb, 1987), hostility over economic or custodial issues may still hold adjustment back at 4 years (Kitson & Holmes, 1992) and at 10 years (Tschann et al., 1989). Persistent guilt was also linked with depression and preoccupied attachment among middle aged people long after divorce (Walters-Champman & Price, 1995).

For some people, divorcing restimulates traumatic issues from childhood, which can be disabling unless they are understood and worked through (Rossiter, 1991).

> *When my husband left I had this panicky feeling which was out of proportion to what was really happening. I was afraid I was being abandoned. . . . I remembered later that the first time I had that feeling was when I had pneumonia and my mother left me in the hospital, in a private room, in the winter. And this picture came back of this hospital and these old gray rooms, and it was winter and every night at five o'clock, when the shadows would come across my bed, my mother would put on her coat and say: "Goodbye, I will see you tomorrow." (Quoted in Weiss, 1979a)*

Divorce or frequent or severe conflicts in the family of origin seemed to "sensitize" adults (especially men) to report greater loneliness and psychological symptoms during and after divorce (Chiriboga et al., 1987). But *deaths* in the family seemed to promote a "hardiness" (or stoicism) that made adults report less suffering from their subsequent divorce (Chiriboga et al., 1991).

The final subtle and enduring issue in divorce is denial of the changes in loyalties and affection or a vague **residual attachment** in the long run. As long as a divorcee does not believe an ex-partner has "stopped loving" him or her, he or she may hold out some hope of an eventual reconciliation and not complete the emotional and psychic divorce processes. As painful as it is, discovering that one's "ex" is dating—and sleeping with—someone new can make the change in affections undeniable and thus promote the stalled adjustment process (Graham, 1997).

> *She can never get back all she lost by going out with that dude. Now I know she was just using me when she said she still cared. Nothing can ever make me turn back now. I just want to get it over and be rid of her as quickly as possible.*

Long-term attachment

What is the outlook for this attachment in the long run? Is it unhealthy to retain any attachment at all? John Bowlby's (1980) theory of attachment (see Chapter 10, Table 10.2) can apply to adult reactions to divorce. We will consider three aspects of attachment, *proximity*, *safe haven*, and *secure base*.

Acute separation distress derives from being unable to gain access to the person you love or need. In divorce, this *proximity* attachment may be fairly easy to shift onto another person after some time, especially when you no longer like being with your ex. This explains how some divorcees latch onto anyone who will have them, as well as the research finding that dating several people aids as much in recovering from a divorce as getting involved with just one person (Spanier & Castro, 1979).

When we are distressed, ill, or afraid, we may still turn to the partner as a *safe haven*, just as we once did to our parents (Hazan, July, 1992). Often ex-spouses will open up and give the needed comfort at such times, because it just feels like the right thing to do.

> *My ex-husband called me last week and I said, "What's the matter?" I can tell from his voice. And he said, "I'm depressed." And I said, "Well, what's wrong?" He said, "You are the only one I know who I can call and complain to." And it's true. No one else would listen or be interested. Not that I am, but I can still pretend.* (Weiss, 1975, p. 93)

In contrast to safe haven, **secure base** attachment can exist with little or no contact at all, because it is a state of mind. Even when a partner is no longer attracted to the spouse and "over" the relationship, there may still be a sense of belonging with him or her. Secure base attachment is a stable internal image of the partner as always accepting and "there" for you (Bowlby, 1980). Thus many ex-mates have made or implied and never explicitly reversed this statement: "Even though I don't want to be around you, in a way I will always love you."

The persistence of Bowlby's attachment types has not been researched. Empirical studies have focused mainly on yearning and grief, which correspond somewhat to the proximity/protest concept. Though 72% of one research sample and 59% of another admitted some attachment to a former partner 2 to 4 years later (Spanier & Castro, 1979; Kitson & Holmes, 1992), this attachment was defined as thinking or love feelings about the ex-spouse or attempts to contact or learn about him or her. Other studies (e.g., Berman, 1985) echo these two in conceiving post-divorce attachment as a preoccupation with the former spouse which is linked to distress, conflict, or depression. However, more benign forms of attachment can persist after divorce as well (Masheter, 1997b).

Should we outgrow attachment to an ex-mate?   Most therapists used to advocate complete severing of all ties between ex-spouses except coparenting (surveyed by Kressel et al., 1978), in order to "recover" from the former attachment and "make room" for a completely fulfilling new love. But experts on grief are now suggesting that at least a *deceased* spouse will normally be a presence to be reckoned with throughout one's subsequent life (Moss & Moss, 1996). Future research is needed to explore what actually happens to attachment after divorce. But we can present an adjustment goal that is theoretically achievable.

We have suggested that secure base attachment has an imprinted quality. Once a person becomes a secure base, he or she can continue to elicit attachment feelings until redefined as having become **intrinsically different** (Weiss, 1975, p. 46).

A middle aged man reports: *It took me 5 years before I found somebody I loved and respected as much as Sandra. I think there was a secret pact that Sandra would take me back if I ever wanted (I was the one that left). It was obvious, because whenever I heard about her, she was dating some guy 5 or 10 years younger than her who hadn't finished college yet. . . . It was neat to know her door to reunion was probably open a crack, even though I didn't want to use it.* [Secure base attachment]

When I finally found somebody . . . I arranged to meet Sandra for a walk. (I always avoided her otherwise.) I told her I thought there was a secret pact that we might some day get back together again, and I wanted to take my name off that pact. I said it had been great and she was right for me while it lasted, but I would never want to get back together, because now I wanted a different kind of woman than she was. She said she thought that pact really did exist, and I wasn't right for her anymore either. [Redefinition of partners]

Three months later she sent me a wedding invitation and mentioned that she met the guy three days after our talk. When I called to congratulate her I said . . . I felt like I ought to be giving away the bride. She said that felt right to her too. [Secure base attachment reconfirmed; phrases in brackets added by text author.]

As the quote above illustrates, finding a new relationship that replaces key elements of the former partnership helps us let go of the proximity and safe haven attachment. The man and woman above probably had a high degree of ego identification and mutuality in thinking, which is likely for people who connect during their identity-forming teens and early twenties. Their mutual ways of thinking seem to have carried over beyond their breakup, so that spoken or unspoken agreements were involved in the post-divorce process.

Should we try to eliminate a past secure base? We don't have to eliminate our attachment to our parents to form a new secure base attachment to a spouse. So why should we need to become completely detached and indifferent to an ex-mate in order to fully recommit ourselves again? Since we may "imprint" our primary caregiver(s), perhaps we may also imprint our first long-term mate. We may be incapable of forming another attachment *exactly* like that. Perhaps the long-lived anger often found among divorcees is partly protest against that first attachment and a heroic effort to destroy it. But a new secure base attachment need not be inferior, since each of our love relationships is unique.

Perhaps the most change-affirming path to pursue with persisting secure base attachment is to *redefine the partner as an old friend or kinsperson*, such as brother- or sister-in-law, who we want to be happy (Kingma, 1987). As adults, we usually need to shift our relations with our parents and siblings to be more equal, more distant, more understanding, and more mutually supportive. Similarly, "modifying" and "de-escalating" marital relating patterns (Masheter, 1997a) to arrive at a stable, separate, and supportive post-divorce relationship could take years of effort, just as it can with family members.

Gains after divorce

For many people, their relief when an oppressive marriage or painful divorce process is over is the first sign that good feelings are still possible. But newly divorced people's struggle with their loneliness and loss often leads them to develop coping skills for taking care of their own needs and moods which can give them pride.

> I woke about four, thinking about [a further rejection by his wife]. . . . I couldn't get back to sleep. I got out of bed and made myself follow my morning routine . . . I got dressed and went out. It was still early so I started to walk, instead of taking the bus. It was a brisk, snowy morning, just after dawn. I suddenly felt happy. I had got myself through the night. I was going to see people during the day. I was all right. It was a fine world. (Weiss, 1979a, p. 206)

Having a positive attitude toward being single can help in building a satisfying lifestyle (Fisher, 1981). Some women develop rituals to celebrate and validate living for themselves instead of taking care of families (Riessman, 1990).

> I'd come home from work, put a chicken in the oven, open a split of champagne, start a fire, put Bach on the stereo, drink champagne, and have a marvelous dinner all to myself. I can spoil myself if I wish and there's no one else I need to think of. (Riessman, 1990, p. 176)

Since being married is normally a component of women's identity, they may have to transform their self-images, or else feel defective until they marry again. Many women create new identities that are more competent, confident, and realistic (Bursik, 1991; Riessman, 1990).

Many men have never faced so many overwhelming emotional situations as during and after divorce. They are very likely to use both work and alcohol as anesthetics. But they may also express emotions more, confide in others more, and reflect more on how they act and what they want in life. One possible result of such soul-searching showed up in an interview study of second marriages that found men more considerate of partners' feelings and needs than their first time around and women more able to define and consider their own feelings (Smith et al., 1990). Some men also broaden their support base to include warmer friendships with both men and women, as well as more sharing of affection with their children (Fisher, 1981).

Thus important gains can arise from coping with the adversity of divorce. Exploration of one's personality, individual self-actualization, and improvements in relating skills can result, if people will look for answers and form supportive relationships.

Post-divorce dating

What types of romantic relationships do we engage in after divorce? Is there a natural progression of such involvements? The popular press has much to say about the adult singles scene, mostly aimed at "Taking Care of Yourself" and "How to Get the Right Man." Since there is little empirical research, we will present descriptions, anecdotes, and some clinically based comments on this important phase in many adults' love lives.

Ihinger-Tallman and Pasley (1987) estimated the average time between divorce and remarriage at 3 to 4 years, but the period between committed romantic relationships can vary from 6 months to 15 or 20 years. At the low end are some people who may have been sick of their marriage for several years or broke it up by having an affair. They may marry quickly because they have been ready to change partners for a long time, or in order to legitimize the affair into new partnership and put their painful divorce episode behind them. At the high end, divorcees may be so stressed and fulfilled with childrearing and/or career or so aversive about romantic relationship, that they have no interest in getting involved until their children leave the nest, their emotional commitment to career wanes, or their attitudes about love radically change.

Stages of dating

In this section we will cover a four-stage sequence in the process of "learning to love again" postulated by Mel Krantzler (1977). These stages are *remembered pain*, *questing-experimenting*, *selective distancing*, and *creative commitment*.

The **remembered pain stage** normally lasts from a few weeks to one year. Some people would not want anything to do with sex or love, except for those in a rapid rebound. At first, it is fear of hurt, a natural tendency to protect our love-wounds, which can lead to a generalized hatred of the opposite sex. As one woman put it:

> In the beginning, I didn't date. And it was just as well because, I think, in those days I would have castrated the man. That's how much hatred was embedded in me. (Weiss, 1979a, p. 202)

Others might go back and forth between this and the next stage, **questing-experimental**, in which one may engage in casual dating and make many new connections but not get personally involved. In this stage, motivated by loneliness, restlessness, or anxiety, we begin to seek company.

> You look for something to fill that emptiness. You start going out. You go out with the girls meeting people. Wrong people, right people, it doesn't make any difference. You start dating, just to get out. When you're not going out, you sit, you talk on the telephone, you read a magazine, but you get tired of it, and

you get disgusted with it. It all builds up inside, and then you go. (Weiss, 1979a, p. 194–195)

Divorced people usually feel uncomfortable when they begin dating, since they haven't dated for a long time. Because they don't know what script to follow, they either try to do what they used to do years ago, or act very reserved and closed down. A woman recalls:

I realized how much I'd changed since the last time I was single. Dating behavior that used to be okay—acting sort of kittenish and deferential—now felt old. I was more evolved. But at the same time, I felt very vulnerable. (Dormen, April, 1992)

When they begin dating, many men are likely to fall back on their young adult script and seek sex to cope with dating anxiety and alleviate their loneliness. As a single father in his thirties put it,

When you disconnect from somebody there's a void. The most pronounced way of filling that void is to have sex. At least that's the way it feels at first. Later on I'd be open to sex on a first date, but I wouldn't push for it.

This stage may typically last somewhat less than another year, according to clinical observations. We find a hint of support in the research finding (Petronio & Endres, 1985/1986) that those divorced less than 2 years were far more likely to view their dates as "on the make" and "superficial" than those who had been divorced longer. Perhaps these judgments about possible partners are partially projections, that is, *it takes one to know one.*

... AFTER THE DIVORCE, COMES SELECTIVE-DISTANCING

Krantzler's next stage is **selective-distancing,** which is characterized by discovering who is more and less fulfilling to spend time with and tentatively approaching deeper involvement and then withdrawing again for fear of being hurt. Moving beyond casual and distant relating, divorcees are likely to get close quickly now, sexually, emotionally, or both. But once they become intimate, they may encounter issues reminiscent of their previous marriage. Highly reactive to these issues, they may either attack them vigorously to "nip it in the bud" and get it right this time or bail out quickly before their remembered misery becomes overwhelming.

A woman says: *My ex-husband wrote the book on controlling. The minute a man starts telling me what I can and cannot do, I'm out of there.*

A man says: *When my wife got upset, there was no dealing with her. I look for girlfriends who are easygoing like I am. I don't mind if a woman gets upset now and then. But if she can't get a handle on it, I'd rather find somebody else. I know there's just going to be more trouble down the road, and I don't want that again.*

During this stage, divorced parents have additional dating difficulties, such as finding a partner who will accept the priority their children have and relate to them as well. In addition to these external restrictions on dating, many of the divorced have long shopping lists of qualifications for a new mate (Weiss, 1979a). A majority of Kitson's (1992) divorced subjects were looking for good companionship, better communication, more common interests, and more sharing. Some wanted more gender equality, while others wanted the husband to dominate more. Women were more likely to seek a good parent and provider, by 30.6% to 7.1% of men who wanted a good parent and homemaker. Men were more likely to want a good sexual partner (50% to 14.3%).

For many, the thrill of new beginnings wears off after a few years. They find they prefer the security of a familiar partner and the imperfections and problems they know to starting over. The intimate communication, resolution of differences, and mutual vulnerability they develop through their experiences of rejoining can give them a sense of hope and durability that is comparable to the resolution stage in marriage (Chapter 4).

In the third or fourth year after the divorce Krantzler observed the final stage, in which people's fears would die down and be succeeded by **creative commitment**. In this hopeful new beginning, they launched a new romantic bond, but explicitly intended to make it work differently than the marriage that had died before. Most are hopeful that they have learned enough from their mistakes to make their new relationship work differently (Kitson & Holmes, 1992; Krantzler, 1977). Many previously divorced people try to hedge their bets by living together before remarrying, hoping to make sure they can work things out before taking the bigger risk. Their numbers are significant, comprising nearly half of all cohabitors in 1980 census data (Spanier, 1983) and almost a third (8.3%) as many as were re-married (28.6%) 4 years after their previous separation in Kitson's 1985–86 sample. In a more middle class, liberal community sample (Ahrons & Wallisch, 1987) 3 years after divorce, 36% of women and 59% of men had remarried and another 28% of women and 19% of men had cohabitation relationships. When asked if living together before marriage makes a lot of sense, 36% of remarried people said yes, compared with only 14% of first-married people (Furstenberg, 1987). Limited research data suggests that cohabiting isn't associated with greater or less subsequent remarital satisfaction (reported in Ihinger-Tallman & Pasley, 1987). But it is possible that "trial cohabitation" may serve to weed out some partnerships that would not stand the test of daily domesticity.

Staying single: Lonely or self-fulfilled?

The cultural stereotype that all divorced adults, unless they are psychologically disturbed or irrecoverably embittered about the opposite sex, want to get repartnered or remarried is no longer true. Between 1970 and 1988 the rate of remarriage after divorce in all age groups dropped more than 40% (Gross, 1992). Some of this drop was due to cohabitation. And some of these people were also single or cohabiting gay men or lesbians who embraced their sexual identities after divorce. But many were also choosing to stay single.

> **Singles Complex**: A psychological condition in which a person feels self-conscious and anxious regarding being unmarried. This condition is most prevalent in single women during parental visits or phone calls, chance meetings with recently married ex-boyfriends, and 20th year high school reunions. (Linn-Desmond, 1992)

The most significant increase in single divorced people is among the middle-aged. In 1970, 1.5 million, or 4.2% of those between 40 and 54, were divorced and not remarried, while in 1991 it was 6.1 million, or 13.8% (Gross, 1992). Older people have less enduring difficulties adjusting to divorce than younger people, partly because they usually have more money, more stable and meaningful work, and no dependent children.

If they are self-reliant and have developed a network of friends, many middle-aged women prefer to live alone. The most important ingredient in a stable, happy single life seems to be a strong network of friends or relatives or both (Freedman, 1978), and more women develop such social bonding than men do. They often view marriage as a bad bargain in which they have to do everything they already do for themselves and take care of a man, too (Gross, 1992). Male companionship is fine in smaller doses, say many of these women:

I've already raised my kids. I don't need to take care of another one.

Indeed, men's special gifts for aggressive confrontation and self-sacrifice on the battlefield and at work are not needed by middle-aged career women. So men may need to become proficient at domestic chores, lest they have nothing left to offer to a mate but companionship, affection, and the likelihood of failing health.

As a group, single divorced men are wealthier, but more prone to illness, accidents, alcoholism, and death than married men or divorced women. But many of the 41% of the single divorcees who are men have the same motivation for staying single as the women. One grandfather in his fifties put it this way:

I like spending a lot of time alone, and I don't like having to bother to compromise with someone. I'd like to have a sexual relationship, but not enough to tie into a permanent relationship. You get tied into their obligations, their friends, and their family, whether you like them or not. I have a few close women friends. When we get together, it's more for quality time than for finances or sex or the lack of it.

Single living offers complete freedom and responsibility for one's own time, with the opportunity to maximize both alone time and quality time with people of one's own choosing. Well-established singles usually have a few intimate friends or relatives whom they can call up and confide in, so they do not stay lonely or upset for long (Weiss, 1979b). A man in his sixties is philosophical:

I'm happy each morning that I wake up. And the rest of the day goes on like that, like tasting fine wine . . . . Of course I get lonely sometimes, and I wonder if it would be better to get married again. But that feeling passes, like a gas pain.

Remarriage: It's not the same

Recent estimates are that about 75% of divorced men remarry, compared to 66% of divorced women (Cherlin, 1992). In contrast, the black remarriage rate has been estimated at around 13% (Furstenberg & Spanier, 1984). Though the remarriage rate has dropped since 1970, post-divorce cohabitation has risen, so the overall repartnering rate has gone up by 7% (Cherlin, 1992). In the first 4 years after separation, women who remarry may be younger and poorer, on the average, than those who don't, while men who remarry may not be significantly younger, but wealthier and higher in status than those who don't (Kitson & Holmes, 1992). Thus, practical concerns are significant in remarriage for women: Since they suffer large financial losses in divorce, most seek to restore their economic condition by remarrying men with more money. In a national survey, 55% of single divorced women said money was either somewhat or very important in choosing a mate (Simenauer & Carroll, 1982). A New York woman's comments suggest that men's money or power may exert an attraction that not all women would acknowledge in a survey questionnaire:

I had to be careful of falling in love with a man because of his prominence or his power or, of course, his money. A woman can fall for a guy who is in this position very easily without realizing that's why it's happening. Money can make you lie to yourself very easy. Whenever I am turned on by a man who is

*very wealthy and secure I must ask myself: Am I turned on to him or am I
turned on to his power and money?* (Simenauer & Carroll, 1982, p. 59)

The men who have that money to offer generally prefer younger
women. Men average 2 to 3 years older than their first wives, but 5 to 8
years older than their second wives (Brehm, 1992). Thus, divorce may nudge
remarriage choices toward security. Women seek financial security, while
men may be seeking emotional security through greater age and economic
power.

The rate of eventual divorce for remarriages, a projected 61% for men
and 54% for women, is higher than that for first marriages, a projected 49%
(Glick, 1984). Since remarried couples reported about the same levels of
satisfaction overall as first-married couples (Vemer, 1989), their higher divorce rate could reflect a greater willingness to divorce when things are
bad—compared to an inestimable percent of those in first marriages whose
beliefs would never let them divorce (Grizzle, 1996).

Remarriage has its own strains. In addition to being less likely to believe in their "soul-matedness," remarried couples may be starting out more
dissimilar and less compatible than first-married couples and perceive each
other less accurately as well (Farrell & Markman, 1986). Better communication may not be consistently better for remarriages, since too much self-
disclosure about the past may reduce marital happiness (Roberts & Price,
1989). Since they often involve blending with children from a former marriage who have not chosen to live with a new stepparent, a host of adjustment problems make remarriages very different from first marriages. For
blending families the honeymoon is likely to be over well before it has
started.

But remarrying parents have a lot to gain from bringing a second parent into their families. They are usually highly motivated to make this new
relationship work, in order both to restore their self-respect as a lovable,
successful mate, and to make a financially and psychologically better life
for their children. People who remarry may be significantly more likely to
have a less traditional orientation toward gender roles than they did in
their first marriage, and to consider their own interests and their partner's
more equally in making the decision to marry (Smith et al., 1990).

There are several keys to successful blending of remarried families,
according to Emily and John Visher (1990):

1. Do not expect parental roles or relations with children to be the
   same as in the nuclear family that either partner had before. Blending a stepparent into a parent role can take 2 years with young
   children and 5 to 6 years with older children (Chapter 6). Build
   step-relationships by developing companionship and love first before gradually taking on a disciplinary role.
2. Take time away from children to build and maintain a strong unified couple relationship.

3. Develop new family events that strengthen belonging and also pre-serve some of the past.
4. Develop a cooperative coalition with ex-spouses, so children are exposed to a maximum of love and a minimum of competition and conflict.

Chapter summary

- Connected to social forces, the divorce rate has leveled off since 1979 at about 50%.
- Lack of communication is the most common of many divorce complaints, and varies in prevalence according to gender. Adultery leaves the longest lasting emotional scars.
- Seven factors influence divorce: alternatives; social networks; overall personal life; idealization of love; psychological issues; closeness and autonomy amid role change; communication and emotional coping skills.
- Six divorce processes: emotional; legal; economic; community; coparental; psychic, with 4 stages of adjustment for each, and with disruptive interactions.
- Alienation and growing apart before divorce can be a 3–5-year long, poorly understood process.
- Blacks are less distressed by divorce due to having a network of support and a tradition of single mothers.
- Women initiate two thirds of divorces, but experience more time-, money- and psychological stresses. Men's economic, employment, and new romance advantages give them a sense of control, but not support networks.
- Perhaps half of coparenting relationships are friendly or cooperative, and half of fathers pay inadequate or no child support.
- Emotional issues in recovery include anger, conflict, and restimulated childhood vulnerability. Safe haven and secure base attachment to the expartner may remain, to be redefined as kinship.
- Psychological gains after divorce include more competent self-images and emotional openness.
- Four stages of dating: remembered pain; experimental; selective-distancing; and creative commitment.
- Singlehood is an increasing lifestyle, with friendship replacing obligations to a romantic partner.
- People remarry for emotional or financial security and coparenting. Their divorce rate is higher, since blended families are difficult, and remarried couples are less comfortable and compatible and know divorce is survivable. With less gender-role expectations, they may develop new personal skills.

Children 6
of divorce

How does parental divorce affect children?

What effects is parental divorce likely to have on children? Are their adult romantic relationships more unstable than those whose parents stayed married? Could knowing about the psychosocial issues they have in common help children of divorce cope with them? Since 25–35% of college students are children of divorce (Johnson & Nelson, 1998), we should seek answers to these questions.

The majority of both clinical and empirical research writings focus on negative effects of divorce on children. But we should *not* conclude that divorce is always disastrous for children, and that most young people will feel some negative effects for a decade or more (Wallerstein, 1989/1991). The current empirical approach of statistically comparing "divorce children" with "nondivorce children," and the clinical focus on psychological problems tend to expose only the darker side of the picture. A fuller description of the long-term effects of parental divorce may emerge when the children of divorce begin to conduct research based on their own life experiences.

The public impact of negative interpretations of divorce research is large and stigmatizing for the children of divorce. Since more social harm than scientific benefit might arise from such research reports, we must keep three key considerations in mind when interpreting the research evidence. First, the statistical differences between large groups of divorce children and nondivorce children are *weak*, rather than *strong*. A meta-analysis of 92 studies found the largest frequently repeated differences (for adolescent conduct problems and relations with fathers) are about 30% as big as the average difference between each individual subject's research test score and the group average, while most other differences are closer to 10% as big (Amato & Keith, 1991a). This means that the *majority* of divorce children do not score significantly differently from nondivorce children on questionnaires about their conduct, well-being, social adjustment, or significant relationships.

Second, the minority of divorce children who do score more negatively on questionnaires (or are observed by others) are likely to have been exposed to more economic hardship and conflictual family processes than the majority, and to have a lower level of educational achievement as well. Both of these factors support a *minimizing* interpretation of differences found in research. They especially encourage college students *not* to apply negative impressions about divorce to themselves since the economic, familial, and educational effects on them are likely to be less than average for children of divorce (see p. 188).

However, the third consideration is more ambiguous in its impact on how we should interpret research. Quantitative research is not a very accurate instrument for illuminating the personal experience of divorce children, either compared to nondivorce children or in its own right. Interviews and personal accounts reveal more of how a person reacts and how family-of-origin experience might be affecting one's attitudes and experience of life and and relationships. These methods yield more qualitative than quantitative results, which lead to generalizations other researchers are quick to criticize. For example, Wallerstein, Corbin, and Lewis's (1988) well-known 10 year follow-up interview research with divorce children is widely faulted for lacking a nondivorce comparison group. Though we cannot fully understand children's reactions to divorce without listening to them (Lee, 1995), we cannot be sure how to interpret what they say either. On one hand, a divorce child might experience less well-being and more difficulty with relationships than a nondivorce child, even if quantitative tests would not show any differences. On the other hand, the stigma of divorce could lead one to a more defensive, distressed, or problem-focused self-expression, so that a divorce child may perceive an experience as more distressing or problematical than would a nondivorce child who encounters the same exact experience (see Brown, 1999, discussed below).

By summarizing research on negative effects of divorce, we are in effect endorsing them as the best information available, when the scarcer, less systematically gathered qualitative reports may give more insight. Therefore we will balance quantitative and qualitative research into the losses and gains that may result from divorce. Then we will conclude with some approaches to converting these effects into personal growth and resilience.

One thing research has shown about children's initial reactions to divorce: the child's age matters. Since children's mental, emotional, and behavioral capabilities change as they grow up, their responses to change vary as well. Because the family is an interactive system (Chapter 11), divorce is not just something parents do to children. Children think, feel, and respond differently by age, sex, temperament, and family role, and these responses affect their parents and influence which of many possible divorce effects are actualized as each child grows up (Ahrons & Rodgers, 1987). The following sections highlight what we have learned about children of divorce in specific age-periods.

Infants and toddlers

Infants and toddlers have one advantage over older children. They usually cannot remember their previous intact family, so they don't need to mourn what they were never aware they had (Peck, 1989). They are likely to take the single parent or remarried family they grow up in for granted and bond with a stepparent who arrives within a few years.

What matters the most is the primary caregiver's life and emotional state, for such young children depend on consistent contact with their mother (or another caregiver) to regulate their emotional states (Kalter, 1990). If the caregiver is upset or warring with the spouse, the child is likely to resonate to those emotions and be unable to distance itself or understand what it is feeling. Thus, if the custodial parent is emotionally unstable, the child's "emotional anchor" is adrift and its emotional development is disorganized.

If the noncustodial father never bonds (Peck, 1989), it is easier for the child to replace him with a stepfather or another male figure. However, during the preschool years a second attachment figure may be vital for helping kids to exist separately from their primary caregiver (Blos, 1979). So the loss of a dependable father relationship might hinder the child's separation–individuation process (Kalter, 1987), reducing his or her autonomy and personal security in adult relationships.

Preschoolers

"...IN ORDER TO COPE WITH THEIR CONCERNS ABOUT BEING AWAY FROM HOME AND PARENTS, CHILDREN CREATE... ORGANIZED FANTASIES..."

Preschool children (ages 3 to 5) have the mental ability to wonder why and how the divorce came about, but not to understand it. According to clinical observations, they are able to create organized *fantasies* but not *realistic scenarios* to cope with their concerns about being separated from parents, about how much effect they have had on family events, and about how lovable they are (Kalter, 1990). Thus, when a father leaves the egocentric world of a young child, the child may believe the father has rejected *him or her*, not the family. If the mother has gone out to work, the child may fantasize that she may be leaving too—perhaps because of something the child has done, or because he or she is unlovable. Though not unique to children of divorce, these fantasies can create deep fears of abandonment and low self-esteem that may last into adulthood.

Young children may psychologically split their reactions and perceptions into the "good" parent and "bad" parent. The "good" parent cares for them on a daily basis and is their secure base. The "bad" parent, who left them, didn't care and is often the target for intense rage. This splitting makes it difficult to view either parent accurately, and later it may color their reactions to intimate partners in adulthood.

Early schoolers

Researchers have found some key elements of children's response to divorce first in early school-age children, aged 6 to 8. This may be because research results are more precise when children begin to communicate more like adults. These children have a multifaceted grief response that is hard for adults to understand and for them to work through until they are older. We will examine some of these reactions, because older children may have them as well (see Table 6.1).

Early school-age children understand more, and their feelings are separate from those of their parents. In school children face new cognitive, emotional, and behavioral challenges, but they experience failure and helplessness at the same time in their **home base**. For their family dynamics, their household routines and economic conditions are all likely to change, usually more than once. The children cannot make parents respond to their feelings when the parents' own needs dictate that they do something else, such as conflict with each other or go away to work. And unlike older children, young children are helpless to escape their family situation on their own or to form other supportive attachments.

TABLE 6.1. Developmental issues for children of divorce in elementary school

Child's situation	Personal development	Results and issues
1. Separate school environment and home base	Conceptual thought	Fantasy influence, irrational conclusions (See Table 6.2)
	Separate feelings	Parents feelings different, so estrangement & lowered contact
	Task mastery orientation	Homebase not under control. Efforts to reunite parents fail. School phobia when child fears separation.
	Bonding with peers	Peers not constant & dependable, so not alternative security.
2. School focus on self-control of emotions and impulses.	Emotional inhibition and deflection.	If self-control succeeds, child is depressed. If self-control fails, child is aggressive and impulsive.
	Emotions mixed with thoughts.	Mental & emotional development may stop, school work & social relations hindered.

Derived from Kalter, 1990.

These children's feelings may be predominantly of loss: loss of harmony in the house due to parental conflict, loss of the security of routine, loss of relationship quality with the overwhelmed caregiver, and reduction or loss of relationship with the parent who moves out. Their efforts to change things will fail, leading to depression from "learned helplessness" (Seligman, 1975) as well as grief. Depressed school children withdraw from friends, lack pleasure, worry about being alone, and are less able to learn (Kalter, 1990).

Not all children suffer all these losses, however. Post-divorce family situations may reduce family conflict and restore routines. Mothers and children may spend almost as much communication time or quality time together in single-parent as in two-parent families (Sanik & Mauldin, 1986). Also, in one study, 20% of elementary and secondary school children of divorce reported higher levels of father support than the average level among two-parent families (Amato, 1987). Fathers' involvement with their children varies a lot in families, and divorce leads some of them to get closer to their kids.

When these children try to make sense out of what happened, their thinking is so immature and fantastic that it leads to erroneous conclusions. Their irrational thinking fits into some categories of Beck's depressive thinking (see Table 6.2).

The comments in Table 6.2 reflect emotion-based thinking. The third shows fear of abandonment. The fourth is embarrassment projected onto friends (i.e., *they* won't want to be with me). The fifth, ("it's something I did") is guilt derived from egocentric thinking, but it also serves to deny the child's utter helplessness in the face of such a life-changing event: If I played a part in causing the divorce, then perhaps I have some power to

TABLE 6.2. Erroneous belief types in children's thinking after divorce

Belief	Description of belief	Children's divorce thinking
Arbitrary inference	Drawing a specific conclusion when the evidence is absent or is contrary to the conclusion.	"Mom and Dad can't care for each other anymore. If they did they wouldn't be getting divorced."
Selective abstraction	Focusing on a detail taken out of context, ignoring other more important features, and conceptualizing the whole experience on the basis of this fragment.	"Dad called Mom today. Maybe they'll get back together soon."
Overgeneralization	Drawing a general rule or conclusion from one or more isolated incidents and applying it to related and unrelated situations.	"Dad said he loves me, but he left. I'll bet Mom is gonna leave someday, too."
Magnification	Exaggerating the meaning or significance of an event.	"I just can't face my friends now. They won't want anything to do with me."
Personalization	Relating external events to the self when there is no basis for making such a connection.	"I know Mom and Dad divorced because of something I did."
Absolutistic dichotomous thinking	Viewing experiences from only one of two opposing perspectives. Same as splitting with people.	"This divorce is either good or bad. It can't be both. It's bad!" "Either mom is good and dad is at fault, or dad's right and mom is wrong."

Expanded slightly from Kurdek, 1988, with descriptions from Beck et al., 1979.

make things better. We will return to the issue of *helplessness* when we consider the long-term effects of divorce.

Other recent theory and research emphasizes the effect of parental conflict that is likely to accompany divorce on children's developing emotional system. Children exposed to frequent parental conflict (usually, but not always present in divorce) may become emotionally sensitized to conflict-related emotions (Davies & Cummings, 1994), as well as less able to concentrate and control themselves when these emotions are occurring (Wilson & Gottman, 1996). This difficulty with emotional control could explain why continuing parental conflict after divorce leads children from ages 4 to 12 to have more behavioral problems, especially if they report being angry and if they seek parental support to control their emotions (Lee, 1997).

Preteens

According to clinical interviews, older elementary school children can understand the divorce better than younger children, by taking a more objective, often cynical view of their parents' troubles (Kalter, 1990). Since they have had more years to become attached to and model on the parent who moves out, they are more likely to experience loyalty conflicts and take sides with one parent or the other. They may be more attached to their previous family life, and many of them have an indelible memory of the first events associated with the divorce, like this college student.

> We were having angel hair spaghetti for dinner, my favorite. I was eager to start eating. My dad set me on his knee. He began to talk about things that I didn't understand and I was only half listening—the smell of the spaghetti was making my stomach growl and I knew that if I didn't eat it soon it would be cold. Then he said it, the words that would drastically change my family's life forever: "Your mom and I are getting a divorce." Everyone suddenly became still as the full force of these words sunk in. . . . If I had to pick a specific time that my childhood ended, it would be that day.

Preteens also have effective psychological defenses that mask and transform their sadness and vulnerability. Boys are more likely than girls to divert their feelings into anger and to become uncooperative at school and take out their anger on other children. They may identify with their noncustodial fathers and act out their hostility toward their mothers (Kalter, 1990). Mothers may unwittingly reinforce these boys' defiance and aggression when they say, "You're acting just like your father." This tendency to *externalize* their reaction to divorce through hostile behavior has been widely documented in research and associated with poorer psychological adjustment than for girls (reviewed in Zaslow, 1989).

Parents report that preadolescent girls are better adjusted to divorce than boys. Their self-esteem is buoyed up if the residential parent's socioeconomic status is high (Howell et al., 1997). But they are more likely to *internalize* or suppress their emotions. They are more likely than boys to utilize the defenses of intellectualization, by understanding what happened without noticing any unpleasant feelings, and reaction formation, by converting anger, fear, and sadness into loving, helpful efforts to restore and promote family harmony (Kalter, 1990). Though both genders may follow these paths, research indicates that girls are generally somewhat better than boys at understanding parental divorce objectively (Kurdek, 1988b), perhaps because their interpersonal intelligence develops earlier (Chapter 7). Girls usually stay closer to their parents and may not confront their negative feelings until puberty. But then many suddenly erupt into defiant, aggressive, and early sexual behavior (Kalter, 1990). By adolescence most quantitative studies find post-divorce effects are about equal among boys and girls (reviewed in Zaslow, 1989).

Children as coparents. Often at least one preteenager or teenager will take on the role of coparent for younger siblings, go-between for warring parents, and confidant, supporter, or sometimes parent for the overloaded single parent, whether it be a mother or a father. The child need not be of the opposite sex to the parent. It could be the first-born, or the closest to the single parent, or a less socially oriented youth who, by temperament, prefers to help out in the home rather than seeking support relationships in the outer world.

This young adjunct parent gains greatly in responsibility and interpersonal sensitivity, both of which are conducive to educational and socioeconomic achievement in adult life. In a thirty year study of Hawaiian at-risk families (many with single parents), male first-borns (most likely to be coparents) were by far the most likely of male children to prove resilient and establish stable jobs and families in their twenties (Werner, 1993).

Some clinicians warn that this maturity may have a price. A "parentified" or "spousified" child may find it difficult to take a path of individual growth because the child feels needed by the custodial parent (Glenwick & Mowrey, 1986; Kissman, 1992). A "spousified" young adult may resist being replaced by a new spouse. He or she may be very slow to commit to a romantic relationship and also prefer to play a similar caretaker role in other relationships.

This student still lives with her caretaking issues, even though she is away at college:

> Many a time the only way Mom talked to Dad, and vice-versa, was through messages sent through me. Even my brother and sister saw the advantages in using me as a courier in getting the things they wanted. . . . I would feel an overwhelming sense of loneliness and desperation, as if no one understood me or would sympathize with my struggles to keep the peace and save the family.
>
> To me, there existed no escape. And as far as I knew, I had not wanted one either. In my forever childish view, I was the backbone of my family, and I did not always fail in "keeping peace". . . . I believe I went far away to college unconsciously, because once I was here, I suffered from guilt in abandoning my family duties, and felt that had I a chance to do it again, I would not have decided to go away to school. . . . [Now after three years] I still feel anger and sadness and loneliness when I see that it is once again my duty to restore the harmony . . . in the family.

"Spousification" has not been researched, so we have no idea how frequently it occurs, or whether it occurs more in divorce families or not. But only-child daughters of divorce, arguably the most likely of daughters to act as partner to a single custodial parent, seem to be the slowest of any daughters to marry (Mueller & Pope, 1977).

Adolescents

Teenagers are likely to respond to the destabilization of their home due to divorce by "growing up fast." Instead of coparenting, they may get away from their family and bond with other youths or families. Many use romantic relationships as a safe haven.

> *Our intimacy was pretty high because my parents had separated in a volatile manner and I got caught up in the crossfire. Spending time with Natasha was a way of evading my problems at home. She also took the time to listen to me and actually admitted that part of her desire was to help me through the tough time I was having with my family.*

During the first year or two of divorce adjustment, parents often don't have the energy to cope with the adolescent's struggles with sexuality, identity, and autonomy. Later they may still not have the time to give adequate supervision (Amato, 1987; Zaslow, 1989). This can lead adolescents to take more responsibility for themselves, and/or to "run wild," as the following two accounts illustrate.

> **A college woman:** *My mother was given sole custody of my sister and me. She tried to compensate for the physical stuff that had gone on before by not disciplining us as much as she should have. She had to work to support us and wasn't home very much to have meals together or talk about things in an adult manner. We all had our different ideas about things and this has caused a lot of arguments among us.*

> **A college man:** *The months that I stayed with my mother still had the day-to-day routine of a traditional family, while my months with my dad were more loose. As I grew older I was given the choice of who to live with when I wanted to. I spent most of my time with my father. I had more freedom to do as I pleased—until I got in trouble with the police. That's when I went to my mother's.*

Compared to nondivorce adolescents, children of divorce engage in more socially deviant behavior, such as truancy, breaking school rules, running away, and encounters with the law (Dornbusch et al., 1985). They are also more susceptible to peer pressure to engage in deviant behavior (Steinberg, 1987). Other studies connect both ongoing parental conflict and parental divorce with lowered self-esteem and increased depression, which is connected to poorer peer relationships and reduced social competence (Armistead et al., 1995; Aseltine, 1996). Four to 6 years after parental divorce, 25% to 30% of girls and 20% of boys are estimated to have clinically significant behavior problems (Grych & Fincham, 1997), which is much more frequent than among nondivorce children. But the majority of divorce children *don't* have these problems.

Several factors sometimes present in post-divorce families have been linked with adolescent conduct problems. Single parents of both sexes are somewhat more likely than two-parent families to be abusive in their punishment (Sack et al., 1985) because of their lack of adult support. Both abusive and non-abusive but coercive disciplinary styles are associated with more antisocial behavior (Patterson & Stouthamer-Loeber, 1984; Patterson, 1986). Continuing parental conflict seems to worsen boys' behavior problems. In fact, high family conflict nondivorce adolescent boys may have more problems than sons of a low conflict divorce (Grych & Fincham, 1997). Inconsistent discipline and lack of parental supervision (Forgatch, Patterson, & Skinner, 1988; Steinberg, 1987) and increased emotional autonomy from parents (Steinberg & Silverberg, 1986) are also conducive to "running wild" and susceptibility to peer pressure. It is not yet clear from research which is more influential, the physical autonomy from low supervision, or the emotional distance from parents that leads some kids to bond more with peers and thus follow their direction rather than that of adults.

Many girls and boys report close, companionate, egalitarian relationships with their single mothers (Fry & Leahey, 1983; Hetherington, 1987). But the behavior problems of adolescent boys are linked to problematical relating patterns with their single mothers, even six years after the divorces. Though single mothers were just as verbally and physically affectionate with their boys as were nondivorced and remarried mothers, they tended to command and criticize more without following through (Hetherington, 1987). They were twice as likely as other mothers to initiate negative verbal or behavioral interchanges, which also lasted longer. On average, this ongoing interactional pattern of nagging and mutual hostile sniping, along with a lack of positive disciplinary control (and with it, boys' problematic social behavior) seems to recede when there is a stepfather in the house. Therefore, we need to consider the effects of remarriage on children and adolescents.

The effects of remarriage

Next to the remarried couple relationship itself, the quality of the stepparent–stepchild connection is the most crucial for positive blended family outcomes (Ganong & Coleman, 1988). There are three key issues involved in the children's development of this bond: (a) the balance of bonding with the new stepparent and with the absent biological parent; (b) the children's behavioral freedom versus parental control (Swenson, 1997); and (c) the shifting balance of closeness and distance with the biological custodial parent.

Children who experience remarriage in their preschool years seem to have the easiest adjustment to bond with the stepparent and replace the absent biological parent. Older children may resist a stepparent because they perceive him or her as replacing their absent biological parent. Even if the absent parent is completely uninvolved, the child may unconsciously resist replacing him or her, because to do so would mean "agreeing" internally that the biological parent was "really" gone when an internal image is actually still cherished. Older children are likely to have enjoyed increased access and intimacy with their custodial parent. Therefore they and their parent both resist the construction of thicker intergenerational boundaries between them to accommodate the new mate's efforts at spousal priority and privacy. The parenting participation by the absent biological parent can also lead to authority conflicts to which the children respond with manipulation or overt rebellion.

The popular fairy-tale motifs of evil stepmother and stepfather and ideal fairy godmother are more than just negative cultural stereotypes (Visher & Visher, 1979). They are psychological images that resonate in the thinking of children as they split up their negative and positive feelings for parent figures (Bettelheim, 1977). Children usually reserve their positive feelings for biological parents with whom they identify themselves and whose enduring love they idealize. Meanwhile, they may project their anger at the betrayal and abandonment of their stable family onto stepparents.

Taking all the factors into account, blending families after a remarriage may be as big an adjustment for children as divorce. Stepparents and stepchildren report less intimacy with each other than do biological parents and children, and some of their relationships may not become closer with more time. In addition, research suggests that when the stepparent brings biological children along into a blended family, a stepchild may feel like a "second-class citizen" and actually be more or less excluded from the inner family unit (Pasley, 1988). Nevertheless, the great majority of adults and children in stepfamilies report life to be almost as positive as do those in biological families, with most of the significant decreases in satisfaction occurring in stepmother families (Furstenberg, 1988).

Stepfather relationships

There is some evidence that it takes about 2 years for children to accept a new stepfather, and that the hardest part is accepting him as having authority and a disciplinary role in the family (Hetherington, 1987). The adjustment may be easier if the biological father was neglectful and the stepfather provides support and companionship that the child never had before. Even if his companionship is desired, most young adults assured a college student interviewer that they preferred stepfathers be more like friends than like parents:

> The problem was that he was trying to be my father and not my friend. Once, he tried to discipline me and I got really irate and I told him, "That's not your job." (Oderberg, 1986, p. 108)

It seems that behind this student's self-righteous rejection is the assumption that he or she has the choice to "not hire" for the job of dad. Some stepfathers don't try to bridge the distance with children, or give up in the face of their resistance.

Five years after the divorce, my mother remarried a wealthy, workaholic businessman. My sister and I resented the fact that he was taking our mother away from us. We were rude to him, but he just ignored it. To this day he isn't that close to us. Talking to him is like talking to a businessman with some concern. He basically married my mother and not our family.

Parenting styles. As table 6.3 indicates, parenting styles vary a lot, but mothers are most likely to be authoritative (warm, involved, and responsively demanding) except when single and dealing with boys, while stepfathers are more likely than biological fathers to be disengaged. Hetherington (1987) points out that the approach that seems to work best for a stepfather is to befriend the children and just support the mother's authority and discipline for the first two years or more. In this way he puts out warmth and support and the children's negative emotional projections are not attracted to him during disciplinary skirmishes. Later, he may take on some authority, along with warmth and closeness, without as much resistance as there might have been before. However, even after two to four years, only a minority of stepfathers may take on an authoritative (13%) or authoritarian (23%) role with teenage boys, while more stepfathers still prefer disengagement (46%), like the businessman in the story above.

TABLE 6.3. Percentages of parents showing four styles of parenting

Family type	Percent permissive		Percent disengaged		Percent authoritarian		Percent authoritative	
	Mother	Dad	Mother	Dad	Mother	Dad	Mother	Father
Nondivorced								
Boys	20	10	13	10	13	27	53	53
Girls	13	3	17	23	13	7	57	67
Divorced moms								
Boys	27		17		33		23	
Girls	27		10		13		50	
Remarried less than 2 years								
Boys	20	17	13	46	27	23	40	13
Girls	20	23	17	33	17	13	46	30
Remarried more than 2 years								
Boys	23	10	17	50	13	13	46	27
Girls	10	3	13	67	13	17	53	13

Permissive parenting: Moderately high warmth, high involvement, low coercion, control, conflict, monitoring and maturity demands.
Disengaged parenting: High hostility; low involvement, warmth, monitoring, control, and responsibility or maturity demands.
Authoritarian parenting: High involvement, control, conflict, monitoring, punitiveness and coercion; low warmth.
Authoritative parenting: High warmth, involvement, monitoring, maturity demands; moderately high but responsive control, low conflict.

Not all colums add to 100% due to rounding error.
Source: Hetherington, 1987.

Both disengaged and permissive parenting styles are associated with children's noncompliant and antisocial behavior, but the correlation is strongest for sons and with parents who are disengaged. Authoritative parenting is associated with the lowest levels of problems both at home and at school, especially in boys (Hetherington, 1987). So it makes sense that boys act out antisocially more if they live with stepfathers than with biological fathers, since the latter were 4 times as likely to be authoritative parents. But boys still act out less with stepfathers than if they live with just their mothers, who have a hard time controlling them alone. Thus, despite boys' initial resistance, stepfathers eventually exert a stabilizing influence in their families. They can certainly relieve mothers of their economic strain and parenting overloads, and they can provide positive guidance, warmth, and companionship for boys as well.

Stepfathers with girls. Surprisingly, research suggests that girls typically resist stepfathers longer and more tenaciously than boys (Furstenberg, 1987; Hetherington, 1987). Girls' negative behavior increases with puberty, and is especially *increased* if a stepfather is present (Zaslow, 1989). Adolescent girls' negative response toward stepfathers rivals boys' negative interaction with single mothers in intensity, and may drive the stepfathers towards the disengagement which grows from one third to two thirds in a few years (Table 6.3). Daughters' hostile attitudes about stepfathers are affected by their bonding and authority attitudes toward their "real" fathers, as in this reaction to a stepfather who entered the picture when the girl was 11.

> My parents were divorced when I was only one year old and I did not see much of my father. . . . The stepfather did try to take over the father position, but all four of us rejected him since the father position had been vacant for ten years. My stepfather was not my friend, nor was he to act like my father. He had no right to discipline me or tell me what to do; that is something that is earned in a parent-child relationship. He did not even come close to earning it, but then again, neither did my biological father.

Daughters clash with stepfathers in spite of the fact that their mothers are carrying out the lion's share of the discipline. This implies that disciplinary issues do not play as major a role in this relationship as they do between single mothers and sons. Certainly, the stepdad in the story above could be catching some hostile feelings the daughter has for her natural dad's betrayal. But why might she long for the dad who was never there for her and reject the stepdad who wants to be there?

Some clinicians argue that the key issue is the adolescent's emerging sexual feelings, which "occur almost routinely in stepfamilies where unrelated teenagers and new stepparents suddenly are expected to relate to each other" (Visher & Visher, 1979). Many biological fathers may distance themselves from their pubescent daughters' budding sexuality to avoid having to cope with their own erotic responses. Yet the daughter's, and even the father's, erotic idealization of each other can flourish not only *in spite of,* but also *because* of the distance between them. Both stepfathers and stepdaughters may withdraw or defend against warm feelings even more vigorously, **because they do not have the pathways of affectionate habits developed over a decade with an infant, preschooler, and little girl to guide and contain their erotic responses during puberty**. Some data on sexual misconduct indirectly supports this theory that a history of affectionate caregiving helps stabilize and contain the erotic energy in father–daughter relationships. Unrelated father substitutes are most likely to have inappropriate sexual contact with girls, while stepfathers are less likely, and natural fathers are least likely. Also, both biological fathers and stepfathers who are sexually inappropriate with their daughters have been minimally or *not* involved with them in earlier years as a caretaker (Gordon & Creighton, 1988).

This suggests that disengagement or open warfare with her stepfather may express a girl's disappointment over the loss of a decade-long affectionate container-relationship with an idealized father—as "daddy's little girl." Another student idealizes her father despite contrary evidence:

> *I must have been the ripe ole age of nine when Mom confided in me that my father was having and did have several adulterous affairs. I was crushed by such revelations, and yet to this day, no matter how much pain Dad has inflicted upon my mother, I can not remove him from the pedestal I had placed him on years before. I could only play the part of a close friend and listen as she denounced the man who put clothes on my back, food on my table, and a roof above my head.*

Developmental psychologists argue further that a pubescent girl may be upset by her remarried mother's obvious "promiscuity" because she is sexual with a new man. If she herself cannot experience enough affection and feminine sexual validation with a safe, warm, idealized male adult, she may try harder to elicit sexual interest from boys. This could lead to battles with her mother over authority and freedom, early sexual behavior, and substance abuse (Kalter, 1989/1991).

Stepmother relationships

Stepmother-child relationships have been harder to study, because only somewhat more than 10% of remarried families consist of custodial fathers and stepmothers (Santrock & Sitterle, 1988). Despite the fact that stepmothers usually have more close contact and give more primary care to children than stepfathers, they may get only a little more (Santrock & Sitterle, 1988) or somewhat less acceptance than stepfathers (Duberman, 1973; Furstenberg, 1988). The pattern of greater maternal involvement in childrearing seems to collide with the children's tendencies to remain attached to biological mothers and direct their negative feelings toward stepparents. A student reports on his best friend's response to a stepmother:

> *I remember Mark telling me numerous times that he did not accept Sheila as his mother because she was a bitch. I think Sheila started to boss Mark around like his father did. Mark told me he was not going to listen to her, which he didn't. Mark's father talked with him and told him he WILL listen to Sheila whether he likes it or not. Mark did what he was told, but he now felt alone and isolated, so he and I planned to run away.*

Both mothers and stepmothers satisfy more basic needs for security, love, and inclusion than fathers. On the one hand, children may be less likely to rate their stepmother relations as "extremely close and caring" than stepfather relations (Furstenberg, 1988), because noncustodial mothers are likely to be more involved with them, more attached, and more competitive than noncustodial fathers (Santrock & Sitterle, 1988). On the other hand, the stepmother's symbolic and actual mothering of stepchildren is very important for their well-being, since children whose stepmothers brought their own biological children into the family reported significantly lower self-worth and greater separation anxiety (Santrock & Sitterle, 1988). Stepmother families are like stepfather families, in that parent–child bonding and discipline seems to proceed more smoothly with same-sex children, that is, stepmoms related well with stepdaughters and stepfathers with stepsons. On the other hand, adolescent sexual feelings might play an unconscious role in distancing stepsons from their stepmothers as it appears to do with stepdaughters and stepfathers.

Long-term results for children of divorce in adulthood

At first researchers thought that the acute effects of divorce on children generally lasted for two or three years, during which almost all children would have emotional distress and learning and behavior problems. Then some longer-term studies found lingering effects five, six, and ten years after divorce (Hetherington, Cox, & Cox, 1985; Guidubaldi, 1988; Wallerstein, 1989/1991). Even in adulthood, children of divorce receive an average of 20% to 25% less financial, emotional, and logistical support from their fathers and 10% to 15% less support from their mothers than children of intact first marriages. Only the financial part of this deficit can be traced to parental income loss. The rest is due to less emotional closeness between parents and offspring (White, 1992). However, the most recent studies emphasize that the family relationships and processes occurring during and after the divorce have a more significant statistical effect on the adult children than the mere fact of the divorce itself. We will outline the more frequently studied negative effects first, highlight the emerging evidence for key family relational factors, and then add what is known about positive effects.

Socioeconomic achievement

Adult children of divorce are likely to achieve somewhat less educationally, occupationally, and financially than socioeconomically matched children of intact marriages (Amato & Keith, 1991a; Mueller & Cooper, 1986). More children of divorce drop out of school, and more are unemployed. Perhaps many children of divorce never make up for their few years of disabled learning during the early divorce adjustment, and their lower average income base fails to support higher education and leads them to settle for less-prestigious, lower-paying jobs. Children of divorce in college represent a significant deviation from the average. So their achievements need not be adversely affected.

Adjustment to adulthood

Since 25–35% of college students are children of divorce, many studies have focused on them. Since college students are the most financially advantaged and academically successful of young adults, however, differences between these students and their nondivorce colleagues should be minimized and not representative of the whole country. For example, Barkley and Procidano (1989) found the only significant difference between divorce and nondivorce students in college was that the former had more **assertive attitudes**; they were highly motivated to "get out and get things done" (p. 84). This attitude may also apply to interpersonal relationships, since divorce daughters in college endorse more Machiavellian attitudes (power-oriented and manipulative) toward other people than nondivorce daughters do (Barber, 1998). Divorce-child students seem to have achieved an independent psychological identity as well or better than nondivorce students (Nelson et al., 1992). Perhaps reflecting some insecurity about their parents' love, they may be more materialistic and engage in more compulsive consumption (Rindfleisch et al., 1997).

Proneness to divorce

Adult children of divorce are significantly more likely than children of intact marriages to get divorced themselves. Divorce children are likely to marry young (Mueller & Pope, 1977), and earliest marriages have the highest divorce rate. So Glenn and Kramer (1987) combined data from 11 national surveys conducted from 1973 through 1985 and adjusted divorce rates for age at first marriage, as well as region of origin, religion, father's occupational prestige, mother's years of education, and respondent's years of education (bottom of Table 6.4). Even with all of these factors equalized, white divorce daughters' rate was over 13% higher than nondivorce daughters, while white sons' and black sons' and daughters' rates were over 5% higher than nondivorce sons and daughters in those categories.

Though these divorce rate increases are less statistically significant for black men and women (due to smaller sample sizes), white women's increase is 52% of the nondivorce daughters' rate and white men's increase is 23%. Several other research studies (Kulka & Weingarten, 1979; Bumpass et al., 1991), including the most recent (Amato, 1996) all corroborate these results. (Remember, that only means that a larger minority of divorce children than nondivorce children get divorces, *not* that most divorce children will get divorces themselves.)

Courtship

Evidence from studies on courtship patterns may help explain this trend toward marital instability. One study of several thousand Midwestern college students (Booth et al., 1984) found children of divorce more likely to be both romantically and sexually active than children from intact marriages. And three factors related to the parental divorce were statistically correlated with further *increases* in the students' romantic activity: (a) the presence of parental conflict after the divorce, (b) deterioration of parent–child relations, and (c) the custodial parent remaining single. Thus, it appears that the more tenuous or insecure the parental bonds may be, the more the children seek bonds of their own. Yet, new, contradictory research finds that a distant or troubled relationship with her father (likely after divorce) may have a significant negative effect on daughter's dating expectations (Butcher et al., 1998), but not on her trust, anxiety, or dating satisfaction (Clark & Kanoy, 1998).

Even though they date a lot, more adult children of divorce may have difficulty forming an intimate relationship than nondivorce children (Johnson & Nelson, 1998). However, the overall quality of family-of-origin functioning (warmth, cohesion, conflict) had a stronger statistical connection to college students' achievement of intimacy than parental divorce by itself. Furthermore, the perceived qualities of college students' current in-

TABLE 6.4. Adjusted percentage of ever-married persons 18 and older who had ever divorced or legally separated, according to their family situation at age 16, by sex, and race: Combined data from 11 U.S. national surveys conducted from 1973 through 1985

Category	Percent lived with both parents at 16	Percent parents divorced or separated at 16	Percent difference
Adjusted for date of survey and years since first marriage			
White males	21.9	34.1	12.2****
White females	24.4	43.0	18.6****
Black males	36.2	46.7	10.5*
Black females	43.2	56.3	13.1**

Adjusted additionally for region of origin, religion in which raised, father's or father substitute's occupational prestige, mother's years of schooling, and respondent's age at first marriage and years of schooling.

White males	22.6	27.8	5.2*
White females	25.1	38.3	13.2****
Black males	36.8	41.9	5.1
Black females	44.7	49.9	5.2

*significant at 10% level **significant at 5% **** significant at 0.1%
Source: Glenn & Kramer, 1987

timacies had larger connections to attitudes conducive to intimacy than did both divorce and family functioning (Johnson & Nelson, 1998; Sprague & Kinney, 1997). Thus, being in a satisfying relationship may help divorce children develop more successful intimate relating styles. Apparently, *divorce children can learn from experience as well as anyone else.*

Divorce children normally have a skeptical view of marriage (Long, 1987; Wallerstein et al., 1988). If their custodial parent stayed single, young women viewed divorce as negative but likely. If their custodial parent remarried, women viewed divorce as even more likely, but more positive, and they wanted to wait longer before marrying themselves (Kinnaird & Gerrard, 1986). Wallerstein and her colleagues (1988) found about a third of young adult divorce daughters were wary of commitment to love and were caught up in short-lived sexual relationships even a decade after their parents' divorce.

Despite the fact that most adolescent and young adult children of divorce are worried about the durability of marriage and vow to marry late or not at all themselves (Wallerstein, 1985), more of them marry young than children whose parents are still married. All this evidence suggests that adult children of divorce have an intensely **ambivalent** attitude toward love and marriage. Glenn and Kramer (1987) conclude that "they seem to be strongly impelled toward marriage while at the same time often feeling highly apprehensive about it" (p. 824).

Though they are more likely to expect and accept divorce than children of intact marriages, children of divorce may be just as committed as anyone else in the beginning of marriage. **But when the going gets tough,** their "learned pessimism" may take over, and they may be more influenced by overwhelming feelings about relational conflict and impending loss than by hope of communicating and working things out (Henry & Holmes, 1998).

When their relationships become troubled, children of divorce may become more emotionally reactive and confused (on the average) than other people, because of emotional conditioning during their parents' distressed marriage and divorce (Hepworth et al., 1984; Wallerstein et al., 1988). Once the reactivity of divorce children is triggered, they may be unfamiliar with negotiating and more inclined to adopt dysfunctional strategies for regaining security and control (Webster et al., 1995). Like other young adults from high-conflict families (Henry & Holmes, 1998), some are more likely than low-conflict nondivorce children to seek control over the partner through domination (Bolgar et al., 1995), aggression (Billingham & Notebaert, 1993), or manipulation. Other divorce children might prefer to escape vulnerability and regain control over themselves through emotionally or physically withdrawing within the relationship or initiating a breakup (Johnson & Nelson, 1998, Brown, 1999; Henry & Holmes, 1998).

Psychological well-being and perceived control over life events

Studies have revealed statistically significant connections, though small, between childhood loss of a parent through either death or divorce and psychological well-being in adult life (Glenn & Kramer, 1985; Rodgers, 1994). A study of older adults found that early parent loss was associated with lower educational achievement, and greater financial strain, which lead to **diminished feelings of personal control** over life (Krause, 1993). Amato (1991) found that early parent loss negatively impacted not only educational achievement and current earned income, but also occupational status and marital status, and *each* of these factors in turn increased adult depression. But even when all of these factors were equalized, early parent loss still increased depression scores in white men and women and black women. (These statistical relationships did not hold for black men or Hispanics.) Thus, a white person's and a black woman's level of achievement and marital status may contribute significantly to happiness. But losing a parent early in life may have a depressive effect on *some* in spite of marriage and personal success.

Perhaps a key psychological factor in this depressive tendency also contributes to these people's ambivalent approach to marriage: **They are hypersensitive to the issue of helplessness and personal control over life events**. Children who lose a parent to death or divorce have been helpless to prevent this loss. A middle aged man calls it a loss of faith:

> When I was twelve, my faith [in relationships] was shattered when I overheard my parents talking about divorce. I prayed for a whole year that it

wouldn't happen, but it did . . . My own marriage lasted nine years, but I thought it was hopeless after the first two. Every time we had a fight, I felt like it was over, and we had plenty of them.

Defending against helplessness. Like a marital partner who has been dumped (Gray & Silver, 1990), children of divorce need to understand what happened in order to alleviate depression (Kurdek, 1988). Being married or in relationship significantly reduces their tendency to feel depressed and their emotional insecurity (Glenn & Kramer, 1987; Rodgers, 1994). They seek the perfectly secure mate to make sure they won't put their children through what they had to suffer.

Parental loss through death or divorce. People who lost a parent through death, tend to marry conservatively and late and stay married as much as nondivorce children do (Hetherington, 1972; Glenn & Kramer, 1987). Because their parent is gone forever, they can complete their grieving process (though often not until adulthood), perhaps with a special relationship to this sadness and vulnerability.

By contrast, the children of divorce are likely to have experienced many happy or unhappy returns of their absent parent after the divorce. Many had him (or her) back for a weekend visit, or could reject *him* when angry. Many had power over both parents by switching loyalties and playing on their love and insecurities (Rivlin, 1985). So they have learned that control tactics might help them get some of the love they want. Where those who lost a parent through death tend to be more hesitant about love relations, children of divorce tend to rush into them in the beginning with enthusiasm (Hetherington, 1972; Brown, 1999). But their optimistic views may be defensively covering up an underlying pessimism about themselves in relationships (Henry & Holmes, 1998). Their struggles between control and helplessness are inevitable, because **love makes us vulnerable and out of control**.

> *It's almost as though every time things start going well between my boyfriend and me, I get scared and feel claustrophobic and do something to destroy it. I get scared because I don't know what's supposed to happen after you fall in love and everything is great. I never, ever, saw my parents express any love towards each other. I can't feel love or express it without scaring myself and becoming confused.*

My own quantitative and qualitative studies of the college love relationships of sons and daughters of divorce compared to those whose parents have not divorced yield a sketchy portrait (Brown, 1999). Divorce children report far more passionate affairs than nondivorce children and they are far more likely to initiate their more serious breakups. Their greatest loves tend toward intensity, ambivalence (both praising and criticizing the partner more), idealization (in the beginning), and disillusionment thereafter, greater felt love and dislike, and self-protective withdrawing and emotional distancing. As a relationship begins, they pursue close emotional closeness with idealism, commitment, and more personal power initiatives. But later they switch from pursuers to distancers to seek control over their hurt and helplessness, even if they are not ready to break up.

Gender differences.   But why is the tendency to divorce so much greater in daughters of divorce than in sons? Two factors already discussed might provide an explanation.

First, at least two thirds of divorces are initiated by women. Men may be just as likely to withdraw from intimacy, but they seem to be less willing to divorce unless they have already found another partner. So it would be statistically anticipated for daughters of divorce to have a higher divorce rate than sons of divorce, if their tendencies to divorce had been equally elevated by some other factor, such as the emotional reactivity and control/ helplessness issues we have raised.

Second, it is usually the **father** whose leaving would be associated with the issues of control, helplessness, abandonment, and depression. So daughters would be more likely to be seized by these issues with their subsequent **husbands** than would sons with their wives. Sons of divorce may develop power and control issues with their single mothers, too, but at least their mothers usually **stayed** when they were young and helpless. Sons of divorce normally retain a far more positive attachment with their mothers than divorce daughters had with their fathers. This suggests that sons might have a more positive internal model of cross-sexual intimate relationships to partially offset the relationally negative effects of their parents' marital distress and dissolution (Henry & Holmes, 1998).

Summary of causative factors from research

There are five main factors influencing children's long-term negative reactions to divorce which have been moderately to strongly supported by American research (reviewed in Amato, 1993). They are

1. absence of the noncustodial parent,
2. adjustment of the custodial parent,
3. interparental conflict,
4. economic hardship, and
5. an increase in other stressful life changes.

According to the bulk of American research, what happens **after** the divorce determines most of the long-term effects on the children, at least after the two years or more of adjusting to the initial disruption. Amato (1993) suggests that we can integrate all of these factors by considering them as a combination of **stressors** and **coping resources**, which we have done in Table 6.5.

TABLE 6.5. Principal stressors and coping resources in children's long-term reactions to divorce

Stressors	Coping resources
Individual personality factors	Child's intelligence
	Emotional regulatory physiology
Absence of noncustodial parent	Parent substitutes available in network
Adjustment and mental health of custodial parent	Secure attachment and authoritative parenting
	Network support for single parent
Post-divorce parental conflict	Family cohesiveness and expressiveness
	Social network buffers and dampens conflicts
Economic hardship	More money makes adjustment easier
	Network provides economic assistance
Increase in other stressful life changes	Community and network provide continuity

Expanded from Amato, 1993.

Parental conflict

The most potent stressor seems to be **ongoing parental conflict**, because it can interfere with the stable love relationships with both parents that are among the child's most valuable coping resources. In fact, a growing body of research (Schwartzberg et al, 1983; Amato & Booth, 1991a; Henry & Holmes, 1998; Sprecher et al., 1998) suggests that chronically conflicting intact marriages may be even more damaging to children's attitudes, relating skills, or self-esteem than divorces. Adult children of conflictual intact marriages are not as reticent to marry as divorce children, **but they expect both their marriages and their childrearing to be problematical** (Long, 1987; Black & Sprenkle, 1991). All this evidence suggests that managing marital conflict maybe is more important to the emotonal well-being of children than staying together for their sake.

Major factors that help with coping

If family conflict, economic hardship, and multiple life changes are the most powerful negative influences on divorce children, parenting styles and security of attachment to at least one parent are the most powerful positive influences. An authoritative and warm parenting style is most conducive to children's psychosocial adjustment, and such parenting is quite possible in a divorce or remarried family, though less frequent than in an intact biological family (Arendell, 1997). In the same vein, young adults with a secure attachment bond to one parent may have very similar attitudes and security levels in relationships, whether they are from intact or divorced families (Face, 1997). Marital conflict and divorce also have a lesser effect on children who have higher intelligence and better physiological regulation of heartbeat (Katz & Gottman, 1997). Abundant economic resources can make adjusting to divorce easier, and poverty can make it more difficult. The positive influence of warmth and expressiveness between divorced family members may be as powerful as continued conflict can be negative (Johnson & Nelson, 1998). Another widely effective coping resource is a solid communal or social network, such as sometimes exists among African Americans or Hispanics (Tienda & Angel, 1987) or in many preindustrial cultures (Bilge & Kaufman, 1983). A communal (or tribal) society can supply more stable love relations, more economic resources, and more support for an overwhelmed parent, and can reduce post-divorce conflict. We can conclude that parental divorce is almost always accompanied by multiple stressors, but this need not spell long-term negative effects for all children.

Positive results of parental divorce

Our intention to provide a balanced view of the effects of divorce on children has been hindered by conceptual problems as well as a lack of empirical research. There are three ways to conceive of positive effects of divorce.

1. Expected negative effects of divorce *fail to show up in research.* But multiple approaches are necessary before we can be sure they don't happen. This brings more *relief* than positivity.
2. Divorce children manifest positively valued characteristics *more* than nondivorce children. But multiple approaches are necessary to develop an integrated picture of personality. (For example, higher assertiveness may be connected to more power–manipulative attitudes.)
3. Existing negative impacts of divorce motivate many to adapt by *growing* in self-knowledge, compassion, and life skills. ("No pain, no gain" or "lemon to lemonade" effect.)

Thus, it is inaccurate to limit our survey of effects of divorce to quantifiable positives and negatives. We draw here a little from empirical, clinical, and anecdotal sources.

Wallerstein (1998) found that 10 years after their parents' divorces, 45% of upper middle class white (hence economically advantaged) young adults "had emerged as competent, compassionate and courageous people," while 41% were "worried, underachieving, self-deprecating and sometimes angry" and the other 14% were "strikingly uneven in how they adjusted to the world" (p. 171). What are some of the advantages this well-adjusted 45% could have?

The extended blended family

If there is good cooperation between remarried ex-spouses, the children can benefit from an increase in loving parents (to 3 or 4) and other relatives, as well as in economic resources. This college student had gained a larger, stronger family.

Both parents are remarried to fabulous people. My step-dad is very compat-
ible with my mom and has been wonderful to me. I couldn't have wished a
better mate for her. The same is true with my step-mom. In fact, these two are
so much alike that it is frightening. Now, mom and dad get along great. Lately,
both families have worked extremely well together to get things done. When
my car died, my dad and step-dad went out together and found a car for me.
They split the cost and my step-dad drove it to me here at school. It's even to
the point where my dad and step-mom's little girl goes to visit my mom.

Gender roles

Research indicates that children brought up in single parent, dual career,
and step families all have more household responsibilities than children in
traditional one-earner families (Amato, 1987). Girls in single-mother families may, in effect, learn the single parent role by performing both male
and female sex-typed tasks, more so than boys (Hilton & Haldeman, 1991).

Growing up fast gave me a head start in life. I developed a very strong sense
of responsibility and confidence which came from taking care of myself and
not coasting through life with my parents there to do everything for me.

Boys in single mother families do some female-role tasks, but they are
often selected for male-role tasks, like automobile and outside maintenance.
Boys' household duties are likely to be less sex-typed in dual career families (Hilton & Haldeman, 1991). Even though they may prefer some of the
traditional division of labor, divorce sons are more accepting of equal power
(Kiecolt & Acock, 1988), as this student asserts:

Since women make up the majority of single parent households, I think this
shows their daughter or son that women don't need to be controlled by or
dependent on a man. This has been supported in many of my relationships,
where women from traditional type families seem to be more dependent on me
and look for me to make most of the decisions. When I've dated women from
single parent homes, they appeared to be less dependent on me and took a lot
less bullshit from me.

Many black and white sons of divorce in college appear to develop
more charming and sophisticated approaches to women's feelings than the
average young man from an intact family. Perhaps many male children in
mother-headed families learned to cope by developing their intuition or
empathic understanding in a way similar to women in male-dominated
families and cultures: "you get good at figuring people out so you can achieve
your own aims despite their power to stop you." Since high levels of
mother-son conflict may lead to greater conflict in sons' romantic relationships (Troyer, 1993), more egalitarian and companionate mother-son relations (Hetherington, 1987) could also be conducive to more egalitarian
relationships.

Early maturation

The well-known tendency of children of divorce to "grow up quickly" (reviewed in Gately & Schwebel, 1992) involves unusual **self-reliance** and **assertiveness.** Through participating in the adult functions of the family and learning many family secrets they may understand **adult and family emotional issues** better and become **skillful negotiators** or **family counselors**. Having a confiding, companionate relationship with each parent individually may allow a young person to develop a **greater tolerance for differences** between their beliefs and personalities. Respecting two different role models can bring **greater freedom to define one's own convictions**, and thus a **greater sense of individuality**. Since father–offspring bonds are normally greatly reduced after divorce (e.g., Henry & Holmes, 1998), divorce sons are less likely than nondivorce sons to identify with their fathers (Evans & Bloom, 1996), so they find it more necessary to "reinvent" themselves. Family therapy theorist Murray Bowen (1978) suggests that individual "I–thou" relationships with each parent are conducive to a greater ability to become intimate with others while respecting differences. Motivated by their approach–avoidance conflict with love, and their tendency to have more premarital and marital intimacies, divorce children can get to know more partners deeply, providing a rich human experience and increased opportunities to develop **wisdom** and **intimacy skills**.

What can children of divorce do to cope with their relationship issues?

Children of divorce can benefit by reviewing their experiences and issues as they enter adulthood in a supportive group atmosphere (McGuire, 1987). McGuire's support group discussed the common issues facing divorce children, in Table 6.6 below, to which we have added some clinical advice.

The table presents a long program of issues and growth directions, which are by no means limited to children of divorce. Many of these issues could be experienced by anyone, whether his or her family of origin was divorced or "dysfunctional" or not. Young adults seeking both intimacy and careers may struggle to have both closeness and personal power, setting up similar strengths and problems in partnership, regardless of having a predisposition based on family background or not (Brown, 1999). We will comment on several issues to conclude this chapter.

Distrust of love and marriage

Children of intact marriages may be just as naively optimistic about love and marriage as children of divorce are naively pessimistic, given the divorce rates in Table 6.4. Marrying later in one's twenties brings down the

TABLE 6.6. Developmental challenges for adult children of divorce

Issue	Coping strategies
<u>Distrust of love</u> and marriage	Respect your cautiousness. Love and marriage can last.
<u>Hostility</u> to mother and father and self-blame	Understand parents and yourself in terms of human strengths and weakness. Talk with parents to express and resolve resentments.
<u>Abandonment fears,</u> especially if opposite sex parent left	Be aware of fear and confusion and seek reassurance or reality check. Discuss any anxieties with partner, confidant, or counselor.
<u>Depression tendency</u>	A. Develop grief processes for losses of parents & disruptive life changes. B. Alleviate depression with exercise, catharsis, pleasing activities, supportive confidantes, re-evaluating situations, & helping others; use antidepressants when needed.
<u>Struggle for control</u> over life, especially over love life	A. Differentiate between what you can and cannot control. B. Aim for what you **can** achieve through self-control: education, understanding of self and relationships, and career prospects (partially under your control). C. Share control in relationships and respect and express your vulnerability.
<u>Seductive, shortlived relationships</u> (women)	A. Gain more realistic understanding of father's characteristics. B. Deal with confusion and feelings when love relationships reach middle stages.
<u>Single-mother boys</u> supernice, charming evasive in relationships	A. Develop an assertive, honest relationship with mother that affirms privacy. B. Develop assertiveness in romantic relationships.
<u>Parents' conflict</u> or use children as <u>go-between</u> or substitute companion	A. Refuse roles of confidant, messenger, peacemaker, or family manager. B. Refuse to discuss complaints about other family members. Insist on relating about yourselves & mutual interests and not about family members C. Redirect parent's companionship needs to other appropriate adults.
<u>Failure-prone character</u> I have inherited or learned my parents' fatal flaws	A Explore both parents' explanations of what didn't work between them. B. What you and they recognize may not be the most important causes of divorce. C. Similar characteristics in interaction could evoke new strengths & weaknesses. D. You cannot eliminate many problematic characteristics. You can cope with them so they are more successful and more responsive to another's reactions.
<u>Undeserved economic</u> and emotional stresses Resentment & wish for stable, nurturing, family love relationships, and religious, interest, or support groups.	A. **Life is unfair.** But psychological wounds can motivate compassion and wisdom. B. Take steps to achieve more nurturing relations and good self-care now. C. Long-term intimacies heal, including peer or adult friendships, and mentorships.

Helping others:	A.	Helping & caring for others is a **good** way to develop
Projecting our desire		compassion and courage and learn from your own wounds.
for nurture by giving it	B.	Nurturing in relationships may lead to mutual caring or just
to someone else who		feeling used, if not reciprocated. Explore prospective helpees'
needs it.		giving and receiving capacities. Experienced
		caregivers allocate their time and energy and are repaid for it.
	C.	Learn to ask for the same warmth and help you are giving.

Sources not previously referred to in this chapter: McGuire, 1987; Guggenbuhl-Craig, 1971; Kast, 1992.

chances of divorce. The wiser course seems to be to stay cautious about marriage, get more preparation for career success, and embrace psychological education and self-awareness through practice in intimate relationships.

Hostility and fear

Divorce children often hang on to their hostility towards absent parents for years, preferring the "strong" feeling of resentment to the "weak" feelings of hurt, sadness, and longing. A few encounters (perhaps skillfully managed by a relative or a counselor) are often enough to melt the barriers of hateful or dismissive words and rediscover the potential for warmth and concern beneath.

Divorce children may unconsciously think their parents didn't love them, because they left—so perhaps they are unlovable. This hampers self-love, since self-esteem is developed first from the love our family gives us (Rice & Rice, 1986). When we are wounded in our self-love, we normally doubt others' love as well. We may be too preoccupied with securing love for ourselves and resentful about the difficulties involved to empathize with another person. As with many other aspects of personality, once we are aware of such a limitation on our empathy, we can consciously go beyond our fear and expand the empathic skills we already have.

Depression, control, and the unfairness of existence

These are the broadest issues, and they impact everyone in one way or another. Most children of divorce did get a "raw deal" and have been subjected to economic and emotional strains that they did not deserve. They normally react with bitterness.

> I was denied my right, as a child, to have a "normal" childhood. I missed out on all of the father–son events. I was an all-star soccer player, and my father was never once at a game. Holidays were nothing but a time of pain and sorrow, longing to be near the parent that we weren't near. I simply won't let that happen to my children . . . parents have no clue what their actions can do to a child.

We all feel happier the more we feel able to exert control over the events in our lives. Yet there are many aspects of our existence over which we have little or no control. We cannot keep ourselves from getting sick or old, or feeling what our biology and socialization have programmed us to feel. Neither can we stop a romantic partner from leaving us, once that person wants to go. We need to distinguish between what we can and cannot control and develop a philosophical approach for both. Our wounds can be a source of courage, compassion, and our most unique personal achievements. Psychology, philosophy, and religion all have valuable approaches to dealing with these issues.

Short-lived relationships for daughters of divorce

Some daughters of divorce have had something similar to long distance romantic relationships with their noncustodial fathers. In order to prove their love and receive love in return, their fathers turned visitations into "dates," showering them with exciting outings, presents, and praise. But at the end of the visit daddy always left, and the daughter had no power to keep him or bring him back.

Girls can incorporate this pattern into their unconscious expectations for romance. Partners may be idealized, but unavailable in some persistent way, such as being married or devoted to a career or alcohol. Or they will be very exciting and loving, and the couple can go to extremes of adventure and romance in weekends or other brief encounters. But if they stay together very long the thrills will dwindle, and problems will arise. Then the excitement of beginning is replaced by anxiety about the end, and it feels better to get out before things get any worse.

These unconscious expectations can lead to rapid, intense beginnings and endings, and the approach–avoidance relating style of that third of the upper middle class daughters in Wallerstein et al.'s (1988) study. Confusion and fear of abandonment may be overwhelming when there is no model for what to do in the middle stages of relationships. People need help relinquishing familiar "affair" patterns (Brown, 1999) and navigating through deepening stages: What is normal in longer relationships? How do I compromise? How bad is this conflict? Friends and counselors can help us make new roadmaps for relating.

Supernice guys

One pattern for sons of single mothers is to repudiate their father's style and behavior in order to be a better family man than their fathers had been. These young men are very sensitive and understanding toward women. But they may give up too much masculine aggression and self-will in order to avoid being "too much like dad." Young women are amazed at first at how considerate they are, but then they often lose their romantic excitement and prefer to be just very good friends. The young men don't understand why their profeminine attitudes and skills are unsuccessful in love and complain that "nice guys finish last."

Charming avoiders, developing Don Juans

Other sons of single mothers learned the same woman-pleasing skills. But they also developed their adolescent masculinity as a rebellion against maternal control. Like the "dating" daughters discussed above, they like to charm and seduce the opposite sex, and also compete with and conquer women through superior skill. Their romantic relationships are similar to the women's, in that they may start off fantastic and then not go anywhere. They often avoid vulnerability and commitment, as this college man admits:

> I sometimes feel as if I have developed a hard edge about me that my girlfriend thinks is preventing me from falling in love with her. I probably have not truly been in love with anyone before, so my pace is slower than she would like.

They are likely to play around with other women during their relationships as well. If their single moms were somewhat authoritarian, as in some African-American families, they may unconsciously fear that long-term commitment means a loss of power. In response they become devious or passive-aggressive. They may yield to and please their partners a lot, but keep "playing around" in secret. In order to change, these men can stop relying on their charm and work on assertiveness and experiencing their vulnerability instead.

Is there a divorce-prone character or gene?

It has been suggested that inheritable abnormal levels of depression, lack of control over negative emotional arousal, and some other interpersonally dysfunctional characteristics might predispose some parents and their children toward divorce (Harris, 1998). But inheritability has not been systematically addressed in research. Learning has been studied, but with mixed results. Lack of adequate gender–role models is not well supported by research as a major cause of divorce (Glenn & Kramer, 1987). Current research suggests that learned insecurities, pessimism about marriage, and dysfunctional coping with conflict could be the most potent factors predisposing children of divorce toward divorcing (Henry & Holmes, 1998). But it seems unlikely that much of this behavior is inherited, or that any one character portrait fits most children of divorce.

Future research and psychoeducation

Henry and Holmes (1998) have begun a promising empirical way to find the key factors in **divorce children's resiliency**. Many children of divorce never get divorced, just as many children of alcoholics never marry problem drinkers or become alcoholics themselves. By comparing those who do and don't divorce, we can explore what they do, think, and feel that is different. For example, negative judgments about divorced parents' faults may lie in wait to become the "kiss of death" when applied to future love partners. Then perhaps revising both negative expectations and ideal images of the opposite sex and striving for a more realistic appraisal of our parents and their divorce might lead us to longer lasting relationships. Perhaps if we could reduce the fear of helplessness, emotional vulnerability, and dysfunctional conflict behavior of many children of divorce, this would help stabilize their relationships.

This and many more questions await future research, and the challenges and opportunities presented by parental divorce are sure to be with us for decades to come.

Chapter summary

- Divorce affects preschoolers first through the behavior and emotions of their caregivers and then via fantasy and splitting. Parental conflict affects self-soothing of negative emotions.
- Young schoolers experience home instability, learned helplessness, and unrealistic thinking.
- Preteen boys externalize and girls internalize feelings; both may become coparents and companions.
- Teenagers separate, act older, and have behavior problems due to conflictual and lacking parenting.
- Stepparents face negativity and resistance to their authority, especially from opposite-sex children.
- Long-term effects of divorce include lower socioeconomic achievement, increased assertiveness, emotional insecurities, depressive tendencies, and concern with helplessness and control.
- Divorce children have more courtships and divorces, perhaps due to learned insecurities, increased pessimism about marriage, acceptance of breakups, reactivity to problems and conflict, and a need for control.
- Principal post-divorce stressors include family conflict, economic hardship, parent loss and parent dysfunction, and disruptive living changes.
- Strengths for post-divorce coping include authoritative parenting, secure attachment, family warmth, and social network support.
- Ten years after divorce about half of adult children may be competent and compassionate. Divorce benefits include extended blended families, gender role flexibility, early maturation, empathic understanding of adult issues, individuation, and intimacy skills.
- Recovery programs for adult children of divorce can focus on distrust of love, hostility and fear, pessimism and control, conflict reactivity, and brief affair patterns, while research explores the factors associated with relationship longevity.

Influences
on relationships

Influences of gender on intimate relating 7

- **Gender Influences Communication**
  Gender-based Stereotypes in Communication
  Actual Differences in Communication
  Differences in Emotional Expressiveness
  Differences in Expressing Empathy
- **Gender Influences the Division of Labor**
  Gender Differences in Participation in Paid Work
  Gender Differences in Domestic Work
- **Gender Influences Relational Power and Decision Making**
  Types of Power
  Preferred Power Tactics
  Three Types of Marital Role Structures
  Power Motivation in Individual Psychology
  Power Motivation in Intimate Relationships
- **Explanations for the Development of Gendered Relationships**
  Structuralist Explanations of Gendered Couple Relations
  Symbolic Interactionist Explanations of Gendered Relations
  Social Exchange Theory
  Exchange and Communalism
- **Cultural Influences**

What are you looking for in a mate? Would you prefer the person to be shorter or taller than you or the same height? Would you want them to be more intelligent, less intelligent, or equal to you? More or less educated, or the same? Older, younger, or the same age? Do you want the person to have a better income, or potential income, than you, or lower or equal income? Asking 300 college students these questions revealed an interesting pattern (Prochaska, 1977). Two-thirds of the women (67%) surveyed reported preferring to marry *only* a male who was *older, more intelligent, better paid, better educated,* and *taller* than they were. Three quarters (75%) of the men reflected the opposite mate preferences. Although you may not agree with these preferences, why do you think there was such consistency?

Many social scientists attribute such distinctive differences in mate preference to biology—women are physiologically attracted to bigger and taller men whom they sense are better protectors (see Chapter 9). Men's

matching attractions, they would contend, are toward evidence of youth, fertility, and nurturance. Other social scientists—predominantly sociologists—put more emphasis on the influence of pre-established gender-linked social patterns and norms, known as **gendered social roles,** which are absorbed from our major cultural institutions (our families, schools, and media). In this view, men's age, height, and education are culturally recognized symbols of success, while intelligence and income only matter when a culture assigns the provider role to men. To understand how cultural norms about gender roles influence our relating, we will examine the current research findings regarding the influence of gender on communication, on the allocation of paid work and "family work," and on the use of power and influence strategies in intimate relationships. Then we consider explanations of how such gender-linked role expectations influence relationship development.

But before we examine the distinctive influence on relationships of societal and cultural norms regarding gender, let us clarify what we mean by **gender role** or **sex role** by making a distinction between gender identity and gender role or sex role. *Gender identity* refers to an individual's emotional or intellectual awareness of being either male or female. Except on rare occasions, gender identity corresponds to the individual's biological sex characteristics, and is believed to be complete by about age three (Hess & Ferree, 1987). In contrast, *gender role* or sex role refers to the personality characteristics, attitudes, and behaviors that a culture or society ascribes to a particular sex. Although societies see gender *identities* similarly (i.e., a penis denotes maleness whether in the Congo or Cleveland), gender *roles* may be viewed differently in different cultures. For example, Italian men are allowed to be emotional but Northern European men are not. *Sexual role* is another aspect of this composite and is concerned with the sexual inclinations and behaviors a person constructs on the basis of a usually already-established gender identity and gender role. Seeing gender as a social role produced in everyday activity, rather than describing gender as an individual property based on biology, allows us to focus on how people in their interactions with others come to perceive each other and each other's behaviors as gender appropriate or inappropriate.

Gender influences communication

Do we expect men and women to communicate differently? Are the differences we see a result of gender role norms (i.e, stereotypes) or are there

actual differences in how men and women communicate in their relationships? Let us look first at research examining the extent to which there are
gender-based stereotypes about men's and women's communication behavior and then review research exploring **actual gender differences** in
their communication.

Gender-based stereotypes in communication

Using a non-experimental approach to address questions concerning gender-based differences in communication, Lakoff (1973) reported that women
and men use language in different ways. Women tend to use weaker, less
forceful expletives (e.g, "Oh Dear" as compared to "Shit"), more tag questions (e.g, "isn't it?" or "you know?" on the end of a statement), a rising
inflection typical of questions when making declarative statements, and
certain adjectives that are reserved for "women's language" (e.g. "sweet,"
"lovely"). Lakoff concluded that women are socialized to use language that
is less meaningful in content, less forceful, and devoid of strong statements.

Consistent with Lakoff's observations, empirical studies have suggested
that certain linguistic features are consistently *perceived* as associated with
either male or female speech. For example, Kramer (1977) reported that
several speech characteristics were stereotyped as masculine or feminine
by both male and female college students. Characteristics listed by subjects
which are associated with male speech included use of swear words and
slang, dominating speech, bluntness, forcefulness, demandingness, and
more open displays of anger. Characteristics more frequently associated
with female speech included proper grammar, politeness, concern for listener, talkativeness, gossip, gibberish, and talk about trivial topics.

Pruett (1989) suggested that expectations of traditional gender roles
impact perceptions of individual communication styles. Reviewing the evidence from a wide range of studies exploring perceptions of male and female communication, Pruett reported that communication by men, as perceived by themselves and others, was generally rated consistent with
traditional masculine gender roles as more powerful, contentious, and dominant. Female communication was reported to be rated in manners consistent with traditionally feminine roles of being attentive, responsive, open,
and friendly. These gender-based expectations also appeared in the communication experiences of married couples. Fitzpatrick and Indvisk (1982),
for example, found that wives perceived themselves as using more "expressive and nurturant" communication styles while husbands saw themselves as being more "task oriented and instrumental" in their communication.

Actual differences in communication

Do men and women actually differ in how they communicate in their relationships? Despite the common belief that women talk more than men,

the bulk of recent research comes to the opposite conclusion! In a review of 63 empirical studies done between 1951 and 1991 (James & Drakich, 1993), 36 of the studies revealed that men talked more overall, or at least in some circumstances, and only 6 reported that women talked more overall or in some circumstances. The difference between scientific and popular opinions becomes clearer when we compare audiences, settings, and topics for conversation. Men definitely talk more in formal groups (such as classes and organizations) and in task-oriented groups. Even more than a third of studies on informal groups of mixed gender found men talked more, though the rest found no significant differences. Women do, however, talk more than men do with their same-sex friends.

If we now compare the topics women and men talk about, studies from 1922 to 1991 document the same gender differences: women talk much more about *people* and *relationships* and about *appearance* (of dwellings or of self), while men talk much more about *work* and *money* and about *sports*. In 70 years the differences may have diminished somewhat, with the main change being a big increase in talk about work and money among women (those who are now working or expecting to work). The lowest gender differences in regard to topics have been found among college students, who are the subjects of two out of three studies enacted since 1950. By combining all these results, we can understand why women are perceived to talk more than men: *(a) it appears that only friendship and couple settings are being considered, and (b) women definitely talk more about people and relationships, which makes many men uncomfortable.* Thus, the popular belief that women talk more than men seems to reflect *men's opinions* about talking more than women's. Men would not notice that they talk more in public and the workplace, because people with higher public status are expected to be more competent and talkative in these arenas (James & Drakich, 1993).

Deborah Tannen (1990) summarizes men's preferred topics and mode of communicaition with the term **report talk,** and women's communication with the term **rapport talk.** That means that while men are often only intending to report on some facts, women are often concerned with establishing rapport, that is, giving and getting signals about how intimate or distant they are with their conversational partners. Communication theorists suggest that every verbal statement has both a report function (i.e., relaying explicit content) and an implication about the relationship between speaker and listener (i.e., a relational message or rapport function). Though both functions may be present, the sexes seem to focus on different aspects (see Chapters 9 and 12).

But how do men and women in love relationships actually talk with each other? In a study involving 20 married couples recruited from a local church, Fitzpatrick and Dindia (1986) compared measures of talk time for individuals in dyadic conversations with their spouses and with strangers. They reported no differences by sex on either the length of time speaking or the percentage of total time holding the floor in conversations with either spouse or strangers. Other studies have also failed to find significant differences between partners on variables related to the amount of time spent talking.

With regard to conflict situations, certain contextual factors appear to contribute to differences in communication between men and women. For example, Heavey, Christensen, and Malamuth (1995) reported that when the topic of a disagreement was initially raised by the woman, compared to the same topic initiated by the man, women were described as more active in the exchange (e.g., starting the conversation, pressuring, nagging) while men were described as interacting less (e.g., becoming withdrawn and silent, refusing to continue the conversation). In contrast, when men initiated the topic of disagreement, the men were more active in the exchange and the women less so.

Difference in emotional expressiveness

If we ask people what emotions they experience, women will be more open in their reports and admit to more intensity of emotional expression than men. Women will report more warmth, happiness, joy, shame, guilt, fear, nervousness, and sadness. In fact, new positron emission tomography (PET) brain scan research found that recalling sad memories activated eight times as much of women's limbic systems as occurred with men (George et al., 1996). Men will report more pride, disgust, and contempt. And both sexes report experiencing anger about equally. The same gender differences show up even more strongly in range of emotional expression, with anger again being the one expression that is most nearly equal. Thus males are more likely than females to internalize, or keep most of their emotions inside. These behavioral differences are consistent with traditional gender roles, since both men and women with more feminine gender-role attitudes or who have traditionally feminine occupations (e.g., teaching and nursing) report more expressiveness than those with more masculine occupations or attitudes (Brody & Hall, 1993).

> Thus the emotions that women display more . . . are related to affiliation, vulnerability and self-consciousness, and are consistent with women's lower status and power, lower physical aggression. . . . Greater male anger, pride and contempt are consistent with the male role of differentiating or competing with others, in which the goals are the minimization of vulnerability in order to maximize the chances of success. (p. 453)

Both family and peer interaction in childhood support the development of these emotional tendencies. Not only mothers, but also fathers discuss more emotions more often with their daughters than with their sons, though mothers still typically avoid anger and fathers avoid disgust. Girls usually play with one or two intimate friends, with whom agreement and cooperation are maximized and hostility is minimized. Boys are more likely to play in larger groups, where competition for leadership and status makes more aggression, hostility, and teasing likely, and vulnerable emotions are detrimental. But that does not mean that all gender differences come from childhood experiences, for some experts have estimated that biologically based tendencies could influence childhood interaction patterns (reviewed in Brody & Hall, 1993). For example, more emotionally sensitive children of both sexes might avoid large groups because ridicule and aggressive interaction are too uncomfortable, so they would develop more harmonious bonds with a few peers (Kagan, Reznick, & Snidman, 1988; Aron & Aron, 1997), and more sensitive people might gravitate toward more expressive and nurturant adult roles as well.

The effects of these emotional differences on relationships can hardly be overestimated, as this example illustrates. Women feel and express the self-punishing emotions (shame and guilt) more than men. A woman may feel guilty about something she thinks might upset her partner, even if he only got angry about it once. So she might torture herself for stopping off for a drink after work, regardless of the fact that he was unaware that anything was "wrong":

> She: I couldn't enjoy myself at the restaurant. I was worried the whole time that you were sitting at home fuming. [She is trying to restore harmony by showing how concerned she was about his feelings.]

> He: That's ridiculous! I don't sit by the door waiting for you to come home! [He resents the implication that he gave her reason to feel dread and guilt, and that he would spend that much time fuming.]

> His effect on her: His hostile, contemptuous response could convince her that he is indeed angry and punishing her for coming home later than she thinks he expected. So her self-punitive feelings are validated when he gives her something like the punishment she feared.

> Her effect on him: He thinks she has gone on an emotional-pain ride without him and blamed him for it. He disrespects her, because she responds emotionally in a way he won't imagine for himself.

But surely we can understand each other better than that, if we just use a little empathy.

Differences in experiencing and expressing empathy

The ability to feel the other's emotion while recognizing it as separate from oneself is considered an essential ingredient for understanding between the sexes. In the days of clearly separate gender roles, it was not as necessary for partners to seek empathic understanding as it is today. People in dominant positions did not need to understand others as much as those in subservient positions, such as minority groups, wives, and children. But now that has changed.

I always tried harder to understand him than he tried to understand me. When I finally started to care as much about myself as I cared about him, he figured out that something was wrong (because I stopped catering to him all the time). But when it came to understanding me, he still didn't have a clue.

In Hite's (1987) volunteer survey, 96% of women believed they were giving more emotional and empathic support than they were getting. In a relationship such as the one above, we can speculate that the woman has specialized for years in taking care of others and of this relationship. So when she changes her mind about what she should get in return for her efforts, she is bound to find her partner way behind on doing his share. Even if he approaches his new task of being empathic with good will, his lack of training and practice will probably keep him behind for a long time.

The following illustrates a typical empathy failure:

Woman: I feel awful . . .

Man: Well, why don't you **do** something about it!

To keep from feeling **dependent**, males prefer to solve their own and others' problems. The man above intends to save the woman from wallowing in despair. But the woman thinks he disapproves of her feeling and does not want to be close. She may simply want to relay her feelings and be empathized with, without desiring a "solution."

Current opinion is divided on whether women are biologically better equipped for empathy or men are equally capable but are just behind in their training. Theorists divide empathy into four steps and raise issues involved with each one:

1. One person broadcasts a feeling state;
2. The receiver "picks up the broadcast" by attending to visual and auditory cues and perhaps by unconsciously mimicking the sender's facial expressions;
3. The receiver feels a bit of the sender's emotion, though his or her emotional associations to the content may be different than the sender's; and
4. The receiver labels his or her own emotional state and realizes that it belongs to the other person (Jordan et al., 1991; Nathanson, 1992).

There are gender-related issues involved in each step: (a) If the sender restricts her or his emotional experience and expression, as men are likely to do, the broadcast will be less effective; (b) the receiver may be either unwilling or unable to read the cues; (c) the receiver may be unwilling or unable to feel similarly to the sender; and (d) the receiver might not know how to label what is being felt or may identify with the resonating feelings as an extension of self (Jordan et al., 1991).

New PET scan research found adult men only 70% accurate in reading sadness on women's faces, compared to 90% accuracy for women—but more of the men's brains lit up during the task. Perhaps "women can't understand why men find it so hard to be sensitive to emotions [because] women's brains didn't have to work as hard to excel at judging emotions" (Begley, March 27, 1995). Men are normally less versatile than women at labeling what they pick up. On the other hand, some women might not clearly differentiate between others' emotions and their own. Even if they can differentiate their feelings from others', their training in "good mothering" may lead them to treat others' needs as if they were their own (Jordan et al., 1991). Some sons of single mothers also may exhibit this attitude.

Current empathy research reveals that men in nurturant, expressive, or artistic professions can be as successful as women at reading emotions from nonverbal cues (reviewed in Tavris & Wade, 1984). But 80% of the studies find men are not as successful at this as women, except when it comes to male anger (Brody & Hall, 1993). This data could imply two things: (a) some men are equipped to become just as empathic as most women, but more men are not; or (b) practicing the processes and skills involved can make everyone equally empathic (as indicated in Ickes, June, 1993). But from infancy on, males are less likely than females to be practicing.

Gender influences the division of labor

Social scientists have long been interested in determining how larger societal expectations and norms affect what men and women choose to *do* in their relationships. Before we look at their findings, look for a moment at  your own ideas about how you think that you should behave in your love relationship by answering the questions pictured in Table 7.1. What differences do you notice in your expectations about behavior and attitudes of men and women? How might these ideas affect the way you might deal with your partner in your intimate relationships?

Gender differences in participation in paid work

Work, both paid and unpaid (i.e., outside and inside the relationship and household) is central to couple and family life. Recent time studies show that the total number of hours married women and men spend as workers (combined paid and family work) is about the same (Berk, 1985; Pleck, 1985). However, more women than men shift their time and invest-

TABLE 7.1. Increasing your awareness of your gender-role expectations

Use the following sentence stems to stimulate your thoughts and feelings. Allow yourself to complete each of these sentences both with your first, spontaneous thought and then, more thoughtfully and reflectively. If done in depth, you may discover that a lot of feelings are wrapped up in your answers. Try not to shy away from these emotions too much since they may provide you with an important source of information about yourself.

The hardest thing about being a man is _____

The hardest thing about being a woman is _____

My favorite "feminine" quality is _____

My favorite "masculine" quality is _____

I would be shocked if I saw a woman _____

I would be shocked if I saw a man _____

Men should_____

Women should_____

A woman's chores should include_____

A man's chores should include_____

What I can't understand about men is_____

What I can't understand about women is _____

To a man, a job _____

To a woman, a job_____

For women, the most important thing about sex is _____

For men, the most important thing about sex is _____

The most aggravating thing about women is _____

The most aggravating thing about men is _____

Source: C. Philpot & J. Borum (1992), *Before You Leap: Premarital Couples Group*

ment back and forth between paid and family/relationship work so that family life is sustained.

What are women's and men's attitudes about providing financially for their relationship? Even though most women do paid work and contribute an average of 30% of the family income, the responsibility and recognition for being family providers still falls to men (Szinovacz, 1984). Although studies indicate overwhelmingly (Baruch & Barnett, 1986; Coleman et al., 1987; Staines & Libby, 1986) that satisfying, well-paid work is related to enhanced well-being for both women and men, the meaning of paid work is often different for them. When asked about their work, women may say, "Work is what I do, not what I am." But men typically offer their occupation first when introducing themselves.

Research indicates that women shape their paid work participation in response to family needs and often respond to increased time demands in the family by cutting back on time spent in paid work (Gerson, 1985; Zavella, 1987). Men typically retain responsibility and recognition for being the family provider even though the wife may be working full time as well (Bernard, 1981; Haas, 1986). Therefore families often give special consideration and support to men, but not to women, as wage earners (Ferree, 1984). Thus, while more than half of all married women are now working outside the home, women (and the men they marry) often continue to give their work secondary status to that of their husbands. One reason for this is that most men bring in more income than their wives. Women continue to get paid only about 70% of the salary men receive for comparable work (Waldenfogel, 1997).

Surprisingly, it is among dual-career working-class couples, rather than among middle-class or upper-class dual-career couples, that men most need their wives' earnings and therefore may most openly recognize them as coproviders. Many of these men recognize that their wives' earnings are essential to their families and take some of the burden of provision off them. They feel sorry for men whose wives nag them for never making enough money (Thompson & Walker, 1989). For example:

> David, a 34 year old carpenter and part-time college student, and his wife, Molly, a registered nurse, have two preschool children. Despite the fact that Molly is currently working part time and earning less than David, he rates Molly's job as more important than his own. He can imagine her as the financial provider if she goes to work full time. (Potuchek, June, 1995)

In her small sample of dual-earner couples, Hood (1983) found wives were recognized as providers only when both partners admitted that their family was dependent on her income and the husband could not say, "Quit if you want." In contrast, evidence is mounting that husbands in middle-class families have the most trouble sharing family provision with their wives. Haas (1986) reported that employed wives whose husbands have the highest earnings are most likely to combine a belief that family provision should be a shared responsibility with a recognition that, in practice, their husbands are the primary providers. Ferree (1984) argues that, in middle-class families, the size of husbands' earnings makes wives' earnings, at best, supplemental and, at worst, unnecessary. Thus, it is easy in such families for husbands to view wives as secondary providers.

In addition, many men oppose their wives' working (Blumstein & Schwartz, 1983; Ulbrich, 1988). Wives engaged in full-time employment hold several distressing symbolic meanings to many a man—either that he is unable to do an adequate job of providing by himself, that he is unable to protect his wife from the "dog-eat-dog" world or both. It is also common for a man to express strong feelings that his wife should "be home for the kids."

Gender differences in domestic work

Responsibilities are reversed when it comes to the work of the home, however. There is clear evidence that husbands and wives perform different types and amounts of family work (i.e., work in the home, childcare, etc.) with women doing much more than men (Warner, 1986). Study after study has shown that attitudes and shared norms continue to define household work as "women's work," and most wives seem satisfied with the small amount of housework that their husbands do (Peplau & Gordon, 1985). In the 1980s husbands did an average of 30% of the family work, compared to their wives who did at least 70%. This represents a change for men from about 20% (Pleck, 1985) in earlier decades. This statistic was not dramatically altered if the wife also was employed full-time outside the home. There are exceptions to this norm, for Berk (1985) reported that 10% of the husbands she sampled did as much family work as their wives.

In summary, it appears that the traditional gender-based division of roles between provider and domestic worker still exists, despite women's massive participation in the paid work force, and a considerably smaller increase in men's contributions at home. Though research studies do not all agree, there is a rough economic "bottom line" that runs through the attitudes about the work roles which we surveyed above. Women and men spend about the same total hours working; on average, men earn 70% of the family income and do about 30% of the domestic work, while women earn 30% of the income and do 70% of the work at home. So it seems that the division of labor is tied to external societal conditions about how men and women are (and should be) compensated for their work. Beyond economics, however, what are the **meanings** that partners give to their work? Do they assume that they are givens, or do partners challenge and renegotiate these task allotments (Knudson-Martin & Mahoney, 1996; Walsh, 1989)?

Changing provider roles.   There is a great deal of change in attitudes about the provider role going on within couples. In 1987–1988, a study found that 46% of the dual-earner couples had substantial disagreement about the provider role in their marriage. Eighty-four percent of those responding 5 years later had made changes in their attitudes about providing, mostly (68%) in response to changes in their actual employment conditions (Potuchek, 1995). Such changes in attitudes and circumstances are leading couples to negotiate the allocation of work tasks in the relationship over and over.

Gender differences in nurturing.   For many women, the ideal of gender equality would be achieved (a) if equal priority were given to women's work or career (regardless of income); (b) if each partner felt equally entitled to have his or her psychological health needs, personal goals, and wishes met; and (c) if low status tasks such as housework were shared equally. However, many women do not often think of the nurturing or "emotional work" of the family—their emotional connections to children and their partner— as things that must be shared equally. Normal gender-role expectations often lead women to approach intimate relationships with an "eye" toward taking on responsibility for maintaining the relationship with their partner and their children (Risman & Johnson-Summerford, 1998). As a result, they are often likely to make more adjustments than men do in an effort to maintain the relationship and family (Brown & Gilligan, 1992).

Nowhere does this show up more vividly than in the meanings attached to motherhood. Closeness and emotional involvement with children that comes with being the primary caregiver is highly valued by most women and seen as a primary aspect of their self definition. It would be unusual to hear a mainstream American woman say: "Being my child's mother is something I do, not part of what I am." Motherhood also normally has so much of an impact on children that few of them would say, "You can quit being my mother if you want." Although sharing the nurturing role seems to work well for many parents, the differential time and energy commitment that comes with primary nurturing (i.e. "mothering" or "involved fathering") is a significant factor in slowing development toward equal sharing of both provider and nurturer roles.

Gender influences relational power and decision making

Are there distinctive differences in how men and women make decisions and resolve conflicts of interest? Research on power relations and decision making among dating couples and married couples reveals an interesting paradox. First, attempts to assess the overall balance of power or the dominance structure in relationships find that many American couples perceive their relationships to be egalitarian; that is, the partners report that decision making is mutual or divided equally. However, as we saw above, workplace and family work responsibilities are not really equally divided between men and women. How do we explain such differences in the outcome of decision making? Because it is unlikely that both spouses are in complete agreement all of the time, we will examine the role that social power plays in the construction of personal gender identities and the development of work role arrangements.

First, let us define what we mean by power. Power can be broadly defined as the ability to get what we want. Social or interpersonal power is the ability of one person to influence another's behavior. Interpersonal power is limited in an important way in couple relationships: One partner's power is not effective if the other partner is not vulnerable and does not accept it (Boulding, 1962). When a "weaker" or more vulnerable partner develops an adequate defense against the specific power, or alters his or her attitude of vulnerability, the "stronger" partner's advantage is reduced or nullified. Then, either a new balance of power is achieved, or a power struggle develops. Since many aspects of couple relationships are now in transition, power struggles are very common today. To better understand them, we will survey the types of power and vulnerability experienced in couples as summarized in Table 7.2.

Types of power

In their classic paper on power and influence, French and Raven (1959) identified five different bases of power, which they distinquished in terms of the casual conditions involved. Because their typology brings together important ideas about the bases, modes, and consequences of power operating in intimate relationships, we will describe each type of power bases.

Legitimate power stems from the belief that another person has a legitimate right to influence me and I have an obligation to accept this influence (French & Raven, 1959). If partners deviate from agreed-upon norms, they are reminded of their responsibilities. If the reminding in and of itself is enough to bring them into line, then the force behind the compliance illustrates legitimate power. The mode of influence will frequently involve restating or reminding the other of the rule. For example, a wife might decide that she would like to take an exercise class that is scheduled during the couple's usual dinnertime. When she tells her husband, he protests that she should make dinner at that time. So she forgoes her plans, believing that her husband is right to demand that she cook dinner at that time and accommodate her dance class to his schedule. After that, it is likely she

TABLE 7.2 Types of power in couples

Type of power	Resources: Basis of power	Vulnerability: People do what you want because . . .	Defenses: People become less vulnerable because . . .
Legitimate power	Authority: legal, social status, religious, gender role	People believe in your authority to direct them.	They disbelieve in your authority and place faith in another or themselves.
Reward power	Rewards: goods, services, love, status, money	People need what you have.	They provide for themselves or get from other sources.
Coercive power	Punishments: Take away goods, hurt people	People fear loss and pain.	They get protection and replacements and stop fearing.
Referent power	Loyalty, respect, continuity, identity, attachment	People want to identify and be close and respected.	Distrust, hatred, and resentment poison respect and closeness.
Expert power	Ability, expertise, knowledge	People need your abilities and help.	They develop their own skills or get help from others.
Information power	Knowledge	People want your information.	They do without or get it for themselves.

Adapted from French & Raven (1959) and Boulding (1962).

will never test the "dinnertime" rule again, whether her husband notices or not.

Reward power denotes one person's ability to reward another person for a certain behavior. Money and material resources are the most obvious rewards. But other rewards can be effective too, such as when a woman buys an expensive outfit and implies to her partner that she will feel more loving and sexual if he approves of her choice and applauds the way she looks.

Coercive power is the flip side of reward power. It is the ability of one person to administer punishments to another if the other fails to do something. Punishments might include disapproval, verbal abuse, physical violence, or withdrawing financial or emotional support or other cooperative actions that enable the partner to lead a normal life. For example, if the man gets upset that the woman has bought a new outfit, she may let him know that she is disappointed in him and wants to be left alone, and so withdraws her attention.

Referent power is based on the love, attachment, belonging, and closeness that partners feel with each other. It is thought to be the preferred type of influence among American couples (Huston, 1983). One partner often wants to fulfill the other's desires, even if they are incompatible with his own, because seeing his partner happy makes him happy too. The more that partners identify with each other and empathize, the less they are involved in open power struggles. For example, the woman who bought a new dress will feel more attractive if her partner finds her attractive in it, and the man might applaud her because making her feel attractive and happy makes him feel attractive and happy.

Expert power is based upon one person's belief that the other has knowledge about a certain area, and is in fact an "expert" in that area. Expert power is usually what you give your teachers or textbooks when you believe what they say or what they write. In marriage, it is typical for each spouse to have certain spheres of expertise in which each can gain the other's ready acceptance without any need to provide reasons or explanations. In a traditional marriage, for example, the husband may unhesitatingly accept the wife's organization of the kitchen or her advice about where to buy refreshments for the office Christmas party. Similarly, she may accept without question his recommendation on car repair or the best route for their vacation trip. Clearly, this type of power is reduced by seeking information and expertise elsewhere.

Informational power exists when one partner's communication enables the other to gain a new understanding of some problem. Thus, if the husband above explained the pros and cons of taking various alternative routes on their vacation so that his wife could recognize the preferred one herself, we would say that he has exercised informational rather than expert power. Rather than saying, "I'm doing this because that's what my husband suggests and he knows best " (expert influence), the wife would say, "I'm doing this because I understand why it is best" (informational influence). Partners, thus, may specialize in the domains within which they acquire information, and hence, each will have convincing material available to buttress their views regarding some matters more than others. For example, a wife who is knowledgeable about cars will be able to explain to her husband the correctness of her diagnosis of a problem with their car.

Preferred power tactics

It appears that the sexes may use somewhat different tactics to try to influence each other. One study (Raven et al., 1975) surveyed power in couples using French and Raven's definitions of social power bases. One significant finding was that women were much more likely to attribute expert power to their husbands than vice versa. Husbands, on the other hand, granted that their wives had referent power because "they are all part of the same family and should see eye to eye with their wives" (p. 224). To further examine gender differences, Falbo and Peplau (1980), evaluated the association between gender, sexual orientation, egalitarianism, and power strategies in a sample of 50 heterosexual women, 40 heterosexual men, 50 lesbians, and 50 homosexual men. After assessing various power strategies and coding them into categories, the authors reported that the heterosexual men were more likely than the two groups of women (i.e., heterosexual and lesbian groups) and the gay men to report using direct and mutual power strategies, such as bargaining or logical arguments. In contrast, both groups of women were more likely than heterosexual men to report using indirect and unilateral strategies such as withdrawing or pouting. The gay men and the two groups of women did not differ significantly from one another in their use of power strategies.

While power issues clearly continue to be a part of intimate relationships, several researchers have begun to go beyond the simple listing of gender differences in power to try to understand how certain combinations of power, task specialization, and styles of conflict resolution are linked together by couples. These researchers argue that rather than look at "across-the-board" differences by gender, there are certain distinctive types of power relations in which men and women organize themselves. Let us look at these different types of marital power relations.

Three types of marital role structures

When we begin to look at how partners structure their roles as a unit (i.e., as an interrelated set), we notice that there is tremendous variety across couples in the way men's and women's roles are structured. Secondly, we notice that there is also variety over time in the same couple in terms of how they structure their couple work tasks and power relations. A third issue concerns the patterning of different aspects of couples' relating (e.g., how self-disclosure, power, and the division of labor are interrelated).

There have been a number of different typologies of family roles, proposed by researchers, that attempt to characterize the gender-role expectations for men and women in marriage. While such typologies usually represent "ideal types" which are abstractions of relationships rather than real life representations, the value of these typologies lies in their attempt to describe how partners' roles fit together in interrelated patterns and to depict the diversity of relationship patterns that now exist in American culture.

Most typologies are drawn from two basic dimensions that are of importance in examining marital/relationship roles. The first concerns the *power relations* between the partners; for example, the extent to which the husband is more dominant over the wife. The second dimension concerns the extent of *role specialization* between the partners. This includes both activities internal to the couple, such as self-disclosure and housework, and activities external to the couple, such as participation in the paid work force.

Peplau's (1983) synthesis of the existing typologies of marital roles provides a useful framework for examining the variety that now exists in the way partners pattern their roles in today's marriages. Drawing heavily upon Pleck's (1976) analysis of male sex roles, Peplau describes three distinctive marital role patterns: the traditional marriage, the modern marriage, and the egalitarian marriage.

The traditional marriage. In traditional couples, as in patriarchal societies, the husband is dominant over the wife and male–female role specialization as "the provider" and "the homemaker" is stronger than in the other two marriage types. Although traditional marriage is not confined to any one social class, most studies examined working-class families in which traditionalists may be more common as a group. A happily married British couple interviewed by Bott (1971) illustrates this traditional pattern:

> Mr. and Mrs. N. took it for granted that men had male interests and women had female interests and that there were few leisure activities that they would naturally share. In their view, a good husband was generous with the housekeeping allowance, did not waste money selfishly on himself, helped his wife with the housework if she got ill, and took an interest in the children. A good wife was a good manager, an affectionate mother, a woman who . . . got along well with her own and her husband's relatives. A good conjugal relationship was one with a harmonious division of labor, but the Ns placed little stress on the importance of joint activities and shared interests. (p. 73)

Traditional partners believe that the husband should have greater authority, and his wife's deference to him is important. A traditional wife often makes decisions about home management and childcare, and both partners discuss major family decisions (Peplau, 1983). Though the husband may delegate certain chores, however, he is the chief executive who has the final say (Scanzoni & Scanzoni, 1976).

Even though American society emphasizes intimate communication, in traditional marriage the widely divergent interests and activities of the sexes may reduce it (Komarovsky, 1962). Furthermore, for traditional men, masculinity means being "tough" and presenting a strong impression to others. Therefore they may neither learn how to disclose feelings nor believe that they should. Traditionally inclined women may be uncomfortable when men deviate from their normal invulnerability, and men may become critical or distant when women express "too many" feelings. Thus, for both sexes same-sex friends and relatives may provide better companionship than a spouse.

A traditional wife may develop her role in three directions: (a) as a "homemaker," her expertise in home management and childrearing gives her influence over her husband's behavior; (b) as a "companion," she cultivates "social graces, personal attractiveness, and personal and sexual responsiveness to her husband, so that she may serve as hostess to his friends and relaxer and refresher to him" (Turner, 1970, p. 269); or (c) as a "humanist." In the humanist role the wife becomes active in community and volunteer work and enhances her status through compassionate service. The development of these roles is affected by social class and education, and women often adopt more than one.

The modern marriage. Modern marriage may be more common among middle and upper classes in America, as well as among Western-influenced upper classes in more patriarchal societies. Male dominance is more muted and role specialization is less pervasive (e.g., Blood & Wolfe, 1960; Scanzoni & Scanzoni, 1976). The Cs illustrate the modern pattern:

> Jill and Charlie C. met in a college drama class 22 years ago. They quickly discovered that they both loved hiking and camping. They spent long hours talking about their feelings and planning a future together. Jill respected Charlie's intelligence and logical arguments and found herself going along with his ideas in most matters. At graduation they married, and Jill worked as a nurse to put Charlie through graduate school. After Charlie got his first teaching job, they started a family and were surprised by the arrival of twins. Jill quit her job to care for the girls. She enjoyed being a full-time homemaker for a while, but went back to work once the children started school. Although the family moved several times to advance Charlie's career, Jill was always able to find new jobs. The Cs feel that their marriage has improved over the years, and they continue to enjoy many joint activities. (Peplau, 1983, p. 250)

In the modern marriage, husbands still tend to lead in decision making, with wives operating more like a junior partner. Role specialization is less pervasive. "The wife has major responsibility for housekeeping and childcare, but the husband is able and willing to help at home. The wife's paid employment is tolerated or even approved and encouraged, but if a conflict arises between their jobs, the man's career comes first. It is also

AN EGALITARIAN MARRIAGE

...HELLO SWEETHEART! DON'T FORGET TO CLEAN OUT THE GORILLA'S DEN! SEE YOU TONIGHT!

understood that the wife's work must not interfere with her responsibilities at home." (Peplau, 1983, p. 250). Thus, the role definitions of modern husbands and wives may be tied to their relative incomes as well as to shifts in gender–role attitudes. Modern roles emphasize togetherness and companionship, with men wanting emotional support rather than deference from their wives (Pleck, 1976). In their leisure time, modern couples typically prefer couple activities over same-sex socializing with friends. They stress compatibility and feel that their relationship with each other should be more important than any separate relations with outsiders (Bott, 1971). Since most modern men do not have close friendships with other men, they channel their desires for companionship into their marriages (Pleck, 1976).

The egalitarian marriage. The egalitarian marriage (e.g., Scanzoni & Scanzoni, 1976; Stapleton & Bright, 1976) is best understood as an ideal that some couples are striving for rather than a common pattern found in American life today. That is why some theorists view America as in transition toward egalitarian marriage, rather than legitimately equal like Sweden and Denmark. "At its core, this pattern rejects the basic tenets of traditional marriage of male dominance and role specialization by gender. In an egalitarian marriage, both partners share equally in power, and gender based role specialization is absent both inside and outside the marriage" (Peplau, 1983, p. 51). Young and Wilmott (1973) call this type of marriage **symmetrical** because gender does not determine the division of labor and because the bases of interdependence are based on **similar** attitudes, skills and abilities rather than **complementary** attitudes, skills and abilities (i.e., different but nesting together). Thus, advocates of egalitarian marriage assume that both biological and socialized gender differences are insignificant compared to individual differences between partners, and that true equality is best achieved when each person's contribution in the traditional provider and homemaker/nurturer roles roughly matches the other's. According to Peplau (1983, p. 251), the wife is no longer the junior partner but a full partner with all the duties and privileges associated with that.

The central theme in egalitarian marriage is a thorough revision of the "gendered" cultural model for marriage which includes some reformulation of what is desirable and possible in men and women as well. In the pursuit of equality, couples develop many alternative patterns for the structuring of married life. Some couples may do housekeeping tasks together, others may take turns, and still others may divide tasks according to personal interests (Risman & Johnson-Summerford, 1998). To support the family financially, partners may alternate holding a paid job, experiment with sharing one job, or prefer that both partners have full-time jobs.

Are those who come closest to living out the egalitarian model today the dual-career couples who both have major commitments for full-time professional careers? Older studies found that while these marriages were often happy, they were seldom truly egalitarian (Bryson et. al, 1976; Holmstrom, 1972; Rapoport & Rapoport, 1976). More recent interviews of 125 dual-career couples revealed that only one third were truly egalitarian in their role structure. In all the others, the wife was responsible for domestic tasks and the husband's job was seen as more important (Peplau, 1993). Thus, even for couples who intellectually endorse an ideal of equality, **both equal decision making power** and **no role specialization** are often not realized.

The key to this problem may be the second goal—elimination of role specialization. This is often too hard to change from an ideal into a reality because of two challenges. First, the connection between income growth, work dedication, and career development benefits couples in which **at least one partner gives high priority to career**, though this need not be the man. Second, the social development of **women** to be mothers usually leads both partners to want them to retain the higher priority nurturing role. However, a small number of couples are challenging both these assumptions.

After interviewing upper middle class couples who had been experimenting with their role allocation for up to 20 years, sociologist Pepper Schwartz (1994) describes a realistic alternative in her book *Peer Marriage*. Couples in peer marriages tend to eliminate the provider complex by valuing their own **intimate friendship** above both **career** and **child raising** and don't make eliminating all role specialization a condition for equality. In a peer marriage,

> the division of labor, like income, may not be precisely equal, (but) it is not greatly unbalanced. No partner takes an . . . uninvolved relationship to the other's territory. There does not need to be a purely androgynous household in which sex role characteristics disappear, but the collaborative nature of the relationship ensures that each person will be strongly represented in the important elements of the couple's everyday life. (p. 127)

To eliminate the "provider complex," both partners accept that responsibility for financial success or failure does not fall primarily on the man. **Some career advantages and financial goals have to be sacrificed** for the good of the family. Flexible work and family time is a key practical objective. Peer partners who are committed to co-parenting and to their demanding careers may not be able to give as much time to children as many one-provider couples or extended families can. Conversely, many peer partners choose to modulate their career involvement in order to make fuller commitments to their family responsibilities.

The three marriage role patterns Peplau (1983) described not only represent different combinations of power allocation and role/task specialization; they also represent different degrees of openness and acceptance of role change and conflict. In traditional marriage, partners assume that both male dominance and clearly specialized roles will not need to change or be contested. In modern marriage, both male dominance and role specialization may need modification, but conflict will be avoided to protect the harmony of the couple and muted male dominance. Egalitarian marriage rejects both male dominance and gender-role specialization. As a result, partners assume that there will inevitably be conflict in resolving their individual personal interests. Peer marriage substitutes deep friendship and responsiveness to one another's desires for dominance and role specialization. But, even among best friends, exercising equal power in such areas as career, money, and parenting can lead to conflict and impasse. Thus, the development of alternative types of marital role agreements over the past three decades has opened up new costs as well as benefits and offered us new challenges to developing our humanity.

Power motivation in individual psychology

What leads an individual to prefer a traditional, modern, egalitarian, or peer style of marriage? Do personal attitudes toward power also affect couple interaction within the types?

Power-motivated people prefer professions in which they can exercise authoritative leadership or influence others, such as teaching, management, law, and politics. They also base their identity on strength, abilities, and mastery, and enjoy accumulating prestige possessions, such as European sports cars. They assert themselves or take risks to have impact on others.

McClelland and colleagues (McClelland et al., 1985) found that norepinephrine may act as a chemical reward system for the power motive. Thus, people get habituated to feeling good when they are feeling powerful. The power motive may be related to fear of weakness (Veroff, 1982; Schafer, 1986) and to having parents who feel deprived of power and status themselves, such as immigrants (McClelland, 1987). Blue collar workers might also have more fear of weakness than college graduates, who have more prestigious jobs available to them (Veroff, 1982). The "pecking order" mechanism may be operating when parents feeling one-down in their world are authoritarian with their children, who then grow up to avoid feeling powerless at all costs. Perhaps having a lengthy experience of helplessness—such as parental divorce or death (Chapter 6), repeated abuse, disease, or disability, or perhaps race or class discrimination—may make us more likely to want control in our adult life and often in our relationships:

> He was a very jealous person, yet he wanted his own space. He wanted to spend almost all of his time with his friends, yet he wanted me to be there so that there was someone next to him that he could grope at and, I guess, feel important with, but at the same time totally ignore.

Power motivation and fear of weakness are related to heavy alcohol use, which gives men a feeling of "magical potency" (McClelland et al., 1972). In contrast, women do not generally feel more potent when drinking; they feel more affectionate instead (Stewart & Chester, 1982). Thus drinking sets the stage for men to make sexual power plays, and for women to respond affectionately. Some of these men approach their love lives as Don Juans making conquests and then moving on (Winter, 1973).

Power motivation in intimate relationships

Highly power motivated men are likely to prefer lower-achieving wives, be more domineering and dissatisfied, and have more affairs and divorces than less power-motivated men (Stewart & Rubin, 1976; McClelland et al., 1972; Winter et al., 1977). Executives have been notorious for pursuing feminine youth and beauty as trophies.

Both men and women who are power-motivated do not like conflict with their partners and friends (McAdams, 1988; Stewart & Rubin, 1976). Yet they often report getting more out of marriage than their spouses (Veroff, 1982). Perhaps they often get their way without conflict by "holding all the high cards" of reward, legitimate, and expert power or by choosing a partner whose vulnerabilities lead her or him to usually give in. Thus power-motivated men normally prefer traditional marriage, especially if their average incomes and/or working class status limits their power and prestige in society. If their incomes were high, they could afford a modern marriage with a wife skillful at romance and ego-support.

Are women any different? Research suggests that "men and women are equally interested in power, although they may express their interest in somewhat different ways" (Stewart & Chester, 1982; Winter, 1988). Power-motivated women with traditional feminine sex-role attitudes are very concerned with their diet, clothes, and appearance, indicating they seek powerful positions and prestige partly through being attractive to others (McClelland, 1987). More nontraditional women expressed their power needs in behavior similar to men's (Stewart & Chester, 1982). Thus, traditional power-motivated women might prefer modern marriage, while nontraditional women might prefer egalitarianism.

Unlike men, power-motivated women do not have unstable dating or marital relationships (Stewart & Rubin, 1976; Winter, 1988). They are likely to marry successful men, avoid extramarital affairs, and keep their marriages stable and satisfying (Veroff, 1982; Winter, 1988). They are not likely to drink a lot, use drugs, be verbally or physically aggressive, gamble, or be more sexually experienced or exploitive. Since many seek status through their relationships, they use their social skills to make their partners feel better, and thus preserve their referent power in rewarding modern-type marriages. For both sexes, taking care of young children during childhood or adulthood is associated more with socially responsible expressions of power, such as leadership roles and career success, and less with impulsive expressions of power, such as drinking, aggression, and sexual promiscuity (McClelland, 1987). Consequently, preferences for a particular type of marriage seem to be related to individual levels of power motivation.

Explanations for the development of gendered relationships

Most couples tend to underestimate the extent to which their particular couple decision making and dynamics are influenced by the generalized gender norms of the larger culture. However, sociologists contend that such social norms influence couples in two ways. Some theorists—known as structuralists—believe that we *take on* the expectations of the culture as to how we are to perform a certain role. In contrast, other theorists—known as symbolic interactionists—believe that we *make up* the roles we play with our role partners through an active process of role evaluation, experimentation, and negotiation that takes place over time.

Structuralist explanations of gendered couple relations

Structuralist sociologists (e.g., Heiss, 1968; Parsons & Bales, 1955) assume that societies recognize certain social categories or positions such as wife or father, and have *norms* (i.e., rules or prescriptions) as to how individuals in these positions should behave. To them, roles are culturally-based norms for behavior that are characteristic of people in a given position in the social structure. Structuralists believe that it is through the process of cultural socialization that we learn to *take on* the reciprocal sets of rights and obligations that comprise our role in a particular social structure such as a dating relationship, a marriage, or a family. From this perspective, the images we have as to how to act as a man or woman or a husband or wife are believed to be a result of our interaction with others in our culture as we grow up. As a child we learn that certain types of duties, activities, beliefs, privileges, values, and attitudes are associated with being a woman or a man, a husband or a wife, a girlfriend or a boyfriend. These expected ways of behaving form a certain package of complementary roles characterized by a particular scripting of behaviors, attitudes, and values. One of the best-known statements of this perspective is found in the work of Parsons and Bales (1955).

Talcott Parsons proposed that there were two separate and distinct roles to be performed in the family, the "instrumental" role and the "expressive" role. He and his collaborator, Robert Bales, believed that it was functional for all small groups to have two "role leaders," one attending to the instrumentality of getting tasks done, the other focusing on the group's social and expressive needs. (Parsons and Bales based these conclusions on research conducted during World War II with bomber crews. It was from this small group research that they generalized to marital and family life.) Since the family is a small group, they argued that it was "largely inevitable . . . that the adult male would play an instrumental role, earning a living outside the family, and that the adult female would play an expressive, nurturing role, located inside the family." They defined these two roles, and hence the positions of men and women, as separate, specialized, complementary, and relatively equal. One young man illustrates these assumptions of specialization and complementarity in his portrayal of his dating relationship:

> I play the reassuring, protective father. She is the faithful, dependent child. Her faith and dependency are a form of reassurance and support for me. But there are days when I would like to come to her, as she comes to me . . . to tell her that I was hurt because my roommate didn't ask if I'd made PhiBet . . . or that I didn't think that my professor liked me anymore . . . but I could never bring myself to talk about such sentimental drivel even though I wanted to. (Cited in Komarovsky, 1976, p. 165)

Structuralists assume that people behave as they do in intimate relationships such as marriage because they have learned that certain norms are appropriate and thus feel a moral obligation to conform. Consequently, any change in one's preferences for how roles are to be structured in an intimate relationship comes from *outside* a couple as a result of a change in cultural values and norms in the larger society. For example, during the 1940s, women were applauded for working in defense factories, but during the 1950s, when the men returned to fill these jobs, women were expected to stay home. Parsons believed it was "dysfunctional" for wives to seek paid employment. Others in the structuralist tradition coined terms like "role strain" to encompass situations that did not fit their model of a strict gender division of labor that allocated women to families and men to outside employment.

There is evidence that the particular family form proposed by Parsons and Bales was idealized and labeled as "normal" in the broader culture during the 1950s and 1960s, although it represented only a cross-section of life in post–World War II middle-class suburban America. Examining the impact of this model on men's and women's expectations for married life in her book, *The Future of Marriage,* Bernard (1972) states: "The sexes get into marriage as they get into bed: with different desires, rhythms, and expectations. Likewise they have entirely different experiences of marriage" (p. 122).

Although the specialized roles that Parsons and Bales proposed as "normal" for the culture may not have been as natural as they claimed, the roles are acknowledged to represent the stereotyped view of the different paths men and women are prescribed to take in American culture. Social expectations that individuals absorb early in life structure distinct domains of social experience (West & Zimmerman, 1991). According to Knudson-Martin & Mahoney (1996) "Women and men bring these gender identities with them into their relationships and sort out and experience their day-to-day interactions through them, often without being fully aware that they are doing so" (p. 141).

A number of writers describing women's socialization contend that women are raised with the expectation that their main goal in life is to take care of others, and thus their lives should be centered around activities that lead to the enhancement of others rather than themselves. Jean Baker Miller (1976, p. 212) observed that a great deal of women's self-worth is associated with giving to others: "Women constantly ask themselves: Am I giving enough? Should I give more? If I had given more would this have happened?" The consequences of not giving enough when others are dependent on them are too frightening to consider.

Many clinicians believe that while responding to the needs of others can provide women with a sense of gratification and pleasure, the price they pay is that they are left to rely on others, particularly their husbands, for their sense of power, status, and authority outside the home. This inequitable recognition of the contribution in the outside world leads to expectations of less power in the marriage relationship itself. Women may find themselves reluctant to ask for what they need, since they don't feel entitled to have their needs met and are afraid of appearing selfish" (Papp, 1988, p. 203).

Many clinicians draw a sharp contrast between this pattern of women's socialization and that of men's. Peggy Papp (1988) writes, "Men's sense of self is based primarily on achievement rather than personal relationships; thus, giving to others is not part of their self image as it is for women. Instead, their self image is connected with doing. Although men are interested in being husbands and fathers, their definition of masculinity comes predominately from their roles outside the family and from their positions of leadership. Success in the working world often requires repressing personal feelings, learning to master passion or weakness, and developing controlled, guarded, and calculated behavior. Mastery of these skills often results in men closing off large areas of their own sensibilities, and inhibits their responsiveness to the needs of others. Intimate relationships are situations to be contained and are often experienced as impediments or traps" (p. 204). Reluctant to acknowledge emotional needs for fear of feeling humiliated or rejected, they wait for the women in their lives to read their feelings and longings for closeness.

Child development. Social scientists Nancy Chodorow (1978) and Carole Gilligan (1982) trace gender differences in relational behavior to early child development. They found an essential gender difference in the fact that mothers can view and treat their daughters essentially like themselves, while their sons are obviously different. As for children, daughters can be continuously close and identify with their mothers, but sons have to separate themselves more and **disidentify** with their mothers in order to develop their gender identity.

There is evidence for the differential approaches to closeness from infancy through adulthood. Already at 3 weeks and 3 months, mothers imitate female babies more than male babies, and female babies are more responsive to their mothers (Moss, 1967, reported in Jordan, 1976b). At six to nine months, mother-daughter pairs were more likely than mother-son pairs to be matched in physiological and emotional states or to notice when they were mismatched and readjust. At nine to twelve months, girls video-taped in a nursery contacted their mothers for attention two and a half times as frequently as boys, had twice as much physical contact with her, imitated her more, shared more activities and feelings with her, and main-tained contact longer (Olesker, 1990).

Probably both parents and children are responsible for these gender differences in separating from mother. A father is more likely to relate more actively to a son than to a daughter unless he does not have a son. He can provide a son, but not a daughter, with a way to be separate from mother by identifying with his gender (Abelin, 1980; Levenson & Harris, 1980). On the son's part, his hormonal balance makes him more active, impul-sive, and aggressive than the average daughter, which takes him further away from his mother. He also conflicts more with her attempts to reel him in or control him (Gjedde, 1988; Olesker, 1990).

The impact of this childhood difference in relating to the mother on later life gender-role expectations can be profound. Generally, males learn to see themselves as more separate from others than do females, whereas women experience themselves primarily through attachments to others and are concerned about their ability to make and maintain relationships (Gilligan, 1982). Consequently, partners enter relationships with different premises, different rules for negotiation, and different ways of interpreting behavior and responding within relationships. Many a snag in relation-ships arises from this difference:

> When I ask Danny if he agrees with me, I'm just trying to get approval. But he usually nit-picks at some minor point, or just acts like the whole subject is too trivial to bother with. Then if I get upset, he tells me I'm too insecure.

Symbolic interactionist explanations of gendered relations

In recent years, this idea of the sexes having distinctly different roles in relationships and that these arrangements are both unchanging and part of the "natural order of things" has begun to be challenged. In contrast to the structuralist perspective explained earlier, many feminist sociologists (Ferree, 1990; Pleck, 1987; Walsh, 1989) argue that the roles we structure in marriage are *diverse and contested* rather than static and uniform. Also, rather than taking on a uniform definition of what it is like to be a man or a woman, a wife or a husband, couples engage in a process of selecting particular cultural roles for themselves, evaluating their applicability to them-selves as a couple, and redesigning them over time. Rather than organizing their relationships in a certain way because of moral obligation (i.e., "This is the right way to do things"), partners organize their behavior to gain personal rewards (i.e., "What do I want to have happen in the relationship?") and avoid personal costs (i.e., "What do I not want to have happen?").

This point of view illustrates the interactionist perspective (as depicted in the work of McCall & Simmons, 1978; Turner, 1978; Turner, 1962, 1970). Rather than merely playing out predetermined cultural scripts, interactionists assume that partners are actively involved in creating and negotiating their roles in the course of their interaction together. The couple depicted below illustrates this process of role structuring:

> Margo: My husband comes from a very, very macho macho family. They think that women are for shit. And so when George got married he thought this was the way to treat a wife. And I said no. His specific phrase was: "I am the master." Doesn't that blow your mind? I said, "Fuck you, baby, there ain't no master here. And if you don't like it, just take a walk." As much as I cared for him, I was not going to take that. Hey, this guy was really foul. He thought this was the way to do it. But he came around. He's been excellent to me.
>
> George: You know she's the established homemaker. I'm established as the breadwinner, the head of the house. That's gotta be. There's only one ball in front of the rack. I'm it. She's the one immediately behind it. She's at my heels. But once in a blue moon, I'll vacuum. Actually I'll do anything she asks me if we're having company and we're pressed for time. If she asks me to clean the dishes, I'll clean the dishes. If she asks me to clean the bathtub, I'll clean the bathtub. I don't think there's anything in the house that's women's work that's demeaning for me to do. This is my home as well as her home. But traditionally she does it all. (Cited in Blumstein & Schwartz, 1983, pp. 374–375)

Interactionists argue that while cultural norms do have an influence in shaping our behavior, these norms are often vague and inconsistent so they do not provide an adequate guide for smooth interaction. Thus, each couple must, as have Margo and George, create their own unique norms for living together as a function of what each prefers (i.e., rewards) and hopes to avoid (i.e., relationship costs). There are many ways of being a couple together. The assumption that there is one right way to allocate responsibilities/tasks in the relationship or to determine who has the power to say who will do what is a myth, particularly in this time of social change. Instead, interactionists argue that most couples must engage in an active process of "role-making" in their relationships rather than on the passive adoption of particular cultural scripts characterized as "role-taking" (Turner, 1962).

Rather than look exclusively at widespread cultural norms, interactionists emphasize that we each develop mental models of ourselves in relationships known as *personal role conceptions*. These are "general-

TABLE 7.3. Your relationship role expectations

Identify your spoken and unspoken expectations about marriage or a committed relationship. Review these on your own. If you have a relationship, you may wish to later review these with your partner and identify areas of compatibility and difference. The following sample questions do not cover every area. Please expand on those areas appropriate to you. Below each subject, some examples are listed to help trigger your thoughts.

ABOUT YOUR PARTNER: What do I expect my partner to provide to me? Support (emotional, financial, physical)? Protection? A buffer against my family? Reassurance about how I look? A parent for my children? Companionship? Help with work? What does my partner expect from me?

DIVISION OF LABOR: Who will be responsible for: Housework? Child care? Yard work? Car maintenance? Shopping? Holiday preparations? Social correspondence? Bill paying? Earning a living? Are there any things that should naturally be done by the man or the woman? How will we decide how tasks should be split up? Is there a difference between who does the work and who is ultimately responsible for that work? Are there any problems with shared responsibilities?

PHYSICAL AND SEXUAL RELATIONS: What characteristics (desired or required) does my partner possess? Is my partner sexually appealing to me? If not, what is lacking? Do I like my partner's sexual attitudes? How do they compare with my own? How often would I like to have physical closeness without sex? What other expressions of affection or physical attention are important to me? To my partner? What are necessary components of a good sex life for me? For my partner? Are there any sexual or affection problems?

SOCIAL RELATIONSHIPS: How independent/dependent will we be on one another? How much time will I spend alone? Will my partner spend alone? How much time will we spend together, just the two of us? How much time will we spend with friends or in other joint activities? Will we share friends or have our own? Will either of us have friends of the opposite sex? How much do I want to be included in my partner's activities? How will I get closeness if I want it? How will I get distance if I want it? What could cause me to feel stifled? Are there any problems with closeness or distance in our relationship?

CONTROL: Who will control what? Who will decide what? Will there be an equal division of power between me and my partner? How do I feel about that division of power? Who will take initiative? Will my partner and I be cooperative or competitive with one another? How will leadership be divided? How will that be decided? If a conflict arises, who will get their way? Are there any problems in the control area?

Source: C. Philpot & J. Borum (1992), *Before You Leap: Premarital Couples Group*

ized and relatively enduring impressions or summary beliefs about the nature of our relationships which shape and organize our experience in relationships" (Peplau, 1983, p. 236). Turner (1978) used the term *working role conception*, to refer to this set of beliefs and meanings people hold as to the characteristics and motives of themselves and their partner. Consider the list of expectations about marriage in Table 7.3.

How readily can you describe your own current working role conceptions/preferences about married or partnered life? Spend a moment and think of what your current preferences are as to what you expect you and your partner are to get from your relationship and how you prefer structuring your roles to do so.

Interactionists do not assume that our role conceptions are that static and unchanging. Instead, they assume that our role preferences and those of our partner emerge over time as we live together. They also believe that the basic way in which we build a set of norms (i.e., agreed upon ways of behaving) emerges through both trial and error and overt and indirect negotiations as people attempt to implement and alter their working role conceptions. A well-known theory emphasizing the nature of this process is social exchange theory.

Social exchange theory

Social exchange theory examines the role of rewards and costs in the development and maintenance of intimate relationships. Although it does not sound at all romantic, social exchange theorists (Blau, 1964; McCall & Simmons, 1969; Thibaut & Kelley, 1959) believe that most of our intimate interaction depends on gaining a reward or profit from the relationship. That is, partners tend to expect certain rewards from their relationships, and remain in them only if they receive those rewards and if there is not a better way of obtaining those same rewards elsewhere. While it may seem very hard-nosed and rational, social exchange theorists assert that love relationships are developed and maintained based on the prospect of certain rewards. As a result, people evaluate their relationships in terms of the value of the consequences of their interactions and engage in certain behaviors only as long as the rewards for the behavior are greater than the costs.

As you might expect, this theory has a basis in both economic theory and behavioral psychology, but the principle of bargaining or exchange has been a part of the common sense lore of marriage for many years. Consider the following description by Walsh (1989) of the bargaining process engaged in by Berber tribesmen:

> In the Atlas Mountains of Morocco sheep herding Berber tribes gather annually, as they have for centuries, for the traditional "Bridal Market" where eligible men shop for wives. As is the custom, each prospective bride strolls through the marketplace, cheeks brightly painted and wearing a headdress that reveals her marital status: her scarf is peaked if she is an unmarried virgin or folded over if she is divorced or widowed. Each carries a blanket she has woven. As a man catches the eye of someone who interests him, she displays her blanket. They examine each other indirectly as they engage in conversation about the merits and flaws of the blanket, and he decides whether he wishes to purchase the blanket as she decides whether or not she wishes to sell it to him. If not in agreement, both move on to other prospects. If their interest in each other is mutual, they then barter over the price of the blanket. If the blanket pleases him enough and he meets her price, the couple goes off to the local official who legalizes their intention to marry. Their families become involved in the bartering process, as sheep and other valuables are weighed in to each side of the bargain. By tradition, the new bride moves into her husband's family tent. . . . Should she fail to meet the

approval of her husband and her mother-in-law, who heads the household, or if she fails to bear a male child, her husband could end the marriage by announcing "I divorce you: I divorce you." (p. 267)

How much does this process parallel that represented by couples in our culture? The comment made by one modern-day wit that "Women marry the best provider they can stomach" or by another that "Marriage is a process by which a man sums up his attributes and suggests to a particular woman that hers are not so much better as to preclude a marriage" reveal that even in current times, couples make some sort of metaphorical *bargain* at the outset of their relationship that is modified over time. Thus, whatever the source of one's ideas, the underlying concept remains the same, that most people engage in some sort of analytical process in developing and staying engaged in their intimate relationships.

Social exchange theory provides a general framework for considering the various facets of this analytical process. There are five major components of this framework: rewards, costs, expectations, perceived alternatives, and investments. We will look at each of these components in turn, but before we begin, look at Figure 7.1, which displays the social exchange "map" as a whole.

Rewards, costs, and relational profit. Relationships may be thought of as involving costs and rewards. Rewards consist of anything that meets a person's needs, such as companionship, love, emotional support in times of distress, sexual gratification, or financial support. Each of us can think of couples whom we have observed who do not appear to derive much pleasure from each other. We may often wonder why they stay together. Couples depicted in the movies or novels such as the warring couple in "Who's Afraid of Virginia Wolf" make us wonder what it could be that each partner is getting from the other. Yet, it is important to keep in mind that rewards differ according to the person. One woman may value her boyfriend because he is supportive of her career ambitions and achievements, another because partners share an interest in athletic activities. Security may keep one person in a relationship, while affection may hold another, and pride may maintain a third. One of the real challenges of building an intimate relationship is discovering what your partner perceives to be rewarding aspects of your relationship and consciously thinking of ways to increase those behaviors. Researchers have found that partners often differ in terms of what they find rewarding in their partner's behavior. For example, Wills and his associates (Wills et al., 1974) reported that women

Rewards	–	Costs	=	Profit
Profit	–	Comparison level	=	Satisfaction
Satisfaction	+	Investments	=	Commitment

FIG. 7.1.
Factors influencing relationship satisfaction and commitment.

are more likely to value affectional response modes that show love and caring (e.g., kissing, hugging, touching), whereas men value instrumental activities (e.g., being cooked a good meal, having their laundry done). Whatever the nature of the rewards valued, the greater the likelihood that the relationship will result in the exchange of certain valued rewards, the more likely it is that the behaviors will be repeated and the relationship will endure.

Intimate relationships involve costs as well—costs such as the time and effort spent to maintain a relationship, the compromises made in one's preferences to keep the relationship going, or the sacrifices made in the way of opportunities that are given up in order to maintain the relationship. Costs are those factors that deter repeating a particular behavior. They also vary from person to person, and relationship to relationship. One of the real challenges of building an intimate relationship is determining what you and your partner are willing to "pay" to maintain the relationship and what you consider to be "fair" in terms of the relative balance of costs for both partners. In an interesting example of the differences in perceived costs across partners, Ross and Sicoly (1979) asked spouses to independently rate how they divided up responsibility for 20 activities relevant to married life (e.g., cleaning the house, caring for children, planning leisure-time activities, etc.). Subjects rated each item by putting a slash at the appropriate point on a straight-line continuum, the endpoints of which were labeled "primarily husband" and "primarily wife." Since having to take responsibility for daily tasks can usually be considered a "cost," each partner was, in effect, saying how much he or she had to "pay" for each mutually

beneficial activity and how much he or she perceived his or her partner was paying. The researchers found that there was very little agreement between the partners in terms of each person's perception of how much he or she was paying (payment being the volume and scope of activities they are willing to assume responsibility for) and their partner's perception of their obligations.

This reward–cost analysis results in the concept of relational profit. Relational profit emerges as a result of reward minus the cost (Profit = Reward – Cost). Thus, you may have heard a friend say: "It's better to put up with this rather than be by myself or try and get a job to support myself," or "It's not worth it to live like this any longer. I'm getting out. Anything would be better than this." People's evaluation of their relational profit and resulting level of satisfaction with their relationship is more complex, however, than a mere summing of profits and costs. In addition to relational profit, people's relationship satisfaction depends upon their current expectations.

Expectations. Social exchange theorists refer to these relationship expectations as the level of comparison between what is expected in the relationship and what is actually experienced. According to Thibaut and Kelley (1959): "The comparison level (or CL) is a standard by which the person evaluates the rewards and costs of a given relationship in terms of what he/she feels he/she deserves" (p. 21). On the basis of past experiences, a person creates a standard against which to judge his or her experience in relationships. The CL is a neutral point between satisfaction and dissatisfaction on one's own mental continuum for judging relationships. One would judge relationships that fall above the CL as satisfactory or attractive, and those that fall below the CL as undesirable. One's comparison level will probably change as one experiences different relationships or different phases of the same relationship. For example, people often report that after a while, as certain expectations or desires are fulfilled, other expectations become relevant and the comparison level is thus raised for one to be satisfied. Thus, satisfaction is a result of a comparison of current profit and existing expectations (Profit – Expectations = Satisfaction).

Perceived alternatives. Commitment to one's current relationship appears to be dependent not only upon one's history in that relationship, but also with the broader social context of the relationship. People are always considering how much profit they experience in a relationship as compared to other potential relationships. Thibaut and Kelley (1959) refer to this as the comparison level for alternatives (or CL alt). CL alt refers to the kind of outcomes people think they would receive if they were involved in some other alternative relationship or lifestyle. Just as CL affects the satisfaction with the relationship, so CL alt affects the ultimate commitment an individual makes to a relationship. If a person perceives that the rewards available from another relationship outweigh his or her current relationship, he or she may be less committed to remaining in the original relationship. Thus, CL alt is the standard one uses to decide whether to remain in or to leave a specific relationship and is based on one's analysis of available alternatives. For example, a woman who remains in a marriage with which she is unhappy may believe that there are no alternatives when her children are small. However, she may leave the relationship when they are older, or if she increases her ability to support herself financially, or if she finds support in another relationship.

Investments. Part of the process of being committed to a relationship involves making an investment. An investment is something that an individual puts into a relationship that he or she cannot recover should that relationship end. A key premise of exchange theory is that: "If a love relationship is to develop into a lasting mutual attachment then the 'lovers' investment' in the relationship—that is their affection for and commitment to one another—must expand at roughly the same pace. If one lover makes significantly greater inputs than the other into the relationship, this invites exploitation or provokes feelings of entrapment, both of which obliterate love. . . . The weak interest of the less committed or the frustrations of the more committed probably will sooner or later prompt one or the other to terminate it" (Blau, 1964, p. 84).

In addition, the process of analyzing the personal costs and rewards of the relationship continues throughout the marriage/relationship. A further consideration in social exchange is the rule of distributive justice which suggests that investments, costs, and rewards should be roughly comparable (e.g., "The more I put in, the more I should get out"). However, long-term relationships often do not have immediate reciprocity built into them. Instead, as relationships progress, an inequality of rewards or costs may often evolve and be tolerated or accepted on the assumption that the burdens or benefits within the relationship will shift at a later time. As Scanzoni (1982) states: ". . . this reciprocity helps to account for marital stability because it sets up a chain of enduring obligations and repayments within a system of roles in which each role contains both rights and duties" (p. 64). Knapp (1984) also suggests that lovers and marital spouses are "less likely to expect a constant balance of rewards and costs because they anticipate that the favors given and received will average out during the course of their relationship" (p. 30). Thus, what appears as a rather straightforward process of exchanging valued outcomes, in fact, is much more subtle and complex than it may first appear.

Exchange and communalism

The exchange perspective comfortably encompasses reward, coercive, expert, and informational power, but not referent power. The **communal** perspective complements exchange theory by adding a non-rational dimension of love, attachment, and compassion (Clark & Grote, June, 1995). **Communal** theory departs from the "this for that" approach to emphasize investments and "we-ness" ("What is good for you is good for me").

The communally oriented person may count rewards and costs occasionally—but helping the partner fulfill needs is often more rewarding than it is costly. Profit and loss are unimportant compared to the **investment** of love and compassion—and hence referent power—in the relationship. Relational profit or loss is not compared to alternatives, because they mean nothing without love and "we-ness." Communal principles can explain some relationships that overstretch the terms of exchange theory:

1. The experience of raising a child, at tremendous cost over at least a quarter of a lifetime, whose main paybacks are not given by her, but by the emotions you feel because of her existence and actions (i.e., "what she puts you through").

2. Caring for your aging and then dying spouse, who can never repay you and sometimes can't even be kind or thankful to you.

Communal theory is not just an ideal. Existing research is compatible with the view that communal attitudes have more influence in close intimate relationships, and exchange attitudes predominate in more superficial connections and in romantic relationships that are just beginning or in decay (reviewed in Brehm, 1992). Perhaps the common denominator across relationship types, stages, and even across cultures is this: *close, stable relationships in a stable context are more communal; changing relationships and changing conditions evoke more exchange attitudes*.

Cultural influences

Rodman (1972) distinguished four different societal patterns for marriage. These are summarized in Table 7.4 and compared to predominant types of power we have discussed.

In the terms of this table, traditional Muslim, Indian, Chinese, Mediterranean, and Latin American societies are **patriarchal**—except for some of the upper classes that are **modified** by westernization. American, British, and some European societies are **transitional egalitarian**, while Denmark and Sweden are considered truly **egalitarian**.

A number of different researchers have evaluated how the resources—skills, competencies, status or knowledge—that the husband or wife brings

TABLE 7.4. Correspondence between types of societies, marriages, norms, and power

Society	Predominant power types	Norm structures	Power need likely (gender)	American marriage types
Patriarchal	Legitimate	Hierarchical	Men	Traditional
Modified patriarchal	Legitimate & referent	Hierarchical & communal	Men	Modern
Transitional egalitarian	Reward/resource & referent	Exchange & communal	Women & men	Egalitarian
Egalitarian	Legitimate equality & referent	Matching & communal	Neither	

Based on Rodman, 1972; Peplau, 1983; Clark & Grote, June, 1995.

to their relationship undergird their amount and relative degree of power. For example, the wife's employment status has been found by several researchers to improve her power in marriage (Safilios-Rothschild, 1967). In addition, the husband's education, occupational status, and income have been positively related to his power in studies conducted in the United States. However, studies conducted in Yugoslavia (Burie & Zecevic, 1967) and in Greece (Safilios-Rothschild, 1967) have found an inverse connection between the same variables and the power of husbands relative to their wives. Rodman (1972) explained these and other contradictory findings by suggesting that the relative influence of resources on marital power is greatest in cultures that are **in transition toward equality**. The cultural context allows (in egalitarian) or prevents (in patriarchal societies) resources from having relevance as causal conditions for marital decisions. Thus, according to Huston (1983): "In strongly patriarchal societies, norms confer authority to the husband independent of the spouses' relative resources. In these societies, such variables as education and occupational prestige are correlated with the husband's exposure to liberal ideas that run counter to life in traditional patriarchy; hence, his high socioeconomic status is inversely related to his reported power. In Western cultures, however, these same properties are seen as resources on which he draws in order to exert influence on his wife" (p. 208).

One of the most interesting studies of marital power which confirms the importance of the broader cultural context was a field study conducted by Strodtbeck (1974) in the late 1940s in the Arizona–New Mexico area with three distinctly different cultural groups: Navaho Indians, homesteading farmers, and Mormon workers. The experimental procedure required each couple to engage in several decision-making situations, and outcomes were analyzed on the basis of the decision-making process itself, as well as on the spouse who won the greater number of decisions in the pair. It was found that the Mormon husbands made a significantly greater number of decisions than Mormon wives (keep in mind that Mormon families are traditionally patriarchal); the farm couples had fairly egalitarian decision-making procedures; and, for the Navaho couples, the wives made more decisions than did the husbands (Navaho women traditionally have had favored positions in their culture). Thus, the study very clearly indicated the strong relationship between one's own power in an intimate relationship and that expected in the larger culture.

Many theorists have argued that the presence of gender roles determines how individual men and women will behave in their intimate relationships, the types of relationships they will develop, and why their relationships will prosper or fade. If men and women wish to be more equal in terms of the balance of power in their relationship, then they must become more conscious of the prevailing gender expectations which undergird our current love relationships, take them with a "grain of salt," and consider ways they may wish to reconceptualize their relationship. This symbolic interactionism describes and studies this renegotiating and reconstructing of relationship agreements.

Chapter summary

- Actual differences in communication are different from stereotypes. Men talk more in public than women, but their talk focuses on providing "reports," while female talk aims for connection or "rapport."
- Women express more warmth, joy, shame, fear, nervousness, and sadness, while men express more pride, disgust, and contempt, and both sexes express anger about equally.
- Most studies find men less able to empathize than women, but the differences may be related to which emotions are transmitted and to the professions of the people studied.
- Work in relationships includes paid employment, domestic labor, and nurturing. Women spend two to three times as much time on domestic work and also nurture the family more. Although employment conditions are changing, men continue to receive more income for their work.
- The six types of social power described are distributed differently in the three most common types of American marriages: traditional, modern, and egalitarian. Peer marriage may be the closest Americans have come in practice to equality in relationship.
- Structuralism teaches that we learn our relationship roles through living up to gender expectations transmitted through social institutions.
- Social interactionism maintains that we renegotiate our roles to cope with limitations of norms. Such negotiation occurs through a process of exchange in which we weigh the relative costs and rewards of being in a relationship compared to other alternatives and add our emotional and financial investments as well.
- Communalism contends that in stable times and satisfied relationships we feel love when supporting both our partners and ourselves, and we count rewards and costs during changes and in new or decaying relationships.

The development of gay and lesbian relationships 8

- **Community Support for Gay Men and Lesbians**
  Friendship
  The Growth of Gay and Lesbian Community

No aspect of human love relations is subject to more myths, misunderstandings, and passionate dislike or support than homosexuality. Among the more than 90% of Americans with heterosexual identities, homosexuality is viewed as an alien "other kind" of sexuality. It is damaging, but common, for humans to **demonize** what is alien to us. As the "other sex," women have been misunderstood and mistrusted at least as far back as we have written documents (DeBeauvoir, 1960; Rogers, 1966). Now men and women are slowly moving beyond demonizing the opposite sex to accommodate both perspectives on what it is to be human. As relationships and perspectives on life of the gay men, lesbian, and bisexual men and women have become better known, public understanding of the full spectrum of intimate relations has grown as well. Demonization of these alternative forms of romantic relating is decreasing as they are becoming accepted into the diversity of American life.

We will explore the current research and expert views on alternative sexual orientations. Only empirical research has a chance of differentiating between one expert's opinion and another's. But almost all research into homosexuality suffers from **volunteer bias**: the social disapproval of homosexuality leads many who engage in homosexual thoughts or behavior to resist participation in research, and to deny their behavior when asked. This biased research results in several ways by (a) underreporting homosexual phenomena, so that they appear to be less frequent than they actually are, and (b) skewing the make-up of research samples because those who choose to participate in studies will be more comfortable with their minority sexual identity, which often means that they are younger, white, highly educated, involved in gay and lesbian communities, and mentally healthy (Klinger, 1996). Though these sampling factors affect results in sometimes unpredictable ways, they can provide some more neutral evidence amid the passionate convictions of more moral or ideological opinions on both sides.

We will explore the origins of alternative sexual orientations and then analyze "homophobia," or fear, aversion, and prejudice directed toward non-heterosexual relating. Then we will follow the experiences of gay, lesbian, and bisexual people through stages of sexual identity formation, attraction and dating, and long-term partnerships. We will conclude by discussing the development of community among non-heterosexual people and of their religious and social recognition in the 1990s.

Same-sex attractions: Inborn, development, or choice?

In both academic and public arenas the basis of alternative sexual orientations has been hotly debated for the last three decades. At first the two sides were called **nature** versus **nurture**. Same-sex romantic or sexual interest was either based on genes, hormones, or brain structures (*nature*), or on child and adolescent development (*nurture*). Recently the experts have shifted their focus to the concepts of **essentialism** and **social constructionism** (Stein, 1996). *Essentialsim* holds that sexual orientation is part of a person's essence—universal, inborn, fixed, and predetermined. *Social constructionism* counters that sexual orientation is defined by societies, developed interactively with sociocultural forces, changeable, and somewhat open to free choice.

The *essentialist* position combines *nature* and *nurture* to conclude that biology and development interact beyond the growing person's understanding to determine a sexual orientation that is an accomplished fact, and the young adult's only options are to cooperate with it or resist. The idea that same-sex orientations are predetermined and fixed is enthusiastically embraced by those who want to include alternative sexual orientations in mainstream society and would like to reduce the influence of homophobic prejudice, conservative religious condemnation, and anti-homosexual legislation. But the scientific evidence for biological bases is only preliminary and very inconclusive (Byne, 1995), and systematic studies of child development in this area are not being undertaken.

In America, the strongest evidence for a more complex *social constructionist* perspective is the confusion about just *what a homosexually oriented person is*. What constitutes a same-sex orientation? Homosexual behavior? Same-gender attractions or sexual fantasies? Or a gay, lesbian, or bisexual identity? Table 8.1 presents the most recent and reliable scientific findings on the frequency of these three aspects of same-sex orientation.

These rates are significantly lower than popularly known estimates, with the most recent reporting 9% of men and 5% of women with homosexual or bisexual identities, and 22% of men and 17% of women admitting they have had some homosexual experience (Janus & Janus, 1992). Other scientific results parallel Table 8.1, with males in exclusively gay rela-

TABLE 8.1. Overal frequency in percentage of those reporting same-gender sexual behavior, desire, or identity in the United States, based on General Social Surveys of 1988–1991 and 1993 and the National Health and Social Life Survey of 1992

Group	Sexual behavior with a partner						Desire		Identity	
	Past year		Past 5 years		Since puberty		Attraction or appeal		Homosexual or bisexual	
	Women	Men	Women	Men	Women	Men	Women	Men	Women	Men
Overall 18–59	1.3%	2.7	2.2	4.1	5.0	9.8	7.5	7.7	1.4	2.8
Ages 18–29	1.6	3.0	2.5	4.2	4.7	7.3	6.7	9.1	1.6	2.9
Ages 50–59	0.4	1.4	0.9	2.5	3.5	9.0	4.6	4.0	0.4	0.5
Race: White	1.2	2.7	1.9	4.0	5.1	10.3	7.6	7.6	1.5	3.0
Black	1.3	3.6	2.9	5.4	4.5	9.5	7.3	7.0	0.4	1.9
Other	2.1	1.4	5.9	1.3	5.6	4.2	7.1	9.4	1.6	1.1
HiSchool Grad	0.8	1.4	1.4	2.7	2.9	7.9	5.3	5.5	0.4	1.8
College Grad	2.5	3.5	3.5	5.4	7.9	11.1	12.8	9.4	3.6	3.3
Live in top 12 CC*	2.1	10.2	3.3	14.3	6.5	15.8	9.7	16.7	2.6	9.2
Suburbs of top CC	1.2	2.7	1.9	5.4	6.2	13.0	9.0	10.3	1.9	4.2
Rural areas*	0.6	1.0	1.0	0.9	2.6	3.1	2.1	7.5	0.0	1.3
Minimum sample	3,255	4,054	1,983	2,512	1,394	1,727	1,394	1,727	1,362	1,692

*CC = Central Cities of 12 largest Standard Metropolitan Statistical Areas. Rural means counties with no towns of 10,000 or more.
Source: Reported by Michaels, 1966.

tionships estimated between 1% and 4%, and exclusively lesbian relationships under 1% (reported in Ellis, 1996a).

Though the newer figures are derived from larger samples more representative of the whole country, they may be underreported due to the social desirability bias against non-heterosexual phenomena. When we guess at the size of this reporting bias by comparing identity figures, we can't help noticing the influence of social groups on the construction of reported sexual orientation. The youngest group reports slightly more than the overall average, while the oldest group's figures are a fourth as high or less (rows 2–3). More Blacks report recent homosexual behavior but less identify with it than Whites (rows 4–5). At least twice as many college grads as high school grads report recent homosexual behavior and 9 times as many women, and almost 2 times as many men identify with it (rows 7–8). Rates in major central cities are 2 to 3 times as high as in their own suburbs, and rural areas report the lowest rates of all. Only the 9.2% frequency for men in the 12 largest central cities matches earlier reports. But while strong communities there could counteract the social bias against reporting alternative sexuality, these communities attract large numbers from other areas, so they are not representative of the country as a whole. So we still do not know what percentages to use, but we can estimate that they are more than the self-identified (1.4% of woman and 2.8% of men), perhaps closer to those reporting homosexual activity in the last 5 years (2.2% of women and 4.1% of men). But the 5% of women and 9.8% of men reporting some homosexual behavior since puberty are not all bisexually or homosexually oriented. For example, people like this 40-year-old married man would not fit:

When I was 13 my best friend and I had a sexual affair. We were just learning about sex, and it was fun. After about a year we just quit. We didn't talk about it, but we both moved on to girls. I don't think of it as gay or right or wrong; it was just good kid stuff.

Cultural attitudes have an immense effect. An inestimable percent of gender-segregated Arab youths reportedly engage in homosexual affairs, normally without ever considering themselves gay (Schmitt & Sofer, 1992). Even a third of those reporting a same-sex partner in the last year (Table 8.1) did not consider themselves to be gay or bisexual, and about a third of those who did identify as gay, lesbian, or bisexual had not had a same-sex partner in the last year (Michaels, 1996). Thus, neither sexual behavior nor sexual thoughts or feelings constitute sexual orientation unless the person *identifies* with them. Therefore, sexual identity is *self-constructed*. And since the numbers vary so much by age, education, race, location, and religion (not shown), we can conclude that the labels for sexual orientation are constructed out of both social influences and personal choice.

Biological influences

There is a growing body of evidence for the possibility of biological predispositions toward alternative sexual orientations. One study has suggested that male homosexuality may be related to a gene sequence carried on the X chromosome in humans, which might mean that it can be inherited from the mother's side of the family (Hamer et al., 1993). Despite the preliminary nature of this study—including a small nonrepresentative sample, lacking control group and numerous issues of genetic inference (McGuire, 1995)—the results immediately hit the news media, causing strong reactions among gays. A middle-aged man said:

*At first, I was very relieved. But then I got really angry—about all those years I was struggling with self-hate. I was frustrated and felt such a loss over all that energy I spent worrying that **I must have done something wrong** or I wouldn't be gay. I can ask, "If you could live your youth all over again, would you do it differently?" But I can't. I don't get that chance.*

This finding supports a smattering of conclusions in other family studies. Two studies reported that identical twins were more likely to both identify as gay than fraternal twins, which implies a genetic component (Bailey & Pillard,1991; Buhrich et al., 1991). A much larger twin study found more agreement of sexual identity for female identical twins than for fraternal twins, but not for males (Hershberger, 1997). But this result might be explained by other research which suggests that greater divergence in *gender behavior* between identical male twins than female twins (and hence, less likelihood of both male twins identifying as gay) could be due to normal masculine competitiveness in twins (Borg, 1997). Other studies suggested that gay men might have a higher-than-average number of gay family members, while lesbians tended to have a higher-than-average number of lesbian family members, compared to estimates of the general population (Bailey & Benishay, 1993; Bailey et al., 1993; Pillard & Weinrich, 1986). However, these family studies rely on small volunteer samples who self-identify their own and their relatives' sexual orientations, and they do not have control groups of heterosexual respondents. Thus, at present, the evidence for a genetic component of homosexual orientation is incomplete (McGuire, 1995). This does not mean that genetics are not involved, but only that scientific research has not yet achieved the certainty that either supporters or opponents of a genetic basis of homosexuality would like to have. McGuire concludes that it would be very difficult to design adequate behavior genetic studies to determine what role genetic, environmental, and random influences might play in the development of homosexuality.

Neurohormones

Animal studies have shown that physical and psychological conditions may create hormonal variations in pregnant females that affect neural maturation of the developing fetus (Ellis & Ames, 1987). During fetal development, the body and the brain are sexually differentiated during specific critical periods. Scientists found that stress-induced hormonal patterns in lab rats can alter adult patterns of "sex-typed" behaviors, such as mounting and grooming (Dorner et al., 1980; Tourney, 1980). Consequently, sex-atypical mating patterns might be "wired-in" to the brain of a creature that has otherwise developed in accord with its genetic sex (i.e., in shape, physical characteristics, and genital organs). Transferring these sexual behavior findings to humans has been very difficult, however. In the eighties, three studies of humans found that males may be more likely develop a homosexual orientation if their mothers experience a severely stressful event during the second trimester of pregnancy, when this sexual differentiation of the brain takes place. However, two more recent studies failed to confirm these results (reviewed in Ellis, 1997). All five studies used small, unrepresentative samples.

Another biological approach to sexual-orientation research relies on animal models and hypothesized brain differences between males and females. Lesbians are believed to have partially-masculinized brains, while gay men are believed to have brains which are not fully masculinized. Research support for these theories has been controversial, because samples have been very small, and the supposed male/female differences in size of certain brain structures are not scientifically established. Gay or lesbian brain structures cannot be considered *intermediate* between men and women, if there are no consistent "normal" differences between the sexes to start with (reviewed in Byne, 1995). Other studies keep coming out with other differences in brain structure or function by sex or by sexual orientation, often conflicting. One test of college students' speed at performing certain verbal and visual tasks with well-documented gender differences found gay males' scores *more extremely male* (i.e., more different from females than those of heterosexual males). This suggests that gay men's brains may function differently from both nongay men and women, but not *intermediate* between them (Halpern & Crothers, 1997). Three neuroscientific reviewers, all writing in reputable, scholarly, homosexuality-oriented books and journals, conclude that a causal connection between hormones and human sexual orientation is not adequately supported yet (Ellis, 1997; Byne, 1995, 1996; Banks & Gartrell, 1995).

Environmental origins

Prior to these physiological findings, researchers explored sexual orientation from a variety of perspectives, including psychoanalytic and social learning approaches (Dannecker, 1984; Minton & McDonald, 1984; Van Tassel Hamilton, 1936). Psychoanalytic views typically focus on internal or overt conflicts with parental figures which are said to lead the child into a gay or lesbian lifestyle (Chodorow, 1978). One study indicates that many gay males were, as children, "mamma's boys" and had rather cold and distant relationships with their fathers (Greund & Blanchard, 1982). Other studies talk about generalized cross-sex identification among gays and lesbians (Meer, 1987):

> **Stephen, 20, describes his childhood.** *"I always identified with the females. You know when you get to elementary school, at lunchtime, the girls sat together and the boys sat together? I always sat with the girls. I was always very androgynous . . . I would get mistaken for a girl. In high school, everybody thought I was gay. I was always called the fag, I was always called the girl, I was called everything."*

> **Mandy recounts a recent conversation with a friend.** *"My friend asked me, 'Don't you remember in grade school the boys used to chase the girls? . . . Mandy, we were with the boys, chasing the girls!' I guess I started liking girls as early as 7 years old."*

The social construction theory holds that Stephen's sexual orientation is partly a reaction to his parents' and others' labeling (Dannecker, 1984).

> *You always hear 'all gay men are good decorators and good cooks' and all that . . . I mean, I'm a secretary. That's pretty stereotypically gay, isn't it? I don't worry about it. Maybe labels and stereotypes influenced me, maybe they didn't . . . I don't know.*

One study suggests that as many as two-thirds of "feminine-identified" male children may pursue homosexual relations in adulthood (Green,

1985). But enough gays *don't* identify with the feminine gender role that a study found only an insignificantly higher average femininity score compared to heterosexuals (Storms, 1980). Though these studies could support psychoanalytic or social-learning theories of sexual orientation, they could also support genetic and neurohormonal theories just as well—feminized behavior could result from a feminized brain. One cannot discern whether boys like Stephen interacted more with mommy and then became "feminine"; whether mommy's substantial interaction with Stephen arose from daddy's rejection of a boy who seemed inherently "unmasculine"; or whether Stephen's own desires to remain close to and model on mommy guided the sequence of events.

A popular belief holds that homosexuality arises from sex segregation or from unpleasant heterosexual experiences in early life. Though the connection is little explored in research, one small study found that 56% of lesbians and 36% of heterosexual women reported traumatic experiences with men (Brannock & Chapman, 1990):

> Lindsay is a survivor of childhood incest. In elementary school, she engaged in sexual activity with other girls (all of whom had also been sexually abused). Lindsay viewed the kissing and touching as "the next step" in close friendships. She wasn't aware that she was "different" until she and a friend kissed in the presence of another girl. When the girl reacted, the two friends began to question their relationship.

Larger studies suggest that 21% of lesbians and 21% of gay men may have been sexually abused, and this may be more than the estimated national average for males, but not for females (reviewed in D'Augelli, 1998, and Klinger & Stein, 1996). But this retrospective report evidence is not enough to convince us that childhood abuse is a likely *cause* of homosexual orientation.

Another interesting theory about sexual orientation suggests that early pubertal sexual experiences may have an *imprinting* effect, whether heterosexual or homosexual (reviewed in Ellis, 1996). Though not yet investigated, this is clearly not always the case, since many gays and lesbians report being aware of same-sex attractions long before puberty.

A small percentage of homosexual behavior may derive from specific social contexts. For example, homosexual behavior may be frequent among exotic dancers or among married women who engage in "swinging" behavior with their husbands (Dixon, 1983). Still, cause and effect are unclear. Did overt displays of female sexuality "teach" the women to admire and eroticize the female body? Or did sexually-liberated attitudes or same-sex inclinations lead the women toward these lifestyles?

There appears that there is no single route to a homosexual orientation, and that predispositions to same-sex attraction may derive from complex interactions between genetics, physiology, social experience, and even some degree of personal choice (DeCecco & Parker, 1995). Current research emphasis on the influence of biological forces in sexual development has served to increase the moral and philosophical acceptance of sexual minorities. Evidence will probably continue to mount that a homosexual orientation is not simply a **choice**, or "sexual preference," but partly an **inborn and biological tendency**. In keeping with postmodern cultural pluralism, this perspective removes homosexual orientation from the realm of sin, psychopathology, and faulty learning, and allows it to be acknowledged as a normal variation of human nature.

Homophobia:
Fear, aversion, or prejudice against homosexuality

The name *homophobia* has been given to a cluster of feelings and attitudes. It may be an irrational discomfort or fear, but it also applies to intolerance, negative attitudes and beliefs toward homosexuals, and anger without discomfort or fear (Monroe et al., 1997). In elementary school, American children normally learn from peer comments that heterosexuality is natural and same-sex attraction is shameful (D'Augelli, 1998). Ninety-five percent of college students report having made or laughed at antihomosexual jokes or having used a derogatory word, and 32% report having done this in front of a gay person (Rey & Gibson, 1997). Gay and lesbian high school students report hearing derogatory words an average of once a day (Jorday et al., 1997). We will not demonize homophobia, the way homosexuality has been demonized, but rather try to understand how it happens and how we can handle it with compassion for both heterosexual and non-heterosexual people.

Table 8.2 shows the percentages of endorsements of pro- and antihomosexual attitudes in a random sample of over 3,500 adults eligible for jury duty in 15 states (Sherrod & Nardi, 1998). Though an average of 39% admitted to having anti-homosexual attitudes or feelings, the proportions depended on the questions asked. On only 1 question was the majority of Americans anti-gay: 59% of males and 62% of females disapproved of considering gayness as a basic civil right comparable to ethnicity and gender. In addition, over 50% of men and 44% of women disliked the idea of gay or lesbian teachers for their children. At the other extreme, only 25% of men and 20% of women felt employment discrimination against gays or lesbians should be legal. Between these extremes, only a third of men and a fourth or a fifth of women would be uncomfortable living or working close to gays or lesbians. Sherrod and Nardi (1998) found that white men held the most apprehensive or hostile views, followed by Latinos, while white women were less homophobic than Latinas or blacks, unless they were Southerners. Religious (especially Protestant) and conservative political ideology is connected with significantly greater homophobia, because these groups condemn homosexuality. Having gay or lesbian friends significantly

TABLE 8.2. Prevalence of attitudes about gays and lesbians. Bold percentages represent fearful or hostile attitudes toward gays and/or lesbians

Attitude questions	Men		Women		Total	
	Yes	No	Yes	No	Yes	No
1. Do you think gay men and lesbians should be allowed to adopt children, just like heterosexuals?	67.9	**32.1**	61.8	**38.2**	64.7	**35.3**
2. Do you think gay men and lesbians should be able to have officially recognized marriages, just like heterosexuals?	63.6	**36.4**	61.0	**39.0**	62.2	**37.8**
3. Would it bother you if a gay or lesbian couple moved into the house or apartment next to you?	**34.4**	65.7	**26.9**	73.1	**30.4**	69.6
4. Would you mind if your child's teacher was a gay man?	**52.8**	47.3	**44.4**	55.6	**48.5**	51.5
5. Would you mind if your child's teacher was a lesbian?	**50.6**	49.4	**44.3**	55.7	**47.4**	52.6
6. Do you think employers should be free to refuse to hire a person because of that person's sexual orientation?	**25.6**	74.4	**19.8**	80.2	**23.6**	76.4
7. Do you think being gay or lesbian is an acceptable lifestyle, just like other lifestyles people lead?	60.6	**39.4**	56.6	**43.4**	58.5	**41.5**
8. Would you feel bothered in any way if you had to work closely with an individual who was gay or lesbian?	**31.7**	68.3	**19.3**	80.7	**25.3**	74.7
9. Do you think a person's sexual orientation should be a civil right that is protected by the government just like a person's ethnicity, religion, or sex?	41.0	**59.0**	37.3	**62.7**	39.1	**60.9**
Average percentage endorsing anti-gay attitudes.:	**40.2**		37.6		39.0	

n = 3500+ in 15 states. Source: Recalculated by Nardi from data in Sherrod & Nardi, 1998.

lowers homophobic attitudes. Having more than high school education does not make a significant difference except for white women.

According to studies, boys' homophobic attitudes rise consistently through the high school years, while girls' drop between the ninth and eleventh grades (Baker & Fishbein, 1997). After high school, homophobic attitudes may decline somewhat with age (Johnson et al., 1997). This slight peak of reactivity among male adolescents offers a clue to the psychological aspects of homophobia.

Psychological aspects of homophobia

On the individual level, homophobia may appear more as an *aversion* than a phobia, since more people admit to aversion or avoidance of homosexuality (as in questions 4, 5, 7, and 9 in Table 8.2) than to apprehensiveness about it (questions 3 and 8). Physiological studies indicate that heterosexual men tend to report uncomfortable feelings and have an aversive sexual response (reduced blood flow to penis) when viewing pictures of nude men, as well as pupil constriction and increased heart rate. But these responses do not occur when homosexual men view pictures of nude women (Hess, 1965; McConaghy, 1967; Freund et al., 1974). Could this aversion be a hostile defense agains a phobia, similar to "I hate snakes"? And why is it strongest in male adolescents?

Freud suggested that all people are physiologically somewhat bisexual (Freud, 1925/1989b; Fenichel, 1945). He thought that homophobic attitudes functioned to shut down homosexual responses and thus channel sexuality toward heterosexual mating and procreation. Intensely anti-homosexual attitudes could deter easily arousable young men in the beginning of their dating years from experimenting with homosexual acts and from connecting sexual feelings to their male friendships. In support of homophobia as a channelizing force, there is evidence that young men's antigay attitudes are lower if they are married (Kunkel & Temple, 1992). Homophobia is higher among men who have the least heterosexual experience (Morin & Garfinkel, 1978), and hence the least established habit paths connecting sexual impulses to heterosexual behavior.

Other studies suggest that homophobia is linked to antisexual attitudes (Brown & Amoroso, 1975), personal guilt about sexuality (Smith, 1971), and anxieties about expression of sexual impulses (Berry & Marks, 1969). People who are uncomfortable with their own sexual feelings have negative attitudes about others, especially homosexuals and prostitutes, because these groups—according to mainstream conceptualizations—are **defined** by their sexual expressiveness. As we have already seen, gay people do not define their lives by their sexual activity any more than do nongay people.

> I'm not gay because of sex. I'm gay because of feelings. I LOVE my partner . . . we talk and eat and sleep and go places just like [heterosexuals] . . . I know people who identify as gay who have NEVER had sex. Still, sex seems to be the only aspect of us that people see. I wish they could just see us as people.

Social aspects of homophobia

The majority of Christian denominations teach that homosexuality is unnatural and sinful, and that one should "love the sinner, but not the sin." A conservative Christian student responded thus to the evidence for genetic influence in homosexual orientation:

> Just as there are tendencies towards alcoholism, there may be tendencies toward homosexuality . . . but you don't justify and condone these actions. You use the will God gave you to resist, and the brain he gave you to seek help.

This text maintains respect for all religions, and we shall not debate the morality of either homosexuality or homophobia.

Led by Unitarians and Episcopalians, many mainstream churches are beginning to adjust their doctrines and policies toward accepting homosexuality as normal. However, history shows us that churches may maintain their moral positions for decades, because they claim a higher source of truth than science or public opinion. Outside of major urban areas, and wherever gay rights organizations do not have much influence, conservative attitudes about homosexuality dominate most public discussion.

Some of the social antagonism toward gays and lesbians focuses on their perceived sexual immorality. Gay men are feared to be psychologically disturbed, child molesters, hypersexual, and aggressive toward unwilling partners (Morin & Garfinkel, 1978), as reflected in the high opposition to gay teachers in Table 8.2. Since the late 1950s evidence has grown that sexual minorities are *not* more likely to be psychologically disturbed than heterosexuals (National Institute of Mental Health Task Force on Homosexuality, 1972), and their tendency toward self-rejection is shared by women, Jews, African-Americans, and some other minorities (Marmor, 1996). There is evidence that gay men are much *less* likely than heterosexually identified men to be child molesters. In a large-scale survey of pedophiles, Groth and Birnbaum (1978) found that **none** of the men were homosexual in adult relationships—**all** were heterosexual.

The confusion about gays and pedophilia may arise because some gay men express attraction to young adult males, admiring their first bloom of manhood. It is just as common for heterosexual men to admire "new-ripeness" or youth in women (Chapter 9) as for gay men to admire youthfulness in men. Clinical treatment experience with sexual offenders suggests that adult sexual exploitation of prepubertal **children** is psychologically quite different from attraction to **adolescents,** and normally derives from the perpetrator's need for power or from his own childhood experiences with sexual excitement. There is also a difference between **feeling** attraction and **acting** in ways known to be illegal or immoral. Thus, molestation of both children and adolescents has more to do with psychological maturity and impulse control than with sexual orientation.

What about hypersexuality and sexual aggression? Gay men may have sex more frequently than heterosexual men and couples, while lesbians have sex less frequently (Blumstein & Schwartz, 1983). And homosexual victimization does occur in prisons, but the perpetrators do not consider themselves gay. It is arguable that heterosexuals' views about gay hypersexuality and aggression are projections of what "evil" male sexuality would be for **themselves**, an exaggeration of their own indiscriminate behavior when aroused. Lesbians face some of the same sexual attitudes as gay men.

> Heterosexuals seem to think that because I'm gay, I want THEM. . . . Once I went to the gynecologist and I heard the woman making homophobic comments outside the door of the examining room . . . like she thought I was lay-

ing there in the stirrups saying 'Oh, baby . . . can you check my cervix one more time!' Heterosexuals need to understand that we don't lust after everyone we see . . . and we do possess the self-restraint to keep sexuality from interfering with our everyday lives.

A cognitive–developmental model of homophobia

A careful look at the relationship between mental development and sexual experience can give us some ideas about how homophobia develops and can be relieved.

Shame plays a major part in gender-role conditioning (Chapter 13). The intensity of shame associated with homosexual behavior may derive from male peer-group conditioning that relies on anti-feminine and anti-homosexual taunts to shame boys into "proper" masculine behavior. Thus, homophobia is emotionally woven into the male gender role via shame-threats to one's self-image (e.g., Fishbein, 1996; Krugman, 1995). Cross-cultural comparison has shown that some cultures with stronger male-dominant sex roles (such as Brazil) also express stronger antigay attitudes (Dunbar et al., 1973)

The two ways to trigger sexual arousal are (a) erogenous stimulation in the body, and (b) sights, sounds, smells, movements, or thoughts that were connected with sexual arousal in previous scenes. Coherent mental-emotional programs or **scripts** connecting thoughts, feelings, sensations, mental images, and actions need to be formed for all sorts of behavior (Tomkins, 1994). Any **unfamiliar** sexual act or imagery, that is, anything sexual which has not yet been connected to our cognitive-emotional scripts for sexuality, will normally evoke some curiosity, but also confusion, discomfort, or aversion. This includes not only homosexual acts but also heterosexual or autosexual acts that we have not yet imagined or tried. Where sexual scripts are lacking, even desired sexual experiences provoke intense anxiety, unless drugs or alcohol are used to anaesthetize it.

I talked a lot about sex, but when it came right down to doing it, I chickened out.

But most adolescent males **don't want** to form any cognitive-emotional scripts about same-sex closeness and any sensual pleasure (except when alcohol-induced), because **that would shame them in their own minds**. The intolerable discomfort of a homophobic reaction might arise as anticipatory anxiety about the prospect of any experience of that anxious/confused state associated with homosexual behavior, as well as the shame-threat to one's self-image if emotional arousal could mean one "liked it." In an effort to avoid this state, we may try to avoid not only homosexual people, but also homosexual imagery and thoughts. This avoidance is typical of the "tolerant" approach to homosexuals:

I don't care what they do, just as long as they keep it away from me.

It is ironic, but not surprising, that the complex of thoughts, imagery, and actions labeled "homosexuality" and our efforts to avoid them evoke so much anxious emotional arousal, that it can powerfully attract our attention at times "in spite of ourselves." This intrusive thinking is just like any other phobia. Being aware of this magnetic "desire to look" at what they do not want to see makes many males and some females secretly dread that they are "latently homosexual," as Freud theorized. We employ several defenses to cope with this secret shame—hostility, ridicule, humor, even pretending exaggerated caricatures of "gayness" to prove we are not afraid of it.

Heterosexual males may also have no repertoire of words and actions (scripts) to deal with unwanted sexual advances. With no script on hand, a male may hate or fear his confused response to gay "come-ons," and may respond aggressively as a way to restore his sense of self-control:

If one of those guys came after me I'd beat him up.

Some people can recall the moments of shame that may accompany their confusion during homosexual advances:

*I felt **humiliated** that the guy came on to me, like I must have looked gay or something. What was it that he saw? I don't want anything feminine or faggoty about me.*

I remember a lesbian coming up to me . . . and she told me she was a lesbian, and I freaked out. I ran over to my roommate and . . . I was all nervous and everything . . . and I said, "Why'd she come up to ME and tell ME that?"

Relieving homophobia. What can we do about our homophobic attitudes? The cognitive developmental explanation suggests a simple response: Familiarity leads to comfort. The more we get to know what gays and lesbians do, say, think, and feel, and the more practice we get in dealing with gay and lesbian behavior and even come-ons, the more we can reduce our anxious arousal level, and the more comfortable we can become. This is precisely what many heterosexuals think they **don't want**. But just as with other typical phobias, such as heights and snakes, familiarity reduces the phobic response, as this student testifies:

Now that I have become much more experienced and much more comfortable with my own heterosexuality, I have become less and less homophobic. At a younger age, a homosexual advance would have provoked me to fight and ridicule that person. Now that I am older and have even had several homosexual friends, I have learned that they are people too. Usually they are better friends as well. If I were to be in a position today in which I was [approached] by a homosexual, I could politely and tactfully decline, and I wouldn't be disgusted. I have been approached several times in my life by homosexuals, and never once was one overbearing. It has always been uncomfortable for me, but it has never been blown out of proportion.

Note that the student above does not claim to be completely "over" his homophobic responses, despite greater familiarity and comfort. Research confirms that the ability to empathize and take the perspective of others is associated with reduced homophobic attitudes (Johnson et al., 1997). Not only friendships, but even courses or public forums about gay and lesbian experience relieve homophobic discomfort for many, even when they don't change some people's convictions about the origins or morality of homosexuality (Ben-Ari, 1998; Nelson & Krieger, 1997).

Does homophobia limit male friendships? The widespread inhibition of positive feelings and physical contact between men in America is frequently linked to homophobia (Lewis, 1978; Roese et al., 1992). Adolescents may learn to deny and distort their warm feelings by substituting aggressive, hostile, and humorous expressions, such as punching, competing with, and ridiculing each other. More homophobic men may have greater reticence to confide with any others intimately (Monroe et al., 1997). This may leave them exclusively dependent upon one relationship with a woman to address and develop their awareness of needs and vulnerabilities (Gulley, 1991). Some women resent this:

> A man's home may seem to be his castle on the outside; inside, it is more often his nursery. (Clair Boothe Luce, American journalist, playwright, and politician)

Women and homophobia

Two explanations have been suggested for why homophobia is not as strong among women as men. First, women do not think sexual thoughts as often as men (Elmer-DeWitt, October, 1994), nor do they learn to link warm feelings with sexual intentions, as men do. Evidence for this includes studies indicating that young men are more likely than women to experience sexual attractions to opposite sex friends (Metts & Cupach, June, 1993; Beard et al., June, 1993). Second, women have more social permission to display affection with each other and no need to act dominant in order to fit into their gender role.

Internalized homophobia

The term *internalized homophobia* is used to describe homophobia experienced by gays, lesbians, and bisexuals. Despite their awareness of their own sexual orientation, they may retain negative opinions about homosexual behavior, as well as a history of alienation and shameful feelings about their differentness (Friedman & Downey, 1995; Kaufman & Raphael,

1996). These self-destructive feelings are very widespread among non-heterosexual high school students, since 47% of one sample reported having considered suicide and 35% had made an attempt (Jordan et al., 1997). In a Massachusetts high school study, approximately 4% of heterosexual and 28% of non-heterosexual boys reported suicide attempts, compared to 14.5% of heterosexual and 20.5% of non-heterosexual girls (Remafedi et al., 1998). In college, non-heterosexual students may use more alcohol than heterosexuals, and their alcohol use was more related to psychological distress as well (DeBord et al., 1998). A middle-aged gay male recounts his experience of chronic shame—or sin—as a youth:

> I went to Catholic school, where they taught that if you didn't confess every sin to the priest and still took communion you were automatically excommunicated from the faith. Well, I knew I couldn't confess that I had sex with a boy, because that was a 'mortal sin'. But I had to go to communion anyway or it would show that I hadn't confessed. So I believed I was excommunicated and going to hell.

Until recently, media images of gays and lesbians reflected almost exclusively the stereotyped "butch" lesbian and "femme" gay male. Most popular films and tabloid news shows include homosexual characters only when they add to the sensationalism of the story. Thus, homosexuals and bisexuals are commonly portrayed as wild, weird, funny, or criminal. But gay and lesbian people are just as diverse as heterosexuals, African Americans, and women. Though more positive and representative role models of gays and lesbians have been introduced into popular television and films, caricatures can still reinforce already internalized negative stereotypes:

SEXUAL IDENTITY A SENSE OF ONE'S SELF AS A HUMAN BEING.

> What you heard about lesbians was all so offensive . . . you heard they were sick and disgusting, and that they were these big bull dykes. . . . I just kept thinking, "God! I don't want to be one of them!"

Lacking positive role models, some gay men and lesbians may spend decades trying to prove to themselves and to their own significant others that they are "good enough," often neglecting their true needs for self-actualization (Gonsiorek, 1988). It is common for them to work long and hard, much to the benefit of their employers and society, and to be especially vulnerable to low self-esteem (Martin & Knox, 1997) unless their efforts are welcomed and recognized by others. Internalized homophobia (or self-shame) can present many obstacles to forming a supportive identity, as we shall see in the next section.

Homosexual identity formation

Identity confusion

Sexual identity refers to one's sense of oneself as a sexual being. Sexual identities can be heterosexual, homosexual, bisexual, and asexual (non-sexual or celibate). Cass (1984; 1990, 1996) has proposed a model of gay, lesbian, and bisexual identity formation which involves six stages. In the first stage, **Identity Confusion**, the individual may question a previously assumed heterosexual identity. Anne describes her first relationship with another woman:

> Just because we fell in love with each other, we thought we were in the wrong damn bodies. She has long hair, she's not butch . . . I'm not butch. Neither one of us could figure out who was in the wrong body because I didn't want to be a man and she didn't want to be a man . . . we were really confused. That's because we'd been conditioned to think about relationships in a specific [heterosexual] way.

Some of one's actions or feelings do not "fit the mold" of one's expectations about heterosexual behavior. Once people begin to realize that their behaviors are in some way "like a homosexual," they may proceed via one of several paths: (a) rejecting the homosexual meaning of experiences, (like the 40-year-old man quoted in the discussion of Table 8.1); (b) accepting the homosexual meaning yet labeling homosexuality as undesirable; or (c) accepting the meaning and acknowledging homosexuality as desirable.

> Because I didn't like sex with men, I thought something was wrong with me. Then when I was with women, I was like "Ahh! There's not something wrong with me . . . it's just that I was with the wrong gender."

Identity comparison

Cass' second stage, **Identity Comparison**, consists of tentatively adopting a homosexual identity, and exploring the implications of being homosexual. Will there be social rejection? Will the family of origin accept the gay or lesbian family member? Will the individual lose old friends? The reactions of straight friends can be quite a shock to a gay person:

> I started really strong, saying, "I just might come out to the whole world now" . . . until [a local gay issue] came up . . . I saw the reaction from coworkers and people . . . and then, boy, it scared me so bad I almost went closeted . . . I was a little worried about even coming down to the bar . . . getting seen out, walking into this bar.

Shame and self-doubt plague many people as they come to a realization of their homosexuality or bisexuality. Furthermore, many of them are rejected by their families when they disclose their sexual identity, which can provoke a severe grief reaction in both young people and their parents. If the undesirable ramifications of a homosexual orientation seem too great, the individual may foreclose and maintain a heterosexual identity:

> I tackled my apprehension about being gay in the usual manner. I became a homophobe that would make Jerry Falwell or Jesse Helms look like Jerry Brown. I figured that if I drew attention away from myself, in the form of negative and condemning behavior, no one would think twice about pointing the finger at me.

Some developing gays and lesbians may cope with negative stigma by identifying as bisexual, as a heterosexual experiencing a "phase," or as a "special case" (Cass, 1990). Stephen recalls his first crush on a classmate in high school:

> I guess I thought 'maybe I'm bisexual.' It was just like 'no, no . . . of course I still like women.' I just hung on to that . . . because I was brought up that way.

Identity tolerance

If the individual is able to reject negative personal stereotypes about gays and lesbians, transition to the third stage, **Identity Tolerance**, can begin. In this stage, the individual acknowledges a homosexual identity, yet still has concerns about the hostility and homophobia in heterosexual society. Some people plan carefully to lessen the social risks of coming out:

> Before I came out, my friend Carol did. She had a network of friends and came out, and then had to rebuild her life from there. So when I came out . . . I did it very gradual, very slow . . . When I went to college, I started talking with different gay people . . . I decided that I was bisexual. . . . It wasn't like I had all these friends here and then telling them I'm gay and them hating me. I didn't know anybody anymore, so I got all new friends. Like going out and buying all new stuff.

Having acknowledged a homosexual aspect of the self, the individual begins to focus upon physical, emotional, and social needs:

> My college had extensive computer facilities . . . so I moved into my own little world, in my own little room, off campus. I sealed myself up inside and didn't leave, even to go to class. Sat on my computer and I hooked up into the gay network. Nobody knew who you were, nobody could see you. And you could talk and talk and 'wig out.' Then someone from my college came on the computer. We said 'let's meet,' and arranged a meeting.

Identity acceptance

In the fourth stage, **Identity Acceptance**, self-esteem and social connections are developing.

> For me it was like someone turned on the light . . . everything made sense.

In this stage of identity development people selectively disclose their homosexual orientation to trusted "insiders," but are, for the most part, "in the closet."

> I have straight friends that have no idea that I'm gay . . . it's mainly a working type relationship. Other than that, all my friends are gay . . . I don't have very many straight friends.

Identity pride

If the secrecy and negative social status are unacceptable, the fifth stage of **Identity Pride** develops. This involves a polarization between people's own positive gay or lesbian identity and their perception of society's negative attitudes toward homosexuals. Anger and pride may develop. Individuals may confront heterosexuals and disclose their personal homosexual identity. If reactions are negative, their beliefs about heterosexuals are confirmed, and they may become entrenched in this stage. Some of the toughest encounters can be with one's own family:

> I didn't have a problem until I told my mother. . . . [Her] being a right-wing, fundamentalist Christian who was expecting grandchildren from me really made things sticky. After two days of the silent treatment, she woke me up one morning and threw me out of the house. . . . We didn't speak for a few months after that. She was planning on my school bills proving to be too overpowering, thus sending me back to her, begging to be let back in at any cost. . . . I did not give in, [and took] a full time job to keep myself in school. Six months later, I sent her a twelve page letter explaining that I was surviving, that her psychological embargo had failed, and if she wanted me as her son, she was to reestablish communication under mutual terms.

Identity synthesis

If enough heterosexuals' reactions to the confrontation and disclosure are positive, individuals may begin to integrate their gay or lesbian aspect and expect the world to be full of supportive as well as hostile people.

Some research has confirmed that many people's minority sexual identity formation goes through these stages (Brady & Busse, 1994; Levine, 1997). Though it is difficult to obtain anything but retrospective data on the first three stages, Levine (1997) found lesbians had typically taken 5 years between first questioning their heterosexuality and entering into an intimate lesbian relationship. In addition, the confrontational attitudes in the identity pride (5th) stage were associated with lower self-esteem than the identity tolerance (4th) stage. The identity synthesis (6th) stage showed the highest self-esteem and personality adjustment. The women in stage 5 were younger than those in stages 4 and 6 as well, which suggests that alienation and confrontation may be common for lesbians who come out in young adulthood, but not necessarily a stage all gays and lesbians will go through.

Sex differences in homosexual identity formation

Women are less likely than men to turn a few homosexual encounters into a homosexual or bisexual identity. To many females, lesbian experiences are simply normal extensions of female affection, and are often outgrowths of intense female friendships (Blumstein & Schwartz, 1977).

Men are more likely than women to discover their homosexuality in adolescence and in casual relationships (Minton & McDonald, 1984):

> [In] middle school . . . we had to take PE. . . . I never took a shower. There was this little hallway where a couple of people would always go and change because they couldn't be around the other people or were too embarrassed or whatever, and I was always one of those people. It started there. And it kinda grew into this admiration type thing, where I wanted to be like him, because he was cute. And then I became consciously aware of it.

In contrast, females are more likely to discover homosexuality in adulthood or when already in love with a female (Cass, 1990). Sheila came out at age 44.

> I was first married when I was 16. During the last five years with my second husband, I had 3 different lesbian relationships. He kept thinking I would change, that I would just have these flings and eventually find out this wasn't what I wanted. We were married almost 14 years . . . I've met at least 20 women in the last year that came out in their forties . . . it's usually after their kids are older, they come out.

Many emerging lesbian women have the supportive benefit of feminist thought and organizations (Paul, 1984). In comparison, teenage males generally experience less support from their lovers than do females, and little support from same-sex friends (Gulley, 1991; Kurdek, 1988a). Men report greater distress than females about a first homosexual experience (Paul, 1984; Schwartz & Blumstein, November, 1976).

> After the first encounter, I felt very ashamed and guilty. I could not sleep that night, and I felt almost like telling my parents. But then I thought that they

would not understand how I felt. While feeling extremely guilty, I told myself that I would never do this again . . . the worse thing was that I enjoyed it.

For most males, sexuality and self-concept develop together during adolescence, when peer groups have a crucial impact. Since male peer groups usually exaggerate their preoccupations with women, a developing gay adolescent can feel very alone:

I think we do feel left out sometimes. Never really being part of a group. I am always striving for that, to fit in. I didn't want to stand out from my peers. I was in a state of confusion, maybe I still am, because I was feeling one way but I could never act on it or express my feelings because no one else felt the way I did. . . . Maybe that's why there is a large number of teenage suicides for kids going through the same thing.

Some gay youths retreated from boys and cultivated friendships with girls instead:

My adolescent friendships were with girls. Boys harassed me. Expressing my emotions was essential to my stability, so I stayed around girls.

If both their peers and their family seem to be anti-gay, gay adolescents may have to postpone their identity development into their late teens or twenties. An advisor to a college gay group reports:

I've overheard a new guy asking one of the leaders what sort of music is gay and what brands of designer clothes to wear. There is so much attachment to symbols of gayness and so much conformity. They almost seem like adolescents.

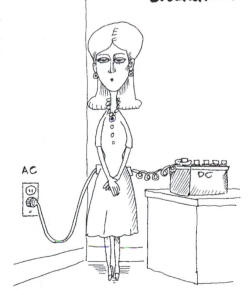

BISEXUALITY

Men who are developing gay identities today may find less hostility and more support than previous generations in America. But they are still likely to experience more turmoil than women do.

Bisexuality

Bisexuality is generally referred to as the capacity for erotic attractions to both males and females. Bisexuals, like homosexual and heterosexual persons, are a diverse population. Both of the following women fit the basic definition:

Linda, who was raised Catholic, has been contentedly married for fifteen years and has two adolescent children. She has recently discovered her attraction to women, and feels ashamed, frightened, and confused. Ashamed, because she has been taught that homosexuality is wrong. Frightened, because she doesn't want to jeopardize her marriage and knows that if she openly starts exploring her feelings toward other women, let alone dates one, her husband will leave her. And confused, because she has always considered herself monogamous, and has believed that you're either one thing or the other: married or single, straight or gay. She is also concerned about the impact her sexual desires might have on her children. However, she feels that unless she explores this other facet of herself, part of her will wither away and die.

Susan knew from an early age that she was attracted to both boys and girls. But by the time she reached her teens she felt scared and alone, because she was aware of the cultural taboo and unable to act on her attraction to women. While still in her teens, she did date several young men, but had reservations about the relationships because her gay side had to be hidden. During her first year of college, Susan was introduced to gay liberation. Now in her thirties, she has been happily and monogamously involved with a woman she met in college. Although Susan is still attracted to men, she feels more free to be herself when she is with another woman. She identifies herself as a lesbian and tells people that she is a lesbian, because she fears that if she says, "I'm bisexual," others will disregard and minimize the homosexual side of her and focus only on the acceptable heterosexual aspect of her orientation.

Both of these women's stories raise this question: Is sexual identity derived from behavior, fantasy, or both? Both women are aware of their attraction to both sexes but won't act on one type of attraction because they stand to lose too much in their interpersonal lives. Gender-role behavior is the key issue for this young man:

From the time he was a small child, Ralph loved playing with dolls, miniature furniture and dishes, and liked to dress himself in skirts and makeup. Although his mother was easygoing about his preferences, his father was furious and yelled that he couldn't stand his "faggot" son, that someday he'd make a "real man" out of Ralph. Now that Ralph is an adult, he is attracted to both women and men, but because of his preferences in dress, people have often considered him to be "less" than a man. "If I'm less than a man," Ralph has reasoned, "I must be a woman. And as a woman, my appropriate sexual partner must be a man." Though he feels attracted to both women and men, Ralph considers himself queer.

Some psychologists would label Ralph as **transsexual**, which designates a person who feels he or she is the opposite sex. Ralph's present homosexual identity may turn out to be a developmental phase for him on the way to a more satisfying bisexuality or transsexuality.

In contrast to the three people we have heard about, Joseph's bisexuality is neither a passing phase nor just a relational **history** of preferring first one sex and then the other. He acts on attractions to both sexes concurrently.

> Joseph's first sexual feelings were directed toward girls, and as an adult, he had many sexual and emotional relationships with women. However, at age 25, Joseph fell in love with a man, his first homosexual connection. Joseph and Howard have been together for five years now in a stable and gratifying "open" relationship where they each see other people, but regard each other as the primary partner. Howard occasionally sees other men. Joseph continues to have love affairs with women, whom he finds more sexually attractive than men. However, he remains devoted to Howard, and declines to label his sexual orientation. Joseph says that when he falls in love, he falls in love with the **person**. Whether the person is male or female isn't an issue.

Thus the label "bisexual" is misleadingly fixed (Blumstein & Schwartz, 1977), for persons who identify as bisexual need not be **equally** attracted to members of both sexes. Joseph is more sexually attracted to women, but possibly more emotionally comfortable and stable with Howard. Do some people need **both** sexes to be satisfied, and get something different from each one? Maybe that's not so crazy: How many heterosexual people are more at ease and satisfied relating to their own sex, even though they are avowedly sexually attracted *only* to the other sex? This idea of needing partners of both sexes for complete satisfaction is not widely expressed among bisexuals, however, since only ten percent endorsed it in one study (Klein, 1978).

The varieties of bisexuality

The concepts of bisexuality are so fluid that they challenge social norms and mainstream thinking about sexuality and identity. Is it behavior, fantasy, self-identification, or a combination of all three factors that determine if someone is bisexual? One Chicago study of men who reported sexual activity with both sexes in the last 3 years combined these factors and grouped them into 8 different bisexual male behavior patterns.

Only 59% of the bisexually active men in Table 8.3 considered themselves bisexual, while 31% identified as homosexual and 10% as heterosexual. This incongruity between identity and sexual behavior supports the grouping of bisexual and homosexual identity together in the most reliable research (Table 8.1). In more popular sexuality research, biased by the volunteer nature of the sample, 5% of men and 3% of women considered themselves bisexual, while only 4% of men and 2% of women identified as homosexual (Janus & Janus, 1992). Only 14% of the sample (bisexual group #7) had been approximately equally active sexually with both sexes, and they were very likely (82%) to currently have a male partner. The three

TABLE 8.3. Eight types of bisexual men in a Chicago study. Percent of sample (n = 443), Percent currently involved with a male or female partner, and description of sexual history

Group identity	Percent of sample	Percent with partner	Description
Gay #1	26	45% male	Gay fantasies; little involvement with women; 3 male partners in 6 months, 21 in lifetime.
Gay #2	5	17% male	Gay fantasies; little involvement with women; 19 male partners in 6 months, 90 in lifetime.
Heterosexual #3	6	48% female	Straight fantasies; 1.7 female partners in 6 months, 13 in lifetime; 0.5 male partners in 6 months, 3.7 in lifetime.
Heterosexual #4	4	65% female	Straight fantasies; 5.4 female partners in 6 months; 35 in lifetime; 1.6 male partners in 6 months, 7 in lifetime.
Bisexual #5	7.7	74% fem / 12% male	Bisexual fantasies; 6.3 female partners in 6 months, 46 in lifetime; 2.5 male partners in 6 months, 18 in lifetime.
Bisexual #6	34	27% fem / 5% male	Bisexual fantasies; 1.3 female partners in 6 months, 12 in lifetime; 3.4 male partners in 6 months, 25 in lifetime
Bisexual #7	14	18% fem / 82% male	Bisexual fantasies; 1.3 female partners in 6 months, 12 in lifetime; 2.2 male partners in 6 months, 19 in lifetime.
Bisexual #8	3	43% fem / 14% male	Bisexual fantasies; 2.4 female partners in 6 months, 26 in lifetime; 31.5 male partners in 6 months, 96 in lifetime.

Source: Combined from Taywaditep & Stokes, 1998.

groups with high numbers of partners (Gay #2, Straight #4, Bisexual #8) had the lowest self-esteem and highest psychological distress and drug problems. Those most likely to be involved with a current partner (Gay #1, Bisexual #5 & #7) had the highest self-esteem and least psychological distress and drug problems (Taywaditep & Stokes, 1998). Even this variety does not encompass all of bisexuality, for the first three out of our four examples of bisexually attracted people would not have volunteered or qualified for the study.

Are there biological bases for bisexuality?

Van Wyck and Geist (1995) suggest two biological factors that might be conducive to bisexuality: high eroticism and high masculinity. They list many research studies that have found that bisexual people engage in sexual fantasies and activities more frequently than either homosexual or heterosexual people. In addition, they report that women exposed to masculinizing hormones before birth may be more likely to engage in *bisexual* behavior as adults, rather than in exclusively *homosexual* behavior. And bisexual women may manifest more masculine sex role characteristics (Storms, 1980) and more masculine and less feminine personality characteristics than either heterosexual or lesbian women. Studies of men also found one genetic and one hormonal feature that might link bisexuality with "hypermasculinity," as well as with impulsivity (VanWyck & Geist, 1995).

Cultural Challenges of Bisexuality

The existence of bisexuality challenges cultural norms by suggesting that sexual desires and sexual identity are fluid and can change. Our identity is a mental construct that serves as an orientation point, so most of us would rather believe we are a fixed sexual entity. Bisexual activists have named this fixed identity **monosexuality**, compared with their **polysexual** choice, which offers more options.

Bisexuality also makes people uneasy who expect monogamy in their relationships. The word "bisexuality" sometimes evokes the image of unpredictable promiscuous behavior, known in the 1970s as "swinging." Although some bisexuals do in fact fit this category, 32% of those in Table 8.3 (Gay #1 and Straight #3) do not. Accepting bisexuality as a normal type of mature sexual identity challenges the mainstream view that stable sexual attractions, sexual identity, and monogamy—or serial monogamy—is the goal of psychosexual development.

We have no comparable quantitative research on bisexuality among women. But we estimate that their behavioral groups and percentages would be very different, since for them, emotional and personality attraction may be more relevant than physical attraction (Bhugra & de Silva, 1998). Women's bisexuality may appear in diverse contexts, including group marriage, prostitution, the women's movement, libertarian ideology, prison relationships, group sex, and friendships which become sexual (Blumstein & Schwartz, 1976).

Anti-bisexual prejudice

Because bisexuals threaten the concept of stable sexual identity, they may experience discrimination from both gay and straight groups (Blumstein & Schwartz, 1976; Paul, 1984). A bisexual woman caught flak from lesbians when she began a serious relationship with a man:

> A few gay women who knew of my relationships with men still considered me a lesbian. Others thought of me as a flake who straddled the fence, frivolously using women and unable to make up her mind. Still others designated me a defective lesbian, a betrayer of the ranks, someone who unfairly had the advantages of heterosexual visibility when she wanted them and enjoyed the "privilege" of being a lesbian, too.

A bisexual man notes:

> When I show up at [the community homosexual] church with a man, I'm greeted warmly and everybody's nice to me. But when I come with a woman, people are cold and ignore me.

Some theorists consider bisexuality a phase in homosexual identity formation, while others accept it as a mature endpoint (Fox, 1996). One study of bisexual men found that the one third who shifted towards gay identity in one year had been more psychologically healthy at the start (Stokes et al., 1997). But this third could correspond closely to the healthier gays (#1) and male-partnered bisexuals (#7) that comprised 40% of the Taywaditep and Stokes (1998) study illustrated in Table 8.3. There is evidence that bisexuals as a group have high self-esteem, autonomy, assertiveness, and mental flexibility (reviewed in Fox, 1996). Many bisexuals claim that their sexual orientation brings a richer, fuller life. Typically, they prefer bisexuality over heterosexual or homosexual lifestyles, and characterize bisexuality as an emotional, creative, and mental advantage (Klein, 1978). "Since we experience both heterosexuality and homosexuality, we are the ultimate expression of human sexual potential, and both heterosexuals and homosexuals could learn from our example to express their full potential" (Shaw, January, 1993, p. 49).

Gay and lesbian relationship development

Researchers estimate that 40% to 60% of gay men (Peplau et al., 1996) and 60% to 80% of lesbians (Klinger, 1996) are currently in relationships. Same-sex and heterosexual couples report similar levels of relationship satisfaction, and both have higher self-esteem and less psychological distress than those who are not in relationships (Peplau et al., 1996). Gay, lesbian, and heterosexual relationships are more similar than they are different. Both the similarities and the differences will concern us as we follow the development of same-sex relationships.

Attraction

Popular stereotypes may lead some to believe that gays like men who are "queeny" or feminine, and lesbians like women who are "butch" or masculine. It is also widely believed that partners in homosexual relationships are gender-role opposites, with one partner taking the feminine role and one partner taking the masculine role. Research indicates that many same-sex couples did adopt traditionally male and female roles in the 1950s, but since the 1970s most gays and lesbians reject this sort of gender role-taking (Peplau et al., 1996).

Research gives us a different picture of homosexual attractions as well. Since everyone has been exposed to the same gender ideals, gays, lesbians, and heterosexuals are often attracted to similar physical attributes considered desirable in the gender of their choice (DeHart & Cunningham, June, 1993). Anne describes what she finds attractive in a woman:

I like a Kim Basinger type. I guess [lesbians are] supposed to like dykes. I like the really pretty, sexy women. . . . My mother says I like hookers. I get criticized for that.

Understanding that gay men are attracted to masculinity rather than "gayness" helped this young athlete cope with a gay advance:

I couldn't believe that a homosexual would be interested in me. I thought I had heterosexual written all over me, but I guess not. Should I change the way I dress? Change my hair? Or what? Then I came to the conclusion that gay men look for the same types of looks in their lovers as the women that like guys. A good-looking man that is appreciated by women is also appreciated by gay men. No matter what I did, they would come up to me regardless, so I just needed a way to tell them no without kicking the hell out of them.

Whether gay or straight, men seem to place more emphasis on sexuality and looks in relationships than do women. In male stranger or group situations, such as computer dating or gay bars, good looks and body beauty seem to be the overriding factor. No matter how attractive or unattractive, assertive or unassertive the research subject was, his liking of another man after a two-hour computer-matched dancing date was directly proportional to the other man's looks (Sergios & Cody, 1986). Many gay men are very concerned with their own looks, since one survey showed half of gay men had below average images of their looks and bodies, compared to only one tenth of straight men (Hagen & Symons, 1979). Some tend to pursue a male "trophy beauty" and feel rejected if they themselves are not beautiful enough (Sergios & Cody, 1986). In the days before AIDS, many gay men acted on new sexual attractions the same night that they met. This combination of sexual freedom and perfectionistic beauty standards could create a lot of suffering when men could come to a party with one partner and go home afterwards with another. Even today, gay men may feel the tyranny of beauty as much as women do:

Being overweight myself, I've had the line "let's just be friends" thrown back at me when I ask for a date, only to see the person cavort off ten minutes later with some nameless pretty-boy. I've been accused of "whining" and "bringing it all on myself" (depression, anger, frustration) when I've confronted friends about discrimination from within the gay community.

Youth is viewed as just as important as beauty in today's gay culture:

[As we] slowly gravitate toward having longer, more committed relationships, it becomes extremely important to find your life partner before you get too old. I have heard the concern expressed amongst my friends in their early to mid thirties that they need to hurry up and find husbands while they are still pretty enough to do so.

Women, lesbian or heterosexual, seem to place more emphasis on personality characteristics and monogamy than men do (Deaux & Hanna, 1984; Bell & Weinberg, 1978). This may be partly due to social influence, since feminist oriented lesbian groups feel that their own attractions and sexual fantasies about "beautiful" women are unwanted influences of a patriarchal culture.

> I had a friend tell me the other day, "You really like pretty, sexy, slutty-looking women." I pride myself on not liking people because of their looks. It's embarrassing for me because I'm a very down-to-earth person. Like it's hypocritical for me to say, "Oh, beauty's not everything" when the only people that catch my interest are . . . you know . . . I don't like it.

Meeting partners

Gays and lesbians have to be very cautious about homosexual attracting behavior, because observers may become hostile or spread gossip. Therefore gay or lesbian social groups and gay bars are the primary meeting places.

> It was 1976 and there was this club . . . a bar . . . and there was a woman's band . . . I started meeting all these people and it was like a whole new world. I didn't realize there were other people like me.

Other gays and lesbians meet in many of the same ways as do heterosexuals: at work, through friends, in college classes, and at cafés. How do they know if someone is gay?

> It's hard to explain. When I talk to this person, it's like heat's coming off her body.

> For me, it's eye contact. There's something about the way our eyes meet. Sometimes you stumble a little . . . like, 'I know he looked at me, but what if I'm wrong?' So then you just keep playing the eye contact game until you're sure. Then you try to strike up a conversation.

> I can pretty much always tell if a guy is gay. It's "gaydar."

Eye contact across a crowded room, shared group activities, a compliment, a question, are ways we all use to meet someone to whom we are attracted.

Gay dating

As with heterosexual partners, some gays and lesbians wait until a relationship is established before engaging in sexual activity. Sometimes this can take quite a while.

I kept thinking 'This is crazy . . . that I've got, like, a crush on her' . . . so I told her I had a crush on her . . . and then she jumps up and says, 'Oh my god, I've had a crush on you the whole time!' . . . so we went for about four months when all we did was hold hands and kiss. And then, finally. I was with her for a year.

Others may "fool around" on dates or engage in "one night stands." Some young men go through a period of promiscuous sex, which is considered normal by many heterosexual men as well. For young gay men the search for sexual conquests may be a response to shame for not being what their families or they themselves expected them to be. They experience themselves as lovable only when other men want them. Some gays report considerable confusion about what is normal when they begin gay dating:

Dating in the gay community seems to be one of those skills that someone has written a book on, but no one owns. . . . I have yet to find a formal means of meeting people to date. I suppose [this is] because [where I live] very few people are 'out' enough, and those that are out are so wary of men out for just a quick roll in the hay, that you're under immediate suspicion if you show interest.

Lesbians have long preferred committed monogamous relationships, and trends of monogamy and safer sexual behaviors are increasing among gays as well (Blumstein & Schwartz, 1990; Juran, 1989).

AIDS isn't a joke, and it only takes one time to get infected. I told him, "If you do not get tested, I do not want to start this relationship."

Developing a partnership

Two processes contribute to the intensity of the early months of gay relationships: blending or merging, and passionate love along with high sexual activity (McWhirter & Mattison, 1984).

In the early stages of involvement both gay and straight relationships are likely to have a lot of physical intimacy and accentuate similarities between the partners. Sometimes passion drives this process, and differences in needs, wants, and interests are overlooked (Nichols, 1982). When this happens, the couple may skip "getting to know each other" and move quickly into an all-consuming partnership. While heterosexual couples normally act out sex-typed roles and participate in differ-

ent recreational activities, gay and lesbian couples are likely to have the same gender attitudes, the same friends, and common values and emotional responses (McWhirter & Mattison, 1984).

If the couple cohabitates, closet space, dresser drawers, and clothes may be shared. As a result, partners' individualities may be submerged and personal space may disappear (Kaufman et al., 1984). Thus merger, or "losing oneself in the other" (McWhirter & Mattison, 1984), can be first a high experience and later a problem for same-sex couples. Since most women have experienced interdependency, closeness, and identity overlap in relation to their mothers (Chodorow, 1998), many lesbians may re-create such female closeness (Lindenbaum, 1985), for they are frequently reputed to merge.

In one study, lesbians reported more couple intimacy but not more fusion of selves than married women (Anderson, 1990). Other studies found that lesbians having more friends and activities together had higher relationship satisfaction (Donaldson, 1993; Eldridge & Gilbert, 1990). Yet lesbian women voice the same concerns about merging as heterosexual women often do:

> I think that's the thing that bothers me most when I'm with a woman. That's what I'm struggling a lot now with . . . I think, "how do I keep from losing myself."

Though the merging may be more extensive in early lesbian relationships, sexual frequency and intensity may be greater in gay male relationships. Needing secrecy in the face of mainstream social disapproval can also keep emotional arousal high in a "Romeo and Juliet effect." For some lesbians, gays, and heterosexuals, the intensity of passionate beginnings is habit-forming, and love is defined as high intensity passion and romance. When that intensity moderates, people may believe their love is fading. This is the most common cause for gay men to end their relationship in the first year (Mattison & McWhirter, 1987). To recover the excitement of sexual intensity, gay men may turn to extra-relationship sex, which can catalyze jealousy and possessiveness. Though many gay relationships accommodate outside sexual affairs, outside lesbian affairs typically develop emotional intimacy and lead to a breakup (Peplau et al., 1996).

The intense blending of new lovers may be emotionally threatening to gay men (Mattison & McWhirter, 1987). Compared to women, gay males are not likely to have enjoyed as much closeness in childhood. Some have felt alienated from everyone and shut down emotionally. They may seek sexual intensity, but be totally unfamiliar with the emotions of intimacy and retreat from them, just as many heterosexual men do.

Nesting

During and following the process of blending, commitment deepens and the shared house becomes a home. Partners find compatibility or

TABLE 8.4. Stages of long-term gay males couple relationships

Stages	Time	Characteristics	Manifestations
1. Blending	First year	Blending Being in love Equal partnership High sexual activity	Sharing similarities, exclusive time together Altered state, passionate yearning for partner Equal financial responsibilities, division of chores Several encounters a week, exclusivity in actions
2. Nesting	1 to 3 years	Homemaking Finding compatibility Decline in passion Ambivalence	Decorating & arranging joint living quarters Create complementary activities & interests Pursuer-distancer dynamics, external sex, jealousy Compatibility & disappointments, security & vulnerability
3. Maintaining	3 to 5 years	Individualization Risk-taking Dealing with conflict Relying on the relationship	Re-emerging individual differences & needs Time apart, separate friendships, self disclosure Tolerating conflict & resolution or avoidance Expecting comfort, familiarity, & dependability
4. Building	5 to 10 years	Collaborating Productivity Establishing independence Partners' dependability	Cooperating, routines, declining communication Individual & mutual career & financial achievement Independent decisions & commitments revitalize each partner, & couple bond retains high priority Steady support, guidance, & affirmation
5. Releasing	10 to 20 years	Trusting Merging money and possessions Constriction Take each other for granted	Accepting partner as imperfect, friendship bond Surrendering & consolidating resources, no separate accounting Boredom, distance from partner, physical decline Relationship ruts, neglecting appreciation & affection
6. Renewing	Over 20 years	Achieving security Shifting perspectives Restoring partnership Remembering	Permanence, emotional & financial security in age Awareness of mortality, aging, lost attractiveness Crises require reexamination, talking, renewal Sharing about mutual history, commentary on life

Sources: McWhirter & Mattison, 1984, 1985.

complementarity of activities and attitudes as new love decreases and emotional openness and vulnerability increase (McWhirter & Mattison, 1984).

> *After a while, we realized that we needed a space that included both of us. We moved into a new apartment, where we both took part in decorating and layout. We each had a place for our own things and our lives were more integrated.*

McWhirter and Mattison (1984, 1987) have organized many of the issues of this and subsequent stages into a model for gay male relationships, included here in Table 8.4. Testing this stage model, Kurdek and Schmitt (1986a) found that couples in their second and third years (nesting stage) reported more stress and disillusionment, less satisfaction with affection and sex, and less shared activity than both those in their first year (blending) and those in their fourth and fifth years (maintaining). Most importantly, these particular stage-specific characteristics were found in **all types of couples—gay, lesbian, heterosexual married, and heterosexual cohabiting**. This is the most extensive stage model for long-term couples anywhere. It was based on interviews with 156 gay male couples. But Kurdek and Schmitt's research suggests that it may provide insights into the life cycles of lesbian and heterosexual couples as well.

Long-term partnerships

Researchers have found that approximately half of gay male couples and about 75% of lesbian couples live together (Blumstein & Schwartz, 1990). Trust, love, and communication tend to be stable relationship values in both same-sex and heterosexual couples (Peplau et al., 1996):

> *Honesty. That's it. That makes it a relationship . . . if you're not honest, what kind of relationship are you having?*

> *Communication is very important to me. Whatever is on my mind, I say it. When I have any type of problem I always tell my partner how I feel.*

Gay males emphasize sexuality in relationships more than heterosexuals do (Kurdek, 1995; Blumstein & Schwartz, 1983). Kurdek (1995) adds that after 10 years together, gay male couples have sex less frequently than heterosexual married couples and frequently devise explicit arrangements for sexual activity outside of the relationship. Acceptance of sexual nonexclusivity is unique to male couples, although this feature may be declining due to the danger of AIDS. McWhirter and Mattison (1984) reported that none of the couples they studied in San Diego in 1979 who were together more than 5 years were sexually exclusive. But later, in a geographically diverse sample, Kurdek (1988a) found 26% of couples together over 10 years did maintain sexual exclusivity. Both exclusive and nonexclusive couples seemed equally satisfied with their relationship, though the exclusive couples reported less tension and more need for closeness and interdependence (Kurdek & Schmitt, 1986b) Why do men seek novel sexual encounters, with more gays (three fourths or more) than straights (a fourth to a third) (Wiederman, 1997) pursuing them, and also more frequently? Men seem to identify sexual satisfaction with sexual intensity, something most likely to be experienced in new love affairs, which we will discuss in Chapter 9. Since gay men do not have wives or childrearing concerns, they can arrange their love lives however it suits them.

In contrast, lesbians report less frequent sex, but emphasize cuddling, companionship, and reciprocal dependence and equality more than heterosexuals (Kurdek & Schmitt, 1986c; Blumstein & Schwartz, 1983). But frequency of orgasms is not an appropriate way to measure women's sexuality. While gay male and heterosexual sex may last for only minutes, lesbian sex is frequently more enduring (Frye, 1990; Schwartz, June, 1991).

Men have foreplay in order to get you ready. With women, foreplay is the whole thing, and women don't want to do anything else . . . they don't want to end it . . . foreplay is what it's all about.

Like gay men, lesbians are unrestricted by the sexual needs and habits of the opposite sex, so they are free to suit themselves.

Gender roles and power

Gays and lesbians also differ from traditional heterosexuals in the roles enacted in a relationship. Research has indicated that gender roles are less prevalent and shared decision making is more common in homosexual relationships (Kurdek & Schmitt, 1986d). Over 90% of gays and lesbians surveyed agree that power in romantic relationships should be "exactly equal." But only about 60% of lesbians and 40% of gay men, compared to 50% of heterosexual married women and 40% of heterosexual married men reported such equality in their current partnership (Peplau et al., 1996). Male couples may be more likely to have an unequal balance of power, because more male partners have large differences in age and income (Blumstein & Schwartz, 1983).

Homosexual relationships in a hostile society

The presence of general social hostility toward homosexuality makes social support for individuals very influential. Finding support is important for both self-esteem and relationship satisfaction (Jordan, 1995; Smith & Brown, 1997). Gays and lesbians are more likely to find acceptance among selected friends than from their families, but support from at least one partner's family may have a more positive impact on their relationship than support from friends (Kurdek, 1988a; Caron & Ulin, 1997).

In order to avoid public hostility, some gays and lesbians simply "stay in the closet." But one partner may wish to be affectionate in public, while the other partner wants to keep the relationship "behind closed doors." Both partners may be dissatisfied.

It's very difficult for me to pretend that my partner is just a friend in public. We're very affectionate at home, and all of a sudden we walk out of the house and I can't touch her. Sometimes you get so used to the [public] distance that you don't even get close at home. Before you know it, that force—that precept against being close—drives the passion out of the relationship.

Members of homosexual partnerships strive for validation in a society which *passive-*

ly fails to acknowledge the legitimacy of their bond (Slater & Mencher, 1991). Same-sex couples are legally barred from marriage, so engagement parties, weddings, and anniversaries are often bypassed without notice. But gays and lesbians have developed their own rituals which celebrate their relationships, support positive self-esteem, and increase warmth and communication with significant others (Manodori, 1997). Though rituals such as birthdays and anniversaries may be borrowed from mainstream culture, they are important because these are the *only* ones the couple may enact (Slater, 1995).

> *I'm big on celebrating every month the anniversary. I feel like we don't have anything else, so every month on that day is like a little mini-celebration . . . For a while, it was every week . . . I would leave flowers on her door.*

Lenore and Jean, like many other homosexual couples, arranged a wedding ceremony:

> *I married Jean at age 21. We had 8 bridesmaids and 8 best men . . . they were all heterosexual couples . . . close friends of ours. . . . We married at a gay bar. Everyone wore white—white tuxes, white dresses. We've been married thirty years now.*

Parenthood

Not only do 20% of lesbians and 10% of gay males have children, but millions of children have at least one homosexual parent (Bozett, 1987; Gottman, 1990). Thus, parenthood is an important issue for many gays and lesbians in committed relationships. Lenore's and Jean's children are from previous partnerships:

> *Jean and I have 26 children and grandchildren together.*

Other same-sex couples have their own children through surrogate motherhood, artificial insemination, or adoption. Though some research has demonstrated that gay or lesbian parents are no more likely than heterosexual parents to raise children who become maladjusted or gay (Allen & Burrell, May, 1994), there is much social hostility against homosexual parents.

> *I was married to my husband when I fell in love with a woman. During the marriage, I always took care of the kids. When I filed for divorce, I told the truth in the court about being a lesbian, and the judge gave my husband custody. I'm still battling for it. You don't give up. You gotta put in that extra effort. I love my kids, and when they visit, it's obvious that he's not really caring for them. I hope [my struggle] helps somebody else, if not me, somebody else down the road.*

Since society is usually very uncomfortable about same-sex couples raising children, baby showers, children's birthday celebrations, and bar mitzvahs are either not held or boycotted by family members. The couple and their children are often not recognized as a family, and partners and stepchildren are often not accepted into each partner's family of origin (Slater & Mencher, 1991). Yet, having same-sex parents may be similar to being raised by a mother and an aunt, or a father and an uncle. In the face of disrespect, gay and lesbian couples must continually struggle to maintain a cohesive family structure.

Durability and dissolution of relationships

Despite the social climate around them, committed same-sex couples may be about as stable as heterosexual couples. In a large study over an 18-month period of couples together for 2 years or less, 4% of married couples and 17% of cohabiting heterosexuals separated, compared to 22% of lesbians and 16% of gays. Among couples together at least 10 years, the separation rate was 4% for married couples, 4% for gays, and 6% for lesbians—there were not enough heterosexual cohabiters to compare (Blumstein & Schwartz, 1983). Thus the most significant difference in the breakup rates was between couples who were married and couples who were not. Therefore we can speculate that the most significant factors that raise separation rates are lack of support for the relationship from family and society and lack of legal support (insurance, medical care, community property) and barriers to separation (divorce laws). In fact, Kurdek (1998a) found that the lack of social forces and legal barriers against breaking up was the *only* difference between lesbians and heterosexual wives that was statistically related to their relationship breakups.

A few social aspects may work together. First, most gay and lesbian relationships remain "couple" relationships, that is, without children or incorporation into an extended family. Sharing a common love for children and family strengthens a couple bond and acts as a barrier to breaking up, as the elevated divorce rate of childless opposite-sex couples indicates. Second, both partners normally have careers, and devotion to career, differences over money, and not pooling finances all make couples more likely to separate (Blumstein & Schwartz, 1983). Since same-sex relationships are likely to follow the model of "best friends" (compare *peer marriage* in Chapter 7), lack of common interests is also listed as a reason for breaking up (Peplau & Gordon, 1983). Other reasons for breaking up echo those most frequently listed by heterosexuals: no communication, alcohol problems, and "she had an affair" (Kurdek, 1991).

Theorists and clinicians have suggested that two further problems may contribute to same-sex couple breakups which are due to male and female socialization (Reece & Segrist, 1981; Roth, 1985). Following from the feminine role as caretakers, many women tend to feel responsible for others in relationships. These women may suppress competitive and aggressive impulses in order to avoid hurting others, and emphasize empathy and care (Kurdek, 1991; Roth, 1985). This combines with the previously mentioned issues of merger and loss of boundaries and the individual sense of self (Lindenbaum, 1985).

> *When I was with her, I think that I focused on what was going on in her life. But I don't need to be in a relationship with someone who wants to be with me 24 hours a day. I think I need to find out who I am, and what I want. I think I was defining what I want by what she could give me.*

At least for younger lesbians, merging can be both fulfilling and stifling. For committed couples mutuality is associated with higher and autonomy with lower satisfaction (Donaldson, 1993), but escape from merger was the most common reason given for breaking up. Half of Peplau and Gordon's (1983) sample said they needed their own independence, and a third saw this need in their partner.

In contrast, as males, many gay men have learned to compete, to suppress feelings, and to value sexuality as a demonstration of masculinity. Researchers have suggested that gays may therefore have more conflicts involving expression of affection, communication, and sexuality in relationships (Kurdek & Schmitt, 1986d; Reece & Segrist, 1981).

Recovering from a breakup

Gays and lesbians typically do not receive as much familial support as do heterosexuals, and they may feel especially uncomfortable disclosing their most vulnerable feelings to friends and relatives (Kurdek, 1988a). Being so alone after so many years with a partner can be devastating.

Kurdek (1991) found that persons who adjusted best to breakups were likely to be more educated, to have not pooled finances, and to have had less commitment to their partners. As with heterosexual relationships, another common problem for gays and lesbians after a breakup is financial disruption. If they owned property together, such as a house, there are no laws (like those for heterosexual divorce) to regulate the separation and protect the partners from wreaking economic vengeance on each other.

> *I've been trying to break up for with Leslie for two years already. But she says she won't leave the house, so I'll have to leave. But she won't buy out my share of the house either—says I'll never get any money out of her if I leave. She's hurt that I want to leave, and I can't afford to move out and lose my biggest life investment.*

Another common problem after a breakup is the relationship with the former partner. The gay/lesbian community is small compared to the heterosexual society, and meeting places for gays and lesbians are limited. Since most partners' friendship networks have been closely intertwined, avoiding contact with these mutual friends may mean avoiding the entire gay or lesbian "scene" in the town. Otherwise, contact with one's ex-partner in the local community seems inevitable, whether it is desired or not.

On the upside, many gays and lesbians surveyed by Kurdek (1991) also expressed positive feelings after relationship dissolution. These included personal growth and relief from conflict.

Community support for gay men and lesbians

We are the only social minority that doesn't get support from their families. We have to become family for each other.

Friendship

Many gay people have lost their trust in most or all of their families, whose closeness, loyalty, and even respect have wavered or ceased. Their **friends** have become their **relatives**. These friends may be straight or gay—what is most important is their trust, loyalty, and respect. Heterosexual friends typically notice and like the exceptional support and loyalty they receive, but they may misunderstand the gay people's feelings.

A college student reports on coming out to his friends.

I told two or three close straight friends, and our relationships have been much better. They know that I don't want them. But they want you to be attracted to them. I said, "You're just not my type." They were disappointed.

Durable friendships are also essential for some gay men who do not have long-term partners. Two middle-aged men assess their relationships:

A gay man says: *You have two different relationships in the gay community, friends and lovers. Friends are points of stability. Lovers may come and go, but friends are the people you can really rely on for the long haul.*

A straight man says: *My friendships with gay men are like the best straight friendships, where the feelings are known—the feeling that you know you like and admire each other. But there's a difference. My gay friend will have feelings I could never expect and don't understand either. When he doesn't show me a feeling, he seems just like any other friend [because straight friends don't show many feelings either]. But when feelings do come out, they can be really hard to deal with.*

Many gays and lesbians form highly nurturing bonds and sublimate any erotic feelings that are present, in the same way as teachers, ministers, counselors, coaches, and other mentors do. In fact, the historical model of **Platonic friendship**, exemplified by Socrates, included erotic feelings which were channeled into nonsexual intimacy, with self-knowledge and personal development as major goals (in Plato's *Phaedrus*). The network of enduring friendships that many gay people develop helps sustain them more than is normal in heterosexual groups, unless they are close ethnic or religious communities. A gay pastor comments:

> *I think we are special people. Gay people have known so much suffering, that they are very willing to share the love that they have.*

The growth of gay and lesbian community

The first generation.   The community of gays, lesbians, and bisexuals in the United States has only been developing since World War II. The "first generation" in the 1940s and 1950s founded the first gay and lesbian social organizations and the first gay church, and established the first gay bars, bath houses, and resort areas as places to meet.

For half a century, mainstream clinical psychology had declared homosexual orientation to be a mental disorder. Police considered gay people and gay businesses appropriate prey for harassment. But in 1969, following raids on five New York City gay bars, a critical mass of organized resentment was reached. When police officers raided the Stonewall Inn in Greenwich Village, they found themselves surrounded and outnumbered by enraged gay people. The Stonewall revolt was the symbolic beginning of an organized gay liberation movement that insisted upon **respect** for gay, lesbian, and bisexual people.

The middle generation.   The "middle generation" came of age during the burst of excitement that followed the Stonewall revolt. In the 1970s and 1980s, the older organizations and meeting places expanded, and new political, artistic, and social groups sprang up. Writers and researchers faced down the hostility toward alternative sexuality in the academic and publishing worlds and sought the truth about homosexual experience. Whole neighborhoods in San Francisco, New York City, Los Angeles, and other large urban areas became centers of gay life.

The influence of the AIDS epidemic.   The AIDS virus decimated this middle generation of active and reflective gay men. It focused the gay community's energy on caring for the sick, on medical research, on the insurance industry, on the government's contribution to the health crisis, and on burying the dead. The spread of AIDS radically transformed what it meant to be gay. But under the burden of this tragedy, the gay community pulled together more than ever before and grew in compassion and spirituality.

Since the media can't resist a tragedy, the mainstream society was touched by the AIDS crisis as it never had been by the gay liberation movement. Heterosexual mainstream reactions ranged from sympathy to horror to hostile triumph. However, major mainstream news media and many businesses have eliminated anti-homosexual prejudice and have begun to treat gay people with respect.

The new generation.   The new generation of post–AIDS gay men and women have seen their issues publicized on the television talk shows. Most take being gay for granted and consider themselves mainstream Americans. They expect to be politically active, both within and outside of the Republican and Democratic Parties (Browning, 1993). As they strive for long-term partnerships, the specter of AIDS may still haunt them like a third person:

> *After about two months, at my request Daniel had an HIV screening. My last lover had been positive, certainly it wouldn't happen twice. Well, it did. When faced with mortality, Daniel went into a funk. He experienced the stages leading to acceptance of his death.*
>
> *During this period, which lasted over a year, my in-love feelings never declined, but Daniel was distant and communication was very poor. I wanted to be the strong one, I wanted him to lean on me, and I needed to lean on him. Independently, we both sought counseling. After hard work by both of us, it was time to repair what had happened to "us."*

Thanks to 50 years of community-building efforts, today many more gays and lesbians in many more places can find strength and support through organizations and institutions. Gay community activities instill a sense of identity, hopefulness, and solidarity.

> *My first conference was a meeting of the National Lesbian and Gay Student Associations. There were hundreds of bright, creative, energetic people—all gay or lesbian or bisexual! There were invited speakers, workshops on love, sex, discrimination, activism, you name it. We all stayed in the same hotel and had parties and discussions in the evenings. It was really very inspirational, and VERY affirming.*

In many cities, gay and lesbian hotlines offer support and referral to appropriate groups, gathering places, and gay-friendly businesses. There are directories of services and festivals across the United States and internationally, such as the *GaYellow Pages* and *The Women's Traveler*. PFLAG (Parents and Friends of Lesbians and Gays) provides a supportive network for heterosexual friends and family members of gay people. Anne adds a final note of reassurance:

> *Never apologize for being yourself. If you're with people that you have to apologize to for being yourself and if you love women, or if you love men and you're a man, never apologize for that, because it's not that unusual. There are a lot of us out there that are just like you, that feel the same way. You're just gay.*

Through stories and research we find some preliminary cognitive road maps for understanding homophobia and homosexual relationships. Our biographical portraits of what it is like to be in a **sexual minority** are similar to the experience of other minority groups. Careful attention to similarities and differences between these experiences and our own could be as illuminating as exploring the contrasting personal experience of women and men. For fully exploring our diversity deepens our insight into human nature and ourselves as a part of it.

Chapter summary

- Nonheterosexual orientation may be essential (inborn) or socially constructed, or both. Less than 2% of women and 3% of men identify as homosexual, but around twice that many have had recent same-sex partners.
- Evidence is mounting, but still inconclusive, for connecting homosexual orientation to genetics, prenatal hormones, and brain structure, as well as environmental influences.
- Sex-atypical behavior or professions and early sexual abuse or imprinting are possible developmental influences. But all these could also be due to inborn tendencies.
- Homophobia is discomfort or aversion or moral opposition to homosexuality, and is connected to gender-role socialization, religion, age, heterosexual experience, and unfounded fears of sexual predation on children.
- Homophobia can be explained as confusion and defensive avoidance reactions arising from unfamiliarity with homosexual behavior. Familiarity reduces it.
- Homophobia among developing gay people brings shame and self-destructive behavior.
- The 6 stages of homosexual identity formation are **identity confusion, identity comparison, identity tolerance**, **identity acceptance**, **identity pride**, and **identity synthesis**.
- While lesbian identity is supported by feminism and often comes through love in adulthood, gay awareness often arises during casual adolescent sex and grows in the midst of hostile peers.
- Bisexuality is a fluid, changing identity which blurs straight and gay categories, and may be connected to a high sex drive.
- Many gay men are attracted to rugged, athletic men, are concerned about their looks (Van Wyk & Geist, 1995, p. 20), and are focused on sex, including some promiscuity. However, AIDS has made gay men more cautious. Lesbians seek feminine partners, affection, and monogamous romantic relationships.
- Lesbians may merge and lose themselves in love. Gay men may seek

sexual intensity, but be overwhelmed by emotional intensity and then seek the thrill of new romance.

- As couples build a nest and configure their relationships, passion abates, and gays may accept external affairs, while lesbians may break up because of them.
- Same-sex couples share power and strive for equality and flexibility of roles, unless age and income are quite different.
- Societal disrespect makes social support crucial, so innovative couple rituals are devised.
- Same-sex couples break up as frequently as do heterosexuals, except that legal and social supports are lacking for either staying together or separating. Additional breakup causes may be lack of children and family, careers, women "losing themselves," and men's inexpressiveness.
- Friendships form the basis of gay and lesbian communities, which have grown since World War II. AIDS shifted awareness toward caring and more rights. Support networks have expanded.

Biosocial and evolutionary perspectives 9

The human sciences regularly attribute our personalities and behavior to two main influences—nature and nurture, or biology and culture. We explore social explanations in Chapter 7. Here we focus on explanations that combine biology and society (i.e., are **biosocial**). We will consider the theoretical framework that attempts to include all of human history at once, **Sociobiology**, and its cousin in psychology, **Evolutionary Psychology**.

Sociobiology is a roughly thirty-year-old hybrid discipline that posits that the Darwinian theory of evolution by genetic variation and natural selection must apply to human nature and human society as well as it does to every other species. Sociobiology seeks a unified theory of human nature and behavior through a **vertical integration** of all the human sciences (Barkow, 1991). This means that research explanations from all levels should fit together. In the last 10 years, some psychologists involved in this new development have named their subfield **evolutionary psychology** (Buss, 1994).

Biosocial theories stir up controversy. They upstage and irritate scientists who study the details of human existence, and then see their findings linked into generalizations about human nature that evoke political controversy (e.g., that women evolved to bear and care for children). However, a conceptual approach that stretches from molecules to world cultures and from couple interaction to the natural selection of genes can liberate us from our own personality-based, ethnocentric, and contemporary biases (here and now is the best or worst of all times). It can also awaken in us a zest for contrast and controversy that arises when many scientific disciplines meet over "the puzzle of human nature." But keep in mind that there is not just one best way for the pieces of human nature to fit together.

Evolutionary psychology of sex and love

Biosocial theory posits these basic principles to explain human nature (Barkow, 1991):

1. Human physiology, thinking, emotions, personality characteristics, and behavior have evolved via genetic mutation and natural selection over hundreds of thousands of years to adapt to the environment.
2. The goals of adaptation are **survival** and **reproductive fitness**, meaning environmental success both for our offspring and ourselves, and have been shaped by evolution.
3. Since humans have only developed agriculture in the last 10,000 years, over 99% of our evolution has been as cooperative hunters and gatherers (Wilson, 1978). Therefore, the human group has always been a vital part of our environment for which we have evolved adaptive characteristics.
4. Because our environments vary and have changed so much, and humans have competed with other predators, we have evolved a **sexual selection** process which promotes a great diversity of genetic mixtures to maximize our chances of success (Daly & Wilson, 1978). Therefore we exist in two types, male and female, who come from different families to mate with each other.

Sex and gender characteristics are at the very heart of biosocial theory. We will consider the gender differences that sociobiology accentuates. Why, for instance, are men more quickly and more visually arousable than women? And why are men often less discriminating in regard to with whom they want to have sex? But before attempting to answer, first let us consider a question of profound significance for human culture:

What's love got to do with it? (Human evolution, that is.)

What's love got to do with human evolution?

The answer, according to Anthony Walsh (1991b), is that love and intelligence developed together in human evolution. These two characteristics have enabled us to dominate over **most** other species (though ants, rats, cockroaches, and viruses are still thriving competitors!). Love and intelligence are also necessary for our own and our world's preservation and harmony into the foreseeable future. Here is how they have evolved:

...DON'T MOVE! WE'VE GOT YOU COVERED!

ANCIENT HOMO SAPIENS WERE ABLE TO COOPERATE ON KILLS WITH SOCIAL HUNTING

1. The first step in the evolution of humanoid primates that would eventually lead to Homo sapiens came when the drought-induced retreat of African forests over 2 million years ago selected for those hominids who were better at adapting to the grassy plains. These ancestors were more comfortable standing upright, better with their eyes and hands, and more clever at making tools and weapons. They could also *cooperate* with each other to kill animals much larger, stronger, and faster than themselves, such as lions and antelope.
2. These hominids steadily increased their intelligence by passing on what they learned to their offspring—and, in the process, evolving complex language and memory. Their brains became larger in relation to the rest of their bodies, growing about one tablespoon in size every thousand years for more than two million years until the emergence of Homo sapiens a quarter of a million years ago (Wilson, 1978).
3. The skull to house such a brain became too big to pass through the birth canal in a pelvis thickened to support two-legged walking. So babies had to be born before their brains were fully developed. Human infants may need about as many months after birth as they had inside the womb just to reach a developmental stage comparable to other mammals at birth (Walsh, 1991b).
4. Human evolution capitalized on this developmental lag and lengthy dependency period. Taking longer to develop self-sufficiency than other animals allows humans to learn (and incorporate into their brain's neuronal configuration) more from caretakers. Humans are thus less restricted by their genetic programming and more adaptable after birth than any other species.

5. Adaptation to this long dependency period involves someone who fulfills the infant's needs reliably and unconditionally. This unconditional nurturing is the most essential form of **love**. Nurturant love is a biological attribute of women, and may be present but less dominant and more flexible in men.

6. Not only reliable care, but face-to-face interaction, environmental stimulation, and both mother's milk and tactile stimulation of the baby's skin contribute significantly to the formation and connection of neuronal pathways in the infant's postnatally incomplete brain (Rice, 1977). The quantity and quality of neuronal connections may be a concrete measure of intellectual capacity in adults (Begley, June, 1993) and of the capacity for future intellectual development in infants. Thus nurturing attention is critical for the development of intelligence in each human being.

7. Mothers of infants needed someone to provide food, shelter, protection, and social support. Either reliable kinfolk or pairbonding with the father (or both) would do. These two different support strategies allow diversity in social structures to support childbearing (see parental investment below).

8. Pairbonding between fathers and mothers borrows biological mechanisms from nurturant love and is facilitated by face-to-face sex with great pleasure attached. For example, oxytocin, a neurochemical associated with breastfeeding and baby-cuddling in women, increases three to five times its normal level in men during sexual climax (Fisher, 1992).

9. Thus the ultimate reason for love between the sexes is to foster **parental investment** of time, energy, material resources, and love in the human infants. The fundamental differences in mating and parenting between humans—in both hunter-gatherer and modern societies—and other primates and mammals are: prolonged juvenile dependence on parents after weaning, parental support of multiple young at different ages, marriage, fathers' continued involvement in child care and support, and a long postreproductive life span with older nonreproductive relatives supporting the younger generation's offspring (Kaplan et al., 1998).

10. Psychophysical systems in animals that evolved for specific environmental adaptations are all interconnected, so the same systems can be redeployed for other purposes. Since humans needed to cooperate to hunt animals, and men needed to leave their wives and babies to hunt for and protect their group, the whole group could help care for the young. The psychophysical systems evolved for sexuality and nurturant love (attachment) could adapt to reinforce reciprocal care among group members. The sex difference in energy investment in children fostered different and somewhat clashing **dual mating strategies** for men and women. Thus, men

TABLE 9.1. Tasks Performed Predominantly by Women and Men in Most Cultures. Tasks predominantly performed by one sex in all known cultures in bold, exclusively in most cultures with asterisk*

Women	Men
Caring for infants	Warfare*
Gathering plants	Metal & weapon making*
Cooking	Hunting, trapping
Fetching water & fuel	Political leadership
Spinning yarn	Fishing, herding, butchering
Making & repairing clothing	Lumbering, mining
Preserving food & dairy	Clearing & preparing land
	Building houses
	Working wood & stone

Sources: Daly & Wilson, 1978; Ember & Levinson, 1991.

and women have evolved to achieve success in both the natural and the social environment, as well as the mating game and the production of successful offspring who carry their genes.

The evolution of women and men

Male/female division of labor

Comparative anthropology has discovered widespread distinctions in the division of labor between women and men, summarized in Table 9.1.

Division of labor seems to proceed from a few tasks that are most essential to survival, namely care of infants (women), physical protection and warfare (men), and provision of food (both sexes). From there men take on the tasks requiring greater distance from children, as well as greater strength, danger, and aggression, and women do things that are closer to home and interruptible, and thus compatible with child care (Ember & Levinson, 1991). *Since humans are inherently flexible in adapting to environments and societies, there is no reason to assume this traditional division of labor is the best for today.* But it can give us clues to adaptive differences between men and women. For example, women's clothing making is related to their greater fine motor coordination. And men's specialization for strength and warfare relates to testosterone, which is also implicated in greater male vulnerability to disease and earlier death (Daly & Wilson, 1978).

"MORE AND MORE IT APPEARS THAT, BIOLOGICALLY, MEN ARE DESIGNED FOR SHORT, BRUTAL LIFES AND WOMEN FOR LONG, MISERABLE ONES,"

Physiological similarities and differences

Average global differences between women and men may be statistically significant but quite small. So women and men are much more similar than different in their abilities. But it is also important to focus in on *what people do with their senses*, such as hearing speech and spatial perception. There we find more pronounced differences that may have a significant impact on both thinking style and psychosocial development (see Table 9.2). We review these differences briefly to note both their pattern as reflective of evolution and their possible effects on couple relationships.

Sensory differences

Women have more sensitive hearing, especially for high-pitched sounds and noise, and they experience the same level of sound as about twice as loud as men do. Because they hear softer sounds even when they are asleep, women are generally lighter sleepers than men. So the average woman is more easily disturbed by snoring, a baby's cry, and loud music. Her better binaural hearing also makes her better at locating their source.

Girls outperformed boys in comprehension of speech and auditory–vocal memory, but boys excel at identifying non-human sounds, whether environmental or animal noises (McGuinness, 1985). Females are more

TABLE 9.2. Gender differences in sense-related activities

Sense	Women excel	Men excel
Hearing	More sensitive, especially soft & high-pitched sounds & noise Prefer 7–9 decibels less loudness Binaural sound location Sound response during sleep Comprehension of speech	Identifying nonhuman sounds
Taste	More sensitive	
Smell	More sensitive, esp human odors Remembering smells Improves at puberty	
Touch	More sensitive Lower pain threshold	
Vision	Adaptation to light Quick adaptation to darkness Movement in peripheral vision Recognizing vague, wide patterns Noticing people (more than objects)	More have abnormal color vision Central vision accuracy Central tracking of movement Binocular distance estimation Noticing objects (more than people)
Spatial orientation	Verbal directions from landmarks Relocating many familiar objects in a realistic setting	Abstract map directions Navigating through a maze Remembering spatial movements

Sources: McGuinness, 1985; McGuinness & Symons, 1977; Velle, 1987; Kimura, 1992; Dabbs et al., 1998.

sensitive to taste and smell than males, which would equip them to develop their children's eating and excretion skills. Variation in these sensitivities is somewhat correlated with the balance of hormones during their menstrual cycles, and increases at puberty, especially for musk-like odors and menstruation-related odors. This suggests a role for smell in mating, as well as mothering, which we will discuss later. Women are better than men at identifying and remembering human body and breath odors (Klutky, 1990), which can assist in diagnosing disease. Men are often impatient with women's greater concern for cleanliness and for socially and sexually desirable smells.

My wife kept raving about how much it stank in the kitchen. I didn't notice anything to complain about. Oh, there were a couple of pieces of food moldering under the sink. But she's always making mountains out of molehills like that.

On the average, women are more sensitive to touch, have lower pain thresholds, and lower tolerance for pain, despite their ability to endure the pain of childbirth (Velle, 1987). Since women are more essential to reproduction than men, they are wired to better notice pain and hence try harder to keep themselves safe and sound. Their touch sensitivity also leads them to give and receive more affection, which babies need. Touch, for women, may be gentler, but more impactful than men can imagine.

The differences in vision are complex, but they can be organized according to hunting versus gathering tasks. Women's greater tolerance for bright light, quicker adaptation to darkness, and greater sensitivity to movement in their peripheral vision (and over the entire retina), combined with finer hearing, equipped them to notice first what might be moving in their environment. Men's more accurate central vision, for tracking stationary and moving objects and for estimating their distance through binocular vision, aided in hunting down and hitting what their women's early warning system detected. Since women are more reactive to movement but less able to track it, they might be more likely to react anxiously to a rapidly moving object, such as a baseball (McGuinness, 1985).

When it comes to the *targets* of vision, males focus more readily on objects and females focus more on people from infancy on (McGuinness, 1985). In a visual tracking experiment, when images of objects and persons were simultaneously presented to separate eyes, males noticed objects significantly more often than they noticed people, while females noticed people more often than they noticed objects (McGuinness & Symonds,

1977). Thus male specialization for objects over people shows up in both vision and hearing, while female preference for attending to people shows up in vision, hearing, and smell.

Gender specialization for hunting versus gathering affect how we relate to our spatial environment. Men are better at finding their way through a maze and orienting themselves with a map (reviewed in Silverman & Eals, 1992) and at remembering spatial details of what they have done (Loftus et al., 1987). But like good foragers, women are better at remembering and relocating a large list of familiar objects in a realistic setting, such as a room or a field, especially (over 60% better) if neither gender was instructed to pay attention to them at the time they were seen (Silverman & Eals, 1992). Men may be better at visualizing an object in space, but women are better at finding it, *if they have seen it in place before* (James & Kimura, 1997; McBurney et al., 1997). When women set out to find their way to a distant place, they normally orient themselves not by abstract directions (north, etc.) or mental manipulation of maps, the way men do, but by applying their own specialized skills, connecting **verbal directions** with a series of located objects (landmarks), such as "turn left at the Shell gas station, then right at Denny's" (Kimura, 1992; Dabbs et al., 1998). Thus, when searching for something by car, men often want few directions, so they can design long-distance movements for themselves, and they want to succeed to prove their competence. The thrill of tracking moving objects and maneuvering through space makes men want to be good at risky driving and sports. In modern times, differences between males and females in sports such as baseball can breed the gender-stereotyping ridicule (discussed in Chapter 13) which boys use to keep each other in line, such as, "You throw like a girl!"

> The father of one girl on the baseball team I'm coaching kept yelling at his daughter to stop throwing like a girl.
> I said, "But she **is** a girl."
> He said, "She doesn't have to throw like one!"

In fact, research indicates boys' elbows are better constructed than girls' for long-distance throwing, which probably derives from their prehistory as spear-throwing hunters (Fisher, 1992). So she probably *does* have to throw like a girl, and her father is inadvertently ridiculing her as would a boy.

Cognitive differences

Small global differences in cognitive ability favoring women in verbal skills (1%) and men in spatial skills (4%) and mathematics (1%) (Hyde, 1981) are based partially on the sensory differences we have outlined. Yet even the millions of above-average girls may not pursue scientific or technical careers, for traditional career-role expectations are alive in both peer groups and school personnel. But many girls may also turn away from career fields that are concerned with objects and abstractions rather than people.

New evidence suggests that women's edge in verbal intelligence may be based on using more parts of their brains. McGuinness (1985) found that women's advantage in auditory processing was partly due to greater ability to form a visual image of a word they had heard. Similarly, PET scan research into language processing has found women's brains, but not men's, active in areas that process **visual** images and **emotional comprehension** and expression (Naylor, in Phillips, 1990; Shaywitz, et al., 1995). Thus the differences in what we mean and what we understand when we speak may contribute to our typical misunderstandings (Tannen, 1990). A man's brain may pay attention to the "report function" of a statement, "just the facts," which he may treat more as objects. But a woman may experience visual imagery and emotional implications that the man does not notice. Which meaning is more accurate, *her* "mountains," or *his* "molehills?" We cannot decide, but we can understand why men remember less spoken words and details of relational events (Loftus et al., 1987) and women resent this.

The most vital impact of all these differences derives from their over-all pattern: that **men are somewhat specialized for the object world and women for the interpersonal world**. These capabilities are the basis for empathy, support-giving, nonverbal sensitivity, **behavioral intelligence**, and the capacity to interpret and respond accurately and appropriately to others' behavior (discussed in Chapter 7). Women consistently excel in behavioral intelligence, by the largest margins of any heavily researched gender difference (Hall, 1998), but it has never been included in standard intelligence tests.

The coming years will see many new discoveries about the ways our brains work. Present indications are that although men and women do a lot of things similarly, they may be doing them with differently configured brain structures, neurotransmitters, and synapses (e.g., Shaywitz et al., 1995; DeVries & Boyle, 1998). However, "it is true of all these sex studies . . . that some of the women's brains [42% in the Shaywitz study] worked like the men's" (Begley, March 27, 1995). If evidence continues to mount for this generalization, then we can conclude that a great many women may be neurologically suited to "men's thinking" (in whatever ways that may be beneficial) as well as "men's work." But we do not know whether the women whose brains process language like men's were born or trained that way. We noted in Chapter 7 that men doing people-oriented work (e.g., counselors, nurses) may have more feelings similar to women's also. So our flexibility is great, whether our brains function exactly alike or not.

The politics of mating: Monogamous or polygamous?

Parental investment theory states that men and women have evolved different and somewhat clashing mating strategies. So what is the clash? Is it this?:

Hogamous higamous, man is polygamous.
Higamous hogamous, woman is monogamous. (Dorothy Parker)

Not quite. To ensure the survival of the species, each man needs to be ready, willing, and able to impregnate as many women as need babies. If warfare were to wipe out most of the men, the few remaining would need to mate profusely to replenish the society. But each woman needs to be much more concerned with providing food, protection, and training for her baby, and hence with securing the continuous loyalty, energy, and resources of the man that impregnates her, or of someone else, or a group. Investment by more than the mother is necessary for raising children, but the father's natural urge to invest in his children is less essential than the mother's is, because he is more replaceable.

Dual mating strategies of men and women. According to parental investment theory, population genetics also affects human mating strategies in a way that contrasts with parental investment. If men and women mate with different partners, they will produce a greater genetic variation among their offspring, which increases the chances of some genetically superior results. But each child needs long-lasting care, protection, and training in order to survive and develop its genetic potential.

Hence the sexes may each have two different mating strategies which apply to different situations. Men may be inspired to mate with as many women as possible, to maximize their chances of fathering successful offspring. Or they may invest their time, energy, and resources in just one or a few wives, depending on their wealth and social status, in order to insure that their offspring have the best advantages as they approach adulthood. Since they are usually highly invested in their children, women are likely to prefer monogamous mating, *unless they have strong resources, childcare, and protection support from kinfolk or village, and/or the available father prospects are all promiscuous.* These strategies are summarized in Table 9.3.

Biosocial scholarship draws from research in many fields to validate

TABLE 9.3. The dual mating strategies of men and women

Mating strategies	Number of partners	Investment in partner	Investment in offspring	Own status & resources	Extracouple sexual behavior
Male monogamy	1 or serial	High	High	High	None, flirting, or secret sex
Male promiscuity	>1 serial or simultaneous	High	Moderate	High	Socially approved sex polygamy, or secret sex
Male promiscuity	>1 serial or simultaneous	Low	Low	Low	Secret or open sex Deserting spouse
Female monogamy	1 or serial	High	High	Variable	None, flirting, or secret sex
Female promiscuity	>1 serial or simultaneous	Low	High	High kin support	Kin approved affairs flirting, or secret sex

these ideas about mating. Since the theory that both promiscuous and monogamous mating may be natural to both sexes is offensive to many Americans, we will explore its meaning and research evidence. First, biosocial theory does not imply that religion or society is "interfering with human nature" and should acquiesce to promiscuity. In fact, leading sociobiologist Edmund Wilson (1998) argues that socially restrictive moral beliefs and strong individual feelings about living by them are present in every culture and therefore natural as well, since they normally promote the harmony, cooperation, and success of the group as a whole.

The evidence for male promiscuity is overwhelming. In the vast majority of human cultures humans are a mildly polygynous species, that is, men are somewhat likely to mate with more than one woman, while women are much less likely to **openly** mate with more than one man. In a survey of 849 human societies (Murdock, 1967, quoted in Daly & Wilson, 1978), strict monogamy was the rule in 137, polygyny was either usual or occasional in 708, and polyandry (multiple husbands or lovers for one woman) was occasional or usual in 4. High-status males can be openly promiscuous or have several wives, while low-status males are more prone to disapproved affairs and desertion. Thus, cultures that allow male polygamy (such as in some Muslim countries) generally require that a man be able to support all of his wives and children.

Though extramarital affairs have become more common among women today in Africa, Europe, North America, and Pacific Islands, they are still much less common than among men. Studies of sexual attitudes and behavior in America (Oliver & Hyde, 1993) and in both industrial and preindustrial cultures all over the world show greater male promiscuity (Symons & Ellis, 1989; Thiessen & Ross, 1990). As the vocal group The Beach Boys put it, in surfers' heaven, there are "two girls for every boy."

Comparing mammals shows that the larger the difference in size (and other physical characteristics) between males and females, the greater is the species' tendency toward multiple wives. Human males are at the mild end on size difference, being from 5% to 12% taller and 8% heavier than females. Men are less promiscuous than other comparatively larger mammalian males, such as gorillas (Daly & Wilson, 1978).

Male mammals who take multiple mates don't survive as well, but not because their wives destroy them. Compared to females, males in more polygynous species have higher conception and mortality rates for embryos, more aggression and competition, higher mortality rates for adolescents and adults, and earlier death than in less polygynous species. As mild polygynists, human males manifest all of these gender differences in aggression and mortality (Alexander et al., 1979).

Lust has a rejuvenating influence on male mammals, known as the Coolidge Effect. Male rats, rams, bulls, and boars will lose interest in copulating with one mate after a while, and even reject her by smell when she is disguised. But once a new fertile female is introduced, the males' sexual interest is completely refreshed, and they will copulate vigorously again, with at least seven successive partners for a bull and twelve for a ram (Symons, 1979). Most men will agree that gazing at a new young woman is energizing. A chorus from Wayne Newton's song about gazing at a nude woman, "You Can Keep Your Hat On," sums it up: "You give me reason to live. You give me reason to live. You give me reason to live."

Can women be promiscuous too? Though women's commitment to their children is unwavering, they are still capable of extrapair liaisons themselves. It has been suggested that this capability, aided by their natural concealment of when they are fertile (through loss of any fertility cycle noticeable by men) and their repertoire of flirtatious expressions, has increased women's power and reproductive success. Women usually initiate flirtatious interaction and have large repertoires of verbal and nonverbal tactics for both flirtation and rejection (reviewed in Trost & Alberts, 1998).

First, flirting and sometimes secretly mating with socially powerful men can secure their additional support and protection for a woman and her offspring (Hrdy, 1986). These men do not have to have sex to become enthusiastic supporters of attractive women, since just flirting is enough to stimulate the Coolidge Effect and make their day.

> *The male students in a relationship class complained that women "use sex"— inviting words, looks, movements, and touches—to get what they want. This frustrated and hurt men, because they didn't like not knowing when a woman "meant it" (that she felt sex or love) and when she didn't. The men wanted to know why women did this.*

> *Most of the women didn't seem to know what to say. But one answer may have spoken for them all: "Because it works."*

Flirting also helps a woman turn her own man away from promiscuous "running around" and toward **constant mate-guarding** motivated by sexual jealousy (Wilson & Daly, 1992).

The male's response to sexual infidelity (Wilson, 1982; Lumsden & Wilson, 1983) is taken as an indication that men are biologically programmed to exchange care for the mother and infant for continued and exclusive sexual relations with the mother. Where sex differences in jealousy have been studied, women seem more concerned about their partners' energy, resources, and attentions, while men are most concerned about sexual loyalty itself (Wilson, 1978; Teisman & Mosher, 1978).

The most convincing evidence that women are capable of multiple mating and that males have evolved in response is found in **sperm competition**. New microscopic films of sperm in action reveal three kinds of sperm cells (Smith, 1984). In addition to those that swim fast in search of an ovum to impregnate, there are two other kinds: **blockers** in large numbers, that link up tails to fend off the advances of alien sperm; and **killers**, that actually attack and disable competitors, which they can distinguish from those of their own "team." Even among monogamous American couples, the number of sperm transferred in a given copulation was not related in a linear way to the time since the last copulation, but rather to the proportion of the time since the last copulation that the pair were out of contact (Baker & Bellis, 1989). Thus their increase in sperm production may be due to an instinct for sperm competition.

Extramarital sex in America

It has been widely accepted that about 50% of married men have had extramarital sex (EMS) (Kinsey et al., 1948; Hite, 1976) and that women's rate has been "catching up" (D'Emilio & Freedman, 1988). But more careful nation-wide sampling techniques combined with interviewing have produced lower estimates. Laumann and colleagues (1994) found that about 37% of men and 20% of women reported ever having had EMS by the time they reached their post-reproductive years. Similarly, relying on the 1994 General Social Survey, Wiederman (1997) found that a maximum of 34% of men and 19.3% of women reported ever having had EMS. Widerman's numbers of men reporting climbed pretty consistently from 15% in their twenties to peak at 29% in their forties, but then reach 34% in their sixties. Women reporting EMS also peaked in their forties, at 19.3%, but there were far fewer in their fifties and sixties (11% and 7.6%, respectively). Presumably, men and women in their forties in 1994 were affected by the peak years of sexual revolution in the late sixties and seventies. Women's EMS rates are clearly affected by prevailing sexual attitudes. And it is possible that social attitudes have encouraged women to "catch up," since slightly over 14% of *both* sexes in their thirties reported EMS. But none of these percentages are as high as they are rumored to be. *So apparently both sexes are capable of EMS, both are influenced by prevailing sexual attitudes, and the vast majority of both never try it while married.*

Ethnic attitudes toward and frequencies of EMS vary considerably. The overall rate among African-American men may be 50% higher than among Whites (Wiederman, 1997), possibly translating to 50% among the oldest men. The Black women's rate is higher than White women's also. According to their reports, over 4 times as many Black men as Whites had EMS in the last year (12.1% to 2.9%), which was similar to the ratio of Black to White women (6.9% to 1.2%). EMS is tolerated, though not approved, among African Americans (Penn et al., 1997). A young married woman says:

> The older women in my church have told me not to worry about my man if he plays around. They say men are just that way. But they'll slow down in their fifties, and then they'll be all the more kind and grateful because you gave them the slack and didn't leave.

Though the sample size of Hispanics and Asians was very small, their EMS rates appear higher than among Whites also, with over three times as many of both men and women reporting activity in the last year. In both groups infidelity should be hidden and is more acceptable for men (Penn et al., 1997). When Whites and minorities are combined, women's recent EMS is most likely to occur in their twenties and thirties, when they are desirable targets, while men's recent EMS peaks in their thirties but continues even past their fifties (Wiederman, 1997).

We can distinguish 4 types of extramarital affairs (Pittman, 1989):

1. a once-only affair, usually brief,
2. an emotionally powerful "falling in love" affair,
3. sexual infidelities in an ongoing marital battle, and
4. recurrent sexual episodes which are considered normal by those involved.

The first type of affair may occur accidentally, perhaps while drunk, alone, on a trip, or frightened. The second type may occur after many years in a placid marriage, when a partner falls in love and then has to wrestle with keeping the affair secret and with staying in the marriage or leaving it. The third type, sexualized marital warfare, may be in a marriage nearing divorce, though not always. The fourth kind, recurrent episodes or affairs, may be part of a "swinging" or open marriage or other sexual behavior tolerated by an ethnic or social group.

It is not clear what percentage of extramarital affairs lead to divorce or are symptoms of imminent divorce, but divorced people are much more likely to have had EMS than those who never divorce (Wiederman, 1997). Affairs of love and vengeance (types 2 and 3) are more likely to lead to divorce than the others. But some clinicians maintain that many couples can "get past" the emotional effects of infidelity if both partners have both the commitment and the patience (Pittman, 1989; Spring, 1996). Whether it's true or not that men react most to their partner's extramarital sex, while women react most to their partner's extramarital love (Buss, 1991), many anecdotes and clinicians testify that the injured partner may never recover all of the marital trust he or she once had, remaining hypervigilant about the EMS partner's activities (Spring, 1996).

Sex and the gender power struggle

It appears that the proverbial "battle of the sexes" is based on clashing mating strategies. Throughout history men have dominated societies and treated women as their property (Levi-Strauss, 1969). The existence of harems and increased polygamy of native chiefs shows that the more power a man has, the more women's sexuality he may try to monopolize.

But some of female evolution may have been driven by countermeasures against male control (Parker, 1987). These include concealed ovulation, continuous sexual receptivity, and unnecessarily large breasts. Since breasts may get as much as 20% larger during sexual arousal, large breasts are an arousal cue for men. A new theory also suggests women's brains may have evolved more effective reaction inhibiting mechanisms than men for both sexual and social situations (Bjorklund & Kipp, 1996). Perhaps such intelligent self-control aided by slower nerve conduction (Tan, 1996) has helped women to control social networks, sense emotional meanings, and flirt effectively to cope with the men who would like to control them.

> God made men stronger, but not necessarily more intelligent. He gave women intuition and femininity. And, used properly, that combination easily jumbles the brain of any man I've ever met. (Farah Fawcett, actress)

In fact, recent PET scan research shows that activating pleasure centers in the brain leads thinking functions in the temporal and parietal lobes to shut down (George et al., 1996). So we really are less mentally active when we are enjoying ourselves.

Contemporary increase in parental investment

Not just moral traditions, but also modern social conditions may influence both sexes to reduce "promiscuity of the fittest" and increase parental investment in their children. In densely populated areas with advanced technology, there is much more competition for jobs, income, and social status, so children need longer and more extensive preparation for adult responsibilities. They then wait longer to reproduce and have fewer children themselves. Fathers' commitment of time, training, and resources to children over this longer pre-adulthood becomes more vital to the success or *fitness* of the children (Kaplan et al., 1998). Mothers' joining the labor force to enhance parental resources—anywhere in the world—also reduces the number of children they produce. This increase in what it takes to make a successful child increases the disadvantages of parental promiscuity, particularly those of divorce and desertion, even if social welfare programs and/or extended family or community support are available (Kaplan et al., 1998). Thus long-term monogamy may be the more successful cross-generational mating strategy for today's competitive world.

Adolescent male sexuality

The evolutionary gender differences in sexuality are strongest during adolescence, when they impact the adult identities that are being formed. Adolescent boys think about sex more than girls, and more of them masturbate (90% of boys, compared to 60% of girls) and they do it more frequently (Jones & Barlow, 1990). They also have intercourse earlier, more frequently, and with more partners (Kinsey et al., 1948, 1953; Oliver & Hyde, 1993).

> About sex especially, men are born unbalanced; we might almost say men are born mad. They scarcely reach sanity till they reach sanctity. (G. K. Chesterton, writer)

Adolescent males' development of feelings for relationship intimacy may be swamped by pubertal sexual feelings, which peer influence often directs into attitudes that are undesirable to women (Jung, 1928/1989). These attitudes can delay their opportunities to learn through romantic relationships. Since identity development is significant in adolescence (Erikson, 1968), adolescent sexuality and the ways it is understood become important elements of a man's identity. By contrast, adolescent women are more likely to be concerned with romance, which involves a more complex relationship with more emotions and less sexuality (Person, 1988). In keeping with their dual mating strategies, men are more likely than women to separate sex from love (Foa et al., 1987).

Stereotype of the hypersexual male

The male sexual drive is widely viewed as naturally overpowering and irresistible. In fact, some American juries have ruled that a woman in alluring clothing or in a compromising situation may have been sufficiently provocative to have her rape case dismissed. This interpretation assumes that men's sexuality is like an on/off switch, while women's is more like a rheostat with gradations. Many people believe that all men want sex most of the time and that satisfactory sex is men's top priority in a relationship (Zilbergeld, 1978). Yet only around 15% of married men and women rate sex as a top priority in their relationship (Schwartz, June, 1991). Apparently male attitudes change in marriage, or perhaps adequate satisfaction in the early married years makes men's priorities change.

Women may be about as capable of responding to visual erotic material as men (Schmidt & Sigusch, 1973). But the "*Playboy* standard of feminine desirability" is an objectification of women's appearance that has more far-reaching effects than any media models for men. Both male- and female-oriented erotica in pornography, leisure media, advertising, and clothing styles have continued to grow in recent decades.

Since male masturbation develops when there is little or no access to girls, adolescent boys and men are more likely than girls and women to develop sexual fantasies and habits which are unrelated to the personality of a real partner (Money, 1980; Jones & Barlow, 1990). Male sex fantasies typically undo or reverse the humiliating experiences of being turned on but powerless to get a partner in adolescence (Stoller, 1987). Thus, the most prevalent fantasy stars the woman who is always ready for sex (Person, 1986b). She mirrors the male's lustful state and empowers him to fulfill his desires, while her obvious appreciation undoes his embarrassment about being turned on. Sexual scenes in both pornographic and mainstream movies emphasize women's arousal, while men are much calmer and in charge. This reassures men that they are not as vulnerable as women. This passage from a pornographic novel about an oversexed teenage girl illustrates the protection against male sexual vulnerability and humiliation:

*Her own body responded, . . . until Mary-Ann began to squeal with fresh de-
lights too great to be held in. Her expressions of joy brought laughter from the
others [all boys].* **Unlike her momentary partner, she was in no way
against showing her delights.** *If they made the others amused and turned
them on, all the better. Besides, it might just enable the boy who was [having]
her to* **save some face.** (Clinton, 1974. Bold print added)

A less popular fantasy features domination over the woman, who willingly accepts and enjoys it, as in the porno scene above (Person, 1986a).
Male domination reverses the male's helplessness over sexual arousal in
everyday life and may ventilate his anger at being unable to succeed with
women he has desired. These fantasies may be involved in male peer group
support for real sexual aggression toward women, including attitudes such
as: "she was asking for it" and "women really like it" (Rapaport & Burkhart,
1984; Wilson et al., 1983). But men's sex fantasies are not more likely to be
aggressive or sadistic than women's (Person, 1986a; Hsu et al., 1994).

Early masturbation habits can also lead men, more often than women,
to feel a compulsive need for sex. A compulsory frequency of sex in marriage leads partners to lose all spontaneity.

*For 27 years I had sex every night with my husband. That was just the way
things were. Then he had his midlife crisis and ran off with a younger woman.
Now she can put up with him.*

Such compulsiveness can lead people to look for love in all the wrong
places, such as bars, baths, parties, and prostitution. Thus, the frequency,
fantasy content, and compulsive power of sexual habits can become major
issues in couple relating.

The experimental/expendable male

Since women are absolutely essential to bearing and raising children, but
men are not (past the point of insemination), it follows that men are more
expendable. Therefore, as demonstrated in our own and numerous other
cultures, it is appropriate that men be specialized for protection and warfare and take on other risky tasks that can get them killed. To prepare them
for this, men should be designed with more testosterone and aggressiveness (Archer, 1988) to carry out these functions.

In order to keep male aggressiveness from running amuck and en-
dangering the survival of human offspring, cultural and perhaps biological
structures are needed to balance aggression with cooperation. Male bonding has been postulated as an inherited tendency (Tiger, 1970). Perhaps we
naturally extend trust and friendship toward those we grow up with and
who look and act like us, and feel caution and mistrust toward those who
seem different. This could provide an innate basis for ethnic prejudice as
well. Whether male bonding is innate or not, males all over the world tend

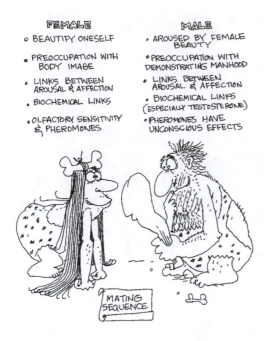

FEMALE

- BEAUTIFY ONESELF
- PREOCCUPATION WITH BODY IMAGE
- LINKS BETWEEN AROUSAL & AFFECTION
- BIOCHEMICAL LINKS
- OLFACTORY SENSITIVITY & PHEROMONES

MALE

- AROUSED BY FEMALE BEAUTY
- PREOCCUPATION WITH DEMONSTRATING MANHOOD
- LINKS BETWEEN AROUSAL & AFFECTION
- BIOCHEMICAL LINKS (ESPECIALLY TESTOSTERONE)
- PHEROMONES HAVE UNCONSCIOUS EFFECTS

MATING SEQUENCE

to play, work, and relate in groups more than females.

The notion that men might be experimental, as well as expendable, rests on evidence of greater variability in male character and abilities compared to women. Though men and women have the same average scores on intelligence tests, the distribution is broader for men than for women, which means there are more men at the genius level as well as among the mentally retarded. Autism, dyslexia, and childhood schizophrenia, as well as unusual artistic, musical, and mathematical talents, and homosexuality are all much more likely in men than in women. The general tendency of men to show more extremes and abnormalities may be associated with the lack of a second X chromosome which could off-set anomalies in the first (Wilson, 1982).

Thus, natural selection might be experimenting with men, creating more abnormalities and mutations because they don't have to be able to carry out the complex and fragile process of conception, gestation, and birth. It is "safer" for the continuation of the species for genetic diversity to be given to men and for women's genes to stray less from what has worked before. Eighteen to twenty-five years of a man's life is enough to display his comparative success in society. Then the more discriminating women will choose the most promising characters—the best protectors, providers, and parental investors—to reproduce the species.

Biosocial factors in the mating sequence

Sociobiology views human mating as an interlocking sequence of events facilitated by inherited tendencies and neurochemical processes as well as by cultural guidelines and individual thoughts and decisions (Eibl-Eibesfeld, 1989; Barkow, 1989). Each gender is thought to be genetically designed for activation of its own mating sequences in reaction to cues presented by the other gender, so the process is interactive. We presented courtship in our own culture in Chapters 1 and 2. Here we will add a selection of biosocial and biochemical factors.

The attractive woman

According to current theory, women make themselves attractive and nurturant (known in America as "nice" or "sweet") to advertise their fertility and quality as child rearers, and men are very responsive to what they see (Symons, 1979). Beauty standards are widely thought to differ by culture. But an intriguing theory suggests that each culture's standards of facial beauty may be derived from images of the **culturally average face**, which can be approximated by superimposing a large number of feminine faces into a computer-composite photograph (Eibl-Eibesfeldt, 1989). These standards show a tendency in diverse cultures in China, Africa, Europe, and the Pacific to favor facial symmetry between the left and right sides (Grammer, 1994) and the fineness and gracefulness of children, as well as their proportionally larger eyes, smaller noses, and smaller chins. Additional favoritism is shown for the adult features of prominent cheekbones and narrow cheeks, along with the expressive features of high eyebrows, large pupils, and broad smile (Cunningham, 1986). Using computer-generated faces Johnston et al. (1997) found males' visual cortex reacted much more strongly to such ideal faces than to average faces, only *half a second* after the images were flashed, before any conscious reflection could have occurred. Since infants also prefer to look at more beautiful female faces, the response to feminine beauty may be partially inborn as well as learned (Langlois et al., 1987). Our cosmetic industry capitalizes on the attractiveness of the childlike attributes to sell women perfumes and soft, smooth skin so they can smell and feel like a child as well.

Symmetry in a woman's body may also convey the message of health and fertility. Specifically, large and symmetrical breasts are indicative of exceptional genetic vitality and correlate with having more children (Manning et al., 1997). Furthermore, asymmetry in a woman's breasts fluctuates during the menstrual cycle, but breast symmetry suddenly increases on

TABLE 9.4. Characteristics of an ideal female mate in preindustrial cultures

1. She will be newly ripe and ready for sexual intercourse, approximately 17 years old. With cosmetics, bras, and contraceptives, she can keep herself looking newly ripe until her twenties when urban cultures prefer to mate (Buss, 1989).
2. She will signal good health, with face and body symmetry and unblemished skin.
3. Her skin will be lighter than the female average for her ethnic group. This preference exists in the majority of cultures world-wide, including many that were not colonized or influenced by white Europeans. But lighter skinned men are not widely preferred (Van den Berghe & Frost, 1986).
4. In most features, such as height, she will be near the midpoint of the female distribution in her group. Her face will be average and young looking.
5. She will have whatever physical features, decorations, and possessions are associated with high social status in her group.
6. She will be a woman with whom the man who is attracted has never had sexual intercourse.
7. She will not be a person with whom the attracted man was raised as a child (Shepher, 1983).

Source: Symons, 1987; Symons & Ellis, 1989, and further elaborated in Buss, 1989; Van den Berghe & Frost, 1986; Shepher, 1983.

the very day of ovulation, as an innate indicator of fertility (Manning et al., 1996). Hip size indicates fertility as well. In many cultures, the ideal female body has a waist-to-hips ratio of 70% (in Buss, 1994), which translates to 30" hips with a 21" waist, or 35" hips with 25" waist. The hip size signals a woman's baby-bearing capacity, while the small waist indicates youth and not having borne a baby before. Symons (1987, 1989) lists the following as possibly standard characteristics of the ideal partner desired by men in preindustrial cultures in the world (Symons, 1987).

Evolution-based tendencies should be strongest when they are most needed, in early mating years, and before mature thinking can assert itself. In fact, modern teenage girls compare their attractiveness, popularity, and romantic relationship success (Benenson & Benarroch, 1998), while teen boys care about athletic success and ogling and pursuing women (DeLamater, 1987). Our theories emphasize **why** beauty standards are what they are, not that they should stay the same when childbearing is not a primary issue.

The attractive man

The need for paternal investment in complex societies generates a longer list of qualities and abilities desired in a man than the male wish-list for women in Table 9.4. Table 9.5 compares three lists of desirable qualities. The first is an anthropologist's estimation of qualities a prehistoric hunter band **leader** would need to have (Wilson, 1978). The second is a summary of what women might look for in a mate in a hypothetical preindustrial culture (Ellis, 1992). The third summarizes the cross-cultural similarities in the qualities ascribed to masculinity in twentieth-century cultures (Gilmore, 1990), to which three group-acceptance qualities—**intelligent**, **prudent**, and **likeable**—have been added (from Kenrick & Trost, 1987).

Though not yet thoroughly researched, there is evidence and specula-tion among experts that a "strong" jaw, prominent brow, tallness, face and body symmetry, and a well-muscled body are all primitive visual cues for dominance. And they are also signs of abundant male hormones in adoles-cence and hence, of genetically-based good health (Cowley, June, 1996; Gangestad & Thornhill, 1997). But at least among American coeds, domi-nant males were not considered more attractive than non-dominant males, unless they were also described as *prosocial*, that is, friendly, cooperative, and helpful (Graziano et al., 1997). Women throughout the world ranked dependable character, emotional stability and maturity, pleasing disposi-tion, intelligence, sociability, and health above ambition and didn't men-tion status and dominance on questionnaires (Buss et al., 1990). But they may actually *look first and most frequently* at signs of status and dominance (Hassebrauck, 1998), before they qualify potential mates for consideration according to other criteria (Townsend & Wasserman, 1998).

Many women have asked, "Why do men always have to keep proving themselves?" Surprisingly, anthropological research indicates that men have

TABLE 9.5. Desirable qualities in males as mates

Hunter group leader	Preindustrial cultural attractiveness	Crosscultural masculinity
Dominant by definition of leader role	Strong social presence, efficacy, and status, tall	Competitive where resources are limited
Proficient in hunting & skillful	Skills and economic capabilities for high status in society	Dominate & organize nature to perpetuate social order
Proficient in self defense	Protective skills	Fights to protect family
Tough	Firm muscle tone, energetic body	Hardy, stoic toward pain
Controlled	Stable & mature	Self discipline, prudence
Cunning, Knowledgeable	Intelligent, ambitious	Intelligent, ambitious
Cooperative	Kind, considerate, generous	Provide for kin Uncomplaining, unhostile
Eloquent	Confident, respected, & liked	Publicly shows character
Attractive to women	Healthy, vital, taller than average Genuinely interested in women	Likeable, successful with women, eager to impregnate
Good with children	Good with children, generous	Protective of family
Relaxed	Ease & freedom of body movement	

Sources: Wilson, 1978; Ellis, 1992; Gilmore, 1990; Kenrick & Trost, 1987.

... FEMALES LEARN HOW EASILY SEXUAL STRATEGY COMES TO MALES!

to keep struggling and stretching themselves in most (though not all) of the world's cultures (Gilmore, 1990). The reasons may be based on the environment, psychology, and evolution, rather than just stupidity.

First, the hierarchical structures of human dominance are both looser and less based on physical prowess than those of most other mammals. Therefore in many cultures competition among males is less controlled by a "pecking order" that regulates how much each man is entitled to achieve by his own efforts. Environments with limited resources, family welfare, or "reproductive success," may depend on male ambition and competitiveness in unrelenting efforts to master the environment and collect resources. Thus, the nearly universal masculine cultural imperatives are *provide, protect,* and *procreate* (Gilmore, 1990). In exceptional settings where resources are always abundant, such as Tahiti, competition to provide, and therefore the need to protect, are greatly reduced, so cultural masculinity is much "softer."

While risking and straining oneself to protect and provide may be thrilling at times, it is not safe, easy, or predominantly pleasurable. As a result, cultures need to guide and prod men to appropriate levels of aggression, competition, and control. Thus, "'real' manhood [is] an inducement for high performance in the social struggle for scarce resources, a code of conduct that advances collective interests by overcoming inner inhibitions"(Gilmore, 1990, p. 223). Gilmore thinks the key inhibiting force to be overcome is childhood passivity and dependence on mother. To become productive and protective men, boys must prioritize self-discipline over indulgence, effort and pain over pleasure, and providing for others over hoarding for themselves. They must resist and condemn their regressive desire for the infant's blissful self-centered dependence on mother.

Biochemical links to attractions and approach

Testosterone is related to both aggressiveness and sexual interest in many animals, including birds, mammals, and humans (Daly & Wilson, 1978). Increases in levels of testosterone can lead to increased fighting and copulating; and copulating and fighting can stimulate increased secretion of testosterone. True to our greater flexibility in actualizing our genetic makeup, human sexual and aggressive behavior is less closely correlated to testosterone than is the case with other animals (Archer, 1991), but the link is there. Testosterone does not directly affect the activity of sexual and aggressive brain centers, but it increases or decreases their receptivity to other neurotransmitters, such as the generally activity-motivating dopamine (Crenshaw & Goldberg, 1996). Thus, testosterone levels make these centers more or less responsive to the other biochemical inputs that trigger the complex sexual and aggressive networks in the brain, though the changes in activity can take days or weeks to appear in behavior (LeVay, 1993).

The evolutionary function of the link between sexual desire and aggression in monkeys is that the dominant male would have the strongest urge to mate. The females would also become more responsive to the signs of dominance, since dominant males would be better able to protect and provide for offspring. In humans there is evidence for higher testosterone levels in male winners of athletic contests than in losers (reviewed in Archer, 1991). Wilson (1982) suggested that the widespread incidence of rape in wartime could be partially caused by the increase in testosterone levels in victorious troops, combined with their high state of physiological arousal through fear and activity.

Testosterone in women increases their aggressiveness and sexual desire as well. But athletic competition may not affect women's testosterone levels as it does men's (Mazur et al., 1997), so they may not biologically link dominance with sexuality as much as men (Fisher, 1992). Studies show two peaks in women's sexual activity, one near ovulation and another a few days before menstruation. The ovulation peak corresponds with peak testosterone and high levels of estrogen. The pre-menstruation peak occurs when postovulatory progesterone, which blocks testosterone effects, drops off, but testosterone is still present (reviewed in Crenshaw & Goldberg, 1996).

Our sense of smell?

Sexual behavior in other mammals is highly related to smells, and the evidence for humans is mounting. Women can recognize their babies by smell within a few hours of birth, and most can differentiate their husbands from other men by smell as well (Eibl-Eibesfeldt, 1989). In modern society, individual odors are covered up by perfumes and deodorants. But they can still affect us, perhaps more than we understand.

Women have a more sensitive sense of smell, while men give off stronger odors. Androstenol and androstenone are odorous substances found in three to ten times higher concentrations in the fatty tissues of men than in women, and in high concentrations in men's perspiration but rarely in women's (Brooksbank et al., 1974). Some societies seem to find human perspiration and genital odors enticing, while others insist they are repulsive (Eibl-Eibesfeldt, 1989; Velle, 1987). In one study, however, Austrian women found androstenone repulsive *except around ovulation*, when their response was neutral (Grammer, 1993). So perhaps men's sweat odors may keep women away except at their peak of fertility.

Smell may be important in women's choice of a mate. While men considered sight and smell equally important in mate choice, smell was most important for women (Herz & Cahill, 1997). In addition, humans can have three different types of blood immunity profiles, which women automatically recognize by smell (Wedekind et al., 1995). When offered male-worn T-shirts to smell, women preferred the T-shirts from wearers whose immunity profiles were *different* than their own. And, unbeknownst to anybody, couples with similar immunity types are more likely than those with different types to be infertile and have spontaneous abortions. So women who heed this smell preference may be choosing for reproductive success.

Human pheromones discovered. Recently, new probable human pheromones have been discovered, along with neural pathways through which they act. Other mammals have two separate olfactory organs in the nose with separate pathways into the brain, both of which affect sexual behavior in males (Halpern, 1987). The nerves from the larger olfactory organ move before the smaller to connect to the limbic system, which is involved in emotions. The smaller olfactory organ, called the vomeronasal organ, has a neural connection directly into the medial preoptic nucleus of the hypothalamus (Moran et al., 1991), which is affected by testosterone in all mammalian brains. The human vomeronasal organ has now been verified as a pair of round pits between 0.2 and 2 millimeters in diameter in the mucous membrane on the floor of the front third of the nose with cells that look and behave chemically like olfactory neurons (Getchell et al., 1993; Monti-Bloch & Grosser, 1991; Stensaas et al., 1991).

Scientists at the University of Utah found that the vomeronasal neurons **did** respond with electrical activity in forty adults, and the responses were both quite distinct from the other olfactory neurons and different for the sexes (Monti-Bloch & Grosser, 1991; Monti-Bloch et al., 1994). The vomeronasal neurons hardly responded at all to "normal" smells, that evoked strong electrical responses in the olfactory neurons, such as clove oil. But they responded from two to ten times as strongly to five other chemicals that were barely detected by normal olfactory neurons and declared odorless by all forty subjects. Women's vomeronasal neurons responded to one of the odorless substances twice as strongly as men's, and men's neurons responded to another substance six times as strongly as women's. Male vomeronasal responses were 80% to 150% stronger to the other three substances, so their overall response was twice as strong as the women's. These substances were pheromones that are specific to each gender.

Such pheromones have been extracted from the skin of people's arms and legs. In placebo-controlled studies, a one second whiff of four artificially synthesized pheromones produced several effects documented in medical labs at the University of Utah and the National Institute of Nutrition in Mexico City (Berliner et al., 1996; Monti-Bloch et al., 1998):

1. After around half a second, heart rate decreased an average of 3.8 beats a minute, for a period of around 2 minutes.
2. Breathing decreased an average of 2 cycles a minute, for a period of around 5 minutes.
3. In half a second the electrical activity changed on the fingers, lasting for around 30 seconds. Electrical skin responses are normally associated with emotional reactions, as in lie detectors. Parasympathetic nervous tone increased. This is the normal speed for nervous reactions, like the brain's reaction to beauty.
4. EEG analysis showed a large increase in alpha brain waves (associated with relaxed concentration), compared to beta waves (busy, scattered activity). The alpha wave increase was present 30 minutes later.
5. Slight but significant increase in core body temperature. (Could that be "the hots?")

6. During a 6 hour test, male pituitary hormone activity that influences the testes was significantly altered. The same pituitary hormone activity in women was altered slightly in the opposite direction, but not significantly.

7. Magnetic Resonance Imaging showed the pheromones activated the hypothalamus, amygdala, thalamus, and two parts of the cortex, the same sites as in animal studies.

A different medical group tested its own synthetic pheromone against a placebo over 6 weeks and found increases in men's sexual behavior with partners, but not with masturbation (Cutler et al., 1998.) The changes in heartbeat, breathing, electrical skin response, brain waves, and some influence on sex hormones and perhaps behavior suggests these pheromones may play a role in "sexual chemistry." MRI shows they do activate parts of the brain that may help us get into the mood for love.

If we sum up the two senses of smell, significant sex differences fit with the contrasting mating strategies we have discussed. Men may be more strongly affected by the pheromones, which act on us without our awareness. But women are more sophisticated in identifying men's odors, which allows them conscious choices about mating and copulating. Thus men may be biologically more impulsive, while women are equipped to be more discriminating in choosing a mate.

Self-esteem

In biosocial theory self-esteem has essential social and evolutionary functions, as well as individual dimensions. Self-esteem is not fixed, but a situation-by-situation estimation of our relative rank and likelihood of attracting and maintaining the attention of significant others. But it can be preformed in childhood. Genetically inferior animal babies are usually rejected and die. If we were comparatively unimportant or unwanted in our childhood, a propensity to shame and withdrawal may become fixed in our personality as a protection against repeating our early (undeserved) social failure. This internalized shame could become a hindrance to self-display and risk when our success and prestige could actually change in a new situation. Thus, self-esteem is our own biased summary of the responses of others. Mastering new skills and choosing groups in which they count is as important as revising child and adolescent failure memories and developing appreciation for our own character and appearance.

Let us now take a look at some of the ways self-esteem comes into play for men and women.

Masculine self-esteem and mating. Men need high self-esteem to risk an overture towards a woman. Barkow (1989, 1991) views a man's self-esteem as his own internalized estimate of his prestige, both within his group and of his group compared to others. Thus part of prestige is competitive comparison (Schwalbe & Staples, 1991). In nonhuman primates, male prestige is derived from physical dominance, and athletic prowess is the first source of preteen boys' comparison and self-esteem (Benenson & Benarroch, 1998). In later adolescence, grades and achievements are indicative of ambition and future success, which can confer self-esteem too. In our closest primate relatives, chimpanzees, relative social standing may depend as much on whom the females pay attention to as it does on physical dominance. Among humans also, both signs of dominance or status and attracting and holding the attention of others are sources of self-esteem (Schwalbe & Staples, 1991, Gilbert et al., 1995). Thus natural selection has fostered our **ongoing awareness of our rank and potential for attracting attention**, which guides our social behavior.

In humans, both wealth and excellence in a variety of skills can substitute for physical prowess, as long as they are valued by the social group. This allows for wide variation in societies, and also lets a man choose a professional group where his particular character and skills are best suited to excel.

Feminine self-esteem and mating. The relationship between self-esteem and coming together with attractive others may be more complex for women. Advertising a woman's attractiveness through flirtatious behavior would require high self-esteem. But one can get attention from others by giving it; and physical dominance is not useful. Shyness and embarrassment lower self-esteem. But we have seen (in Chapter 1) that displays of unsureness can make both sexes more approachable and that shyness and withdrawal can invite an interested other into the pursuer–distancer dance.

Women's self-esteem is also based either on social status (the dominance and resources of their family or group) or on their ability to attract and maintain the attention of significant people in their group. Therefore, at all ages, girls and women are more concerned and self-critical about how they look (Pliner, et al., 1990; O'Brien, 1991). Women's self-esteem may also relate more than men's to **being included** and liked in families and groups, which is a more supportive than competitive process. Thus, women score higher than men in self-perceived lovableness and likability (O'Brien, 1991) and their self-esteem is more affected by the level of love they feel from others (Walsh & Balazs, 1990). Mastering skills and careers can certainly support self-esteem. But research into women's supposed "fear of success" found that they were actually **not** afraid of **success**, but of disapproval and exclusion by their significant groups if they achieved beyond the others' expectations (reported on in Wade & Tavris, 1990; American Association of University Women [AAUW], 1991b).

A massive study of teenagers (AAUW, 1991a, 1991b) found a drop in girls' self-esteem around the beginnings of puberty. A similar drop began 2 years later in boys, but this left girls with lower average scores throughout the period. The boy's drop is more closely related to losing confidence in being "good at a lot of things," while the girl's self-esteem changes parallel their liking for "the way I look" (raw data in AAUW, 1991a). This was attributed to schools, because African-American girls did not have the same drop, and they were also not as interested in their schools. From grade school to grad school, girls may talk less and receive less attention and useful feedback from teachers than boys (Sadker & Sadker, 1992).

But gender-role socialization and schooling experiences can be understood in a biosocial framework which includes **pubertal hormones** as essential factors. One study suggests that girls' self-esteem is likely to be lower a year after beginning to menstruate than after only six months (Lackovic-Grgin et al., 1994). Male behavior is influenced by hormones as well. For example, the male predominance in classroom talking could be based on having more testosterone and less monoamine oxidase (MAO). Differences in both neurochemicals have been linked to males' greater susceptibility to boredom and tendency to seek high sensation levels (Walsh, 1991a), such as risk-taking. Thus teachers are responding to the male students because they are most insistent on making something happen. Sensation seeking and sexual discomfort may also motivate boys' harassment of girls.

Perhaps there are two sources of change in women's self-esteem at puberty. First, perhaps the composition of the group to which the girls wish to belong changes so that they no longer rate themselves as highly. Second, perhaps their estimate of what they might need to do to be included and liked changes as well.

First, since pubertal hormones lead girls to turn to **boys** for attention, their self-esteem is in for a bumpy ride! As girls approach puberty, their passionate interest in boys climbs, while the boys' interest plummets (Hatfield et al., 1988). Comparing the graphs of male and female self-esteem scale means and passion scale means by age (Figure 9.1) shows this relationship clearly.

The girls' major drop in self-esteem (ages 9 to 13) corresponds roughly to the boys' greatest drop in passion (ages 10 to 12). But girls' self-esteem changes are not as clearly parallel to boys' passion changes as they are *mirror opposites* of their own passion changes (correlation –.5, with less than 1% chance probability). Girls' self-esteem in Catholic all-girls schools drops too, though their self-concepts are higher in comparison with girls attending coed Catholic schools, a difference not found among boys (Lee & Bryk, 1986). So the presence and feelings of boys and the school activities and attitudes that support boys may weaken girls' self-esteem. **But girls' self-esteem goes down even without boys around**, and *may be more corre-*

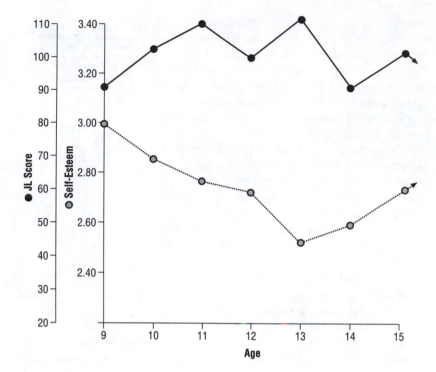

FIG. 9.1a.
Self-esteem vs
passionate love scales
overlayed (girls).

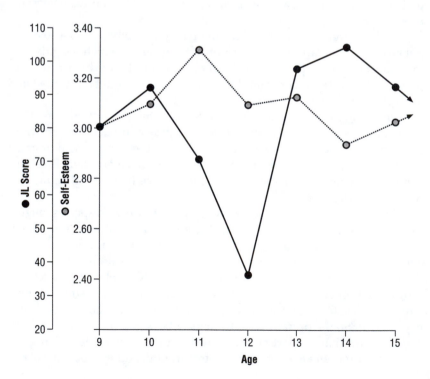

FIG. 9.1b.
Self-esteem vs
passionate love scales
overlayed (boys).

lated with girls' own juvenile love for boys than with the boys' feelings for them. Boys' self-esteem changes are also roughly opposite to their juvenile love scores (though less strongly, correlated –.3), which suggests that they, too, become more insecure as their mating interest grows in their teens. Why should this process become much more influential at puberty?

There is some biological evidence that serotonin levels drop with puberty (McBride et al., 1998), which may be related to body image distortion (Neumarker & Bartsch, 1998), as well as rejection sensitivity and applause hunger (Nathanson & Pfrommer, 1993; see Chemistry of Courtship below and Shame Biochemistry in Chapter 13). Perhaps girls are designed to become reproductive adults much more quickly than boys, because in our prehistory people could die so young that teenage motherhood was a necessity. Perhaps early teenage girls are programmed to be particularly attuned to societal cues about how to act, think, and feel, as well as how to mate, so they can absorb **their society's model of a good mother** in just a few years.

Lowering young college women's self-esteem experimentally by giving them embarrassingly negative results on personality tests may make them more receptive to a male student's invitation for a date compared to other subjects whose self-esteem was supported or unaffected (Walster, 1965). Our biosocial interpretation suggests that **what we call low self-esteem may function biologically to promote female receptiveness to mating and hence to reproduction and motherhood.**

> I feel sure that no girl could go to the altar, and would probably refuse,
> if she knew all. (Queen Victoria)

So why don't African-American girls show this dip in self-esteem? The researchers argued that the majority of Black teenage girls have strong female role models and play an adjunct parent role in their families, so their self-esteem is already anchored in family responsibilities, instead of adolescent ideals (AAUW, 1991a, 1991b). And a biological study suggests that these girls might have higher serotonin levels than Whites as well (McBride et al., 1998).

This biosocial theory gives us three ideas about girls' present social situation. First, cleansing American schools of antifeminine socialization practices may not be enough. It might work better to segregate the sexes than to train the boys to be nice during their early aggressive and un-passionate years. Second, girls' naive emulation of imagined feminine ideals may not cease, but their immediate experience of exemplary adults might be alterable. Both feminine mentoring and fatherly support might help when girls' need is greatest for reassurance of their worth and for learning about their biological and social directions in life. Third, we can see that our society's bid to postpone reproduction for 5 to 10 years is meeting with resistance from our biological nature. So we can be more sober and less condemning as we continue our efforts.

Courtship: Flirtation, salesmanship, and sales resistance

As prospective mates are approaching each other, women need to keep cueing men to approach while holding back from too much intimacy or sexual contact. Meanwhile, men try to "sell" their special brands of excellence and seek exclusive sexual favors as proof of their success. Since much of American society does not regulate women's mate choice, they need to choose very carefully. They must entice men into showing off their resources and qualities and decide quickly which of many potentially interested men to encourage.

> *The male students in my [the first author's] class were angry that women said they judged them as good or bad prospects for a serious involvement in the very first meeting. They felt it was unfair and prejudiced, since they preferred to jump in and get casually involved and then "just see what happens."*

Why can't women "just go with the flow?" The answer can be derived from **the dual mating strategies of men**. If unrestrained, many young males pursue a comparatively promiscuous, uncommitted strategy of mating which may include deceiving themselves and their partners about their intentions (Kenrick & Trost, 1987; Paul & Hirsch, 1996).

> *My relationships usually never lasted more than a week. I would be a perfect gentleman when I meet the girl or when I ask her out. As soon as we get alone, I get carried away and try to have sex. This leads the woman astray, and I usually never see her again. I tend to feel unattracted to her right after sex. This causes the girl to want me, but I do not want anything to do with her. It sounds harsh, but it's the way I feel.*

HEIGHT IS AN ATTRACTIVE QUALITY IN MEN

Since both sexes are capable of both purely passionate mating and more monogamous cultural mating norms, the cues people give during courtship determine which mating strategy each participant will pursue. If a woman must try to mate with a man who will stick around, she must also appear to be interested in **only** that man from very early in their contact. Sexual reticence and fidelity are principal signals of monogamous mating strategy, and men are very reactive to them. If a woman seems to be just as interested in other men as she is in him, a monogamously inclined man may automatically "lose faith" in her as a potential mate. Then he may shift into a promiscuous mating strategy—trying to copulate with her quickly, and investing as little emotion and resources as he can.

Women learn how easily these dual mating strategies come to men. The female "virtues" of reticence and disinterest in other men reflect women's desire to preserve their ability to choose a partner who will respond with parental investment and not simply seduction and abandonment. On the other hand, if she lives with her extended family, and the available men don't have much social status or resources (Table 9.3), a woman may join in less committed passionate mating and thus keep her options open for higher status providers in the future. In relatively impoverished minority subcultures, **matrilocal**, or mother-centered, social structure compensates for temporary paternal investment by organizing kin support (Kurland, 1979).

The biochemistry of romance

Courtship has its own highly pleasant brain chemistry that does not depend on intercourse for its appeal.

> If you can stay in love for more than two years, you're on something.
> (Fran Lebowitz)

Researchers are beginning to discover which neurochemicals may make being in love so powerfully blissful. Table 9.6 lists some aspects of the in-love state (expanded from Table 2.1) compared to known facets of the neurotransmitter groups known as dopamine, serotonin, and phenylethylamine.

TABLE 9.6. Symptoms of being in love compared to selected neurotransmitter effects

In-love symptoms & behaviors	Neurotransmitter groups identified
Exhilaration, euphoria, spiritual union	High dopamine, high norepinephrine
Increased energy, appetite loss	Dopamine, norepinephrine, high serotonin
Wakefulness	Dopamine, norepinephrine, low serotonin
Anxious arousal: trembling, pallor, flushing, butterflies, sweaty palms, weakness, pounding heart, rapid breathing, dizziness	Dopamine
Anxiety: fear with beloved, uncertainty, emotional hyperreactivity, shyness, fear of awkwardness, rejection	Dopamine, low serotonin
Separation anxiety, despair, missing beloved	Low endorphins
Intense focus: long eye contact, pupil dilation	Possibly dopamine, norephinephrine
Heightened attention: preoccupation, idealization, hope, fantasies of beloved, heightened memory	Dopamine, norepinephrine, low serotonin
Motivation to reorder priorities, possessiveness	Dopamine

Sources: Fisher, 1998; Liebowitz, 1983; Crenshaw & Goldberg, 1996.

The dopamine family of neurotransmitters are perhaps the most important for experiencing pleasure, reward, motivation, and attraction. Dopamine and norepinephrine both energize the brain for intense activity, though they affect many different sites in the brain in different ways. These chemicals also play a role in sexual motivation and arousal. The attention-focusing feature of these neurotransmitters is designed to facilitate targeting and guidance for our energized activity, and it can show up as obsessive preoccupation and, perhaps, a human version of imprinting (Tennov, 1997; Fisher, 1998).

Gazing at an attractive person (and, for women, at a baby), unbroken eye contact, and gazing at another's dilated pupils all produce dilated pupils (Hess, 1965; Hess & Petrovich, 1987); and electrical brain activity increases as eye contact is made at closer range (Gale et al., 1978). Eye contact also stimulates unstable emotional reactivity, as threat, shame, hypnotic trance, or mutual admiration. So dopamine effects are probably present here too.

Serotonin acts in some ways contrary to dopamine, contributing to the satisfaction of sexual satiation rather than arousal (Crenshaw & Goldberg, 1996). Serotonin acts as somewhat of a brake on the excitatory influence of dopamine. So problems associated with excitement, such as obsession, anxiety, and shyness, can be alleviated by the family of antidepressants that increase available serotonin [selective serotonin reuptake inhibitors (SSRIs), such as Prozac]—but the result is often reduced sexual excitement and retardation or prevention of orgasm.

Another likely candidate is phenylethylamine, or PEA, which enjoyed brief public fame as the "falling in love" drug (Liebowitz, 1983). PEA is a neurotransmitter in the brain whose molecular structure makes it part of the amphetamine family. Like other amphetamines, PEA makes us feel energized, excited, euphoric, capable, and optimistic—in short, "on top of the world." Amphetamines can lower the threshold of stimulation required to produce pleasure in animal brains, so PEA might facilitate pleasure for humans as well. Scientific evidence has linked fluctuating PEA to manic-depressive mood swings (Sabelli & Javaid, 1995), and new love is similar to manic behavior.

> I met her at a party, and we didn't spend much time together. But the next evening she came over. We talked, watched a movie on the VCR, drank a bottle of wine, and talked some more. Before I knew it, we had talked the entire night away. Neither one of us was tired at all, and I couldn't wait to see her again and pick up where we left off.

Current biochemical research indicates that PEA, dopamine, norepinephrine, and perhaps other neurotransmitters may act together to produce the in-love state, as well as sexual desire. In fact, many chemicals can influence sexual behavior (see Table 9.7), and their intricate interactions have yet to be pinpointed (Crenshaw & Goldberg, 1996).

TABLE 9.7. Some naturally-occurring substances with generally excitatory or inhibitory effects on sexual behavior

Excitatory substances	Inhibitory substances
Norepinephrine	Cortisol (emergency-stress)
Dopamine	Monoamine oxidase (MAO)
Estrogen (in female)	Estrogen (in males)
Phenylethylamine (PEA)	Opioids (and endorphins)
Oxytocin	Progesterone
Testosterone	Serotonin
Vasopressin	Alcohol (large doses)

Source: Derived from Crenshaw & Goldberg, 1996.

What is striking about the chemicals in Table 9.7 is that many of the inhibitory substances can act to **balance** the excitatory substances and thus either facilitate or shut down sexual feelings and behavior. Cortisol helps us gear up to deal with stressful situations, but depresses sexual desire. Monoamine oxidase (MAO) breaks down and disposes of norepinephrine, dopamine, serotonin, and PEA. Men have 20% less MAO than women and are more likely to be high sensation seekers. They are also less likely to suffer from depression and more likely to use alcohol to manage their emotions. Alcohol probably soothes the anxious edge of PEA's invigorating effect (Mutovkina & Lapin, 1990), as well as that of dopamine and norepinephrine, by acting like an endorphin in the brain (Crenshaw & Goldberg, 1996).

A neurotransmitter theory of love euphoria explains why it could be more exciting to have a drawn-out courtship, rather than proceeding to sex immediately and then staying together. If we generate increasing levels of excitement by meeting every day, we may rapidly reach our maximum neurotransmitter levels and then plateau out, rather than keep reaching new peaks (Milkman & Sunderwirth, 1987). On the other hand, temporary separation from our new love can trigger separation distress (low endorphins) and further obsessive thinking that may facilitate imprinting the beloved in our memory. The greatest pleasure of passion may come not from the **amount** of excitatory chemicals, but from increases in their secretion, as when you increase the **dose** of a psychoactive drug (Liebowitz, 1983).

Does it spoil all the mystery and fun to think that falling in love might really just be a neurochemical drug trip? Though this explanation is only a scientific possibility at present, it could be helpful to us in several ways. First, we can better understand why we don't stay "in love" as long as we want to. Romantic passion is designed to motivate us for bonding and childrearing, through shifting neurotransmitter balances. Since dopamine and norepinephrine respond to novel and achievable challenges, once we get habituated to our partner these and PEA production probably taper off. Many of us have listened to complaints about a relationship, concluding with these fateful words: "Well, I love him, but I'm not *in love* with him."

The speaker thinks there must be something wrong. And if the in-love feelings don't come back soon, then it may be time to start breaking up, especially if you are young and not married. Changing our mate or finding a new one seem to be the only options for bringing "that old black magic" back again.

Better living through chemistry?   Perhaps a biochemical understanding of in-love states can give us more freedom of choice. If you were hopelessly in love, and you knew it was destructive, you could treat your condition as a biochemical addiction. Perhaps you could even choose to "fall out of love" again, by changing your brain chemistry. If you were constantly miserable when not head over heels in love or when any lover pushed you away, perhaps you would be healthier and happier if a medication could alleviate your withdrawal response.

Though little scientific effort has been expended toward finding a "falling out of love drug," the anti-manic drug lithium may help some people. And antidepressant drugs that inhibit monoamine oxidase (MAOI antidepressants), alleviate withdrawal symptoms from amphetamines and from PEA (Liebowitz, 1983) by increasing supplies of noradrenalin, dopamine, and serotonin, as well as PEA. Since these neurotransmitters are in short supply when we are depressed, taking MAOI antidepressants may perhaps make some people less dependent on infatuation to feel good. SSRI antidepressants that inhibit the reabsorption of serotonin may work also (Nathanson, 1992). But tinkering with brain chemistry often not only alleviates depression, but also can send some people into mania or excessive anxiety (Sabelli et al., 1990).

How long does passion last?   Since human evolution naturally selects qualities in us necessary for raising successful children, passionate adult love need only last long enough to produce a child, after which it could interfere with fulfilling the needs of the child. A stable, durable **attachment** that soothes our responses to external events and makes us distressed when we interrupt or destabilize our relationships would serve the survival of our offspring better than a passionate excitement that kept parents grabbing each other and sneaking off to make love (Fisher, 1992).

The normal duration of romantic passion may be about **3 years,** according to various empirical and anecdotal sources:

1. Interviews with around 800 lovers established that being in love normally lasted between 18 months and 3 years (Tennov, 1979).
2. Sex researcher John Money (1980) also estimated that passionate love normally lasts 2 to 3 years.
3. According to United Nations divorce statistics, the largest proportion (statistical mode) of divorces occurred in the largest number of societies (in which divorce was comparatively easy to obtain) between the second and fourth years of marriage (Fisher, 1992).

4. A government official from Botswana, where divorce is still infrequent, said: "When a couple gets married, they are frequently told that this feeling you have now will evaporate in 2 or 3 years. You are married for your families, not for this feeling."
5. According to recent research, engaging in exciting activities may improve marital satisfaction (perhaps due to doses of dopamine and norepinephrine). But couples married less than 3 years were not likely to boost their satisfaction through excitement, since it was usually high already (Aron & Aron, 1996).

Neurochemicals for sex and bonding. Sex is linked with two specific neurochemicals, **oxytocin** and **vasopressin**, which are known to be connected to parental behavior and social bonding in both sexes (Insel, 1992; Winslow et al., 1993; Crenshaw & Goldberg, 1996; Uvnas-Moberg, 1997). Research has shown that oxytocin levels are highest at orgasm, but they also increase during intercourse, stroking, cuddling, and birth labor, lactation, and breast-feeding. Oxytocin facilitates male erection and both sexes' nervous sensitivity, working synergistically with dopamine and other neurotransmitters to increase the pleasure of all of these activities. But it is secreted in brief spurts, breaks down in 5 to 10 minutes, and stops working in both animals and humans if injected for 10 days in a row. Repeated injection with oxytocin lowered rats' blood pressure and caused females to start gaining weight. So it is possible that sex is not only good for our health, but it also triggers women's bodies to prepare for pregnancy.

The interactions between oxytocin and other neurotransmitters are complex. But its interaction with endogenous opioids, or *endorphins* is worth noting. Endorphins can inhibit secretion of oxytocin, but injected oxytocin can accomplish the same temporary relief of pain as endorphins (Yang, 1994). Thus sex- and touch-stimulated oxytocin is a temporary pain-killer too. Apparently oxytocin helps overcome the inhibitory effect of opiates and endorphins on sexual intercourse, and alcohol (which acts similarly to opiates in some ways) partially reduces oxytocin secretion in women due to breast stimulation (Coira et al., 1992). But since its effects are brief, oxytocin seems to foster the production of endorphins afterwards (Crenshaw & Goldberg, 1996). Thus oxytocin fosters affection and bonding in ways that are both antagonistic and synergistic with our endorphin system (see below). Since its "cuddle-chemical" effects are designed for sexual and touch pleasure and for maternal nurturing, our oxytocin system seems well designed to bring sex, love, affection, and nurturance together.

Though present in both sexes, vasopressin is stimulated in male humans and other mammals especially during sexual arousal and dream-sleep. It helps control brain temperature in the hypothalamus, where both pheromones and dreaming may lead to temporary temperature surges—perhaps as reflected in slang: "I'm hot for him/her." In males of a monogamous species of rodents, prairie voles, vasopressin helps bring about long-lasting pairbonding, mate guarding, parental involvement with pups, and aggression towards strangers (Insel 1997). These links between vasopressin and behavior did not occur in female prairie voles or in males of a similar but non-pairbonding species, mountain voles. Apparently mating stimulates vasopressin secretion, which may set off an irreversible change in patterns of neurochemical receptors, resulting in enduring pairbonding, protective, and perhaps nurturant behavior. Whether sexual arousal and these mated and parental behaviors are as closely linked in human males or not remains for future research to explore. But this vole research suggests a biochemical basis for men's loyalty, mate competition, and "mate guarding," that is, possessiveness.

Oxytocin disrupts learning and memory in both men and women, while vasopressin enhances them. Crenshaw and Goldberg (1996) speculate that the pleasure of sex, birthing, and cuddling may help people forget what is negative and thus promote enduring peaceable relations useful for parenting.

Relationship maintenance through attachment. The connection between pair bonding and mother-child love is developed in adult attachment theory (Bowlby, 1969; Shaver et al., 1988). We have suggested that passionate love seems to normally last two to three years, long enough to have and perhaps wean a child. After this both sexes are biochemically capable of developing passion for a new partner (Fisher, 1992). But this is long enough for attachment to the mate to build up, since it may take an average of two years to develop (Hazan, July, 1992).

Oxytocin and vasopressin *promote* bonding with a mate or a child. But biopsychology postulates that **our brain's own internal opiates, called endorphins** may be more involved in *maintaining* attachment (Panksepp et al., 1997). Compared to passion, attachment is a milder feeling, in which the presence of one's partner, relative, (or mother for an infant) has a pleasant effect which also soothes pain. Endorphins are secreted to counteract both physical and emotional pain, giving us "runner's high," helping us cope with stress, and soothing us when we cry.

The importance of these neurochemical "good-feelings" has been shown in experiments with several mammalian species. The distress of rat pups separated from their mothers is soothed by both opiates, such as heroin, and synthetic endorphins. Chemically blocking the endorphin receptors makes them more distressed and more motivated to seek affectionate contact but less soothed by it (Keverne et al., 1989; Panksepp et al., 1980). Similarly, human parents, children, and mates may feel mildly pleasant when together, but when sick, injured, or threatened, they seek each other to trigger the endorphins that soothe their distress. When separated, couples' symptoms of endorphin withdrawal can include sleeplessness, hypervigilance, and desperation, as painful as they are for a child.

But endorphins, like opiates and alcohol, don't just soothe our pain and separation distress. They also suppress the production of oxytocin. Thus it is possible that the biochemistry of attachment tends to sideline the biochemistry of passion in those with enduring close relationships. This might be a biological basis for the comparative lack of sexual intercourse among family members and children raised together, as well as for the decline in frequency and importance of sex among long-term mates.

Since attachment cues in our endorphins, enduring intimate relationships function as a support against the struggles and setbacks of life. They are a "secure base" amidst a sea of troubles (Bowlby, 1980) that reliably triggers our brain's own tranquilizing and restorative forces. If romantic **passion** functions to bring two people together into a love bond, **attachment** may gradually supercede passion and make it painful to break up. Since these endorphin processes are the same between adult partners as between parents and children, attachment may well serve to bind whole families together, in contrast to passion, which excludes all but the euphoric pair.

Divorce

According to evolutionary theory, people should be designed to be capable of divorce, especially to get rid of an uninvested, dangerous, infertile, or dysfunctional man or woman. Almost every society has some sort of arrangement for divorce (Price & McKenry, 1988) and some preindustrial societies have divorce rates nearly as high as our own (reviewed in Fisher, 1992). In 160 preindustrial societies (Chapter 5, Table 5.2), the common reasons for seeking a divorce fit this model. The most common is blatant extramarital sexual affairs (cited also in 25–50% of divorces in industrialized countries), particularly by the wife. Affairs would convince the husband that he could not count on rearing children with his own genes. Infertility comes second, followed by cruelty, particularly by the husband. After this come complaints about the partner's character, nonsupport by the husband, sexual neglect, and desertion (Betzig, 1989). In cultures where divorcing is comparatively easy, (North America, Northern Europe, but also Fiji), the divorce rate reaches a slight peak between the second and fourth years of marriage (Fisher, 1992).

It appears that the decline in passion by the second or third year of consistent togetherness sets up the riskiest transition a relationship must face. If there were no children by this time to require and evoke attachment, then attachment processes might not be a strong successor to romantic passion. Since birth control did not exist until recently, couples could assume they were infertile. If their culture also accepts as "natural" that sexual loyalties can shift, then either separation or extramarital affairs are likely. Thus, affairs, sexual neglect, and desertion are divorce-worthy signs that the romantic passion has died or moved on.

In America, the divorce rate was 3–4 times higher among childless couples than among parents a hundred years ago, and it is still higher today (Kenrick & Trost, 1987). Though children may decrease the quality and quantity of marital interactions, they nevertheless increase marital commitment, perhaps via attachment processes as well as economic and cultural barriers to divorce. In statistics from 45 societies, 39% of divorcing couples had no dependent children, 26% had one dependent child, and 19% had two, but only 7% had three and it dropped off from there (Hoffman & Manis, 1978).

Financial resources for parental investment clearly affect our tendency to divorce. For males, higher incomes reduce the risk of divorce (Kenrick & Trost, 1987), while greater individual control of resources by women increases it (Fisher, 1992). Gender reactions to sexual infidelity are probably affected by economics, since women might be unlikely to show their reactions to male infidelity where men control most of the economic resources (Hupka & Ryan, 1990).

Critique of the biosocial perspective

We must remember that biosocial theories are not a definitive scientific explanation of human nature. Even though evidence may have been drawn from many different arenas, such as physiology, neurochemistry, history, paleoanthropology, and comparative animal studies, it still does not guarantee that a theory is correct. The vastness of the field of comparative studies makes it likely that even the best theorists may "mix and match" the evidence that supports their ideas, rather than insist that **any contradictory evidence proves that our present explanation is inadequate**. Critics point out that many biosocial theorists rush to assume genetic and biological universals of human nature, without giving adequate consideration to environmental and social forces that may be even more compelling (Bem, 1993). It is particularly tempting and questionable to conclude that contemporary American college students' attitudes and dating/mating behavior represent evolutionary mechanisms without first seeking corroboration from many other cultures and scientific disciplines. David Gilmore (1990) accentuates sociocultural considerations when he argues that cultural and psychological masculinity may derive not so much from testosterone as from nearly world-wide competition for scarce resources and the consequent need to resist psychological urges toward passivity and maternal comfort. Biosocial theory responds with "Yes, both environmental and psychosocial forces led men to evolve their biological mechanisms for dominance, competition, and collaboration."

Let us also consider what sorts of inferences are appropriate to make from these theories and what sorts are not. Establishing a theory of evolutionary psychology based on paleoanthropology does not mean that what worked for prehistoric hunter-gatherer groups is best for us now. Neither should the data that mothers have always been primary caregivers to infants convince us that "a woman's place is in (or near) the home." For we can supplement the vital aspects of her infant care (breast milk, attachment, tactile stimulation, reliable need fulfillment) through other people.

But human nature changes a lot more slowly than we want it to, and the combined effect of social, environmental, and evolutionary forces may lead us to develop in ways we cannot presently understand. Though there is enough evidence for when and where our species evolved, there are still many holes and weaknesses in evolutionary theory that must be addressed as we proceed toward a unification of human sciences.

Our cultural ethnocentrism has an age-old tendency to project our own attitudes and traits backward onto the evolutionary past and then search for evidence to "retrofit" contemporary traits onto biological human nature. Thus evolutionary theory resonates with current social controversies, where **mate-guarding** means male domination, **autopredation** means the inevitability of male-initiated wars, and **concealed ovulation** signals female deception and manipulation in the battle of the sexes. There is a huge difference between the pace of *cultural* evolution that impacts our current thoughts and behavior and the *biological* evolution that forms our basic psychological structure. We need to understand that our ideals, such as equal rights and treatment for all people, and our inherited biopsychological strategies for survival and propagation are two different things. If we adjust our expectations to include them both, we may approach the task of improving human society with more patience and humility.

Chapter summary

- In biosocial theory human characteristics are designed by natural selection for survival and reproductive success, which involves flexible strategies for living and mating.
- Nurturant love stimulates intelligence, and both are vital to our evolutionary success, because our larger, slower developing brains require longer parental care.
- Romantic love evolved to stabilize parental investment in offspring. But groups provide alternative support, thus allowing both monogamous and promiscuous mating strategies.
- The survival-based division of labor influenced gender differences in sensory and cognitive abilities. Men specialized in the object world, while women specialized in interpersonal abilities.
- Male and female mating strategies often clash, with men more impulsive, promiscuous, and domineering and women more cautious,

alluring, and intuitive. Relative gender size also suggests mild polygyny, along with male traits of dominance, aggression, and increased mortality.

- Male possessiveness seeks certainty of genetic fatherhood. Female jealousy may be more concerned with losing parental investment than with sexuality.
- Cultural standards of feminine beauty emphasize health, fertility, and "new ripeness."
- Testosterone influences sex and aggression in males more than females.
- Women identify the scents of their mates and children, as well as potentially healthy matches.
- Though not consciously smelled, human pheromones catalyze warmth, emotional skin response, and alpha brain waves, affecting men more strongly than women.
- Girls' self-esteem may become much more sensitive to socially desirable qualities during puberty. Lowered self-esteem may predispose girls to seek courtship.
- Women's expression of monogamous romantic interest attracts a high-investing mate, while flirtatiousness may invite low-investment promiscuity.
- Cultural masculinity includes striving to provide, protect, procreate, and endure pain and adversity, in order to succeed in environments with limited resources and competitive groups.
- Dopamine, norepinephrine, and phenylethylamine are conducive to excitement of love and sex.
- Generated in sex, touch, and nursing, oxytocin promotes pleasurable attachment. Vasopressin instigates pairbonding, mateguarding, and parental nurture in some male rodents and perhaps men.
- Endorphins reinforce attachment by soothing pain and by causing separation distress in their absence. They reduce oxytocin and sexual desire, perhaps helping attachment supercede sex. Shared with both children and mate, attachment preserves families better than passionate love.
- The peak in divorces after 2–4 years of marriage may be due to a normal decline in passion but weaker attachment in the absence of children, since infidelity and infertility are among the top reasons for divorce.
- Biosocial theorizing should not assume that hunter-gatherer sex roles are "natural," that current society is either the leading edge of evolution or the key to perennial human nature, or that human biology will quickly mold itself to our present hopes and ideals.

Theoretical perspectives on relationships ‖‖

Some of the travelers seek to systematically understand the elements of ships and how to build them. They may concentrate on the varieties of basic structures, properties of individual parts, ways they are held and work together, or historical development of models that have worked. Others study the ecology of ships in the sea, the varieties of early training, and prior experience of crew members. What they all have in common is the desire to understand how certain basic elements lead to ships' behavior on their voyages. They are searching for what makes ships strong, effective, and durable so that they can advise each other on how to proceed in every weather.

Part III explains how the emotional lessons we incorporate as children shape our later emotional and intimate behavior, moving us toward some ways of relating and away from others. Chapter 10 reviews some history and several types of individual, cognitive, and developmental psychology, while Chapter 11 concentrates on family systems theories.

Perspectives on intimacy in psychology 10

The Origins of Western romantic love

The source of our ideal image of romantic love that has attracted the most scholarly interest for centuries is **courtly love**, or "fin amors," which apparently arose in Southern French courts and began to leave its mark in

"MAYBE REAL-LIFE LOVE WOULD BE LIKE REAL-LIFE ROMANCE, IF WE ATE MORE **POPCORN!** JUST SPENDING TIME IN THE DARK HASN'T HELPED."

literature in the mid-twelfth century. It is the source of polite behavior we call courtesy or chivalry. Courtly love departed strikingly from Christian views of the time by radically increasing the value assigned to women and to sexual love. It also has so many features similar to mystical religion, that it is sometimes called a "religion of love."

Four factors that were unique in courtly love (Singer, 1984) are still important today. First, sexual love between men and women was seen to be in itself something wonderful, an ideal worth striving for. In contrast, the ancient Romans and Greeks viewed sex as trivial, and passionate love as an affliction, a madness from which one should recover. Second, romantic love was believed to ennoble both the lover and the beloved. (In the movie "As Good as it Gets" the courting novelist tells his beloved at their first dinner date, "You make me want to be a better man.") Third, romantic love was elevated to being an ethical and aesthetic achievement which cannot be reduced to a mere sexual impulse—what moderns call "true love." Fourth, love was seen as an intense relationship that establishes a holy oneness between two persons. This view comes from Plato's "soul mate" myth in The Symposium, and is now celebrated in Christian marriage.

The most explicit description of courtly love was written by Andreas Capellanus, a Church-educated official at the feudal court of Aquitaine (1184/1941). Capellanus' *The Art of Courtly Love* follows the medieval rhetorical custom of presenting both sides of an issue by praising and explaining love for two books and then condemning it as unChristian in the third. His catalogue of "rules of love" is full of psychological insights and clues to the twelfth-century attitudes toward love:

1. Marriage is no real excuse for not loving. (Medieval courtly love was generally viewed as not possible, or not very likely, in marriage [De Rougement, 1940; Singer, 1984].)
2. He who is not jealous cannot love.
3. No one can be bound by a double love.
4. It is well known that love is always increasing or decreasing.
5. That which a lover takes against the will of his beloved has no relish.
6. Boys do not love until they arrive at the age of maturity.
7. When one lover dies, a widowhood of two years is required of the survivor.
8. Love is always a stranger in the home of avarice.

9. It is not proper to love any woman whom one would be ashamed to seek to marry.
10. A true lover does not desire to embrace in love anyone except his beloved.
11. When made public love rarely endures.
12. The easy attainment of love makes it of little value; difficulty of attainment makes it prized.
13. Every lover regularly turns pale in the presence of his beloved.
14. When a lover suddenly catches sight of his beloved his heart palpitates.
15. A new love puts to flight an old one.
16. Good character alone makes any man worthy of love.
17. If love diminishes, it quickly fails and rarely revives.
18. A man in love is always apprehensive.
19. Real jealousy always increases the feeling of love.
20. Jealousy, and therefore love, are increased when one suspects his beloved.
21. He whom the thought of love vexes eats and sleeps very little.
22. A true lover considers nothing good except what he thinks will please his beloved.
23. A lover can never have enough of the solaces of his beloved.
24. A true lover is constantly and without intermission possessed by the thought of his beloved.

We find several of the above phenomena connected to the arousal theory for attraction (Chapter 1), including items 4, and 17 through 21, as well as item 11 (secrecy), item 12 (difficulty) and item 23 (endless sexual anticipation). There are also many symptoms of physical distress and mental obsession which were derived from medieval Arab medical descriptions of "ishq," or love-sickness (Boase, 1977), including items 10, 13, 14, 21, 23, and 24. "A new love puts to flight an old one" argues for the chemical primacy of courtship over long-term attachment (Chapter 9).

Theories of real and ideal love

If this love seems too good to be real, it is. From what is known about the medieval nobility in Southern France, courtly romantic love existed in poetry and fiction, but not in real life. The real courtly ladies were trapped in arranged marriages with older feudal lords who would punish any extramarital affairs with death. Capellanus attributed this explanation for why love cannot occur in marriage to his patroness, Marie de Champagne:

> Love cannot exert its powers between two people who are married to each other. For lovers give each other everything freely, under no compulsion or necessity, but married people are in duty bound to give in to each other's desires. (Capellanus, 1184/1941)

Romantic love requires individual freedom, but medieval women were made to marry against their will. *Thus, **the medieval Western concept of romantic love may have originated as a make-believe emancipation from the economically based practice of arranged marriage**. Courtly audiences probably knew this romantic love was only make-believe. Americans embrace romantic love as an ideal today and celebrate it in fiction and film too, but for different reasons.

Industrialization and the idealization of romantic intimacy

Changes in community and personality brought about by industrialization in the nineteenth century are the social foundation for the rise of the modern intimate relationship. The key change was the separation of the work world from the home, so each working person was isolated from family and community for most of the day. Now freed from the controlling influences of family and community, each person was increasingly subjected to the tantalizing influences of entertainment, exposure to strangers from diverse backgrounds, and the market economy. One historian of intimate relationships suggests:

> People must have panicked at the flood of unchecked impulse that suddenly became their own responsibility. The dilemma of these people, it seems, is that at the same time they were threatened from within by their own impulses they were also isolated from the very people from whom they had come to expect not only restraint and control but warmth, intimacy, and in general the gratification of emotional needs. (Gadlin, 1977)

Thus, people began to develop "private lives," along with new needs for intimacy, support, and moral guidelines. The concept of romantic intimacy grew to include many interpersonal needs formerly fulfilled by the extended family and the community. Industrialized North America and Europe now lead the world in viewing emotional intimacy and friendship as a primary expectation in marriage.

Romantic intimacy is idealized today as a counterforce to the alienation of individuals in industrial society. Love plots in the movies frequently revolve around the values of kindness, self-sacrifice, and trust against the more self-serving and competitive qualities fostered in the work world.

Therefore we do not expect our media-based conceptions of love to be real-istic—any more than courtly romances were realistic in their day. For in Hollywood's "fairy tale" tradition, our romantic and adventurous fictions give us imaginary relief from the reality of materialism and inspire us to believe in more communal values in spite of everything.

Our modern conceptions of love are inevitably idealizations, because they are not derived from life, but from literature and film, and because they are meant to inspire us to be better than we usually are. But will we be better off if we drop our idealization of love and base our relationships on good sex and good, equitable exchanges of support and services? Marriage would not need to last, since sex and services can be replaced pretty easily as long as one's "mate market value" is high. But perhaps idealizing the immediate experience of love is necessary for people's psychospiritual health, because it fosters values that transcend material happiness (Lindholm, 1998). Perhaps people need to idealize and transcend ordinary reality somehow, whether through religion, charismatic cults, state-wor-ship (nationalistic fervor), or romantic love.

Three components of love

We saw in Chapter 2 that it is very helpful to conceive of love as consisting of **passion**, **intimacy**, and **commitment** (Sternberg, 1988). Sternberg places these three components into a triangle, which facilitates the conceptual organization of several different kinds of love, as Figure 10.1 indicates.

One helpful insight of the triangular diagram is that we might **experience** romantic love (intimacy plus passion) even without admitting that we are in love, or that we want our present mental state to continue. Since Americans associate love with commitment and duration (Fehr, 1988), we may deny that our emotions are really love when we are unwilling to com-

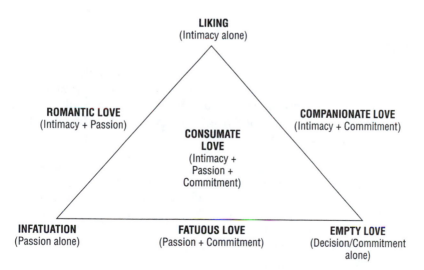

FIG. 10.1. Triangular representation of three components of love.

mit to a future (casual relationships, Chapter 1). The other positions along the triangle describe significant versions of love as well. **Companionate love** and **empty love** describe what long-term spousal love can be like when passion has dwindled. **Fatuous love** (passion and commitment) can occur when two people's needs and emotions fit well together (such as when people are rebounding from breakups) and they commit and move in or marry without getting to know each other.

Research shows (Sternberg, 1987) that relationship satisfaction is associated with the degree to which each partner's actual experience of each of the three factors (passion, intimacy, and commitment) approximates his or her ideal expectations. That means either that partners who see or experience more or less passion, intimacy, or commitment than they want will be dissatisfied, or that dissatisfied partners are likely to report more or less of these than they want. It also suggests that couples whose ideal expectations for these three factors differ are likely to experience dissatisfactions that are not easy to resolve.

We can get beyond simplistic concepts of love by dividing it into thinking, feeling, and acting. Sternberg reserves passion for passionate love and intimacy for companionate feelings and actions. But it is conceptually simpler to class all love *feelings* under passion and consider intimacy as a category for shared *behaviors* and not the emotions that sometimes motivate them. *Thinking* aspects of love extend beyond the term commitment, as we will see when we consider more theories below. The American cultural bias for **intimacy** is reflected in the positive names for all combinations that include it and the negative names for all combinations that don't include it: "infatuation," "fatuous love," and "empty love." Our culture substitutes couple intimacy for the community continuity and interdependence we are lacking, but that doesn't make intimacy the key factor that makes a relationship "good." Indeed, the courtly tradition discussed earlier emphasizes the ennobling power of passionate feelings combined with a commitment not to act on them in any intimate ways.

Colors of love

The "colors of love" approach (Lee, 1973; Hendrick & Hendrick, 1992b) avoids value judgments and covers a wider variety of love attitudes. Lee (1998) points out that not only individuals but classes, entire cultures, and eras are likely to think that one style of loving is "true love," while others are delusional or inadequate:

> Some have argued that love must be unselfish and concerned only for the beloved . . . others have said love should be self-fulfilling and realistic. Some even apply a Puritan work ethic, arguing that true love must be productive [as in Fromm's *Art of Loving*, 1956] or contribute to growth and development. . . . Would it not be equally valid to argue that love should be more fun? (Lee, 1988, p. 41)

Lee sorted out six different basic love styles and found that many also regularly occurred in combination. They are **eros**, **ludus**, **storge**, **mania**, **pragma**, and **agape**. Eros is a passionate attraction that is closely linked to perceiving the partner as ideally beautiful (as in Plato's *Phaedrus*). Our present knowledge of pheromones and the power of specific cues in attraction suggests there are other sources of erotic euphoria besides visual beauty. This student reports on an eros love at first sight:

> I was working at a local grocery store when she walked in one night with her family. At that exact moment I knew that this girl was the right one for me and I was determined that she was going to be mine no matter what. Passion may have played the biggest role in my impulsive decision. She is blond with hazy blue eyes and a great pair of legs, all of which are traits that I have imagined that my wife-to-be would possess.

Unlike the single-minded passion of **eros**, **ludus** (Latin for play) plays at love as a delightful game, often with more than one partner at the same time. The purpose is not possession of the beloved or commitment, but to get the most excitement and fun out of the moment. Frequently criticized today as "game-playing" and "player" love, ludic loving (taught to Romans in Ovid's *Art of Love*) is more common among today's men than women and is reduced when people acknowledge that they are "really" in love (Hendrick & Hendrick, 1988, 1992b). **Storge** is the ancient Greek word for friendly love between siblings and playmates. It is common in farming areas where everyone grows up together and eventually settles down in companionate marriages. It is central in peer marriage (Chapter 7) and in the belief that your partner should be your best friend. **Mania** is love as a madness (Capellanus and ishq), complete with obsessive preoccupation, jealousy, possessiveness, insecurity, physical symptoms, and a roller-coaster of positive and negative emotions. Many psychologists insist that manic lovers are psychologically disturbed. But mania often erupts in first love or in combination with eros, and it captivates in movies as it once did in courtly romance.

Pragma lovers seek similar religious, ethnic, economic, and social class backgrounds first, then may add compatible interests, goals, and gender roles, all before considering any feelings. It is pragmatic mate-choice with emphasis on compatibility and a socially appropriate match. Pragmatic mating has been desirable among the social elite throughout history. In some cultures arranged marriages serve this purpose, while in ours it can be approximated by computer dating agencies or social clubs. **Agape** is selfless, altruistic, generous love, of the sort that is advocated by Christianity and Christian authors, such as Leo Buscaglia (*Love*, 1985) and M. Scott Peck (*The Road Less Traveled*, 1984). You can estimate the relative values you give to each of these six love styles by totaling your scores on the questionnaire in Table 10.1.

TABLE 10.1. Love attitudes scale: From Hendrick & Hendrick, 1992

For each statement indicate how much you agree or disagree. The items refer to a specific love relationship. Whenever possible, answer the questions with your current partner in mind. If you are not currently in relationship, answer with your most recent partner in mind. If you have never been in love, answer in terms of what you think your responses would most likely be. For each statement:

> 1 = Strongly disagree with the statement.
> 2 = Moderately disagree with the statement.
> 3 = Neutral—neither agree nor disagree.
> 4 = Moderately agree with the statement.
> 5 = Strongly agree with the statement.

1. My partner and I were attracted to each other immediately after we first met.
2. My partner and I have the right physical "chemistry" between us.
3. Our lovemaking is very intense and satisfying.
4. I feel that my partner and I were meant for each other.
5. My partner and I became emotionally involved rather quickly.
6. My partner and I really understand each other.
7. My partner fits my ideal standards of physical beauty/handsomeness.
8. I try to keep my partner a little uncertain about my commitment to him or her.
9. I believe that what my partner doesn't know about me won't hurt him or her.
10. I have sometimes had to keep my partner from finding out about other partners.
11. I could get over my affair with my partner pretty easily and quickly.
12. My partner would get upset if he or she knew of some of the things I've done with other people.
13. When my partner gets too dependent on me, I want to back off a little.
14. I enjoy playing the "game of love" with my partner and a number of other partners.
15. It is hard for me to say exactly when our friendship turned into love.
16. To be genuine, our love first required caring for a while.
17. I expect to always be friends with my partner.
18. Our love is the best kind because it grew out of a long friendship.
19. Our friendship merged gradually into love over time.
20. Our love is really a deep friendship, not a mysterious, mystical emotion.
21. Our love relationship is the most satisfying because it developed from a good friendship.
22. I considered what my partner was going to become in life before I committed myself to him or her.
23. I tried to plan my life carefully before choosing my partner.
24. In choosing my partner, I believed it was best to love someone with a similar background.
25. A main consideration in choosing my partner was how he or she would reflect on my family.
26. An important factor in choosing my partner was whether or not he or she would be a good parent.
27. One consideration in choosing my partner was how he or she would reflect on my career.

TABLE 10.1. *Continued*

28. Before getting very involved with my partner, I tried to figure out how compatible our hereditary backgrounds would be.
29. When things aren't right with my partner and me, my stomach gets upset.
30. If my partner and I break up, I would get so depressed that I would even think of suicide.
31. Sometimes I get so excited about being in love with my partner that I can't sleep.
32. When my partner doesn't pay attention to me, I feel sick all over.
33. Since I've been in love with my partner, I've had trouble concentrating on anything else.
34. I cannot relax if I suspect that my partner is with someone else.
35. If my partner ignores me for a while, I sometimes do stupid things to try to get his or her attention back.
36. I try to always help my partner through difficult times.
37. I would rather suffer myself than let my partner suffer.
38. I cannot be happy unless I place my partner's happiness before my own.
39. I am usually willing to sacrifice my own wishes to let my partner achieve his or hers.
40. Whatever I own is my partner's to use as he or she chooses.
41. When my partner gets angry with me, I still love him or her fully and unconditionally.
42. I would endure all things for the sake of my partner.

Score the first 7 questions for eros, the next 7 for ludus, then 7 for storge, 7 for pragma, 7 for mania, and the last 7 for agape. Over 21 points gives an endorsing attitude for each love style. Capellanus' *The Art of Courtly Love* (1184/1941) suggests that love is inspired by eros, felt as mania, and promises agape, though it may be carried out according to a ludic "game-plan."

Some of Lee's styles resemble Sternberg's: **eros** is close to romantic love; **mania** to infatuation; **storge** to liking and companionate love; and **pragma** to empty love. **Ludic** lovers play with passion, while manic lovers' reactiveness makes them the playthings of passion. **Agape** is related to a communal, rather than exchange orientation (Chapter 7), even giving our partner's needs a higher priority than our own.

Gender-difference studies show males as more ludic and slightly more erotic. Women's reputation for being more affected by romance comes from their greater reports of manic symptoms. But they also place more value on both friendship (storgic) and pragmatic considerations, so women may be more practical than men, if they are not "love-struck" (Hendrick et al., 1988). These gender differences fit with the male and female dual mating strategies (Chapter 9) as well. Lee suggests (1988) that lovers will understand and respect each other better if their favored love styles match, and that love styles can change for different partners and also change with the same partner over time. Women are somewhat more likely to proceed from friendship toward more erotic love, with an earlier focus on practical issues, including commitment. Men are somewhat more likely to start with erotic excitement and let friendship come later. In fact, research has found that both male and female students tend to prefer an unknown potential partner whose dominant love style is similar to their own, but **storge** and **agape** were most consistently desired (Hahn & Blass, 1997). In existing relationships satisfaction and commitment levels may be most related to **erotic** and **agapic** love scores (Morrow et al., 1995). This suggests that unselfish generosity and friendly intimacy are most attractive, while passion and idealization are also likely to foster relationship satisfaction.

Social psychological theories

In addition to Sternberg's factors and Lee's colors, social psychologists have explored and theorized about many aspects of love. Focusing primarily on cognitive behavior for the last two to three decades, researchers have expanded on the ways that our thinking shapes and influences our close relationships.

Steve Duck (May, 1991) emphasizes the importance of **making meaning together.** According to his theory, two people develop similar interpretations of their life together and who they are in relation to each other. Even without defining their relationship as love, two people can develop their mental closeness as they weave more and more interpretations of their worlds and their experiences into a common pool of stories and symbols. This theory implies a slow development of closeness that emphasizes **intimate communication** and friendship love without a big role for passionate feelings.

Two-factor theories. Other social psychologists have pursued a "two-factor theory" of love, assuming that both emotion and thinking play vital parts. Arthur and Elaine Aron (1986, 1994; Aron et al., 1991) emphasize the importance of emotional or physiological arousal in love and posit a basic *motivation* that is beneath consciousness. Focusing on a couple's mental experience of union, they contend that loving arises from a motivation to expand oneself. Couples construct overlapping self concepts and unconsciously include parts of the other in themselves. If I love someone, I admire her qualities, and I am motivated to incorporate her and those qualities into myself. Thus love impulses serve a drive toward self actualization through expanding our experience, abilities, and qualities. This theory could apply to both friendly and passionate relationships, and it prioritizes nonconscious process over mental acts of making meaning. Derived from Indian Vedantic psychology, love as expansion of the self is also closely related to the Jungian ideas that a romantic partner may be a projection of one's own unrealized opposite sex qualities and that passionate feelings accompany each new growth we aspire to in the course of **individuation**, or actualizing our potential.

Focusing more on emotions, Elaine Hatfield (1988) defines passionate love as "a state of intense longing for union with another. Reciprocated love (union with the other) is associated with fulfillment and ecstasy. Unrequited love (separation) with emptiness, anxiety, or despair. A state of profound physiological arousal" (p. 191). Thus passionate love is primarily emotional and physiological arousal. But there are cognitive and behavioral components as well. Cognitive features include intrusive thinking or preoccupation with the partner, idealization of the partner or the relationship, and desire to know the other and be known. Behavioral features include actions toward maintaining physical closeness and toward determining the other's feelings, studying the other person, and service to the other. Searching for the emotional sources of falling in love, Hatfield finds conditions of low self-esteem, dependency, anxiety, separation and loss, and neediness (Hatfield & Rapson, 1993). Hatfield views love as rooted in childhood attachments, so "anything that makes adults feel as helpless and dependent as they were as children, anything that makes them fear separation and loss, should increase their passionate craving to merge with the other" (Hatfield & Rapson, 1993, p. 45).

While agreeing that such "deficient" personality states can lead us to fall in love, Sharon Brehm (1992) adds that high self esteem and effectiveness conditions are also conducive to passionate involvement. Brehm emphasizes the role of mental concentration in increasing passion. She cites a study (Tesser & Paulus, 1976) that suggests that the causal relationship between thought and romantic arousal goes both ways: "the more you love someone, the more you will think about him or her; the more you think about someone you love, the more you will love him or her" (Tesser & Paulus, 1976, p. 103). Drawing from the nineteenth century French novelist Stendhal and the sixteenth century Spanish mystic, St. Teresa of Avila, Brehm proposes that "the core of passionate love lies in the capacity to construct in one's imagination an elaborated vision of a future state of perfect happiness" (Brehm, 1988, p. 253). Thus idealization is the key cognitive component of love. A study of both dating and marital couples found that idealizing the partner and the future was associated with higher love and satisfaction and with dating couples staying together and increasing in satisfaction at a later time (Murray & Holmes, 1997). Interviews with couples married over 20 years found that partners had preserved an idealized (romanticized) image of each other, often associated with early romance memories, next to their more sober images with faults and aging (Wallerstein & Blakeslee, 1995). Thus idealizing the beloved and the relationship helps love flourish, and negative re-imaging occurs in marital decay (Chapter 4) and before and after divorce (Chapter 5).

The two-factor theory rebalanced. Brehm's ideas and subsequent research reemphasize the theme of idealization that began with courtly love. But we know more about how thinking may influence emotions than about how emotions and physiological arousal may influence thought and imagination. Research into biochemical mechanisms of attraction and bonding in Chapter 9 suggest that the **emotional factor** in love may be strong enough to grow on us, whether it is set in motion and guided by conscious thinking or not. The power of testosterone, dopamine, phenylethylamine, seroto-nin, oxytocin, vasopressin, and endorphins suggests that passionate emotions will naturally grow as a function of **time** and **intensity** focused on a potential partner (Capellanus' "excessive meditation"). Passionate emotional processes are not under the control of conscious thinking, though they can be influenced.

> If it is your time love will track you down like a Cruise missile. If you say 'No! I don't want it right now', that's when you'll get it for sure. Love will make a way out of no way. Love is exploding cigar which we willingly smoke. (Lynda Barry, cartoonist)

How do the cognitive and emotional factors interact? If we concentrate on our partner and our feelings, we are giving more time and heightening our intensity. If we concentrate on something else, such as work, studies, or more than one romantic interest, we may divert or dilute our intensity and thus retard the growth of passion. On the other hand, idealizing of the relationship may be an automatic response to the euphoric passionate state, unless we have emotional resistance to the in-love feelings. But despite the natural growth dynamics of romantic bliss, we may be able to **choose** which thoughts about our relationship to value and repeat. We can label our early responses attraction, lust, love, infatuation, or even nervousness or discomfort. We can focus on idealization or on criticizing and disqualifying our partner as unworthy of our love.

Thus, naturally growing emotions may be biologically more primary, with conscious cognition able to "ride herd" on them by restimulating and reinforcing or by diluting or misconstruing them. Mystery and unusual conditions would foster passion by attracting more attention. If biochemical and emotional responses can develop independently of our thinking, we can explain how love feelings can develop in spite of our labeling them "just friends" or "just lust" or holding off sex or commitments.

Early love and unrequited love

The relative importance of sexual activity versus concentration on our feelings and images is particularly noticeable in early love experiences. Children report passionate feelings for peers from age 4 on up, with no relationship to sexual activity (Hatfield et al., 1988). One student reports on his earliest passion, which he nurtured from the second through the fourth grade:

> I met her in the second grade and was captivated at her beauty. There were about 6 of us trying to win the attentions of the most beautiful girl in class. In fourth grade she gave [us] all attention, including myself. During the summer I actually got the nerve to call her, but hung up when she answered the phone (pretty silly). I was CRUSHED in 5th grade when I couldn't find her anywhere . . . she was switched to a PRIVATE school. I didn't see Judy again

until 9 years later in her father's orthodontist office. She still had that 'look' in her face, but she was sorta fat now. I still would have loved to talk to her for more than the few minutes I got to.

This is **unrequited love**: loving someone who does not reciprocate or may not even know about our love. Though typically regarded as psychologically abnormal in our happiness-oriented culture, unrequited love is a mixture of misery and bliss, which perhaps three fourths of college students have already experienced at least once (Aron & Aron, 1991). The intensity of unrequited passion most students reported was related to how wonderful they thought the relationship would really be—Brehm's *idealization*. But for others, the intensity of their love was more related to the extent to which they considered it to be a desirable thing to be in love.

Fantasy love is much better than reality love. Never doing it is exciting. The most exciting attractions are between two opposites that never meet. (Andy Warhol, artist)

Some psychologists teach that it is an addiction for us to be "in love with love" (Peele, 1975). But it is important to distinguish between love in a real relationship and in one person's mind and heart. Suppose we are relating to someone who wants and needs things from us, but our highest priority is keeping our love feelings as intense as we like them. This would qualify as an addictive behavior. But if our contact and expectations with each other are minimal—as were the liaisons of the chivalrous knights in much of courtly romance—then we can dwell on our love without hindering or disappointing anyone. We can call this **virginal** or **chaste love**, because it admires and may seek closeness with the beloved in spirit, but not in body or behavior. This is the way many Muslim and Christian mystics and devotees have loved God. Contemporary research shows another side of unrequited love—that unrequited lovers are likely to wrestle with low self-esteem because of feeling rejected (Baumeister & Wotman, 1992). The would-be lover's estimation of his or her **probability** of acceptance by the beloved is associated with his or her self-esteem.

He was a [high school] senior, the girl a sophomore, and his supposedly superior status compounded the humiliation of her rejection of him. . . . He concluded his account by saying, 'to look back on it, I feel so stupid for the naive way I came off and how much ass-kissing I did.' (Baumeister & Wotman, 1992, p. 99)

Since this lover believes himself socially worthy of acceptance by his beloved, he feels her rejection is "personal." The biosocial explanations of self-esteem in Chapter 9 and shame in Chapter 13 suggest that if the prospective partner is socially distant, whether by age, status, or ethnic group membership, the lover's estimation of his or her probability of success will be low, so rejection will feel less humiliating. Desiring a person who is obviously inaccessible may be inspiring, and bring with it no humiliation of personal rejection. This seems to be as true of the courtly knight's devotion to his [usually married] highborn lady as of a fan's love for a movie, sports, or music star. It also fits for a proverbial young "social nobody's" love for a social celebrity, such as a cheerleader or acknowledged campus political, sports, or group leader.

Unrequited love can serve as a rehearsal for first love (Harms, 1992). Alapack (1984) notes that adolescent first love normally includes the same elements of spiritual union we have found both unrequited lovers and religious mystics yearning for and imagining. These include (a) **pervasive presence of the beloved**, (b) **absolute and extreme terms of expression**, (c) **uniqueness**, (d) **perfection**, (e) dream-laden **idealism**, (f) soul-mate **togetherness**, and (g) **orientation to the future**.

> *The feeling of loving Kiane, and of knowing that Kiane was in love with me, was the closest thing there could be to heaven . . . And the incredible thing was that it kept getting stronger, more beautiful and more perfect every day.* (Alapack, 1984, p. 103)

> *I am never alone. He is always with me in spirit even if he isn't at my side.* (p. 105)

Unrequited love can substitute for a real romantic relationship when no acceptable partner is in sight, or when we don't have the time or desire to share ourselves with anyone who might hurt us.

Why do we love particular people?

Perhaps this is too complicated for scientific theories, or there is too much chance involved. Perhaps we don't want to find out, because we prefer to experience a mysterious force in love—though that might increase our chances of divorcing (Chapter 5).

A comprehensive theory locates this mysterious force in the nonconscious thinking and feeling aspects of our own minds and in events and people in our world that "come to meet" and fit with our own tendencies. One explanation for our loving particular people has three parts: (a) the situation, (b) readiness—based on our personal development and recent events in our lives, and (c) desirable characteristics such as reminiscences, ideals, and growth factors.

The most extensive explanations for loving **particular** people have been developed in the psychodynamic tradition begun by Freud, Jung, and others. Contemporary marital therapist Harville Hendrix (1988), sexologist John Money (1980), and psychobiologist Anthony Walsh (1991b) all propose that unconscious memory residues of significant people and experiences of childhood (which Hendrix calls the "imago") provide a mass of cues, some of which "light up" when we perceive similar characteristics. Starting with Freud, psychotherapists have noticed that we transfer feelings and expectations from our significant childhood relationships onto adult relationships with similar meaning. Most of us have heard someone say, "I was cheated/burned/hurt/disappointed by my last (or most important) partner (or mother or father), so I don't trust anybody now (because they're all like that)." We've also heard, "My mother/father was unreliable, overreactive, vicious, alcoholic, crazy, or cold, and my partner was just the same way." Both of these cases reveal a *transference* of feelings and expectations which are obvious, because they are negative reactions of which the speaker is already aware.

Though the popular view assumes that psychoanalysts believe we look for mates who remind us of our opposite sex parent (Murstein, 1986), the mainstream Freudian view is far more complex (Fenichel, 1945). Our attractions may transfer characteristics and expectations from either parent, or from siblings or other persons in the childhood environment, or from more than one of these people at the same time. For example, you might be attracted to a person with your brother's sense of humor, your mother's untiring devotion, and your father's quietness. The actual characteristics of these people do not matter as much as the way you receive and react to them. Thus if you are the child of an alcoholic, you might mate with either a drinker or a nondrinker whose emotional extremes, unreliability, or excessive shows of affection could be similar to your experience of your alcoholic parent. Though our attraction to negative characteristics shocks us, positively valued characteristics from early experience may be just as influential in adult life—such as constant companionship, unfaltering attention, playfulness, or nurturant touch.

> My wife told me she was initially attracted to my kindness. I could not understand that, because nobody had ever called me "kind" before. But then I found out that she considered her father, who died when she was young, kind. She thought her mother, who is still living, was selfish and unkind. I guess I'm lucky I resembled an idealized memory at first, rather than a living disappointment.

In addition to transferring attraction from early significant others, we can also be attracted to characteristics that are like ourselves. Since we were each once the center of our own universe, creating a "mutual admiration society" with someone who resembles us strengthens our self-love. Both types of characteristics, those reminiscent of ourselves and those imprinted from early significant others, can show up in three ways: (a) a **positive** way, in which we are attracted to similarity to self or other, (b) in a **negative** way, in which we avoid similarity by choosing characteristics that are opposite from self or other, or (c) in an **ideal** way, in which we seek characteristics we have wished for in ourselves or others.

Transference and empirical research

The bulk of empirical research into attraction could support the theory that one prefers partners who are similar to oneself (3A in Figure 10.2), which Freud (1914/1989) called narcissistic. But some studies indicate that similarity to one's ideal of self (3C) may be a more potent motivation for attraction and may be confusing the data wherever it was not asked (Wetzel & Insko, 1982; LaPrelle et al., 1990). In one large-scale study, Jedlicka (1980) found that children in Hawaii of racially distinct parents (such as Japanese or white American and Hawaiian native) were much more likely to marry someone of the same race as their opposite-sex parent than of their same sex parent, or of any other race. This supports Freud's early idea that our "Oedipal" love for our opposite-sex parent (a subset of 2A) has an important influence in mate choice.

A study of **relationship** characteristics (in contrast to looks or personality) that newlyweds valued in their mates found more similarity to the mother (1A in Figure 10.2) among both sexes (Aron et al., 1974). Apparently we seek to duplicate in marriage the characteristics of our first love relationship (with our mothers). Or at least we are likely to believe they are present at the time we marry.

Contemporary relationship theorist Harville Hendrix offers an intriguing twist to the ideal type of attraction. He finds that we search for a partner who will help us recover our "lost self" (Hendrix, 1988, p. 30)—that is, those thoughts, feelings, and behaviors that we had to give up to adapt to our families and to society. Most of us had to become less sexual and less aggressive to please our parents, and many of us learned to be less outgoing, inquisitive, active, intuitive, imaginative, exhibitionistic, or less of many other characteristics as well. If another person appears to have our lost qualities, we can attempt to "recover" them through joining with that person as a couple. An example of "lost self" attraction would be Australian outback movie hero Crocodile Dundee, whose unspoiled, "noble primitive" spirit captivated sophisticated urban audiences. Sometimes such "lost self" attractions can be problematical, however. Appealing uncivilized qualities actually may be antisocial, as in the imprisoned criminals with whom some female penpals become fascinated enough to marry.

Another unexplored source of desirable features may be our **first great love**. In grade school, high school, college, or the first marriage this be-

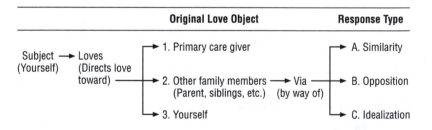

FIG. 10.2.

loved image might be "imprinted" with great magnetism (Perper, 1985). This **partner-image** may incorporate some features of early caregiver, family, and self, but combine and recreate them in the colors of passionate young adult love. This glorious dawn of love might then be **idealized** as "what love could be"—more developed than childhood reminiscences, but still little tarnished by the compromises of adult life.

The unconscious connections of our attractions may be as likely to come **after** as **before** the situational and readiness factors and generic characteristics, such as looks, intelligence, or kindness. For it is also possible that projecting important past relationships, characteristics, and ideals onto a partner occurs as a mental "retrofitting" once we have a relationship. Thus each new romantic relationship may stir up varying reminiscences of childhood relationships, as our minds ferret out ways to connect present perceptions and experiences with analogous aspects of our past.

Why "psychoanalyze" our attractions in all these ways? First, many of us have learned from our culture that we must be experiencing "true love" if we cannot find any reasons for an attraction that make sense to our conscious minds (see Myth 13 later in this chapter). If we study our present and past love relationships, we can discover the roles played by specific unconscious reminiscences and earlier loves in them. Once we are aware, we can gain more freedom to choose how much power these unconscious motivations will have to determine **which attractions we will pursue**. For example, if we discover that **unreliability** has a fascination for us that is reminiscent of a parent or a first love, we can hold ourselves back from future "fatal attractions" (Chapter 3) to unreliable people. We might search for "unreliability" in a more mature form, such as **spontaneity** paired with responsibility. Or we might loosen up a compulsion to date tall men, short women, blondes, or people with dark skin or foreign accents, once we recognize it as a relic of our first love. Second, if we discover we are attracted to a particular quality we cannot find in ourselves, such as generosity, boldness, or gracefulness, we might set out to develop the missing aspect for ourselves. Third, it may also be important for us to develop a quality our attractions are avoiding, such as argumentativeness or high self-love. Thus, greater awareness of the personal roots of our attractions can help us grow more through relationships and love less blindly, so that we suffer less severe disillusionments.

The chemistry of transformation

Love expands our consciousness. By living in **dialogue** with a partner, we add some of his or her perspective to our own (Fromm, 1956; Person, 1988). Thus our beloved can also become an inner conversation partner who is consulted subconsciously about many things that happen. New love requires us to restructure competing connections, such as with parents, bud-

dies, former lovers, beloved activities (Chapter 2), or even favorite drugs.

I used to party a lot with my buddies. But my girl-friend changed all that. First I found myself spending more and more time with her instead of them. Then I drank less when I went out with her, because she didn't want me to be that drunk. I really didn't miss drinking when I was with her, because we were having so much fun.

The power of loving gives us the **courage** (which literally means "heart-stuff") and energy to expand ourselves by trying new things. Jung (1946/1954; 1925/1971) explained this as an al-chemical process (analogous to chemistry) which produced transformation. The emotional relationship should be kept carefully **contained** by reducing external emotional ties and ener-getic or passionate pursuits. Then the emotional energy (or "eros") produced by two people's interaction would not dissipate, but would "heat up" the crucible of their intimacy so that their personalities would "chemi-cally" change. This theory positively interprets the lovers' process of acti-vating and reacting to each other's personality issues. When their person-alities start to get in the way of intense intimacy, they will either have to back off, or their old selves will begin to decompose and change.

This analogy of chemical combustion helps explain what may happen when two people get together for a casual relationship and/or recreational sex. After a while their "emotional chemistry" begins to heat up. Then they have to "cool it off" by reducing their intimate time, and dissipate their excitement by redirecting their emotional intensity toward other people and other projects. Thus, a budding erotic bond can be weakened both by "playing the field" and by passionate commitment to one's career or stud-ies. But if erotic energy is continuously concentrated in one container—whether a relationship or a demanding pursuit—**there is a chemical effect that leads eventually to crises and transformations in character**.

Child development and love: Attachment

Since World War II, scientific observation of infants has begun to replace the earlier theories constructed from reminiscences of adult patients. Some of the observations have been combined into a theoretical construct called **attachment**. Attachment theory is based on British psychoanalyst John Bowlby's theoretical synthesis of animal infant development research and psychoanalysis, and on American psychologist Mary Ainsworth's research observations of human infants in Africa and America. Bowlby (1969) applied to human infants the concept of animal imprinting during a sensitive period, as in the example of newborn goslings attaching themselves to the first moving object they see. Bowlby's attachment system of behavior consists of crying, smiling, calling, following, clinging, and sucking. These newborn and infant behaviors are all designed to increase or restore contact with the primary caregiver, and they all appear much more frequently with that person than with anyone else. The sensitive period for attachment as posited by Bowlby and Ainsworth begins at six to sixteen weeks and ends at around twelve months.

The response of the primary caregiver (also called "attachment object") is vitally important for the **mental working model**, or stable unconscious expectations the infant builds for future relationships with others. What Erik Erikson (1943) called trust and mistrust of the environment (to be achieved in infancy), Bowlby called secure and insecure attachment. Ainsworth found three different attitudes toward self and others determined by early attachment experiences. **Securely attached** infants over one year old exhibit distress (e.g., crying, clinging, following) briefly when separated from their primary caregiver, but otherwise seem comfortable exploring the world and other people in her absence (Ainsworth et al., 1978). These infants seem to have a stable expectation that the caregiver is accessible and reliable in her response, so she can be treated as a **secure base** from which to venture forth and encounter the unknown (Bowlby, 1969). Attachment behavior can still be activated in an infant by fatigue, hunger, illness, or unusual and alarming circumstances, at which point it will protest the caregiver's leaving or continued absence (Ainsworth et al., 1978). Ainsworth found two thirds of the infants she observed (66%) to be securely attached.

Insecurely attached infants can be divided into two types, **anxious/ambivalent** and **avoidant**. The 10% of Ainsworth's sample who were **anxious/ambivalent** infants acted as if they were reacting to the caregiver's recent departure much of the time. Apparently hooked by the fact that she gave good mothering some of the time, but not reliably, the anxious/ambivalent infants cried, clung, and searched for the caregiver in her absence, instead of tackling the rest of the world with confidence from her internalized secure base (Ainsworth et al., 1978). But sometimes these infants also resisted or attacked the caregiver, as if in frustration that evoked attachment needs are inconsistently filled. The 24% of **avoidant** infants in Ainsworth's sample didn't show much attachment behavior, whether the caregiver was just leaving or just returning. They didn't seem to use their caregivers as a secure base, and they even rejected her advances when she showed interest in them. They seemed detached and defensive toward caring contact. In contrast to the anxious/ambivalent children, whose maternal care was observed to be warm and genuine, but unreliable, the mothers of avoidant children were rated by observers as more interfering, rejecting, or neglectful.

Attachment theory is important in contemporary psychology because its basic elements are not hypothetical internal drives or states, but observable behaviors that are widespread beyond infancy. For example, attachment behaviors are apparent in grief reactions, in which the anxious/ambivalent type corresponds to the protest, crying and searching during acute grief. The defensive detachment of the avoidant type occurs during the later grief stage of depression and withdrawal from others (Bowlby, 1973). As another example, as early as age 4, childhood friends who are both securely attached to their mothers have more positive and more coordinated interactions than friendship pairs in which one is insecurely attached (Kerns, 1994).

What does all this have to do with adult love relationships? Attachment is arguably the most primitive and basic form of all love bonds. A table compiled by Shaver, Hazan, and Bradshaw (1988) from over two dozen research publications reveals an astonishing number of similarities between attachment behavior and adult romantic love.

Comparing attachment with romantic behaviors when the primary relationship is insecure or interrupted (items 4, 5, 6, 7, 12, and 15 in Table 10.2) sheds light on some of our popular criticisms of lovers. Thus "insecure," "possessive," or "mania" love appear to be fundamental, rather than abnormal forms of love. For intermittent and uncontrollable separations normally elicit attachment behaviors such as search (e.g., hypervigilance, following), protest (e.g., possessive anger), clinging, and grief. Yet it is possible for adults to feel only a little and to neither express nor act on these basic reactions, at least when healthy and not threatened. The key to such a **secure attachment style** may be internalizing a **secure base** attachment to another person, and/or a solid secure base from our childhood attachment.

These similarities between adult love and infant attachment can explain the correlation Aron and his colleagues (1974) found between some characteristics (especially dominance, responsiveness, and trust) of both sexes' newlywed relationships and the kind of relationship they had with their mothers. Thus, regardless of what influences our attractions, our first attachment may well provide the raw material for each person's **internal working model** of self and other (Bowlby, 1969), that is our expectation of what we and our partners should be like in a love relationship.

The three attachment styles Ainsworth found in infants are also found in college students and middle-aged adults, with about the same percentage of avoidant style (25% compared with 24% of infants) and 10% less of securely attached style (56%) and more of anxious/ambivalent style (19% compared with 10% of infants) (Shaver et al., 1988). Perhaps some people become more **anxious/ambivalent** after infancy. But older adults were more likely to become secure, which suggests that there may also be ways to become more secure through adult love experience. Though upbringing may teach girls to be more anxious, and boys more avoidant (see Gilligan, 1982; Olesker, 1990), there were no gender differences in percentages of

TABLE 10.2. Features of infant attachment and adult romantic love compared

Attachment	Romantic love
1. Formation and quality of the attachment bond depends on the attachment object's sensitivity and responsiveness.	Love feelings are related to an intense desire for the love object's real or imagined interest and reciprocation.
2. Attachment object provides a secure base and infant feels competent to explore the world.	Love object's real or imagined reciprocation provides a secure base and causes lover to feel confident and secure.
3. When attachment object is present, infant is happier, has a higher threshold for distress and is less afraid of strangers.	When beloved is viewed as reciprocating, the lover is happier, more positive, and more outgoing and kind.
4. When attachment object is not available or not sensitive, infant is anxious, preoccupied, and unable to explore freely.	When beloved acts uninterested or rejecting, lover is anxious, preoccupied, and unable to concentrate.
5. Behaviors: proximity- and contact-seeking; holding, laughing, touching, caressing, kissing, rocking, smiling, crying, following, clinging.	Behaviors: desiring time together; holding, touching, caressing, kissing and making love; smiling and crying, clinging, and fearing separation.
6. When afraid, distressed, sick, or threatened, infants seek physical contact with caregiver.	When afraid, distressed, sick, or threatened, lovers like to be held and comforted by their beloved.
7. Distress at separation: crying, calling and searching for attachment object, sad if reunion seems impossible.	Distress at separation or loss: crying, calling and searching for beloved, sad and listless if reunion seems impossible.
8. At reunion, infants smile, greet caregiver with positive cry, bounce and jiggle, approach, or reach to be picked up.	At reunion with beloved, or when beloved reciprocates after reciprocation was in doubt, lover feels ecstatic, greets beloved positively, with hugs, etc.
9. Infant shares toys and discoveries with attachment object.	Lovers share experiences and gifts and imagine how beloved would react to interesting sights or events.
10. Infant makes prolonged eye contact with caregiver, enjoys touching nose, ears, hair.	Lovers make prolonged eye contact, fascinated with each other's features, and enjoy exploring noses, ears, hair.
11. Though infant can be attached to more than one person, there is one key relationship, and a hierarchy of attachments.	Some believe they can love more than one person, but love normally occurs with only one partner at a time.
12. Separations and nonresponsiveness, up to a point, increase the intensity of attachment behaviors: proximity-seeking, protest, clinging, calling, etc.	Adversity (social disapproval, separations, intermittent nonreciprocation), up to a point, increases intensity of the lover's feelings and commitment for the other.
13. Infant coos, sings, talks baby talk; mother talks a combination of baby talk and motherese. Much nonverbal communication.	Lovers coo, sing, talk baby talk, use soft nurturing tones, and much communication is nonverbal.

Continued

TABLE 10.2. *Continued*

14. Responsive mother senses infant's needs and "reads the infant's mind." Origin of empathy.	Lovers feel almost magically understood and sympathized with. Empathy sought and shared.
15. When relationship is not going well, infant is anxious and hypervigilant to cues of attachment object's approval or disapproval.	When relationship is not yet secure or not going well, lover is hypersensitive to cues of beloved's reciprocation or nonreciprocation, and feelings of ecstasy and despair are dependent on these cues.
16. Infant appears to get great pleasure from caregiver's approval, applause, and attention.	At least early on, lover gets great happiness from beloved's approval, applause, and attention.

Adapted from Shaver, Hazan, and Bradshaw, 1988.

college students or adults reporting an anxious/ambivalent or avoidant attachment style (Shaver et al., 1988; Collins & Read, 1990).

Current research is exploring the effects of these three attachment styles on romantic relationships. For instance, most people would prefer to have a partner with a secure attachment style, whether they share that style or not. Young adults with a secure attachment style report the longest, and anxious/ambivalent subjects report the shortest, love relationships (Feeney & Noller, 1990). Secure students in relationships are most likely to be still satisfied with their relationships 3 years later (Kirkpatrick & Davis, 1994). Anxious adults in relationships are just as likely as secure adults to stay in the same pair for 4 years, but secure adults are more likely to have married (Kirkpatrick & Hazan, 1994). Avoidant subjects were likely to report lower intensity of love experiences and less being in love. Both anxious/ambivalent and avoidant partners are more likely than secure partners to report diminishing satisfaction as a relationship progresses (Keelan et al., 1994).

Adult attachment styles contain three basic dimensions: comfort with closeness, belief in the dependability of others, and anxiety about abandonment or losing love (Collins & Read, 1990). Some of these attachment dimensions may be similar toward one's opposite sex parent and current dating partner, but not toward the same sex parent. Men who rated their mothers cold or inconsistent were very likely to be dating an anxious partner. Women who rated their fathers the same way were very unlikely to be dating men who believed in others' dependability, and somewhat likely to be with men who were uncomfortable with closeness. So it appears that insecurely attached men are likely to seek security with women who are obviously eager for closeness, but this turns out to be due to the women's anxiety. In contrast, the women with cold fathers appear to gravitate toward men who are also untrusting and who back away from closeness. Men had more significantly negative reactions to anxiety in their love partners than to any variations in partners' attitudes toward closeness or dependability. Women were most significantly affected (but positively) by their partners' comfort with closeness. This pair of contrasting reactions seems to reflect both sexes' relationships with primary caregivers, as outlined by Gilligan (1982): Men need to independently regulate their own closeness, after distancing themselves from their mothers, so they would dislike an anxious partner's need for reassurance and closeness. Women seek closeness and warmth to duplicate their closeness to mother, but if their fathers were cold, they keep finding themselves with somewhat avoidant men. And perhaps both sexes experience their partners through the same eyes as they experienced their parent.

Thus, attachment-style research is finding more empirical links between both mothers and opposite sex parents and the experience of romantic relationships. Twin studies suggest that attachment style is not strongly inherited (Brussoni et al., 1996). But biosocial theorists suggest that all 3 styles could be influenced by the parents' *environment* and foster the success of our species in those environments (Belsky, 1997; Keller, 1997): The secure style would derive from a *stable, predictable, economically adequate* existence for the parents, which is conducive to secure-base parenting (Chisholm, 1996). This would foster in the offspring stable "quality" young adult bonding and high, enduring parental investment in their own offspring. The avoidant style would derive from *unstable, unpredictable, comparatively impoverished* environments for the parents, in which multiple partners (second mating strategy) and lower investment/involvement parenting might produce greater chances of some successful offspring. Such parenting could foster in the offspring avoidant, opportunistic "quantity" relations and low-investment parenting (at least by men) in their own children.

Elements of development and their impact on adult intimacy

Early childhood development

Those who systematically observe children have been trying for decades to find the key factors involved in the development of healthy, resilient selves and fulfilling love relationships. In the 1970s and 1980s two different but comparable stage theories emerged, both of which are based on observation of both normal and disturbed children. The first was Margaret Mahler's theory of **separation/individuation** (Mahler et al., 1975). The second was Daniel Stern's theory of **interpersonal development of the self** (Stern, 1985). Taken together, these theories help us understand two central aspects of love relationships—connection and individual autonomy. Table 10.3 depicts the stages of infancy and toddlerhood according to both theories.

Mahler's theory of **symbiosis**, **separation/individuation**, **refueling**, and **object constancy** explains how both secure attachment and autonomy can

TABLE 10.3. Stages of infant development according to Mahler and Stern.

Mahler's stages	Age (mos)	Stern's senses of self	Age (mos)
Normal Autism	0–1m	Emergent sense of self	0–2/3m
Symbiosis (with mother)	1–5/6m	Core (physical) sense of self	3–7/9m
Separation/individuation	(6–36+m)		
Differentiating (from mother)	5–7/10m		
Practicing (exploring activities	7/10–15m	Subjective sense of self (Emotional attunement: Empathy)	9–15m
Rapprochement crisis (negotiating security and freedom)	16–25m		
On the road to object constancy	26–36+m	Verbal sense of self (Word meanings, mental models)	15–30+m

Sources: Mahler, Pine, & Bergman, 1975; Stern, 1985.

come about. Mahler's newborn is not aware of the external world (autistic stage), but soon enters an infantile experience of **symbiotic** interdependence with its caregiver. The mother is supposed to be the infant's entire world, since it depends on her reliable attention and can only see far enough to recognize the face of the person who is nursing it. The maternal side of this interdependence is supported by mechanisms such as cry and smell recognition, pupil dilation (indicative of a pleasurable state of consciousness), and lactation (with oxytocin to stimulate and reward closeness).

For Mahler, the direction of early childhood development is from a dual-entity with the caregiver towards progressively greater separation and self-directed goals and behavior. (This reflects the Western male model of development—as distinguished by Gilligan (1982)—in that it views separateness and individualism as more mature than closeness and relatedness.) For this reason Mahler's last four stages are part of the **separation/individuation** phase. **Separation** means achieving the ability to exist and take care of our needs at a distance from our caregiver. **Individuation** means becoming a unique individual instead of a part of the caregiver's identity. Each move the infant makes away from its caregiver may trigger both excitement about something new and anxiety about separation. For the child's security, the caregiver must be physically and emotionally available to **refuel** the child whenever it needs food, diapering, or other intangible services, such as comfort, praise, contact or reassurance. It may be more difficult and less fulfilling for mothers to give the child room to separate and explore, while hovering nearby (as if tethered to its movements). Yet matching the mother's responsiveness to the child's rhythms is significant, for attachment research indicates that intrusive mothers who interfere with separation efforts are likely to produce **anxious/ambivalent** children, while maternal neglect can produce **avoidant** children (Main et al., 1985).

The first subphase of separation/individuation is **differentiation**, during which the infant explores its own body and that of its caregiver and discovers the differences between self, caregiver, and environment. The second subphase, **practicing**, emphasizes the excitement of discovery as the toddler practices using its new movement skills, first crawling, then walking, and has its first "love affair with the world" (Mahler, 1979a).

The third and fourth subphases, rapproachment crises and developing object constancy, are less important for our purposes than their result. The final goal of separation/individuation is for the child to develop an **internal stable image** of its own identity and of a separate but supportive and positively valued mother-equivalent to attachment theory's **internal working models**. **Object constancy**, the faith that mother will consistently love and support one, no matter what happens, is a combined mental and emotional construct in the child's mind equivalent to attachment theory's **secure base**. This faith can be re-experienced in future relationships as the basis for feeling safe to be ourselves without fear of losing the other person's love (Ables & Brandsma, 1984). Thus, the result of successful separation-individuation is **object constancy** and a **secure attachment style**.

Stern (1985) eliminated the **symbiotic** stage and emphasized **emotional attunement** instead. His theory of infant development does not proceed from maximal closeness toward individuality—from "oneness in the womb" to "standing [alone] on your own." Instead, closeness (or relatedness) develops at the same time as separateness, with physical, emotional, and verbal (mental) components. The key feature of mother–infant closeness is not present (for the child) in the beginning, but arises between the ages of 9 and 15 months through **emotional attunement**.

At about 9 months, Stern observed infants beginning to read the expressions on faces, as well as body position and movement to find out if others share their own intentions and inner states. While developing its emotional or **subjective sense of self,** the toddler relies on its perception of being emotionally understood, which depends on the caregiver showing **emotional attunement—**the root of **empathy**. Mother's and infant's facial mimicry of emotions is part of attunement. This attunement may be the actual experience which adults later imagine to be symbiosis or "merger of selves."

Development through young adulthood

For developmentalists, Mahler's and Stern's stages may provide a basis, but adolescent development also contributes to the psychology of relationships. Erik Erikson (1980) named his young adulthood stage (ages 18 to 25) **intimacy versus isolation**, and we will consider it here. Since he assumed success with each stage was a substantial support for subsequent stages, Erikson argued that we have to develop a secure **identity** before we can embrace the closeness and intensity of **intimacy**. But young women did not seem to proceed in the same way. He wondered if women's young adult identity was less complete than men's, or perhaps they had a separate developmental sequence in which intimacy could precede identity (Franz & White, 1985). He thought young women might be including their love partner in their identity of themselves, which is close to the theories of Carl Jung (1959) and Arthur and Elaine Aron (1986).

> All this is a little more complicated with women because women, at least in yesterday's cultures, had to keep their identities incomplete until they knew their man. Yet, I would think that a woman's identity develops out of the very way in which she looks around and selects the person with whose budding identity she can polarize her own. Her selection is already an expression of her identity, even if she seems to become totally absorbed in somebody else's life. (Erikson in Evans, 1967, p. 49)

We can see such absorption and a contemporary reaction to it in a 19-year-old college sophomore's report of how she lost her identity to her previous boyfriend:

> *Over the years John and I had been writing, he had built up this image of his ideal partner and had given her my name. Then, when I couldn't live up to that ideal, he wanted me to change. I wanted to believe that I could be perfect for someone, so I would do almost anything John asked in order to make him happy. The problem was, every time I changed because he wanted me to, a little part of me was taken away. I wasn't even a shadow of the person I used to be.*

Without guidance in struggling for her autonomy, she tries to "be perfect," by incorporating an external image of herself—which her 19-year-old conscience now considers a sell-out. This is similar to what we saw twelve-year-old girls beginning to do in our discussion of self-esteem (Chapter 9). Thus, romantic intimacy and a couple identity might be dominant elements of a woman's identity, if she mated during her adolescence. But they might be less potent if she went to college and developed a professional identity first. By their twenties, women's years of cognitive development may allow them to override their biological sensitivity to absorbing cultural messages, and help them to discriminate between external expectations of them which fit their own interests and those which don't. With more freedom today, some women start a long-term relationship early, between 15 and 21 years old, and after several years reject the husband or boyfriend as an "identity package" and dominant influence. After breaking up they begin developing a new adult identity for themselves.

Erikson's stages of development have been criticized as male-centered, since autonomy and individualism is typically more important to men than women. But according to Stern's theory, our connectedness develops throughout childhood along with our individuality. We could revise popular individualistic cliches such as "You have to stand on your own two feet *before* you can join with somebody else," or "You have to love yourself *before* you can love anyone else." We could say instead, "You *learn to love* in relationships, and you *discover yourself* in relation to your life and your companions."

Applications of developmental theory to romantic relationships

Mahler's individuation theory has been applied to intimate relationships in two ways. First, achievement of object constancy is posited as a prerequisite for the ability to relate to a love partner as a separate but trustworthy individual, as discussed above. Second, theorists believe that major aspects of the separation-individuation process are relived during adolescence and again in long-lasting love relationships. Let us explore separation/individuation, differentiation, refueling, and attunement.

Differentness and trust: Do I have to give up me to be loved by you?

The ability to express an attitude or take an action that contrasts or conflicts with one's companion rests on achievements of separation/individuation. First, we must perceive our thoughts, feelings, and desires as **different** from the other person's. This awareness develops in Stern's subjective self phase and becomes intense during Mahler's rapprochement stage—known as the terrible twos—when toddler's and mother's aims conflict. But it is **object constancy** that forms the unconscious faith that conflicting with a loved one will not destroy the love bond between us. Without the implicit sense that we are lovable and that love normally lasts, we will neither initiate anything unless we expect that our companion wants it, nor say no to something the other wants. A divorced woman puts it this way:

> "Not my will, but your will be done," was my motto. "Your moods are my commands," was another basic rule. Everything **he** thought was important, but nothing **I** thought mattered. When I first realized what was going on, I thought he was a terrible tyrant. But then I discovered that I didn't have any idea what I felt when he was around, except that I was anxious to make sure he still loved me.

Differentness in Adolescence. In adolescence it is so important to belong and be like the group, that asserting our differences and saying **no** to others may be a neglected skill. Thus, college students are typically unsure of how to assert their differences with either peers or romantic partners. Setting a limit that is reinforced by social customs is comparatively easy, such as asking someone to stop smoking in a theater with No Smoking signs. But setting a limit that is purely one person's preference against another's can be emotionally tense, because hostile reactions and damage to the relationship are quite possible. In addition, culture often limits our freedom to say no by pathologizing stinginess, selfishness, insensitivity, etc. In college relationships, a student might feel uncomfortable giving help to someone who does not give back, or accepting help or close contact from someone who wants to become romantic. Or we might dislike a partner's drinking, sports-watching, cooking, or support needs, or not feel like praising something the partner wants praised—yet to disappoint the other person is very uncomfortable.

In theory, internalized **object constancy** would tend to counterbalance conformity urges. We would be predisposed to expect others to be different from ourselves in some vital ways, yet likely to care for us through most any conflict that occurs. But sensitivity to maintaining harmony with peers should be strong in adolescence, according to biosocial theory, because in the long course of our evolution, we needed to develop solidarity, conformity, and reciprocal support with our group for our survival. So "being yourself" and interdependence are both supported by respectable theories.

Separation/individuation and adolescence. We start from the premise that the personality characteristics developed during the first cycle of bonding and separation/individuation in infancy act as a foundation for each person's style of relating. But relating style can be further developed in subsequent cycles, including in adolescence (Blos, 1979) and in love relationships. Adolescents often make efforts to differentiate themselves from their parents by argumentation and "practicing" nonconforming behavior and values. They identify with peers, idols, and love partners and then differentiate from these replacement models as well. There is a need for **refueling** through recognition and reliable logistical, financial, and **secure base** family support.

The late adolescent separation/individuation process impacts our study because it occurs during the development of young adult intimacy. The timing of adjustments in autonomy and closeness with parents often affects these romantic relationships. The relationship between development in autonomy and closeness with parents and length and depth of interpersonal relationships has typically been stronger for men than for women (Levitz-Jones & Orlofsky, 1985). But students of both sexes who are increasing their autonomy with regard to parents may prefer "practicing" through extended casual dating to a long-term union or merging. This "no commitment, no strings" attitude has been called **counterdependence**: One's self-concept is **dependent** on feeling **independent**. One study of female college eighteen- and nineteen-year-olds (Levitz-Jones & Orlofsky, 1985) found that the 80% not involved in mature love relationships had significantly more problems with separation/individuation (as measured on a

Separation Anxiety Test) than the 20% who had achieved a more mature level of intimacy. In addition, 50% who fit the classification of "merger-style" relaters were arguably not as far advanced in their second round of separation/individuation as the 20% high-intimacy group, because their need for contact and closeness was not balanced by a strong drive for autonomy and pleasure in independent functioning. This does not mean it is "better" to have high intimacy relationships at a younger age, as peer competition among women, but not men, might suggest. But young adult separation/individuation developments may effect relationships.

Attunement and separation/individuation in love relationships

Again, in most **long** love relationships, we may go through a cycle of initially **increasing psychological union**, followed by renewed **separation/individuation**, which can be stabilized by **object constancy** (Gilfillan, 1985; Bader & Pearson, 1988).

Individuation in adulthood.   Jung (1964; Guggenbuehl-Craig, 1977) postulates an essential need for continued development throughout adulthood. For Jung, **individuation** is the process of coming into conscious awareness of potential parts of our personality, with the consequence that these parts are developed, integrated, and often actualized in the world. According to human potential psychology, this means that we each have an inborn drive to experience and develop our unique potential by "rising to" the internal and external situations we encounter. An intimate relationship can be a powerful means for growth, as we develop love, generosity, and numerous other qualities. We can also grow in awareness of the dark sides of our partners and ourselves by visiting the inferno of frustration and hostility as we live together over the years (Denninger-Polster, 1987).

At first, our new growth appears as emotion, turmoil, passion, and energy directed toward increasing intimacy. But later the partners may develop parts of themselves that are not involved in their relationship. These aspects may be even contrary to or exclusive of the relationship, such as playing a musical instrument, doing a project, or developing a career or fruitful relationships with other people.

> Picture each individual person as a rosebush. In our seed-DNA is all our unique potential for growth. The environment we grow in, with its variations of soil, weather, water, food, and neighboring plants, will contribute to how we actualize our different possibilities. But they are all there, encoded in our seed. Each time we put out a new branch, the force of our emotional energy is concentrated in that green sprout. When we start to love somebody, we grow a branch toward that person's bush, as if toward the sun. Our green force is passionately intense, until our branches have reached each other and intertwined. But later other

branches need to grow, and our growing force enters them as eagerly as it once swelled our romance branches. These other new self-actualization branches sprout thorns, too. And they resist anyone's efforts to bend them around to suit partnership needs.

Though our partnership is not the primary focus of our passion, this does not mean that the "love has died" in our relationship. Passion is felt at the points of *new* growth. But passion is only part of love, and intimacy, attachment, and commitment are important, too. When it is possible to bring some of a partner's new growth into the relationship it may cause some turmoil and change there. Then new passion can be felt between the partners, as it was when they were each other's growth goal before.

Union and differentiation in relationship.   The **attunement** or **union** stage and the **differentiating** stage that follows are major stages our developmental theory can help us understand. In Chapter 4 these two stages were described as **expansion** and **contraction**. Here we will explore their psychological underpinnings from a developmental perspective.

Union is more than finding another person overwhelmingly attractive and spending lots of time together. For a sense of union to endure, a **secure base** of trust or **object constancy** must be established. Since couple trust is beyond rational explanation (Holmes & Rempel, 1989), a trusting partner may experience the secure feelings of **object constancy** that were developed in early childhood. Perhaps the experience of **empathy** or **emotional attunement** is what leads adults to expect object constancy from each other. When our partner seems to "resonate" to most of the feelings we express, our experience may well be reminiscent of mother-child attunement. This resonance may be as important to a "we-ness" for the couple as their commitments and shared verbal constructions of their worlds. Partners in love also tend to construct their own sense of what they feel in response to their emotional resonance, just as they did as children with their caregivers. That may be the basis for one responding sooner or more to one's partner's feelings than to one's own.

Many relationships can remain in the "we-ness" **expansion** state without much individuation of either partner for many years. But there is a cost to prolonging this idyllic state. Partners become less aware of their own feelings and more anxious or hostile about any separate activity that raises the possibility of seeing oneself or the other as fundamentally different (Bader & Pearson, 1988). They may avoid all conflict and shun any growth and change unless one can convince the other to change in the same way and thus preserve their belief in "growing together." One example of such a compromise that appears to preserve mutuality while fostering separation is a common deal that partners make: "Why don't you go out with the girls on the nights when I go out with the boys?"

Hostile–dependent relationships.   In time, the paradise of union can also turn into a hell if the partners' needs are inappropriate or excessive (Solomon, 1989; Bader & Pearson, 1988). A partner who received inadequate positive response in childhood may require constant positive reflection from the spouse and be hypersensitive to any disappointment or differentness. Mind-reading and matching of feelings is expected, and any less-then-affirming feeling the partner expresses is taken as an attack. What was at first a narcissistic paradise of feeling praised "just for being me" becomes a bitter disappointment and reproach: "You don't love me anymore!" More socially competent people who have this reaction are likely to break up and try to find somebody who will love them better and longer. But the less confident will stay together in the classic bind: "Can't live with you and can't live without you."

From union to differentiation.   Differentiation between partners is positive, because each of us have our unique life path to follow. Differences in needs, responses, and behavior are not mistakes, neuroses, or childish leftovers that a partner can change if enough effort is exerted. They are aspects of each person that won't disappear, but must grow and develop **with** the person (Bader & Pearson, 1988). But losing the fond hope of a perfect fit can be a bitter disappointment that leads to a long **contraction** period in a relationship. The need to grieve for the loss of the fantasy of a perfect fit is often obscured by recurrent bickering over the personality and behavior differences themselves. We can approach differentiating positively by focusing on the list of individual tasks in Table 10.4.

TABLE 10.4. Tasks of differentiating self from partner

A. Differentiating of the Self.

1. Knowing and expressing one's own thoughts, feelings, and desires.
2. Diminishing emotional contagion: not getting pulled into having to feel the same feelings as the partner at the same time.
3. Developing awareness of what works for oneself in solving conflicts.
4. Handling "alone time," including private thoughts and private physical spaces.
5. Developing individual goals.

B. Differentiating from Others.

1. Developing more balanced perceptions of the partner and being able to give empathic responses even at times of disagreement.
2. Handling discrepancies in desires for closeness.
3. Developing mechanisms for resolving conflicts with the partner.
4. Developing mechanisms for "how we do things as a couple."
5. Recognizing and handling different value systems.

C. Establishing Boundaries.

1. Developing separate friendships.
2. Delineating separate areas of family, domestic, and financial responsibility.
3. Planning for separate activities.
4. Developing the capacity to handle privacy within the relationship.

Source: Bader & Pearson, 1988, p. 126.

It is normal to encounter A.1 and 2 together, when I need to get in touch with what I think and feel as distinct from what I know and can feel of my partner's feelings. For example, when my partner wants to tell me about something or ask me to participate in something she is excited about, I need to find out what *I* feel about it in addition to her excitement. I may need to express my caution, irritation, or disappointment, even though it doesn't match her emotional state. Task B.1 also suggests that I should not need to exclude my partner's excitement (or other feelings) from my awareness in order to value what I feel, but I could value her emotional state and subjective truth as different from mine and yet enriching. Enjoying alone time (A.4) involves developing my own thoughts and pursuits, so that my times of being without my partner aren't full of helplessness, jealousy, or fears of abandonment.

There are a great many potential discrepancies in people's desires for closeness (B.2), because there are many different kinds of closeness that are sought and valued differently by different people, as illustrated in Table 10.5.

Most of us wouldn't *want* to share all these types of intimacy with one person. As if all these distinct kinds of intimacy weren't enough ways to be different, in each category a couple's desired behaviors, intensity, duration, and timing can differ. For example, one partner may want more or different physical or sexual closeness while the other wants more or different communication or emotion. Or one partner may have "overdosed" on human contact at work and just want to be left alone. Each couple may discover they have half a dozen "closeness mismatches" which are typical for them. Handling them may require working out a different strategy for each mismatch. You can evaluate your "intimacy profile" by marking each type of intimacy with 1, 2, or 3 for high, medium, and low priority for you, including who you want that category with. Mark "No" if you don't like to

TABLE 10.5. Types of closeness or intimacy

1. **Physical:** Familiarity and closeness with another's body in work and play, medical care, touch, massage.
2. **Sexual:** Erotic pleasure sharing.
3. **Emotional:** Empathic attunement and expressing emotions.
4. **Intellectual:** Sharing spheres of ideas.
5. **Aesthetic:** Sharing experiences of beauty.
6. **Creative:** Sharing in acts of creating together.
7. **Recreation:** Sharing experiences of fun, sports, and play.
8. **Work:** Sharing or cooperating in tasks.
9. **Crisis:** Facing crises, problems, and pain together.
10. **Conflict:** Facing and struggling with differences.
11. **Commitment:** Trust and mutuality from common investments of self.
12. **Spiritual:** Sharing religious and transpersonal concerns.
13. **Communication:** Verbal sharing and understanding.

Adapted from Oden, 1974.

share a type with your partner. Estimate the amount of time you spend or want to spend on each in a week (or month). Comparing profiles with your partner would reveal your mismatches for discussion. You can also consider your intimacy preferences and alternatives as a whole.

The union–differentiating couple.   Differentiating may be a normal and psychologically necessary, though disruptive development in a couple's life together. But it is particularly painful and threatening when one partner starts on this path before the other. Once a person resumes a highly valued pursuit outside the relationship, she may discover that she no longer believes that "we can share almost everything, every thought and feeling with each other." When she "opens the door" to keeping some thoughts or responses private, her thoughts may approach subjects she had automatically avoided before, because they didn't fit into the shared "we-ness" of the relationship.

Problems arise in both partners, however. The other partner usually notices the differentiator's shift in energy and may react as if abandoned: "It seems like you don't love me as much anymore." The differentiating partner may feel guilty, because it is true. If loving has been defined as focusing mental and emotional energy on the partner, the differentiator is now doing it less, while the union-oriented partner is still doing it as much as before. Thus the couple may begin a pursuer–distancer dance, trading accusations of "selfishness" and "overdependence" (Figure 10.3).

The differentiating couple.   The best solution to the problems discussed above, according to Bader and Pearson (1988), is for both partners to embark on the task of differentiation. Since their greater separation reduces their security with each other for a while, they need to be reliable and reassuring for each other. They need to **refuel** each other with calls, gifts, praise, affection, and comfort, without assuming that a refueling need expressed at an inopportune time is "too insecure." Each partner's specific needs for refueling normally derive from similar processes in their families of origin. To deal with differences, the couple needs to develop a conflict style that allows for expression of anger and disappointment without uncontainable

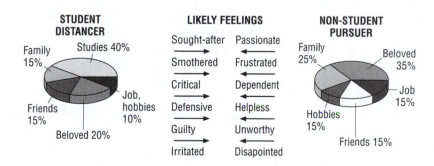

FIG. 10.3.
Distancer–pursuer.

escalation. They must foster mutual respect and understanding for differences and aim for resolutions that give reason for hope.

Fairness of exchange versus communalism. Differentiating partners may apply an abstract principle of **"fairness"** as a simple rule for judging disputes, which can lead to an **exchange** mentality (Chapter 7): "I'll give you something if you give me something." Such a tradeoff is usually quite successful for everyday problem-solving: "I'll cook if you clean up afterwards." But relying on fairness may undermine the process of **differential** self–awareness and self-development if we assume: "You can take a step on your individuation path, if I get something out of it, or get to take one on my path at the same time." The principle of strictly equal "give and take" in relationships can be a reaction to losing the feeling of perfect harmony, and can be summed up in this way:

> "If I can't have everything I need from you (and give you everything you need) just naturally, without having to think about it, then I'll have to keep score. Then I can use your desires and my generosity for leverage to bargain for what I most need from you."

Supporting a partner's process of self-development, even when it involves focusing energy away from the union, may mean getting over the loss of the perfect fit and setting our own desires aside to witness and facilitate a growth trajectory that is fundamentally **different** from our own. Our partner's growth toward self-actualization may have a different starting point, different blockages (from upbringing, culture, abilities, and gender role expectations), different current issues, and a different direction from our own. Our investment of ourselves in support of our partner's differential development may be **unfair** or **inequitable** in the long run, as well as the short run, because two different developmental trajectories may require unequal balances of giving and receiving. This puts a **communal**, **agapic** love orientation to the test.

The traditional gender roles that required women to sacrifice themselves for their husband's external success are being widely rejected today. Some men have chosen to sacrifice their aspirations to support their wives' development. But individual differences represent an important limitation for any social theory that postulates equality for everyone. Accepting an equal right to self-development for both sexes does not mean that the ideal relationship balance consists of equal amounts of giving and receiving, of self-actualization and self-sacrifice on both sides. Ongoing differences in needs, directions, timing, and goals are best approached through the integrative model of conflict resolution discussed in the conflict chapter: **Both partners do not strive for an abstract ideal of equality, but devote themselves to maximally supporting both their own and their partner's unique journey through life.**

Myths of love and marriage and their meanings

Much current psychology debunks popular myths about love and marriage as dangerous to relationship health. When carefully considered, however, most of these myths are partially true and partially false. Table 10.6 outlines many popular myths, along with some of their cultural functions and psychological meanings. By paying attention to their clues as to how our minds work (Stevens, 1982), we may study these myths with the respect their psychological power deserves, while not falling prey to either blind faith or unconsidered rejection. We will comment on a few.

Happily ever after

The assumption that love and sex can be joined and will continue throughout marriage at the same passionate level (Myth 1) can only lead to disillusionment (Crosby, 1991). Since the biochemistry of new love is normally more powerful than old love (Chapter 9), this myth sets us up for serial monogamy, assuming that a new attraction would deliver a more enduring passionate high.

But the **idea** that love and sex can be good for a lifetime fosters commitment to durable monogamy. Our memories of romance and passion act as mental cues in which love doesn't change, so we can find renewal when the marital going gets boring or rough. Americans fondly believe in the possibility of putting romance and passion back into marriage, and are instructed weekly by popular magazines on just how to do it.

Holy marriage

Several myths combine in the common psychological predilection to experience pair bonding as a timeless, perfect, and paradisiacal union (Jung, 1949/1954). This union shows up in dreams, myths, folk tales, tabloid newspapers, and films as the marriage of the prince and princess or of pop stars, or the hero winning the beautiful girl. It is also symbolized in countless elaborate "dream weddings." Calling the "perfect couple" a cultural stereotype cannot explain away its power in our imagination.

Love conquers all

Love usually does not literally conquer all obstacles. Neglecting contemporary couple issues under the banner of "love is the answer" may lead to unconscious resentment that can destroy relationships. But love does have a power that is beyond rational understanding and acts to transform thoughts, attitudes, and issues in the direction of mutual respect and devotion to the partner's happiness. The American concept of love usually includes commitment (Fehr, 1988), and the willpower involved in commit-

TABLE 10.6. Purposes and meanings of love and marriage myths

Myth	Cultural purpose	Psychological meanings
1. Love and sex will be stable and happy ever after.	Emotional and sexual constancy, fidelity, and commitment.	Paradisical feeling of holy marriage, security.
2. Marriage is a sacred covenant.	Religion and society unite in support.	Coupling participates in divine meaning and energies.
3. Love conquers all.	Commitment conquers adversity and obstacles.	Love-force transforms people and issues.
4. Loving means no anger or conflict.	Mutual submission to pair bond: "honor and obey."	Union entails harmony; in-love stage represses anger.
5. Magical knowing of partner's feelings, thoughts and needs.	Foster attending to and complying with needs.	Union is a partial merger, dwelling with partner's consciousness and needs.
6. Love leads to marriage.	Love is a premier criterion for mate choice.	Love conjures longing for permanent union.
7. Love is dying or dead if one is attracted to others.	Love maintains the bond but mates are replaceable.	New love chases away old. In-love stage usually precludes attractions.
8. Marriage partner will meet all needs.	Spousal role specifications.	Union is harmony and primordial paradise.
9. Marriage gives us identity.	Social role specifications.	Identify with symbol of holy couple.
10. Marriage makes me feel good about myself.	Couple formation serves cultural cohesion	Developmental step furthers personal growth.
11. Relationship is antidote for loneliness. Togetherness equals closeness.	Cohesion is better than isolation and individual anomie.	Partner is symbolic security. Imagined closeness is reassuring.
12. Good relationships come naturally.	Cultural norms are part of natural order.	Union equals harmony.
13. There is a Right partner for me.	Certainty is possible in mate choice.	Belief in "soul-mate" helps to lower defensive boundaries and allow dependency.
14. The Perfect Fit wants the same intimacy, power sharing, and love expressions	Personalities match both symmetrical and complementary behavioral needs.	Union equals harmonious and reciprocal paradise.
15. Marriage starts new life: you don't marry the family.	American mobility and generational role shift.	Symbolic adulthood, new power for individual growth.
16. Children cement the marital bond.	Protection of children.	Child symbolizes partners' union and fosters parental devotion.

Myths adapted from Crosby, 1991, and Anderson et al., 1989. Interpretations by first author.

ment can counterbalance both external physical and social obstacles and internal shifts in
thought and feeling (May, 1969).

Magical knowing

The expectation of magical knowing is that lovers can literally read each other's minds, taking care of many physical, emotional, and
sexual needs without ever mentioning them
and occasionally bursting out with "I was just
thinking that!" Though occasionally possible
when feelings are strong, mind-reading is very
unlikely to be accurate all the time. With their
higher emotional intelligence, women may be
more proficient than men, as expected in Indian and Japanese cultures. In addition, when
we have differentiated out of our early union,
we may wish to pursue personal rather than couple interests much of the
time, so we don't want to know what our partner is thinking.

Misunderstandings over mind-reading often involve the **fundamental
attribution error**, which holds that my own actions are probably the result
of many **changeable** factors, while **yours** are proof of your unchanging character traits. This skews my mind-reading results, because I assume that if
you once acted or reacted in a certain way, you will do the same thing every
time a similar situation comes up. Also, if you **don't** read my mind, then
you probably don't want to.

> The students in Relationship Skills Lab tangled over the men's com-
> plaint that girlfriends sometimes expect them to know "what's wrong"
> when the women are upset, but "don't want to talk about it."
>   The women explained that their unhappiness usually stems from a
> recent incident [which her partner **did not remember with the same
> emotional emphasis** as she did]. But the woman may think that if her
> partner does not remember her feelings, then he either "doesn't have
> the sensitivity of a snail," or "just doesn't care."

The current counter-myth is that magical knowing is impossible, and
you should always spell out what you want in words. Yet there are numerous couple needs that are regularly fulfilled without being expressed, such
as being fed, praised, and listened to, as well as financial and emotional
security and sex. Verbal communication is not universally necessary, and
judicious editing of what one says is also an important intimacy skill
(Gottman et al., 1976).

Myths of marriage

Relationship is certainly not an automatic antidote for loneliness. But the image of ourselves as coupled and loved can serve as a **secure base** and cue in our endorphin system. Believing our partner is "there for us" can provide all the internal security we need.

The myth that good relationships "just come naturally" (12) is now opposed by countermyth that marriages require a lot of hard work. But couples still want their bond to be a "natural" haven of comfort, harmony, and unconditional acceptance. Denying relationship problems until they become overwhelming is just as common as it is normal. The success of the **minimizer** style (Chapter 4) shows that ignoring issues and accentuating the positive can greatly extend the life of relationships, as long as **both** partners use this approach.

The 'right partner' myth

The myth that there is one "right" partner for each of us (myth 13) is supported by the assurance that we will be sure when he or she comes along, because we'll "just know." Since the properties of this intuitive certainty and the methods for obtaining it are rarely discussed, many lovers are perplexed when faced with the decision to marry. If you are no longer so intensely in love that every moment together is blissful, and both your prospective mate and the compatibility between you are clearly less than perfect (myth 14), how do you know if "this is really **the one**?" You can rationally weigh the pros and cons. But does your lack of certainty mean your heart is not voting, and therefore this may not be "the one?"

Perhaps intuitive certainty is possible, but neither inevitable nor essential to a good partnership. A sense of physical, mental, and spiritual communion is an aspect of the "holy marriage" that may be evoked by emotional attunement. But this experience can occur at any time during a relationship, so we don't need a premonition of "rightness" to guarantee the future of our bond. The myth of Mr. or Ms. "Right" fulfills a psychological function, and there are at least two ways for the feeling of intuitive certainty to develop.

Our intuition of "rightness" helps us relax our defensive boundaries, share our innermost secrets and needs, and give ourselves to our partners without counting the cost. This intuitive "click" when we are first getting to know someone may have a historical source in memory cues from earlier relationships. Feeling familiar makes uniting with this person seem like rejoining with a forgotten part of ourselves. But we can also develop shared meanings and emotional attunement in a long relationship, without ever noticing that we feel "made for each other." Such unions may seem more "made right" than "born right," but they can feel just as good.

Then is there only one Mr. or Ms. "Right" for each of us? Since there is probably no "perfect fit" (myth 14) for us, there is no **rational** reason to

Table 10.7. Types of love stories

"Love is" . . .	Modes of thought and behavior	Typical views on relationships	Complementary roles
1. Addiction	Anxious attachment, clingy Fear of loss	"I couldn't live without . ."	1. Addict 2. Codependent
2. Art	Partner's attractiveness Emphasis on looking good	"—is the most beautiful person I could ever find."	1. Art admirer 2. Work of art
3. Business	Working for couple goals Money is power, work roles	"We're in this business together."	2 business partners or CEO and employee
4. Cookbook	Do things by a recipe and relationship will work out.	"We succeed because we always . ."	1. Cook 2. Second cook or diner
5. Gardening	Continually nurturing the relationship	"I tend to my relationship the way I would to a rose."	1. Gardener 2. Garden
6. Home	Centered in the home: emphasis on comfortable living	"Our home/family is the center of our life."	1. Caretaker 2. Caretaker's partner
7. Humor	Love is strange and funny	"Nothing works right and that's hilarious."	1. Comedian 2. Audience
8. Mystery	Love is mysterious, don't reveal too much of yourself.	"I keep my secrets and keep my partner guessing."	1. Sleuth 2. Mystery figure
9. Pornography	Love is a pornographic performance, often degrading	"Let's do my thing."	1. Sex/porn addict 2. Sex/porn object
10. Religion	Love is a religion or a set of activities set by religion	"Loving devotedly is my path to salvation."	1. Love mystic, striver 2. Object of devotion
11. Science Fiction	Partner is like an alien, weird, incomprehensible	"He/she is from a different planet."	1. Human 2. Alien (totally different)
12. Theater	Love is a dramatic performance with scripted scenes and lines	"This is great drama."	1. Actor/actress 2. Co-star or audience
13. Travel Adventure	Love is a journey; you don't know what might come next.	"We're always in the process of becoming."	1. Traveler, navigator 2. Traveler, conavigator
14. War	Love is a series of battles in a war that can't be won.	"I'll fight for what is right and for my dignity."	1. Aggressor 2. Defender

Excerpted from Sternberg, 1996.

believe that only one partner could be "right," so everyone else must be "wrong." But we prefer believing in the special rightness of our long-term partner as a support for a **more than rational** commitment. Many people in their second marriages may know there are "other fish in the sea," but they elevate their present relationship to exclusive "rightness" by demoting their first marriages as "a mistake" (Westoff, 1977). Thus, the ability to unite deeply with another rests on unconscious as well as conscious factors, and there is more than one way to arrive at an intuitive sense of "right" partnership.

The development of individual relationship myths

In addition to the collective myths, we each inspire ourselves with individual visions of what our partner and our relationship means. In our episodic memory we each weave a selection of our relationship events and reactions into a unique web of meaning (Duck, May, 1991), just as we construct our own identity (McAdams, 1985). Thus both our conceptions of ourselves and of our relationships are actually working models—or myths—that inspire and guide our thoughts and actions.

We construct our early visions of ourselves and partners in our new relationships out of hopes and projections. This "myth of origin" of the relationship points to both the growth possibilities and the potential problems to come. We might experience ourselves as kind and wise helpers or as star performers or brave adventurers. Then we may keep trying to repeat "helper," "star," or "hero" roles. But our partners keep outgrowing their "victim," "admirer," or "sidekick" parts.

Relationship stories

Robert Sternberg (1996) offers two dozen types of "relationship stories" which we have sampled in Table 10.7. According to Sternberg, from individual, family, and cultural experience we unconsciously construct a few of these stories in our minds. Each one structures our thinking about what should happen in a relationship. We will embrace and stay with a partner who fulfills the complementary role in a potent story, even if he or she experiences the relationship as a different story. All stories have advantages and disadvantages, but some are more flexible and may lead to more durable coupling than others. When roles or stories clash, relationships will most likely fail.

Without debunking these visions of our partners and ourselves, we need to recognize the difference between imagination and reality and endure the tension that results (Kast, 1987). If the meaning and possibilities in our original relationship myths wear out, they cease to inspire us. If we do not acknowledge this change, we may search for our myth in new lovers or spend years in resentment and efforts to revivify it. Once we recognize our mythic inspiration, we can either find other ways to enact it or develop new facets of ourselves in new roles. We can also let go of and grieve over our visions of each other, *instead of confusing our vision with the person onto whom it was projected*.

Thus the branches of individual psychology offer us many theories of how and why we love. They also give us explanations of processes involved in adult development and in relationship change. These theories cannot offer the promise of scientific certainty that many of us would like to have. But they offer approaches to understanding ourselves that respect the unconscious, non-rational, and non-commonsensical aspects of ourselves. Some of them attempt to explain mysteries of our nature. Others only *show* us our mysteries, without solving them. Yet when theories are extended to become coherent stories, we may integrate them to make meanings and guidelines for our lives.

Chapter summary

- Three components—passion (emotional), intimacy (behavioral), and commitment (cognitive)—combine into many types of love. Comparing their experienced and expected levels may affect satisfaction.
- Lee found 6 love styles: Eros (passionate euphoria), Ludus (playing with love), Storge (friendship), Mania (roller-coaster feelings), Pragma (practical mate-choice), and Agape (selfless concern). Men report more ludic tendencies, while women report more manic, storgic, and pragmatic.
- One cognitive theory suggests that partners gradually build up shared definitions and meanings. Another says love aims at expanding our self inclusion of elements of the partner in our self-concept.
- Two-factor theories stress emotion and thinking, as preoccupation with or idealization of the partner. Emotion and thinking may be partially independent. Focus on the partner increases feelings, while distracting from, mislabeling, or criticizing feelings can weaken them.
- In early and unrequited loves, we may prefer to enjoy love's uplifting power without mixing it with the uncertainty of intimate interaction.
- Love for particular people may transfer characteristics from our caregiver, family members, ourselves, and first loves. We may seek features which are similar, opposite, or idealized versions of these.
- Love adds dialogue with another person to our consciousness and gives us energy and courage to make changes. Unbalanced emotional investment predisposes partners to emotional struggles.

- Attachment is a behavioral system developed in early life. Reliable support makes securely attached infants treat their caregiver as a secure base. Anxious/ambivalent infants are insecure and easily upset about caregiver's intermittent support, while avoidants are indifferent or hostile toward closeness.
- In relationships, differences between secure and insecure attachment styles show up in comfort with closeness, belief in others' dependability, and anxiety about losing love. Women are pleased when men are more comfortable with closeness, while men dislike women's anxiety about losing love.
- Mahler's model proceeds from symbiosis with mother to separation/individuation. Individuation proceeds from differentiation of self, through practicing autonomous activities with "refueling," to object constancy–an internal working model of a loving caregiver as secure base.
- Stern's observed emotional attunement with mother is important, because it may provide an emergent sense of self as a dual-entity and the basis of experiences of union and a paradise of love.
- Erikson puzzled that many women put intimacy first and form some identity around a partner. Sensitivity to cultural guidelines may power their adolescent absorption of a wife identity, which they can later alter or outgrow. Individuation and interdependence may develop together for both sexes.
- To express a difference, we must differentiate our responses from the other's and have faith that conflicting would not destroy the bond between us. Adolescents normally avoid asserting differences.
- Young adults repeat some separation/individuation. When individuating from family, they may shy away from union and commitment and prefer practicing-style relationships.
- Adult individuation means developing potential parts of personality, which lovers do by developing coupling-related abilities. Once they have grown together, they may then grow in other directions too.
- Emotional attunement is felt when lovers "resonate." This facilitates nonrational trust, identification, and developing emotions similar to our partner's.
- When preserved too long, union can make us stagnate. And hostile-dependent partners may become insatiable for praise and emotional resonance.
- Differentiation of selves may bring disillusionment and power struggles. There are many tasks involved, including differentiating and expressing feelings, while remaining receptive to the partner.
- Partners are likely to differ in priorities for the 13 types of intimacy and in intensity and timing for fulfilling those intimacy needs.
- In a union–differentiating couple, the differentiating partner may

feel guilty for turning energy elsewhere, while the union partner feels betrayed and fears abandonment.

- If both partners are differentiating, abstract fairness may not work as well as supporting both their own and their partner's unique paths in life.
- Myths of love, sex, and marriage are windows onto our culture and psychology, and are often partly true but damaging if we live by them. "Forever after," "love conquers all," and "holy marriage" myths symbolize superhuman strength and durability.
- Personal myths about our relationships guide and inspire our actions. We may unconsciously prefer certain roles in standard love stories and stay with lovers who resonate to them. But our visions can wear out, and they are different from the partners on whom we project them.

A family systems perspective on intimate relating

11

I never saw my mother and father openly disagree. Instead I can remember sensing my mother's or father's withdrawal from each other when they were upset. It was as if the warm, loving side of them that I was used to was turned off and there was a cold distance there instead. Consequently, I found myself often holding back in my family when I was angry, not saying what was on my mind, and being very careful when I did disagree with either of them. When I got married, I found myself falling into the same patterns with my husband of avoiding open disagreement even when I felt strongly about something. Instead of directly informing him when I was angry or disagreeing with him openly, I signaled it indirectly by my withdrawal.

Family systems theory finds its roots in general systems theory, the premises of which are:

1. One part of a system does not affect another part in a linear way, like one billiard ball hitting another.

2. Instead, all parts affect and are affected by each other simultaneously. Feedback loops connect each part (in our case, each person), so all influence is reciprocal.
3. Any change in one part (person) in a system affects the whole system, just as changing the movement of one planet in our solar system would affect all the other planets.
4. A system tends to maintain its equilibrium through feedback aimed at dampening any unusual activity by any one part (person).

Family systems theorists contend that our experiences in the system of our *family-of-origin*, the family in which each of us was raised, are crucial to the development of our own style of relating and our ideas about the nature of the intimate relationships we wish to form. It is from experiencing how our family members relate to us and how they relate to each other that we develop our views about: (a) what we have to do in order to be loved, accepted, and cared for; (b) what we feel it is important to do or avoid doing in life; (c) what we feel we can safely reveal about ourselves to another person; and (d) how we can communicate what we feel when we feel threatened in some way. Each of us develops our own internal picture of the "way people should act when they love each other" or "how a partner should act" primarily as a result of our repeated exposure to models of relating in our families of origin. These ideas become the standards against which any mate's behavior is measured.

Thus the family-of-origin is the "main base against and around which most current family blueprints are designed." (Satir, 1972, p. 200). Although many of us may desire a relationship and family life different from the one we grew up in, Satir suggests that "it is easy to duplicate in your family (or intimate relationship) the same things that happened in your growing up. This is true whether your family was a nurturing or a troubled one." (p. 200) Familiarity exerts a powerful pull.

But what are the family patterns we follow so unthinkingly? And how exactly do they affect the type of intimate relationships we construct for ourselves? In this chapter we will explore the habits in our intimate relationships which family systems theorists assume are shaped by the close

relationships we experience in our families of origin. We will then examine the theory and research describing several different styles of intimate relating found in families.

Acquiring habits of intimate relating

Family systems theorists believe that the influence of our family patterns on our lives is subtle and complex, yet touches all areas of our lives in deep and hidden ways. An analogy from the world of computers clarifies how our habits of thinking, feeling, and behaving are encoded from our experience in our family. As you probably know, some processing programs have a function named "Reveal Codes." Activating this function displays on the screen, in brackets, all the programmed commands that structure how the words are arranged on the electronic screen. Just as the computer memory holds the encoding of decisions to paragraph or tabulate, you hold within your own memory a wealth of organizing information that can help you understand your current style of intimate relating. Once the codes (i.e., assumptions) of your family's interactional patterns are revealed, you can recognize how these patterns are operating in your own love relationships, consider whether they are helpful or not, and decide whether you want to try to substitute new codes, new information, and new actions.

We are usually unaware of habits of thinking, feeling, and acting in a love relationship until we experience something different. For example, one woman discovered that her own ideas about how affection and closeness should be communicated were quite different from those of her partner:

> It was not until I became closely involved with my husband's family that I realized that the amount and type of touching and other forms of physical contact people have with one another can differ greatly. Rarely, in my husband's home, will another person reach for someone else's hand, put their arms around another's shoulder, walk arm in arm, or kiss or hug for no special reason. Instead, hugs are only given for greetings and occasional comfort. Men do not often touch each other except for a handshake. When people sit down, they sit apart and give each other lots of space.
>
> In contrast, in my home, touching was a natural occurrence. Our mornings usually began with hugs and kisses in the kitchen as everyone was getting their breakfast. When we talked or watched television we rarely hesitated to cuddle up next to someone, run our hands through the other's hair, or tickle whomever happened to be within reach.

As this example illustrates, two partners can have very different expectations as to how affection and closeness are communicated to one another. When they notice such differences, partners often believe the other's habits and beliefs are wrong, dysfunctional, or old-fashioned. But are they? Or is it just a matter of that with which we are familiar or comfortable? What are your family's expectations about when and how much partners should touch and like to be touched? Are there other ways your family has of expressing their affection and closeness for one another? Many researchers (Gottman, 1994a; Kantor & Lehr, 1975; Nugent & Constantine, 1988) studying couple and family life have reported that there are distinctively different "styles" by which family members interact, and different beliefs undergirding these ways of interacting. Furthermore, each of these "styles" of interaction is viewed as quite satisfying by the family members involved.

Table 11.1 depicts beliefs and practices of 3 different styles of couple and family interaction: the Avoider style, the Passionate Volatile style, and the Validator style. These statements are based on Gottman's (1994c) longitudinal study of couple interactional patterns and marital satisfaction discussed in Chapter 4. Notice how familiar or unfamiliar they are to you. You can easily see how a partner who believes in avoiding conflict or disagreement would be uncomfortable living with someone who believes it is important to "hash things out" on a regular basis.

Viewing interpersonal intimate relationships as rule-governed systems

Do we merely find that one "right person" who fits our internal expectations about intimate relating? (The same question applies to Sternberg's "love stories" in Chapter 10.) Family systems theorists contend that, in reality, the process of coupling is much more complex. How then can we shift from considering our relationships as merely the amalgamation of both partners' separate sets of preferences for intimate partner behavior to explaining partners' interaction patterns over time? Human systems theory, family systems theory in particular, provides us with a lens for looking at **the patterns of action between people**.

In contrast to individual psychology's focus on behavior as primarily a result of the interplay of **forces** internal to the individual, systems theorists postulate that each of us is a part of a larger set of relationships known as a family which is organized in a coherent way. **Information about the nature of the interpersonal relationships** among this group of persons explains the actions of any member. The individual and the family systems approaches need not be incompatible or prove each other wrong. But they can lead to different practical approaches to change.

Rather than assuming that people do what they do because of what goes on in their heads **individually**, family systems theory posits that the actions of individuals are determined by the social contexts in which they find themselves. These contexts lead people to play roles that fit with roles of others. If you take someone out of a particular relational network for therapy, and then return that person to the same network, the individual will quickly begin to conform to that context once again. To maintain changes, the person must be coached on changing reactions and behavior in response to others. That means that you cannot understand behavior exclusively by studying the **parts** (individual partners) of a relationship system because the parts only make sense in the **context of the whole**. Thus, intrapsychic thinking looks at the person as a whole consisting of internal parts, such as the Freudian superego, ego, and id, and explains the behavior of the whole person in terms of these parts. In contrast, family systems

TABLE 11.1. Evaluating your family's interactional style

Do these statements fit your experience of life within your family?

Avoider style

1. We often hide our feelings to avoid upsetting each other.
2. We believe that a lot of talking about disagreements often makes matters worse.
3. It seems like we accept most of the things in our family that we can't change rather than make a big fuss about them.
4. We often agree not to talk about things we disagree about.
5. We believe that there is not much that can be gained by getting openly angry with each other.
6. I think that most of us prefer to work out any negative feelings we might have about each other on our own.
7. When we talk about our problems we find they just aren't that important in the overall picture of our family life.
8. A lot of talking about disagreements often makes matters worse.
9. Men and women ought to have separate roles in a marriage and family.
10. We hardly ever have much to argue about.
11. When we have some difference of opinion we often just drop the topic.
12. When I'm moody I prefer to be left alone until I get over it.
13. Many of our family conflicts can be solved with just the passing of time.
14. There are some personal areas in my life that I prefer not to discuss with my family.
15. In our family there is a fairly clear line between our roles so that we don't need to resolve disagreements about how to do things.

Passionate volatile style

1. We often do things separately.
2. When we have a disagreement, we enjoy trying to persuade each other to see things our way.
3. We feel comfortable with a strong expression of negative feelings.
4. There is nothing personal I would not think of sharing with my family.
5. We believe in honestly confronting disagreements, whatever the issue.
6. We believe we should be direct and honest with each other no matter what the results.
7. Sometimes we enjoy a good argument in my family.
8. We argue but only about important issues.
9. We think it's a good idea for all of us to have a lot of separate friends.
10. My parents have a romantic side they show.
11. We enjoy working out our values through our arguments.

Validator style

1. My family has a real feeling of togetherness.
2. The religious and other beliefs we share are basic to our family.
3. We cultivate a sense of we-ness in our family life.
4. We share with each other what's happening with us personally and emotionally.
5. There are few issues in married or family life which are worth arguing about.
6. My parents seem to have a strong sense of togetherness in their married life.
7. We are comfortable with only a moderate amount of emotional expression.
8. My family believes that one should argue only about important issues.

Adapted from Gottman, 1994c.

thinkers see the person as **a part of a larger whole**, (i.e., a web of relationships). For example, to understand the woman's style of demonstrating her anger and disappointment with her husband depicted in the opening anecdote, the family systems therapist would not just listen to the woman's story about her past history. The therapist would also observe the current patterns of interaction between the woman and her husband and the current meanings they give to these interactions.

Establishing a relationship system

But if it is not simply a matter of finding that one "right person" who fits our ideas as to what the relationship should look like, how do people decide to become involved and committed to one another? Although you may not be aware of it, when you become involved in an intimate relationship with another person, together you develop relatively predictable patterns of behaving together. According to family systems theorists, these predictable patterns of interaction develop as partners reveal to each other their preferred ways of relating, of expressing their ideas and feelings, giving and receiving nurturing and affection, and performing the tasks of living. Thus living together might be seen as a process of working out **shared agreements** (which are, for the most part, not overtly discussed) concerning how you and your partner are to live with one another (i.e., how you design your dance). These shared agreements result in certain agreed-upon **limitations** to acceptable ranges of behaviors in the relationship. Such agreed-upon limits develop over time, outside the awareness of the participants.

The development of such agreements as to how the relationship will function have been termed the **rules** of the relationship by family systems theorists such as Jackson (1965) and others (Watzlawick et al., 1967). This concept of "rules" may be viewed as a metaphor for how each partner offers the other a definition of their relationship (and therefore a self-definition within the relationship.) Obviously there are a wide array of areas of living together with which couples must become comfortable and thus for which they must construct rules. For example, is a woman to decide what sort of work she will do, or will her partner's wishes to be the sole provider dictate her involvement in employment outside the home? Is the man to comfort his partner when she is unhappy, or is he expected to become exasperated with her? There are a multitude of different issues which couples confront in the process of living together for which they establish some order and predictability. (Some partner expectations clash, and the couple rule may be that these behaviors continue to be disputed.)

Family systems theorists such as Jay Haley (1963, 1972, 1976) contend that each of the situations that a couple faces is dealt with by establishing explicit or implicit rules to follow in a particular situation. When they meet a similar situation again, the rules for relating they establish are either reinforced or changed. For example, in the following dialogue we see the rules for relating followed by a husband and wife:

Husband: I wish you would get yourself some new clothes. Take $75 and buy yourself a new outfit. Spiff yourself up!

Wife: I'm sorry, dear, but I don't think we can afford it right now.

Husband: #@$%! But I want to spend it on you!

Wife: I know, dear, but there are all these bills and things. (Jackson, 1965, p. 82)

If we look beyond the $75 they are talking about, we can see the rules for relating they have worked out. The husband is allowed to complain about the wife and act in charge, but the wife indicates she does not intend to follow his orders; that in fact his orders are of questionable value. Also, because she sets no time conditions, we do not know if she will ever get a new outfit or not. This is one clue to the rules for their relationship. Jackson (1965) explains: "Rather than executing a piece of action, the couple is going through a repetitive exchange which defines and redefines the nature of their relationship" (p. 21). Thus, on another occasion, we hear this same couple:

Husband: Hey, I can't find any dress shirts!

Wife: I'm sorry, dear, they're not ironed yet.

Husband: Why don't you send them to the laundry! I need ironed shirts! I don't care what it costs!

Wife: We spend so much on groceries and entertainment. I felt I should try to save a few dollars here and there.

Husband. Listen, for Pete sakes, I need shirts for work!

Wife: Yes, dear, I'll try to get to it. (Jackson, 1965, p. 83)

Notice that just as the wife does not specify *when*, nor whether she is really saying yes or no, the husband does not insist on a clear, definite agreement. Family systems theory would not attribute individual motives to their behavior, such as that the husband likes to bluster or the wife likes to frustrate him. Instead they propose that what these exchanges illustrate is the predictable pattern of interaction which both the husband and wife establish and participate in, which often has a life of its own.

According to Haley (1963), these rules for relating may differ in the extent to which a couple is aware of their existence. There may, for example, be rules which a couple would readily announce, such as the expectation that each partner can have a night out with friends each week. In addition, there may be rules that the couple would not mention but would agree to if they were pointed out, such as the rule that each partner consults the other when faced with major decisions. Finally, there are those rules an observer could notice but the couple would probably deny, such as the rule that one partner is to always have the upper hand in a disagreement and the other is to be on the defensive. Establishing these various rules for relating cannot be avoided. Whenever two people complete an interaction, a rule is being established. Even if the partners should decide to behave entirely spontaneously, *they would be establishing the rule that they are going to behave in that way*. Not only must couples set rules, they must also reach agreement on which of them is to be the one to set the rules in each area of their life together. This process of working out a particular rule always occurs within a context of resolving who is setting the rule (Haley, 1963, p. 34).

For example, a wife might not object to her husband inviting a friend over for dinner. But if he does not consult her about his wish to invite his friend to their home, he implies that she has no say in the matter. Then she might strongly object, but her objection would be at a different level and would concern the emerging rule that she was given no say. Similarly, a husband might not protest if his wife purchases an expensive piece of furniture, unless she does so without consulting him first.

In the early stages of a relationship each partner might graciously let the other be identified as the one in charge of various aspects of the relationship, but ultimately a struggle will set in over who is to set the rules in which areas of their life together. As a part of the struggle to reach agreement on rules for living with each other, a couple inevitably establishes another set of rules—those rules to be followed about how to create new rules, eliminate old rules, change rules, or resolve disagreements about which rules to follow. This set of rules for creating and changing rules becomes a set of **meta-rules**, or rules for making and breaking rules.

Over time as their frustration and disappointment in not resolving certain issues mount, these partners may grow discontented with this particular rule of relating and seek to learn ways to handle disagreement differently. A viable meta-rule structure for this couple might be that the person who is most upset may seek out resources (e.g., a friend, book, marital counselor) who might help them negotiate a new rule about expressing disagreement—such as "taking a time out" to talk about having differing ideas or feelings about an issue. This would be a new set of meta-rules that can enable the couple to change and adapt their rules for relating as they chafe against the limits inherent in their current ways of operating. Family systems theorists contend that in well-functioning relationships even the meta-rules change over time. Couples who do not have such a meta-rule structure often become stuck in ways of doing things that no longer fit their changed circumstances and become dissatisfied.

How do such rules and meta-rules develop? If an intimate relationship could be worked out by the application of agreement on rules, who is to make them, and how to make them, relationships such as marriage could be quite rational affairs. Obviously they are not. According to Haley (1963):

> Couples find themselves struggling with strong feelings over minor matters. One major source [of such feelings] is the fact that each partner

was raised in a family and given long and thorough training in the explicit and implicit rules for how people should deal with each other. However, each of us joins up in a marriage or committed relationship with a person who was given training in a different family with its own *differing* set of rules and expectations. Thus, as a couple, one must immediately try to reconcile different sets of long-term expectations each having the emotional force of immutable laws of nature. (p. 36)

Take, for example, a wife raised in a family in which, if disagreement begins to mount and personal thoughts and feelings are expressed, the other party is to leave the room to consider it carefully and refrain from a spontaneous response. Let us say that her husband has been raised in a family in which the expected response to such a situation is to be emotionally supportive, and leaving the room would indicate total rejection. You can imagine how each partner would interpret the other's behavior during a disagreement. It would take discovering that these actions have different meanings to each partner before new relational patterns and rules could be developed.

It is often difficult to realize how subtle are the patterns we learn in our families of origin, where we are exposed to millions of messages over time about how we are to behave with each other. It is often only in experiencing differences with one's partner concerning how certain situations are to be handled that we come to realize that we have learned set ways of handling certain situations. If not questioned, these ways of doing things are passed on from generation to generation.

> In my family growing up, money was considered a very private matter. Decisions about money were not talked about with the children, much less with those outside the family. Thus, I was very upset when my wife talked about our salaries and mortgage payment with some of our friends during dinner out one night. When she did it a second time, I blew my top and let her know how upset I was. Only after we talked did I realize that not everyone operated the way I had been taught to operate about money matters.

Family systems theorists contend that when two people come together in a relationship, they begin to create a **new system** of rules that regulate their interaction together. This new system is somewhat different from that of either of their families of origin. This new system of interaction is formed through a process of **mutual influence** and joint creation of meta-rules. Thus, when two sisters from a family, which has the rule that you should never fight openly with your mate, marry, we may find that one sister and her new husband will go to great lengths to avoid fighting, while the other sister and her new husband will fight openly on certain issues and not on others. Family systems theorists believe that it is the unique combination of rules and meta-rules from both partners' families of origin which blend together to form the couple's new rules for relating.

Changing relationship rules over time

Although most couples make some sort of bargain at the outset of their relationship about how they will relate with one another, this bargain is usually modified several times over by the demands of their family life cycle, the development of each individual, and the broader social context in which they live. As a matter of fact, the very process of becoming married often changes partners' expectations about their acceptable behavior with each other. Then, if a couple has a baby, the presence of a third party changes the nature of their intimate connections again.

> *Ray and I had Mindy after eight years of marriage. We had a grand time. We went out when we wanted to. We traveled when we wanted to. We were probably spoiled in that we had so much freedom. Then, after Mindy was born, I (the wife) stayed home with her for a year and just when I was thinking of going back to work, we got pregnant with Tommy. We knew that we did not want anyone else raising our kids when they were little, so I have chosen to stay home with them until they are in school. But I tell you, after eight years of freedom, to be strapped down! When children are born it changes your lifestyle dramatically.*

Several researchers (Crohan, 1996; Johnson & Huston, 1998) contend that the transition to parenthood is one of the most challenging and difficult of the family life cycle and has a high potential for both personal and marital change. Adding a third member to a preexisting dyad necessarily changes the social organization of the family and having a child often influences the division of domestic labor, power, communication, and conflict within the marital system. Studying African-American and white couples, Crohan (1996) reported that after the birth of the first child the marital relationships of both groups had more frequent negative interactions and fewer positive ones than before. In addition, gender roles tended to become more traditional because the women became more psychologically and physically involved in their parental role than did the men. Moreover, couples experienced less leisure time together, sexual relationships declined, and patterns of intimacy and communication were often disrupted. Johnson and Huston (1998) reported a similar pattern of wives developing child care preferences more like their husbands' preferences, after the birth of their first child.

Another major change in a couple's life is the loss of members of the couple's intimate circle, such as the launching of young adult children. This transition provides an opportunity for partners to redefine their relationship at midlife. Researchers studying couples during the "empty nest phase" of the couple life cycle (Aldous, 1978; Becker, 1986; Becker et al., 1977; White et al., 1986) report that couples report greater marital satisfaction as children become young adults and families move into the middle years prior to retirement. Even those couples having adult children leave and move back in with them due to financial or personal difficulties report high marital satisfaction (Mitchell & Gee, 1996).

In addition, demands for change in a couple's rules for relating are spawned by the psychological development of individual partners. The famous "seven-year itch" and "20-year review" (Carl Whitaker, in Neil & Kniskern, 1982)—which triggers the desire in many couples to redefine their lives and their relationships—can be thought of as crises over the degree of separateness versus connectedness and/or stability versus change individuals seek in their lives and relationships. Partners have many markers to measure whether they are "on time" or "off time" (Neugartern, 1979) in their personal conceptualization of how well they are doing in their adult lives.

Finally, changes in life circumstances such as changed job status (e.g., underemployment or unemployment) or residence, changes in one's own or one's children's health (e.g., infertility or the death of a child), or dealing with a physical attack or a life threatening illness may further complicate a couple's attempts to balance separateness with connectedness and to find a comfortable mix of continuity and variety in their rules for relating.

> *I am a college graduate and a high-level manager of a very successful women's wear corporation. My husband, Dave, is a freelance artist. Over the eight years of our marriage, at first largely supported by my earnings, my husband has gained more and more acclaim for his art work, and traveled widely overseas. We've each given ourselves a lot of space to do our own thing. But now I'm not sure what we want to do. We both seem to want to be together more, but can't seem to decide whose path to follow. He recently received an offer to work overseas in France, and is eager for us to move to France, at least temporarily. But this would mean I would have to give up my job. Traveling in Europe with him is not what I had in mind. I was really hoping to convince him that now is the time to have a baby. After all, I am not getting any younger.*

In summary, the basic assumptions that undergird family systems explanations of how intimate relationships develop are relatively simple:

1. We each grow up learning a certain way of interacting in close proximity with others from our own families of origin. This shows up as a set of beliefs or "rules for relating" that, among other things, define what is "safe" and what is "unsafe" in our emotional relating.
2. We each, where possible, choose a partner whose rules or model for relating "fit" our own, a person who shares a similar belief system about what is "safe" and "unsafe" in emotional relating.

3. Together with our partner we develop a shared set of agreements or rules for relating which has elements of both partners' preferred rules woven together in a unique way. These rules are often not consciously arrived at, but they signal the permissible ranges of our behavior with each other.
4. Our rules of connection evolve over time in response to pressures from inside or outside of our relationship.
5. Those partners having the greatest difficulty in fitting their rules together or in altering their rules as circumstances demand, will have the lowest probability of surviving as a couple over time.

Research on the family systems perspective

Hardly anyone would deny that experiences in our own family have an influence on our expectations and preferences for intimate relating. The evidence for exactly **how** our family experiences influence our intimate relating is somewhat limited, however, and takes several different forms. As we stated earlier, many family systems theorists (Bowen, 1978; Lerner, 1989) believe that the manner in which intimate partners relate to each other emotionally is similar to the manner in which partners related emotionally in their families of origin. In studying how early family experiences affect our current relating, researchers have followed one of two tracks: (a) They have examined how people describe their ways of relating (i.e., their patterns or "rules" for relating) to their families of origin and how such rules are reflected in their current patterns of relating to an intimate partner; (b) They have examined the degree of similarity and compatibility of personal "relationship rules" between intimate partners and how this "relative fit" of rules is related to the degree of satisfaction partners report experiencing with their relationship.

Most researchers who have explored the first track have done so from a clinical perspective in which patterns of relating were conceptualized on a continuum from functional ones to dysfunctional ones. The research of Williamson (1981) and Bray and his associates (1984, 1993) is illustrative of this approach. These researchers assessed the level of **differentiation** individuals reported they experienced in their early family relationships and in their current love relationships. Differentiation was defined as the extent to which a person reported being able to identify and express personal thoughts and feelings with other persons, including "former parents," in an emotionally non-reactive way. Each person's level of differentiation was measured by their responses to a questionnaire known as the PAFS (Personal Authority in the Family System). The PAFS measures a person's perception of the quality of their family relationships (i.e., parent to parent, parent to adult child, adult child to intimate partner). Table 11.2 shows a sampling of the items found in the PAFS.

Many different aspects of emotional relating are tapped: (a) the respon-

TABLE 11.2. The personal authority in the family system (PAFS) questionnaire: Sample questions

1. I share my true feelings with my parents about the significant events in my life.
2. My parents and I are important people in each other's lives.
3. I get together with my parents from time to time for conversation and recreation.
4. I take my parents' thoughts and feelings seriously, but do not always agree or behave in the same way.
5. I openly show tenderness toward my parents.
6. I am fair in my relationships with my parents.
7. I can trust my parents with things we share.
8. My parents and I have mutual respect for others.
9. I am fond of my parents.
10. My parents do things that embarrass me.
11. My present-day problems would be fewer or less severe if my parents had acted or behaved differently.
12. My parents frequently try to change some aspect of my personality.
13. I sometimes wonder how much my parents really love me.
14. I am usually able to disagree with my parents without losing my temper.
15. I often get so emotional with my parents that I cannot think straight.
16. I usually help my parents understand me by telling them how I think, feel, and believe.
17. My parents say one thing to me and really mean another.
18. How comfortable are you having sexual relations in the privacy of your own bedroom when your parents are in your home?
19. How comfortable are you talking to your mother and father about the private and personal story of growing up in their family of origin and extended family (i.e., talking about perceptions, thoughts, and feelings about their relationships with father, mother, siblings, aunts, uncles, etc.)?
20. How comfortable are you talking to your mother and father about family secrets both real and imagined, and about skeletons in the family closet?
21. How comfortable are you talking to your father and mother about specific mistakes or wrong decisions which they made in the past and would like to do again differently (e.g., marriage, marriage partner, occupation)?
22. How comfortable are you talking to your opposite-sex parent about the fact that that parent is no longer the #1 love in your life?
23. How comfortable are you talking to your same-sex parent to declare openly the ways in which you are different from that parent in your beliefs, values, attitudes, and behavior?

Source: Williamson et al., 1982.

dent's perceptions of how he/she initiates or receives intimacy from a partner, (b) perceptions of how he/she perceives the parents initiating and receiving intimacy with each other, (c) the extent to which family members thoughts and feelings are influenced by the thoughts and feelings of their parents as well as significant others—a dimension they term emotional fusion, (d) the extent to which the respondent often feels "triangled" into the relationship between his/her parents, and (e) the degree to which his/her parents' wishes continue to be a strong source of pressure or influence in decision making, which they call interpersonal intimidation.

Studies using the PAFS have revealed a strong relationship between respondents' levels of expressed intimacy, degree of triangulation, emotional fusion, and interpersonal intimidation in their own intimate relationships and the levels of these aspects perceived in their parent-child relationship. For example, among college undergraduates, the higher the extent of fusion and intimidation reported in their relationships with their parents, the higher the level reported in their own current intimate relationships (Bray et al., 1984; Lawson et al., 1993). Wilcoxon & Hovestadt (1983) asked partners to assess the health of their family of origin experiences and their perceived adjustment as a couple. They found that the greater the discrepancy between partners' PAFS scores for their family of origin, the lower the level of marital adjustment reported.

The second approach to assessing the impact of one's family rules for relating on one's current relating has been taken by researchers such as Larry Constantine (Nugent & Constantine, 1988), David Kantor and William Lehr (1975), David Reiss and his associates (1981), and John Gottman (1994c). Each of these theorists propose that it is the degree of similarity or compatibility of the partners' **belief systems** or **paradigms** about their relationship that is a key predictor of marital satisfaction. They do not assume that there is one best, or "healthiest" way to interact as a couple and one best set of guiding images each partner holds that serve as a reference model for the relationship, as the **personal differentiation** model suggests. Instead they assume that there are many styles of couple interaction partners find satisfying, and that the key to understanding couple satisfaction is in looking at the relative "fit" between both partners' ideas and preferred styles of intimate relating. Thus, contemporary conflicts between traditional and egalitarian belief systems are viewed as "culture clashes" instead of the morally "good" versus the "not so good." In this tradition, Nugent and Constantine (1988) assessed the marital paradigms of 103 couples seen in marital therapy to determine whether the similarity of **paradigm** was related to success in treatment of marital difficulties. They reported that while 92% of those couples sharing the same basic relationship paradigm were successfully treated in marital therapy, only 60% of the couples in which the partners had different paradigms were considered successful in their marital counseling outcome. Thus the relative success in resolving marital difficulties via therapy was strongly related to the "fit" of the partners' paradigms.

Investigating the degree of partner similarity has been the focus of a number of different research studies. Byrne and Blaylock (1963) found that satisfied marital couples tended to share the same attitudes and preferences for emotional closeness. Furthermore, satisfied couples often report greater agreement and consensus than they in fact have (Acitelli et al., 1993). Marital partners' perceptions of intimacy may be based on three sources: (a) a person's own view of intimate experience; (b) a culturally based view in which husbands and wives enact two separate co-cultures; and (c) the couple's joint construction of what intimacy is (Kenny & Acitelli, 1994). Heller and Wood (1998) extended this study by using a more objective index of similarity and understanding between spouses, and found that those couples who reported the greatest level of similarity of intimacy with their spouse reported the greatest level of understanding of their spouse and satisfaction with their relationship.

Typologies of couple and family interaction

The family paradigm approach provides a framework for understanding why couples who interact quite differently from one another report their relationships to be satisfying. Some family system theorists assume that our relating systems regulate two basic dimensions of our interaction: the degree of **connectedness** versus separateness and the degree of **adaptability** to change. Here are some aspects of each dimension:

Connectedness versus Separateness
1. how much partners prefer to spend their time on activities apart from their partner versus together;
2. how much they prefer to communicate about personal problems and solve relational problems with their partner versus "on their own";
3. how much they see their partners as their primary source of companionship versus have an array of other persons as companions.

Adaptability to Change
1. how much partners have predictable roles and routines versus negotiate and shift responsibilities and routines around;
2. how much partners prefer to challenge the cultural status quo in their role expectations versus follow culturally desired role patterns.

Other theorists (Bagarozzi & Anderson, 1989; Olson et al., 1983a; 1983b) have further subdivided couples' preferences for connectedness into two areas: (a) their preferences for expressing and following self interests versus relationship interests and (b) their preferences for communicating love, value, and worth. Adaptability is also subdivided into two areas: (a) couples' preferences or rules for sharing and structuring power, influence, and leadership, and (b) habits for searching out and responding to variety and change in life circumstances. Using these two general dimensions (of connectedness and adaptability), a two-by-two table can be constructed reflecting four possible combinations of preferred styles of connectedness and adaptability. When this is done, the typologies of couple and family paradigms proposed by Constantine (1986) parallel the couple interactional styles reported by Gottman (1994a, 1994c, Chapter 4) and the couple types described by Fitzpatrick (1988c). Figure 11.1 shows these similarities.

Constantine's relationship paradigms

Building on the pioneering work of Kantor and Lehr (1975) and Reiss and his associates (1981), Larry Constantine (1986) organized the basic dimensions of interpersonal connectedness and adaptability into a four part system.

Constantine proposed that partners operate with each other as if guided

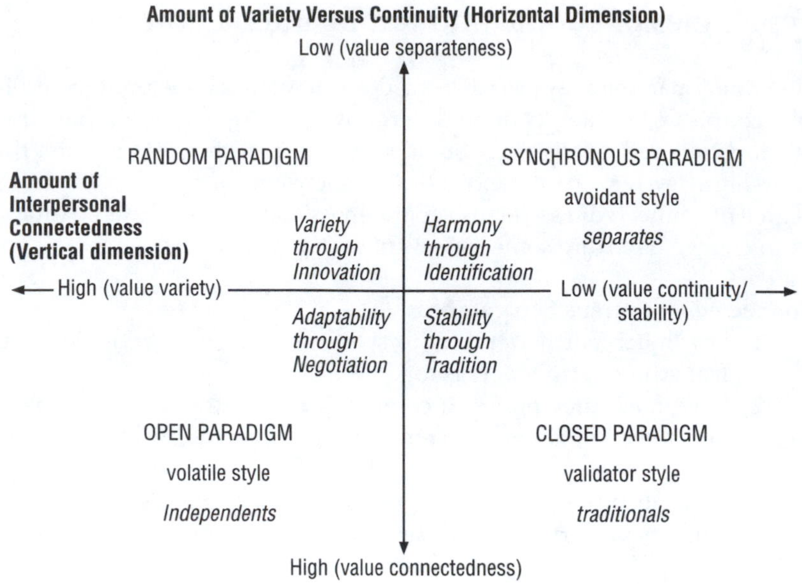

Amount of Variety Versus Continuity (Horizontal Dimension)

Low (value separateness)

| RANDOM PARADIGM | | SYNCHRONOUS PARADIGM |

Amount of Interpersonal Connectedness (Vertical dimension)

◄— High (value variety)

Variety through Innovation — *Harmony through Identification*

avoidant style

separates

Low (value continuity/ stability) —►

Adaptability through Negotiation — *Stability through Tradition*

OPEN PARADIGM

volatile style

Independents

CLOSED PARADIGM

validator style

traditionals

High (value connectedness)

FIG. 11.1. Comparison of Constantine's paradigm, Gottman's styles, and Fitzpatrick marital types.

by a **family paradigm**, an overarching image of their relationship and of marriage and families in general, which influences the rules for relating that they develop. These images function as points of reference against which partners check their experience with each other, define their priorities among competing ends, and develop the guidelines for their everyday actions and judgments. Thus a paradigm is not only a model of what an intimate relationship is, can, and should be but also a lens through which experiences in relationships and with the world are interpreted (Reiss, 1981).

The four distinctive paradigms of couple and family life proposed and researched by Constantine and his associates are: (a) the **closed** paradigm, (b) the **random** paradigm, (c) the **synchronous** paradigm, and (d) the **open** paradigm. The divergent goals and preferred strategies of each of the different types of paradigms enable each one to be good at dealing with certain life situations and prone to specific difficulties in others. Thus each paradigm can be seen as having inherent strengths and vulnerabilities. Obviously real couples are more variable than might be accounted for by the four types. Nevertheless, the typology suggests some fundamental distinctions in the way couples organize their lives together and establishes the range of themes upon which unique variations are built by couples. Figure 11.1 has sketched four major goals (harmony, stability, adaptability, and variety) and operating strategies for reaching them (identification, tradition, negotiation, and innovation) which highlight the ways the paradigms differ from one another. Table 11.3 outlines some of the defining features and the probable strengths and limitations of each paradigm.

The closed or traditional paradigm.   The core values of the closed or traditional paradigm are those of stability, security, and belonging. Partners guided by a closed paradigm prefer stability whenever possible, and operate to correct deviations from their established patterns. Because continuity and uniformity are given priority, the couple relationship tends to value structures that are hierarchical and grounded in tradition and authority. Thus the couple may have many traditions that they respect and repeat. Leadership is clear, it is often hierarchical in nature leaving no doubt about who has the final authority and responsibility for decisions in a particular area. Others—including children, friends, extended family members, and outsiders—are considered but are expected to fall in line and support their decisions. Such relationships depend on "respect" and willingness to sacrifice individual needs and wishes "for the good of the relationship." The following couple, married for thirty years, appears to operate from this paradigm.

> Kevin: We're very good about being on the same wavelength with the kids. In other words, they can't go to one person to get one answer and then go to the other and get the other answer. Discipline per se is rare. I may occasionally put my foot down, but usually if we get a chance to talk about things ahead of time, we're going to handle it the same way. She's really the expert in handling the kids and I follow her lead.

> Jean: Yeah, and we don't disagree much. He'd probably like to live on a boat. I can't do that because I get seasick. But at this point in life, we don't disagree. We just sort of laugh over it. I've told him to go get another girl and go live on a boat (she laughs). But we really never fight. We never go to bed mad. We learned never to do that. We had a little thing last week. He bought a convertible as an investment and I thought it was a little screwy. And I thought, "Well, what can I go out and spend money on?" But that's not a real disagreement. I laughed and thought, "Well, wonderful, he has a new toy." (Blumstein & Schwartz, 1983, p. 379)

We can imagine this couple constructing a dance similar to a **waltz** as their image of relationship life. The steps are predictable, there is a high level of coordination or connection, and not much discontinuity or change in the dance step. There is a clear leader and follower, although possibly a different one depending upon the arena of family life. Couples with this paradigm may resemble the television couples of the 1950s (e.g., *Leave it to Beaver* or *Father Knows Best*) where the husband's leadership is consistent. Even if the leader consults and discusses matters with his mate, no doubt remains as to who has final authority and responsibility for each decision. As these couples interact with their own families of origin, or create families of their own, their internal organization might resemble that of a football team. There is a high degree of coordination of actions among the various players, predictability (fixedness) as to who will do what role, and a

TABLE 11.3. Defining features, strengths, and limitations of marital and family paradigms

	Closed/traditional	Random/individualistic	Open/verbal	Synchronous/serene
Individual and relationship	Relationship or group comes first.	Individual comes before relationship.	Merges both individual and relationship needs.	Neither takes priority, needs are identical.
Stability and change	Builds stability.	Creates change.	Generates flexibility; combines stability and change.	Timelessness.
Decision making	Based in authority, tradition; commands, directions passed	Based in originality; spontaneity; autonomous actions.	Based in consensus; open communication; negotiation.	Based in tacit agreement, mutual identification; automatic.
Power and control	Hierarchy, fixed roles.	Anarchic, egalitarian, independent solutions.	Mutual collaboration, joint solution.	Indirect or covert, implied understandings.
Provides	Security, belonging.	Freedom, variety.	Intimacy, adaptiveness.	Tranquility.
Promotes	Comformity, loyalty.	Individuality, independence.	Mutuality, cooperation.	Harmonious identification.
May sacrifice	Individuality, variety.	Security, stability.	Tranquility.	Intimacy, involvement.
Probable direction of failure	Rigidity, over-involvement.	Chaos, under-involvement.	Chaos, over-involvement.	Rigidity, under-involvement.

Source: Nugent, M. D., & Constantine, L. (1988).

clear leader who makes decisions and expects them to be followed in a "top down" style. In such couples, roles between the mates are often complementary—that is, one's actions do not repeat or compete with the other.

The image of couple interaction depicted in the **closed** paradigm closely resembles Gottman's validating style of couple interaction (1994a). Marriage partners tend to pick their battles carefully and to follow a particular pattern of **validation, persuasion, and compromise** during their conflicts. Thus the flare-ups that do occur sound more like a problem-solving discussion rather than an all out attack. Each not only presents their opinion, but listens to their mate's, before attempting to persuade their partner of a particular option. Gottman and his colleagues (1989; Gottman, 1994a) report other interesting features of couples demonstrating this style. One is that there seems to be a fair amount of traditional sex role behavior with each spouse having a separate sphere of influence—the wife is in charge of the home and children, and husband is usually the final decision maker (see Chapter 5). This structure minimizes conflict, since each predictably defers to the other in dealing with issues in their sphere of influence.

The closed paradigm of couple life is also similar to the **traditionals** described by Fitzpatrick and her colleagues at the University of Wisconsin (Fitzpatrick, 1984, 1988c). Traditional couples demonstrate a high value for "we-ness" (e.g., cohesion) over individual goals and values. They also highly value verbal openness, shared time and shared activities, being in love, and displaying affection.

One of the pitfalls of this style of relating is that the balance between personal development and togetherness may get too skewed toward togetherness. Partners may sometimes feel guilty if they wish to follow interests that do not include the partner or family. Another built-in vulnerability of this style of relating is that things can become too "humdrum" and passionless, limiting the excitement and smoothing out the edges too much in their partnership.

The random or individualistic paradigm. In contrast to the closed or traditional paradigm, the **random** marital paradigm is oriented toward variety and change. Couples operating within this paradigm value maximizing change and value novelty, creativity, individuality, and autonomy. The couple depicted below, both aspiring young actors in their late twenties, share this paradigm:

> Abbey: One of the reasons we get along so
> well is that we are both busy and we don't

get on each other's case a lot. It's not a problem, because he's in the theater. If he had a regular nine-to-five job, then it might be.

Biff: (Nodding his head in agreement). We've established a certain SOP—standard operating procedure. The girl that I was married to before could never have dealt with it. I may call Abbey at three in the afternoon and say, "I'm going to be at the theater at six to take care of some things. I should be home by seven, seven thirty"—and then not get home till midnight. I may not remember to call, whatever—it doesn't bother Abbey. But my ex-wife would have killed me for that or tracked me down by three-ten. That's what I mean when I said we have a partnership here. We both understand the business, and we operate within it, without consulting each other very much . . . I have friends who have problems. One has a structured job and the wife does not, and they can't keep the relationship. We, on the other hand, seem very adaptable. (Blumstein & Schwartz, 1983, p. 400)

Freedom and the desires of the individual partner come before those of the couple. Thus "do your own thing" is a typical motto of partners favoring this paradigm. Independence of thought and actions, and separate solutions to the problems of couple and family life are the norm. Thus it might be commonplace for couples embracing this paradigm to decide that they do not need to agree on what they will have for dinner or where they might go on vacation. Such couples may enjoy experimentation and try to create new ways of doing things.

Such a relationship can be most exciting, but it can also degenerate into chaotic independence and leave partners isolated. It can also be problematic if children are added to the scene who demand heavy amounts of time and energy for their rearing. Families operating with this paradigm might be likened to a golf team, in that each member is considered an individual performer in their own right, and each person's satisfaction is not viewed as dependent on that of any other. Independent solutions are valued over coordinated action. Decision making is either egalitarian or anarchic. Whenever possible, couples guided by this paradigm will opt for novelty and change rather than stable continuity, which they may see as too dull and routinized. Because of this highly individualized style of interaction, these couples often tolerate a high degree of conflict with each other and utilize an impressive array of individual versus joint problem solving skills. Surprisingly, neither Gottman (1994c) nor Fitzpatrick (1984, 1988c) reported a couple style or type that parallels this paradigm. But children of divorce who experienced a great deal of freedom and less than normal dependence on either parent might operate from this paradigm.

The open or collaborative paradigm.   Partners who are guided by an **open** model of relating tend to value talking things through and trying to resolve an issue to everyone's satisfaction. Thus partners may try actively to solicit the other's viewpoint, share their ideas, and take time to check out the other's feelings and reactions. Interactions in this style are often quite emotionally intense and challenging. Since the partners have a deep commitment to fairness and equal rights and responsibilities, great value is placed on making decisions through consensus and negotiation, and considering possible solutions that address the needs of both the individual partners and the relationship. Decision making is designed to promote adapting to different needs through flexibility and innovation. Leadership is shared, assertiveness is valued, and no one solution is consistently preferred. To return to the sports world, this paradigm might fit a basketball team, where both coordination and flexibility in roles and decision making are highly valued to optimize success.

These couples are similar to the group Fitzpatrick (1988c) called **independents**. The couples tend to debate and argue irrespective of the importance of the issue and "demand compliance and react negatively if their partner attempts to withdraw from the conflict" (p. 335). They tend to value autonomy very highly and use the pronoun "I" much more than "we." They are also much more likely to support a nontraditional sex role arrangement, such as both partners following careers and sharing childcare.

Since they operate with assertiveness, couples embracing an open paradigm may develop the volatile style described by Gottman—jumping right in to advocate their position instead of listening to their partner's opinion first. Though they may want to give careful attention to each other's opinions, like **traditionals**, the more volatile **open** couples may proceed more like a democratic group with no fixed traditions except to stay together. Persuasion may take precedence over laws, so they can veer from one course to another. They are good at allowing for change, and they welcome new energy, but may consume much of it by constantly "working things out."

The synchronous or serene paradigm.   Partners with a **synchronous** paradigm value a peaceful, harmonious relationship. They tend to avoid any open disagreement or dispute, and solve problems primarily by applying endless amounts of patience and an implicit faith that things will work themselves out if left alone. Partners operating within this paradigm often make decisions more by tacit agreement or a mutual identification with a valued outcome than by direct comments or an overt search for consensus. There is often a belief in a common vision to guide action, but not much intensity of connection. The partners in the following interview depict this set of beliefs.

> Tom: I think we both feel pretty strongly that we both should work and both of us should be involved in raising the kids. We always knew that we were pretty committed to our careers as well as to our children, so there's never been a lot of talking or haggling about who would do what. It just worked out because we have a basic commitment to being married and to each other.

Belle: I see it that way too. We have always known what we want, and we both work to make it happen. Sometimes there have been times when I think we are killing ourselves by working so hard and we both complain about it, but then I don't think we would know what to do with ourselves if we didn't have to work.

These partners assume that they each know their part in the total dance, whose pattern is relatively stable and can be carried out with little interchange or alteration, like a square dance. Their interactions are determined by stable forces—their career(s), families, social groups, communities, or religious prescriptions. If such a couple constructs a family life together, it might operate with members having separate spheres of action and a common identity and mission. In sports, this most resembles a baseball team's operation, especially since the players always play complementary positions and keep the appropriate distance between them. Because a common mission and harmony are highly valued, little initiative is taken for independent action or solutions that require direct negotiation.

This fits Fitzpatrick's **separates** (1988c) and Gottman's **conflict avoiders** (1994a). As discussed in Chapter 4, they tend to step around conflict, and smooth over or ignore differences rather than confront them head on. Of course, these coordinated separates have vulnerabilities too. Because conflict is not usually handled directly, partners may have real difficulty dealing with differences resulting from changed life circumstances that cannot be avoided. For example, if the husband loses his job and the wife must work, resolving that issue may be monumental for them. They may also long for closeness now and then. But their planned events—such as attending church—may be stiff or non-intimate, while their unprogrammed "close encounters" may be more awkward and stressful than fulfilling.

The exaggeration principle.　Constantine suggests that each of these paradigms is characterized by a set of preferred ways of responding to the world that can lead to relationship disablement as well as strength. The best name which might be given to this principle is the **exaggeration principle.** Constantine discusses it as such:

> The basic principle behind the paradigmatic view of disablement is very simple, although its implications are myriad and complex. Confronted by problems, [couples or] families do whatever they do best, with the [couple] family typically applying their usual way of problem-solving. When this doesn't work they try harder. "Trying harder" is itself defined paradigmatically; families try harder by doing more of the same. Thus, by using the resources of its relationship structure and remaining true to its paradigm *each [couple] family under stress has a natural tendency toward exaggeration of its own special character*.
>
> The more difficult the situation, the more extreme are the measures that will be taken, extreme, that is, in a way consistent with the [couple or] family paradigm. The longer an impasse is sustained, the greater the

degree of exaggeration. (Constantine, 1986, pp. 182–183). (The word couple was added to highlight the application of this principle to couples as well as families.)

This exaggeration disables each paradigm according to their unique way of dealing with stress and turmoil. **Closed** couples grow more isolated from the world, more strongly and intensely focused internally, and more rigid as they become increasingly disabled. The **random** family or couple tends toward greater separateness and chaos. **Open** couples go around in circles. If the problem cannot be solved, they become increasingly involved in a process of gathering information and hashing things out that in the end creates chaos. The **synchronous** couple relies on consensus, and when this fails, the separateness between the partners grows despite their attempts to ignore it. As they become more disabled, they are disconnected from their problems and turn into a "dead" couple (Constantine, 1986, pp. 182–183). The challenge for stressed families is to "borrow" management strategies from another paradigm. Thus, for example, random couples can gain from some sense of traditional structure and reliability or from a sense of harmony and purpose that comes from beyond the two of them.

Constantine's, Gottman's, and Fitzpatrick's typologies have many implications. First, many people believe that one style of life is more successful or appropriate (usually either the traditional or the open style). But researchers have found that there are many ways a couple can relate that can be quite successful. Second, the concept of relationship or family paradigm also suggests that we may not be able to change our ideas and ways of relating too quickly. But studying the paradigm of our earlier family life can make us more aware of how we are used to relating emotionally in close relationships. This student notices the clash of his own traditional paradigm with his girlfriend's and her daughter's more random style:

> I made dinner for the three of us last week (a chore that I hate). When I was just putting the plates on the table, Michelle (her daughter) announced, "I am going outside for a little bit," and ran out the door. I screamed, "Get back here!" but she didn't hear me. Sarah (the mother) looked horrified. She wanted to know why I was so upset. Wasn't it obvious? It was just incredibly **rude** to run out like that. Sarah didn't see it that way, and when she came back, neither did Michelle. My idea that meals should be eaten together just doesn't fit into the way their family does business. Even when I explained to her that I thought it was rude to run out after I had gone to the effort of cooking, I could tell that she still thought I was being silly.

Personal interaction styles related to family paradigms

An implication of Constantine's exaggeration principle is that it can help us guess how children growing up in each family paradigm might tend to cope personally with emotionally challenging interactions. Figure 11.2 depicts the typical interactional styles fostered by responses to stressful situations in each paradigm.

The **traditional closed** family fosters mutual adherence to agreed-on guidelines. It is normal to be a good **follower** and to be better able to respond to what the whole family (or group) has decided on as proper for a situation than to be aware of or respond to our own thoughts and feelings. The traditional mother is the ultimate follower and harmonizer, as she exerts herself to make everyone comfortable and teach the children to be good troopers. But even the traditional father is only leading according to the guidelines he has been taught for responding to the world and his family's needs. Others may see family members as **nice** and reliable, but often lacking in spontaneity and playfulness. With friends and partners, a person from a traditional family is likely to be more aware of what delights and bothers the other person than what he feels or needs for himself.

Under stress, **traditionals** are likely to **placate**, putting others' satisfaction before their own needs: "I do everything to make you happy." They may be valued as devoted, unselfish partners or friends. But they are prone to depression and to episodic outbursts of anger: "Why don't you ever treat me as well as I treat you?"

The **random** family fosters creative innovation in opposition to traditions. Both adolescents and adults from random families may yearn for some structure and stability in relationships, but still **oppose** those who expect reliable service from them. They may deny the effects of a relation-

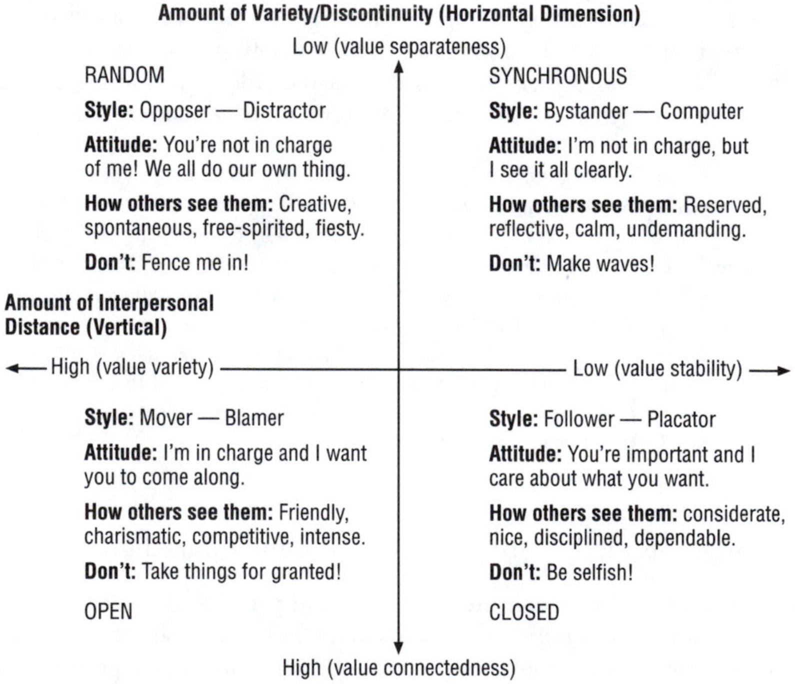

Amount of Variety/Discontinuity (Horizontal Dimension)

Low (value separateness)

RANDOM

Style: Opposer — Distractor

Attitude: You're not in charge of me! We all do our own thing.

How others see them: Creative, spontaneous, free-spirited, fiesty.

Don't: Fence me in!

SYNCHRONOUS

Style: Bystander — Computer

Attitude: I'm not in charge, but I see it all clearly.

How others see them: Reserved, reflective, calm, undemanding.

Don't: Make waves!

Amount of Interpersonal Distance (Vertical)

← High (value variety) —————————————— Low (value stability) →

Style: Mover — Blamer

Attitude: I'm in charge and I want you to come along.

How others see them: Friendly, charismatic, competitive, intense.

Don't: Take things for granted!

OPEN

Style: Follower — Placator

Attitude: You're important and I care about what you want.

How others see them: considerate, nice, disciplined, dependable.

Don't: Be selfish!

CLOSED

High (value connectedness)

FIG. 11.2.
Influence of paradigms on members' interpersonal styles.

ship crisis by **distracting** and escaping conflict into humor, alcohol, or unrelated activities (such as music or TV), or by creating diversionary dramas, such as conflicts with outsiders or authorities. A decade or more of "doing my own thing" unrelated to others may leave them reluctant or even unable to tune in to either their own or anyone else's real feelings in an interpersonal conflict. But they can be great to have fun with.

The **open** family rewards the assertiveness and energetic initiative of a **mover**. The mover exudes charisma and persuasion to get others involved in her activities. Since she is good at motivation, she often carries the ball with friends and lovers. When the competition gets stressful, she may expect her partner to assert his own feelings, as she does hers. Though she may appreciate a friend or partner who gets his way through asserting like she does, she may **blame** others who are less self-aware and "don't take care of themselves" as she has learned to do. Though often well liked, her intensity and strong focus on verbal intimacy may be too much for others, who may back away from feeling dominated.

The **synchronous** but **separate** paradigm supports self-control and perfectionism. Some introverted children of single or two-career parents start trying to be successful, responsible, "super-reasonable" adults at an early age, and do not "run wild" in search of peer companionship. It is their way of keeping their idea of the family alive. In place of the rough and tumble of intimate encounters, family members are keen observers of others, with the **distance** for intelligent analysis—but often without the interpersonal confidence and skills to apply their insights to interaction. They make good students—of life or any other subject—but they tend toward reflection rather than action. In adult relationships, they may appear easygoing, but feel left out because they don't know how to get emotionally involved. They **won't risk mistakes** and may prefer their closest relationships to be on a mental level or with computers and the Internet.

No matter which family paradigm you grew up with, you will probably feel that your way of responding to others is the best. Hence **traditionals** have little patience for selfishness and disrespect. **Individualists** criticize conformity and "boring" consistency. **Open** family members think everyone ought to be open and competitive. And so on.

Perhaps you are asking yourself why you fit into more than one category. First, most families don't fit **exclusively** into one paradigm. In fact, Constantine thought they were more likely to become dysfunctional if they did. Family paradigms can also shift over time, such as from traditional via divorce or career development to random, open, or synchronous, as in this report.

> When my mother went to work for the first time since I was born, decision making started to change. My father would work from 11 pm to 7 am and sleep most of the day. This led to him partially losing touch with the family. My mother would work from 8 am to 5 pm and later. Everyone was busy and the time for family togetherness was dwindling. The decisions were being made separately, [but] not to interfere or cause rifts with any other family member.

We all tried to avoid any open disagreement or dispute. Subconsciously I knew if a problem arose it would work its way out, if I left it alone.

Second, individual members of most families tend to "specialize" in one or two of the four interactional types we have discussed, rather than all being purely the type reinforced by the dominant paradigm. You may be moved to diverge from your family's "normal" personality type by a combination of innate temperament, birth order, and needs for attention and recognition of your own uniqueness, rather than your cooperation in the "family business."

Each paradigm's Achilles heel

Among divergent personalities, each family type may have at least one "shadow type" or Achilles heel. This personality style evokes the greatest conflict or discomfort and is considered most "abnormal" (i.e., unsuited for the family paradigm). But it is often secretly effective for challenging the family to move beyond their systemic restrictions toward greater viability and mental health. Thus the **traditional** family often gets its **rebel** (**opposer** type), who unconsciously seeks to enliven the group by moving in new directions. Both **random** and **separate** families can't cope with a kid who is dependent and needs to evoke the closeness of a **traditional** or **open** system. The much idealized **open** family is not very supportive for an introverted, highly sensitive child who is not assertive. Preprogrammed **synchronous** families are disturbed by both individualistic spontaneity and assertive attention-seeking. And so on.

To put all this together, Table 11.4 shows you how to become more aware of your own personal interaction types in action.

Understanding family processes

In addition to evaluating the impact of your family paradigm(s), you can review the personalities and behavior of your family members to find out

---

TABLE 11.4. Your interpersonal interaction types

1. Which paradigm(s) have been dominant in your family?
2. Which interaction styles predominate for you when you are normally relating to (a) family, (b) a close friend, (c) a lover?
3. Which style do you adopt with (a) family, (b) friend, (c) beloved in a crisis or conflict?
4. Which style of yours was (is) most reinforced by your family? How does that style make you feel now?
5. Which style of yours was (is) least welcomed in your family? What thoughts and feelings did (does) that evoke?
6. Which family member were you most intrigued by or attracted to? What style(s) and family interaction did (does) that person have? How did the family respond?
7. How have you reacted to romantic attractions or partners with each interaction style?
8. What are the interaction styles of your best friend(s)?

---

what you have learned from them about the ways an intimate relationship or a life is or should be structured. For example, you may recall never seeing your parents argue, and feel you never learned how to argue. You may have learned that you were not given support to be envious or jealous, so that if you were you certainly could not tell anybody. There may be certain things you would change if you could about your ways of relating, with what you know now. In addition, there may have been certain decisions you made about what you wanted to be or not be or what you wanted to have for yourself in a life or relationship which were based on watching and being involved in specific family relationships. For example, you may discover that you feel safest or most comfortable when you play a particular role—such as the caretaker, provider, or "cheerer-upper" ("In my family I was hired to be cheerful")—even when there is a part of you that is tired of the responsibilities that go with this role.

Relationship triangles

Not only do particular people and pair relationships influence us, but **triangular** relationships do too. For example, you have a relationship with your father and a relationship with your mother, but you also were part of a three-person or **triangular** relationship with them. Families have many possible **triangles**, and in each you may play a very different role. In one triangle, involving your sister, your mother, and you, you may have had to learn to deal with competitiveness and jealousy, feeling special, and feeling left out. In another triangle, involving your mother, father, and yourself, you may have seen your mother taking all of the responsibility for child rearing and allowing your father to dictate the schedule and needs that were to be met in the family. You may have learned early on that to win the love and approval of your parents you must demonstrate concern for the needs of significant others. Thus, you may feel in your current intimate relationships that you cannot speak up openly about what you want, that you have yet to learn how to make demands for yourself, to argue for equitable and fair treatment for yourself, or even to explore sexually what you like. To illustrate the ways family triangles can work, let us explore one of the most widely influential triangles in families—husband, wife, and daughter—with its consequences for the daughter's romantic life.

MOTHER - DAUGHTER TRIANGLES

Mother–daughter triangles. We have already pointed out that mother–daughter bonds are often more intimate and enduring than those of mother and son (Chapter 7), and that mother–child love is more essential to human evolution than husband–wife love (Chapter 9). Since mother–daughter love can rival husband–wife love, it is not surprising that a mother often finds her daughter more available and compatible, and less powerful and frustrating than her husband—and hence a better companion and confidant. Thus she may **"triangle in"** her daughter to fulfill intimacy needs which she first sought from her husband (Bowen, 1979). Shifting a wife's intimacy needs to her daughter takes the "heat" off of a husband who is too over-worked, distracted, or uncomfortable to provide them. But the wife may be uninterested in her husband's own needs for closeness when he shows them, if she already has a safer and more reliable closeness with her daughter. And she may be very reluctant to let her daughter grow up and leave her for a man—or even for college, as this college senior writes:

> *Since I have been away from home, my mother feels a part of her is lost. She calls me almost every day telling me she misses me and she can't wait for me to come home for the summer. I miss being home but I also enjoy being on my own and working towards my career goals. Recently I have realized that my mother depends on me too much at times. I feel like I have to deal with her problems along with mine.*

The persistence of the mother–daughter bond can lead to a major tug-of-war between mother and the daughter's boyfriend or husband and could be the source of the classic husband/mother-in-law antagonism, popularized in many television sit-coms.

Cultures everywhere have had to find ways to deal with mothers who have to give up their daughters to a man from a different family. The parents of American brides typically pay for the wedding. And they hope to keep their daughter near when they say, "We're losing a daughter, but we're gaining a son." A mother's grief can be very confusing for her daughter, who may be torn between her supportive, familiar, and often undemanding maternal relationship and her sexual love for a man, which is a powerful, but unfamiliar and often disappointing intimacy.

To some extent, every boyfriend and husband may put an end to everyday mother–daughter intimacy. The mother's struggle against letting her daughter go—and trying to get her back—may go on for years, even for a lifetime. It is also a lengthy and complex task for a young woman to find her own identity beyond "daughter" and "wife." The coed below depicts the strategies women use to get more distance in their family relationships.

> *I was babied because I was the last child and I wasn't given much responsibility. This made it harder for me to become an independent person and break away from my family to have a serious relationship. I was the child to be triangled into my parents' marital problems. . . . I was able to extricate myself easily after my sister graduated from college because she took over my responsibility. I believe that she's afraid to go out into the real world and begin on her own. I'm glad to be rid of my position but am also sorry for my sister, because I know that she's afraid to leave and that my mom is making it too easy for her to stay because she needs someone there to rely on.*

These triangles with mother and romantic partner can be problematic for men, too. In many patriarchal cultures, such as African groups, India, and Taiwan, extensive steps are taken to "divorce" a new wife from her own mother and compel her submission to her husband's mother instead. Because her son may be her only economic support in her old age, the husband's mother does not want conjugal love to have as much power over her son as she does. Even without clear cultural rules, some American women have felt their partner's mother's power reach out, as this coed did:

> My parents were flying down to spend Thanksgiving with us (I'm an only child). So I asked Bill if he would postpone his flight to his parents until Friday. It was the only way he could be with both his and my parents, and I had spent the last holiday at his place. Well, he asked his mom, and she hit the roof. She didn't just lay a massive guilt trip on him, she called **me** up and chewed me out for being so selfish and immature and trying to keep her son from doing what **he** really wanted to do.
>
> I couldn't believe it, and didn't want to talk back to her the way she was talking to me. She got what she wanted, too, because Bill had to make the final decision about when he would fly home. And he didn't have the guts to stand her up. I was furious! [This one-and-a-half-year romance died over Christmas vacation.]

Detriangling.   Family therapy pioneer Murray Bowen (1978), used to coach students on how to extricate themselves from family triangles. Here are his basic ideas for "**detriangling**":

1. Don't allow yourself to be used as a substitute for another family member, especially not for a spouse. If another's need for companionship, confiding, comfort, and validation from you feels excessive, say so. Ask about the availability of the other's primary love partner. Advise the other to redirect energy toward such a person and pull back.
2. Don't allow yourself to be used as a go-between. Do not carry messages or keep secrets when asked, but tell the person that is not what you want in your relationship, so you will not carry out such expectations.
3. Establish one-to-one relationships with individual family members, emphasizing the here-and-now and the unique thoughts and feelings of "I" and "you." Spend time in pairs, so other persons' reactions are not immediately involved. Talk about your own life and interests, not family gossip or your issues with other relatives.
4. Do not form lasting alliances with a few relatives or against others, because sooner or later such loyalties will lead you to be untrue to your own thoughts and feelings "to keep the peace." Build your one-to-one relationships on openness and authenticity, **for** the two of you, but not **against** someone with whom you haven't yet connected.

These prescriptions are admittedly a bit idealistic and peaceful-warrior-like. They were developed for students of family therapy, who honed their professional skills by using them on their own family relationships. The process of dismantling triangles easily takes decades, and can never be completed—but you can get good at keeping your own connections free from third-party interference.

Emotional distancing and cut-offs

In many families some members are "cut off" from one another, either through divorce or separation or a longstanding feud or rift. Family system theorists believe that when there is a cut-off in a person's family past, and particularly if there is a cut-off in that person's present life, it affects their current relating with persons outside the family as much as with persons inside the family.

> Whether it's through death or through emotional or geographical distancing, you can think of a cut-off as being like an amputation—in which the flow that normally goes through a limb is blocked, but pain remains in the phantom limb. When a relationship is cut off, the energy that was meant to flow toward it can't go there anymore. The flow either is diverted, frozen, or dried up. When an important relationship ends, and whatever feelings you had tied up in that person get suspended, your ability to be emotionally open and trusting in future relationships may be limited. Alternatively, if you are cut off from expressing your feelings about an important relationship in an open, direct and healthy way, the energy and feelings tied up in that first relationship may be displaced onto any future relationship that evokes the **memory** of the cut-off relationship. The unresolved and unexpressed feelings seek out a person or situation that gives them a channel for expression and may leak out in inappropriate ways. (Gordon, 1993, p. 177)

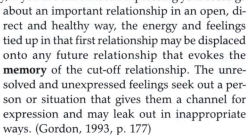

Emotional cut-offs are particularly common with fathers, since they are typically the most distant of important relationships and also less flexible and responsive to emotional difficulties.

> After five years of talking about rocky romances in my men's group, we developed a saying: Before you get deeply involved with a woman, find out about her relationship with her father. If it was bad, you're in for a rough relationship. For you will bend over backwards to make her feel better and convince her you are a better man—but then you'll be too "nice" and wimpy to fill his shoes.

Men can be just as affected by emotional cut-offs with their fathers as women. Their unexpressed feelings and unfinished issues can surface in personal, mentoring, and authority relationships.

It is not easy to resolve difficulties resulting from triangling or emotional cut-offs in your family. But becoming aware of them and what lessons they have taught us is a first step in beginning to change these patterns.

Limitations of the family systems perspective

Several different research approaches have tested the influence of the family of origin on one's current relationship problems or issues. Because most family systems theorists have been clinicians, they have been more interested in helping partners change their ways of relating than in exploring empirically the relationships between early family life and current relating. Therefore the limited empirical research has been from this "problem/nonproblem" framework. Although it appears that family-of-origin experiences have some effect on an individual's current intimate relating preferences, it is also clear that these past experiences in our families of origin are not straitjackets preventing change. Researchers have reported instances in which individuals reporting very problematic early family of origin experiences have developed very functional and satisfying marriages (Lewis, 1986). Thus there is some evidence supporting the family systems perspective. But it is by no means substantial enough for us to conclude that family systems explanations for relationship development are more powerful than any other theoretical viewpoint, or that our early family systems experience is the key predictor of how we will behave later.

Chapter summary

- Our standards and preferences for intimate relating may develop in our families of origin as a set of beliefs or "rules for relating" defining what feels right, wrong, and unsafe.
- The principle of family systems is that each action or communication by one member affects all the others by disturbing the balance of the system.
- People choose a lover/partner whose model for relating "fits" their own. Partners who report being most similar in customs, values, and styles of emotional expression and conflict resolution report the highest satisfaction.
- Partners' invisible "rules" evolve in response to normal developmental changes such as the birth of children or the death of parents, or traumatic events such as chronic illness or job loss.

- Those partners having the greatest difficulty in altering their relationship "rules" as circumstances demand may have the lowest relationship satisfaction.
- Typologies of family interactional patterns place couples on two dimensions: connectedness or distance, and continuity or variety expected in roles, decision making, and conflict resolution styles.
- The *closed/traditional* paradigm thrives on follower/placator behavior and validator style conflict. The *random* paradigm fosters opposer/distractor behavior. The *open/independent* paradigm thrives on mover/blamer/assertive behavior and volatile/passionate-style conflict. The *synchonous/separate* paradigm fosters bystander/super-reasonable behavior and minimizing/avoiding conflict. Each family type's strengths and weaknesses are exaggerated in times of crisis.
- Personal feeling and interaction processes are shaped in triadic as well as dyadic relationships. Triangular relations, especially involving one parent's emotional connection to a grown-up child, can limit the young person's growing room and set up a tug-of-war with his or her romantic partner.
- Escaping family connections through emotional cut-offs may leave the family force-field quite active below consciousness.

Practical skills for relationship enhancement IV

Communication: Sharing ourselves 12

- **The Communication Process**
  Understanding the Transactional Nature of Communication
- **Analyzing Communication**
- **Improving Communication**
  Self-disclosure
- **Listening and Affirmation**
  The Art of Empathic Listening

My husband and I met in a strange way. We had each separately made an appointment to look at an old house which we hoped to rent and arrived there at the same time. We started talking about who should have first say at renting the house (which we both loved) and then shifted to talking about ourselves. We decided that I had first crack at the house and then we went and had breakfast together and sat and talked the whole day. We shared our backgrounds, values, wishes, and fears. He was such a fun-loving and open person and was so comfortable talking about these things, that he made me comfortable sharing similar types of information. That was 24 years ago and we are still able to share the important aspects of our lives easily with one another.

Each of you probably has a similar special story about the beginning of the most important friendship or romantic relationship that you have experienced in your life. In thinking about how such relationships began, most of you would probably emphasize the value or comfort you derived from each of you *sharing information* about yourselves in a give-and-take fashion—not just letting one person make all the effort, do all the talking, or take all the risks. Most couples who are pleased with their relationship report that as their relationship developed, each of them made an effort to talk about themselves and learn about the other. In contrast, couples who have become dissatisfied with their relationship often report feeling "shut out" or misunderstood by their partner (Burleson & Denton, 1997).

In this chapter we will examine the ways communication helps develop and enrich intimate relationships. First, we define what we mean by communication and explore the various aspects of the communication process. Then, we introduce you to two aspects of communication which couples report are necessary to developing and enhancing intimacy—revealing one-self and one's assumptions and practicing empathic listening.

The communication process

While the quality of a couple's communication has been recognized as an important element in fulfilling intimate relationships, social scientists and clinicians who work with couples struggle to define precisely what about communication makes it so important and how exactly it operates in successful relationships. There are at least three different ways communication has been conceptualized by social science researchers and clinicians.

Most of the earliest researchers of intimate relationships looked primarily at the *amount* of information transmitted between partners. They focused on knowing *how much* self-disclosure persons are willing to demonstrate with an intimate partner; *what kinds of things* people are willing to disclose to their partners; and *whether the level of disclosure changes* over the course of a love relationship. Researchers and clinicians believed that by merely increasing the range and scope of communication between partners relationship satisfaction would be enhanced. Self-help book authors often instructed couples to "tell all." When partners shared more thoughts, feelings, and ideas, satisfaction was thought to be higher; when they disclosed less, satisfaction was lower (Broderick, 1984).

A second perspective on communication emerged with the growth of the electronic age. According to Burr, Day, and Bahr (1993): "the process of sending and receiving electronic messages became a useful metaphor for describing partners' communication. Instead of volume (i.e., amount), partners were instructed to pay attention to the *clarity* of the message. Messages needed to be 'encoded,' 'transmitted,' and 'decoded' without any 'distortion'" (p. 231). In this perspective, terms and metaphors used to describe couple communication parallel those used to describe how radio and television signals are sent and received. Researchers and clinicians view communication as falling along a continuum from clear to distorted. "Clear communication refers to the clear and successful exchange of information between partners. It includes the necessity of 'checking out' communication in order to clarify meaning or intention. In contrast, the lack of clear communication refers to vague or confusing exchanges of information and the inability to 'check out' meaning" (Barnhill, 1979, p. 98). These experts believe that dissatisfied partners demonstrate significant skill deficits in sending and receiving messages while satisfied partners more accurately receive and interpret their partner's messages and clearly express their own.

Although this second perspective widened the lens to include both partners' communication behavior, couple communication research

(Burleson & Denton, 1997; Gottman et al., 1998) has revealed that there is much more to couple communication than the clear transmission and reception of messages. A third perspective has emerged as researchers and clinicians increasingly recognized the impact of the relationship history and meaning system they construct together on a couple's communication. In this perspective, couple communication is viewed as: "a *symbolic, transactional process* of constructing shared meanings which evolve over time" (Galvin & Brommel, 1982, p. 6, emphasis added). Saying that communication is *symbolic* means that partners utilize a wide variety of symbols ranging from verbal behavior (i.e., words) to nonverbal behaviors (e.g., facial expressions, eye contact, and body language) to express themselves. These symbols *develop shared meanings* for a couple. If these meanings are not mutually understood, it is very difficult for partners to communicate effectively.

In believing that communication is *transactional*, these scientists mean that when partners communicate they have an impact on each other's construction of the meanings given their behavior. That is, the meaning each partner gives to a particular act both influences and is influenced by the current and past set of shared meanings which partners have constructed about their relationship. This is similar to viewing a communicating couple as an **interactive system** (described in the beginning of Chapter 11). For example, a wife who constantly praises her husband for his thoughtfulness and sensitivity, who notices the good things about his efforts, may change her husband's perception of himself and his subsequent behavior with her and with other people. On the other hand, a wife who constantly complains about or objects to her husband's parenting behavior may erode his sense of competence in his parenting and change his behavior toward her and their children. This example illustrates a key assumption of this transactional perspective: that our beliefs about a person and our subsequent responses to him or her can actually change the behavior of the person with whom we interact. Each of us creates a context of meanings about and for our partner, and we relate to our partner within that context. The content and style of our communication with our partner vary according to the meaning each of us gives to our own and our partner's actions, and the subsequent expectations we have for ourselves and our partners. Thus, to determine the outcome of a particular communication, the transactional view stresses the importance of examining the perceptions and meanings partners give to their own and their partner's actions (i.e., the pattern of relationship practices or "rules" within which we comfortably operate).

By saying that communication is a *process*, these experts are emphasizing that not just one specific communication act or sequence of acts is important. Instead each act or sequence of acts must be understood in the broader context of the ongoing relationship. Consequently, in this third perspective both the shared meanings about the nature of the relationship and the content and clarity of the message are the focus of examination.

We will explore couple communication through the lens offered by this third perspective. We assume that to assess or improve your communication with a partner you must look at how you and your partner transmit information between yourselves. And, in addition, you must consider the unique system of meanings about your relationship you and your partner have constructed about your relationship.

Understanding the transactional nature of communication

There are several key ideas for understanding communication through this transactional lens. First, we assume that communication is multi-leveled. Second, we assume that how people communicate is influenced by the *mental model* or set of meanings and practices (i.e., the rules for relating) that partners develop as to how they must feel, think, or interact for the relationship to survive. Third, we assume that we can *discover and change this set of meanings and practices* (i.e., relationship rules) by reflecting on the ways we believe we should interact.

Communication is multi-leveled.   Communication occurs on many different levels at the same time. According to Watzlawick, Bavelas, and Jackson (1967), each message can have four general parts: (1) a subject telling us *who* the action of the message is about, (2) a predicate telling the receiver *what* action is being done, (3) an object telling to *whom* the action is directed; and (4) the *relationship context* of the action (i.e., who I am in relationship to you and you to me). Researchers and clinicians often assess the effectiveness of people's communication by examining the extent to which these various elements of a message are present and form a consistent versus contradictory message. The inherent consistency of a sender's message can be examined by assessing the fit between the *digital or content level* of a message (the first three message elements described above) and the *analogic or relationship level* of a message (the relationship context element).

Digital/content level.   This is the verbal information being transmitted. It consists of the tangible, concrete issue or topic one person might be relating to another. For example, I might say: "I feel tired." There may be many areas of confusion within this level alone since people often cover several topics of information which do not hang together in a logical way. For example, I might say: " I feel tired. Do you think it will rain tonight?" The connection between these two topics may not be that clear to a listener. In addition, people can shift their point of reference in their report from one time to another and not tell their listener. For example, they may start talking about something that happened yesterday and before you know it, the speaker's reference point may shift to a similar situation that occurred 2 years ago. Or people can have totally different pictures of the same experience and get bogged down in who is right rather than just exploring each person's picture of the incident and how the discrepancies occurred. The digital/content level involves the words themselves and what the message is about on the surface—the specific topics discussed, regardless of whether these topics are related to one another.

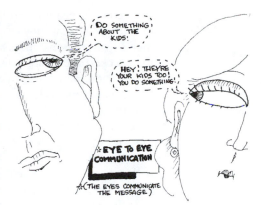

Analogic/relationship context level. The analogic level of a message conveys a message about the nature of the relationship between sender and receiver. This was formerly called the **metamessage**, or what is transmitted *beyond the message*. The analogic message is often expressed through nonverbal or paraverbal behaviors such as voice tone, posture, body language, or gaze. For example, the *way* in which a person says "How are you?" conveys an analogic message about the relationship. If the tone, words, and manner are distant and perfunctory, it may be congruent with a relationship that is the same, or it may imply some unresolved conflict in a relationship that is normally warm and intimate. The response to "How are you?" also depends on the relationship history between the two people.

These aspects of communication often have multiple meanings. Paraverbal communication is ambiguous, because the meaning of a message often depends on the meanings developed by the participants in their relationship. Suppose, for example, that a wife is lying on the couch watching one of her favorite television shows. She sees her husband getting up and going toward the kitchen and she says "Please bring me some iced tea, Babe." This message defines one as "helper" and the other as "helpee." If the husband accepts her request and brings her a glass of tea he is participating in defining their relationship in a way that is different than if he ignores her request. Thus, a communication not only carries a digital content message (i.e., Please bring me some iced tea, Babe), it also offers a certain definition of the nature of the relationship between the speaker and listener that can be accepted or rejected by the listener.

The analogic or relationship context level of a message can affirm or disconfirm what is being said on the digital/content level. One of the most common difficulties in communication between couples occurs in the sending of mixed or double messages in which the content and relationship levels of a message contradict one another. That is, we may say one thing at a content level, a second thing at a nonverbal level, and yet a third thing at a relationship context level. Mixed or double messages occur frequently in most communication. Problems occur when the persons involved are totally unaware that they are giving mixed messages and will not take comments from their listeners about this confusing circumstance without feeling attacked and depreciated. Partners must have ways of letting each other know when mixed messages are being delivered.

For example, a husband may phone his wife to tell her that he is planning to stop over after work and have a drink with some friends. If she says "okay" to his plan but in fact is quite unhappy that he is not coming home to spend time with her, she may communicate her "okay" in a depressed or hopeless tone which sends two different messages: A verbal "yes" it's okay with me, and a nonverbal signal of unhappiness. Her husband needs to clarify what she actually wants to communicate. The particular practices (i.e., the relationship rules) for reporting self that this couple has developed may either permit this "checking out" to occur or block it. As can be seen in Table 12.1, each message you make to another defines your relationship with him or her in some way (e.g., as one that is supportive and cooperative, combative and competitive, distant or close, etc.).

The influence of mental models on communication. Each of us brings certain beliefs and expectations as to how we should relate in a love relationship. These expectations form a ***mental model*** of how people "in love" are supposed to feel, think, and behave. The mental model we have of ourselves and a partner in a love relationship is usually quite different from the one we have of ourselves in a child-parent relationship. This mental model—based on conclusions we make from our current observations and our past experiences—serves as a reference point for interpreting our expe-

TABLE 12.1. Digital and analogic meanings

Building closeness

Digital message:	"I finally got that raise."
Analogic message:	This message defines the relationship as a close one where the person can reveal the frustration of delayed recognition without fear of criticism.

Creating or maintaining distance

Digital message:	"I'm really far behind on that term paper and I need to work on it all weekend."
Analogic message:	One meaning might be that you are indirectly signaling that you do not want to plan something with your partner for the weekend.

Specifying ownership or responsibility

Digital message:	"I'm really not sure why I got so angry last night while we were trying to balance the checkbook. "
Analogic message:	Bringing up this topic may mean you have enough of a sense of safety and trust about your partner that you are willing to discuss this with your partner and accept responsibility for your part in the interaction.

riences in a love relationship. According to Gordon (1993), "We usually expect that the person who professes to love us will give us their undivided attention; show their love through their words and gestures; be loyal, constant, and companionable at all times; and also be agreeable, friendly, faithful, honest, trustworthy, respectful and sexy" (p. 97). Though not something we necessarily think about, when these expectations are unfulfilled it may make us feel angry, disappointed, hurt, or resentful—feelings which subsequently show up in our interactions with our partner. Because our mental model of our love relationship is usually outside of our awareness, we often neither realize how it shapes our behavior nor test out our assumptions about ourselves or those we love.

Over time we learn more about each other and discover what our partners' "comfort zones" are, that is, what our partners are comfortable sharing of themselves with us and how they wish to share themselves, and they learn similar information about us. We often develop a shared set of standards or rules for relating. This shared mental model and set of rules for relating helps coordinate actions as partners work out joint ways of acting and communicating together. As Altman and Taylor (1973) state: "Whether it be in a superficial conversation or in lovemaking, the well developed relationship functions in a meshed fashion without verbal or physical stumbling" (p. 133).

The development of this shared set of assumptions and "rules" for relating also allows you and your partner to create a boundary between your relationship and the outside world. You usually do this through the development of a *unique* code or shorthand of meanings. Small nonverbal behaviors such as a raised eyebrow or a terse comment like: "I don't want another Washington trip" might reflect a shared image of a miserable vacation with a broken-down camper, bad weather, and poor motel accommodations. These message systems are usually idiosyncratic to you as a couple. Through this special code, verbal expressions take on new meanings, and certain types of vocal tones, facial expressions, or body movements come to have unique meanings understood only by the partners. Thus when a partner asserts that he needs time to "chill out," his partner may willingly withdraw and leave him alone while an outsider might wonder what getting cold has to do with time to relax alone. By interviewing 112 cohabiting couples about their personal idioms, Hopper, Knapp, and Scott (1981) found that there were several different functions served through the development of a couple's own idiosyncratic vocabulary. These functions were: (a) conveying teasing insults only the partners knew about; (b) developing a unique style of signaling confrontation or expressing affection; (c) making a sexual invitation through unique sexual references or euphemisms; (d) making requests and triggering routines; or (e) developing special partner nicknames and names for other persons.

These "coded ways" for conveying meaning to one another can have both positive and negative impacts. For example, a woman may experience that every time her boyfriend says "that's a good idea" in a sarcastic voice in response to a suggestion she makes, it is a signal that he does not like the idea and wants her to drop it. Or it could be that the word "movie" may be coded for a man in a certain negative way because every time he and his girlfriend have gone to a movie in the past month, they have had a fight. As a result, when his girlfriend asks to go to a movie, he may hear it as an invitation to another fight rather than a chance to be together. These are illustrations of how certain meanings given to our partner's communications can shorten the speed of transmission but can also increase the possibility for errors in meaning. Thus, while partners do develop their own highly efficient and unique message system, they must also develop ways of checking out meanings and clarifying misunderstandings.

Finally, these rules for relating which we develop in our intimate relationships often provide the mechanisms to allow for change and greater richness in the ways we interact together. For example, within love relationships that are secure, partners often find they can share negative and positive judgments about one another in order to resolve problem areas. In contrast, in relationships which are less secure, partners may feel that they cannot threaten the relationship by airing negative feelings. Thus, they often hold back and do not openly deal with areas with which they are dissatisfied.

Analyzing communication

To understand how our communication is influenced by our personal mental model and shared relationship rules, let us analyze the communication between two people, examining it step by step as though it were occurring in a slow-motion film. Let's imagine that it is noontime on Friday and Peter and Tina (a dating couple in their early 20s) are sitting and facing each other over the lunch table in the College Student Union. They have been dating each other exclusively for the past three semesters, and have talked about marrying in a year and a half when they graduate from college. Tina says: "I'd like to go to a movie tonight. What about you?" Her words are an invitation, but her tone is sullen. Peter notes the difference between her words and tone, but does not say anything about it. He assumes that she is still annoyed by the fact that he had had to work on a term paper for the last two weekends and she is sending him the message that she wants to go to a movie but knows he is too tied up in his term paper to cut loose and take her. He responds as though this internal assumption was true and says: "You're never satisfied! You want me to do well in school, but then you won't let me take the time to do well!" Tina is outraged. She feels (inside) that she has made a simple, conciliatory request and he has hit below the belt. She says, "Damn it! You don't appreciate anything I do!" And they are off and running in a major conflict.

For purposes of illustration, let us depict the exchange between Tina and Peter in Figure 12.1. as a complete unit of communication consisting of fourteen parts.

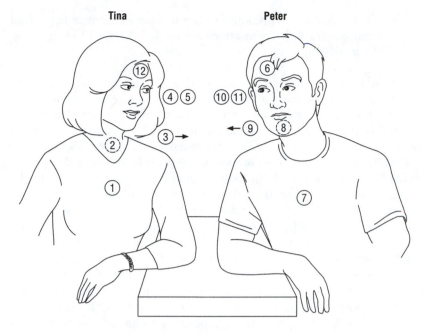

Tina   Peter

FIG. 12.1.
Schematic drawing of
elements of
communication cycle
between Tina and
Peter.

1. Internal assumptions Tina has developed about their relationship which shape
   the meaning she intends by her message.
2. Message intended by Tina
3. Verbal message sent by Tina
4. Nonverbal message sent by Tina
5. Message about the relationship context (i.e., analogic message) sent by Tina
6. Message interpreted by listener (i.e., Peter)
7. Internal assumptions Peter has developed about the nature of their relationship
   which shape his interpretations
8. Response message intended by Peter
9. Verbal respone sent by Peter
10. Nonverbal response sent by Peter
11. Message about the relationship context sent by Peter
12. Tina's interpretation of Peter's message

As depicted in Figure 12.1, we can consider any single act of communication between two people as including a pair of internal and external events for each participant:

1. the expression of an external verbal and nonverbal message sent by the speaker (e.g., Tina's external message, "I'd like to go to a movie tonight. What about you?");
2. an internal interpretation by the listener (i.e., Peter's interpretation of her nonverbal message that she is annoyed with him);
3. the listener's response based on the internal assumption (i.e., "You're never satisfied! You want me to do well in school, but then you won't let me take the time to do well!");

4. the speaker's interpretation of the listener's response (e.g., Tina feeling outraged). These are elements 3, 6, 7, and 12 in the schematic drawing.

As you can see, the first element (coded 1 in the drawing) of a single communication is the internal assumptions made by the speaker about the current situation. The second element is the message intended by the speaker. In Figure 12.1 this second element has been figuratively placed into the speaker's throat, because it is not what is actually said. Instead, it is what the speaker might get around to saying if he or she had the time, undivided attention, and ability to discover and express everything that he or she really has to say on the subject. There is a dotted line around this element for two reasons. First, what the speaker intends to say is often vague. It is not normally worked out in advance in words, unless it has been previously written or spoken. The speaker normally discovers and develops what she or he intends to say during the act of saying it, and not before. Second, the boundary around what the speaker intends to say is porous; thoughts and feelings can seep into it from both the speaker's unconscious mind (coded as 1 in Figure 12.1) and from her or his reactions to the way the listener appears to be responding to her or him at the time (coded as 8, 9, 10) and in the past (not schematically represented except in 1 and 12).

The internal assumptions (i.e., mental model of the speaker) (coded as 1 in Figure 12.1) include the feelings, memories, and thoughts which relate to and potentially could affect the content of the message the speaker intends to get across. The longer the speaker speaks and thinks and focuses on the topic of the message, the more of these associated thoughts and feelings may rise up into consciousness, either directly or by interfering and disrupting the rest of the message intended. These shape the speaker's idea as to the message he or she decides to send (coded 2). Thus, communication can be a powerful means of becoming aware of what is unconscious and potential inside of you, if you express yourself while concentrating on one topic.

The third aspect of communication (coded as 3 in Figure 12.1) is what the speaker actually says. This is all that is immediately accessible for any person or audio tape recorder outside of the speaker. It is usually less than what the speaker intends to say, though its meaning to the speaker may approximate his or her intentions. The message sent is certainly far less than what would come out if much of the mental assumptions of the speaker were to be brought to the surface and expressed also.

The nonverbal elements of the speaker's message, the fourth aspect (coded as 4 in Figure 12.1), are expressed along with the verbal message. These include facial expressions, body language, rhythm, and tone of voice. These elements may express aspects of the speaker's internal experience. The speaker is unlikely to become aware of what she or he is thus expressing nonverbally unless the listener brings it up. However, listeners don't normally comment on the nonverbal aspects of the message coming their way. They may respond unconsciously with their own nonverbal behaviors (coded as 10 in Figure 12.1). Listeners normally respond verbally only when they are powerfully affected (e.g., hurt) by the nonverbal message sent or when they are trying to help speakers become more conscious and aware of themselves.

The fifth element of the speaker communication depicted in Figure 12.1 is the speaker's message about the relationship context (i.e., the analogic or metamessage). This is an unspoken but implied message about the relationship between the speaker and the listener as seen by the speaker. Expressing a message to a person in a specific situation implies something about the relationship. It is a message about the message sent, which is why it is called the relationship/analogic or metamessage. For example, Tina's comment, "I'd like to go to a movie tonight. How about you?" implies that the speaker has the right to offer the listener a suggestion about entertainment and deserves a response to the offer. While an awareness of the relationship metamessage is not necessary to normal communication, the concept of relationship message, or *metamessage*, is helpful when one reaches a moment of change in a relationship. Since the message about the relationship expresses the speaker's understanding of the nature of the relationship, a strong reaction to it or a change in what one sends can signal a crisis or change in the relationship.

For example, one standard aspect of the relationship message in most communications is "The speaker has the right to speak in this way to the listener." Both the speaker and the listener are usually unaware of such a relationship message because it is part of their habitual assumptions about the relationship. Even so, the relationship message will affect the listener's interpretation of the message sent (coded as 6 in Figure 12.1). But if this relationship message is brand new to the listener, it will jump into awareness. It may come as such a shock that the comprehension of the message is impaired, and the listener will respond to the **metamessage** more than the message. If a man who is usually loving tells his girlfriend," Fuck off!" he is likely to get something like "How dare you talk to me like that!" If a student casually greets a fellow student with "I love you," he is likely to be met with fear and defensiveness. (Women have greater permission to use this message, however.)

One aspect of maturing in relationship to members of your own family (as well as to a lover) is becoming aware of the implicit relationship messages that spell out the unspoken rules for relating. For example, parents are usually supposed to judge children's behavior but not vice versa, and children are usually not supposed to comment on parents' behavior, whether it be pleasing or painful. Thus it would be changing a relationship rule (and might bring on a family crisis) if a college student said to a parent: "I don't think you have enough information and experience to judge whether I'm doing well enough at school or not," or "Why do you usually seem to ignore mother (sister, brother, etc.) when she or he speaks?" The new relationship rule being proposed is that I (the grown student) have the ability to judge my own behavior from close up better than you do from a distance. In addition I can perceive something disturbing in your behavior, and I want you to explain it to me.

The message received (coded as 6 in Figure 12.1) is what the listener actually hears and what he or she picks up of the nonverbal accompaniment. Because of the selectivity and limitations of human senses, as well as for reasons inherent in each specific situation (such as distractions both inside and outside the listener), the message received is not always the same as the message sent.

The message understood (coded as 6 in Figure 12.1) is the meaning the listener makes. Making meaning is an active process, involving the listener's comprehension skills, mental set, and many unconscious thoughts, beliefs, and feelings. Thus, the same message could mean different things to different listeners, and the chances are good that it won't mean exactly the same thing to the listener as it would to the speaker.

The listener's internal/unconscious assumptions (coded as 7 in Figure 12.1) to the message received can be triggered by the words, nonverbal elements of delivery, the metamessages, the person, whom and what he or she reminds one of, and the history of the relationship. All of these reactions affect both the process of making meaning out of the message received and the creation of the listener's intended response. The response intended by the listener (coded as 8 in Figure 12.1) is also not formulated in words unless it has been previously rehearsed, which is very unlikely. Some responses are rehearsed, however, particularly those meant to be encouraging (e.g., mm-hm, really, wow, eager look) or noncommittal (e.g., hmm, a nod, or attentive look). In this case the listener attempts to keep 8 from influencing 9 or 10.

The response sent (coded as 9 in Figure 12.1) is often not quite the same as the response intended, since we usually say less than we might want to say. The listener's nonverbal response (coded as 10 in the figure) includes facial expression, body language, and tone and rhythm of voice. The relationship metamessage is the listener's feedback (i.e., the listener's version of the relationship between them, coded as 11 in Figure 12.1), the unspoken, implied message about the speaker's message. It can reinforce or dispute the nature of the relationship as implied by the speaker (5 in Figure 12.1). If the listener's response content or style conveys consistency with the speaker's relationship message, then it consolidates and validates the speaker's view of the relationship. Even rebellion against the content of a message ("You're never satisfied! . . . ") can still support the original message about the relationship (I'm trying to get you to do things according to my schedule, but I know you won't change). On the other hand, a listener's response that changes the subject MAY imply that the message sent was not received, or that it was rejected, *along with its metamessage about rights of the participants to discuss the topic*.

The message actually received and interpreted by the speaker (coded as 12 in the figure) is usually not quite the same as the message that was sent (12 does not = 10), because the situation as well as the speaker's internal state influence the making of the meaning. Finally, the listener's message understood by the speaker (coded as 12 in the figure) is also not the same as what was received, because the making of meaning *is* an active and subjective process, as was explained earlier.

There are at least two basic responses to a message: a noncommittal response or a subjective reaction. Noncommittal responses such as a smile, a nod, "mm-hm" or an attentive look lead the speaker to assume he or she has been properly heard and understood. The speaker then assumes the message intended (coded as 1) equals the message understood (coded as 6), which is normally AT BEST only partially true. (It is possible for 1 = 6, in cases of accurate mind-reading or very kindred spirits. The longer couples know each other the more frequently this wondrous event can occur.) The advantage of these noncommittal confirming responses is that the speaker may continue speaking and thus explain more of what he or she really needs to say. The disadvantage is that the speaker believes the listener not only knows but also agrees with his or her thoughts, which is most likely not true.

On the other hand, subjective responses lead to a more lively two-way conversation. But since the message intended is often so different from the message understood (2 does not equal 6) and the listener's reactions are likely to be quite different than what motivates the speaker (2 does not equal 8), "honest, spontaneous, authentic" subjective responses are often quite unlike what the speaker intended to say or evoke in the listener. The exchange often goes quickly away from what the speaker wanted, and miscommunication can occur. In summary, in normal communication, 1 does not equal 3 does not equal 6 because the message intended has been altered two or three times in the process of transmission and interpretation of its meaning. With all this room for error, it is no wonder that we are often misunderstood. And it is no wonder that most conversations do not reach the depths of communion possible were both participants able to express more of both their intended messages and their unconscious aspects. Many arguments, such as the one between Tina and Peter, occur because the speaker's multiple messages are not clarified, but the listener assumes he or she has understood correctly. Rather than discovering what their partner actually meant, both Tina and Peter carried on a private dialogue inside themselves almost as if the other person were not there. Each made assumptions based on the other partner's words or behavior; went through several explanations inside, decided what the message meant, and then acted on those conclusions as though they were a reality. How does one keep from jumping to such conclusions?

Improving communication

What do persons in satisfying love relationships say about their communication? Although there have been some studies of communication behavior between intimates who are dating and not married, the majority of studies on couple communication have focused on married couples and have contrasted those who are happily married with those who view their marriage as dissatisfying or problematic. We can either study how couples *believe* they communicate, or we can observe and analyze their *actual behavior*. Let us look first at how couples believe they communicate with each other.

To discover the aspects of communication which couples typically say are important, take a moment to complete the questionnaire in Table 12.2 about a current relationship or close friendship.

What did you notice about how you and your partner communicate? What do you expect satisfied couples would say compared to dissatisfied couples? Using this very questionnaire, Leslie Navran (1967) found that happily married people differed from those who were unhappily married in specific ways. Here are some of them, listed in descending order of importance:

- Happy couples much more frequently talked over pleasant things that happened during the day
- They more frequently felt listened to and understood by their spouses (i.e., that their messages were getting across to their spouses)
- They discussed things that were shared interests
- They were less likely to break off their communication or inhibit it by pouting
- They made more frequent use of words that have a private meaning for them as a couple
- They generally talked most things over together, including personal problems
- They were more sensitive to each other's feelings and made adjustment to take their partner's feelings into account when they spoke
- They relied to a greater extent on nonverbal communication (such as the exchange of glances)

By observing the actual behavior of married couples researchers also found major differences between the ways happily married partners and unhappily married partners communicated (Burleson & Denton, 1997; Donohue & Crouch, 1996; Gottman, et al., 1998). First, they differ signifi-

TABLE 12.2. Navran's Partner Communication Inventory (PCI)

Below is a list of items on communication between you and your partner. Using the scale described here, fill in the blank space next to each item with the number which best represents the extent to which you and your spouse behave in the specified way.

1 = Never; 2 = Seldom; 3 = Occasionally; 4 = Frequently; or 5 = Very frequently

____ 1. How often do you and your partner talk over pleasant things that happen during the day?

____ 2.. How often do you and your partner talk over unpleasant things that happen during the day?

____ 3. Do you and your spouse talk over things you disagree about or have difficulties over?

____ 4. Do you and your spouse talk over things in which you are both interested?

____ 5. Does your spouse adjust what he/she says and how he/she says it to the way you seem to feel at the moment?

____ 6. When you start to ask a question, does you spouse know what it is before you ask it?

____ 7. Do you know the feelings of your spouse from his/her facial and bodily gestures?

____ 8. Do you and your spouse avoid certain subjects in conversation?

____ 9. Does your spouse explain or express himself/herself to you through a glance or gesture?

____ 10. Do you and your spouse discuss things together before making an important decision?

____ 11. Can your spouse tell what kind of day you have had without asking?

____ 12. Your spouse wants to visit some close friends or relatives. You don't particularly enjoy their company. Would you tell him/her this?

____ 13. Does your spouse discuss matters of sex with you?

____ 14. Do you and your spouse use words which have a special meaning not understood by outsiders?

____ 15. How often does your spouse sulk or pout?

____ 16. Can you and your spouse discuss your most sacred beliefs without feeling of restraint or embarrassment?

____ 17. Do you avoid telling your spouse things that put you in a bad light?

____ 18. You and your spouse are visiting friends. Something is said by the friends which causes you to glance at each other. Would you understand each other?

____ 19. How often can you tell as much from the tone of voice of your spouse as from what he/she actually says?

____ 20. How often do you and your spouse talk with each other about personal problems?

____ 21. Do you feel that in most matters your spouse knows what you are trying to say?

____ 22. Would you rather talk about intimate matters with your spouse than with some other person?

____ 23. Do you understand the meaning of your spouse's facial expressions?

____ 24. If you and your spouse are visiting friends or relatives and one of you starts to say someting, does the other take over the conversation without the feeling of interrupting?

____ 25. During marriage, have you and your spouse, in general, talked most things over together?

Source: Navran L. (1967).

cantly in the *nature of their self-disclosure to their partner*: Satisfied partners *express themselves much more freely* to each other on a much wider range of topics, both positive and negative, than dissatisfied partners do. Second, satisfied partners demonstrate a significantly *greater amount of emotional sensitivity and responsiveness* to each other. Third, satisfied partners show a much *greater willingness to send and receive positive messages* from their partners than dissatisfied couples do. Recent research indicates that these communication qualities appear to be based not on significant differences in skill, but on significant differences in *willingness to self disclose and listen responsively* (Burleson & Denton, 1997). Let us look at the research about these two aspects of couple communication in greater depth.

Self-disclosure

How free do you feel to express positive and negative feelings to the people you know and like/love? Do you believe that you should reveal everything to your partner, or are there some things better left unsaid or unknown? Self-disclosure occurs "when one person voluntarily tells another things about oneself which the other is unlikely to discover from other sources" (Pearce & Sharp, 1973, p. 414). It involves honestly offering one's thoughts and feelings for the other's examination, hoping that acknowledgment and reciprocity will follow. For many years, social scientists and clinicians believed that partners who were more open would achieve greater levels of intimacy and bonding. Sidney Jourard (1971) was one of the first psychologists to develop the area of self-disclosure for discussion and research. He stated that: "The optimum marriage relationship . . . is a relationship between I and Thou, where each partner discloses himself *without reserve*" (p. 67). Jourard believed that when we hide our innermost feelings and thoughts from others, we tend to lose touch with ourselves, resulting in both physical illness and interpersonal estrangement.

In recent years, however, social scientists and clinicians have begun to question this "tell all" philosophy as accumulating evidence shows that what one discloses and how one discloses are important considerations influencing the quality of relationships (Gilbert 1976). Many clinicians now feel that "telling all" with blunt honesty can be hurtful. Instead there is a need to consider when and how to self disclose to people we wish to get to know better or with those whom we are involved in a love relationship. Thus, learning how to share oneself with others may not be as easy as it looks.

But how important is the practice of self-disclosure in building an intimate relationship?

SELF DISCLOSURE
WHEN SOMEONE OPENS THEMSELVES UP TO ANOTHER

Researchers regularly report that partners who consider themselves to be happy in their marriage seem to have a much broader "comfort zone" of mutual self-disclosure. Jorgenson and Gaudy (1980) reported that the scores on marital adjustment measures of 150 couples improved systematically as the couples' reports of self-disclosure about fears, anger, depression, and sex, and their perceptions of their partner's willingness to self disclose these same feelings increased.

In a similar vein, Burke, Weir, and Harrison (1976) found that spouses who reported turning to their partner most often when dealing with problems and disclosing more to their partner than to anyone else also reported greater marital and general life satisfaction than those who did not. In a study of 51 couples, Hendrick (1981) also reported a strong positive relationship between a couple's marital satisfaction and high self-disclosure, and also that there was a positive relationship between each individual spouse's self-disclosure and the other spouse's marital satisfaction. The more the wife disclosed, the more satisfied the husband reported himself to be and vice versa.

In contrast, problematic couples appear to share with each other on a much narrower range of topics and put a much greater emphasis on discussing only negative feelings—satisfied couples tend to focus on positive feelings (Levinger & Senn, 1967; Davidson et al., 1983). Anger, rather than expressions of love, dominates communication in unhappy couples. Dissatisfied husbands and wives may differ from satisfied husbands and wives in the amount of negative nonverbal behavior that accompanies their verbal reports. Dissatisfied couples were more likely to express their negative feelings about a problem, to incorrectly attribute negative intentions to their partners, and to signal agreement or disagreement all with the same negative affect (Stanley et al., 1995).

There is much evidence that men and women tend to react to emotional situations and deal with conflict in different ways. *But these differences between the sexes appear to play a much more significant role in problem marriages than in happily married ones*. For example, Komarovsky (1962) found in working-class marriages that the greater the willingness to share oneself with one's spouse, the higher the level of reciprocity between spouses. (That is, if one spouse engaged in extensive self-disclosure, his or her spouse was also likely to engage in high levels of disclosure.) She also found that spouses' levels of self-disclosure, whether high or low, seemed to depend mostly on their perceptions of their spouse's interest and responsiveness to them. If they viewed their spouse as disinterested and unresponsive it tended to inhibit their self-disclosure. Third, she found that husbands and wives differed in the areas in which they did not express themselves freely to their spouses, what she called "emotional reserve." Wives held back most in "personal areas" (i.e., worries about health, dissatisfactions with self, hurts, dreams for herself and family, and reminiscences). Husbands, in contrast, held back most in areas concerned with work and money (i.e., worries about bills and economic concerns in general). These husbands told Komarovsky that they did not think it was "manly" to complain about work, to bring the job home, or to worry the family. There were also differences between the sexes in the network of intimates to whom partners disclosed. The wives in the study disclosed to a fairly wide support network that included their husbands, their close female friends, and their close relatives. In contrast, husbands disclosed only to their wives in happy marriages and to no one in unhappy marriages.

There is also clear evidence that the way in which husbands and wives express themselves emotionally to their spouse is different among dissatisfied spouses than satisfied ones. Dissatisfied wives often appear more emotionally expressive than their mates, but this is not always a good thing. Studies show that wives demonstrate more direct expression of their feelings and more criticisms designed to hurt or express dislike or disapproval (Hahlweg et al., 1984). They also tend to express more negativity than their husbands (Margolin & Wampold, 1981; Noller, 1993; Gottman, et al., 1977).

What is particularly interesting is that *these differences in levels of self-disclosure between the sexes hailed in much of the popular press are most evident in couples experiencing problems.* In satisfied couples, both partners tend to have similarly high levels of disclosure. Illustrating this finding, Gottman and Levenson (1988) reanalyzed Komarovsky's data on self-disclosure in working-class marriages and found that the differences between the sexes in levels of self-disclosure were strongest for couples low in marital adjustment. Husbands in happy marriages appeared to disclose as much as their wives did, while husbands in unhappy marriages disclose very little, and much less than their wives do. Thus Gottman and Levenson's evidence suggests that self-disclosure for men is strongly related to the climate of their marriage. Husbands in happy marriages self-disclose, but only to their wives, while husbands in unhappy marriages disclose to no one.

In summary, there is considerable research evidence accumulating that indicates that the range and style of self-disclosure is strongly related to partner satisfaction. In addition, the media depiction of significant differences in the ways men and women react to emotional situations and deal with conflict appears to be much more characteristic of problem marriages than of happily married couples.

The practice of self-disclosure.   One way to develop a new relationship or enrich an existing one is to share yourself and get to know your partner better. This involves both talking and listening. Whether you have been married for twenty years or have known each other for less than a week, the basic concept remains the same: You have to get beyond the superficial small talk often used as a substitute for conversation. Frequently at the beginning of a relationship, partners may fear baring their soul to another or may believe that they need to withhold information about themselves to maintain mystery or allure or to retain control over the relationship ("keep them guessing"). Others believe that they need to put their best face forward and stay away from sensitive questions that might make them look bad. We have learned, however, that one way you can learn to trust a person is to begin to *gradually* risk disclosing information about yourself, and see how your partner responds. Self-disclosure is a way to let your partner know who you are—your areas of interest, hidden talents, and hopes. Sharing yourself also allows you to build trust in your partner and to increase your awareness of yourself . When you discuss your hopes, dreams, and beliefs with others, you clarify these ideas for yourself. But how do you decide when and how to disclose?

First, *self-disclosure usually occurs incrementally*. Clinicians such as Gordon (1993), Satir and Baldwin (1983), and Hendrix (1988) have described the progressive levels of personal information that people feel comfortable disclosing as they become more intimate with their partner. The first level is emotionally neutral information that reveals your thoughts, attitudes, and opinions about certain socially approved areas, but little of your inner emotional life. At this level you might reveal your personal and professional goals, where you might like to take a dream vacation, what people have most influenced your life, what you like best and least about school or your work, and what your views are on world hunger, world peace, abortion, religion, or divorce. (See the first part of Table 12.3 for a sampling of these topics.)

TABLE 12.3. Self disclosure topics

Level 1: Less risky feelings, attitudes and opinions

1. The personal and professional goals I want to accomplish in the next year are . . .
2. The three people who have most influenced my personal values are . . .
3. My feelings about abortion are . . .
4. What I would or would not like about having children . . .
5. What I believe my partner and I should do about caring for our home (e.g., housework) is . . .
6. What my religious beliefs are . . .
7. My feelings about divorce . . .
8. What my fears are about getting married . . .
9. What qualities I most like in a close friend . . .

Level 2: Vulnerabilities about self and partner

1. The two biggest personal challenges I am facing in my life at present are . . .
2. What I am most worried/concerned about this week is . . .
3. An important change I want to see in myself . . .
4. If I could change one thing about the way I was raised, it would be . . .
5. Personal living or work habits I would like to change in myself are . . .
6. What I am most afraid of is . . .
7. My greatest anxieties are . . .
8. What I like most about our relationship . . .
9. An important change I want to see in our relationship is . . .

Level 3: Secrets and uncertainties about self and partner
1. Parts of my body and appearance I dislike the most are . . .
2. The most negative behavior quality I notice in you is . . .
3. The way I would feel more loved by you is . . .
4. Fears and inhibitions I have and don't want known are . . .
5. I've been secretly resentful in our relationship about . . .
6. Two specific things I don't want you to know about me are . . .
7. My biggest disappointments in life are . . .
8. My biggest failures in life are . . .
9. My biggest, darkest secret is . . .

At a somewhat deeper level, partners reveal their feelings and desires on more personal topics. For example, you are more willing to share when you feel frustrated by a particular incident, when you are worried or concerned about something, what you are afraid of, and, to a very limited extent, what you might want to change in yourself or in the relationship. (Second section of Table 12.3.)

The deepest level of intimacy is characterized by much more openness and risk-taking. Partners more comfortably share their feelings about themselves, their partner, and the relationship, and open up about some of their "deepest, darkest secrets." They may reveal to their partners thoughts about which they are embarrassed or ashamed, areas where they feel threatened by their partner, resent him/her, or wish he/she would change. Obviously, these deepest levels of intimate information represent a territory of hidden and troubled feelings and take a great amount of trust and courage to reveal. (Final section of Table 12.3.)

Considering what is necessary in order to have such deep levels of self-revelation illustrates the second major principle of self-disclosure, that **self-disclosure** (especially the deeper levels of personal sharing) **occurs in a context of a safe, caring, trusting social relationship.** In order for people to risk disclosing such personal information they must feel they will be heard and understood, believe that they will not have that information used against them in any way, and must feel that their listener is concerned and committed to their welfare. The deeper the level of personal disclosure in a relationship, the more that relationship is characterized by trust, reciprocal openness, empathy, caring, and commitment to the other.

Finally, we have learned that in satisfying relationships **self-disclosure is usually reciprocal**. If I am open with you and reveal my fears or worries to you, I assume that you will respond at a similar level of openness about yourself. If this does not occur, it may be because you are not comfortable or ready to share yourself at the same level. (Note: This is a very vivid illustration of the rules for relating that we establish together with another person.) If you wish to change your current rules for relating—to become more disclosing—it may be a good idea for you to check out both your and your partner's comfort with this level of disclosure through the use of gentle questions. It is important that each partner not be intimidated by the level of self-disclosure, or he or she may attribute a different meaning to the disclosure than what was intended.

Think for a moment about a current love relationship, a close friendship, or a family relationship. Review the list of potential topical areas of information pictured in Table 12.3 and indicate on which you have disclosed or would feel comfortable disclosing and on which you have not and would not. Then reflect on which topics the other person has disclosed to you. You will probably notice that your levels of self-disclosure closely parallel each other. If you only feel comfortable sharing information up to a certain category with your friend or partner that is probably what he or she is comfortable with. Obviously, the more puzzling or upsetting the information is to you, the more you must be able to trust your listener to keep this information in the strictest confidence.

Guidelines for deepening self-disclosure. How would you go about deepening the level of closeness and intimacy you have in a relationship? What are you willing to disclose to that person to deepen the level of intimacy between you? To decide these, you will need to consider the following issues:

- WHO AM I SELF-DISCLOSING TO? Relationships develop in stages, therefore your level of self-disclosure will often depend on how comfortable you feel with the other person (and he or she with you). What stage of relating are we in?
- WHAT IS THE RISK OF SELF-DISCLOSING? You must evaluate whether your listener demonstrates enough trustworthiness, openness, and listening ability to make your disclosure productive. Burleson and Denton (1997) suggest that the qualities of trustworthiness, sincerity, likability, good listening skills, warmth, and openness are important aspects to assess. You may need to be patient since it may take time for you or your partner to evaluate whether each of you has these qualities.
- IS THIS THE RIGHT TIME FOR SELF-DISCLOSURE? Obviously there may be some times when you are exhausted and just need to be by yourself. Having someone make a demand on your time and attention is not what you want at that moment. You always need to evaluate your own mood and that of your partner. You may feel open to disclosure at one time and not another. Finally, the social context places constraints on when you disclose, because deeper levels of disclosure typically happen when a couple is alone.
- WHAT IS THE PURPOSE OF THE SELF-DISCLOSURE? Sometimes people reveal information about themselves at times where such disclosures do not seem relevant or where the listener is unsure how the speaker wishes them to respond. To maximize getting the response you want from your listener, consider whether the topic of your self-disclosure is relevant to the situation and if you have let your listener know your intention in making this disclosure. Is it because you want emotional support, information, advice, or help with joint problem-solving?

Listening and affirmation

You may recall reading in Chapter 4 that couples in satisfied marriages reported that they experienced their partners as someone they could trust and open up to. Furthermore, a key feature among satisfied couples, regardless of their interactional style (Gottman et al., 1994b; 1998), was the 5

"UNHAPPY" COUPLES CONSISTENTLY MISINTERPRET EACH OTHER'S STATEMENTS AS MORE NEGATIVE THAN THEY WERE MEANT TO BE.

...THIS COFFEE IS BITTER!

HE'S SAYING OUR MARRIAGE IS BITTER!

to 1 ratio of positive to negative exchanges in discussions of differences.

Think for a moment about an important relationship in which you are now involved. What is it that makes you feel comfortable confiding your feelings in that relationship? What is it that your partner does that makes you feel understood and helps you share your own inner thoughts and feelings? In all likelihood, a key aspect of that experience is the way that your partner listens to you and affirms both you and the value of your message. Affirming that we have been "heard" or understood by another is a powerful way in which our listener communicates acceptance and value of us as persons. If you remember the distinction we made earlier between the content and relationship levels of a message, you will remember that what people say and how they respond not only is an exchange of information but confirms the nature of the emotional connection between them. In recent research examining how couples manage conflict (Gottman et al., 1998), Gottman and his associates found that one of the most powerful predictors of the successful resolution of conflict was the extent to which a husband signaled his willingness to hear his wife's point of view. Such an action conveyed the relationship message that he was willing to accept influence from his wife by treating his wife's needs and concerns as legitimate. The way in which each partner listened to the other (i.e., by affirming, disconfirming, or ignoring their message) signaled what value the person and the relationship had.

Consequently, misunderstanding a partner's message or disconfirming its value sends the relationship message that the relationship is not a valued one. Such a message is likely to affect a couple's relationship in many different areas—in their day-to-day conversations, in their expression of both positive and negative emotions, and in their decision making, problem solving, or conflict resolution.

Evidence from a number of studies shows that couples high in marital satisfaction are more likely to perceive accurately each other's message and to predict each other's reactions than are couples low in marital satisfaction. This difference is visible in partners' abilities to accurately understand each other's verbal messages (Gottman et al., 1976), nonverbal messages (Kahn, 1970; Noller, 1980), and intentions. Is this simply a matter of happy couples "being on the right wave length"? Researchers who examine the ways such couples communicate say "NO, it is not just magic, karma, or luck." Instead, there are specific behaviors in which dissatisfied couples engage that satisfied couples do not and vice versa. In a study of 21 maritally satisfied couples and 21 maritally dissatisfied couples, Kahn (1970) reported that "dissatisfied husbands and wives are particularly prone to misinterpreting each other's nonverbal signals . . . and to attribute negative connotations to their partners' attempts to communicate affection, happiness and playfulness" (p. 455). Attempting to observe what behaviors distinguished distressed and nondistressed couples, Gottman and his associates (1977) also concluded that the misinterpretation of nonverbal messages was an important key. They reported that: "Distressed couples were more likely to *mindread* incorrectly and negatively (that is, to assume incorrectly that the intent of their partner's message was negative), and to disagree, all based on negative nonverbal behavior" (pp. 467–468.)

However, the idea that poor communication skills are the cause of marital distress and that all couples need to do is communicate better is currently challenged by research. Much of prior marital communication research (Floyd & Markham, 1983; Noller & Gallois, 1988) assumed that good communication enhances marital quality, so communication skill should be enhanced. But recent research on couples in their first few years of marriage (Burleson & Denton, 1997; Gottman et al., 1998) reveals a much more complex picture. Comparing the communication behaviors, motives, and skills of 60 distressed and satisfied couples, Burleson and Denton (1997) found no significant differences in skill levels in four areas: (a) communication effectiveness of the speaker, (b) perceptual accuracy of the listener, (c) predictive accuracy about the listener's response, and (d) interpersonal cognitive complexity. However, distressed couples did express significantly more negative intentions toward each other than the non-distressed couples. As a result, these authors suggest that: "This pattern of results raises the possibility that the negative communication behaviors that are frequently observed in distressed spouses *may result more from ill will than poor skill*" (p. 897, emphasis added).

This does not mean that communication skill (such as accurate and affirmative listening) is unrelated to marital satisfaction, however. Researchers report that this relationship between communication skill and marital satisfaction seems to differ as a function of marital distress and gender. For example, among the couples who reported high levels of satisfaction with their marriage, the husband's marital satisfaction increased as his wife's levels of skills in communication effectiveness, perceptual accuracy, and response predictive accuracy increased (Burleson & Denton, 1997). However, among distressed husbands, this relationship was reversed; that is, the more skilled his wife became, the more dissatisfied was the husband. Furthermore, non-distressed husbands' skills apparently had no effect on non-distressed wives' satisfaction—except for their accuracy in predicting the wives' listening response. These findings are not consistent with previous research evidence about the differences between the sexes in their effectiveness in the sending of positive messages. Noller and Gallois (1988) had reported that across various types of negative, positive, and neutral message communication tasks, wives tend to send clearer messages to their mates than did husbands. In addition, they reported that when spouses were asked to decode a videotape of men and women unknown to them performing a similar message-sending task, both sexes obtained higher scores for perceptual accuracy regarding the females' versus the males' positive message (providing further support for females' superior ability to send positive messages). However, husbands who were happily married were significantly more accurate senders of positive messages than were husbands low in marital satisfaction. An earlier study of sex-role orientation showed that husbands in well-adjusted marriages tended to have many more expressive qualities than did other husbands (Antill, 1983) and did not fit the stereotype of the inexpressive male (Balswick & Peek, 1971).

In contrast to the positive message-sending tasks, negative message sending was generally very accurate for both husbands and wives. Neither group appeared to have problems getting across their negative messages (Guthrie & Noller, 1988). However neutral messages were very difficult for spouses to decode and spouses low in marital adjustment had significantly more difficulty accurately perceiving the neutral messages from their spouse than did those high in marital adjustment. In looking more closely at why such differences in sending messages emerged, Noller and Gallois (1988) reported that most of the wives used quite different behaviors for sending positive and negative messages, while husbands used the same behavior for both types of messages. However, husbands who were more satisfied were more likely to use more diverse and effective nonverbals as did their wives, such as an open smile or sustained gaze/look for positive messages and an eyebrow flashed for negative. Husbands from less satisfied marriages tended to use the eyebrow flash for both positive and negative messages.

There were also major differences noted in the extent to which distressed or non-distressed partners could accurately interpret the meaning of their partner's message. Wives in non-distressed marriages more often used nonverbal behavior to indicate whether they understood their partner's meaning than did both distressed wives and husbands. Husbands in non-distressed marriages also more accurately predicted the meaning of the message sent by their spouse than did husbands in distressed marriages. According to Noller and Gallois (1988): "Low adjustment couples have a number of problems in their communication: they are inaccurate in understanding the messages sent by their spouse, especially the positive ones; they inaccurately assume that their spouse will understand a particular message when they do not, and they often do not realize that they have been misunderstood by their spouse" (p. 76). Thus, partners' interpretation and assumptions about the content of their spouse's message appear to be handled quite differently by happy and unhappy couples.

A crucial difference which social scientists have repeatedly provided evidence for is the use of affirming versus a non-confirming style of listening. Compared to dissatisfied wives and husbands, happily married people demonstrate significantly greater sensitivity and willingness to respond to their partner's communications and to ascribe positive intentions to their spouse's actions (Floyd & Markman, 1983; Gottman et al., 1976). They signal interest in listening to what their partner has to say; respond to negative comments from their partner by de-escalating rather than engaging in counter-blaming and counter-attacking; and demonstrate willingness to engage openly in dealing with emotionally charged issues by using "softening" or "low-escalation" strategies rather than passively avoiding them (Gottman et al., 1998). In addition, satisfied partners are much more likely to know what type of response is preferred by their spouse in an emotional situation (i.e., to predict accurately their spouse's reaction). In a major study of 225 couples and their families, Fisher and her associates (1992) reported that satisfied wives handled conflict situations in a way that did not lead to stubbornness, complaints, or eventual withdrawal on the part of their husbands. In contrast, dissatisfied wives tended to verbally attack their mates, which resulted in a striking tendency for the husbands to clam up in the face of conflict. Fisher describes these men's reaction:

> . . . when confronted with a marriage conflict, a greater proportion of the dissatisfied husbands than the wives withdraw, either physically or psychologically, by such means as walking out of the house ("I say what I have to say and then I go zoom out of the house") or by silence ("I don't pay any attention until she cools off"). (p. 193)

Similarly, husbands in satisfying marriages frequently *accepted their wives' influence* by staying with the conflict situation rather than distancing or avoiding emotion, and signaling an active interest in reconciling rather than escaping their partner's concerns. "Both spouses signal a willingness to engage actively or to 'move toward' resolving issues rather than to avoid or 'move away' from them" (Fisher et al., 1992, p. 278).

We have seen (here and in Chapter 4) that both partners in satisfactory marriages are often quite knowledgeable and sensitive about each other, demonstrate a high level of predictive accuracy about their partner's response to a message from them, and use that knowledge to confirm the positiveness of their relationship (Shapiro & Swensen, 1969). In contrast, the more accurately dissatisfied wives could predict their husbands response to them, the more negatively they perceived them (Burleson & Denton, 1997; Kurdek, 1995). Such results confirm that the relationship between communication skill and relationship satisfaction is not just a function of how efficiently or effectively a message is sent, but also of what the partners expect to be the analogic message or metamessage about the nature of the relationship. Is it one in which people expect to be affirmed and supported by their listener or one in which they expect to be judged and criticized? In the next section we will discuss how you can use your listening practices to build a context of affirmation and support.

The art of empathic listening

So what are your listening habits? Do you really pay attention to what your partner is saying or do you tend to listen with an ear for when in the conversation you can make your own points? Do you listen for the meaning things have for you or do you listen for the meaning things have for your partner? Building a close, intimate relationship means that you feel heard and understood by the other person. It also means that he or she can count on the same kind of listening from you. This requires you to give your undivided attention and to listen with empathy; that is, with attention to how things are from your partner's perspective rather than from your own.

This type of listening is not as common as it might appear. Most of us have been trained to listen by inference rather than to really try to understand what our partner is attempting to convey. We often assume that we *understand* what others are saying. But, in fact, we often *infer* what we *think* they are saying by their tone of voice and body language. In short, we often do not truly listen to what they have to say. How many times have you said something and had your listener misinterpret it? The following exchange between one couple depicts how a lack of listening can make one's meaning go awry:

> Speaker: The game is on tonight, so I'll call you late.
>
> Listener. Thanks a lot! Why don't you just skip calling me all together! (Listener's interpretation: He does not enjoy spending time with me. The game is more important to him than our relationship!)
>
> Speaker: What are you getting so upset for? You know I always watch football on Monday night! (Speaker's intended meaning: Games are my alone time. I do not think she will enjoy it so I'll just get together with her after the game.)
>
> Listener: Sure! And every other night you have a chance!
>
> Speaker: What's the point of talking with you at all. I can't do anything right as far as you are concerned!

Neither of these persons may be aware of what had led to their argument. Their interaction has progressed into a conflict even though it started with the speaker's attempt to be thoughtful and to inform the listener of his plans. All that would have been needed was for either to ask what the other meant (without defending their own actions). Perhaps, for example, the speaker could have said "You seemed upset when I said I was going to watch TV. How is that upsetting you?" To interrupt a cycle of misunderstandings, one needs to ask questions designed to clarify what is meant. Such questions help us to explore and expand the meaning that the words and events have for someone.

Even after asking questions that invite our partner to share their perspective, we cannot always be sure that we have understood what the other meant. Therefore, using questions to double-check our understanding and to convey to our listener that we understand them is often quite useful.

> Speaker: I'm exhausted. I need to go to bed early tonight. What time were you planning to come over?
>
> Listener: It sounds like you are real tired and would like to get to sleep early. Should we re-schedule for another night?
>
> Speaker: I'd love to do that, but is that okay with you?
>
> Listener: Sure.

Probably the greatest impediments to being able to really listen are our own self-interest and our self-protective mechanisms. Most of us tend to listen for what is of interest to us or for what will enhance or affirm our own position or qualities. Therefore we often hear what we want to hear or listen defensively. That is, we focus on how we can rebut, defend, or contradict what has been said, rather than on what our partner wants us to understand about his or her experience. While this is perfectly natural, this type of listening is a barrier to intimacy. It often causes us to respond with judgments about the rightness or wrongness of our partner's experience rather than conveying our understanding of it. To listen empathically, we need to inquire into what our partner is telling us, as well as to advocate for our perspective. This is not easy to do, especially when emotions are running high and you need yours to be the "right" perspective. However, there are some real benefits to learning how to inquire into your partner's perspective as well as advocate for your own perspective.

One benefit is that you can deepen the communication you have with one another. When you attempt to make your own implicit interpretations and assumptions and those of your partner more explicit, you evoke much greater interest and integrity in your dialogue. This is likely to make both of you nervous many times, but it will increase the verbal and emotional intimacy that you have. *In many relationships you may not want to increase the honesty or intimacy*, and we are not suggesting that you always *should*. Young people, especially young men, are often rather frightened by such an experience, even if they also desire it. Unable to predict or control what might happen, they are afraid of the possible embarrassment, mistakes, or rejection they might experience. However, increasing your intimacy with another person is good for your maturation, whether with a friend, relative, or lover. This is because intimate communication is a vehicle for becoming more aware of your own internal mental models and more comfortable with aspects of your own and other people's humanity.

Becoming more intimate does not obligate you to marry your lover or stay loyal to a friend or relative, though it does make it more likely that your bond will endure.

Guidelines for empathic listening. Remember that if you are going to listen empathically you cannot let the speaker go on for too long before you attempt to summarize the most important points. If you let the message go on for five minutes or even one minute without responding, you are likely either to miss the most important points or to slant your selection in a way the speaker doesn't like. As a result, you must interrupt the speaker and explain that you don't want to miss anything important and that you will need to be told the story in more bite-sized chunks. The speaker will soon learn not to overburden you with details if he wants to be fully understood.

You will also learn to notice when you are tired of paying such exclusive attention to the other person. You will be less likely to keep listening when you don't want to anymore. You may stop pretending to listen to people when you are tuning out and decide to be more honest about when you are listening and when you are not. This can have valuable benefits, because you will stop letting yourself be talked at and start listening more attentively when you want to. If you are truly trying to understand what is being said, you will not settle for just listening and then parroting back the words that were said. A parrot does *not* understand what it is saying. If you really want to understand both mentally and emotionally what is being said, then you will ask about any words and any feelings that do not make sense to you. You will interpret and respond to nonverbal cues that accompany the message they seem to add to or change. You might paraphrase the verbal message and then add, "You also seem to be worried about how I'll react to what you are saying. Is that so?" Or you could say, "And this prospect seems to be making you very happy (or nervous, etc.)." This focus on identifying and inquiring into feelings and assumptions is appropriate whenever real feelings (and not just socially acceptable ones) are accepted in a relationship. Obviously, it is much easier to be an empathic listener when a problem/situation your partner is telling you about does not involve you directly. But the closer and deeper the bond becomes between two people the greater the chance that upsetting situations will involve the speaker and the listener. This requires a much greater amount of patience and forbearance to listen openly to how the other person is thinking and feeling about a situation rather than try to convince him or her of the rightness of your perspective.

There are a number of important principles to keep in mind when you try to listen empathetically:

1. *Decide whether you can devote your utmost attention to your partner at this time.* If not, schedule a time as soon as possible to listen. Because this type of listening takes time, thought, and energy, you can't expect to be available for this style of listening all the time. However, postponing such exchanges too long may signal to your partner that you want to avoid them or do not care.

2. *When your partner is speaking, do not interrupt.* When you hear something that causes an emotional reaction in you, it is tempting to jump in and defend yourself with explanations, excuses, or challenges to the accuracy of your partner's point of view. Try instead to be quiet, (you might need to have them pause for a moment so that you can take a deep breath and refocus yourself) and to invite them to talk further.

3. *Do not rush your speaker.* To experience being really listened to and heard, you should not rush your partner to tell you about their experience (so that you can get to your part). Relax and try and put yourself in as receptive a mind set as possible.

4. *Don't be defiant or jump to conclusions.* Often we believe that we know what our partner is going to say before he or she even says it, or internally tune out what they have to say to defend ourselves from a message our partner is giving us that we do not want to hear. This attitude of resistance stands in the way of genuine listening. We must have an open mind and heart if we really want to learn about another's insides.

5. *Give your partner your undivided attention.* Most of us have a bad habit of listening to others while we are doing something else. We often half-listen, our mind occupied by a number of different things. Try to structure your attempt to listen empathically by setting aside a time and place where you will not be interrupted or distracted by other things.

6. *Be committed to understanding how your partner thinks and feels.* This does not mean you have to agree. But trying to understand how they think and feel and acknowledging and accepting those thoughts and feelings are most important.

7. *Accept your partner's feelings and point of view without judgment.* The power of empathic listening is the signal you send to your partner that says you value his or her point of view as a person with unique perceptions, needs, and wants. Listening and confirming that you understand what he or she has experienced or wants is not the same thing as agreeing to see things the same way. You have your own perspective and desires, but there are often many "right" viewpoints. To view the world the way another person views

it, it may be necessary to gain an understanding of how they are interpreting the situation and how their previous experiences in relating (with friends, lovers, or family) may have shaped their interpretations of the current situation.

8. ***Examine your own assumptions about and interpretations of your partner's behavior.*** We often hold a number of problematic assumptions and expectations for our love relationships that can hinder our ability to build warm, loving relationships. These beliefs and expectations become evident only when we find ourselves in situations where we are feeling angry, hurt, or disappointed by our lover. Gordon (1990) has identified a number of these troublesome beliefs, such as "If you loved me you would behave in a certain way (e.g., not interrupt me when I am busy, or know what I want and feel) or "Loving me means not forcing me to do what you want." These beliefs may sound strange, but they are based upon the myths of romantic love that we have all grown up on and that convey the idea that the beloved places us at the center of his or her universe.

Exploring our mental model of relationships

These expectations and assumptions are aspects of our mental model about romantic relationships. We often only become aware of these when they are set off by the way our partner deals with us or how we or our partners express feelings of anger and pain. Digging out these expectations and assumptions can be difficult because the situations we find ourselves in can trigger a series of internal negative emotional reactions. As the emotion builds, it is easy to blame the other person for our tension. We may say to ourselves: " This would not have happened if my partner (or myself) were different!" To make progress we must be willing to accept our feeling as something that comes from inside us, even though perhaps triggered by an outside event. Then we can explore what particular ideas and expectations we hold that are linked to our current feelings.

One method for exploring how our own internal assumptions shape our feelings and thoughts about our partners is the Left-Hand Column Exercise, developed by Argyris and Schon (1978), which is depicted in Table 12.4. This exercise allows us to track backward from: (a) the actions in a situation, (b) to our reactions, thoughts, and feelings about it, (c) to our underlying assumptions and standards about the relationship—our basis for interpreting the situation. This three-part assessment provides a useful framework for organizing how one might reveal internal experiences and assumptions to a partner or ask about a partner's experience. Although it is scary, revealing your perceptions, feelings, and assumptions about a given situation and asking for your partner's honest response in return is a powerful way to grow mentally and emotionally intimate.

When you share this information, it is important to remember that

TABLE 12.4. The left-hand column exercise

STEP 1: Choosing a problem

Select a problem you've been involved with during the last few months, the kind of tough interpersonal difficulty that many of us try to ignore. It may be:

- You can't reach agreement with your partner.
- You feel your partner is not pulling his or her weight.
- You believe your partner is treating you unfairly.
- Your partner is resisting—or may resist—a change you want to implement.
- You believe your partner is not paying attention to the most crucial problem.

Write a brief paragraph describing the situation. What are you trying to accomplish? Who or what is blocking you? What might happen?

STEP 2: The right hand column (what was said)

Now recall a frustrating conversation you had over this situation—or imagine the conversation that you would have if you brought up the problem. Take several pieces of paper and draw a line down the center. (You can use a word processor with a two-column feature.) In the right column, write out the dialogue that actually occurred. Or write the dialogue you think would occur if you raised the issue. The dialogue may go on for several pages. Leave the left-hand column blank until you're finished.

STEP 3: The left-hand column (what you were thinking)

Now in the left column, write out what you were thinking and feeling, but not saying.

STEP 4: Reflection: Using your left-hand column as a resource

You can learn just from the act of writing out a situation, putting it away for a week, and then reading it again. Now you can examine your own thinking, as if you were looking at the thinking of someone else. As you reflect on your thinking and actions, ask yourself:

- What has really led me to think and feel this way?
- What was my intention? What was I trying to accomplish?
- Did I achieve the results I intended?
- How might my comments have contributed to the difficulties?
- Why didn't I say what was in my left-hand column?
- What assumptions am I making about the other person or people?
- What were the costs of operating this way? What were the payoffs?
- What prevented me from acting differently?
- How can I use my left-hand column as a resource to improve our communication?

Example: I have developed a way of describing my left-hand column to others in a nonaccusatory way. I'll use language like this: "Look, I feel like I'm between a rock and a hard spot. The rock is our conversation, my right-hand column. You're saying you want to . . . on the other hand, my own thoughts, my left-hand column, say that if we do what you want, we are likely to lose . . . I'm leery about raising this with you because in the past, when I've asked you about this for other reasons, you've gotten upset with me." In other cases, leverage lies with the conversation itself. Begin by rewriting the previous conversation as you might have held it. How could your right-hand column (what you said) bring some of your important left-hand column thinking to the surface? How could you have revealed your thoughts in a way that would contribute to the situation turning out the way you wanted? What could you have said that would effectively inquire into the other person's left-hand column?

Source: Adapted form Argyris & Schon, 1978.

while some of your assumptions may be faulty or unrealistic, your feelings are not faulty. Often when we share our internal experience, our partners may have a hard time listening and may try to defend themselves. This type of personal self-disclosure is probably the riskiest mode of disclosing. Obviously, it has to be engaged in not with an eye to blaming the other person and punishing them, but with letting them in on your effort to understand yourself and what gets triggered in your interaction together.

In addition to enhancing positive interactions, there are a number of ways to use listening to manage negative interaction: as damage control in the midst of a conflict, and to clear the air in a pre-announced "unfinished business meeting." In the next two chapters we will describe how partners manage their emotions and resolve disagreements and conflicts.

Chapter summary

- Communication is a complex, multi-level, transactional process in which partners convey information and construct their relationship through the meanings they give to messages they exchange.
- We can analyze communication into the speaker's intent, the actual content, the relational metamessage, and the listener's interpretation of both message levels.
- Differences in self-disclosure among distressed and non-distressed couples affect the self- and relationship meanings they construct. Non-distressed couples are more self-revealing and know more about their spouse than distressed couples.
- Couple satisfaction appears to be influenced more by the perception of motives of the partner than by communication skill alone.
- Gender differences exist in the relationship between satisfaction and communication skill. Wives' communication skills are a good predictor of husbands' satisfaction in non-distressed but not distressed couples. In non-distressed couples, communication skill is more related to husbands being satisfied and liking their wives than to wives being satisfied and liking their husbands.
- Consequently, communication problems may be better viewed as a *symptom* of couple difficulties *rather than their cause*.
- Satisfied couples affirm the speaker's message and value it. Distressed couples send and reinforce negative messages while disconfirming positive ones.
- Empathic listening as well as reflecting on and inquiring into the underlying assumptions that partners use to interpret a message are useful pathways to enhancing partner intimacy.

Understanding and coping with emotions 13

Neither scientific knowledge about human nature nor careful training in communication skills can guarantee our success in a particular situation. In order to manage our own lives, we have to know ourselves. That means paying attention to what we are thinking, feeling, and doing as well as what we see going on around us, creating a balance between monitoring others, and monitoring ourselves. **The key inner skill for adeptness in in-**

timate relationships is a good collaboration between our thinking and feeling. This includes respecting, naming, and remembering our feelings, thinking carefully about the feelings we have, and discovering the feelings that underlie our thoughts.

This chapter presents research, theories, and practical advice for understanding and coping with emotions. This is a frontier area for research (Perlman, October, 1998). As a result, our popular language and understandings may interfere with developing more systematic knowledge of emotions. We will classify and rename some emotions in order to better understand them. We will present an overview of emotion theory and focus on the relational emotions that are least understood—interest and shame. Then we will apply our understanding to coping with four major emotions—shame, shyness, jealousy, and anger. Some major ideas introduced in this chapter may be new to you. They include:

1. Treating emotions as primary movers in our lives, as powerful as thinking.
2. A biosocial model of 9 basic families of emotions and an introduction into how some of them may interact to construct our experience and personalities.
3. Shame affect is much more than just a "shameful" undesirable emotion. It plays a fundamental role in inhibiting and regulating emotions and social behavior, with a role in shyness, attraction, jealousy, and anger.
4. A flow chart model of relationships, with each emotional communication connected in an endless chain of relational events.

We have seen strong support for the centrality of emotions in relationships from the contraction and resolution stages and the five-to-one ratio in Chapter 4, to current research on communication among distressed and non-distressed couples in Chapter 12. Therefore, we will delve deeply into affect, even though much future research is needed to provide the empirical support social science seeks.

The reason and emotion dance

Reasoning seeks **definitive statements** about attitudes and behavior that will always be valid. But emotions are often quite fluid and changeable, which can make people uncomfortable.

Women are so neurotic, always changing their minds! They're insistent about one thing one minute, and then in the next, they feel something totally different.

In many two-person encounters, one person is less aware of emotions and acts more calmly, while the other expresses more emotion. The calmer person may consider him- or herself "reasonable," while the other person gets labeled "emotional." The reasonable person often comes up with more facts and reasons, while the emotional person is more intense about the direction of the encounter.

Two basic ideas from emotion theory and research can clarify the interaction of these two roles. First, **emotion can take priority in the brain** and determine what we will perceive and think, directing us toward action or expression. Second, **emotions are contagious when expressed**—the more intense, the more contagious. This contagiousness is partly due to **motor mimicry**. We unintentionally mimic others' facial expressions, breathing, and body rhythms (Bavelas et al., 1987), which makes us feel a bit of what they are feeling (Ekman, 1992). PET–scan research also finds intense emotion reduces blood flow to some cognitive processing sectors of the brain, while intense concentration reduces blood flow to some emotion centers (Devrets & Raichle, 1998). So the emotional "dancer" may be temporarily less capable of attending to thinking, with the reasonable "dancer" similarly unprepared for feeling.

When one person's "emotional alert" takes over the other person's agenda, the reasonable person may not like it. For example, when we don't want to feel another's anxiety or anger, we stay rational and minimize the emotion, trying to "solve the problem" as soon as possible. We may also try to regain control of the interaction and show that our reasonable responses are the best. It takes two to do this tango, but the reasonable dancer may feel superior, believing the emotional dancer has "lost control." Meanwhile, the emotional dancer may believe the reasonable partner doesn't value the issue or care about his or her core concerns.

Thus, the reasonable-versus-emotional dance is a normal pattern set in motion when an emotional state takes priority in one person. Both sexes can be in either role. We can be more respectful when we understand both roles and realize that: **(a) there is a kernel of truth in nearly every emotion, and (b) the contrasting reasonable versus emotional attitudes are catalyzed by their normal interaction and may not be permanent characteristics of either person involved**. The combination of reasoning and emotion is the key to a healthy and developing relationship.

A basic scientific theory of emotions

Emotion theory and research is a fascinating, underdeveloped field combining many social and biological sciences, much more complex than our popular understanding. We will outline a **biosocial** theory of emotions that is emerging from a spectrum of respected theorists. Our approach is based mainly on the work of Silvan Tompkins, Carroll Izard, Robert Plutchik, Paul Ekman, Jaak Panksepp, and Donald Nathanson. But many other contemporary researchers are converging on similar ideas.

Because theories are caught up in the words used to describe them, we must define a few basic words. Though we will use **emotion** as our generic term, the basic building blocks of neuronal and bodily events involved are called **affects**. Then **emotions** are defined as the more developed combinations of affects with cognitions, and **feelings** are what we notice when we become aware of an emotion. Thus many **emotions** represent sequences of different **affects** in succession and are connected to a collection of events that has occurred with these affects in the person's past. While **affects** belong to the realm of biology, **emotions** are indivisibly connected to biography (Nathanson, 1992). Each emotion can be a complex and idiosyncratic sequence that is not entirely comprehensible without the images of past events. Yet when a complex **emotion** enters consciousness, we may give the **feeling** a simple name, such as jealousy.

Emotions are so similar across cultures and persistent in spite of molding by social forces, that they must be anchored in our evolution as a species (Tomkins, 1962; Panksepp et al., 1998; Porges, 1997). Each basic **affect** has the following characteristics (Izard, 1992):

1. An inborn neurological foundation, consisting of neuronal pathways and neurochemicals, as well as numerous interconnected parts of the brain.
2. A unique and universally recognized facial expression (and probably a unique pattern of bodily changes as well).
3. A biological and/or social function, that is a set of behaviors that helps us survive and succeed and/or have a desirable effect on others.
4. A possible role in human evolution.
5. Appearance very soon after birth, before much thinking could be involved in constructing the affect. There is controversy whether all affects appear so early.

In addition, Ekman (1992) adds several other distinctive features worthy of note, including: (a) presence in other primates, (b) quick onset, (c) brief duration, (d) "uncalled-for" occurrence, and (e) automatic mental processing (at least non-conscious, with conscious processing—that is thinking—possible but not necessary).

Most theorists categorize between eight and ten basic affects. Compare the characteristics listed above to the nine affects categorized by Silvan Tomkins (1962, 1963) in Table 13.1

The basic internal effect of affects is to **amplify** specific stimuli, **prioritize** our consciousness, and **motivate** and **guide** our brain's response in **specific directions**. This table raises a few questions:

TABLE 13.1. Basic emotions in biosocial theory

Affect emotion	Neural system (Panksepp)	Near birth	Recognizable expression	Biological and/or social function	Role in evolution
Surprise Startle	(Probable)	Yes	Wide eyes	Orient to new perception	Protection from intrusion.
Interest Excitement	Desire Approach	Yes	Eager look	Extend attention span, learn, play; motivate and extend contact with others.	Investigate surroundings, pursue novel encounters.
Joy Enjoyment	(Probable)	Yes	Smile Laughter	Motivate repetition, relieve tension; give pleasure, motivate interpersonal contact.	Reward system for maternal and social bonding.
Distress Anguish	Separation Distress	Yes	Crying	Relieve emotional overload, protest loss; evoke nurture and help.	Summon caretaker, restore interpersonal connections.
Anger Rage	Attack/Rage	Yes	Anger Face	Energize for fight; intimidate attackers. Defend against physical/emotional injury.	Eliminate threats, kill prey. Defend dominance and resources.
Fear Terror	Fear	Yes	Fear Face	Energize for flight or avoidance; alert others, evoke protection.	Protect self and others. Avoid danger.
Dis-smell (Contempt)	(Probable)	Yes	Upturned Nose and lips	Reject dangerous or tabu smells. Avoid strange-smelling species & tribes.	Protect from contamination.
Disgust	(Probable)	Yes	Downturned Mouth, expulsion	Avoid dangerous foods. Social aversion.	Protect from poisoning.
Shame Humiliation	(Separation)	Few Months	Blush, avert eyes, hide	Limit emotional expression; retreat from inappropriate or rejecting people; privacy.	Keep to one's place in social group and vis-a-vis strangers.

Sources: Tomkins, 1982; Izard, 1992; Panksepp, 1982, 1992.

1. Can we "have" emotions when we are not aware of any? Yes. The most common purposes of human emotions are to motivate action or expression to others, and awareness or thinking is not necessary for these purposes.
2. Can emotions arise without being catalyzed by a thought process? Yes, despite much valuable theory and research into cognitive effects on emotional expression (e.g., Lazarus, 1991; Mandler, 1997) and valuable intervention strategies to change emotions by changing thinking (e.g., Beck, 1976). Thinking and emotional structures in the brain can be interdependent, and they can also function independently of each other (LeDoux, 1989, 1992).
3. Can we keep our emotions to ourselves? Yes, but only if we shut down or mask our facial expressions. Most emotions naturally broadcast themselves to other people.

4. Is sadness not a basic affect? Sadness is either viewed as synonymous with separation distress (Ackerman et al., 1998; Panksepp et al., 1998) or as a compound of distress and shame (Tomkins, 1982).

5. Is love not a basic affect? Probably not, since there is neither a unique and universally recognizable facial expression, nor an emergence in the first few months of life. Both love and attachment *may* have some unique biochemical constituents, but their expressions are not reliably distinguishable from combinations of excitement, joy, shame, and distress.

Our prospects for altering emotions can be clarified through understanding the independence and interdependence of thinking and emotion. We cannot change some uncomfortable emotional reactions by changing our appraisal of an input **before** it becomes an affect. But we can sometimes hold up our emotional actions and expressions in order to increase our awareness of what is happening and our options of what to do about it—such as in counting to ten when angry. Once new habits are formed, new emotional experiences might overwrite the memories of some prior experience and thus change our stored patterns for emotions. After all, children do learn to suppress and change many reactions as they grow up. But some emotion-connected memories (perhaps particularly early or traumatic) may alter our neuronal or biochemical structure and thus persist along with the cognitive adjustments we have devised to cope with them. Thus we can respect the power of our emotions, even as we employ thinking strategies for dealing with them.

The shame family of emotions

The most important affects (or emotion families) for understanding romantic relating are *interest/excitement*, *joy*, and *shame/humiliation*. We do not have room to analyze all three affects, so we will focus on the least understood, shame/humiliation. Shame is not considered a basic affect by all theorists, and it is not popularly understood as broadly and deeply as we shall explain it here. However, this new understanding can greatly advance our approach to many other emotions and to familiar situations in relationships.

The importance of shame was first recognized by Silvan Tomkins (1963, 1982). Tomkins' most revolutionary idea was that *shame affect evolved to oppose excitement and joy when they are impeded* in any way. So this inborn affect *acts as a braking force on the positive affects, and thus regulates our social emotions*, like a brake on a car. In order to survive, infants and children must broadcast emotions derived from interest, joy, anger, fear, and distress to get the attention of adults. But adults in every human culture have learned to *dampen* or hold back their emotions. Cognitive theorists (e.g., Lazarus, 1991) believe that impulsive emotions are brought under cognitive control by learning. But Tomkins asserted that cognition is not enough at first to hold back emotions *by itself*. To give thinking time to take over, a primary affect is needed during child development that can act as a braking force on other affects, emotion counteracting emotion—this universal response we call shame affect. For example, suddenly blocking an exciting activity for 2–4 month old infants produced slumping down, gaze aversion, confusion, and other signs of primitive shame (Papousek & Papousek, 1975), as did failure to elicit facial joy and interest from their mothers (Cohn & Tronick, 1983).

A small child meeting strangers shows shame affect in action. Her initial excitement falters against the strangeness and is quickly inhibited (shyness). She may blush, hang her head, avert her eyes, and even try to hide behind a safe known companion or in a familiar activity. Shame responses have reduced but not eliminated her interest in the newcomer. She retreats until the attention shifts away from her and she can slowly become more familiar with the new person. It is striking that similar shyness dynamics also occur when an adolescent or adult encounters an attractive person who evokes more interest/excitement than he or she feels comfortable expressing or enacting. (See below.)

Shame's evolutionary social function

Public attention clearly makes shame affect more intense. It is an unlearned, universal affective response to "want to hide" when we are publicly "seen" acting inappropriately. It also occurs when we are not familiar with what we are feeling and "don't know what to do" and when we know we have made a mistake, even if no one else has seen it. Since we dislike being aware of our discomfort, shame amplifies itself in time, just as interest, fear, and other affects do (Tomkins, 1962). Therefore, shame affect is a vital negative motivator for socialization, manners, morality, continued social learning, and striving for excellence. Shame motivates us to keep some things to ourselves, thus forming a basis for a separate self (Nathanson, 1992). By comparing ourselves to ideals and others, we also learn to inhibit showing and acting on anger, fear, sadness, and even disgust.

A mother comments on her five-year-old's struggle to suppress distress:

She has that same sore throat feeling that I did all through school. She said she fell down on the playground and it hurt really bad, but she just had an awful sore throat instead of crying, because she knew the other kids would make fun of her if she cried.

The evolutionary function of emotions is to impel us toward action or self-expression that will enhance our survival, success, and reproduction. The basic function of shame affect is to interrupt and inhibit emotional processes that are *not* enhancing our survival and success so we can redirect our energies toward another approach. Shame affect plays many other evolutionary social roles, including fostering acceptance of tribal hierarchy and male self-other comparisons to evaluate one's fitness for competing for mates (Parker, 1998).

The biochemistry of shame

Shame and pride have been linked to serotonin and its influence over submission and dominance in humans and primates (Weisfeld, 1997). Leaders have higher levels of serotonin than followers. Shame affect promotes the appeasement behavior of those who do not dominate. As modesty, inhibition, and shyness, it protects against potential aggression by others through anticipatory appeasement; as shame, guilt, and embarrassment, it seeks reconciliation after mistakes through reparative appeasement (Keltner et al., 1997). Among the least dominant are the depressed, whose high levels of anxiety, rejection sensitivity, and applause hunger relate to shame. Serotonin-enhancing Prozac-type antidepressants can alleviate these symptoms, as well as social phobias and the avoidant, borderline, and obsessive-compulsive personality disorders, all of which include actions and/or other defensive reactions to chronic shame, as well as avoiding people and public scenes (Nathanson & Pfrommer, 1993).

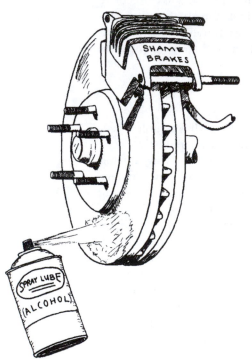

Shame is our affective braking system for social situations, while fear functions similarly for physical situations. Much of our "anxiety" about social situations may be more related to shame emotions than to fear. In fact, two biological theorists have grouped some neurological mechanisms for these two emotion families together and called them **behavioral inhibition system** (Gray, 1991) or **harm avoidance system** (Cloninger, 1986). Alcohol ("liquid courage") disables both fear and shame ("better judgment") by blocking an alarm transmission in the brain (Gray, 1987).

The role shame plays with other emotions has been inadequately understood, because the complexity of interacting affects has not been systematically investigated. This lack may be partly due to our natural response to turn away from shame affect in others and to "get past" it quickly in ourselves. However, scientific attention is now increasing for shame emotions as a group (Tangney & Fischer, 1995; Weisfeld, 1997). Popular psychology has also focused on shame (Bradshaw, 1988), but has often implied it is mainly devastatingly bad for us. Despite the pain it causes, shame affect is as valuable to our system of emotions as brakes are to a car!

As Table 13.2 indicates, shame emotions warn us about disruptions in the flow of our acting and expressing emotion with others. Shame emo-

TABLE 13.2. Functions of the shame family of emotions

Emotion	Function for person having the emotion	Restorative actions (some signalled by showing emotion)
Shame	Signals social failure; breaks visual contact with those around; stops action or emotional expression.	Leave the scene; avoid repeating the experience; change action or expression.
Humiliation	Signals that others are actively asserting the inappropriateness of your action or expression.	Eliminate or avoid the others or change action or expression.
Embarassment	Signals inappropriate or unsuccessful action or expression in public.	Avoid the public or make oneself more appropriate or successful (improve).
Shyness Inhibition	Warns of lack of connection and rapport with others; protects against potentially socially inappropriate approach or emotional expression.	Seek social rapport; learn appropriate behavior and emotional expressions to enhance rapport.
Guilt Remorse	Signals actual or potential unpleasant or unacceptable consequences of an action or expression. Signals you are not meeting your expectations of yourself.	Do not repeat action; seek forgiveness and make amends; improve your future actions and expressions. Or change expectations of yourself.
Hurt	Signals lack or disruption of responsive emotional rapport with another person. Signals the other person is not meeting your expectations.	Alert other about the disruption; communicate expectations; distance yourself, or change expectations to reduce hurt.
Sadness Grief	Contact is disrupted/lost, but *interest affect* is still strong, so shame persists until *distress affect* builds up to the emotional pain of *separation distress*.	Alert self to effort to restore contact; if not successful, amplify interest and distress until self turns away to another focus.
Vulnerability Insecurity	Warns that understanding and rapport with someone are not assured, or that mental-emotional processes are inadequately organized.	Seek greater understanding and rapport, alert other about this need, or hold back on feelings or expectations.

tions feel so "bad" that we are compelled to take action to avoid or overcome our interpersonal difficulty. The key function of the shame affect family for our purposes is also a central feature of the relational psychology of women, as developed by Jean Baker-Miller, Judith Jordan, and the other theorists of the Stone Center at Wellesley College (Jordan et al., 1991; Jordan, 1997b): *Shame emotions signal and respond to the failure of empathic connection or interpersonal rapport*.

We are not used to thinking of grief, hurt, vulnerability, or insecurity as shame-related emotions. Tomkins (1963) viewed grief as a compound of shame and distress: with a relationship loss shame affect is triggered by the rupture of a valued connection, and separation distress arises when we cannot "get past" the uncomfortable shame because we keep on wanting the other person to come back. Thus we find some of the typical responses to shame emotions will occur during grief, including social withdrawal, hanging one's head and hiding one's eyes, self-blame, depression, avoidance, and angry blaming (see the Compass of Shame below). Furthermore, grief gradually goes away when we turn our interest toward new life and other people, but it returns when we remember (temporarily restore our interest in) the lost person or object. *The presence of grief, hurt, or any other form or combination of shame affect suggests that a moment of interest/excitement or joy was felt too.* (Kelly, 1996).

Just as embarrassment and shyness reflect a lack of public emotional rapport, so do hurt and insecurity signal disruptions in more intimate rapport. We feel hurt in a personal relationship when a person with whom we have assumed an empathic rapport does not respond as we expect. Feeling insecure or vulnerable is an anticipatory warning about inadequate rapport with the other person for the risk of self-expression. This student views his girlfriend's insecurity in a new light.

> *It annoyed me when I would ask my girlfriend what was wrong and she would always say "Nothing." Now I realize that when she says "nothing," she is embarrassed about her feelings and scared about how I might react. This brings me one step closer to understanding women.*

Our embarrassment, shyness, and vulnerability or insecurity are influenced by two other factors besides our present situation: familiarity/competence, and past experience. First, if we are not familiar with and competent at handling the sights, sounds, thoughts, emotions, and actions combined in the moment, our "shame-brakes" may come on automatically. Second, since most emotional responses are pre-scripted by memory, painful failures and past shame experiences can make our shame-brakes come on as well.

The compass of shame: Responses to shame affect

According to Nathanson (1992), we can picture the normal responses to shame affect as a 360-degree **compass**, whose four basic directions appear in Figure 13.1.

WITHDRAW

ATTACK OTHER ◄——————— (Shame) ———————► ATTACK SELF

AVOID
(Overcompensate)

FIG. 13.1.
The compass of shame
responses.

Any response in a specific situation could shift between directions, or be a mixture of two directions, such as *attack-other and withdraw* ("He's not worth my attention, so I'll stay away from him.") This means that any time you notice a behavior or attitude that could fit on this **compass**, it could be a response to a shame emotion. We will examine each direction individually.

Withdraw. The primary reaction to shame is **withdrawal**—breaking off human contact and hiding ourselves from scrutiny. Its positive social function is to prevent further "mistakes" from occurring. Social politeness and shyness are mild forms of withdrawal. Politely we refrain from looking at others too long or too directly, from expressing ourselves too openly, and from gazing at others when they are doing something socially inappropriate. Not to restrict our behavior in these ways is considered "shameless." Withdrawal occurs in college classes every hour, when students do not speak up or show any interest or excitement "for fear of looking stupid."

Attack-self. Withdrawal is likely to involve confused thinking and negative self-evaluation, or **attacking of the self**. This temporary low self-esteem or self-blaming can develop into depression (Nathanson 1987, 1992). In affect theory, "low self-esteem" is a setting of our self-comparing thermostat for triggering inhibition-shame emotions in situations we have come to associate with low acceptance or low hierarchical position (Kaufman, 1996). The positive social function of the **attack-self** response comes out in apologizing: We appease the other and restore favorable contact by admitting to a mistake and soothing any hurt feelings. Deference toward others, conformity, making jokes against ourselves, guilt rumination, and the extreme of masochism are all submissive behavior aimed at restoring acceptance from others and ourselves.

This young man's recollection of a high school breakup shows a central role of shame-affect, which he calls "uncomfortable" and to which he responds in the **withdrawal** and **attack-self** modes (shame words in bold).

> When she would kiss me in school I would feel tremendously **uncomfortable**.
> I didn't want to be **rude**, so I let her do it. . . . It was very difficult to break up

*with her. I didn't even have the **courage** to do it **face to face**, so I broke up with her over the phone. When I did it, I felt like the **biggest piece of dirt** in the whole world. I also felt very relieved. The breakup was definitely the result of what my friends would say to me if they found out that we were dating. I was **afraid** to kiss her in school because of what my **friends would think** if they **saw** us.*

Avoid. Unlike the discomfort of reversing **withdrawal** and **attack-self** responses, the **avoid** and **attack-other** responses are reversing psychological defenses against being aware of shame. At the opposite pole from withdrawal, **avoidance** is normally accomplished by distracting others and ourselves from any moment of shame affect. We automatically shift attention to something highly positive about ourselves, seeking positive attention to eliminate any possible negative exposure (Morrison & Stolorow, 1997). We can call this accentuation of self-pride the narcissistic solution (Nathanson, 1992) or **overcompensation**. Seeking academic, physical, or social achievements or skills and making ourselves powerful, wealthy, famous, or attractive all protect us from feeling shame by drawing attention away from inadequacies and social failures.

> *Burying myself deep in sports in high school placed me in the group of boys that because of **sporting achievements** didn't have time to participate in courting activities, instead of the group that couldn't find a girlfriend.*

Making conquests can also overcompensate for feelings of inadequacy, as this 22 year-old realized:

> *As most people know, I have spent my active sexual life with more than numerous partners. I always wondered why I had done it. I would tell myself that I wouldn't have any more "one night stands," but the next night I'd do the same thing.*
> *About fourteen months ago, I started serious weight training. It made me feel good about myself to see my strength go up and my body look better. About that time, I gave up on the cheap sex. What I was doing was using the number of "sexual conquests" to make myself feel good.*

Gay male promiscuity may be partly an **avoidance strategy** too. Perhaps gay emphasis on **sexual attractiveness** compensates for one's early shame response to being **sexually different** from what one's parents and most everyone around expect. This man is aware that attractiveness (**avoidance**) can feel better than internalized homophobia (**attack-self**).

> *Among gay men appearance is everything . . . the **degrading of self-concepts** which may be attributed to such social pressures may be a factor in gay men's promiscuity. I believe it has been a factor in conquests of my own sexual past. If I can have him, then I must be similarly attractive.*

Attack-other. This response turns the tables to humiliate the other person for triggering our shame. Controlling, dominating, and verbally or physically attacking the other person shifts the burden of shame and helplessness (vulnerability) away from ourselves. This response risks triggering escalating attacks back and forth or being publicly censured for hostile actions. We will show how domestic violence is related to shame later in this chapter.

Attack-self and **attack-other** are prevalent in humor. Much of male bantering with humorous put-downs mixes the two, with group acceptance as the reward for proving one can "dish it out as well as take it." In a ridiculing tradition since before the Civil War, African Americans have made fun of each other as ugly and of their families as poor and low class, as a toughening mechanism against shame reactions to the condition of second-class citizens. A high-school lover resorted to **attack-other** as a "cost-escalation" termination when he felt anxious and confused about how to deal with his relationship.

> *I got sick of her and started to act like more of an asshole, hoping that she would break up with me, because I couldn't break up with her.*

Shame in gender-role conditioning

Women's shame. Both sexes are shamed for lacking self-control, being too emotional, childish, awkward, or naive. But there are gender differences in shaming. Girls can be shamed for "unfeminine activities," such as aggressiveness, domination, anger, persistence, competitiveness, and being uncaring, unloving, or selfish. However, they are not called "brother" or "boy," but "bitch," a negative feminine-gendered term.

Women may be more susceptible to shame than men (Lewis, 1987) because of greater awareness of feelings and more persistent orientation toward relationships. This leads to greater response to interrupted rapport or threats of loss—popularly called **insecurity**. But women's shame awareness is due to their tendency to blame themselves (**attack-self**) for relationship difficulties, which may date back to age 1 (Olesker, 1990), and is noted by a college senior:

> *I believe women are more emotional when in fights because we feel that something is directly wrong with us.*

Men appear less shame-prone, because they automatically tend to **avoid** awareness of broken connections by focusing on something else positive.

Patriarchal society's valuation of masculine over feminine traits may imply a basic defective differentness for women.

> As a result of prevailing male standards and the silencing of women's reality, for women there is a broad and widespread sense of "being"

...ONE OF THESE DAYS I'M GOING TO ASK WHAT CODEPENDENCY MEANS...

wrong; that is, one's **being** is wrong. One's reality is not right, one looks for the wrong things in life, one's cognitive capacities are not developed in the right direction. Such a pervasive sense of deviance and inferiority leads to a profound disempowerment, and one loses the ability to represent one's own reality, ultimately, to even know one's truth . . . in **shame** we lose our ability to speak, initiate, and expect respect. (Jordan, 1997a)

We saw in Chapter 9 that adolescent girls' epidemic of low self-esteem may be partly socially influenced and partly a biologically programmed pubertal shift toward social competence as reproductive females. Young women may focus on looking beautiful and acting "sweet," because beauty and caring, nurturant behavior are universally admired feminine characteristics. Thus exerting herself to be **beautiful** and **a good mother/caretaker** can help a woman **avoid** and compensate for any shame feelings from her "otherness" or personal past.

But striving to be always **nice** means exaggerating nurturant impulses and denying one's hostile impulses. We don't expect **men** to be all "good," or to show "badness" only in ways that **women** find appealing (the way men picture "bad girls"). Accentuating beauty and nurturance provides shaky defenses against shame emotions that easily collapse. Any new perception of imperfection in her looks is likely to plunge a woman into distress (i.e., from happy **avoidance** back to **attack-self**). Many mainstream American women project their underlying shame onto feeling fat or ugly (Silberstein et al., 1987). Similarly, mainstream American mothers are prone to feeling guilty (**attack-self**) about not being a good enough mother, no matter how much they are doing.

Thus the extremely helpful, unrelenting efforts of "super-wife" and "super-mom" may be **avoidance** responses too. The frequently broken rapport with a dysfunctional partner and the frustration of positive couple and family expectations trigger shame—and many women's **attack-self** response ("it's partly my fault") leads them to overprotecting, overworking, and "loving too much," or **codependency** (Beattie, 1987).

Men's shame. Boys are much more openly shamed for acting "feminine" ("sissy") than girls are shamed for acting "masculine." Not only peers but also parents and other adults participate in molding boys into men by disapproving of or ridiculing "unmasculine activities" with labels like "sissy" and "girl."

The first time I remember feeling "shamed" was when my mother told me to stop crying because "big boys don't cry." At that point where I was corrected for crying, I felt ashamed because I was guilty of acting like a girl, not a boy.

Men emphasize the **avoid** and **attack-other** responses more than women, whose greater depression-proneness indicates greater **attack-self** (Sethi & Nolen-Hoeksema, 1997). Men can not allow themselves to feel or act "weak" without feeling ahsamed. They learn through "kidding" interaction to laugh off (**avoid**) their shame emotions and to retaliate in kind (**attack-other**) or with anger, which deflects the focus from shame onto fight-or-flight responses. Males also emphasize **avoidance** of shame, by developing **self-confidence** or **pride** as its opposite. **But this makes men as defensive about their pride** (or "big egos" as seen by women), **as women are prone to feeling inadequate about their appearance and "niceness."** This man remembers how his pride developed:

During high school, I was very susceptible to shame or embarrassment . . . I was concerned with what other people thought of me and felt humiliated when someone would criticize my appearance . . .

*My development of pride to counteract shame has sometimes allowed others to think of it as being detached from my feelings. Some people (especially girlfriends) say that I hesitate to show my emotions or discuss my feelings openly. While **it doesn't bother me**, I think that it is the result of wanting to avoid shame and embarrassment over what others think of my feelings.*

One clinical theorist contends that many male psychological issues derive from a frequently inadequate transformation of overwhelming childhood shame-as-global-unworthiness into adult shame-as-signal that some behavior needs to be altered (Krugman, 1995). Since many boys learn to bypass shame awareness with both peers and family, they do not learn to cope with it. So they may defend themselves vigorously against what feels like a potentially unsurvivable global failure of their selves. Therefore, they deny any vulnerability and choose external action, impulsivity, and sensation-seeking to stay out of the emotional thickets of close relating. A man explains why he can't cry as an adult:

*When I was a young boy I was easily brought to tears and it frustrated me immensely. Every fist fight I was in up until high school I would be crying and fighting at the same time. **How embarrassing**, it would appear that I was being beat in the fight because of the tears, when it was just the overload of emotions that was making me cry.*

*I have become very good at controlling my emotions, especially crying. In fact, I cannot remember the last time I cried. This is one reason I despise sad movies so much. I find myself concentrating on other things outside of the movie [**avoidance**] so that I don't have this feeling of crying.*

Men are more likely than women to need narcissistic "specialness" ("I'm terrific") and to react with rage when "shown up" or feeling shame (Heiserman & Cook, 1998), which sets the stage for much violent conflict. They are also more likely to **avoid** shame awareness with **alcohol** or passionately seeking to **be right** all of the time.

Male/female differences in shame responses

Many misunderstandings between the sexes may arise from typical differences outlined above. For example, when a disappointment or disconnection in relationship occurs, a woman is likely to criticize herself, which may be comfortable for her man. But she may also expect him to search himself for fault too and become annoyed when he does not. Following his avoidance and attack-other strategies, the man may have ignored the issue or assumed she's just picky or insecure. He wants her to be like him and just "get past it," while she attacks him for being insensitive and uncaring.

Journeys of the heart:
Emotional coping in romantic relationships

We do not come equipped with ready-made patterns for thinking, feeling, and acting in romantic relationships. We have to learn how to cope with our experiences through observation, trial, and error. Each of our relationships is a unique journey and adventure for our minds and hearts. But most romantic journeys have enough in common that we can symbolize our emotional experience as pathways or **flowcharts**. The flow-chart model applies to the "local" level of individual emotions and relationship scenes and to the "macro" or "global" level of the life cycle of a whole relationship. Dealing successfully with individual complex emotions-in-context involves developing adequate mental pathways or procedures to "go with the flow." The process of initiating, developing, maintaining, and ending relationships includes dozens (if not hundreds) of situations or "relationship scenes" that give rise to affects and emotions. By developing our natural procedures for coping with these scenes, we can improve our experience of the whole journey.

In each unfamiliar relationship scene, disorganized combinations of perceptions, thoughts, affects, and actions can arise. If there are no appropriate memory traces, our unla-

COPING WITH AN EMOTION CAN BE LIKE DEALING WITH AN OCEAN WAVE

beled emotions may not make any "sense." ***Coping with an emotion can be like learning to deal with an ocean wave.*** Waves of emotion will come whether we want them or not. We either have to get out of the water (by avoiding relationships) or deal with them in some way. When we have no experience with the emotional forces involved, we are likely to get dunked or tumbled onto our heads, which may make us want to retreat from the water. But with practice we can learn to surf the waves and even enjoy the play of forces around and through us.

The analogy of surfing, however, implies more competence and control over the elemental forces of the water than we should assume for coping with relational emotions. For there are other people involved whose reactions to our emotions and actions are not as predictable as waves. For example, you may have an expressive way of "surfing" on a wave of excitement that works for you. But the person you are excited about could be frightened, stimulated, or irritated in ways that don't mesh well with you, because of personality differences and a past history you know nothing about.

Thus, learning to cope with emotion in a specific type of relationship scene, such as initiating contact, expressing affection, or dealing with differences, involves connecting up sights and sounds with thoughts, internal imagery, memory traces, and emotions into a coherent mental process, so that we are "riding the wave." When our emotional procedure is unorganized, or the other's response doesn't fit into it, shame affect may put the brakes on automatically. Then we are forced to deal with the disruption in the flow of our thought and emotion in addition to the uncomfortable situation.

Emotional detours

Much of what goes awry in relationships can be viewed as relationship scenes in which one person is unable to cope with the emotions involved or copes in a way that the other person cannot accept. A college senior illustrates this:

> *This 10 days was the most consistent time I have ever spent with any one person I was romantically involved with, and it was great. But then it came time for me to move to another state to do my second internship. I broke up with her again. When I broke up with her both times, I was overwhelmed with emotions I had just started to experience. Since I thought I felt okay when I was single, I broke it off.*

This man's apparent "fear of intimacy" is actually discomfort in the face of emotional scenes for which he does not have a satisfactory procedure (perhaps as a **withdrawal** response to shame affect triggered by the coming impediment to his excitement and joy). Luckily for him, his girlfriend did not allow his relationship **detour** to become a **derailment**:

*She wasn't going to let me go without a fight. She told me she was coming to visit no matter what I said and I had better be at the airport to pick her up! We had a great four days together. With the two of us working as a team instead of separate, I have learned that when I start to get those feelings again I will let her know without flinching away like before. We have always been intimate in our conversations, but now we plan to include our **fears of losing the relationship** as well.*

Since they are usually influenced by shame-braking, relationship detours often appear as a **withdrawal**, like the one above. By risking rejection to go after him, the young woman gave him incentive and helped him begin to expand his repertoire of **known feelings** and coping strategies. In addition to such abrupt withdrawals, many other normal relationship behaviors can be understood as shame-affect-based disruptions or detours. These include "backing off," inhibitions, and "turn-offs" (all **withdrawals**); showing off, making oneself important, flirting with outsiders, and power-plays (overcompensating **avoidances**); shyness, apologies, and reassurance-seeking (**attack-self**); and arguments, betrayals, and personal attacks (**attack-other**).

Shyness

Though shyness and inhibition are widely considered undesirable in today's extraverted society, they are valuable when approaching the opposite sex. As we saw in Chapter 9, shyness and reticence in approaching opposite sex strangers is very adaptive for mate selection. It is difficult to assess a stranger's social status, so at first, two people may not know how they compare socially. But if a man approaches a woman from the wrong group or of the wrong social level, he could be rejected or physically attacked (by other men in the woman's group). And if a woman approaches a man in the wrong group or of the wrong status, she could be rejected or exploited sexually. Therefore, inhibitions on romantic excitement have helped men and women gather more information about prospective mates and thus stay alive and procreate more successfully.

It's much easier for me to talk to a girl who is a friend. When I want her for my girlfriend, I just totally freeze up.

Both sexes may feel more shy the more "turned on" they are, because more shame-braking is needed to hold their excitement back. And since shame emotions interfere with thinking, we have good reason to expect that we will sound confused or stupid if we try to talk. A student talks about women's shame reactions when a man with whom they have spent some time has said he would call, but does not:

> For the first few days, you're hopeful, but worried that you didn't handle everything right, like gave him too much or too little encouragement. Then you really start to trash yourself—"I'm ugly, I'm a klutz, I'm not good enough for him or anybody else either." You could call **him**, but by this time, your negative thoughts far outweigh your hopes. When you speak to your girl-friends about it, they tell you **he's** a jerk and a fake, and you're fine. That helps, to attack him for a while. But you keep going back to attacking yourself, because it doesn't matter what girls think. It's only what guys think that really counts. And with guys, you're a loser.

A comparison of defense mechanisms used by shy versus non-shy students found that shy students experienced more social anxiety (shame-discomfort), turned more aggression inward against themselves (**attack-self**), and also used **less** denial and repression (**avoid**) than non-shy students (Foley et al., 1986). Perhaps the non-shy students denied or repressed their distress through humor, flirtation, and other self-confident behavior (all **avoidance** strategies). This student moves from **withdrawal** to **attack-self** and overcompensating **avoidance** during a spring break that was a "dream come true."

> To my surprise, we were looking forward to living with five girls for three weeks. The day of arrival finally came, and out of this van stepped five extreme-ly beautiful girls. Mark, my roommate, knew all of them from home and high school, so he felt comfortable around them. I watched . . . but as soon as one of them said something to me I kind of just smiled and said yes. I got in my car and went to class, even though it was an hour earlier than I usually go [**with-draw**]. It wasn't like I thought I was ugly or anything. It was that I thought they were too good looking for me. I felt like a poor boy in a rich girlfriend's house [**attack-self**].
>
> While I was at school all I could think about was going home and facing the five of them. I went through every step in my head, how to act, how to talk, how to respond, and even how to walk . . . We all started talking. First came the twenty questions [**embarrassment**]. I made it sound like my life was so boring compared to theirs. All I did was smile and agree to every comment they made. They could have said they liked killing dogs and I would have agreed with them. I must have looked pitiful [**attack-self**].
>
> [After about a week] my roommate said he overheard two of them saying that they thought I was cute. . . . Now that I had this inside information, I concentrated on the one I found most appealing . . . I made myself look like big stuff [**avoid**] while she agreed to everything I said. I would tell her the most unbelievable bullshit and she would think I was God. I would tell her

things like my dad was a millionaire and I was going to inherit all of it when he died, stupid things like that.

Shyness may have an inborn physiological basis and be increased by childhood experiences. Especially shy and socially inhibited children may be more easily excited than others in their heart rates, pupil dilation, and muscle tension in their throats (Kagan et al., 1988). Two thirds of especially shy children were not first borns (Kagan et al., 1988), and especially shy men were much more likely to remember being bullied and betrayed as children than men of average shyness (Gilmartin, 1987). Thus, temperamental excitability and experiences of being dominated seem to increase this type of emotional inhibition.

Shyness may also arise from **high sensitivity** to sensory stimuli, present in 15–20% of people (Aron & Aron, 1997). This may result from higher than average amplification of stimuli in the brain (Eysenck, 1991). Thus, some people may appear shy partly because they need to retire from overstimulating circumstances—**not** because they are **frightened,** but in order to process mentally what they have taken in.

The Arons' research showed that highly sensitive people usually like watching people and spending at least 1 hour a day in quiet. They are also likely to be highly intuitive, play a musical instrument, appreciate their dreams and subtle aesthetics, and **fall in love "hard"** (see Table 13.3). Their tendency to experience sensory overarousal can make for difficulties in relationships, however. For in today's fast-paced society, highly sensitive people may want their love relationship to act as a comfort zone and haven *from* **overstimulation**. This may lead to friction with a more "outgoing" or sensation-seeking partner who may want the relationship to provide, rather than protect from, excitement. Thus, partners with widely differing scores on the sensitivity test may need to adjust to their different optimal arousal levels in relationship.

Fear of rejection

According to affect theory, shyness with a particular person is **not** caused by "fear of rejection." Instead it is the painful awareness of shame-affect acting as a brake against our excitement about the person. We label it "fear of rejection" by connecting our emotional state to the most catastrophic consequence we can imagine under the circumstances. But rejection is actually **not** the worst thing that can happen. For once rejected, we can turn our amorous attention off or direct it elsewhere. The worst fate is to be left hanging, neither accepted nor rejected, like the student whose romantic interest does not call, or in this high school account.

There was a girl whom I was fairly passionate about, but she did not reciprocate my feelings. One day, I approached her by a locker and asked her if she would like to go out. She didn't say no, but persisted in saying something that

TABLE 13.3. The highly sensitive person scale

1. Are you easily overwhelmed by strong sensory input?
2. Do you seem to be aware of subtleties in your environment?
3. Do other people's moods affect you?
4. Do you tend to be more sensitive to pain?
5. Do you find yourself needing to withdraw during busy days into a darkened room or any place where you can have some privacy and relief from stimulation?
6. Are you particularly sensitive to the effects of caffeine?
7. Are you easily overwhelmed by things like bright lights, strong smells, coarse fabrics, or sirens close by?
8. Do you have a rich, complex inner life?
9. Are you made uncomfortable by loud noises?
10. Are you deeply moved by the arts or music?
11. Does your nervous system sometimes feel so frazzled that you just have to get off by yourself?
12. Are you conscientious?
13. Do you startle easily?
14. Do you get rattled when you have a lot to do in a short amount of time?
15. When people are uncomfortable in an environment do you tend to know what needs to be done to make it more comfortable (like changing lighting or seating)?
16. Are you annoyed when people try to get you to do too many things at once?
17. Do you try hard to avoid making mistakes or forgetting things?
18. Do you make a point to avoid violent movies and TV shows?
19. Do you become unpleasantly aroused when a lot is going on around you?
20. Does being very hungry create a strong reaction in you, disrupting your concentration or mood?
21. Do changes in your life shake you up?
22. Do you notice and enjoy delicate or fine scents, tastes, sounds, works of art?
23. Do you find it unpleasant to have a lot going on at once?
24. Do you make it a high priority to arrange your life to avoid upsetting or overwhelming situations?
25. Are you bothered by intense stimuli, like loud noises or chaotic scenes?
26. When you must compete or be observed while performing a task, do you become so nervous or shaky that you do much worse than you would otherwise?
27. When you were a child, did parents or teachers see you as sensitive or shy?

Source: Aron & Aron, 1997.

> to this day makes me feel uneasy about myself, "I will think about it." I can
> still remember the feeling of loneliness and bitter shame as I stood in that student-
> filled hallway with a bright red face. Weeks passed and she never said anything.
> However by saying "I will think about it," she still left a glimmer of hope in
> my mind. It would have been easier on my psyche if she had just said no.

Along with his "glimmer of hope," his shame-brakes must have stayed on for weeks, which is why he still remembers so well. Table 13.4 suggests strategies for riding the waves of romantic excitement and shyness.

Shyness and falling in love

We have described shyness as a dynamic tension between the propelling force of attraction and the inhibiting force of shame. Reciprocal liking may

TABLE 13.4. Recommendations for dealing with shyness

1. **Examine your attitudes about yourself** in relation to others for beliefs that increase your inhibitions. Rethink and discuss any self-defeating beliefs with trusted friends.
   A. If some beliefs might be realistic, check them out. Being too fat/thin, short/tall, or plain, passive, domineering, or hostile can make problems which you can approach and improve.
   B. Your assumed defects probably matter less to potential friends and partners than to you. Giving too much attention to your defects weakens your incentive to seek new contacts.
   C. The strengths and achievements you emphasize to make yourself feel good also matter less to others than they do to you. Trying to impress others with your strengths may convince them that only strengths like yours matter to you (narcissistic solution), so they don't meet your standards.

2. To transform the shame-braking of your excitement, **establish emotional rapport** with the person.
   A. Meet the person in a group with whom you are already comfortable, so you can forget your strangeness and include the new person in your comfort zone.
   B. Pretend you already have rapport with the new person, and that you are a very comfortable, loyal, and supportive friend to him or her.
   C. Use humor to release the tension of inhibited excitement. Notice if your humor is belittling to either yourself or your potential partner.
   D. A go-between can transmit favorable impressions and insure comfort. She/he can also check out possible impediments in potential partners' attitudes, readiness, or competing relationships to reduce the chances that initial enthusiasm will quickly fade into an uncomfortable limbo-rejection, technically known as a "fizzle."
   E. If even rapport with friends is difficult, you may need to rework expectations of distrust or victimization through desensitization, experimentation with new friends, and counseling.

3. **Planning your moves in an approach** can help you form imagery, thoughts, and feelings in advance. The more you plan, the more your experience will feel familiar to you, so there will be less shame affect when you are riding your emotional waves.
   A. Visualize imaginary scenes of what you would like to have happen.
   B. Whenever uncomfortable feelings arise in your fantasy scenes, take a few relaxing breaths and visualize how they could dissipate or be handled with techniques such as 2B or 2C above. Then rerun the same fantasy until you can relax and enjoy it.
   C. Create images of **mutual attraction** and **rapport** with your prospect. You could imagine that you two are walking or dancing with your movements effortlessly synchronized, or that you are reacting to each other with mutual generosity, joy, and supportiveness.
   D. If a catastrophic possibility arises when you are fantasizing your procedure, imagine how you would deal with it. Use relaxing breathing while reviewing such scenes, until you get the level of discomfort you feel down from "unbearable" to a "midrange" feeling, from a 10 to a 5 or so. But your possible catastrophe may not happen at all, so replacing it up with a positive acceptance scene is just as realistic and helpful for you.

4. Practice dating is a good way to **develop the scripts and social skills** to make initiating relationships more comfortable. College counseling centers often organize social skills training in small groups, where you can practice interacting in pairs. "Going out as friends" also serves as practice with less interest-versus-shyness to raise anxiety.

Sources: Berger & Bell, 1988; Gilmartin, 1987; Hope & Heimberg, 1990; Sprecher & McKinney, 1987; and the authors.

be the most frequent trigger for falling in love (Aron et al., 1989), because expressed or rumored liking by a possible partner raises our expectation of emotional reciprocity and rapport, which relieves our shame-brakes. Then whatever romantic interest was present in dynamic equilibrium can suddenly burst forward. If one person's previously inhibited interest was weak, the rush of romance may be brief. Its early passing may evoke renewed embarrassment and hurt in both persons. That is why prospective lovers regularly disguise their romantic advances in "plausibly deniable" half-steps.

> *I saw the girl that had told me the other girl wasn't interested at a party soon after that. She **had been drinking**, and . . . she was interested even though her friend was not. . . . Although we had only kissed for a while, I told her I wanted her for a girlfriend and was very excited about it . . . she said that we should date for a while. I thought "God I'm stupid, that was stupid to come on that strong" (**attack-self**) . . . But I was thrilled that a girl had an interest in me.*

We have seen that alcohol inactivates our shame-brakes (also known as our better judgment), making it the most popular social and romantic lubricant. Now it is clear why many shy people say they "fall in love hard." Strong shame-brakes allow attraction to build up to an overwhelming outburst, sometimes triggered by alcohol. Perhaps shyness or other shame-affect responses to social obstacles play an important role in building up romantic feelings in many cases of rapid **falling in love**.

Further along on the flow-chart of romantic relationships we consider another emotion that also involves shame and rapport: jealousy.

Jealousy: Threatened rapport

Contemporary social research distinguishes two types of jealousy: social comparison jealousy (envy) and romantic jealousy (Salovey & Rothman, 1991). For our purposes, we will concentrate on the second type of jealousy.

Romantic jealousy

Romantic jealousy may be an innate emotion whose purpose is to preserve the pair bond (Daly & Wilson, 1982). Sibling rivalry is a jealous response to when mother turns her attention to another child, which begins at about age two. By age four, children show possessive jealousy when their same-sex playmate goes away to play with someone else. Thus, our earliest scenarios of jealousy involve a perceived threat to our bond of mutual attention and a potential loss of love. This reaction is probably innate, since protesting the interruption of maternal rapport would have a high survival value. One research project found that reported romantic jealousy responds to perceptions of the threat to the pair bond and is not affected by prior sibling rivalry (Clanton & Kosins, 1991), so that could be inborn as well.

Both love and friendship involve the expectation of attention and understanding, which we have called **affective resonance** or **rapport** (Chapter 10). We have already defined **vulnerability** or **insecurity** as a shame-based emotion that warns us that our interpersonal rapport may be inadequate to insure an accepting response. Thus, jealousy involves shame affect, because it arises from a feeling of intolerable **vulnerability** in relationship to our partner. Research studies have related jealousy to feeling *anger, sadness, anxiety, hurt,* threatened, *betrayed,* invaded, pressured, *confused, insecure, helpless,* aroused, *embarrassed, rejected, frustrated, mistrustful,* and *envious,* with all italicized words part of or responsive to shame affect. Other research also connects it to love, happiness, and sexual arousal or passion, which represent the excitement and joy whose interruptions trigger shame affect (reviewed in Guerrero & Anderson, 1998).

It is easy to assume jealousy comes from **insecurity**, because it is a **feeling state** that may be expressed through insecure thoughts. It is also convenient and sensible to attribute jealousy to the prospect of possibly losing our partner's love. But in our affective explanation the key trigger for jealousy is not personal insecurity, but **an awareness of interrupted rapport in the present**. If affects come first, then the normal theories of perceived threat to the bond (e.g., Guerrero & Anderson, 1998) and fear of possible future loss are both learned cognitive interpretations of this impediment to our interest-and-joy connection.

Thus, if we are unaware of any interruption in our rapport, or if we immediately interpret a temporary interruption (such as our partner's going to work) as no threat to future rapport, then we can **avoid** any experience of jealousy. "Out of sight, out of mind," self-reassurances, and redirecting our attention to something rewarding should save us from the torment of jealousy.

Widespread stories attest to some people's intuitive ability to sense when their romantic partner is sexually or passionately involved with someone else, in spite of a lack of evidence, and in spite of consistent reassurances that everything is fine. Some of us get "a funny feeling" about some of our partner's friends or ex-partners and not about others. Others dream of the partner's infidelity or get sick when the partner has a sexual escapade while hundreds of miles away on a trip. As widespread as such intuitive sensing of pair-bond threats may be, it would be difficult to test through research. Suspecting our partners with no factual basis occurs more often—yet its *affective* basis is still real.

Jealousy and control

Being vulnerable means I cannot prevent myself from having uncomfortable emotions in my situation. But if I'm used to being in control of myself, I may attempt to control **your** behavior to reduce my discomfort. I may try to prevent you from having rapport with another person. Patriarchal social patterns encourage males to assert such control. And men may be less comfortable with intimacy-related emotions and more defensive to **avoid** such vulnerability as well. But both sexes can attempt to reduce their vulnerability by possessive strategies. Neuroendocrine research (reviewed by Henry, 1986) suggests that such efforts at continued control are associated with anger-proneness (and increased norepinephrine secretion). So jealous people often seek to make their partners wrong and instigate verbal and even physical attacks (**attack-other** response).

> We were spending every free moment together and beginning to talk of marriage. Tom became very insistent that I inform him of where I was going, what I was doing, who else might be there, and the purpose of my going. It was as if I had another parent. He became very enraged when I talked with other people, especially males. He had turned into a possessive maniac. I told him many times that we . . . should end it, but he would only threaten me with his life, as well as possibly mine.

If I don't have confidence about controlling my situation, I may experience more anxiety than anger. Then I may reveal my **insecurity** and seek reassurance that I am your highest priority and am not ever being shut out of rapport ("Do you miss me?"). I may also give you more of what you want, as long as that means more rapport between us. This submissive approach may provoke resistance to my "weak" attempt at control. Thus your irritated reactions could reinforce my fear that I'm losing both rapport and respect. This young woman was miserable when she was trying to control her soldier-lover from a position of weakness:

> Whenever Robert would have an assignment at another base for a few days I would be so jealous, wondering what he was doing and who he was with. It used to drive me crazy, not knowing what to think . . . I would use anything I could to have some kind of control over him . . . I'd do all kinds of things for him just so he'd feel in my debt, like cook, clean, and do his laundry . . . There were many times I wanted to say no but never did.

A less obviously jealous response is to **withdraw** from the relationship, thinking perhaps, "It's not safe for me with him; he has hurt me and will probably do it again," or "This relationship would probably fail anyway." If I am lucky and you care about our rapport as much as I do, you may come after me to find out what is the matter. Then I might tell you how hurt I am. If we stay with hurt and **attack-self** instead of anger or guilt-induction, then we may end up restoring our rapport, as this student found.

> *The other day she had to meet some friends to play volleyball for a tournament. I notice that one of the guys obviously likes my girlfriend. He is constantly . . . touching her all over. When he tells her, "Oh, too bad, nice try," followed with a high five, he grabs her hand and pulls her arm up and over his shoulders so she has her arm around him. I was getting* **pissed but for no real reason.** *. . . Later she knew something was bothering me as hard as* **I tried to hide it.** *So I told her* **I felt stupid** *about being jealous over something so petty. She was relieved. She was ecstatic and mauled me on the bed and told me I had nothing to worry about.*

The **avoid** response eliminates any awareness of vulnerability. I could distract myself by concentrating on my work, adventures, or food or drug indulgence, particularly if they make me feel powerful, victorious, and **invulnerable** (such as may occur with alcohol and "upper" drugs like amphetamine and cocaine). Making myself impressive and desirable to others and denying my desire for rapport would help too:

> In a jealousy role-play, a student's live-in partner was asked out to dinner by her ex-boyfriend, who was in town for a visit. The current boyfriend refused to show his partner that he was threatened. The woman was expecting his jealousy to show how much he cared for her. He explained that he could get **hurt** if he felt threatened or showed it. So he only asked her to bring him home some dessert, as a subtle way of asking her to keep thinking about him.
>   While she was out to dinner, he said he would go work out at the gym [power, impressiveness]. Afterwards he'd go out for some drinks and maybe flirt with some women [restoring his romantic potential].

Current research is based on people's own reports of their jealous feelings, either before or after they have occurred, because it is so difficult to track emotional responses when they actually happen. Many of the factors that have been found to increase or decrease subjects' reported jealousy point to either **perceived vulnerability** or cognitive strategies to prevent jealous feelings before they occur or to eliminate them afterwards, as in Table 13.5, below:

Admitted dependency in the relationship (item 1) was associated with admitted jealousy, but only among women. Perhaps men don't admit dependence, whether they are affected by it or not. Desire for exclusivity (item 2) was conducive to jealousy, no matter how long or important the relationship (items 4 and 5) or how dependent the partner seemed to be (item 3) (Salovey & Rodin, 1989). Thus, whenever we desire exclusive rapport we become **vulnerable** to losing it. Popular opinion is correct that jealousy can be connected to general insecurity (items 9 and 10) (White & Helbick, 1988).

TABLE 13.5. Personal & relational factors associated with reported jealousy

Personal or relational factors	Research correlation with reported jealousy
Relational factors	
1. Admitted dependency in relationship	Women only (positive correlation)
2. Desire for exclusive romantic relationship	Men and Women (positive correlation)
3. Perceived dependence of the partner	None
4. Length of the relationship	None
5. Reported type of relationship (casual, serious, married, etc.)	None
6. Perceived dissatisfaction of the partner	Both sexes (more dissatisfaction=more jealousy)
7. Perception of partner's attraction to another person	Both sexes (More jealousy)
8. Perception of lower emotional involvement by partner than by oneself	Both sexes (More jealousy)
Personal factors (less connected to relationship)	
9. Low Self Esteem, insecurity	Both sexes (lower=more jealousy)
10. Lack of Control over our situation in life	Both (less control=more jealousy)
11. Estimates of one's own physical attractiveness compared to partner's	Both (lower in comparison=more jealousy)
12. Estimated access to opposite sex friends compared to partner's	Both (less access=more jealousy)
13. Personal intention for extrarelationship sex	Both (more intention=less jealousy)
14. Attachment style: Secure	More anger at partner than insecure styles
15. Attachment style: Anxious	More jealousy; suppress anger more
16. Attachment style: Avoidant	Less jealousy, more anger at rival
17. Unfamiliarity and difficulty with own emotions in relationship	No research

Sources: Salovey & Rodin, 1989; White & Helbick, 1988; Sharpsteen & Kirkpatrick, 1997; Guerrero & Anderson, 1998.

But so, too, is perceiving that the partner is dissatisfied with the relationship (item 6), attracted to someone else (item 7), or relatively less emotionally involved (item 8) (Salovey & Rodin, 1989).

The factors of our own physical attractiveness compared to our partner's (item 11), our relative access to opposite-sex friends compared to our partner's (item 12), and our own sexual intentions (item 13) all work to lower jealousy via the **avoidance** strategy. They assure us that we don't need a single emotionally resonant bond and that we have many such bonds from which to choose.

A survey of relationship therapists (reviewed in White & Helbick, 1988) found that jealousy was mentioned more frequently in troubled relationships among young couples (59% of those under 30) than among older couples (39% of those 30–45, 21% of those 46–60, and 13% of those over 60). There are several appealing explanations for this fact. First, mate guarding should be strongest in our prime years of fertility, and could weaken considerably for humans over 45. Second, our skills for coping with jealous feelings could improve with age and practice. Partners' urges to engage in sexual affairs normally decrease as well. Finally, experience leads to greater control over our lives and hence more self-affirming ways to refocus our attention away from dependence on relationship for satisfaction.

Possessive, controlling behavior based on difficulties with handling emotions

Difficulties coping with our emotional responses to life as a couple (item 17 in Table 13.5) have not been studied directly, because they are usually out of research subjects' awareness. However *alexithymia,* the inability to find words and coping strategies for emotions and moods, has been related to an overcontrolling personality style (Haviland & Reise, 1996) and to abusive relationships (Yelsma, 1996), in which both jealousy and shame are likely factors (Barnett et al., 1995; Dutton et al., 1996). This brings us back to our central theme in this chapter, **experiences of learning to ride the waves of emotions life gives us**.

Thus if my mental processes for riding emotional waves are undeveloped or disorganized, or if my stored program-fragments for coping are contradictory, I may feel **confused** and **vulnerable**. I may respond with either possessive controlling, verbal or physical attacks, impressiveness, submissiveness, or withdrawal. Controlling and attacking responses look like jealousy.

When jealous behaviors stem from lack of emotional coping skills, I may be criticized for clinging, smothering, controlling, or insecurity. If I try to make sense out of the situation by invoking **perceived threats or fear of rejection**, my partner will say: "What's the matter, don't you trust me?"

It is not a matter of trusting my partner. I don't understand my own feelings, so I can't have faith in my **own** actions. My partner's behavior evokes states in me that I can not cope with. It's like taking a blind walk and not knowing where the emotional cliffs are. This situation was depicted in a dream of a 21-year-old male student who was just beginning a romantic relationship:

> I'm driving on the onramp to a freeway in a Volkswagen bug. When I merge into traffic, I suddenly can't see a thing. I'm terrified, because I could get hit at any moment or hit something myself. I can't stand driving blind, so I pull over onto the shoulder. Once I stop I can see everything whizzing by on the freeway. But when I start up again, everything goes blank. I wake up in terror, because I can't go forward like this.

The dream shows how helpless and **vulnerable** the dreamer feels initiating a journey in a tiny, crushable vehicle. He can make sense out of his life when he **withdraws** to the sidelines, but not when he gets into the flow of the relationship. Both his unaccustomed **vulnerability** of lacking imagery (vision) to guide him and the rapid, unpredictable ways that new relationship scenes occur make him want to escape.

Dealing with jealousy

Both jealousy research and affect theory provide numerous clues for dealing with jealousy. White and Helbick (1988) provide a list of strategies people typically follow:

1. improve the relationship;
2. interfere with actual or potential rival relationships;
3. deny the threatening implications of the partner's or a rival's feelings and behavior;
4. develop romantic or non-romantic alternatives to the relationship;
5. think or speak negatively of the rival or the partner;
6. reflectively examine our own role in the jealous drama;
7. demand or negotiate for greater commitment.

Obviously, these strategies vary in their approaches and results. Two could move us toward greater rapport (items 1 and 7), one attempts to reduce real threats (item 2), two are avoidance strategies (items 3 and 4), one attacks the other(s) (item 5), and one seeks greater self-awareness (item 6).

The purpose of affect is to amplify an experience until it commands enough of our conscious attention that we take steps to do something about it (Tomkins, 1962). Therefore the two avoidance responses and one attack-other strategy above (items 3, 4, and 5) could be unproductive if they kept us from becoming aware of our vulnerable emotions. Another way to gain self-awareness is to assume whenever our partner complains of feeling restricted or controlled that we **might** be reacting to some emotional confusion, vulnerability, or threat, though we are not aware of it. It does not mean our partner is "right" to want more freedom and we are "wrong" to want more reliable rapport. But our needs are momentarily different, and both negotiation and coping strategies should be explored. Some of these are in Table 13.6.

Suggestions 1 through 3 focus on negotiating explicit guidelines for our relationships, such as this student couple created:

> I have a female friend that I've known for seven years . . . It sort of became an annual summertime thing that we went to islands like Nantucket for the day. [My girlfriend] was very jealous of this, because she thought we were somehow bonding, and she and I should be doing those things. I didn't really realize how she felt until she went on a formal dinner cruise with another guy. That was a "slap-in-the-face" wakeup call. I found out exactly how she had been feeling, and we very informally agreed to try to spend "special times" only with each other.

TABLE 13.6. Strategies for dealing with jealousy and vulnerability

1. PRIORITY OF RAPPORT AND EXCEPTIONS. Explore with your partner situations in which each of you feels cut off from emotional rapport. Discuss cases of when someone else (such as a parent or friend) has a higher priority for attention. Listen to how each of you experiences such situations and search for ways of handling them. Just trying to reach agreements for handling interruptions in your rapport supports your sense of priority with each other.

2. EXCLUSIVITY AND RIGHT TO KNOW. Make agreements with your partner about what romantic exclusivity means in your relationship and your right to inquire about outside friendships. If you have not agreed on exclusivity and on the right to then don't inquire. If lack of exclusivity leads to jealous feelings, withdrawal or avoidance may be in order. That means reducing the relationship or finding self-enhancing activities or flirting or warm friendship with others.

3. SPECIFIC BEHAVIORAL LIMITS. Jealous incidents indicate that you may need more specific relationship rules. Find out what behaviors make each of you jealous, and make agreements about each one. For example, you may agree that some disconcerting behavior, such as casual flirting, is OK, or OK if the partner does not know about it. But other actions, such as kissing, keeping secrets, or some kinds of emotional involvement, may be off limits at any time. Respect your differences in what makes each of you emotionally uncomfortable. Concern for each other's emotional tolerance is a sign of respect and priority for your partner.

4. AREAS LACKING IN FULFILLMENT. Discover any dissatisfaction with the relationship, or with other aspects of your lives, such as work or family. These dissatisfactions could lead one to wish for the excitement and distraction of new romantic interest. If you are attracted to someone else, that person may have specific characteristics or behave in ways that are missing in your relationship. You may be able to discuss what you want to improve in your relationship without mentioning your outside attraction and hurting each other. How could you bring these aspects into your present relationship? It may work better to change your own goals and activities, rather than what you do together.

5. CULTURAL EXPECTATIONS FOR JEALOUSY. Be aware of what your culture, parents, and peer groups think are proper relationship rules and reasons for jealousy. What do you think you should feel and do, as a person of your upbringing? Some of the reasons you "should" feel jealous may not be realistic in your situation, and some of your judgments about when you "should not" feel jealous may not match your experience. You need to accept that you do feel what you feel, **before** you decide what to do about it.

6. NEED FOR SELF ESTEEM. Notice those parts of your life you feel good about. Then look for ways to improve your good feelings in those and other areas of your life, such as work, environment, physical and financial condition, friendships, and meaningful leisure, aesthetic, learning, and spiritual activities. Start your life developing in any of these ways, and you will feel more alive and attractive to others.

7. NEED FOR POWER AND EQUAL INVESTMENT. Do you feel equally powerful and invested in the relationship? If you feel that you are contributing more and/or do not have equal power in decisions, you may need to assert yourself more in order to reduce your tendency to feel jealous.

8. DEPENDENCE ON THE RELATIONSHIP. Ask yourself what your life would be like if your relationship ended. If you can't think of much to look forward to without your partner in the center of your life, your dependence may be making you vulnerable and easily threatened. Begin the process of rediscovering your own life by remembering what you used to do before your relationship took center stage, and by branching out in areas mentioned in #6 above.

TABLE 13.6. *Continued*

---

9. LEARN ABOUT DIFFICULT EMOTIONAL EVENTS. Discover what relationship scenes and emotional events in your life might have been too uncomfortable. Then seek help from someone you trust to learn how to experience, understand, and respond to those events. That person might be your partner, a friend, relative, counselor, or mentor who would know those events from experience. Ask your partner to be especially kind and understanding when you open up about your unfamiliar, vulnerable scenes and feeling states. Relationships will probably always offer us new scenes with which we don't know how to cope. But the less experienced we are, the more frequently such scenes will come our way.

The other suggestions focus on exploring dissatisfactions and inequalities (items 4 and 7) and monitoring ourselves for cultural expectations, self-esteem, dependence, and difficulty with emotional experience (items 5, 6, 8, and 9). Thus, in order to cope with jealousy, we may need to open several windows onto our relationships and ourselves. We also must find words for unfamiliar feelings, even though they could easily be misunderstood by the very person whose understanding matters the most. It takes courage to embark on such a course of transforming our jealousy from a wrecker of relationships to a catalyst for personal and relationship growth. But the results are well worth the risk.

Anger

Anger is the most dangerous and controversial of the affects. Anger is the most insistent about going beyond the boundaries of the individual to affect others, so society is most insistent about moralizing about and controlling it. We will go beyond opinions about how we **should** cope with anger to provide a broader, more neutral picture of it in relationships. Proceeding from some sources of anger, we will sketch several different styles of dealing with it, along with some of their consequences. Mapping alternative pathways for experiencing anger can help us discern when and how it can be both **useful** and **destructive**. This road map may help us to make responsible choices about how to cope with each situation we encounter.

What is anger for?

The connection between anger (an emotion) and aggression (an action) has been much debated. The most effective aggressive acts, such as hunting, warfare, or business maneuvers are often "cold" and calculated, rather than angry. But anger is a rapid start-up mechanism for spontaneous, spur-of-the-moment defensive and aggressive acts. **Anger arises regularly, though not always, in response to physical or emotional threats or injuries, especially if there seems to be a chance of gaining control of the situation** (Henry, 1986).

When he broke my favorite bowl, I saw red and started screaming at him.

When we examine the occurrence of anger in interpersonal situations, the positive purpose seems to be **to defend against attack or bring about change by making present conditions intolerable**. When focused within a relationship, anger responds as **attack-other** to shame affect due to disconnection or violated expectations, and it aims to either **restore** or **destroy** the bond. Anger naturally makes continuation of "business as usual" impossible, so that some change must take place. Whether the bond is improved or damaged depends on both people. For the partner may experience the "new" personality of the angry person as intolerable, and therefore back away from the relationship. And sometimes we ourselves wait to express our anger until matters have become so intolerable, that we don't know whether we want the relationship to improve or end.

Sometimes we may also find ourselves bickering and seething when we have not been wronged, simply because we are out of balance in the relationship or with ourselves. We need time out from the relationship to resume our own pursuits without being concerned about someone else. Thus our anger may sometimes function to reduce (i.e., partially or temporarily destroy) our relationship, whether we are aware of this intention or not. As one woman put it,

> *Sometimes I would start criticizing my boyfriend for trivial things. He would get mad, and I would get mad, and we'd both stomp off. Almost as soon as he was gone I'd start feeling ten pounds lighter, and I wouldn't care about what we argued about at all. After this happened several times, I decided I wasn't really mad at him, I just needed to blow him out of my space for a while.*

We often need to mobilize anger after a breakup as well, in order to keep our distance and counteract the urges born of loneliness and separation distress that draw us back together.

> *The first time I broke up with Robert, I knew I was doing the right thing. But I missed him so much. He told me he loved me and wanted to get back together so bad, that I gave in. Things didn't get any better. So I broke it off again. The same things happened, but this time my friends kept reminding me of all the nasty things he had done. I stayed mad, instead of feeling sorry for him, and I wouldn't take him back. I deserve better than him.*

Since **angry action** seeks to alter the conditions of a relationship, **anger in awareness** lets us know that some aspect of ourselves or our relationship is not working. It may be a consistent pattern, and it may be something more or different than the "last straw" incidents that trigger our reaction. In order to understand where such anger might be coming from, let us explore several sources for our anger in relationships.

Sources of anger

Four interpersonal sources for anger in couples are reviewed in the next chapter. Here we will consider the connections to **couple dances**, **depression and fear**, and **shame-affect**.

Couple Dances.   One type of accumulating annoyance is repetitive interaction patterns or "couple dances." In these behavior sequences, each person's typical actions have a way of evoking (or provoking) the other person's responses with monotonous regularity. Each person thinks the **other** person is causing the problem by doing something **first** that sets the whole vicious circle in motion:

> She: You interrupt me every time I try to talk about what's bothering me!
>
> He: That's because you always spring it on me when I've just walked in the door!
>
> She: You wouldn't let me talk to you any other time, so I have to catch you when you first come in. You just don't want to talk about it period!
>
> He: If you didn't always come on so strong, like the house is on fire, I might be more willing to listen to your gripes!
>
> She: By the time I finally get your attention about what's bothering me, I've complained so many times that I'm ready to explode.

We have discussed two couple dances before, the **pursuer–distancer dance** (Chapter 2) and the **reasonable–emotional dance** at the beginning of this chapter. These two duets often occur together, since the pursuer may become more and more emotionally expressive over the distancer's dodging and minimizing the issue. The distancer in the example above may normally suppress his own emotions because the other's "gripes" trigger **shame** over the perceived accusation of wrongdoing. This time the distancer above is not very reasonable, but is rejecting shame by **attacking** the emotional person's behavior.

It is important to recognize that the reasonable partner's tendency to view his or her thinking as superior to the emotional partner's may be influenced by **shame-avoidance**. **The reasonable–emotional dance goes better if reason dances _with_ emotion instead of _against_ it**. Instead of assuming that the emotional person's intense focus is irrelevant and overblown, it is more fruitful to assume that **every emotional expression contains a grain of valuable truth**. Adopting this simple rule can help us get past our reasonable-person defense and concentrate on discovering what is emotionally important. By assuming there is some truth and value to the other's emotion, we respect, rather than discount it. Thus we preserve our end of the rapport between us. Discounting, ignoring, or acting condescending toward the other's emotions is likely to trigger hurt and shame, which could escalate the disconnection and anger in the relationship.

The **underfunctioner–overfunctioner dance** is another couple game that can lead to anger (Lerner, 1986). One type of overfunctioner can be a woman whose gender-role expectation includes taking care of most domestic chores, tending to her partner's social and emotional life issues, and keeping the relationship working well. The man may be highly competent at work or other aspects of life, but appear unmotivated in housekeeping and emotional relating. The woman might demand that he do more, but still criticize his comparatively incompetent efforts to respond to her desires. Overfunctioners get angry because underfunctioners are not sufficiently grateful for what is done for them, and they don't improve enough. Underfunctioners may get rebellious about feeling shamed whether they try to comply or not.

> I don't know how many times I've told or showed Bill how to do the dishes right. But I still keep finding plates that aren't clean and glasses with smudges on them. He can't be that incompetent! He just doesn't care. I don't know how many times I've blown a fuse over this. But it just doesn't seem to do any good.

Anger connected to depression and fear.   Anger can be a liberating force when one has lived in a prison of either depression or fear. Recent research (reviewed in Henry, 1986, and Carlson & Hatfield, 1992) indicates that unpleasant or threatening situations trigger *anger* if we perceive ourselves as having some control, or *fear* if we don't have control. If neither fight nor flight strategies are successful over time, then we become lethargic and *depressed* and perceive ourselves as helpless to affect our situation. These three emotional states involve different neurochemical balances, with anger highest in norepinephrine and testosterone, fear highest in epinephrine, and depression highest in cortisol, ACTH, and also **endorphins**. Endorphins make depression comfortably numb, compared to the fight or flight activation of anger or fear. Depression in humans may be similar to the apathy in animals caught by a predator that enables them to stop struggling and submit to being killed.

Anger reanimates us by raising our epinephrine and norepinephrine levels and fostering efforts toward control. It may or may not be appropriate to aim this anger at a relationship partner. But if we were frightened and controlled by our parents, we may live in a psychological prison that our partners do not suspect. Our abilities to protest and protect ourselves may have been frozen because we were not allowed to defend ourselves. We may have developed pleasing "false selves" that seem to thrive on **doing the right thing** for others. Outside the family, we may have learned to be "cool" or "nice" conformists to fit in. But these false selves become increasingly frustrating to our satisfaction in our adult years. When these "false selves" crack in adulthood, we may surprise ourselves and others with how "uncool" and unreasonable we can be.

Anger connected to shame emotions. We have already connected the shame family of emotions with anger via **attack-other**. Much current research connects anger to shame, whether it proceeds from affect theory or not. From childhood through old age, shame proneness is related to maladaptive anger, including malevolent intentions, and direct, indirect, displaced, and self-directed aggression (Tangney et al., 1996). Clinical research has found internalized shame related to anger and antisocial behavior in several alcohol-related personality patterns (Cook, 1997) and has emphasized the experience of intense shame emotions before violent outbursts (Thomas, 1995).

In popular psychology the most common emotional precursor of anger is **hurt**, due to criticism, betrayal, or rejection of a desire. We normally consider hurt to be like sadness, which is distress affect connected to a loss. But hurt shows up at first as gaze aversion, desire to withdraw and hide, and disorganized thinking. This affective response may be extremely brief, less than a second, before it is replaced with anger (Retzinger, 1991). Or, if not quickly transformed into **avoid** or **attack-other** responses, hurt becomes intolerable and may evoke distress and crying. Thus, when acknowledged, hurt appears like sadness, rather than anger. These alternative affect sequences are central in conflicts.

Trying to be **right** is an **avoid** response to the discomfort of ruptured rapport, whether objective criteria for "rightness" exist or not. If a person is **right**, he or she will feel righteous and strong, instead of bad about disharmony. But pushing right and wrong back and forth becomes a desperate struggle to **avoid** feeling bad.

Researchers Thomas Scheff and Suzanne Retzinger (1991) videotaped and then slowed down spontaneous conflictual interactions in couples and discovered that shame (or hurt) and anger alternated in every encounter. In fact, if shame signs did not occur, then anger was short-lived and did not return. **Unacknowledged** shame (e.g., bypassed hurt) occurred before each episode of angry escalation. Detailed monitoring of a complex system of verbal and nonverbal signs of both shame and anger revealed that in all the couple conflicts together, there were twice as many indications of shame as there were of anger. One student recalls how boys are trained to substitute anger for hurt:

> *If a guy gets hurt by a girl he will usually not let on. He will likely go off on a rampage in a way to hide his true feelings. I see it in my friends, too. They joke or poke fun at others so that they may change their thoughts. Males usually grow up with the notion that they cannot let their emotions come out or they'll get trampled on.*

According to Scheff and Retzinger, the anger that responds to hurt often shows up indirectly as **disrespectful treatment**. This triggers more hurt (shame) in the other person and thus perpetuates the cycle. Table 13.7 lists the signs of shame from their videotapes.

TABLE 13.7. Cues of shame affect in communicative behavior

Verbal Statements:

References to being ridiculed, put down.
References to feeling inadequate, deficient, ashamed, embarrassed, humiliated, exposed.
Negative comparison of self to others, negative thoughts about one's appearance.
Obsessive thinking about what one might have said or done.
Feelings of disconnectedness to significant others: rejection, desertion, abandonment, ostracism, exclusion, isolation, and loss of support or love.

Vocal behavior in conversation:

Vagueness ("It was sort of strange").
Minimizing, attempting to diminish the force of statements (It was just. . .").
Exaggeration, expansion, grandiosity ("Everything is going wrong," "I'm doing FINE!").
Denial, defensiveness ("That's NOT what happened," "I KNOW I'm right!").
Vocal manner indicating vocal *withdrawal*, *hiding*, and *disorganized thought*, such as:
    Oversoft speech, irregular speech rhythm, hesitation, self-interruption, self-censorship, self-doubt ("I don't know"), pauses and filled pauses ("I - uh - wish").
    Stammering and stuttering (We feel embarrassed "for" someone who is stuttering from an impediment, because their disorganized speech confuses our thinking and mimics shame affect).
    Fragmented speech, rapid condensed speech, laughed words.

Gestures:

Hiding behavior: Hand covers or touches parts of face. Turning eyes away or turning eyes down.
Crossing legs, crossing arms, turning head and body away. Fidgeting.
Blushing. Struggling for control: Turning lips in, tensing, biting or licking lips; biting tongue.
Facial masking of feelings: "Wiping off a smile"; false smiling and laughing to cover negative feelings.

Triggering shame in the partner: Disrespectful behavior.

Interrupting, disregarding, and invalidating the partner's statements.
Imitating the partner ("You simply can't STAND it any more!").
Revising, and correcting the partner's statements ("You mean YOU aren't satisfied!").
Interrogating, asking questions whose answers are already known, or questions that are designed to put the other in an already invalidated position ("Didn't you KNOW that would happen?").
Name-calling, sarcasm, degrading tone of voice ("Aren't YOU the world's expert on shame and hurt!").

Adapted from Scheff and Retzinger, 1991.

By becoming aware of these signs of shame or behaviors that trigger it, we may be able to interrupt and deescalate our angry interchanges. We can shift to noticing and perhaps expressing confusion, embarrassment, helplessness, and hurt. That may mean saying, "I'm embarrassed," or "That hurts!" Unfortunately, moments of shame, hurt, helplessness, and confusion usually pass by too quickly and are followed by anger. But after the incident is over we can review what happened and discover a moment of our own shame response. Then we can say something like: "I realize now, that I got confused when you interrupted me, and that's when I got mad. I can't stand being interrupted." Later we can be more aware of similar moments and have a chance to interrupting the spiral of anger at that point.

Reviewing our quarrels is not meant to help us "keep score" or decide who did the worst things. Communication theory shows that our interactions form an endless chain extending backward and forward for months and even years. We are not trying to find out who did what **first**, as children do: "She hit me first!" But we can interrupt an angry spiral at **any** place by opening up a moment of shame affect. **If we can name and respect either our own or our partner's moment of hurt, isolation, or confusion, we can head off future rounds of angry escalation**. A married student describes one such moment with his wife:

> When I get mad at my wife, she gets upset and won't talk. This only makes me angrier because I want to settle the issue. Now I understand that I am feeling shame for making my wife feel bad. [She has also withdrawn from rapport, triggering shame from disconnection.]

In an argument the hardest part of recognizing a shame-family emotion is that it feels **weak**, even **helpless**, to feel hurt, confusion, or embarrassment. It feels stronger to be mad or just **right** about something. It takes courage to dwell on a shame feeling long enough to understand and express it. The husband above could try to stop this escalation by saying what he now realizes:

> I hate it when you clam up. I don't want you to feel bad. I want to work this out. Feeling cut off from you is the worst thing for me.

Discussing a shame moment even once may stop it from trapping us into automatic anger again. Even examining our own previous moments of shame, hurt, and disrespectful behavior through writing can help us proceed more carefully with this fast-moving chain of emotions.

Barriers to experiencing and expressing anger

If anger was totally absent in our family of origin and our parents were always reasonable around us, we may feel extremely embarrassed about showing any anger, assuming that it is always "out of place." Or anger may have been experienced as very destructive or as worse than useless, that is, damaging to the person who got angry. Then we may expect our own anger to be just as damaging, so we will try to avoid it.

Some barriers to anger are more typical for males. Having thrown tantrums as toddlers (Chapter 9), many boys later learn from peers that anger leads to a fight. But fighting with **girls** is heavily shamed in most cultural groups. Many grown men have no socially accepted anger expression and try to never express anger toward women, at least not strong anger. They don't know what to do with strong anger anymore, as this student's experience of a simulated argument illustrates:

*As soon as we started arguing I knew I was in trouble. She had that "woman's" tone of voice, the sound of someone who knows they're right, knows they're winning the argument, is rubbing your nose in your own failure and enjoys doing so. Whenever I almost had an appropriate response and would try to say it, she would cut me off and change the subject with that quick and antagonizing tone of hers. This kept me constantly **off balance** and **so upset** that it was hard for me to fight back.*

I was brought up in an average country household and taught to always be especially nice to women. Therefore, no matter how ugly the scene became, I just couldn't force myself to fight on her level for fear of being rude and hurting her feelings.

Finally, when all of my options had run out, I thought about how "might makes right." I wondered just how many punches it would take to shut her up. I've never hit a woman before and I don't believe I ever will. But the more I lost in the argument, the more I thought about it. I maintained my nice-guy status, though, since thinking about something and actually doing it are two different things.

Since this student will not try any of the tactics he mentions, he feels like a helpless loser. In that state of shame he notices that "might makes (him feel) right." If a man is *also* too uncomfortable with shame, then the shame brakes of morality can fail and lead to tantrum-like violence, toward either a partner or inanimate objects.

In a past relationship I got so angry at the girl, I didn't know how to act or what to say. I punched the mirror in my truck and broke it, which made me feel good for a moment. But I realized this was unacceptable and scared the girl and probably ended the relationship.

Women often face a different bind. They may be more used to attacking themselves and regard showing anger as unfemale or as too dangerous with men. They may learn that it is more acceptable to be nice and conciliatory rather than angry. Such "friendliness" often works better to defuse a conflict, and sometimes to get more of what we want from the other person (Tavris, 1989).

*One thing that I have learned about men is that they prefer it if you yell and hit them in an argument. They know how to handle that. But as soon as you throw them that curve and act really nice to them, they get **scared** and they don't know how to respond. This in turn causes the **guilt**, and then nine out of ten times, we get what we want.*

Though winning through kindness may be more frequently socialized in women, men can learn it too, by being punished for anger expression and rewarded for friendliness (Hokansen, 1970). Masking angry feelings with a friendly manner becomes a habit (i.e., *reaction-formation*) which helps in many conflictual situations. But when it does not work, one may have no familiar way to become angry or insistent on one's own behalf.

Undermining another's anger

The expression of anger has to be tolerable to both members of a couple for it to succeed in improving their relationship. If one partner is too uncomfortable, he may **undermine** the other's expression. Families of origin may model various forms of anger expression and habitual responses that may put the shame-brakes on or undermine others' anger. Since the partners come from different families, one person's normal angry expression or anger reduction habits may either escalate, reduce, or undermine another's normal expression (See Table 13.8).

Any determined effort to impose extensive punishment on a partner for expressing anger can stifle it by rendering it counterproductive. Two such punishments are lengthy silent treatments and strictly refusing to respond to any demands made in anger. **Intimidating** responses are often effective because they have also been used by parents to squash their children's anger, as in "Don't you DARE talk back again, or you'll wish you hadn't!"

Collapsing in tears or giving premature apologies can turn anger into guilt.

> *Before I could tell him off for what he did, he apologized. And then he acted like the matter was all settled, and I'd be out of line if I said anything more about it. Supposedly I got what I wanted, but I still felt cheated, and somehow he'd won, because now I felt like the bad guy for still being mad.*

TABLE 13.8. Ways of undermining anger in another

Actions	Reactions by angry person
Ultimatums: "If you EVER yell at (insult, etc.) me again, it's over!"	Suppress anger expression while ultimatum remembered; feel **powerless** and **shamed**; seek retaliation; find another way to be angry.
Relational Punishment: Long **silent treatment**, blocking any improvement *because* anger was openly expressed; make anger unproductive.	**Helplessness**, **bitterness**, **depression**; seek support, intervention, and renewal outside the couple. Spiraling **distance** and disaffection.
Intimidation: Show more **extreme anger**, superior force, **violence**, destructiveness.	Terror, **withdrawal**, **depression**, deviousness, flight, retaliation, police intervention.
Collapse: Cowering, tears, **self-blame**; giving in, **apologizing** prematurely, no presentation of own position or understanding for partner's.	Hollow victory; **no** sense of understanding or **respect**; **guilt** for hurting partner. May try toning down expression to seek understanding.
Disrespect: **Laughing at** partner's anger, joking about the issues; **distracting** from subject; ultra-calm; **responding like a parent** to a child.	Feeling **humiliated** or toyed with, **shamed**; being pursuing distractor, retaliating; feeling **one-down** and **resenting** partner's **superiority**.

Words in bold print are likely to be responses to shame-affect.

ANGER

... OKAY, OKAY SO YOU'RE ANGRY. WHO CARES? YOU BETTER COOL OFF OR I'LL SHOW YOU REAL ANGER!

TAP TAP TAP TAP TAP

Though some angry people will settle for compliance out of fear, most really want **respect** for their feelings and consideration for the merits of their desires. If we stop undermining each other's anger, we can develop both respect and compatibility. With practice, we can learn to express anger without being physically threatening. And we can also learn not to be frightened of our partner's expression. Giving and receiving anger is a two-person dance that couples design first without conscious reflection. But with growing awareness, we can re-choreograph our angry interchanges so that we are more predictable, safe, and effective. By using our awareness to reduce both barriers and insults and by respecting our moments of shame, we have a better chance of creating angry interchanges that lead to mutual **respect** for both our needs and our emotionality.

Levels of anger: Is there a <u>right</u> way to be angry?

There is no single **right** way to deal with anger, or, for that matter, with any other emotion. We will map out six levels of the experience of anger (Table 13.9) and explore some of their consequences.

TABLE 13.9. Ways of coping with emotions categorized by level of direct expression

Emotion level	Internal handling (Keeping it to yourself)	External handling (Social manifestation)
Most restrained level	**Repression** (No awareness) Feeling obliterated Defenses dominant	**Acting Out** (No conscious link with original emotion): **Avoid** (Distract by self-enhancing experience); **Attack Other** (Reduce, belittle, destroy).
Intermediate restraint level	**Suppression** (Emotional awareness mixed with mental override on behalf of other priorities). Thoughts may contain all four shame reaction styles.	**Reporting:** Communicating about emotion without physically showing it. May include all four reaction styles.
Least restrained level	**Feeling** and **Dwelling on**: (Emotional awareness predominates). Thoughts reflect original emotion and may include shame reaction styles due to inaction.	**Expressing, dramatizing** Being filled with and expressing the original emotion, including shame reaction styles if connected to emotion's history.

Note: These coping strategies apply to anger and most other emotions as well.

The first key decision regarding anger is to either **approach** or **avoid** it. Approaching anger may mean risking the future of the relationship in hopes of improving it. Avoiding anger puts off this threat of deterioration. But we usually must reduce our intimacy to avoid the irritating issue. Thus, approaching anger intensifies the relationship, while avoiding anger may preserve it in a limited form, or foster pulling away and contraction (Chapter 4).

Repressing. To avoid anger completely, we **repress** it or **act it out**. **Repressing**, or forgetting, anger has the advantage of avoiding any disturbance in the flow of interaction between us. Repression of anger is supported by **denying** it ("I'm not mad at all") or **projecting** ("You're sure negative today"). Simple repression is aided by changing the subject, obsessively concentrating on something else, eating, or just losing consciousness.

> *When I'm bothered by something, I like to oversleep. Sometimes I feel that sleep will make it better. Remember the expression, "Things will be better tomorrow after a good night's sleep"? Sometimes it turns out that way.*

Acting out. Repressed anger can be expressed outwardly in disguised ways through acting out. **Compensation** (**avoid** response to shame) involves trying to cover up the unwanted anger by accentuating some other area in which one feels good. Some people throw themselves into sports or lifting weights, while others may work on developing some knowledge or skill or go shopping, where they can get attention and be in charge. In **displacement**, one "takes out" anger on a racketball or at a sports event, or by acting belligerent in sports or at a bar. **Fantasy** and **identification** can sometime satisfy backed-up anger, as when we revel in the hero's violence in movies, or when some dwell on the destructive power of Hitler or Satanism. **Reaction formation** may mask dangerous anger by substituting "niceness," as we have described before.

Passive aggression is another way to act out and still avoid anger. It involves giving in to another's demands, or failing to mention one's own thoughts and feelings. Then, later one "unknowingly" does something that violates what one has agreed to, such as forgetting to take out the trash. True **passive aggression** is an unintentional betrayal of expectations, an unconscious enactment of the saying: "Don't get mad, get even." What triggers passive-aggressive behavior may be feeling powerless and not entitled to one's own view or anger, which is a shame–anger bind.

As the **target** of passive aggression, we are likely to feel betrayed and furious. What can we do? If we are able to speak calmly, we might say: "I'm pretty upset and confused about what has been happening. Are you upset and confused too?" If we just get angry, our anger may "burn through" to our partner's anger. We can still seek understanding after tempers cool. On the other side, what if we have accidentally hurt or let someone down, and he or she seems angry but confused? We can look for what we could be upset about if we had done our accidental deed on purpose. It takes courage to look at a shame–anger bind and speak openly in spite of it.

Suppressing. **Suppressing** anger has an advantage over repression. We still know we are upset, so we do not do (or undo, or forget) things without recognizing the anger that may be motivating us. We are able to take care of our business and even act friendly, without having anger take over our priorities and affect how others perceive us. In many situations we need to suppress anger, because the cost of expression is too high. For instance, in most business and employment, conciliatory friendliness is probably the only safe path to take. Even assertive negotiating presupposes a basic equality, which may be unavailable.

> When I was in the military, I used to express my opinions openly to my supervisors, and many times I would get in trouble for doing so. We were supposed to do our jobs their way and not question their authority. I never liked that, but I really didn't have a choice.

Cardiovascular studies have shown that suppressing anger may pose a greater health risk than expressing it (Tsuda et al., 1988). If we cannot avoid **feeling** anger, we face a dilemma. Expressing anger puts our relationships, jobs, and reputations at risk. And it can be habit-forming, thus increasing our angry states (Tavris, 1989). What should we do?

When we **suppress** our anger, we often try to gather evidence to decide whether our issue is important enough to deal with. Though we may rationalize away our annoyances as too trivial to bring up, we may also keep them in a "gunnysack" full of festering complaints. Suppressing these emotional issues means avoiding discussions of gripes, which encourages our partner to build up a "gunnysack" as well.

> She wanted to talk about it, and I was always looking for a quick way out of it. Since I didn't make an effort to confront all the changes that were going on in our relationship, she also tried to forget or ignore it. Every so often little signs of anger, frustration, or discontent would leak out, but I didn't pay attention to them. Until something would happen (that she would get mad about) that would light the fuse on the stack and . . . Every single thing, no matter how small or large, would come out, and she would really get carried away. My only purpose at that point was to say or do whatever it took to make everything okay. I really hated that, because it left me very unsatisfied and nothing got accomplished.

The student above notes that smoothing over his partner's outbursts didn't work, once the issues had built up beyond ignoring. When suppressed anger does not explode, it can poison our thoughts and collect grievances until they become sufficient justification for breaking up, without the partner ever knowing what was building up. A college man describes a "staining" effect that suppressed hurt and anger have had in the development of his relationships.

> I am easily hurt by the "bad" things my partner has to say about me. Time and time again I have felt torn up inside by seemingly insignificant actions or words. In order to combat this I have managed to suppress the smaller incidents with some success. Although I still feel a little hurt I am usually able to let it slide.
>
> However, if these things occur early in the relationship, it tends to retard the growth of my feelings for that person. It's almost like she has left a major stain on a so far perfectly white sheet. I will always notice it, and it may form the basis for my starting to dislike her (although I don't usually realize it), but still going through the steps of forming the relationship.

Reporting.   On the positive side, **suppressing** anger means maintaining control over it, so that we can **report** on it in a careful way. **Reporting** emotions means standing outside of them and naming them, rather than being overwhelmed by them. Reporting greatly reduces both physical and vocal expressions of anger and its effect on our thinking. Thus reporting reduces the likelihood that our anger will either infect or threaten the person we are confronting. We can also choose our words carefully in hopes of maximizing the effect we want to have. This makes reasonable negotiation and solutions easier to achieve. Reporting anger is preferable in situations that require diplomacy, which includes most public and professional encounters. But reported anger is sometimes not impressive enough on a visceral level for the other person to take it seriously. For example, announcing you are disappointed that your partner is denying or avoiding obligations may have little effect until you get mad about it.

Dwelling on anger.   Dwelling on anger means "stewing" about it without expressing it to anyone else. It is useful for thinking about options for acting on it. We can write letters expressing our anger to help get it off our chests and discover what really matters. After rereading our words, we can decide what we actually want to do or say, with less pressure to explode or exaggerate. On the other hand, if we only dwell on our anger, we may magnify it until we are too bitter to act or interact with others; we may do nothing to change the situations that frustrate us again and again.

Expressing and dramatizing.   Expressing anger puts the issue at center stage, but it can evoke more escalating conflict over the expression than over the issue itself. There is a distinction between **expressing** and **dramatizing**. Though somewhat out of control, anger expression is usually quite patterned. One person's pattern of spontaneous anger may seem like an exaggerated "drama" to another person, whose family expressed anger in more restrained ways. We are very likely to judge anger styles that are different than our own as offensive (**attack-other**). But if we respect the angry person's basic intent, which is to make life better for himself, we can dampen

our reaction to his style, as long as it is not destructive of life or property.

Raising and lowering our levels of angry expression

Our choices for experiencing anger can be expanded by developing the six levels we have discussed. The same approaches can be applied to other emotions as well.

For people who don't have much contact with their anger (or fear, joy, sadness, etc.), **dwelling on** it is a good approach. At selected points during each day, write down in a notebook every instance of your anger, irritation, sarcasm, superiority, and negative judgments. Also note when someone else did something wrong or showed anger in some way and how you reacted. A second important method for getting in touch with anger is **reporting** your emotional awarenesses to another person. Such sharing may seem normal for women for most emotions, but unusual for men. If it is awkward for you, make an explicit "buddy contract" with someone, so that each of you reports a type of emotional experience to the other on a daily basis. This basic behavior modification strategy rewards your awareness and reporting with your buddy's attention, interest, and supportive comments.

For people who may be able to **report**, but not **express** anger, popular therapies have developed many strategies to practice expressing. You can practice evoking and maintaining anger by glaring and arguing six feet apart from a partner and just expressing "yes" versus "no," with an attitude difference in mind. Or you can simulate generic or specific angry situations. There are physical exercises, such as deep breathing with an angry face, pounding pillows, and swinging foam bats. The purpose of these exercises is not to train us to do those things when we are angry, but to experience our own loss of control in anger as relieving it and not destructive to either ourselves or others. Then we will be more comfortable with intense anger, both in ourselves and in others.

Finally, for those who cannot restrain their tendency to blow up every time they get mad, there are interruption methods, such as counting to ten and leaving the scene. But just avoiding an outburst is not enough. We need to experiment with suppressing and reporting to give us more options. While **dwelling on** our anger, we can write about our feelings and imagine other ways to react without blowing up. We can learn **reporting** from what we write and by practicing scripted words, such as "I am angry at you because . . . "

As important as expressing anger can be, it is equally vital that we respond to it without either undermining it or escalating beyond the partners' tolerance. Since angry confrontations are so often a couple dance, it may be necessary for one partner to raise the level of intensity she or he can receive and express, while the other moderates and changes his or her expressive style.

Violence

Research reports violence in from 22% to 40% of dating couples, 38% of engaged couples, and over 25% of married couples (Cate et al., 1982; Gryl et al., 1991). Men are more likely to get violent than women and more likely to hit, push, and shake, or use a weapon. Women resort more to slapping and throwing things (Hatfield & Rapson, 1993). A flood of new research into couple violence promises to validate some of the strategies we use to cope with it.

Current research findings (Lloyd & Emery, June, 1993) are consistent with suggestions that, although couple violence may arise in a variety of ways, the most common and best understood trajectory is the same shame–rage connection we have already discussed. Wife abusers' shame proneness may be developed by parental shaming through public scolding, random punishment, and general criticism, which produces disturbances of identity and rage (Dutton et al., 1995). In a clinical case study, Lansky (1987) traces a history that begins with coercive parenting with criticism and physical punishment and stifling the child's attempts at self-defense as "talking back." Children thus become silent, helpless, and mentally confused, all prime signs of the shame state. Sooner or later, the growing person discovers that aggressive fury provides a sense of power that wipes out the helpless shame, and **attack-other** is born. A father reports on a neighborhood delinquency problem:

> There is a father on our street who verbally threatened *me* when the pitch of my voice went up on the phone. I can imagine how heavy he must be with his son! The 11-year-old has screamed obscenities at four parents on the block when they criticized his behavior. Then he runs into his house, where there is no parent at home. He's venting his fury at the rest of us, because he can get away with it.

An adult who experienced heavy-handed shaming as a child is likely to be hypersensitive to criticism, as well as to advice and any sort of failure. For example, failure at work can lead to attacking others at home via the "kicking the dog syndrome."

> Whenever my dad had a bad day at work he would start picking on mom as soon as he walked in the door. "This place is a mess! What have you been doing all day long?" She wouldn't defend herself, so after a while he would start in on me, but I would fight back.

Once a disconnection or hurt occurs, even if the shaming was not intended, a humiliation-sensitive adult may go beyond blaming to violence.

First, the experience of criticism causes a complete disorganization of thinking and feeling, and the person may lapse into a passive silence similar to a reprimanded child:

> *Every time I try to explain my point of view, she interrupts to say something I said is wrong. I lose my train of thought. I don't know where I was. It's like I can't even think straight when she's around.* (Lansky, 1987)

For wife abusers, the intense shame may be experienced as a tight throat, nausea, stomach pain, and a feeling as though one's chest and abdomen are collapsing, exploding, or imploding (Thomas, 1995). After anything from a moment to several hours the person breaks out of the shame state by yelling, threatening, or striking out. During the violence he feels powerful, and afterwards he may justify himself: "It's almost like I have to hit her to get her attention" (Lansky, 1987, p. 344). But he may also struggle with guilt for hurting someone, and with helplessness and shame for being out of control and doing something unacceptable. From guilt and shame come inhibition and confusion, and the cycle of shame, passivity, and violence can begin again.

How can we break the cycle? The most immediate intervention is to interrupt the cycle by leaving the scene. Afterwards the initiators of violence often try to minimize their own shame: "Let's forget it ever happened." But such avoidance may allow both the conflictual issue and the violent acts to remain as barriers between the partners. If the shame and hurt on both sides go unexpressed, it will be hard to avoid the alienation and sensitivity to humiliation of the perpetrator and the victim's fear of repeating the cycle.

Specialists in treating battering and familial abuse (e.g., Madanes, 1997; Browne et al., 1997) point to several principal goals for change:

1. The perpetrator needs to feel his shame and express it, no matter how difficult that may be.
2. Empathic connection is the most potent healing agent for shame, and for interpersonal violence as well. The perpetrator needs to feel the feelings of his victim, because that fosters emotional investment that will work against future violence.
3. His disconnection will lessen if he feels like making amends and the victim expresses some possibility of accepting them.
4. He may benefit from exploring the childhood roots of his sex-role expectations and shame-based behavior.
5. And he needs to learn words for his feelings (alleviating alexithymia) and alternative ways of responding to them.

If a couple tries to resolve a violent episode by themselves, admitting shame, apologizing and making amends are a good beginning. If partners don't want the violence to happen again, they can try to pinpoint what triggered the loss of control. But they need to keep some distance from their feelings, as if they were examining the events in an accident. Sometimes the conscious awareness of **shame–rage triggers** reduces their power to "set us off." Talking over a simple procedure for dealing with volatile emotional situations can help potentially violent reactors through the confusion of overwhelming hurt and shame. If the person attacked felt severely threatened, however, she or he may feel intimidated on many subsequent occasions, until a nonviolent conflict habit is thoroughly established.

If violence occurs more than once, or if both partners are violent, getting away from the situation is not enough. Intervention by a third person is essential, and a professional counselor trained in conflict management would be best. This makes intimate violence somewhat **public,** and that scrutiny activates their shame inhibitions against violence. Partners are likely to reduce their provocation and disrespect toward each other when they know that a neutral person will be reviewing every one of their actions. (Thus shame is very useful in the public regulation of behavior.) When violence is occurring, we should not hesitate to call in a housemate, a neighbor, or the police. But children are not independent or powerful enough to act as witnesses. They are normally viewed as weaker and controllable by a violent adult, and they may be traumatized by the incident.

If alcohol is involved, professional help is needed. Since alcohol interferes with shame affect, remorse and promises to reform are rarely sufficient to change patterns that combine intoxication and violence. Community intervention is usually necessary, combining professional counseling with engagement of friends and relatives and substance abuse support groups. Police, punishment, and domestic abuse shelters are important emergency resources. Victims of physical abuse often feel as embarrassed about "going public" as the perpetrators. But public embarrassment can provide the necessary emotional inhibition to make continued private violence unlikely. Professional counseling and retraining can help change the patterns. But personal support from friends and relatives is needed to relieve the stress of fear, anger, and shame that both violence and public intervention can generate. Many cases of domestic violence are only resolved when the partners divorce and are separated by restraining orders and vigilant friends and relatives. Intimate violence typically arises from personal shame, disruption of rapport, and the inability to cope with emotions. So whether the couple stays together or separates, these problems are best resolved through **emotional connections** with others outside the couple and retraining of emotional coping strategies.

To improve our understanding and handling of emotions, we have provided a biosocial theory of emotions. We studied the shame emotions because they are pivotal regulators of interpersonal behavior. With a new understanding of shame affect, we can refine present explanations of shyness, jealousy, and anger and understand many approaches to coping with them.

Chapter summary

- Emotions set priorities for consciousness, continually fluctuate, and are contagious. Thinking can contain them, but in a reasonable–emotional dance assume that every emotion contains a kernel of valuable truth.
- In technical language, emotions are biological affects combined with personal history. Feelings are emotions we think about, rather than merely express or act on.
- Basic emotions are inborn, quick, brief, unbidden, automatically processed, and universally recognizable on faces. Also present in other primates, they have been selected in our evolution. They include surprise, interest/excitement, joy, distress, fear, anger, disgust, dis-smell, and shame.
- Shame affect is a brake that responds to any impediment in interest/excitement or joy and to interpersonal disconnections, and thus regulates our contact with others. Its biological function is to interrupt and inhibit behavior that is not enhancing our survival and success.
- Shame emotions such as embarrassment, shyness, insecurity, and guilt signal social danger or incorrectness and trigger confusion and desire to withdraw from view.
- We can ignore and replace shame by focusing on a self-flattering compensation or by attacking someone else. Or we can distort them through withdrawal and self-critical depression. Undefensive shame awareness can motive apologizing, improving, and making amends.
- Men may repress shame and shame each other with feminine words, retarding their development of adult shame. Women and minorities may be more aware of shame and feel that their nature is defined as second-class. Men strive for pride and rightness. Women often feel inadequate about looks and mothering.
- Emotions come like waves which we can embrace and learn how to ride. Whether we proceed, detour, or derail in relationship scenes depends on how we ride the waves and how we respond to shame when our rapport is interrupted.
- Shyness is based not on fear of rejection, but on perceived lack of rapport. It may be influenced by inborn and developmental sensitivity. It may predispose us to fall in love suddenly and "hard."
- Jealousy perceives a potential loss of love, which may be an interpretation of weakened or interrupted rapport in the present. Possessive controlling may be an attempt to prevent our beloved from triggering uncomfortable emotions we don't know how to ride. Controlling our partner's behavior and feelings defends us against our own disorganized emotional processes.
- We can cope with jealousy by negotiating relationship guidelines and exploring relationship dissatisfactions and inequalities, as well

as our own cultural expectations, self-esteem, dependence, and difficulties with experiencing emotions.

- Interpersonal anger seeks to make change necessary by preventing continuation of business as usual. Anger can motivate useful individual distance or keep ex-lovers from trying again.
- The reasonable/emotional dance and the underfunctioning/overfunctioning dance feed anger. Bypassed shame and hurt and disorganized, inexpressible emotions trigger anger escalation. So expressing hurt can deescalate arguments.
- Anger expression can be undermined if associated with physical fights, long-lasting retaliatory punishments, intimidation, collapsing in hurt or fear, or premature apologies.
- We can cope with emotions through repression, acting out, suppression, reporting, dwelling-on, and expressing. No one of them is best, but each has consequences in human interaction.
- Avoiding anger may reduce the quality of a relationship, but expressing it risks termination. Repressing anger can result in unconsciously sabotaging our agreements or displacing it onto other actions.
- Suppressing anger helps get along with others and focus on other priorities. But stored up dissatisfactions may trigger surprise-attacks or poison our attitude toward the partner. Reporting suppressed anger is the preferred public and professional way to negotiate over divisive issues.
- We can increase our varieties of anger awareness and expression and also re-choreograph our anger-dance so that it is less damaging and more productive and satisfying.
- Much of interpersonal violence arises from the shame–rage connection, in which confusion, helpless frustration, and alexithymia are replaced by angry action. Intervention and retraining are necessary to change the cycle of violence. Empathy, shame expression, and new behavior can help relieve the violent reactors' confusion and initiate nonviolent habits.

Facing and resolving conflicts 14

My girlfriend and I go round and round about how much I need to work around our apartment. I think that I really am quite reasonable about pitching in and doing what I see needs to be done. She complains that she always has to tell me what to do that I don't just see it and do it without her reminders. Doesn't she know I have more on my mind than noticing whether the toilet needs to be cleaned again? We never seem to be able to settle this!

Why does it often seem to be a standoff between what you want to do and what your partner wants you to do? Over and over you may catch yourself thinking that if your partner would just **agree** with you things would go so much more smoothly! One of the realities of living as a couple is that you must always grapple with the question: How are we going to run the show—your way or mine? Partnering means learning to face and "work through" the inevitable differences and power struggles of living together. But learning how to both "give and take" in a relationship is no simple matter. In this chapter we will examine the current theory and research about how couples face and resolve the day-to-day differences, conflicts, and power struggles that are a natural part of any relationship.

The inevitability of conflict in intimate relationships

Shouldn't people who love each other not have to disagree or fight? Apparently, the answer is *no*. Social scientists who study intimate relationships have found that conflicts appear to be an inevitable part of most couples' lives together. Not only are they reported by couples experiencing distress in their relationships, they appear to be equally present in successfully functioning relationships (Billings, 1979; Koren et al., 1980; Raush et al., 1974; Gottman et al., 1998; White, 1989; Zvonkovic et al., 1996). Various researchers and theorists cite a number of reasons to explain this inevitability (Peterson, 1983; Zvonkovic, et al., 1996).

First, the more emotionally invested two people are in each other, the more powerful each person's influence is on the other. In a casual relationship, it is easy to "abandon ship" without worrying about how to resolve certain differences. With increased investment in a relationship comes a greater potential for anger and more vulnerability to hurt. The more they **mean** to each other, the more each partner tends to "play for keeps" in dealing with each other because each knows that he or she must live with the consequences of his or her own behavior, and that those consequences will have a significant impact on both partners. They have a history and a future together.

Second, people in intimate relationships typically spend a great deal of time together. When people are together day by day, disagreements can be expected. If one partner sees another only once a week, it might be much more possible to tolerate an irritating personal habit or behavior than when they live with each other every day. The more frequently persons interact with one another, the greater the potential for conflicts to arise.

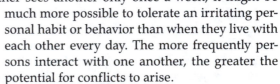

But experiencing conflict and resolving it effectively are two different things. Too often, partners either avoid conflict or let it manifest as nonproductive, bitter fights from which no one emerges the victor. To understand how to resolve conflicts in your intimate relationship, it is important to know how conflict develops, what paths conflict can take, what factors influence conflict, and what methods are available for effectively managing it. In this chapter we will seek to address each of these issues.

Defining conflict

For some of us (Coser, 1985; Mack & Snyder, 1957), conflict between intimates means an open struggle, either verbal or physical. Others (Boulding, 1962; Stagner, 1967) consider conflict to be **any** psychological antagonism even without its expression in open battle. Here we will draw from the latter meaning and will define conflict as **an interpersonal process that occurs whenever the actions and desires of one person interfere with the actions and desires of another.** For example, Susan may believe that John is expecting her to do too many of the housekeeping chores. Because his desire for her to do housework interferes with her desire to do other things, she is experiencing conflict whether she expresses it or not. Conflict can also develop over a difference in preferred attitudes or values. John may not believe in sternly disciplining Susan's children by her first marriage as she expects. Conflict happens when one person's actions or desires for action block those of the other partner resulting in "a struggle over values, behaviors, power, and resources in which each partner seeks to achieve his/her goals usually at some expense to the other" (Scanzoni, 1982b, p. 31).

Stages of conflictual interaction

The first step to understanding conflict in intimate relationships is to learn how it develops. Most researchers on conflict consider that the actual confrontation, or "fight," expressed in a shouting match, calm discussion, or other fashion, is really part of a larger process, which consists of a prior conditions stage, a beginning, a middle, an ending, and an aftermath stage (Galvin & Brommel, 1982). These stages in the conflict process are depicted in Figure 14.1. Donald Peterson (1983) provides an interesting perspective on the various types of interactions that trigger conflict, the divergent responses individuals might possibly make to these situations, and the various types of endings which may result from these responses.

The prior conditions stage

Conflict does not usually occur without some prior reason or connection to a past experience both partners have shared. As they say, "It takes two to tango." Conflict originates in each participant's interpretation of his partner's message about the conditions or "rules" of the relationship within the context of the current situation. (Remember the idea of content and relational messages from Chapter 12). Prior conditions might include: ambiguity about each partner's responsibilities and role expectations; competition over money, affection, or time; past experiences in sharing and conflict resolution; and the quantity of previously unresolved conflicts (Galvin & Brommel, 1982, pp. 8–12). For example, Brian may believe that Sandra is

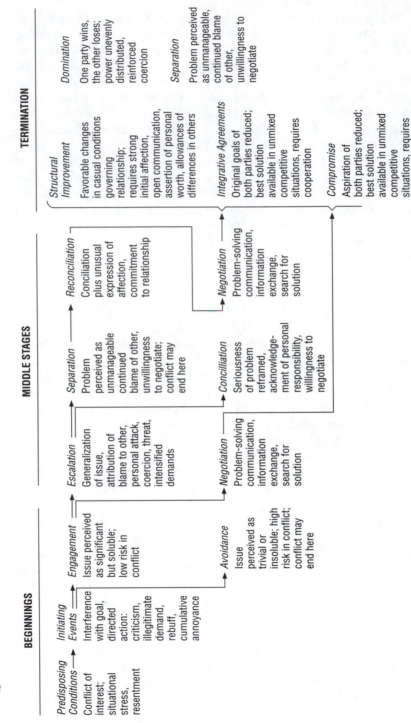

FIG.14.1.
The possible courses of conflict. Source: Peterson, 1983.

The possible courses of conflict, showing the progression through stages:

BEGINNINGS

Predisposing Conditions → Conflict of interest; situational stress, resentment

Initiating Events → Interference with goal, directed action: criticism, illegitimate demand, rebuff, cumulative annoyance

Engagement → Issue perceived as significant but soluble; low risk in conflict

Avoidance — Issue perceived as trivial or insoluble; high risk in conflict; conflict may end here

MIDDLE STAGES

Escalation → Generalization of issue, attribution of blame to other, personal attack, coercion, threat, intensified demands

Negotiation → Problem-solving communication, information exchange, search for solution

Separation → Problem perceived as unmanageable, continued blame of other, unwillingness to negotiate; conflict may end here

Conciliation → Seriousness of problem reframed, acknowledgement of personal responsibility, willingness to negotiate

Reconciliation → Conciliation plus unusual expression of affection, commitment to relationship

Negotiation → Problem-solving communication, information exchange, search for solution

TERMINATION

Structural Improvement — Favorable changes in casual conditions governing relationship; requires strong initial affection, open communication, assertion of personal worth, allowances of differences in others

Domination — One party wins, the other loses; power unevenly distributed, reinforced coercion

Separation — Problem perceived as unmanageable, continued blame of other, unwillingness to negotiate

Integrative Agreements — Original goals of both parties reduced; best solution available in unmixed competitive situations, requires cooperation

Compromise — Aspiration of both parties reduced; best solution available in unmixed competitive situations, requires cooperation

not interested in spending time with him on the weekend because she twice turned him down when he asked her to go to dinner on Friday night and went out with her girlfriends instead. As a result of this prior condition, when he asks again and she suggests that they include another couple she knows, he may view it as more evidence of her rejection of him, feel hurt, and engage in an argument with her about this.

Clearly, past experiences have set the groundwork for new tensions. Because each couple has a history of having succeeded or failed in effectively resolving past conflicts, each disagreement is handled in a historical context of what has gone before (e.g., who is entitled to what given what has been resolved or remains unresolved). In addition, each partner develops a set of beliefs and expectations about the other partner that undergirds their perceptions of how the other will respond to them and how they should respond back. Couples structure their life with each other around these beliefs. A perceived threat to or violation of these relationship "rules" results in frustration.

The frustration awareness stage

The second stage in the conflict process, the beginning, is when one or both partners become frustrated when they perceive the other as blocking them from satisfying some need or concern. They begin to believe that they are being attacked or threatened by something they have seen or heard in regard to one another. A number of different types of conditions or circumstances can lead to such a feeling.

Types of frustrating conditions.   When married couples were asked by Peterson (1979) to give detailed accounts of specific events that precipitated conflicts in their marital relationships, their answers could be grouped into four types: criticism, illegitimate demands, rebuffs, and cumulative annoyances. Looking at **criticism** first, "It does not seem to matter much whether an act is intended to be critical, the important condition is that the behavior is **interpreted as critical**. If the remark or act leads to a feeling of injury and injustice on the part of the offended person, that person is likely either to retaliate with some form of aggression or to withdraw" (Peterson, 1983, p. 371; See also the section on Shame in Chapter 13). A wife recounts such an incident, when she and her husband were playing tennis together:

> We were playing tennis. Both of us were rather tired and hot. Neither of us was having a particularly good game. When Tony overshot two serves, I said somewhat facetiously, "You're not with it today, are you?" He seemed to see that as criticism (and I guess it was) and he got ticked off. He snapped something back at me about how I wasn't playing so hot either!

A second type of event that commonly triggers conflict is an **illegitimate demand**, such as the one depicted in the following story:

I asked Jim if he would do the dishes—to get them out of the way—while I fixed the handle of the teapot so we could have some tea. There were negative vibrations from Jim who immediately suggested that we do the dishes together, implying that I should wash. I asked if he would like to wash them and he said, " Well, I would if it were just the dinner dishes, but there's all that other stuff in the sink." (Peterson, 1983, p. 371)

Peterson (1983) reports that among his married respondents, the demands that seemed especially likely to produce serious conflict were those that were perceived as **unjust,** that is, outside the expected demands each person has agreed the other can make on him or her. For example, a husband who expects his wife to support his need for a career redirection by temporarily becoming the sole breadwinner for the family, or a wife who expects her husband to take over the purchasing of the family groceries due to new responsibilities of her own may trigger conflict if they do not take the time to examine these expectations with their partner and make them more explicit. However, if the partner on whom the new demand is placed feels that it is unfair, the intent and legitimacy of the demand will have little importance to that partner, possibly resulting in open conflict (Peterson, 1983).

A third kind of action that can trigger confict is the **rebuff**, which is when one person appeals to another for a particular reaction, and the other fails to respond as expected:

I was worried about a situation at work, and unsure of how to handle it. I started talking with Sue about what happened to me at work. She kept on peeling the potatoes and did not even look at me. Talk about a turnoff! I stomped out of the kitchen and slammed the door.

As depicted above, it is typical for the person perceiving a rebuff to feel disconnected and devalued, and to respond either by becoming angry or withdrawing or both (shame responses).

The fourth kind of initiating event is the **cumulative annoyance**. With this type, the person often reports that a series of actions have occurred and have irritiated the person but have not been commented upon. Then, for some reason, one "final straw" exceeds the threshold, and the fight is on, as seen in the following report:

I asked him to help me with the house. He agreed . . . and we even set up a schedule of things for him to do . . . but each day I had to remind him. It got to be such a hassle, that after four weeks of hassling him I finally blew up, and told him he needed to find someone else to be his maid, I was through doing it all!

We can understand how these different types of events have the power to trigger conflict when we view criticism and illegitimate demands as potential violations of personal norms and perceived threats or attacks against a person's self-image.

Deciding to avoid or engage.   When one partner experiences an event as a threat or attack, both must decide whether to engage the other and confront the conflict or to avoid it. This decision is based on the couple's previous history of conflict resolution, the impact the current conflict might have on their sense of emotional closeness and commitment as a couple, current perceptions of power within the relationship, and the relative importance of the current issue to each partner. Based on previous experience, a partner may decide that he or she will lose more by pushing the issue than by sidestepping it. Or, a person may arrive at the conclusion that the issues are either not important enough to jeopardize the relationship or that the disagreement will create too much distress, at least for the moment.

If a conflict is initiated, it is likely that at least one person has weighed whether the issue is important enough to confront it at the present time and also whether a positive outcome is more likely from dealing with the issue than from avoiding it. As might be expected, researchers (Christensen & Heavey, 1990; Klinetob & Smith, 1996) have found that the individual who feels most discontented with current circumstances is often the one who initiates engagement about an issue. In addition, the strategies used to initiate conflict often differ, depending on the relative power of the partners. Although many researchers (Peterson, 1983; Scanzoni, 1982) report that the more powerful partner tends to engage in conflict more readily than the less powerful, the very willingness to engage in conflict may indicate a certain level of frustration in a relationship. Wives often control fewer economic and social resources, have fewer alternatives, and may perceive themselves as less powerful than husbands (See section on Power in Chapter 7). This might explain why women are much more likely than men to use indirect coercive strategies in initiating conflict situations (White, 1989). Often, a less powerful partner may decide to engage in open disagreement if she feels that she has reached the limit of what she can tolerate and that the risks of losing are not as damaging as staying in the current situation.

In addition, the level of frustration and the decision to try to resolve an irritating situation may rest upon the power an individual has (or perceives he or she has) in their relationship. For example, a woman who grows more and more discontented about the allocation of housework or childcare (i.e., accumulated annoyance) may engage her partner in an attempt to distribute the tasks "more fairly" (Kluwer et al., 1997; Zvonkovic et al., 1996). Although this woman feels the division of tasks is unfair, a wife with a more traditional view of marriage might have no problem with a similar arrangement.

The active engagement stage

According to Peterson (1983), once open conflict begins, it appears to take one of three paths: (a) toward direct negotiation and problem resolution, (b) toward escalation and intensification of conflict, or (c) toward deescalation by means of conciliation and then negotiation. Figure 14.1 depicts these divergent paths of conflict.

Direct negotiation. In this path, each person states his or her position in a straightforward way and seeks validation of his or her position or perspective by the other. Once this has been obtained, problem solving can begin, in which the couple generates possible solutions, considers the "pros" and "cons" of each solution alternative, and selects one on a trial basis. In these exchanges, partners usually feel that the other cares about their preferences and is interested in working toward a solution that is acceptable to both.

Escalation. Some conflicts quickly grow out of control. One partner blames or verbally attacks the other who then responds in kind. Both partners belligerently threaten and intimidate the other as a means of trying to force the other to see things (or do things) their way. Researchers and clinicians (Gottman et al., 1998; Heavey, Christensen, & Malamuth, 1995) have identified a number of key processes that characterize these escalating conflicts. Certain responses—blaming, counter-attacking, condemning—create a pattern of escalating emotional intensity in the interactions of distressed partners (see Chapter 13). For example, in one study Gottman and his colleagues (1998) videotaped couples, establishing a play-by-play account of how these couples tried to resolve their most serious problem. The researchers discovered that distressed and non-distressed couples differed significantly in how the complaining partner presented his or her complaint and how his or her partner responded to it. Non-distressed partners began "gently" with an initial agenda-building stage where they laid out their perspective and complaints (without blaming) and invited the speaker to express his or her perspective or feelings about the problem before deciding what to do. In contrast, distressed couples immediately moved into an arguing

phase in which the speaker complained about the situation and the listener immediately discredited the speaker's perspective by arguing about the facts of the case. This led to an escalating cycle where the more the speaker complained, the more the listener felt attacked and responded with blame, resulting in the speaker feeling that his or her perspective was not valued or accepted, which caused the speaker to push harder to be heard. Consequently, most of the distressed couples never moved to a negotiation phase where problem solving, informational exchanges, and comments of agreement occurred.

This escalating pattern often consists of **cross-blaming and criticizing** where one partner expresses a complaint and the other partner, rather than acknowledging the complaint, counters it with a complaint of his or her own. Witness the following exchange between Gail and Dick, a young married couple in their early twenties, discussing the pressures put on the couple by their family members:

Dick: But boy, no matter how much pressure my sister puts on you, you know . . .

Gail: You don't accept the fact that I can be pressured . . .

Dick: I do accept that . . .

Gail: Or that it's intolerable for me . . .

Dick: Well, You never said it was. and I defended you against my sister . . .

Gail: Not in front of me.

Dick: I did. I did behind you, and I also . . .

Gail: Well, I did behind you and that's what you complained about . . .

Dick: I asked you and you said you didn't.

Gail: What—defended you?

Dick: Yeah.

Gail: The hell I didn't, I did. I did plenty.

Dick: Well, this is news.

Gail: It's not news.

Dick It's news. At any rate, if I don't make the money and if I don't pull things together and if I don't find employment . . .

Gail: Except that I'm trying to find a job too, Dick. I'm anxious to get a job just as much as I was before . . .

Dick: Yeah, but you're not expected to by anyone else but me. I really take issue with you on this. I think that pressure does come on me to get a job and be the breadwinner. You know divorces come about through this, "He's a lousy husband." "All he does is run around and play and do nothing . . . " (Rogers, 1972, p. 44)

You will note how, rather than acknowledging the partner's comment, each feels compelled to defend his or her position by offering a new complaint as a defense against the criticism of the other. Both Dick and Gail blame the other for the current situation and argue that the problems are all the other's responsibility rather than shared. As a result, each feels that he or she has been attacked by the other. To make matters worse, each person brings in several other issues in addition to the original complaint.

Gail's shift in topics from dealing with what her husband was first discussing was her way of defending herself from the implicit blame in his remark. However, it had the effect of devaluing the husband's experience rather than inviting them to work through his initial complaint to some resolution. The couple ends their discussion neither resolving their disagreement nor quite knowing how the discussion escalated so rapidly in a negative direction.

In contrast, research shows that non-distressed couples engage in conflict quite differently (Gottman et al., 1998). First, the speaker does not shift immediately into angry, blaming criticism. Second, the listener does not counter the speaker's complaints with complaints of his or her own, as we saw above, or argue about the legitimacy of the speaker's perspective. Instead, the listener tends to employ responses that calm his or her partner and deescalate the situation. So, if a wife were to express a complaint, her husband might acknowledge her perspective by making a statement like: "I didn't know this was bothering you. What do you think we should do about this?"

Many clinicians assume that non-distressed partners use "active listening" to deescalate a conflict, but Gottman and his associates (1998) reported in a recent study of 130 newlywed couples that non-distressed couples do not use active listening during their conflicts any more frequently than distressed couples do. Gottman indicated that active listening techniques may be much more than most people can handle when faced with a conflict in which they are held responsible for the other's distress. In fact, non-distressed couples engage in three specific patterns: (a) they signal a willingness to accept the legitimacy of the other's influence in deciding that this is an issue that needs resolution; (b) they use "gentle" rather than intensely confrontational tactics to approach a conflictual topic; and (c) they respond to complaints with strategies, such as conciliation, that calm and soothe the other as well as help resolve the conflict.

Conciliation.   When a conflict "heats up" to a high level of emotional intensity, it is often very difficult to move to rational problem solving or negotiation. Thus, to make this move possible, a conciliatory action is usually necessary. This is designed to soothe and **deescalate** the negative feelings of the partner by expressing a willingness to work toward resolution of the problem. The most common conciliatory strategies reported by married couples (Gottman et al., 1979; Peterson, 1979) consist of two elements. First, at least one partner reframes the conflictual issue as less important than maintaining the relationship (e.g., "I don't want to fight you on this"). Second, the person who first moves toward conciliation **takes some personal responsibility** for the conflict, rather than blaming the other for all of it, and also takes some personal responsibility for trying to resolve the conflict (e.g., "This probably is at least partly my fault. What can I do to resolve it?").

To be effective in lowering the intensity of the conflict (i.e., deescalation), these conciliatory moves must be accepted by the other partner and followed by reciprocal conciliation from him or her. The result is a reduction in the intensity of the emotions and the ability of the partners to move together toward using more rational means (i.e., negotiation, compromise, etc.) to resolve the conflict.

Positive sentiment override. Many couples deescalate their conflicts without explicitly addressing the issues in conciliatory statements. They can allow emotions to cool by pausing for a drink or taking a bathroom break. Or they can shift the course of the argument and soothe negative emotions by engaging in **"positive sentiment override"** (Gottman, July, 1996). Many couples have behaviors they often use to invoke positive feelings and interrupt the negatives: a joke, a touch of concern, an activity in which partners collaborate (like cleaning house), or a pleasant activity (like taking a walk or playing with their dog). Once negative emotional arousal is reduced and some positive feelings have been recruited, moving the couple back toward the "magic" 5-to-1 ratio (see Chapter 4), rational approaches toward the conflict are possible.

The conflict ending stage and types of endings

One way or another, all conflicts end, although they may not be resolved. Often, people just withdraw from one another without a clear resolution of their difficulties. Peterson (1983) reports five different kinds of endings used by married partners to close their conflicts with one another: separation, domination, compromise, integrative agreement, and structural improvement. (See Figure 14.1)

Separation. The separation, or "standoff," is characterized by the withdrawal of one or both parties without immediate resolution of the conflict. Under some conditions, separation is a useful step in attaining later resolution because it allows partners to "cool off" and get some distance from one another, giving them time to think of a better way of dealing with their differences. But at other times separation may not be helpful at all. If it is a brusque departure accompanied by insults rather than an effort to deal with the conflict in a thoughtful way, it arouses a different emotional response in one's adversary. Withdrawal can also have a damaging effect if it is *not* followed by more effective efforts to resolve differences.

Researchers report that aggression, withdrawal, and nonresolution characterize the interaction of distressed couples. Moreover, in the most extreme forms of marital distress, couples tend to operate as if all their conflicts as irresolvable (Beavers & Lewis, 1985). There is often a mood of despair and discouragement, and couples appear to rely on disengagement or withdrawal as the only ways to avoid disagreement in their lives. Spouses who are extremely angry and disappointed with their mates often create an "island of invulnerability" through withdrawal (Guerin et al., 1987).

Gottman and Krokoff (1989) report a similar pattern in highly distressed couples that develop "parallel lives" in which they might live as if they are in a boarding house, occupying the same house but totally withdrawn from each other's lives (discussed in Chapter 5).

Domination/submission.   Some conflicts end by conquest. One person pushes for a certain line of action leading to his or her personal goals, and the other gives in. This might be called a "steamroller-style of conflict resolution": I push to get agreement from you and you allow me. Consider the following conversation between Susan and Tom, a young, dual-career couple in their late twenties who met and married while both were in graduate school. Susan wishes to discuss her potential job change with Tom:

> Susan: Tom, I've been thinking a lot lately about my job, and I've decided that I've just got to look for some other kind of position.
>
> Tom: (looking at his newspaper) Um.
>
> Susan: I've realized that I won't get hired at the university. I guess I thought I would be so bright a star that they would make an exception to my graduating from here, but that is not going to happen. I can go on looking for grants and writing jobs for myself, but I don't want to do that.
>
> Tom: (Looking up). Well, what do you want to do?
>
> Susan: I would like to look for an academic position at a university. I've been talking to some of my friends at Montana State. They have a position open and seem real interested in having me interview for it.
>
> Tom: Well, I don't know, I have to see if there is a job for me there. Montana doesn't have many people, I don't know if they could support another lawyer.
>
> Susan: But you don't understand! This sounds like a really good position. I don't think you realize how few and far between academic positions are right now.
>
> Tom: But I thought that when you were looking you would consider towns big enough for me to get a job in too!
>
> Susan: I just don't think you really want to move—you don't want to leave your job here, do you?
>
> Tom: Oh, go ahead and talk to them. I know you won't get off my back until you do what you want anyway!

As you can imagine, there are often significant costs to the relationship over time with this pattern. Ignoring one partner's wishes in order to gain victory at any cost often results in the losing party psychologically withdrawing from the decision making and, ultimately, from the relationship.

Compromise.   Compromise is usually conceived as a solution to conflict in which both parties reduce their aspirations until a mutually acceptable alternative is found (Peterson, 1983). Although compromise might be the best outcome, participants often feel like "no one wins" because the final outcome is not satisfying to either partner (Bach & Wyden, 1968; Fisher & Ury, 1981). For example, Frank and Sue are arguing about how they will spend their summer vacation. One wants to stay home and sit by the pool and the other wants to visit France. They might decide to compromise and arrange to spend a weekend at a resort several hours drive from their home. However, in such an arrangement, neither of them may feel that they are spending their vacation as they would like.

Integrative agreements.   In contrast to compromise, a number of professionals involved in negotiation and conflict resolution training with couples suggest that partners look for a solution that represents elements of both people's goals and aspirations. They distinguish several principles by which such agreements can be reached (Pruitt & Carnevale, 1980; Fisher & Ury 1981). First, couples must commit time to exploring both the goals and costs of various options so that each partner can get a clearer picture of the other's preferences. Second, partners consider ways of inventing new options that may lead to connecting their divergent goals. Third, they try to find ways of cutting the costs of particular options to one or both parties. Demands, goals, and aspirations, as Pruitt and Carnevale (1980) say, often " . . . come in bundles, and in order for concessions to be seen as acceptable, it is usually necessary to *unlink* or separate the goals cognitively so that some may be modified while others are kept unchanged." Consider how Tom and Susan, the couple depicted earlier, might use this approach to work toward an integrative agreement about a possible job change:

> Susan: Tom, I've been thinking a lot lately about my job and about what I want to be doing in a job. I'd like to talk with you about what I've been grappling with. Is now a good time for you and I to talk?
>
> Tom: (Reading the newspaper). I guess this is as good a time as any.
>
> Susan: You sure?
>
> Tom: (Looking at her) Yeah.
>
> Susan: I've been thinking about the grant job I now have. This is the second year of doing this grant and I guess it is finally dawning on me that I won't be hired by the department. I guess I always knew they wouldn't hire their own graduates, but I thought I could be a bright enough star that they would make an exception. I realize that that just is not going to happen.
>
> Tom: So what does that mean?
>
> Susan: Well, I can keep on writing, looking for grants, but I don't think I want to do that forever. What I would really like is to teach at a university . . . a real faculty position.

Tom: You mean move from here?

Susan: That's probably what it would take since I can't get hired on here. I'm wondering what that would be like for you, moving?

Tom: Well, it isn't something I've thought of . . . I'm just getting established here in my practice . . . it would be rough, starting all over again.

Susan: I know. You've got a base of people who know you here.

Tom: And if we moved out of state, I would have to take the Bar exams again. That would be a real bitch . . .

Susan: Yeah. It was miserable enough to go through the first time, wasn't it?

Tom: You really think there's no hope of getting what you want here?

Susan: I really do. I kept on thinking I might get one, but I guess I'm finally realizing I'll have to go someplace else if I want a faculty position.

Tom: Well, where would you want to go or look?

Susan: I haven't even thought that far. I first wanted to see what your reactions were to this.

Tom: I guess it wouldn't hurt to look, but it would be important to me that we begin to think together about what we want. Where would you want to start looking?

Susan: Well, definitely not up North. I don't like those cold slushy winters. Maybe someplace here in the South if it wasn't too backward. Or maybe some place out West. My convention is coming up and I could see what jobs there were available and what the possibilities are, then get back with you and see what you think about the places.

Tom: Check it out. Out West might be fun. Then we can figure out what I might be able to do. I guess right now I have a little more flexibility with a law degree than you do to get started.

Susan: Great!

Although Tom and Susan are still a long way off from hammering out an integrative agreement, they clearly depict the first step, that of beginning to explore and assess each other's wants and needs. The key to attaining integrative agreement is to **treat the situation as a solvable problem** for which two cooperating parties can seek a mutually acceptable solution (Pruitt & Carnevale, 1980). This orientation contrasts with the competitive "win–lose" orientation in which one party tries to press the other toward his or her preferred outcome. "For this to work, the parties must be stubborn about their basic goals, but flexible about means for attaining these goals" (Fisher & Ury, 1981). This process obviously requires cooperative problem-solving and a problem that is serious, but not overly conflictual: "If the conflict is trivial, the people involved tend to choose an easier option. . . . If the conflict is too severe, they may be unable to stay in this cooperative problem-solving mode long enough to work out a cooperative solution" (Peterson, 1983, p. 380).

Structural improvement.   An important unintended result of conflict is that it can lead to profound changes in the way two partners structure their relationship. They may also discover qualities in themselves or the other that may be surprising or disturbing. The following story describes an example of such relationship restructuring:

> Debbie and Sean were a couple in their mid thirties who met while both were in school. Both of them were employed in demanding professional jobs . . . Married for ten years, they had two boys ages 3 and 9. In their first visit for marriage counseling they both seemed angry and scared. Each reported feeling that the other was so involved in work and parenting that there was little real caring reflected in their day-to-day life together. As they spoke, they quickly moved to attacking each other for being so immersed in other people and things, and for each ignoring the other. Neither expressed the hurt and disappointment they experienced, or the fear that the other "did not love them anymore." Instead, they presented evidence of instances in which the other had been uncaring. As their counselor gently coaxed each of them in turn to express to the other their sense of hurt and wants of greater closeness, each partner noticeably softened. It was obvious that neither had considered that beneath the surface attacks, both of them were feeling hurt and lonely, unsure of whether the other loved them. Expressing how they felt changed each partner's perception of the other's behavior, and resulted in more carefully examining how they might try to more openly signal when they were feeling unheard or unappreciated rather than withdraw or attack the other.

As illustrated, shifting how one responds to a conflict may result in a tighter or a looser couple bond. According to Peterson (1983), a tighter bond is more likely to result when "highly important but previously unrecognized issues are discussed and *reconciled*" (emphasis added). This leads to each partner knowing more about the other, increasing trust and the ability to approach other unacknowledged issues in a more productive manner. For such structural improvement to result, "flexible rigidity" may be needed. Each person must be firm in asserting his or her own personal worth, yet also accepting of the other's qualities, even when they contrast with one's own values.

Follow-up stage

The final, follow-up stage could also be called the aftermath because it includes the subsequent reactions of partners following a conflict. The outcome may be either positive or negative. There may be a sense of increased closeness and commitment to the other and to the relationship as a result of the conflict experience. Or, the grudges, hurt feelings, or resentments may fester and seed increased alienation. **But there will always be more encounters in the future, so reconciliation, agreements, and impasses are all temporary and subject to revisiting and revising.**

Factors affecting couple conflict

Are some ways of resolving conflict more strongly associated with relationship distress than with satisfaction? Do men and women differ in the ways they deal with interpersonal conflict? Do couples change their ways of resolving conflicts over time or across particular situations? Finally, how does ethnicity affect a couple's conflict-resolution efforts? In this section we will examine current efforts to answer these questions.

Couple conflict styles

A number of fascinating attempts have been made to determine whether over time couples develop a preferred "fight style" or patterned way of resolving conflicts. Several researchers have reported that couples do develop a "fight style," that they develop it early in their relationship, and that they use it across a wide variety of conflict situations. For example, in their study of conflict in couples at an early stage of marriage, Raush and his associates (1974) reported that, even after only four months of marriage, each of the couples they studied seemed to intermesh as a unit and formed their own "style." Not only did both partners share a communication style (e.g., the pace at which they spoke, and length of speaking), they also shared a distinctive conflict-resolution style. In turn, these styles appear to be jointly constructed and maintained. Each couple's manner of dealing with conflict "remained quite consistent across time" (p. 204).

What do these "fight styles" look like? Recent investigators (Fitzpatrick, 1988c; Constantine, 1986; Gottman, 1994, 1998) have identified three distinctively different styles that *satisfied* couples use to handle conflicts: (a) a **competitive** style, (b) a **cooperative** one, and (c) an **avoidant** one (see Chapter 4). Couples using a **competitive** style (referred to by Fitzpatrick, 1988, as "independents") tend to value individual autonomy and avoid too much interdependence. They readily engage in conflict to resolve differences in terms of relative privileges and power. Those using a **cooperative** style (Fitzpatrick's "traditionals" or referred to by Constantine, 1986, as "closed") structure their relationship in terms of a great deal of physical and psychological sharing. These couples value interdependence of thought, routines, and actions and place a lesser value on individual autonomy than "independents" do. Thus, while they will engage in conflict, they would rather avoid it if possible, and tend to use rationality to limit conflict escalation. In contrast to both of these groups, partners using an **avoidant** style (Fitzpatrick's "separates" or Constantine's "synchronous") maintain a certain distance from people and problems, even those of their mate. They value predictability of routines and schedules, have more need for psychological space, and tend to avoid conflict to a significant degree. They tend to engage in role–task segregation rather than role sharing, and minimize conflict through denial and disqualification.

Conflict styles and relationship satisfaction

A number of researchers (Gottman, 1991; Raush et al., 1974; Ravich, 1972, 1985) examined how people in a committed relationship manage the inevitable differences that arise between them over time and what the costs and benefits of using a particular conflict resolution style are to each partner. Raush and his associates (1976) organized partners' responses to interpersonal conflict into three broad categories: (a) **cognitive** acts (entailing neutral actions, suggestions, and rational arguments) (b) **affiliative** acts (involving conciliation, attention to the emotional impact of the conflict on the other, or appeals to the other's investment in the relationship or sense of fair play) and (c) **coercive** acts (characterized by rejection of the other or personal attacks and intimidation of the other). These categories are depicted in Table 14.1.

Dissatisfied couples tend to consistently exchange many more coercive responses in conflicts than satisfied couples. In contrast, satisfied couples tend to use more affiliative and cognitive responses to resolve their conflicts. Looking closely at how distressed couples interacted during conflicts, Gottman and his associates (1998) reported that unhappy partners frequently engage in personal attacks and threats in attempting to get their way. Their partners respond with counter-threats and attacks that frequently *escalate* the conflict. Neither partner assumes responsibility for dampening the heat between them by using cognitive responses or collaborative approaches. Thus, one partner's negative, coercive remarks seemed to always be reciprocated by negative, coercive responses from the other. In contrast, satisfied couples use twice as many cognitive responses in their conflicts, as well as routinely use many more affiliative actions to deescalate or dampen the negativity of escalating conflicts (i.e., **positive sentiment override**). Moreover, husbands in satisfied marriages tended to acknowledge the wife's influence and worth in the relationship rather than to ignore or reject her influence.

Gottman and his associates (1998), as well as other researchers (Houts et al., 1996; Kurdek, 1994; Talmadge & Dabbs, 1990) have also observed that distressed couples consistently interpret each other's statements or motives as more negative than they are meant to be. Such couples often perceive that the other does not truly care about their wants or needs. Consequently they tend to interpret their partner's actions, even those which are positive, in a negative way, which *invalidates* their partner's efforts or ideas. For example, after having had an argument about the allocation of housekeeping chores the night before, one husband got up early to cook

TABLE 14.1. Types of couple conflict-resolution responses

COGNITIVE RESPONSES

1. **Opening an issue:** Opens an area for discussion or primes the other for a course of action (e.g., "There is something we need to talk about").
2. **Seeking factual information:** Attempts to find out factual information (e.g., "Tell me more").
3. **Giving factual information:** (e.g., "I'm finishing the dishes").
4. **Withholding information:** Concealing or disguising plans or feelings that the other wishes to know about (e.g., "I'm not telling. I've got a surprise.")
5. **Suggesting a course of action:** Proposing a plan of action either by means of a question or statement (e.g., "Let's stay home" or "How about going out to dinner").
6. **Agreeing with the other's statement:** (e.g., "Okay" or "M-hm").
7. **Giving cognitive reasons:** Providing reasons for a course of action either of one's own or one's partner's (e.g., "There are three reasons why we should do this").
8. **Exploring the consequences:** Examining the consequences of a course of action (e.g., "What will happen if we do __").
9. **Denying the validity of the other's argument:** Denying other's argument with or without use of counterarguments (e.g., "Yes, but . . . ", or "I see no reason for . . . ", or "I don't agree with that").

AFFILIATIVE RESPONSES
Reconciling responses

1. **Changing the subject:** Attempt to deal or effect a pause in the conflict by shifting the topic of conversation (e.g., "Let's talk about something else" or in the midst of an argument ask "Did you put the dog out?").
2. **Using humor:** Use humor to temper the conflict (e.g., "I'm going to trade you in").
3. **Accepting the other's plans, actions, ideas, motives, or feelings:** Indicate acceptance of what the other had said (e.g., "That's a good idea" or "You have a point there").
4. **Diverting the other's attention:** Redirecting other's attention as a maneuver to win one's point in an argument (e.g., "Where did you learn to argue so well" or "You're cute even when you're angry").
5. **Introducing a compromise:** As an attempt to include each person's aim in an overall solution (e.g., "I'll make a deal with you" or "Let's do it this way now. Next time we'll do it your way").
6. **Offering to collaborate in planning:** To offer to help adopt a solution or work together to plan a solution (e.g., "Let's work this out" or "Well, let's look at it both ways").

Resolving responses

1. **Avoiding blame or responsibility:** Partner acts to make the other realize "It's not my fault." or "I've no control over it." (e.g., "I didn't want to bring work home, but I can't help it" or "I didn't bring it up, he brought it up").
2. **Accepting the blame or responsibility:** Appealing for forgiveness or reconciliation (e.g., "I'm sorry" or "I admit I'm wrong").
3. **Showing concern for the other's feelings:** Exploring the other's affect or emotional investment in an issue/goal (e.g., "What's bothering you, honey?" or "Are you really satisfied?").
4. **Seeking reassurance:** Evoking reassurance from the other directly or indirectly (e.g., "You're not mad at me, are you?" "Forgive me?").
5. **Attempting to make up:** Trying to soothe or smooth over emotional differences, to restore good feelings in the relationship (e.g., "Maybe we are both wrong" or "Now give me a kiss, and let's forget it").
6. **Offering help or reassurance:** Assuring through word or gesture one's positive feeling toward the other (e.g., "So long as we can work it out, that's what counts . . . " or "Here—I'll help you with that").

TABLE 14.1. *Continued*

Appealing responses

1. **Appealing to fairness:** Attempting to obtain one's goal by appealing to the other's sense of fair play (e.g., "Do you realize I've had a busy day too?" or "We always do what you want to do").
2. **Appealing to the other's motives:** Attempting to convince the other of the benefits the other would achieve by accepting the sender's plans (e.g., "You'll really like this, dear" or "Doing __ would be of benefit to both of us").
3. **Offering something else as a way of winning one's goal:** Offering partner something in return for his agreement (e.g., "You won't get your present unless you do __").
4. **Appealing to the love of the other:** Exerting pressure on the other by capitalizing on the affiliate relationship (e.g., "Do it for me" or "If you love (respect, think well of) me, you will __").
5. **Pleading and coaxing:** Either passively (pleasing) or actively (coaxing and prodding) attempting to convince the other without making explicit the motivation to which the appeal is made (e.g., "Come on, honey, do it just this once").

COERCIVE RESPONSES

Rejecting responses

1. **Giving up or leaving the field:** Making statements such as "I give up" or "I quit" or "I'm going to bed" which are a genuine giving up rather than a tactic to force the other to give in to one's demands.
2. **Calling the other's hand:** Recognizing the other's move as a strategy or calling the other's bluff (e.g., "You're not going to get away with this!" or "You can't win that way" or, in response to one partner saying "I'm going to leave you" the other responds "I'll see you when you get back!").
3. **Rejecting the other person:** Signal you reject the other person versus the other's ideas (e.g., "I don't want to talk with you!" or "No, I would rather be alone").

Coercive responses or personal attacks

1. **Appeals to authority/correctness:** Using an outside authority or set of circumstances to force the other to agree (e.g., "The boss is expecting us" or "We said we would do this").
2. **Commanding:** Ordering or forcing the other to do what one wishes (e.g., "I don't care what you want. We're going to do __" or "Put that book down!").
3. **Demanding compensation:** Demands a price from the other for yielding on an issue (e.g., "I'll let you do what your way, but by damm you'll have to __").
4. **Inducing guilt or attacking the other's motives:** Putting the other on the defensive by attacking, revealing or interpreting the other's motives or behavior as not measuring up to a supposed ideal standard (e.g., "You don't really want to do __, you're just being spiteful (mean, stubborn)" or "You're doing things to upset me. You know I don't like this, but you do it anyway").
5. **Disparaging the other:** Attacking the person, or the character or talents of the other (e.g., "That's a stupid thing to say" or "You're acting like a dumb jerk").
6. **Threatening the other:** (e.g., "Just try and get away with this" or "If you keep acting this way, I'll leave").

Source: Summary of information found in Raush et al., 1974.

breakfast for his wife the next morning. However, the wife interpreted this as demonstrating his resentment of her sleeping in and not getting up to cook for him. Thus, the husband's conciliatory act became more ammunition for the wife in future conflicts.

On the other hand, satisfied couples operate as if they have "money in the bank" concerning their relationship with their partner. That is, even though a partner may say something upsetting or painful, the other interprets his or her partner's responses through a more favorable lens. In addition, satisfied partners repeatedly interpret their partners' motives as positive and affirm their partner's intentions and actions as a result (see also Chapter 12).

Another difference is that a number of dissatisfied couples demonstrate a pattern where one partner tries to avoid conflict completely and the other attempts to engage him or her in conflict (Christensen & Heavey, 1990; Heavey et al., 1995). This withdrawal from conflict where one partner provides no overt disagreement or conflict, always agreeable and compliant, was associated with marital deterioration over time. The usual pattern of this type is where one spouse attempts to open an issue for discussion (most frequently the wife), while the other (typically the husband) withdraws as a listener, a **pursuer–distancer** dance that Gottman (1991) calls **stonewalling**. That is when the listener is rigid or moves slightly and does not use typical listener responses, like nodding or vocalizations that indicate the listener is tracking. When the husband stonewalls in response to his wife's disagreement, he emotionally withdraws from the conflict. The wife then attempts to re-engage her husband. When she fails, she grows more critical and emotionally detached from him over time, and they begin to live separate emotional lives. This eventually results in a second stage where partners lead quite detached parallel lives: *"as if they were living side by side like two railroad tracks that run in the same direction but never touch . . . When both withdraw and are defensive, the marriage is on its way to separation and divorce."* (Gottman, 1991, p. 195, emphasis added).

The conflict style of these husbands may derive from their childhood learning about conflict resolution. Their only socialized method of conflicting involves threatening violence and such high emotional arousal that it is not entirely under rational control and also totally unsuited to dealing with women. Therefore, as men, they back away from open conflict with women until they are cornered in the task of maintaining their distance.

Gender Differences in Conflict Resolution

Although popular lore would have us believe that men and women differ greatly in how they communicate and deal with conflict, research on couples' conflict reveals a much more complicated picture in real life. In Chapter 12 we found that there are no significant gender differences in the ways men and women in satisfied marriages tend to respond to each other. In contrast, men and women in unhappy marriages engage in marital conflict in markedly different ways that are more gender specific (White, 1989). The findings of White's study that examined differences by gender in couples' patterns of communication during conflict are shown in Table 14.2.

According to White's results, while husbands and wives in the satis-

TABLE 14.2. Means of affiliative and coercive behavior scores exhibited by males and females, sorted on the basis of self or spouse marital satisfaction

Interactive behavior	Satisfied Husbands	Wives	Unsatisfied Husbands	Wives
Male affiliation	33.9	33.4	28.0	28.3
Male coerciveness	9.3	8.4	16.9	17.2
Female affiliation	28.0	30.5	38.1	36.0
Female coerciveness	18.2	15.5	14.4	17.0

Source: White, 1989.

fied group were fairly equally matched on the levels of coercive and affiliative statements they made, the husbands and wives in the dissatisfied group exhibited opposite strategies in response to conflict. Dissatisfied males were significantly more coercive than their wives, and dissatisfied females were significantly more affiliative, while their coercive behaviors remained at the same level as that of their husbands. Thus it appears that wives in dissatisfied relationships are typically more sensitive and responsive to their husband's messages during conflict than husbands are to them (White, 1989). In addition, wives tend to reciprocate their partners' positive and negative speech more than husbands do (Notarius & Johnson, 1982) and are much more likely than their partners to work to develop the topics raised by the other in conversation (Fishman, 1978).

Although the differences in how satisfied wives and husbands handle conflict are small, they do have areas of complementary behavior (Gottman et al., 1998; Kelley, 1979; Gottman & Krokoff, 1983; Rauch et al., 1974; Rubin, 1983). Many researchers have noted that, even among satisfied couples, wives initiate discussion about a conflict more often than their husbands do and tend to use emotional appeals. In turn, satisfied husbands tend to remain reasonable and calm when presented with conflict and use problem-oriented and conciliatory strategies in an attempt to resolve, postpone, or end the dispute. Wives, more than husbands, appear to determine the affective atmosphere of an argument by the way they start a conflict. Wives are usually the ones who build a climate of agreement, or more importantly, escalate or deescalate the conflict with their verbal and nonverbal negativity. However, husbands' messages and emotions make a crucial contribution to the course of the conflict in how they respond to their wives' messages and emotions.

The pivotal role of the wife in monitoring the relationship and *initiating conflict* is borne out in several other studies. Holtzworth-Munroe and Jacobsen (1985) contend that wives are always monitoring their relationship, whereas husbands only do so when things are not proceeding smoothly. In marriages that eventually ended in separation or divorce, women usually knew the relationship was in trouble long before their partners did (Hagestag & Smyer, 1980). Pearlin and Johnson (1977) reported that ignoring the unpleasant aspects of marriage was related to *reduced* psychological health for wives in their sample, but not for husbands. Other researchers have confirmed this pattern of women's greater involvement. Several researchers (Blumstein & Schwartz, 1983; Krokoff, 1987) report that wives tended to be more sensitive and responsive than their husbands to the distressing aspects of marriage, and therefore, were more likely than their husbands to bring up and confront an issue. A different study claims that both men and women saw the women as performing more negative behavior in a relationship than the men did (Orvis et al., 1976). These results were confirmed by Hendrick (1981), who found that, "although husbands and wives agreed on the problems that wives contributed to the marriage relationship, there was very low agreement on the problems that husbands contributed" (p. 206). One possible explanation for why both husbands and wives tended to see wives as "causing" the marital problems may well reside in the traditional sex roles in marriage. Wives have traditionally assumed responsibility for keeping marriages functioning smoothly and, thus, have often accepted a major share of the blame for marital problems.

In a study of married couples, Fitzpatrick (1988b) found that **distressed** husbands tended to attribute their own positive and negative behaviors during conflict to stable, internal causes. This attribution enabled them to take credit for positive behaviors and resist requests that they change negative behaviors because "it's just the way I am." In contrast, the husbands typically gave their wives little credit for positive behaviors and pushed their wives to change what they saw as malleable negative behaviors. Fitzpatrick suggested that this attribution process affords these distressed husbands a greater sense of control over interpersonal events. On the other hand, non-distressed husbands tended to make the same attributions about their wives that they made about themselves.

Consequently, although we may believe that many of the differences women and men display in their conflicts may be attributed to gender-specific modes of conflict resolution, it is noteworthy that satisfied partners do not fit this pattern. One might infer that these non-distressed couples have been able to move beyond the gender stereotypes reflected in the current social reality of the United States (as described in Chapter 7). To some extent, couple conflict-resolution patterns for distressed couples of male control and female affiliation and sensitivity to the health of the relationship reflect this social imbalance of power.

Another possible explanation for gender differences in conflict styles may be our cultural attitudes toward reason and emotion. Western culture teaches that reason is right, accurate, and realistic, while emotion is weak and often dangerous. Men are brought up to control their emotions, and even women may believe that getting upset means that they are causing problems. Both men and women can grow up believing that only reasonableness is a valid way to contend for truth and power, and that whoever gets emotional is confessing to the weaker argument and, therefore, deserves to lose.

Cross-cultural differences

It appears that what constitutes acceptable ways of communicating about marital problems varies across different cultures. Researchers discovered that Israeli couples living in the U.S.A. reported higher levels of expressing negative emotions such as anger or disagreement than did Anglo-Saxon American couples (Winkler & Doherty, 1983). However, although Anglo-Saxon couples were calmer and more reasonable in verbal behavior, Israelis were substantially less violent than the Americans. Surprisingly, the high level of negative emotions Israeli couples expressed was not associated with marital dissatisfaction or violence. In contrast, among the Americans, calm, reasonable communication was associated with higher marital satisfaction while more impulsive, angry behavior was associated with lower marital satisfaction.

One study examined cross-cultural differences in conflict resolution between satisfied and dissatisfied German and Australian couples and discovered striking cultural differences in the way couples responded to a negative comment by their partner (Halford, Hahlweg, and Dunne, 1990). Satisfied Australian couples tended to use affiliative responses in response to a negative comment (such as accepting or agreeing with it). However, while satisfied German couples used affiliative responses to a certain extent, they were much more likely to counter-refuse or criticize in response to a refusal than were the satisfied Australian couples. In addition, dissatisfied German couples most frequently counter-refused, while dissatisfied Australian couples provided neutral information. Thus, Australian couples, satisfied Australian couples in particular, were more likely to respond with positive or neutral responses to their partner's verbal negativity than were German couples.

Racial differences

Most research on couple conflict resolution has been conducted with white, middle class married couples, although some limited research (Crohan, 1996; Oggins, Veroff, & Leber, 1993) examining the effects of ethnicity on intimate relationships has been conducted. An analysis of the data from one of the few large surveys on conflict in which a significant number of African American couples were interviewed (Straus & Gelles, 1986, 1990; Stets, 1990) revealed that a larger proportion of African Americans engage in both physical and verbal aggression than whites do (Stets, 1990). This pattern held for both African-American women and men. In addition, African-American women reported inflicting higher rates of verbal and severe physical aggression than men did.

In considering these findings it is important to keep in mind that the majority of this sample of African-American respondents were from the lower socioeconomic class, and so, the findings are not reflective of African Americans in general. Class structural theory states that individuals of a lower socioeconomic class are more likely than upper-class individuals to experience frustration, stress, and strain, and, in response, aggression, regardless of race. Therefore, the differences in the use of verbal and physical aggression among white and African-American women and men in the studies cited may be due to both socioeconomic differences and racial minority issues.

Principles for resolving conflict constructively

Much time and attention has been devoted in recent years to assisting couples in learning how to resolve their conflicts more effectively. As a result, clinicians have developed a variety of approaches (Bach & Wyden, 1968; Fisher & Brown, 1988; Gottman et al., 1976; Guerney, 1977; Miller et al., 1975, 1991; Stuart, 1980) to help couples resolve their differences. Each approach seems to offer a combination of methods for helping couples change their **views** (on the nature of conflict, their partner actions/liabilities, and the conflict resolution process) as well as their **actions** (related to initiating conflicts) as a way to effectively resolve conflict. Among the first approaches were Bach and Wyden (1968), who emphasized the need for couples to consider the value of developing "fair fighting rules." They said that conflict is unavoidable. The difficulties people have come not so much from the conflict itself, nor even from the issues over which conflict arises, but from the failure to develop effective ways of resolving conflict. Thus, they stressed the need for couples to examine their own patterns of managing conflict and to bring these more under voluntary control by developing and adhering to rules that are more constructive for conducting their conflicts.

We will discuss a series of twelve principles that represent an integration of the conflict resolution methods developed by Bach and Wyden (1968) and other clinicians (see Table 14.3). Three assumptions are implicit in the formulation of these principles: (a) conflict and conflict resolution are not the same thing, (b) utilizing rational ways to resolve conflicts introduces a much-needed sense of control into a relationship, and (c) it is preferable that partners jointly decide to develop and try out a set of ground rules together.

Developing basic ground rules

We offer you a set of four basic ground rules that can help you and your partner acquire a more "rational" way of "controlling" the negative forms of conflict engagement. These are not the only way to effectively deal with conflict, but they can have a significantly beneficial effect on the quality of the relationship. These ground rules are as follows:

Complain with a spirit of good will and friendship. Can you trust each other, and not be afraid that you or your partner will exploit the other's

TABLE 14.3. Principles of constructive conflict resolution

Basic ground rules

1. Complain with a spirit of good will.
2. Admit your feelings.
3. Avoid attacking each other.
4. Elicit and validate the other's point of view.

Specific techniques

5. Select an appropriate time.
6. Be specific, focus on the here and now, and ask for a reasonable change.
7. Deal with one issue at a time.
8. Listen empathically.
9. Use a "stop action" rule.

Finding a solution

10. Think, explore, reflect.
11. Invent options for mutual gain.
12. Use objective criteria.

weaknesses? To build such a feeling of mutual trust, you must <u>first</u> be willing to view any problem or grievance that arises as a problem that belongs to the relationship and not to your partner. That is, it is important that you view the problem as something that you must both "unpack" and look at, with both of you sitting together on the same side of the table and trying to figure out what to do about it. See this as a process of joint control and problem-solving rather than attempt to demand what the other should do to correct the problem.

Second, you must consider that the aim of an argument or altercation is not agreement, but understanding and closeness. Most couples believe that their differences are settled by reaching agreement. Often, however, there are aspects of an agreement or accord about which either party has some reservations or that has been overlooked, which can fester and erupt at a later date. The true purpose of a discussion or argument should be for each person to understand the other's thoughts, feelings, wants, and needs more clearly. To do so means being willing to present your issues and to inquire into the other's thoughts and feelings.

Admit your feelings.   Both of you must be able to lay out your position in order for it to be accessible to problem resolution. This means that, as a first step, you must be open to telling your partner if something is bothering you. Too many exchanges between intimates sound like the following:

Tom: What's wrong?

Linda: Nothing!

Tom: But you're stomping around and acting mad. What's wrong?

Linda: If you don't know, there's no use telling you.

Even the most sensitive of partners is not a mind reader. Blaming your partner for not "knowing" encourages unproductive dialogue. Often you may not know what is really bothering you. It may be that your worries about work or discomfort brought on by illness or fatigue are displaced on your partner. Learning to sort out the components of an angry mood can often be difficult, but this is the first step toward dealing with it constructively rather than just exploding or letting the anger feed on itself.

As a second step, you must be willing to describe the stand you have taken without trying to sound right. Most of us normally try to sound right when we are angry. We have had all the years of our childhood to learn that angry confrontations are always about right and wrong. Whenever our parents showed anger at us, they let us know we were wrong in some way. So it is no wonder that whenever we get angry at our partner, we automatically assume that one of us (preferably ourselves) must be right, and the other must be wrong. However, in adult quarrels there is very little that is factually right or wrong. Most arguments are about what suits me and my beliefs, and therefore feels right, versus what suits you. According to affect theory (see Chapter 13), believing we are right helps us **avoid** feeling bad (shame affect) for being in disharmony with the other person. Furthermore, **attacking the other** for being wrong makes us feel strong. In sum, it is not surprising that we approach intimate conflict in these ways, even though the result is likely to be enduring resentment.

Therefore, after you express what first comes to your head, namely your righteous anger, you'll need to understand that your partner may feel just as righteous about being angry as you do. You will need to find and express the other feelings you have underneath in order to lead the discussion toward a more successful outcome for all. You must try to express your feelings rather than build a case for your point of view. If you can explain why you are afraid or what makes you uncomfortable rather than what you demand, this can make it much easier for your partner to join with you to resolve the issue.

Learning to talk clearly about your feelings can be difficult. One way to promote more honesty and clarity in your personal expression of your position is to use personal "I" statements (e.g., "I feel . . . ", "I need . . . ", "I am afraid . . . ", "I think . . . "). Such statements are self-representing and tell about you. However, be careful not to use opinionated "I" statements, such as "I think you should . . . ", "I feel you hurt me when . . . ". These are not useful because they indirectly attack or blame the other for your situation. The object is to discover and share your own feelings. Such a careful discussion of the feelings behind one's reactions requires some control that we do not always have and may sometimes need to approach conflicts.

Avoid attacking each other.   It is easy to find yourself "upping the ante" and attacking the character of your partner when he or she fails to hear your complaints, or to discount them "out of hand." Moreover, most partners have a collection of insults and sarcastic remarks that can be used to instantly dramatize the intensity of their feelings. However, sarcasm, insults, name-calling, and attacks on one's family or one's character elicit only feelings of anger and revenge, not cooperation. Once initiated, most attacks are met by counter-attacks, thus snowballing into a fight of increasing viciousness. The couple below depicts this process:

> Justin: (Opening his soft-boiled egg) Why in hell don't you ever put out napkins for breakfast?
>
> Sara: (Pouring coffee for Justin) Because it isn't necessary, I never spill anything on myself.
>
> Justin: (Getting madder) So what? I like to wipe my mouth after I eat.
>
> Sara: (Superior) No! That's not it at all. I know what it is. You just like to nag me!
>
> Justin: (Stops eating) That's ridiculous! You want to be nagged. That's why I can't get a goddamned napkin unless I yell about it.
>
> Sara: But don't you really like it?
>
> Justin: What, to wipe my mouth?
>
> Sara: (Losing her temper) No, you jerk, I mean yelling at me!
>
> Justin: (Getting up from the table, furious) Oh, to hell with it! I'm going to have breakfast at McDonald's. (He grabs his briefcase and leaves)
>
> Sara: (Yelling after him) You're totally insensitive to what I try and do for you. You just complain!

If Justin and Sara attempted to air their differences without attacking each other, it might sound something like this:

> Justin: (Annoyed) Honey, this may not be a big deal to you, but I would like to use a napkin with my meals. Would you mind laying one out for me? You too, if you want.
>
> Sara: (Primly) I didn't think we needed napkins. We're both neat.
>
> Justin: (Patient but firm) Well, you may be, but I would just like to use one.

Sara: But why?

Justin: I grew up with napkins laid out on the table, and I guess I'm really used to them. It meant the table was set right.

Sara: And so you're saying I don't set the table right.

Justin: No, I'd just like you to put out napkins.

Sara: Well, if it means that much to you. But why can't you put out your own napkin?

Justin: I guess I could do that.

In the first of these disagreements, each partner attempted to be **right** and to get his or her way. When their positions were not immediately met with agreement, they attributed all sorts of negative motives to each other and implied the other was to blame for their difficulties. The more the other resisted, the more each attempted to overwhelm the other with criticism. In the second conversation, the partners kept closer to the issue at hand and did not try to justify their position by attacking the other. In this process they exchanged information with each other, understanding more clearly what each wanted around the issue. Thus, both partners emerged winners. This principle, as well as the preceding one, is the essence of assertive communication. Table 14.4 summarizes the key steps in assertive communication.

Elicit and validate each other's point of view. Are you ready to listen as well as to complain? It is often very difficult to be willing to hear your partner's perspective on an issue, much less solicit it, but this is an essential part of good negotiation. Rather than attempt to "steamroll" your partner into seeing things the way you do or "tune out" when he or she has a grievance, you need to give each other an opportunity to be heard. To be open to practicing this it is important to keep in mind that no two people—no matter how much they love each other—perceive things the same way. We view the world through different glasses, and each person may define very differently what we may call the same thing (e.g., being thoughtful). Unless we acknowledge our different perceptions about ourselves, our partner, and our relationship in the present and future, these differences will interfere with conflict resolution (Fisher & Brown, 1988). To build a strong intimate relationship it pays to recognize that your partner and you will perceive the world differently.

In addition to soliciting your partner's point of view, it is important to accept it. The following statement from a 40-year-old man illustrates the value of accepting an intimate's feelings:

> *We've been married for fifteen years and have two children. One guide we have used for working out our differences is that when either of us has some feeling about something, we treat it as just valid as the other person's. For*

TABLE 14.4. Steps in assertive communication

I. **YOU NEED TO CONSIDER BEFORE YOU START THAT:**

1. **ASSERTING IS NOT CONTROLLING OUTCOMES**. Assertive communication is stating your own feelings and/or desires as clearly as possible, while insuring the other person's right to differ and letting go of your expectation of any particular outcome.

2. **ASSERTION IS DESIGNED FOR EQUAL POWER NEGOTIATION**. Assertive communication is designed for situations in which your cultural norms do not determine what you can and cannot do to get what you want, or in which you want to go against cultural norms. Assertiveness implies, and attempts to create, an interaction between two people with equal power. So when you do not want to endure punishment because of violating cultural norms, or because of presuming equal rights with someone who wields more power (such as a teacher or boss), you must express yourself more diplomatically than pure assertiveness would require.

3. **THERE MAY BE BARRIERS AND CONSEQUENCES**. It is important to consider your reasons for not wanting to assert yourself before going ahead. Besides feeling inhibited or lacking the skills, you may wish to behave unassertively because of religious beliefs, intense caring for or fear of losing the other person, fatigue, concern for your social acceptance, high probability of punishment, and lack of concern for the outcome. We may also consider short- and long-term effectiveness of assertive responses for maintaining or enhancing the relationship, as well as for your own self-respect. You are always risking the future of a relationship when you assert. You are risking your own happiness and peace of mind when you do not.

II. **WHEN YOU ARE GETTING STARTED YOU NEED TO REMEMBER TO:**

1. **SEPARATE YOURSELF**. In order to get in touch with your own feelings, you need to **separate** yourself from the emotional effects of the others involved. You may be so used to feeling within a "force-field" of what the other feels and wants, that you need to get both mentally and physically away from influence to find out what you really think and feel, instead of what you are supposed/used to thinking and feeling. This may mean responding to another's request with "I don't know, let me think about it," and going away for enough time to feel separate.

2. **DISCOVER YOUR FEELINGS**. In order to **discover your feelings** about an issue or situation, you can remember past instances and imagine what a future instance would be like. It may be useful to imagine facing the issue with someone you are not at all attached to or worried about, to see if your reactions are different from those you have toward the person actually involved. Once you know your feelings, you can proceed to what you want on the basis of those feelings and other concerns. Both what you would feel and want if you didn't care about the other's reaction and what you feel/want when you **do** care about the other's reaction may be equally important to formulating your assertive communication.

3. **SEPARATE FEELINGS FROM OUTCOMES**. Sometimes you don't know what you could want or are not sure what you feel. Asserting a feeling (such as "I really like you," "That makes me anxious," or "I'm confused") does not have to be attached to a desired outcome (such as "Squeeze me," "Stop it!" or "Tell me what's happening"). You can express a feeling (such as "I felt embarrassed, helpless, and lonely when you got drunk"), even when you are sure its implied desire ("Please control yourself") would be angrily rejected, as always. You can never be sure when or how someone will change, nor can you judge by the past that someone will never change. It is valuable to assert your own truth and being, even when you are sure it "won't do any good." At least the other will not forget how you feel.

Continued

TABLE 14.4. *Continued*

III. **WHEN YOU ARE ASSERTING AND INTERACTING BE SURE TO**:

1. **EXPRESS YOURSELF AND SUPPORT YOUR LISTENER'S FREEDOM**. Clearly express what you feel and/or want, while stating that the other's position counts for you in the eventual outcome of the issue. ("I don't know what you think, but I'm fed up with hamburgers every day").

2. **FOLLOW THROUGH**. If the other person does not respond adequately, or apparently agrees with you, but does not act on it, do not silently condemn him. Keep repeating the assertion until you are taken seriously. Nobody is perfect. There are at least 4 ways to follow through:

   a. **REPEAT YOUR INITIATIVE**: "I know you've heard this before, but . . . " Use humor, use notes; keep trying. Don't mind being called a nag: "I'm letting you know what is important to me, so that it becomes important to you too."

   b. If your patience wears out, **SHOW YOUR ANGER**. That may get the attention you didn't get before. But your anger should be directed *only at starting the negotiation*, not at winning or denigrating. (Appropriate: "Stop ignoring me and start dealing with my issue!" Inappropriate: "You never paid any attention before, so you can take it or leave it, my way, from now on!")

   c. If you have repeated verbal initiatives several times, and shown your anger (if you can do that), all without success, you can **WITHDRAW COOPERATION** in some significant way from your relationship. This stops business as usual and makes something go wrong for the other person. It can be dangerous, because you are intentionally sabotaging your cooperation. The activity, goods, or service you interrupt or sabotage should be important enough to compel attention, but not so devastating that the person goes crazy or escalations and reprisals overshadow the original issue. Examples of cooperation areas: cooking, paying bills, sex, cleaning, supportive words or actions.) Once your sabotage is noticed, you need to explain its purpose: "I'm sorry I had to do this to you, but I can't keep on cooperating with you until you start cooperating with me by dealing with my issue." You are threatening the relationship trust by violating your normal rules, so don't use this method very much, or you could permanently damage your partner's trust in you.

   d. Ultimately, you can **WITHDRAW COMPLETELY** from the relationship and say: "When you are ready to deal with my issue, give me a call." Or you can threaten to leave as an ultimatum. Every time you rock the relationship boat, termination becomes a possible consequence. Using this "ultimate weapon" even occasionally leads to a power-struggle, roller-coaster relationship in which passion is exaggerated by the threat of loss, and participants cannot do much else with their lives. So it is better to do this only once, when you really intend to leave.

3. **NEGOTIATE** with both people's desires in mind. Be flexible. You will discover what your bottom line is through trial and error. You can't know what will really work for you until you try it. So don't be embarrassed to **RENEGOTIATE** your resolutions after trying them out. Everybody is imperfect and changeable. (For example, one might say: "I was wrong about what I need. Let's rethink this"). Use the follow-through methods above when actions don't match agreements made.

---

example, I was the type of person who did not squeeze the toothpaste tube at the bottom, but would squeeze it any which way. That used to drive my wife crazy. There was no question of whether or not it **should** *drive her up the wall. It just did. So this is one way I gave in, and tried to remember to squeeze it from the bottom as she liked. I changed gradually because I knew it bothered her.*

Take time to explore what each of you is thinking and feeling without putting each other on the defensive by dictating how he or she should think or feel. As much as possible, avoid using the word "why." For most people, "why" is associated with overtones of blame and demands for justification. Consequently, it elicits defensiveness. Try to stick with the facts, rather than attribute motives to your partner or try to read your partner's mind. Focus on understanding your partner's perspective. Keep in mind that there is always more than one way to view reality. Thus, you can accept and explore your partner's point of view without having to change your own.

Specific techniques for resolving conflicts

Below are some techniques that people use to improve their conflict resolution skills.

Select an appropriate time. It is much more likely that your partner will be cooperative if you select a mutually convenient time to discuss a grievance. If you bring up a matter when one of you is angry, when nothing can be done about it (e.g., the middle of the night, right before guests are due, or when one of you is in the shower), or when concentration is impossible (e.g., when your partner is trying to study for an important exam or balance the checkbook), you minimize the chances of having a productive discussion. When your partner is fatigued, sick, or under special pressure, try to postpone dealing with the conflict. Unfortunately, irritation and conflict often emerge during such stressful circumstances, and a "hit-and-run" tactic is often commonplace. For example, Pete and Linda have just gotten into bed after attending a dinner party at his boss's house. It is 1:00 A.M. and he has to catch an early plane in the morning:

> Pete: (Interested in some sex with Linda) How about some fun before I leave?
>
> Linda: No. (Pulling away)
>
> Pete: Is something wrong?
>
> Linda: Yes! There are some things you do that I want to talk to you about!
>
> Pete: What?
>
> Linda: You always ignore me at these dinner parties! I'm left to fend for myself. It's as if you don't even want to be around me! What's the matter, aren't you proud of me?
>
> Pete: Whoa! What are you talking about? I take you to the party don't I?!
>
> Linda: But you just bring me in and spend the rest of the evening talking with everyone else. You pay much more attention to the other women there than to me!

Pete: Listen, I can't deal with this now. I've got a plane to catch early in the morning. Can't we deal with this some other time.

Linda: No, I want to settle this now. I'm hurt and angry with the way you treat me!

Pete: Linda, I'm not going to stay up half the night arguing with you about this now.

The argument continues to escalate as they argue not only about the inattention, but also the lack of agreement about when to discuss it. Unfortunately, when one feels hurt or angry with one's partner, it is tempting to deal with the issue right then (remember the adage "Never go to bed angry"). However, admitting that something is bothering you and making a mutual promise to discuss the problem at a later, better time can keep the argument from escalating. This gives both of you the time to reflect on your feelings, decide what needs to be said, and discuss the problem under better conditions. Setting up an appointment a short time in the future can give you an opportunity to eliminate as many distractions (e.g., the telephone, the television, other people) and immediate obligations (e.g., making dinner, minding the children) as possible. Conveying that you are willing to commit energy to working out your differences goes a long way toward improving the situation and providing hope that a solution can be found.

Be specific, focus on the here and now, and ask for a reasonable change. To convey effectively to your partner what is upsetting about his or her behavior, you need to be specific about what is making you angry or upset. Be as concrete as possible and avoid making generalizations. Rather than assume that your partner knows what you mean by your complaint, you need to be very specific about what you want him or her to do. Thinking about what is making you angry, and focusing on the specific actions, feelings, and attitudes you are experiencing in the anger-producing situation helps make your complaint more understandable to your partner.

Hudson and O'Hanlon (1991) encourage their clients to use "videotalk" as a way of being specific and concrete. Videotalk means not going beyond describing what one could see or hear on a videotape of the situation. It is an alternative to using vague words that are open to different interpretations or telling other people one's interpretations of the situation. Couples often generalize about their partners in ways that trigger defensiveness and prevent understanding, and videotalk is a way to focus on what the situation looks or sounds like without interpretation. For example, a wife complains that her husband "never" engages in loving behavior and that he "always" seems preoccupied by his work and outside interests. When her husband counters by saying that was not true and that "just the other day I heard you drive in and went out and helped you carry in your groceries!" she responds with, "Anyone can carry in groceries, that's not being loving!" In order for him to meet her expectations, she needs to pinpoint what *specific* actions would be evidence of loving behavior in her mind and to work out a way of attaining these together.

It is also important to focus your complaint on here-and-now behavior. Do not bring in issues and grievances from the past. Dredging up the past usually confuses the issue at hand by serving as ammunition for convincing the person that you are right. Neither of these tactics makes your partner more open to your point of view. Ask yourself the question, "Are you prepared to confine yourself to the here-and-now and not to delve into the past?"

Finally, it is important to consider what really is upsetting you. What do you really want from your partner? Often a person explodes at his or her partner with little understanding of what he or she really wants changed. The person berates his or her partner about how awful things are but does not have in mind a concrete action for changing things. In fact, most unfocused criticism impedes the progress toward a constructive solution. If a problem requires change, talk about your feelings of needing to come to some solution and elicit your partner's help in trying to solve the problem. Give him or her a chance to voice his or her own ideas. A college woman living with her boyfriend described the following:

> Tom and I were both in school and working. But somehow I ended up doing most of the cooking and cleaning. I found myself exhausted and angry and felt I had the lion's share to do. I began to resent the fact that Tom did not do more and began to criticize him for being sloppy. Finally, during one of our fights, I said I was tired of doing the housework and really needed some help. We spoke about the situation, and Tom offered to prepare some of the meals and help with some of the housecleaning. As a result, I feel a lot more loving toward him.

Keep in mind that what you suggest might be the start of some ideas of how things can change or be improved. Focus on your interests and needs, not your position. Do not rigidly cling to your idea. See what else might emerge.

Deal with one issue at a time. You can deal more effectively with conflict if you focus on one grievance at a time and avoid other topics. This sounds simple enough, but it is not what usually happens. Most people greatly fear getting embroiled in conflicts with their partner, so they put off letting their partner know what is irritating them until they can no longer contain their irritation. This process is called "**gunnysacking**" by clinicians (Bach & Wyden, 1968; Gottman et al., 1976). It results when one or both partners store up many unexpressed

resentments because they do not want to "rock the boat" when things are going well and because they tend to ignore dissatisfaction when feeling good. Then when a fight erupts, the sack is suddenly opened and dumped out. Rather than dealing just with the issue at hand, every other irritation and hurt that they have not verbalized up to this point may be brought out. Overloaded with grievances, the partners often become confused and angry, feeling the situation is hopeless. To avoid this situation, couples counselors suggest that it is important as a long-range strategy to regularly "clear the air" with one's partner. As a short run strategy, it is important to ask oneself "What is really bothering me?" "Is this issue that might seem somewhat trivial actually related to something very important?"

Another way to accept gunnysacking or holding back on complaints might be to consider it as normal behavior in most relationships (couples, families, workplace, friendships, etc.). Therefore, when someone dumps out all of his or her grievances, we could refrain from criticizing that person for storing them up. Instead, we could say: "Hey! That's a lot of complaints all at once! I didn't know you were still bothered by all that. But we can only deal with a few things now. What's really important to you right now?" The rest of the list can be brought up at another time or allowed to recede back into the gunnysack. *But at least both people now know what is inside.*

Listen empathically.   Most clinicians consider good listening skills a cornerstone of effective conflict management. Thus, much of what we addressed in the chapter on communication concerning efforts to "share self" and to listen empathically to one's partner are valuable ingredients for effective conflict resolution. If you recall, empathic listening requires that you listen without judging and try to hear the feelings behind a remark. This entails hearing accurately what the other is saying and responding by acknowledging that you heard those feelings. Comments such as "I can tell you are angry" or "I am hearing you say that I did not listen to what you wanted," indicate that you are attempting to understand your partner's experience, rather than thinking "How can I best shut this down (so it doesn't get worse!)." In the following exchange, Tom is not listening empathically to Ann:

> Ann: I'm furious that you agreed for John and Martha to use our cottage on the Fourth of July weekend. Why didn't you consult me?

> Tom: I didn't think we would be out there that weekend, and I knew it would just be empty.

Ann: But how did you know I didn't want to make plans for us to be out there?

Tom: Well, we haven't had time to be out there the last two months, what with you working so much. Why was that weekend going to be any different?

Ann: Now you are going to lay a guilt trip on me about my working! You're avoiding the question!

In the exchange above, neither Ann nor Tom are attempting to understand "where their partner is coming from" (i.e., what they are concerned about and want the other to do differently). Attempting to listen empathically to what the other person is saying can help resolve such differences rather than escalate them:

Ann: I'm furious that you agreed for John and Martha to use our cottage on the Fourth of July weekend. Why didn't you consult me?

Tom: You sound angry. Want to talk about this?

Ann: Yes, I was upset when I heard you agree to let John and Martha use the cottage, because I wanted us to go out there that weekend.

Tom: Gee, I didn't know you had that in mind. That would have been nice. I guess I assumed that you would be working again that weekend and we wouldn't be able to plan anything.

Ann: But that's just the point! I know we haven't had much time together and I really miss it. I had wanted that to be a time the two of us could just relax and play.

Tom: I'm sorry I made you feel angry. I agree we have to talk about it, because I don't want to do that to you, but I obviously have done it this time. Let's talk about it again on Saturday morning to see what we can do about it.

The second conversation between Tom and Ann goes in a completely different direction when Tom signals his willingness to hear Ann's feelings about the incident. Instead of increasing the sense of resentment and distance between them, acknowledging Ann's feelings and signaling his willingness to listen lets Ann reveal many of her feelings behind her initial anger. Asking questions to draw out the other person, giving feedback by restating what your partner has said, and checking out your assumptions as to what they mean or feel by their statements are all ways in which you signal to your partner that you are listening to what he or she is saying.

Use a "stop action" rule.   Conflicts often become so heated that listening to each other's position is not possible. To function in such times, it is useful to develop a "stop action" rule—where you and your partner agree to call a time-out during your discussion to cool things down. You may stop and decide to set a later time to talk further about the issue. Or you may decide to stop and wait until each of you has calmed down before deciding on a time when you can get back together to resolve the issue. It is important **not** to see that as a withdrawal or stalling tactic. You and your partner need to return to the issue at some time and try to resolve it in order to maintain your trust that this is not a stall tactic. Many couples have "stop action" moves already choreographed into their conflict behavior (see the section on Conciliation earlier in this chapter). But even if you do not, you can agree to introduce them for your future arguments.

Finding a solution

It is often difficult when one is in the midst of a disagreement to think of alternative ways of resolving the disagreement. The following three principles are useful for building effective solutions:

Think, explore, and reflect.   Have you learned something about your partner or yourself from your conflict that you did not know before? Has all the information related to an issue been explored? Have you identified the true issue and are not doing battle about a trivial matter that is camouflaging a deeper grievance? What do you really want to see changed? It is important to examine your own feelings and thoughts about what your partner has said as well as what you have said to him or her. You may often need time to figure out what to do and may not be able to come up with a solution together right away. Would thinking about an issue and finishing the discussion in a day or two be helpful? Often taking time to reflect alone or together on possible solutions to the problem is helpful. This particular principle is a key "damage-control strategy." You may wish to review the others depicted in the Damage-Control Kit (Table 14.5).

Invent options for mutual gain.   In a conflict, we all believe that we know the right answer and that our solution should be adopted. Often the only creative solution is to suggest a compromise that, unfortunately, leaves neither partner satisfied. This occurs when partners think of negotiating along only one dimension. However, there are a number of dimensions to consider that can lead to different options for resolving a couple's difficulty. Regrettably, these options are usually not readily evident to either partner. Partners end up like the proverbial sisters who quarreled over an orange. After the sisters finally agreed to divide the orange in half, the first sister took her half, ate the fruit, and threw away the peel, while the other threw away the fruit and used the peel from her half in baking a cake. All too often, partners end up with half an orange for each side instead of the whole fruit for one and the whole peel for the other. Why? First, most people assume that there is one best solution and that discussing multiple options only confuses things. Second, most people see the world as "win/lose" rather

TABLE 14.5. Damage-control kit for couple conflicts.

Type of damage	Response tool* (with sample phrasing)
Avoiding issues and confrontation; Minimizing or stonewalling.	Ask for an appointment time to deal with issues. Repeat initiatives until response is adequate for progress. Be proud of the "Nag" label.
Silent treatment (as punishment)	Allow some recovery time (e.g., 1 day). Then use humor, or initiatives, and ask for an appointment time.
Sarcasm or sniping (nonconfrontive unconnected stinging comments).	"I feel stung/attacked by you. What's bothering you?" "What can I do to make you happier?"
"Hit and run" (hostile remark on the way out the door).	Later: "What did you mean by that last remark? Is something bothering you?"
Passive-aggressive sabotage: No anger, but accidental getting even.	"I'm boiling over what you did (or didn't do). Were you disappointed or irritated about that matter, or about some other aspect of our relationship?"
Undermining your anger: Being superreasonable, emotionally hurt, or fearful, or prematurely apologizing or (apparently) giving in.	"I'm mad now, so don't distract me and hear me out." "Don't fix it or flip out until I'm finished." "Your apology is not enough, until you **understand** what bothers me and what I want you to do about it."
Inappropriate timing (e.g., bedtime)	Make an appointment for the earliest convenient time.
"Gunnysacking" (dumping many stored-up complaints all at once in an argument).	"It's important to know what all is bothering you. But let's work on the **most important** issue now and note down the others for later." Focus on issues most tied to current feeling state, and others may shrink as emotionally connected, but merely past landmarks.
Magnifying minor irritations or arguing over everything.	Someone may need time free, or irritations may symbolize a long standing unresolved issue or power struggle. "Is there some common thread in all these issues of something that bothers you about our relationship?" If it is an unchanging power struggle, you and your partner may benefit from external intervention and counseling.
"Vesuvius" type sudden outbursts and anger.	These may be ventilating anger from sources outside your relationship. After the exploder has simmered down, discuss sources and ways to either reduce the outbursts, or keep them from being too intimidating–such as keeping safe distance and eliminating verbal and physical threats.
Competitive arguing: Win/lose or right/wrong struggles.	"I don't think one of us is **right** and the other **wrong** on this issue. I want to understand what feels right and wrong to you and get you to understand what feels right and wrong to me. I want us both to **win** this argument if we can find a way."

Continued

TABLE 14.5. *Continued*

Type of damage	Response tool* (with sample phrasing)
"Low blows" (Name calling, and statements that drive someone out of control and thus derail the process of mutual listening and understanding	After tempers have calmed, bring up the offending actions, and say: "That makes me so upset and hurt that I can't deal with anything else. Whether you mean it or not, it hits me like a low blow. So please don't use that in an argument. Did I do or say anything that hits you that way?" (e.g. We may want to discuss our embarrassing shadow-qualities or our behavioral similarity to a disliked relative at some time, but **not** during an argument.)
Ultimatums ("If you don't shut up, give in, etc.), I'll never speak, see you, etc. again."	Treat like low blows: "It makes me crazy when you threaten to end it. So please don't use that on me. Do you really feel that way? Let's figure out what we can do about your feeling."
Emotional escalation: Trading accusations and insults.	Use **stop action and conciliation**: "Wait! This is getting out of hand! We're just hurting each other. You're too important to me to ruin things over this argument. I must be partly responsible for this problem. Let's cool down a little and start listening to each other."
Physical violence.	Ultimatums are in order (e.g. "If I can't be certain that I will never be touched violently again, I have to get out of the relationship to protect myself.") Involve public authorities to deter repetition. If it happens again, or alcohol is involved, get away from the scene and get professional help.
A pattern of intimidation through violence, threats of violence, explosiveness, and/or rigid control.	Get enough authorities, friends, and family involved to provide for safety and leave. Involve the police. If your behavior with your partner may contribute to escalation, stop it.
Repeating clashes over the same issue that don't lead to changes but instead poison mutual respect and harmony.	Redefine the problem in a broader way, to include more aspects of life, so that an integrative resolution could combine them and/or initiate change in relationship rules and structure. Or encapsulate the problem as an incompatibility and insulate it with mutual respect and humor.

* These are not the only or the best methods of coping with the danger of the conditions listed. They reflect current cultural norms and psychological thinking. For consideration of your own unique personalities and conditions, consult with local social services or mental health professionals.

than "win/win." Why bother to invent if all the options are obvious and I can satisfy you only at my own expense? It is important for the partners to look with an eye towards mutual gain. To do this requires talking about one's wants and needs, identifying common ones and pinpointing differing ones. Consider the couple, Tom and Susan, described earlier in the chapter who were discussing a career move. They looked carefully at what might be various dimensions of the solution and considered how to dove-tail their various interests.

Use objective criteria. Are there some standards or procedures (e.g., of fairness, efficiency, communal benefit, etc.) by which you can evaluate the merits of the resolution at which you arrive? The more you and your part-ner are able to agree to standards by which you judge your methods for resolving a conflict, the more likely you are to produce a solution with which both of you can live. What kinds of standards can be applied to judging the value of a solution? You might want to consider resources in-vested, such as time, money, or thought. Potential payoffs and rewards should also be considered. However, some life-changing issues, such as childbearing or psychological development, have a powerful **non-rational** motivation for many people. In this case, the rational, objective criteria may organize, but cannot completely contain, the life-changing experience being considered.

What if it does not work?

Research indicates that when highly aroused physiologically, people are not able to use empathic listening and negotiation skills very much (Gottman et al., 1998). Under high arousal, one's mental processing ability narrows down to habitual ways of coping with threatening circumstances. So you need to know that you are not a failure when you are too upset to use the guidelines we have described here. Just remember three things, in the midst of conflict or afterwards:

1. Your partner is just like you, with a genuinely human personal his-tory, thoughts, and feelings. These lead him or her to the desires and expressions that you cannot understand or appreciate during the heat of an argument.
2. After you calm down you can still apologize for your hurtful ac-tions and show your partner the respect you also want for yourself.
3. Remember that *every scene in a couple's life is connected to an endless chain of prior and subsequent encounters*. So there are potentially many more opportunities to approach a resolution, to minimize the damage of uncomfortable differences, and to revise your ways of dealing with conflicts.

It is **not** essential that you **never get too angry** to follow constructive guidelines. Instead, the key to containing couple conflict is to develop hab-its for interrupting emotional escalation and reconnecting with positive feelings. Once we restore our faith and good will toward each other we can resume effective negotiation and problem solving.

Chapter summary

- Conflict is defined as an interpersonal process that occurs whenever the actions and desires of one person interfere with the actions and desires of another.
- Conflict is a process consisting of: a prior conditions stage, a frustration awareness stage, an active engagement or avoidance stage, a conflict-ending stage, and a follow up stage.
- Conflicts can end in: separation, domination and submission, compromise, integrative agreements, and structural improvement.
- In contrast to distressed couples, satisfied couples consciously deescalate conflict to facilitate problem resolution.
- Rather than one "good" style, there are at least three different conflict resolution styles among satisfied couples:(a) competitive (volatile), (b) cooperative (validating), and (c) avoidant (minimizing).
- The most distinctive gender differences in conflict resolution style are demonstrated by distressed couples, in which men avoid and are inexpressive and women pursue and initiate more.
- Although cross-cultural studies of conflict reveal couple differences in emotional expressiveness, our limited evidence on racial differences in America suggests that black/white differences may be due to class, power, and culture.
- Practical approaches to constructive conflict style emphasize developing basic ground rules and using conciliation, pausing, and positive sentiment override to deescalate emotionality.

Conclusion

What is love?

Let us summarize some of the main explanations and theories about romantic love discussed in this book. We have approached love through the concepts of *attraction, passion, intimacy, commitment,* and *attachment.* Attraction may arise from excitement, shyness, or other emotional arousal; from beauty or features similar to previous romantic or familial loves; and from unusual or intimate situations. Out of attraction may arise passion, with its yearning and separation distress, its obsessive focus on and idealization of the partner, and the altered state of being together, along with its emotional fulfillment through intimate gaze, touch, and sharing, as well as sex. Love may grow through developing intimacy as behavioral closeness and sharing in various (but usually not all) areas of experience. Commitment to love is an act of will, but other cognitive aspects may include developing "we-ness" and shared ways of viewing life and the world. Because of some unconscious inclusion of the partner as a part of oneself, cultural love myths and personal images of lover roles and love stories may serve as unexamined guidelines for relating. The maturing of love may bring a gradual lowering of passionate intensity and the development of milder emotions of attachment in two or three years, which foster child rearing and family cohesion more than passion. In fact, serial monogamy and polygamy are also fulfilling, because new attraction has a rejuvenating effect and new passion can be more potent than enduring attachment.

What have we learned about satisfying relationships?

We cannot give you a manual for successful relationships, as you will find in many popular relationship books. We don't want to forget the scientifically neutral methods employed in researching this book and declare how good relationships *should* be. But we will select some of the many aspects that have been discussed, which might help you conduct the kind of relationships you yourself want to have.

The idealization involved in romantic attraction is a support for relationship longevity, if we can preserve it *next to* a more realistic image of our partner that respects his or her faults (Chapters 1, 4, 10). Having experience with a lot of partners may make it more difficult to idealize any one of them who doesn't have more "best" aspects than all the rest.

The tug-of-war of relationship loyalties includes friends and ex-partners with whom we have some remaining romantic (or hostile) feelings. Also included are parents, who may continue as either supportive or rival attachments for a lifetime, depending on the needs and intimate sharing both the parent(s) and grown son or daughter have with each other (Chapters 2, 11). While there is no best way to experience sex in intimacy, performance attitudes can interfere with the pleasure, comfort, and caring that are its most common meanings.

While separation distress after breaking up may indicate that we really love our expartner, it does little to help painful or dysfunctional relationships improve. It is valuable to learn as much as we can from each breakup (Chapter 3), but some painful lessons about what to do or avoid may be not as applicable to future partners as we expect.

Relationship satisfaction derives from the sum of both positive and negative aspects of our relationships. These two "piles" may normally be considered separately or even partially ignored, depending on how we feel (Chapter 4). So remember the positive before you dwell too long on feeling negative. Find out what your partner considers rewarding and increase it without being asked. When your "we-ness" is low and your sense of separateness and distrust high—in the contraction stage or on the road to divorce (Chapter 5)—remember to consider family, community, and life-cycle aspects of your life, as well as couple satisfaction. And remember that couples regularly move beyond to greater acceptance even after years of bitterness and estrangement.

Divorce recovery and new love are normal, but are often slowly developing processes (Chapter 5). Post-divorce cooperation between parents and their individual relationships with children are important for the children's well-being (Chapter 6).

Expecting love relationships to fail is as naive as expecting them to "just come natural" and last forever. Pay attention to the pursuer-distancer dance and ask if your motivation for either pursuing or distancing might be to maintain control over your feeling and your relationship (Chapter 2, 6, 13). Though dramas of control versus closeness may make passion run high, allowing the partner equal control builds more trust. And love is *not* controllable anyway.

Recognize the differences between you and your partner, whether based on gender role expectations; on sensory, cognitive, and emotional awareness and functioning; or on the uniqueness of your sensitivity and family experience (Chapters 7, 9, 10, 11). Since we may unconsciously include our partner in ourselves, we may naively assume that our partner is and does just like us (by projection of "we-ness"). Or if he or she is *different*, that shock means either the partner is defective or we are. We can extend our awareness of being human by attempting to understand what our partner feels, thinks, and does—and thus remove the shame-based assumption that somebody must be *right* and somebody *wrong* whenever a painful difference exists. For example, men must be insensitive and minimize everything emotional, except what affects their sex or power. Women, however, make emotional mountains out of molehills and bypass facts to perceive relational meanings where there are none.

Be aware of the potential for crises during the second, third, and fourth years of togetherness, when many relationships begin to shift their emotional basis from predominantly passion toward more mild attachment (Chapter 9). Discover how cultural myths and your gender role expectations about sex and love may influence your adaptation to this shift (Chapters 7, 10).

Talk or write about your arguments after they happen, so you can develop more awareness of what happens and move toward a conflict style that is compatible—even though not "comfortable"—for both partners (Chapters 4, 14).

Discover what types of intimacy you want to share with your partner and what you would keep for yourself or other relationships (Chapter 10). Find ways to balance your intimacy needs with contact with others and your own self-actualization. Fairness may be a narrower standard for satisfying relationships than a communal interest in both partners' personal development and self-actualization.

Explore both your own and your partner's predominant family paradigms and personal relating styles in tense situations. Then consider ways to broaden your repertoire of expectations and behavior (Chapter 11). Consider ways to extricate yourself from triangular relationships that may interfere with your one-to-one relationship with your partner—and solicit your partner's feeling about the triangle as well.

Whenever you think your partner is implying a negative nonverbal or relational message (in a double message), check it out with him or her (Chapter 12). This can stop negative assumptions about each other from building up. Disclose your thoughts, feelings, and personal history to build intimacy in the early years of a partnership, but consider and respect your reasons for being reluctant to share all of yourself as well.

Emotions are central in relationships, but what they are and how they work are just beginning to be studied. Expect to find kernels of truth in both emotion and reason—and respect them equally (Chapter 13). Awareness of the dynamics of shame affect and its family of emotions may be a skeleton key for opening up a wide variety of interpersonal emotional phenomena. This awareness may lead us toward more conscious emotional coping and more intended outcomes in all relationships. When you experience jealousy, look for several personal and relationship issues underneath, and treat them with respect. Understand the wide spectrum of anger experience, from bound-up or repressed to dramatic or violent. Broaden or change your repertoire of expression and develop your anger dance with your partner.

Develop the ability to express conciliation statements in the thick of a conflict (Chapter 14) or override the negativity with some positive interpersonal sentiment so that you and your partner can deescalate conflict on both the content and emotional levels. Agreeing on some rules for fair fighting can help keep your differences from poisoning your intimate rapport.

Future journeys of the heart

We have seen in Chapters 5, 7, and 9 that changing economic conditions and diversifying roles for women beyond child rearing have shifted marital roles toward equal power and flexible responses to employment and financial conditions. These contemporary forces in the United States have also lowered birth rates, increased divorce rates, and supported the growth of serial monogamy and stable singlehood.

Thus, there are now not one but several major paths for journeys of the heart to follow. In addition to the three main heterosexual paths, gay, lesbian, and bisexual relationship paths can be similar, include multiple romances, or other alternative, more polysexual patterns. Gays and lesbians have done a lot to create communities of mutual support and have thus begun to restore the communalism that has withered in the face of industrialization and modernization.

As we each pursue one or more of these paths in the course of our lives, we are collectively gathering the experience to *reinvent* couple relationships. While some of us want our paths to converge toward increasing intimacy, other pursue parallel paths of coordinated effort or potentially divergent paths of self-actualization. By experimenting with these convergent, parallel, and divergent paths of the heart, we may discover many new insights and develop new strategies for being in relationships. Our present profusion of different paths might contribute to our evolution, for diversity of cultures and flexible adaptation to environment and society are essential strengths of human nature. And when we have room for multiple perspectives on reality and many approaches to living, we set the stage for creative innovations in cultural design that no single perspective could foresee. Therefore, many of us may experience turmoil, excitement, and new discoveries in our lifetime of relationships that we cannot even imagine today.

References

Abbey, A., McAuslan, P., & Ross, L. T. (1998). Sexual assault perpetration by college men: The role of alcohol, misperception of sexual intent, and sexual beliefs and experiences. *Journal of Social and Clinical Psychology, 17*(2), 167–195.

Abelin, E. L. (1980). Triangulation, the role of the father and the origins of core gender identity through the rapprochement subphase. In R. Lax, S. Bach, & J. Burland (Eds.), *Rapprochement* (pp. 151–167). New York: Jason Aronson.

Ables, B. S., & Brandsma, J. M. (1984). *Therapy for couples. A clinician's guide for effective treatment.* San Francisco: Jossey-Bass.

Acitelli, L. K., Douvan, E., & Veroff, J. (1993). Perceptions of conflict in the first year of marriage. How important are similarity and understanding? *Journal of Social and Personal Relationships, 10*, 5–19.

Ackerman, B. P., Abe, J. A., & Izard, C. E. (1998). Differential emotions theory and emotional development: Mindful of modularity. In M. F. Mascolo & S. Griffin (Eds.), *What develops in emotional development?* (pp. 85–108). New York: Plenum.

Acklin, M. W., Bibb, J. L., Boyer, P., & Jain, V. (1991). Early memories as expressions of relationship paradigms: A preliminary investigation. *Journal of Personality Assessment, 57*(1), 177–192.

Ade-Ridder, L., & Brubaker, T. (1983). The quality of long term marriages. In T. Brubaker (Ed.), *Family relationships in later life* (pp. 21–30). Beverly Hills, CA: Sage.

Adams, J. M., & Jones, W. H. (1997). The conceptualization of marital commitment: An integrative analysis. *Journal of personality and social psychology, 72*, 1177–1196

Afifi, W. A., & Burgoon, J. K. (1998). "We never talk about that"; A comparison of cross-sex friendships and dating relationships on uncertainty and topic avoidance. *Personal Relationships, 5*(3), 255–272.

Ahrons, C. R. (1994). *The good divorce: Keeping your family together when your marriage falls apart.* New York: Harper-Perennial.

Ahrons, C. R., & Rodgers, R. H. (1987). *Divorced families: A multidisciplinary developmental view.* New York: W. W. Norton.

Ahrons, C. R., & Wallisch, L. S. (1986). The relationship between former spouses. In S. Duck & D. Perlman (Eds.), *Close relationships: Development, dynamics, and deterioration* (pp. 269–296). Beverly Hills, CA: Sage.

Ahrons, C. R., & Wallisch, L. S. (1987). Parenting in the binuclear family: Relationships between biological and stepparents. In K. Pasley & M. Ihinger-Tallman (Eds.), *Remarriage and stepparenting: Current research and theory.* New York: Guilford.

Ainsworth, M. D. S. (1989). Attachments beyond infancy. *American Psychologist, 44*(4), 709–716.

Ainsworth, M. D. S., Blehar, M. C., Waters, E., & Wall, S. (1978). *Patterns of attachment: A psychological study of the strange situation.* Hillsdale, NJ: Lawrence Erlbaum.

Alapack, R. J. (1984). Adolescent first love. *Studies in the Social Sciences, 23,* 101–117.

Aldous, J. (1978). *Family careers: Developmental change in families.* New York: John Wiley & Sons.

Alexander, R. D., Hoogland, J. L., Howard, R. D., Noonan, K. M., & Sherman, P. W. (1979). Sexual dimorphisms and breeding systems in pinnipeds, ungulates, primates, and humans. In N. A. Chagnon & W. Irons (Eds.), *Evolutionary biology and human social behavior: An anthropological perspective.* North Scituate, MA: Duxbury Press.

Allen, J. B., Kenrick, D. T., Lindner, D. E., & McCall, M. A. (1989). Arousal and attribution: A response facilitation alternative to misattribution and negative-reinforcement models. *Journal of Personality and Social Psychology, 57,* 261–270.

Allen, M., & Burrell, N. (1994, May). *Comparing the impact of homosexual and heterosexual parents on children: Meta-analysis of existing research.* Paper presented at the conference of International Network on Personal Relationships, Iowa City, Iowa.

Altman, I., & Taylor, D. (1973). *Social penetration.* New York: Holt, Rinehart, Winston.

Amato, P. R. (1987). Family processes in one-parent, stepparent, and intact families: The child's point of view. *Journal of Marriage and the Family, 49,* 327–337.

Altman, I., Vinsel, A. & Brown, B. A. (1981). Dialectic conceptions in social psychology: An application to social penetration and privacy regulation. In L. Berkowitz (Ed.), *Advances in experimental social psychology, vol. 14.* New York: Academic Press.

Amato, P. R. (1991). Parental absence during childhood and depression in later life. *The Sociological Quarterly, 32,* 543–556.

Amato, P. R. (1993). Children's adjustment to divorce: Theories, hypotheses, and empirical support. *Journal of Marriage and the Family, 55,* 23–39.

Amato, P. R. (1996). Explaining the intergenerational transmission of divorce. *Journal of Marriage and the Family, 58,* 628–640.

Amato, P. R., & Booth, A. (1991a). Consequences of parental divorce and marital unhappiness for adult well-being. *Social Forces, 69,* 895–914.

Amato, P. R., & Booth, A. (1991b). The consequences of divorce for attitudes toward divorce and gender roles. *Journal of Family Issues, 12,* 305–322.

Amato, P. R., & Keith, B. (1991a). Parental divorce and the well-being of children: A meta-analysis. *Psychological Bulletin, 11,* 26–46.

Amato, P. R., & Keith, B. (1991b). Separation from a parent during childhood and adult socioeconomic attainment. *Social Forces, 760,* 187–206.

Amato, P. R., & Rogers, S. J. (1997). A longitudinal study of marital problems and subsequent divorce. *Journal of Marriage and the Family, 59,* 612–624.

American Association of University Women. (1991a). *Expectations and aspirations: Gender roles and self-esteem.* Washington, DC: Greenberg-Lake Analysis Group.

American Association of University Women. (1991b). *Shortchanging girls, shortchanging America.* Washington, DC: Author.

American Psychiatric Association. (1994). *Diagnostic and statistical manual of mental disorders* (4th ed.). Washington, DC: Author.

Anderson, K. K. (1990). Intimacy, fusion, and relationship quality of women in lesbian and heterosexual relationships. (Doctoral dissertation, Oklahoma State University, 1990.) Dissertation Abstracts International, 50, 4814B.

Anderson, K. L. (1997). Gender, status, and domestic violence: An integration of feminist and family violence approaches. *Journal of Marriage and the Family, 59,* 655–669.

Anderson, P. B. (1996). Correlates of college women's self-reports of heterosexual aggression. *Sexual Abuse Journal of Research and Treatment, 8*(2), 121–131.

Antill, J. (1983). Sex role complementarity vs similarity in married couples. *Journal of Personality and Social Psychology, 45,* 145–155.

Archer, J. (1991). The influence of testosterone on human aggression. *British Journal of Psychology, 82,* 1–28.

Arditti, J. A. (1991). Child support noncompliance and divorced fathers: Rethinking the role of paternal involvement. *Journal of Divorce and Remarriage, 14*(3–4), 107–119.

Arendell, T. (1997). Divorce and remarriage. In T. Arendell (Ed.), *Contemporary parenting: Challenges and issues* (pp. 154–195). Thousand Oaks, CA: Sage.

Argyris, C., & Schon, D. (1978). *Organizational learning: A theory of action perspective.* Reading, MA: Addison-Wesley.

Aries, E. J., & Olver, R. R. (1985). Sex differences in the development of a separate sense of self during infancy: Directions for future research. *Psychology of Women Quarterly, 9,* 515–532.

Armistead, L., Forehand, R., Beach, S. R. H., & Brody, G. H. (1995). Predicting interpersonal competence in young adulthood: The roles of family, self, and peer systems during adolescence. *Journal of Child and Family Studies, 4*(4), 445–460.

Aron, A., Ain, R., Anderson, J. A., Burd, H., Filman, G., McCallum, R., O'Reilly, E., Rose, A., Stichmann, L., Tamari, Z., Wawro, J., Weinberg, L., & Winesauker, J. (1974). Relationships with opposite-sexed parents and mate choice. *Human Relations, 27,* 17–24.

Aron, A., & Aron, E. (1986). *Love and the expansion of self: Understanding attraction and satisfaction.* New York: Hemisphere.

Aron, A., & Aron, E. (1991, May). Motivational structures of types of unrequited love. Paper presented at the conference of the International Network on Personal relationships, Normal/Bloomington, IL.

Aron, A., & Aron, E. (1994). Love. In A. Weber & J. H. Harvey (Eds.), *Perspectives on close relationships* (pp. 131–152). Boston: Allyn & Bacon.

Aron, A., Aron, E. N., Tudor, M., & Nelson, G. (1991). Close relationships as including other in the self. *Journal of Personality and Social Psychology, 60*(2), 241–253.

Aron, A., Dutton, D. G., Aron, E. N., & Iverson, A. (1989). Experiences of falling in love. *Journal of Social and Personal Relationships, 6,* 243–257.

Aron, A., Paris, M., & Aron, E. N. (1995). Falling in love: Prospective studies of self-concept change. *Journal of Personality and Social Psychology, 69*(6), 1102–1112.

Aron, E. N., & Aron, A. (1996). Love and expansion of the self: The state of the model. *Personal Relationships, 3*(1), 45–58.

Aron, E. N., & Aron, A. (1997). Sensory-processing sensitivity and its relation to introversion and emotionality. *Journal of Personality and Social Psychology, 73*(2), 343–368.

Aseltine, R. H., Jr. (1996). Pathways linking parental divorce with adolescent depression. *Journal of Health & Social Behavior, 37*(2), 133–148.

Aune, K. S., Buller, D. B., & Aune, R. K. (1996). Display rule development in romantic relationships: Emotion management and perceived appropriateness of emotions across relationship stages. *Human Communication Research, 23*(1), 115–145.

Avioli, P. S., & Kaplan, E. (1992). A panel study of married women's work patterns. *Sex Roles, 26,* 227–242.

Bach, G. R., & Wyden, P. (1968). *The intimate enemy.* New York: Morrow.

Bader, E., & Pearson, P. T. (1988). *In quest of the mythical mate: A developmental approach to diagnosis and treatment in couples therapy.* New York: Brunner/Mazel.

Bagarozzi, D., & Anderson, S. (1989). *Personal, marital and family myths: Theoretical formulations and clinical strategies.* New York: Norton.

Bailey, J. M., & Benishay, D. S. (1993). Familial aggregation of female sexual orientation. *American Journal of Psychiatry, 150,* 272–277.

Bailey, J. M., & Pillard, R. C. (1991). A genetic study of male sexual orientation. *Archives of General Psychiatry, 48,* 1089–1092.

Bailey, J. M., Pillard, R. C., Neale, M. C., & Agyei, Y. (1993). Heritable factors influence sexual orientation in women. *Archives of General Psychiatry, 50,* 217–223.

Baker, J. G., & Fishbein, H. D. (1998). The development of prejudice towards gays and lesbians by adolescents. *Journal of Homosexuality, 36*(1), 89–100.

Baldwin, D. V., & Skinner, M. L. (1988). Structural model for antisocial behavior: Generalization to single-mother families. *Developmental Psychology, 25*(1), 45–50.

Ball, F. L. , Cowan, P. & Cowan, C. P. (1995). Who's got the power? Gender differences in partner's perception of influence during marital problem-solving discussions. *Family Process, 34,* 303–321.

Balswick, J., & Peek, C. (1971). The inexpressive male: A tragedy of American society. *The Family Coordinator, 20,* 363–368.

Banks, A., & Gartrell, N. K. (1995). Hormones and sexual orientation: A questionable link. *Journal of Homosexuality, 28*(3/4), 247–268.

Barber, N. (1998). Sex differences in disposition towards kin, security of adult attachment, and sociosexuality as a function of parental divorce. *Evolution and Human Behavior, 19,* 125–132.

Barkley, T. J., & Procidano, M. E. (1989). College-age children of divorce: Are effects evident in early adulthood? *Journal of College Student Psychotherapy, 4*(2), 77–87.

Barkow, J. H. (1989). *Darwin, sex, and status: Biological approaches to mind and culture.* Toronto: University of Toronto Press.

Barkow, J. H. (1991). Precis of Darwin, sex and status: Biological approaches to mind and culture. *Behavioral and Brain Sciences, 14,* 295–334.

Barnett, O. W., Martinez, T. E., & Bluestein, B. W. (1995). Jealousy and romantic attachment in maritally violent and nonviolent men. *Journal of Interpersonal Violence, 10,* 473-486.

Barnhill, L. (1979). Healthy family processes. *Family Coordinator, 28,* 94–100.

Bart, P. B., & O'Brien, P. H. (1985). *Stopping rape: Effective avoidance strategies.* New York: Pergamon.

Baruch, G. K., & Barnett, R. C. (1986). Consequences of fathers' participation in family work: Parents' role strain and well-being. *Journal of Personality and Social Psychology, 51,* 982–983.

Baucom, D. H. ,& Adams, A. N. (1987). Assessing communication in marital interaction. In K. D. O'Leary (Ed.), *Assessment of marital discord: An integration for research and clinical practice* (pp. 139–181). Hillsdale, NJ: Lawrence Erlbaum.

Baumeister, R. F., & Wotman, S. R. (1992). *Breaking hearts: The two sides of unrequited love*. New York: Guilford Press.

Bavelas, J. B., Black, A., Lemmery, C. R., & Mullett, J. (1987). Motor mimicry as primitive empathy. In N. Eisenberg & J. Strayer (Eds.), *Empathy and its development* (pp. 317–338). New York: Cambridge University Press.

Baxter, L. A. (1983). Relationship disengagement: An examination of the reversal hypotheses. *Western Journal of Speech Communication, 47*, 85–89.

Baxter, L. A. (1984). Trajectories of relationship disengagement. *Journal of Social and Personal Relationships, 1*, 29–48.

Baxter, L. A. (1986). Gender differences in the heterosexual relationship rules embedded in break-up accounts. *Journal of Social and Personal Relationships, 3*, 289–306.

Baxter, L. A. (1990). Dialectical contradictions in relationship development. *Journal of Social and Personal Relationships, 7*(1), 69–88.

Baxter, L. A. (1991, May). *Thinking dialogically about personal relationships*. Invited address to the conference of the International Network on Personal Relationships, Bloomington, IL.

Baxter, L. A., & Bullis, C. (1986). Turning points developing romantic relationships. *Human Communication Research, 12*(4), 469–493

Baxter, L. A., & Wilmot, W. W. (1985). Taboo topics in close relationships. *Journal of Social and Personal Relationships, 2*, 253–269.

Beard, C., Harris, B., Kurzweil, N., & Monsour, M. (1993, June). *An empirical investigation of challenges confronting cross-sex friendships*. Paper presented at the conference of the International Network on Personal Relationships, Milwaukee, WI.

Beattie, M. (1987). *Codependent no more: How to stop controlling others and start caring for yourself*. New York: Harper & Row/Hazelden.

Beavers, W. A., & Lewis, R. (1985). *No single thread*. New York: Guilford.

Beck, T. A. *Cognitive therapy in the emotional disorders*. New York: International Universities Press.

Becker, G. S. (1986). *A treatise on the family*. Cambridge, MA: Harvard University Press.

Becker, G. S., Landes, E., & Michael, R. T. (1977). An economic analysis of marital instability. *Journal of Political Economy, 85*, 1141–1187.

Begley, S. (1993, June 28). The puzzle of genius. *Newsweek, 121*(26) 46–51.

Begley, S. (1995, March 27). Gray matters. *Newsweek, 125*(13), 48–54.

Belcastro, P. A. (1982). A comparison of latent sexual behavior patterns between raped and never raped females. *Victimology, 7*, 24–230.

Bell, A., & Weinberg, M. (1978). *Homosexualities: A study of diversity among men and women*. New York: Simon & Schuster.

Bellis, M. A., & Baker, R. R. (1990). Do females promote sperm competition? Data for humans. *Animal Behaviour, 40*(5), 997–999.

Belsky, J. (1997). Attachment, mating, and parenting. An evolutionary interpretation. *Human Nature, 8*(4), 361–381.

Bem, S. L. (1993). *The lenses of gender: Transforming the debate on sexual inequality*. New Haven, CT: Yale University Press.

Ben-Ari, A. T. (1998). An experiential attitude change: Social work students and homosexuality. *Journal of Homosexuality, 36*(2), 59–71.

Benenson, J. F., & Benarroch, D. (1998). Gender differences in responses to friends' hypothetical greater success. *Journal of Early Adolescence, 18*(2), 192–208.

Berg, J. H., & McQuinn, R. D. (1986). Attraction and exchange in continuing and noncontinuing dating relationships. *Journal of Personality and Social Psychology, 50,* 942–952.

Berger, C. R., & Bell, R. A. (1988). Plans and the initiation of social relationships. *Human Communication Research, 15*(2), 217–235.

Berger, R. M. (1990). Passing: The impact on the quality of same-sex couple relationships. *Social Work, 35,* 328–332.

Berk, S. (1985). *The gender factory: The apportionment of work in American households.* New York: Plenum.

Berliner, D. L., Monti-Bloch, L., Jennings-White, C., & Diaz-Sanchez, V. (1996). The functionality of the human vomeronasal organ (VNO): Evidence for steroid receptors. *Journal of Steroid Biochemistry and Molecular Biology, 58*(3), 259–265.

Berman, & Leif, (1975). Marital therapy from a psychiatric perspective: An overview. *American Journal of Psychiatry, 132*(6), 583–592.

Berman, W. H., & Turk, D. C. (1981). Adaptation to divorce: Problems and coping strategies. *Journal of Marriage and the Family, 43*(1), 179–189.

Bernard, J. (1972). *The future of marriage.* New York: Free.

Bernard, J. (1981). The good provider role: Its rise and fall. *American Psychologist, 36,* 1–12.

Bernard, J. L., Bernard, S. L., & Bernard, M. L. (1985). Courtship violence and sex-typing. *Family Relations, 34,* 573–576.

Berry, D. F., & Marks, F. (1969). Antihomosexual prejudice as a function of attitudes toward own sexuality. *Proceedings of the 77th Annual Convention of the American Psychological Association, 4,* 573–574.

Berscheid, E. (1986). Mea culpas and lamentations: Sir Francis, Sir Isaac, and "the slow progress of soft psychology." In R. Gilmour & S. Duck (Eds.), *The emerging field of personal relationships.* Hillsdale, NJ: Lawrence Erlbaum.

Berscheid, E., & Peplau, L. A. (1983). The emerging science of relationships. In H. H. Kelley, E. Berscheid, A. Christensen, J. H. Harvey, T. L. Huston, G. Levinger, E. McClintock, L. A. Peplau, & D. R. Peterson (Eds.), *Close Relationships* (pp. 1–19). New York: W. H. Freeman.

Berscheid, E., & Walster, E. (1974). A little bit about love. In T. Huston (Ed.), *Foundations of interpersonal attraction* (pp. 355–381). New York: Academic Press.

Berscheid, E., Walster, E., & Campbell, R. (1972). *Grow old along with me.* Unpublished manuscript, Department of Psychology, University of Minnesota.

Betcher, K., & Pollack, W. (1993). *In a time for fallen heroes: The recreation of masculinity.* New York: Guilford.

Bettelheim, B. (1977). *The uses of enchantment: The meaning and importance of fairy tales.* New York: Random House.

Betzig, L. (1989). Causes of conjugal dissolution: A cross-cultural study. *Current Anthropology, 30,* 654–676.

Bhugra, D., & de Silva, P. (1998). Dimensions of bisexuality: An exploratory study using focus groups of male and female bisexuals. *Sexual & Marital Therapy, 13*(2), 145–157.

Biblarz, T. J., & Raftery, A. E. (1993). The effects of family disruption on social mobility. *American Sociological Review, 58,* 97–109.

Bilge, & Kaufman, G. (1983). Children of divorce and one-parent families: Cross-cultural perspectives. *Family Relations, 32,* 59–71.

Billingham, R. E., & Notebaert, N. L. (1993). Divorce and dating violence revisited: Multivariate analyses using Straus's conflict tactics subscores. *Psychological Reports, 73,* 679–684.

Billings, A. (1979). Conflict resolution in distressed and non-distressed married couples. *Journal of Consulting and Clinical Psychology, 47,* 368–376.

Bisagni, G. M., & Eckenrode, J. (1995). The role of work identity in women's adjustment to divorce. *American Journal of Orthopsychiatry, 65*(4), 574–583.

Bjorklund, D. F., & Kipp, K. (1996). Parental investment theory and gender differences in the evolution of inhibition mechanisms. *Psychological Bulletin, 120*(2), 163–188.

Black, L. E., & Sprenkle, D. H. (1991). Gender differences in college students' attitudes toward divorce and their willingness to marry. *Journal of Divorce and Remarriage, 14*(3–4), 47–60.

Blanck, R., & Blanck, G. (1968). *Marriage and personal development.* New York: Columbia University Press.

Blau, P. M. (1964). *Exchange and power in social life.* New York: Wiley.

Blood, R. O., & Wolfe, D. M. (1960). *Husbands and wives: The dynamics of married living.* New York: Free.

Blos, P. (1979). *The adolescent passage: Developmental issues.* New York: International Universities Press.

Blumstein, P. W., & Schwartz, P. (1976). Bisexuality in men. *Urban Life, 5,* 339–358.

Blumstein, P. W., & Schwartz, P. (1977). Bisexuality: Some social psychological issues. *Journal of Social Issues, 33,* 30–45.

Blumstein, P. W., & Schwartz, P. (1983). *American couples: Money, work and sex.* New York: William Morrow.

Blumstein, P. W., & Schwartz, P. (1990). Intimate relationships and the creation of sexuality. In D. McWhirter, S. Sanders, Y. J. Reinisch (Eds.), *Homosexuality/ heterosexuality.* New York: Oxford University Press.

Boase, R. (1977). The origin and meaning of courtly love: A critical study of European scholarship. Manchester, UK: Manchester University Press.

Bogolub, E. B. (1991). Women and mid-life divorce: Some practice issues. *Social Work, 36,* 429–433.

Bohannon, P. (1970). The six stations of divorce. In P. Bohannon (Ed.), *Divorce and after* (pp. 29–55). Garden City, NY: Doubleday.

Bohannon, P. (1970a). *Divorce and after.* Garden City, NY: Doubleday.

Bolgar, R., Zweig-Frank, H., & Paris, J. (1995). Childhood antecedents of interpersonal problems in young adult children of divorce. *Journal of the American Academy of Child and Adolescent Psychiatry, 34*(2), 143–150.

Booth, A., & Edwards, J. N. (1989). Transmission of marital and family quality over the generations: The effect of parental divorce and unhappiness. *Journal of Divorce, 13*(2), 41–58.

Booth, A., Brinkerhoff, D. B., & White, L. K. (1984). The impact of parental divorce on courtship. *Journal of Marriage and the Family, 46,* 85–94.

Borg, J. G. (1997). Are differences between twins a result of mutual rivalry? *Acta Geneticae Medicae et Gemellologiae: Twin Research 46*(1), 23–36.

Borg, S., & Lasker, J. (1981). *When pregnancy fails.* Boston: Beacon Press.

Bott, E. (1971). *Family and social networks* (2nd ed.). New York: Free.

Botwin, M. D., Buss, D. M., & Shackelford, T. K. (1997). Personality and mate preferences: Five factors in mate selection and marital satisfaction. *Journal of Personality, 65*(1), 107–136.

Boulding, K. (1962). *Conflict and defense: A general theory.* New York: Harper.

Bowen, M. (1978). *Family therapy in clinical practice.* New York: Jason Aronson.

Bowlby, J. (1969). *Attachment and loss: Vol. 1. Attachment*. New York: Basic Books.

Bowlby, J. (1973). *Attachment and loss: Vol. 2. Separation*. New York: Basic Books.

Bowlby, J. (1980). *Attachment and loss: Vol. 3. Loss, sadness, and depression*. New York: Basic Books.

Bozett, F. (1987). Children of gay fathers. In F. Bozett (Ed.), *Gay and lesbian parents* (pp. 38–57). New York: Praeger.

Bradbury, T. N., & Fincham, F. D. (1990). Attributions in marriage: Review and critique. *Psychological Bulletin, 107*, 3–33.

Bradshaw, J. (1988). *Healing the shame that binds you*. New York: Health Communications.

Brady, S., & Busse, W. J. (1994). The gay identity questionnaire: A brief measure of homosexual identity formation. *Journal of Homosexuality, 26*(4), 1–22.

Braiker, H. B., & Kelly, H. H. (1979). Conflict in the development of close relationships. In R. L. Burgess & T. L. Huston (Eds.), *Social exchange in developing relations* (pp. 135–168). New York: Academic Press.

Brannock, J. C., & Chapman, B. E. (1990). Negative sexual experiences with men among heterosexual women and lesbians. *Journal of Homosexuality, 19*, 105–110.

Braverman, L. (1991). The dilemma of housework: A feminist response to Gottman, Napier, and Pittman. *Journal of Marital and Family Therapy, 17*(1), 25–28.

Bray, J., Williamson, D., & Malone, P. (1984). Personal authority in the family system: Development of a questionnaire to measure personal authority in intergenerational family processes. *Journal of Marital and Family Therapy, 10*, 167–178.

Bray, J. H., & Hetherington, E. M. (1993). Families in transition. *Journal of Family Psychology, 7*, 3–8.

Brehm, S. (1985). *Intimate relationships*. New York: McGraw-Hill.

Brehm, S. S. (1988). Passionate love. In R. J. Sternberg & M. L. Barnes (Eds.), *The Psychology of Love* (pp. 232–263). New Haven, CT: Yale University Press.

Brehm, S. S. (1992). *Intimate relationships* (2nd ed.). New York: McGraw-Hill.

Broderick, C. (1984). *Marriage and the family*. Englewood Cliffs, NJ: Prentice-Hall.

Brody, L. R., & Hall, J. A. (1993). Gender and emotion. In M. Lewis & J. M. Haviland (Eds.), *Handbook of emotions* (pp. 447–460). New York: Guilford Press.

Brown, L. M., & Gilligan, C. (1992). *Meeting at the crossroads: Women's psychology and girl's development*. Cambridge, MA: Harvard University Press.

Brown, N. M. (1993). Conversation topics among casual and serious daters. Unpublished data.

Brown, N. M. (1993a). What do students talk about in relationships? Unpublished raw data.

Brown, N. M. (1999). *Love relationships of children of divorce: How are they different?* Doctoral dissertation at Union Institute, Cincinnati, OH.

Brown, M., & Amoroso, D. M. (1975). Attitudes toward homosexuality among West Indian male and female college students. *Journal of Social Psychology, 97*, 163–168.

Browne, K. G., Saunders, D. G., & Staecker, K. M. (1997). Process-psychodynamic groups for men who batter: A brief treatment model. *Families in Society, 78*(3), 265–271.

Browning, F. (1993). *The culture of desire*. New York: Vintage Books.

Bruess, C. J. S., Dellinger, C., & Sahlman, J. (1993, June). *"I'll mow the grass; you fix dinner": Engaged couples' expectations of task sharing in marriage*. Paper presented at the conference of the International Network on Personal Relationships, Milwaukee, Wisconsin.

Brussoni, M., Jang, K. L., BacBeth, T. M., Clark, M., & Livesley, W. J. (1996, June). *Nature and nurture in adult attachment relationships: A twin study.* Poster session presented at the conference of the International Network on Personal Relationships, Seattle, WA.

Bryson, R. B., Bryson, J. B., Licht, M. H., & Licht, B. G. (1976). The professional pair: Husband and wife psychologists. *American Psychologist, 31,* 10–16.

Buckle, L., Gallup, G. G., & Rodd, Z. A. (1996). Marriage as a reproductive contract: Patterns of marriage, divorce, and remarriage. *Ethology and Sociobiology, 17,* 363–377.

Buhrich, N., Bailey, J. M., & Martin, N. G. (1991). Sexual orientation, sexual identity, and sex-dimorphic behaviors in male twins. *Behavior Genetics, 21,* 75–96.

Bumpass, L. L., Martin, T. C., & Sweet, J. A. (1991). The impact of family background and early marital factors on marital disruption. *Journal of Family Issues, 12*(1), 22–42.

Burger, A. L., & Jacobson, N. S. (1979). The relationship between sex role characteristics, couple satisfaction, and couple problem-solving skills. *American Journal of Family Therapy, 7,* 52–60.

Burgess, E., & Locke, H. (1960). *The family: From institution to companionship* (2nd ed.). New York: American.

Burgoon, J. K., Buller, D. B., Hale, J. L., & deTurck, M. A. (1984). Relational messages associated with nonverbal behaviors. *Human Communications Research, 10*(3), 351–378.

Burie, P., & Zecevic, A. (1967). Family authority, marital satisfaction and the social network in Yugoslavia. *Journal of Marriage and the Family, 29,* 325–336.

Burke, R. J., Weir, T., & Harrison, D. (1976). Disclosure of problems and tensions experienced by marital partners. *Psychological Reports, 38,* 531–542.

Burleson, B. R., & Denton, W. H. (1992). A new look at similarity and attraction in marriage: Similarities in social-cognitive and communication skills as predictors of attraction and satisfaction. *Communication Monographs, 59,* 259–268.

Burleson, B. R., & Denton, W. H. (1997). The relationship between communication skill and marital satisfaction: Some moderating effects. *Journal of Marriage and the Family, 59*(4), 884–902.

Burr, W. R., Day, R. D., & Bahr, K. S. (1993). *Family Science.* Pacific Grove, CA: Brooks/Cole.

Bursik, K. (1990). Correlates of women's adjustment during the separation and divorce process. *Journal of Divorce and Remarriage, 14*(3/4), 137–162.

Bursik, K. (1991). Adaptation to divorce and ego development in adult women. *Journal of Personality and Social Psychology, 50,* 300–305.

Buscaglia, L. F. (1986). *Loving each other.* New York: Fawcett.

Buss, D. M. (1989). Sex differences in human mate preferences: Evolutionary hypotheses tested in 37 cultures. *Behavioral and Brain Sciences, 12,* 1–49.

Buss, D. M. (1992). Mate preference mechanisms: Consequences for partner choice and intrasexual competition. In J. H. Barkow, L. Cosmides, & J. Tooby (Eds.), *The adapted mind: Evolutionary psychology and the generation of culture* (pp. 249–266). New York: Oxford University Press.

Buss, D. M. (1994) *The evolution of desire.* New York: Basic Books.

Buss, D. M., Abbott, M, Angleitner, A., Asherian, A., et al., (1990). International preferences in selecting mates: A study of 37 cultures. *Journal of Cross-cultural Psychology, 21*(1), 5–47.

Butcher, K. H., Campbell, V. L., Drake, B. J., Utermark, T. L., & Raiff, G. W. (1998).

Relationships with parents and college women's dating motivation and romantic exploration. Paper presentation at the conference of the International Network on Personal Relationships, Oxford, OH.

Byers, E. S., & Heinlein, L. (1989). Predicting initiations and refusals of sexual activities in married and cohabiting heterosexual couples. *Journal of Sex Research, 26,* 210–231.

Byne, W. (1995). Science and belief: Psychobiological research on sexual orientation. *Journal of Homosexuality, 28,* 303–344.

Byne, W. (1996). Biology and homosexuality: Implications of neuroendocrinological and neuroanatomical studies. In R. P. Cabaj & T. S. Stein (Eds.), *Textbook of homosexuality and mental health* (pp. 129–146). Washington, DC: American Psychiatric Press.

Byrne, D. & Blaylock, B. (1963). Similiarity and assumed similarity of attitudes between husbands and wives. *Journal of Abnormal and Social Psychology, 67*(6), 636–640.

Cacioppo, J. T., & Tassinary, L. G. (Eds.). (1990). *Principles of psychophysiology: Physical, social, and inferential elements.* New York: Cambridge University Press.

Cahn, D. D. (1990). Intimates in conflict: A research review. In D. D. Cahn (Ed.), *Intimates in conflict: A communication perspective* (pp. 1–22). Hillsdale, NJ: Lawrence Erlbaum.

Campagna, A. F. (1985–1986). Fantasy and sexual arousal in college men: Normative and functional aspects. *Imagination, Cognition, and Personality, 5,* 3–20.

Campbell, J., & Moyers, W. (1988). *The power of myth.* New York: Viking.

Canary, D. J., & Cupach, W. R. (1988). Relational and episodic characteristics associated with conflict tactics. *Journal of Social and Personal Relationships, 5,* 305–325.

Capellanus, A. (1184/1941). *The art of courtly love* (J. J. Parry, Trans.). New York: W. W. Norton.

Cappella, J. N., & Palmer, M. T. (1990). Attitude similarity, relational history, and attraction: The mediating effects of kinesic and vocal behaviors. *Communication Monographs, 57,* 161–183.

Carlson, J. G., & Hatfield, E. (1992). *Psychology of emotion.* New York: Harcourt Brace Jovanovich.

Caron, S. L., & Ulin, F. (1997). Closeting and the quality of lesbian relationships. *Families in Society: The Journal of Contemporary Human Services, 78,* 413–419.

Carter, E., & McGoldrick, M. (1989). *The changing family life cycle.* (2nd ed.) Boston: Allyn Bacon.

Cass, V. (1996). Sexual orientation identity formation: A Western phenomenon. In R. P. Cabaj & T. S. Stein (Eds.), *Textbook of homosexuality and mental health* (pp. 227–251). Washington, DC: American Psychiatric Press.

Cass, V. C. (1984). Homosexual identity: A concept in need of a definition. *Journal of Homosexuality,* 105–127.

Cass, V. C. (1990). The implication of homosexual identity formation for the Kinsey model and scale of sexual preference. In D. McWhirter, S. Sanders, & Y. J. Reinisch (Eds.), *Homosexuality/heterosexuality.* New York: Oxford University Press.

Cate, R. M. (1991, May). *Relationship thinking: A measure and some initial studies.* Paper presented at the conference of the International Network on Personal Relationships, Bloomington, IL.

Cate, R. M., Henton, J., Koval, J., Christopher, F. S., & Lloyd, S. A. (1982). Premarital abuse: A social psychological perspective. *Journal of Family Issues, 3,* 79–90.

Cate, R. M., Huston, T. L., & Nesselroade, J. R. (1986). Premarital relationships: Toward the identification of alternative pathways to marriage. *Journal of Social and Clinical Psychology, 4*(1), 3–22.

Cate, R. M., & Lloyd, S. A. (1992). *Courtship*. Newbury Park, CA: Sage.

Cazenave, N. (1979). Middle income black fathers: An analysis of the provider role. *Family Coordinator, 32,* 341–350.

Centers for Disease Control. (1993, February). HIV/AIDS surveillance report: Year-end edition, U. S. AIDS cases reported through December 1992. Washington, DC: Author.

Cheek, J. V. P., & Malamuth, N. M. (1983). Sex role stereotyping and reactions to depictions of stranger versus acquaintance rape. *Journal of Personality and Social Psychology, 45*(2), 344–356.

Cherlin, A. J. (1992). *Marriage, divorce and remarriage* (2nd ed.). Cambridge, MA: Harvard University Press.

Chick, D., & Gold, S. R. (1987–1988). A review of influences on sexual fantasy: Attitudes, experience, guilt, and gender. *Imagination, Cognition, and Personality, 7*(1), 61–76.

Chiriboga, D. A., Catron, L. S., & Associates (1991). *Divorce: Crisis, challenge or relief?* New York: New York University Press.

Chiriboga, D., Catron, L., & Weller, P. (1987). Childhood stress and adult functioning during marital separation. *Family Relations, 36,* 163–167.

Chodorow, N. (1978). *The reproduction of mothering: Psychoanalysis and the sociology of gender.* Berkeley, CA: University of California Press.

Christensen, A. (1990). Gender and social structure in the demand/withdrawal pattern of marital conflict. *Journal of Personality and Social Psychology, 59,* 73–81.

Christensen, A. & Heavey, C. L. (1990). Gender and social structure in the demand/withdraw pattern of marital conflict. *Journal of Personality and Social Psycholgy, 59,* 73–82.

Christensen, A., & Noller, P. (1992, July). *Nonverbal behavior and the demand-withdraw pattern in married couples.* Paper presented at the conference of the International Society for the Study of Personal Relationships, Orono, ME.

Christensen, A. & Shenk, J. L. (1991). Communication, conflict, and psychological distance in nondistressed, clinic , and divorcing couples. *Journal of Consulting and Clinical Psychology, 59,* 458–463.

Christopher, F. S. (1988). An initial investigation into a continuum of premarital sexual pressure. *Journal of Sex Research, 25*(2), 255–266.

Christopher, F. S., & Cate, R. M. (1985). Premarital sexual pathways and relationship development. *Journal of Social and Personal Relationships, 2,* 271–288.

Christopher, F. S., & Cate, R. M. (1988). Premarital sexual involvement: A developmental investigation of relational correlates. *Adolescence, 13*(92), 793–803.

Christopher, F. S., & Frandsen, M. M. (1990). Strategies of influence in sex and dating. *Journal of Social and Personal Relationships, 7,* 89–105.

Clanton, G., & Kosins, D. J. (1991). Developmental correlates of jealousy. In P. Salovey (Ed.), *The psychology of jealousy and envy*. New York: Guilford Press.

Clark, D. A. (1992). Understanding the development of the concept of suicide through the use of early memory technique. *Death Studies, 16*(4), 299–316.

Clark, K. J., & Kanoy, K. (1998). Parents' marital status, father-daughter intimacy and young adult females' dating relationships. *Journal of Divorce and Remarriage, 29*(1–2), 167–179.

Clark, M. S., & Grote, N. (1995, June). *Can we make sense of the literature on use of justice rules in intimate relationships?* Paper presented at the conference of the International Network on Personal Relationships, Williamsburg, VA.

Clarke-Stewart, K. A., & Bailey, B. L. (1989). Adjustment to divorce: Why do men have it easier? *Journal of Divorce, 13*(2) 75–94.

Clinton, C. (1974). *A student depraved.* San Diego, CA: Manchester.

Cloninger, C. R. (1986). A unified biosocial theory of personality and its role in the development of anxiety states. *Psychiatric Developments, 3,* 167–224.

Cloninger, C. R. (1988). *Personality and psychopathology: Neuroadaptive processes.* Oxford: Oxford University Press.

Cobliner, W. G. (1988). The exclusion of intimacy in the sexuality of the contemporary college-age population. *Adolescence, 23*(89), 99–113.

Cochran, S. D., & Peplau, L. A. (1985). Value orientations in heterosexual relationships. *Psychology of Women Quarterly, 9,* 477–488.

Cohen, L. L., & Shotland, R. L. (1996). Timing of first sexual intercourse in a relationship: Expectations, experiences, and perceptions of others. *Journal of Sex Research, 33*(4), 291–299.

Cohn, J. F., & Tronick, E. Z. (1983). Three-month-old infants' reaction to simulated maternal depression. *Child Development, 54,* 185–193.

Coira, V., Alboni, A., Gramellini, D., Cigarini, C., Bianconi, L., Pignatti, D., Volpi, R., & Chiodera, P. (1992). Inhibition by ethanol of the oxytocin response to breast stimulation in normal women and the role of endogenous opioids. *Acta Endocrinologia, 126*(3), 213–216.

Coleman, L. M., Antonucci, T., Adelmann, P., & Crohan, S. (1987). Social roles in the lives of middle-aged and older black women. *Journal of Marriage and the Family, 49,* 761–771.

Coleman, M., & Ganong, L. H. (1992). Financial responsibility for children following divorce and remarriage. *Journal of Family and Economic Issues, 13*(4), 445–455.

Colgrove, M., Bloomfield, H., & McWilliams, P. (1991b). *Surviving, healing & growing.* Los Angeles: Prelude.

Collins, N. L., & Read, S. J. (1990). Adult attachment, working models, and relationship quality in dating couples. *Journal of Personality and Social Psychology, 58*(4), 644–663.

Combrick-Graham, L. (1985). A developmental model for family systems. *Family Process, 24,* 139–150.

Comfort, A. (1972). *The joy of sex: A gourmet guide to lovemaking.* New York: Simon & Schuster.

Comstock, G. (1991). *Violence against lesbians and gay men.* New York: Columbia University Press.

Constantine, L. (1986) *Family paradigms: The practice of theory in family therapy.* New York: Guilford Press.

Cook, D. R. (1997). Shame and anger scripts in men: An empirical study. Unpublished manuscript.

Cook, M., & McHenry, R. (1978). *Sexual attraction.* Oxford, UK: Pergamon Press.

Coser, L. A. (1956). *The functions of social conflict.* New York: Free.

Covey, L. S., & Tam, D. (1990). Depressive mood, the single-parent home, and adolescent cigarette smoking. *American Journal of Public Health, 80,* 1330–1333.

Cowley, G. (1996, June 3). The biology of beauty. *Newsweek, 127*(23), 60–66.

Coysh, W. S., Johnston, J. R., Tschann, J. M., Wallerstein, J. S., & Kline, M. (1989). Parental postdivorce adjustment in joint and sole physical custody families. *Journal of Family Issues, 10*(1) 52–71.

Crenshaw, T. L., & Goldberg, J. P. (1996). *Sexual pharmacology. Drugs that affect sexual functioning*. New York: W. W. Norton.

Critelli, J. W., & Waid, D. R. (1980). Physical attractiveness, romantic love, and equity restoration in dating relationships. *Journal of Personality Assessment, 44*, 624–629.

Crohan, S. F. (1996). Marital quality and conflict across the transition to parenthood in African American and white couples. *Journal of Marriage and the Family, 58*, 933–944.

Crosby, J. F. (1991). *Illusion and disillusion: The self in love and marriage* (4th ed.). Belmont, CA: Wadsworth.

Crosby, J. F., Lybarger, S. K., & Mason, R. L. (1987). The grief resolution process in divorce: Phase II. *Journal of Divorce, 11*(1), 17–40.

Crown, C. L. (1991). Coordinated interpersonal timing of vision and voice as a function of interpersonal attraction. *Journal of Language and Social Psychology, 10*(1), 29–46.

Cunningham, J. D., Braiker, H., & Kelley, H. (1982). Marital status and sex differences in problems reported by married and cohabiting couples. *Psychology of Women Quarterly, 6*, 415–427.

Cunningham, M. R. (1986). Measuring the physical in physical attractiveness: Quasi-experiments on the sociobiology of female facial beauty. *Journal of Personality and Social Psychology, 50*, 925–935,

Cunningham, M. R., Druen, P. B., & Barbee, A. P. (1997). Angels, mentors, and friends: Trade-offs among evolutionary, social, and individual variables in physical appearance. In J. A. Simpson & D. T. Kenrick (Eds.), *Evolutionary social psychology*, (pp. 109–140). Mahwah, NJ: Lawrence Erlbaum.

Cupach, W. R., & Metts, S. (1986). Accounts of relational dissolution: A comparison of marital and non-marital relationships. *Communication Monographs, 53*(4) 311–334.

Cupach, W. R., & Metts, S. (1991). Sexuality and communication in close relationships. In K. McKinney & S. Sprecher (Eds.), *Sexuality in close relationships* (pp. 93–109). Hillsdale, NJ: Lawrence Erlbaum.

Cutler, W. B., Friedmann, E., & McCoy, N. L. (1998). Pheromonal influences on sociosexual behavior in men. *Archives of Sexual Behavior, 27*(1), 1–13.

D'Emilio, J., & Freedman, E. B. (1988). *Intimate matters: A history of sexuality in America*. New York: Harper & Row.

Dabbs, J. M., Jr., Chang, E., Strong, R. A., & Milun, R. (1998). Spatial ability, navigation strategy, and geographic knowledge among men and women. *Evolution and Human Behavior, 19*(2), 89–98.

Daly, M., & Wilson, M. (1978). *Sex, evolution, and behavior*. North Scituate, MA: Duxbury Press.

Daly, M., Wilson, M., & Weghorst, S. J. (1982). Male sexual jealousy. *Ethology and Sociobiology, 3*, 11–27.

Dannecker, M. (1984). Towards a theory of homosexuality: Socio-historical perspectives. *Journal of Homosexuality, 9*, 1–8.

Darwin, C. (1872/1965). *The expression of the emotions in man and animals*. Chicago: University of Chicago Press.

D'Augelli, A. R. (1998). Developmental implications of victimization of lesbian, gay, and bisexual youths. In G. M. Herek (Ed.), *Stigma and sexual orientation: Understanding prejudice against lesbians, gay men, and bisexuals* (pp. 187–210). Thousand Oaks, CA: Sage.

Davidson, B., Balswick, J., & Halverson, C. (1983). Affective self-disclosure and marital adjustment: A test of equity theory. *Journal of Marriage and the Family, 45*, 93–102.

Davies, P. T., & Cummings, E. M. (1994). Marital conflict and child adjustment: An emotional security hypothesis. *Psychological Bulletin, 116*(3), 387–411.

Davis, J. D. (1978). When boy meets girl: Sex roles and the negotiation of intimacy in an acquaintance exercise. *Journal of Personality and Social Psychology, 36*(7), 684–692.

Davis, K. E., & Todd, M. J. (1982). Friendship and love relationships. In K. E. Davis (Ed.), *Advances in Descriptive Psychology* (Vol 2). Greenwich, CT: JAI Press.

Davis, M. S. (1973). *Intimate relations.* New York: Free Press.

De Beauvoir, S. (1953). *The second sex.* (H. M. Parshley Trans.). New York: Knopf.

Deaux, K., & Hanna, R. (1984). Courtship in the personals column: The influence of gender and sexual orientation. *Sex Roles, 11*, 363–375.

DeBord, K. A., Wood, P. K., Sher, K. J., & Good, G. E. (1998). The relevance of sexual orientation to substance abuse and psychological distress among college students. *Journal of College Student Development, 39*(2), 157–168.

DeCecco, J. P., & Parker, D. A. (1995). The biology of homosexuality: Sexual orientation or sexual preference? *Journal of Homosexuality, 28*(1–2), 1–27.

DeHart, D. D., & Cunningham, M. R. (1993, June). *Evolutionary theories of physical attractiveness: Do the standards hold for non-heterosexuals?* Paper presented at the conference of the International Network on Personal Relationships, Milwaukee, WI.

DeLamater, J. (1991). Emotions and sexuality. In K. McKinney & S. Sprecher (Eds.), *Sexuality in close relationships* (pp. 49–70). Hillsdale, NJ: Lawrence Erlbaum.

DeLamater, J. (1987). Gender differences in sexual scenarios. In K. Kelley (Ed.), *Females, males, and sexuality: Theories and research.* Albany, NY: State University of New York Press.

DeMunck, V. C. (1998). Introduction. In V. C. DeMunck (Ed.), *Romantic love and sexual behavior: Perspectives from the social sciences.* Westport, CT: Praeger.

Deninger-Polzer, G. (1987). *Der fruchtbare streit in der paarbeziehung* [Fruitful conflict in couple relationships.] In G. Pfluger (Ed.), *Das paar-mythos und wirklichkeit* [The pair-myth and reality], (pp. 39–60). Olten, Germany: Walter Verlag.

Denton, W. H., Burleson, B. R., & Sprenkle, D. H. (1995a). Association of interpersonal cognitive complexity and communication in marriage: Moderating effects of marital distress. *Family Process, 34*, 101–111.

Denton, W. H. , Burleson, B. R., & Sprenkle, D. H. (1995b). Motivation in marital communication: Comparison of distressed and nondistressed husbands and wives. *American Journal of Family Therapy, 22*, 17–26.

Derlega, V. J., Metts, S., Petronio, S., & Margulis, S. T. (1993). *Self-disclosure.* Newbury Park, CA: Sage.

Derlega, V. J., Winstead, B. A., Wong, P. T. P., & Hunter, S. (1985). Gender effects in an initial encounter: A case where men exceed women in disclosure. *Journal of Social and Personal Relationships, 2*, 25–44.

Desrochers, S. (1995). What types of men are most attractive and most repulsive to women? *Sex-Roles, 32*(5–6), 375–391.

DeVries, G. J., & Boyle, P. A. (1998). Double duty for sex differences in the brain. *Behavioral Brain Research, 92*, 205–213.

Dickson, L. (1993). The future of marriage and family in Black America. *Journal of Black Studies, 23*(4), 472–491.

Diedrick, P. (1991). Gender differences in divorce adjustment. *Journal of Divorce and Remarriage, 15*, 33–45.

Dion, K., Berscheid, E., & Hatfield, E. (1972). What is beautiful is good. *Journal of Personality and Social Psychology, 24*, 285–290.

Dixon, J. K. (1983). The commencement of bisexual activity in swinging married women over age thirty. *Journal of Sex Research, 20*, 71–90.

Donaldson, C. (1993). *Correlates of relationship satisfaction for lesbian couples.* (Doctoral dissertation, Hofstra University, 1993). Dissertation Abstracts International, 54-08B, 4369.

Donohue, W., & Crouch, J. (1996). Marital therapy and gender-linked factors in communication. *Journal of Marital and Family Therapy, 22*, 87–101.

Dormen, L. (1992, April). Second chance at love: A divorced woman's guide to dating. *Redbook*, 50–56.

Dornbusch, S., Carlsmith, J., Bushwall, S., Ritter, P., Leiderman, H., Hastorf, A., & Gross, R. (1985). Single parents, extended households, and the control of adolescents. *Child Development, 56*, 326–341.

Dorner, G., Geier, T., Ahrens, L., Krell, L., Munx, G., Sieler, H., Kittner, E., & Muller, H. (1980). Prenatal stress as a possible aetiogenetic factor of homosexuality in human males. *Endokrinologie, 75*, 365–368.

Dosser, D. A., Jr., Balswick, J. O., & Halverson, C. F., Jr. (1983). Situational context of emotional expressiveness. *Journal of Counseling Psychology, 30*(3), 376–387.

Dosser, D. A., Jr., Balswick, J. O., & Halverson, C. F., Jr. (1986). Male inexpressiveness and relationships. *Journal of Social and Personal Relationships, 3*, 241–258.

Douglas, W. (1987). Affinity-testing in initial interactions. *Journal of Social and Personal Relationships, 4*, 3–15.

Drevets, W. C., & Raichle, M. E. (1998). Reciprocal suppression of regional cerebral blood flow during emotional versus higher cognitive processes: Implications for interactions between emotions and cognition. *Cognition and Emotion, 12*(3), 353–385.

Drigotas, S. M., & Rusbult, C. E. (1992). Should I stay or should I go? A dependence model of breakups. *Journal of Personality and Social Psychology, 62*(1), 62–87.

Druen, P. B., Cunningham, M. R., Turner-Clark, S., & Persinger, B. (1993, June). *From first date to last mate: Learning about self, partners, and relationships.* Paper presented at the conference of the International Network on Personal Relationships, Milwaukee, WI.

Duberman, L. (1973). Step-kin relationships. *Journal of Marriage and the Family, 35*, 283–292.

Duck, S. W. (1982). A topography of relationship disengagement and dissolution. In S. W. Duck (Ed.), *Personal relationships. 4: Dissolving personal relationships.* New York: Academic Press.

Duck, S. W. (1991, May). *New lamps for old: A new theory of relationships and a fresh look at some old research.* Paper presented at the conference of the International Network on Personal Relationships. Normal/Bloomington, IL.

Duck, S. W., & Pond, K. (1989). Friends, Romans, countrymen, lend me your retrospective data: Rhetoric and reality in personal relationships. In C. Hendrick (Ed.), *Review of social psychology and personality, Vol. 10: Close relationships* (pp. 3–27). Newbury Park, CA: Sage.

Duck, S. W., Pond, K., & Leatham, G. (1991, May). *Remembering as a context for being in relationships: Different perspectives on the same interaction.* Paper presented at the conference of the International Network on Personal Relationships, Normal/Bloomington, IL.

Duck, S. W., Rutt, D. J., Hurst, M., & Strejc, H. (1991). Some evident truths about communication in everyday relationships: All communications are not created equal. *Human Communication Research, 18,* 55–71.

Dudley, J. R. (1996). Noncustodial fathers speak about their parent roles. *Family & Conciliation Courts Review, 34*(3), 410–426.

Dunbar, J., Brown, M., & Vuorinen, S. (1973). Attitudes toward homosexuality among Brazilian and Canadian college students. *Journal of Social Psychology, 90,* 173–183.

Duran-Aydintug, C. (1997). Adult children of divorce revisited: When they speak up. *Journal of Divorce and Remarriage, 27*(1–2), 71–83.

Dutton, D., & Aron, A. (1974). Some evidence for heightened sexual attraction under conditions of high anxiety. *Journal of Personality and Social Psychology, 20,* 510–517.

Dutton, D., & Aron, A. (1989). Romantic attraction and generalized liking for others who are sources of conflict-based arousal. *Canadian Journal of Behavioural Science, 21,* 246–257.

Dutton, D., & Painter, S. L. (1981). Traumatic bonding: The development of emotional attachments in battered women and other relationships of intermittent abuse. *Victimology: An International Journal, 6,* 139–155.

Dutton, D. G., van Ginkel, C., & Landolt, M. A. (1996). Jealousy, intimate abusiveness, and intrusiveness. *Journal of Family Violence, 11*(4), 411–423.

Dutton, D. G., van Ginkel, C., & Starzon (1995). The role of shame and guilt in the intergenerational transmission of abusiveness. *Violence and Victims, 10*(2), 121–131.

Dym, B., & Glenn, M. L. (1993). *Couples: Understanding the cycles of intimate relationships.* New York: Harper-Collins.

Ehrlich, H. S. (1986). Denial in adolescence. *The Psychoanalytic Study of the Child, 41,* 315–336.

Eibl-Eibesfeldt, I. (1989). *Human ethology.* Hawthorne, NY: Aldine de Gruyter.

Ekman, P. (1992). Are there basic emotions? *Psychological Review, 99*(3), 550–553.

Eldrige, N. A., & Gilbert, L. A. (1990). Correlates of relationship satisfaction in lesbian couples. *Psychology of Women Quarterly, 14,* 43–62.

Eliot, T. S. (1922/1936). The waste land. In *Collected poems 1909–1935.* New York: Harcourt, Brace, & World.

Ellis, B. J. (1992). The evolution of sexual attraction: Evaluative mechanisms in women. In J. H. Barkow, L. Cosmides, & J. Tooby (Eds.), *The adapted mind: Evolutionary psychology and the generation of culture.* New York: Oxford University Press.

Ellis, L. (1996a). Theories of homosexuality. In R. C. Savin-Williams & K. M. Cohen (Eds.), *The lives of lesbians, gays, and bisexuals: Children to adults* (pp. 11–34). Fort Worth, TX: Harcourt Brace.

Ellis, L. (1996b). The role of perinatal factors in determining sexual orientation. In R. C. Savin-Williams & K. M. Cohen (Eds.), *The lives of lesbians, gays, and bisexuals: Children to adults* (pp. 35–70). Fort Worth, TX: Harcourt Brace.

Ellis, L. (1997). Perinatal influences on behavior and health, with special emphasis on sexual orientation and other sex-linked behavior. In L. Ellis & L. Ebertx (Eds.), *Sexual orientation. Toward biological understanding* (pp. 71–90). Westport, CT: Praeger.

Ellis, L., & Ames, M. A. (1987). Neurohormonal functioning and sexual orientation: A theory of homosexuality-heterosexuality. *Psychological Bulletin, 101*, 233–258.

Elmer-Dewitt, P. (1994, October 17). Now for the truth about Americans and sex: The first comprehensive survey since Kinsey smashes some of our most intimate myths. *Time*, 62–70.

Ember, C. R., & Levinson, D. (1991). The substantive contributions of worldwide cross-cultural studies using secondary data. *Behavior Science Research, 25*(1–4), 79–140.

Ephron, N. (1983). *Heartburn*. New York: Alfred A. Knopf.

Erikson, E. H. (1963). *Childhood and society*, 2nd ed. New York: W.W. Norton.

Erikson, E. H. (1968). *Identity, youth and crisis*. New York: W. W. Norton.

Evans, R. (1967). *Dialogue with Erik Erikson*. New York: Harper & Row.

Evans, J. J., & Bloom, B. L. (1996). Effects of parental divorce among college undergraduates. *Journal of Divorce & Remarriage, 26*(1/2), 69–91.

Ewart, C. K., Taylor, C. B., Kraemer, H. C., & Agras, W. S. (1991). High blood pressure and marital discord: Not being nasty matters more than being nice. *Health Psychology, 10*(3), 155–163.

Eysenck, H. J. (1967). *The biological basis of personality*. Springfield, IL: Thomas.

Eysenck, H. J. (1991). Biological dimensions of personality. In L. A. Pervin (Ed.), *Handbook of personality* (pp. 244–276). New York: Guilford.

Face, J. (1997). *The relationship between attachment style and experiencing a parental divorce during childhood with courtship attitudes and behaviors in young adulthood.* (Doctoral Dissertation, Virginia Commonwealth University.)

Falbo, T., & Peplau, L. A. (1980). Power strategies in intimate relationships. *Journal of Personality and Social Psychology, 38*, 618–628.

Farrell, J., & Markman, H. J. (1986). Individual and interpersonal factors in the etiology of marital distress: The example of remarital couples. In R. Gilmour & S. Duck (Eds.), *The emerging field of personal relationships*. Hillsdale, NJ: Lawrence Erlbaum.

Feeney, J. A., & Noller, P. (1990). Attachment style as a predictor of adult romantic relationships. *Journal of Personality and Social Psychology, 58*(2), 218–291.

Fehr, B. (1988). Prototype analysis of the concepts of love and commitment. *Journal of Personality and Social Psychology, 55*(4), 557–579.

Fein, S., & Spencer, J. S. (1997). Prejudice as self-image maintenance: Affirming the self through derogating others. *Journal of Personality and Social Psychology, 73*(1), 31–44.

Feingold, A. (1990). Gender differences in effects of physical attractiveness on romantic attraction: A comparison across five research paradigms. *Journal of Personality and Social Psychology, 59*, 981–993.

Felmlee, D. H. (1995). Fatal attractions: Affection and disaffection in intimate relationships. *Journal of Social and Personal Relationships, 12*(2), 295–311.

Felmlee, D. H. (1998). "Be careful what you wish for . . .": A quantitative and qualitative investigation of "fatal attractions." *Personal Relationships 5*(3), 235–254.

Felmlee, D. H., Sprecher, S., & Bassin, E. (1990). The dissolution of intimate relationships: A hazard model. *Social Psychology Quarterly, 53*(1), 13–30.

Fenichel, O. (1945). *The psychoanalytic theory of neuroses*. New York: W. W. Norton.

Ferree, M. M. (1984). The view from below: Women's employment and gender equality in working class families. In B. Hess & M. Sussman (Eds.), *Women and the family: Two decades of change* (pp. 57–75). New York: Haworth.

Ferree, M. (1990). Beyond separate spheres: Feminism and family research. *Journal of Marriage and the Family, 52,* 866–884.

Fields, N. (1983). Satisfaction in long term marriages. *Social Work, 39,* 37–41.

Fincham, F. D., & Bradbury, T. N. (1991). Cognition in marriage. In W. H. Jones & D. Perlman (Eds.), *Advances in personal relationships, Vol 2* (pp. 159–203). London: Kingsley.

Fincham, F. D., & Linfield, K. J. (1997). A new look at marital quality: Can spouses feel positive and negative about their marriage? *Journal of Family Psychology, 11*(4), 489–502.

Fincham, F. D., & O'Leary, K. D. (1983). Causal inferences for spouses behavior in maritally distressed and nondistressed couples. *Journal of Clinical and Social Psychology, 1,* 42–57.

Filley, A. C. (1975). *Interpersonal conflict resolution.* Glenview, IL: Scott, Foresman.

Fishbein, H. D. (1996). *Peer prejudice and discrimination.* Boulder, CO: Westview Press.

Fisher, B. (1981). *Rebuilding when your relationship ends.* San Luis Obispo, CA: Impact.

Fisher, B. (1992). *Rebuilding when your relationship ends, (2nd ed.).* San Luis Obispo, CA: Impact.

Fisher, H. E. (1991). Monogamy, adultery and divorce in cross-species perspective. In M. H. Robinson & L. Tiger (Eds.), *Man and beast revisited.* Washington, DC: Smithsonian Institution Press.

Fisher, H. E. (1992). *Anatomy of love: The natural history of monogamy, adultery, and divorce.* New York: W. W. Norton.

Fisher, H. E. (1998). Lust, attraction, and attachment in mammalian reproduction. *Human Nature, 9*(1), 23–52.

Fisher, L., Nakell, L., Terry, H., & Ransom, D. (1992) The California family health project: III. Family emotion management and adult health. *Family Process, 31,* 269–287.

Fisher, R., & Brown, S. (1988). *Getting together: Building relationships as we negotiate.* New York: Penguin.

Fisher, R., & Ury, W. (1981). *Getting to yes: Negotiating agreement without giving in.* New York: Penguin.

Fishman, P. M. (1978). Interaction: The work women do. *Social Problems, 25,* 397–406.

Fitzpatrick, M. A. (1984). A typological approach to marital interaction: Recent theory and research. Chapter in L. Berkowitz (Ed.), *Advances in Experimental Social Psychology. Vol 18,* Orlando, FL: Academic Press, pp. 1–47.

Fitzpatrick, M. A. (1988a). *Between husbands and wives.* Newbury Park, CA: Sage.

Fitzpatrick, M. A. (1988b). Negotiation, problem solving and conflict in various types of marriages. In P. Noller & M. A. Fitzpatrick (Eds.), *Perspectives on marital interaction* (pp. 245–270). Clevedon, England: Multilingual Matters.

Fitzpatrick, M. A. (1990). Models of marital interaction. In H. Giles &W. Robinson (Eds.), *Handbook of Language and Social Psychology* (pp 433–451). Chichester, UK: John Wiley & Sons.

Fitzpatrick, M., & Dindia, K. (1986). Couples and other strangers: Talk time in spouse-stranger interaction. *Communication Research, 13,* 525–652.

Fitzpatrick, M., & Indvisk, J. (1982). The instrumental and expressive domains of marital communication. *Human Communication Research, 8,* 195–213.

Fletcher, G. J., Fincham, F. O., Cramer, L., & Heron, N. (1987). The role of attributions in the development of dating relationships. *Journal of Personality and Social Psychology, 53*(3), 481–489.

Flinn, M. (1988). Mate guarding in a Caribbean village. *Ethology & Sociobiology, 9,* 1–28.

Foa, U. G., Anderson, B, Converse, J., Jr., Urbansky, W. A., & Cawley, M. J., III. (1987). Gender-related sexual attitudes: Some crosscultural similarities and differences. *Sex Roles, 16*(9/10), 511–519.

Foley, F. W., Heath, R. F., & Chabot, D. R. (1986). Shyness and defensive style. *Psychological Reports, 58*(3), 967–973.

Forgas, J. P. (1991). Affect and cognition in close relationships. In G. J. O. Fletcher & F. D. Fincham (Eds.), *Cognition in close relationships* (pp. 151–202). Hillsdale, NJ: Lawrence Erlbaum.

Forgatch, M. S., Patterson, G. R., & Skinner, M. L. (1988). A mediational model for the effect of divorce on antisocial behavior in boys. In E. M. Hetherington & J. D. Arasteh (Eds.), *Impact of divorce, single parenting and stepparenting on children* (pp. 135–154). Hillsdale, NJ: Lawrence Erlbaum.

Fowers, B. J., Montel, K. H., & Olson, D. H. (1996). Predicting marital success for premarital couple types based on PREPARE. *Journal of Marital and Family Therapy, 22*(1), 103–119.

Fox, R. (1972). Alliance and constraint: Sexual selection and the evolution of human kinship systems. In B. Campbell (Ed.), *Sexual selection and the descent of man 1871–1971.* Chicago: Aldine.

Fox, R. C. (1996). Bisexuality. An examination of theory and research. In R. P. Cabaj & T. S. Stein (Eds.), *Textbook of homosexuality and mental health* (pp. 147–171). Washington, DC: American Psychiatric Press.

Frank, S. J., Avery, C. B., & Laman, M. S. (1988). Young adults' perceptions of their relationships with their parents: Individual differences in connectedness, competence, and emotional autonomy. *Developmental Psychology, 24*(5), 729–737.

Franz, C. E., & White, K. M. (1985). Individuation and attachment in personality development: Extending Erikson's theory. *Journal of Personality, 53,* 224–256.

Frazier, P. A., & Byer, A. (May, 1991). *Initial attraction as a function of adult attachment style.* Poster presented at the conference of the International Network on Personal Relationships, Bloomington, IL.

Frazier, P. A., & Esterly, E. (1990). Correlates of relationship beliefs: Gender, relationship experience and relationship satisfaction. *Journal of Social and Personal Relationships, 7,* 331–352.

Freedman, J. (1978). *Happy people: What happiness is, who has it, and why.* New York: Harcourt Brace Jovanovich.

French, J. R., & Raven, B. (1959). The bases of social power. In D. Cartwright & A. Zander (Eds.), *Group dynamics: Research and theory* (3rd ed.). New York: Harper & Row.

Freud, S. (1914/1989). On narcissism: An introduction. In P. Gay (Ed.), *The Freud reader* (pp. 545–562). New York: W. W. Norton.

Freud, S. (1925/1989a). Three essays on the theory of sexuality. In P. Gay (Ed.), *The Freud reader* (pp. 239–293). New York: W. W. Norton.

Freud, S. (1930). *Civilization and its discontents.* (J. Strachey, Trans.). London: Hogarth Press.

Freund, K., Langevin, R., & Zajac, Y. (1974). Heterosexual aversion in homosexual males. *British Journal of Psychiatry, 125,* 177–180.

Friedman, B. J. (1977, January). Sex and the lonely guy. *Esquire Magazine* (pp. 71–75).

Friedman, R. C., & Downey, J. (1995). Internalized homophobia and the negative therapeutic reaction. *Journal of the American Academy of Psychoanalysis, 23*(1), 99–113.

Fromm, E. (1956). *Art of loving*. New York: Perennial Library/Harper and Row.

Fry, P. S., & Leahey, M. (1983). Children's perceptions of major positive and negative events and factors in single-parent families. *Journal of Applied Developmental Psychology, 4,* 371–388.

Frye, M. (1990). Lesbian "sex". In J. Allen (Ed.), *Lesbian philosophies and cultures* (pp. 305–315). Albany, NY: State University of New York Press.

Furstenberg, F. F., Jr. (1988). The new extended family: The experience of parents and children after remarriage. In K. Pasley & M. Ihinger-Tallman (Eds.), *Remarriage and stepparenting: Current research and theory*. New York: Guilford Press.

Furstenberg, F., & Spanier, G. B. (1984). *Recycling the family*. Beverly Hills, CA: Sage.

Gadlin, H. (1977). Private lives and public order: A critical view of the history of intimate relations in the United States. In G. Levinger & H. L. Raush (Eds.), *Close relationships: Perspectives on the meaning of intimacy* (pp. 33–72). Amherst, MA: University of Massachusetts Press.

Gagnon, J. H., & Greenblatt, C. S. (1978). *Life designs: Individuals, marriages and families*. Glenview, IL: Scott, Foresman.

Gale, A., Kingley, E., Brookes, S., & Smith, D. (1978). Cortical arousal and social intimacy in the human female under different conditions of eye contact. *Behavioural Processes, 3,* 271–275.

Galea, L. M., & Kimura, D. (1993). Sex differences in route-learning. *Personality and Individual Differences, 14*(1) 53–65.

Galvin, K., & Brommel, B. (1982). *Family communication: Cohesion and change*. Glenview, IL: Scott, Foresman.

Gangestad, S. W., & Thornhill, R. (1997). The evolutionary psychology of extrapair sex: The role of fluctuating asymmetry. *Evolution and Human Behavior, 18*(2), 69–88.

Gangon, J. J., & Simon, W. (1973) *Sexual conduct: The social sources of human sexuality*. Chicago: Aldine.

Ganong, L. H., & Coleman, M. (1988). Effects of parental remarriage on children: An updated comparision of theories, methods, and findings from clinical and empirical research. In K. Pasley & M. Ihinger-Tallman (Eds.), *Remarriage and stepparenting: Current research and theory*. New York: Guilford Press.

Gately, D., & Schwebel, A. I. (1992). Favorable outcomes in children after parental divorce. *Journal of Divorce and Remarriage, 18*(3/4), 57–78.

Gauvin, D. V., Harland, R. D., Michaelis, R. C., & Holloway, F. A. (1989). Caffeine-phenylethylamine combinations mimic the cocaine discriminative cue. *Life Sciences, 44,* 67–73.

George, M. S., Ketter, T. A., Parekh, P. I., Horwitz, B., Herscovitch, P., & Post, R. M. (1995). Brain activity during transient sadness and happiness in healthy women. *American Journal of Psychiatry, 152*(3), 341–351.

George, M. S., Ketter, T. A., Parekh, P. I., Horwitz, B., Herscovitch, P., & Post, R. M. (1996). Gender differences in regional cerebral blood flow during transient self-induced sadness or happiness. *Biological Psychiatry, 40*(9), 859–871.

Gerson, K. (1985). Hard choices: How women decide about work, career and motherhood. Berkeley, CA: University of California Press.

Gibran, K. (1923/1982). *The prophet*. New York: Alfred A. Knopf.

Gilbert, P., Price, J., & Allan, S. (1995). Social comparison, social attractiveness and evolution: How might they be related? *New Ideas in Psychology, 13*(2), 149–165.

Gilbert, S. (1976). Self disclosure, intimacy, and communication in families. *Family Coordinator, 25*, 221–229.

Gilfillan, S. S. (1985). Adult intimate love relationships as new editions of symbiosis and the separation-individuation process. *Smith College Studies in Social Work, 55*(3), 183–196.

Gilligan, C. (1982). *In a different voice: Psychological theory and women's development*. Cambridge, MA: Harvard University Press.

Gilmartin, B. G. (1987). Peer group antecedents of severe love-shyness in males. *Journal of Personality, 55*(3), 467–489.

Gilmore, D. D. (1990). *Manhood in the making: Cultural concepts of masculinity*. New Haven, CT: Yale University Press.

Givens, D. B. (1978). The nonverbal basis of attraction: Flirtation, courtship, and seduction. *Psychiatry, 41*, 346–360.

Givens, D. B. (1983). *Love signals: How to attract a mate*. New York: Crown Publishers.

Gjedde, P. F. (1988). Parental concordance on child rearing and the interactive emphases of parents: Sex-differentiated relationships during the preschool years. *Developmental Psychology, 24*(5), 700–706.

Gladue, B. A., & Delaney, H. J. (1990). Gender differences in perception of attractiveness of men and women in bars. *Personality and Social Psychology Bulletin, 16*, 378–391.

Glass, S. P., & Wright, T. L. (1988). Clinical implications of research on extramarital involvement. In R. A. Brown & J. R. Field (Eds.), *Treatment of sexual problems in individual and couples therapy* (pp. 301–346). New York: PMA Publishing.

Glenn, N. D., & Kramer, K. B. (1985). The psychological well-being of adult children of divorce. *Journal of Marriage and the Family, 47*, 905–912.

Glenn, N. D., & Kramer, K. B. (1987). The marriages and divorces of the children of divorce. *Journal of Marriage and the Family, 49*, 811–825.

Glenwick, D. S., & Mowrey, J. D. (1986). When parent becomes peer: Loss of intergenerational boundaries in single parent families. *Family Relations, 35*, 57–62.

Glick, P. C. (1984). Marriage, divorce, and living arrangements. *Journal of Family Issues, 5*, 7–26.

Glick, P. C. (1985). Orientation toward relationships: Choosing a situation in which to begin a relationship. *Journal of Experimental Social Psychology, 21*, 544–562.

Goldberg, H. (1987). *The inner male: Overcoming roadblocks to intimacy*. New York: Signet.

Gonsiorek, J. C. (1988). Mental health issues of gay and lesbian adolescents. *Journal of Adolescent Health Care, 9*, 114–122.

Goode, W. (1956). *Women in Divorce*. New York: Free Press.

Gordon, M., & Creighton, S. J. (1988). Natal and non-natal fathers as sexual abusers in the United Kingdom: A comparative analysis. *Journal of Marriage and the Family, 50*, 99–105.

Gordon, L. (1993). *Passage to intimacy*. New York: Simon and Schuster.

Gottman, J. M. (1990). Children of gay and lesbian parents. *Marriage and Family Review, 14*, 177–196.

Gottman, J. M. (1994a). *What predicts divorce?The relationship between marital processes and marital outcomes.* Hillsdale, NJ: Lawrence Erlbaum.

Gottman, J. M. (1994b) Why marriages fail. *Family Networker, 18*(3), 40–49.

Gottman, J. M. (1994c). *Why marriages succeed or fail.* New York: Simon & Schuster.

Gottman, J. M. (1996, July). *Against empathy.* Panel presentation at International Network on Personal Relationships conference, Seattle, WA.

Gottman, J. M., Coan, J., Carrere, S. & Swanson, C. (1998). Predicting marital happiness and stability from newlywed interactions. *Journal of Marriage and the Family, 60,* 5–22.

Gottman J. M., & Krokoff, L. J. (1989). The relationship between marital interaction and marital satisfaction: A longitudinal view. *Journal of Consulting and Clinical Psycholgy, 57,* 47–52.

Gottman, J. M., & Levenson, R. S. (1988). The social psychophysiology of marriage. In P. Noller & M. A. Fitzpatrick (Eds.), *Perspectives in Marital Interaction* (pp. 182–202). Clevedon, England, & Philadelphia: Multilingual Matters.

Gottman, J. M., Markman, H., & Notarius, C. (1977). The topography of marital conflict: A sequential analysis of verbal and nonverbal behavior. *Journal of Marriage and the Family, 39,* 461–477.

Gottman, J. M., Notarius, C., Gonso, J., & Markman, H. J. (1976). *A couple's guide to communication.* Champaign, IL: Research Press.

Goudy, T. C. (1980). Self disclosure and satisfaction in marriage: The relation examined. *Family Relations 29,* 281–287.

Gove, W. R., & Shin, H. (1989). The psychological well-being of divorced and widowed men and women: An empirical analysis. *Journal of Family Issues, 10*(1) 122–144.

Graham, E. E. (1997). Turning points and commitment in post-divorce relationships. *Communication Monographs, 64*(4), 350–368.

Grammer, K. (1989). Human courtship behaviour: Biological basis and cognitive processing. In A. E. Rasa, C. Vogel, & E. Voland (Eds.), *The sociobiology of sexual and reproductive strategies.* London: Chapman & Hall.

Grammer, K. (1990). Strangers meet: Laughter and nonverbal signs of interest in opposite-sex encounters. *Journal of Nonverbal Behavior, 14*(4), 209–236.

Grammer K., & Thornhill, R. (1994). Human (homo sapiens) facial attractiveness and sexual selection: The role of symmetry and averageness. *Journal of Comparative Psychology, 108*(3), 233–242.

Gray, J. A. (1987). Perspectives on anxiety and impulsivity: A commentary. *Journal of Research in Personality, 21*(4), 493–509.

Gray, J. A. (1991). The neuropsychology of temperament. In J. Strelau & A. Angleitner (Eds.), *Explorations in temperament: International perspectives on theory and measurement* (pp. 105–128). New York: Plenum.

Gray, J. D., & Silver, R. C. (1990). Opposite sides of the same coin: Former spouses' divergent perspectives in coping with their divorce. *Journal of Personality and Social Psychology, 59*(6) 1180–1191.

Graziano, W. G., Jensen-Campbell, L. A., Todd, M., & Finch, J. E. (1997). Interpersonal attraction from an evolutionary perspective: Women's reactions to dominant and prosocial men. In J. A. Simpson & D. T. Kenrick (Eds.), *Evolutionary social psychology* (pp. 141–167). Mahwah, NJ: Lawrence Erlbaum.

Grebe, S. C. (1986). Mediation at different stages of the divorce process. *Divorce and Family Mediation,* 34–47.

Green, R. (1985). Gender identity in childhood and later sexual orientation: Follow-up of 78 males. *American Journal of Psychiatry, 142,* 339–341.

Green S. K., & Sandos, P. (1983). Perceptions of male and female initiators of relationships. *Sex Roles, 9*(8), 849–852.

Greene, R. M., & Leslie, L. A. (1989). Mothers' behavior and sons' adjustment following divorce. In T. W. Miller (Ed.), *Stressful life events* (pp. 498–512). Madison, CT: International Universities Press.

Greenstein, T. M. (1996). Husbands' participation in domestic labor: Interactive effects of wives' and hubands' gender ideologies. *Journal of Marriage and the Family, 58(3),* 585–595.

Greif, G. L. (1992). Lone fathers in the United States: An overview and practice implications. *British Journal of Social Work, 22,* 565–574.

Greif, G. L. (1985). Single fathers rearing children. *Journal of Marriage and the Family, 47,* 185–191.

Greund, K., & Blanchard, R. (1982). Is the distant relationship of fathers and homosexual sons related to the sons' erotic preference for male partners, or to the sons' atypical gender identity, or both? *Journal of Homosexuality,* 7–25.

Grizzle, G. L. (1996). Remarriage as an incomplete institutions: Cherlin's (1978) views and why we should be cautious about accepting them. *Journal of Divorce and Remarriage, 26*(1–2), 191–201.

Gross, J. (1992, December 31). Single: Happiness is being alone, or is it? *New York Times* News Service.

Groth, A. N., & Birnbaum, H. J. (1978). Adult sexual orientation and attraction to underaged persons. *Archives of Sexual Behavior, 7,* 175–181.

Grych, J. H., & Fincham, F. D. (1997). Children's adaptation to divorce: From description to explanation. In S. A. Wolchik & I. N. Sandler (Eds.), *Handbook of children's coping: Linking theory and intervention* (pp. 159–193). New York: Plenum Press.

Gryl, F. E., Stith, S. M., & Bird, G. W. (1991). Close dating relationships among college students: Differences by use of violence and by gender. *Journal of Social and Personal Relationships, 8,* 147–165.

Guerney, B. G., Jr. (1977). *Relationship enhancement: Skill training programs for therapy, problem prevention, and enrichment.* San Francisco: Jossey-Bass.

Guerrero, L. K., & Afifi, W. A. (1995). Some things are better left unsaid: Topic avoidance in family relationships. *Communication Quarterly, 43,* 276–296.

Guerrero, L. K., & Anderson, P. A. (1998). Jealousy experience and expression in romantic relationships. In P. A. Anderson & L. K. Guerrero (Eds.), *Handbook of communication and emotions: Research, theory, application and contexts.* New York: Academic Press.

Guggenbuhl-Craig, A. (1977). *Marriage—Dead or alive.* (M. Stein, Trans.) Dallas, TX: Spring.

Guidubaldi, J. (1988). Differences in children's divorce adjustment across grade level and gender: A report from the NASP-Kent State nationwide project. In S. A. Wolchik & P. Karoly (Eds.), *Children of divorce: Empirical perspectives on adjustment.* New York: Gardner.

Guldner, G. T. (1996). Long-distance romantic relationships: Prevalence and separation-related symptoms in college students. *Journal of College Student Development, 37*(3), 289–296.

Gulley, M. (1991). *Support seeking and interactive coping among same-sex friends, opposite sex friends, and romantic partners.* Unpublished master's thesis.

Guthrie, D. M., & Noller, P. (1988). Spouses' perceptions of one another in emotional situations. In P. Noller & M. A. Fitzpatrick (Eds.), *Perspectives in Marital Interaction* (pp. 153–181). Clevedon, England: Multilingual Matters.

Gutman, D. (1987). *Reclaimed powers: Toward a new psychology of men and women in later life*. New York: Basic Books.

Gwartney-Gibbs, P. A., Stockard, J., & Bohmer, S. (1987). Learning courtship aggression: The influence of parents, peers, and personal experiences. *Family Relations, 36*, 276–282.

Haas, L. (1986). Wives' orientation toward breadwinning. *Journal of Family Issues, 7*, 358–381.

Hackel, L. & Ruble, D. N. (1992). Changes in the marital relationship after the first baby is born: Predicting the impact of expectancy disconfirmation. *Journal of Personality and Social Psychology, 62*, 944–957.

Hagemeyer, S. (1986). Making sense of divorce grief. *Pastoral Psychology, 34*(4) 237–250.

Hagestag, G. O., & Smyer, M. A. (1980). *Divorce in mid-life: Implications for parent caring*. Presented at meetings of the American Orthopsychiatric Association.

Hagen, J., & Symons, A. (1986). Beauty report. In S. Sprecher & E. Hatfield, *Mirror, mirror on the wall* (p. 25). Honolulu: University of Hawaii Press.

Hahlweg, K. L., Revenstorf, D., & Schindler, L. (1984). Effects of behavioral marital therapy on couples communication and problem solving skills. *Journal of Personality and Social Psychology , 40*, 1150–1159.

Hahn, J., & Blass, T. (1997). Dating partner preferences: A function of similarity of love styles. *Journal of Social Behavior and Personality, 12*(3), 595–610.

Haley, J. (1963). Marriage therapy. *Archives of general psychiatry, 8*, 213–234.

Haley, J. (1972). Marriage therapy. In G. Erickson & Y. T. Hogan (Eds.), *Family therapy: An introduction to theory and technique* (pp. 180–210). Belmont, CA: Wadsworth.

Haley, J. (1976). *Problem solving therapy*. San Francisco, CA: Jossey-Bass.

Halford, W. K., Hahlweg, K., & Dunne, M. (1990). The cross-cultural consistency of marital communication associated with marital distress. *Journal of Marriage and the Family, 52*, 487–500.

Hall, G. C., & Barongan, C. (1997). Prevention of sexual aggression: Sociocultural risk and protective factors. *American Psychologist, 52*(1), 5–14.

Hall, J. A. (1998). How big are the nonverbal sex differences? The case of smiling and sensitivity to nonverbal cues. In *Sex differences and similarities in communication. Critical essays and empirical investigations of sex and gender in interaction* (pp. 155–178). Mahwah, NJ: Lawrence Erlbaum.

Halpern, D. F., & Crothers, M. (1997). Sex, sexual orientation, and cognition. In L. Ellis & L. Ebertx (Eds.), *Sexual orientation. Toward biological understanding* (pp. 181–198). Westport, CT: Praeger.

Halpern, M. (1987). The organization and function of the vomeronasal system. *Annual Review of Neuroscience, 10*, 325–362.

Hamer, D. H., Hu, S., Magnuson, V. L., Hu, N., & Pattatucci, A. M. L. (1993). A linkage between DNA markers on the X chromosome and male sexual orientation. *Science, 261*, 321–327.

Hariton, E. B., & Singer, J. L. (1974). Women's fantasies during marital intercourse: Normative and theoretical implications. *Journal of Consulting and Clinical Psychology, 2*(8), 50–56.

Harms, V. (1992). *The inner lover*. Boston, MA: Shambhala.

Harrington, N. T., & Leitenberg, H. (1994). Relationship between alcohol consumption and victim behaviors immediately preceding sexual aggression by an acquaintance. *Violence and Victims, 9*(4), 315–324.

Harris, J. R. (1998). *The nurture assumption: Why children turn out the way they do; Parents matter less than you think and peers matter more.* New York: Free.

Harry, J. H. (1983). *Gay children grow up.* New York: Praeger.

Harter, S., Waters, P. L., Pettitt, L. M. Whitesell, N., Kofkin, J., & Jordan, J. (1997). Autonomy and connectedness as dimensions of relationship styles in men and women. *Journal of Social and Personal Relationships, 14,* 147–164.

Harvey, J. H. (1989). People's naive understandings of their close relationships: Attributional and personal construct perspectives. *International Journal of Personal Construct Psychology, 2,* 37–48.

Harvey, J. (May, 1991). *House of Pain and Hope: Accounts of Loss.* Paper presented at the Conference of the International Network on Personal Relationships, Normal/Bloomington, IL.

Harvey, J. H., Agostinelli, G., & Weber, A. L. (1989). Account-making and the formation of expectations about close relationships. In C. Hendrick (Ed.) *Review of personality and social psychology, Vol. 10* (pp 39–62). Newbury Park, CA: Sage.

Harvey, J. H., Flanary, R., & Morgan, M. (1986). Vivid memories of vivid loves gone by. *Journal of Social and Personal Relationships, 3,* 359–373.

Hassebrauck, M. (1998). The visual process method: A new method to study physical attractiveness. *Evolution and Human Behavior, 19*(2), 111–123.

Hatfield, E. (1988). Passionate and companionate love. In R. J. Sternberg & M. L. Barnes (Eds.), *The psychology of love* (pp. 191–217). New Haven, CT: Yale University Press.

Hatfield, E., Schmitz, E., Cornelius, J., & Rapson, R. L. (1988). Passionate love: How early does it begin? *Journal of Psychology & Human Sexuality, 1*(1), 35–51.

Hatfield, E., & Rapson, R. L. (1993). *Love, sex, and intimacy: Their psychology, biology, and history.* New York: HarperCollins.

Hatfield, E., & Sprecher, S. (1986). *Mirror, mirror . . . The importance of looks in everyday life.* Albany, NY: State University of New York Press.

Hause, K. S. (1995, June). *Friendship after marriage: Can it ever be the same?* Paper presented at the conference of International Network on Personal Relationships, Williamsburg, VA.

Haviland, M. G., & Reise, S. P. (1996). A California Q-sort alexithymia prototype and its relationship to ego-control and ego-resiliency. *Journal of Psychosomatic Research, 41*(6), 597–608.

Hazan, C. (1992, July). *Attachment formation and transfer: Tests of two models.* Paper presented at the conference of the International Society for the Study of Personal Relationships, Orono, ME.

Heavey, C. L., Christensen, A., & Malamuth, N. M. (1995). The longitudindal impact of demand and withdraw during marital conflict. *Journal of Consulting and Clinical Psychology, 63,* 797–801.

Heavey, C. L., Layne, C., & Christensen, A. (1993). Gender and conflict structure in marital interaction: A replication and extension. *Journal of Consulting and Clinical Psychology, 61,* 16–27.

Heiserman, A., & Cook, H. (1998). Narcissism, affect, and gender: An empirical examination of Kernberg's and Kohut's theories of narcissism. *Psychoanalytic Psychology, 15*(1), 74–92.

Heiss, J. (1968). An introduction to the elements of role theory. In J. Heiss (Ed.), *Family Roles and Interaction* (pp. 3–27). Chicago: Rand McNally.

Heiss, J. (1986). Wives' orientation toward breadwinning. *Journal of Family Issues, 7,* 358–381.

Heller, P., & Wood, B. (1998). The process of intimacy: Similarity, understanding and gender. *Journal of Marital and Family therapy, 24*(3), 273–288.

Hendin, H. (1975). *The age of sensation.* New York: W. W. Norton.

Hendrick, C., Hendrick, S., Foote, F. H., & Slapion-Foote, M. J. (1984). Do men and women love differently? *Journal of Social and Personal Relationships, 1,* 177–195.

Hendrick, C., & Hendrick, S. S. (1988). Lovers wear rose colored glasses. *Journal of Social and Personal Relationships, 5*(2), 161–183.

Hendrick, S. (1981). Self-disclosure and marital saticfaction. *Journal of Personality and Social Psychology, 40,* 1150–1159.

Hendrick, S. S., & Hendrick, C. (1992a). *Romantic love.* Newbury Park, CA: Sage.

Hendrick, S. S., & Hendrick, C. (1992b). *Liking, loving & relating* (2nd ed.). Pacific Grove, CA: Brooks/Cole.

Hendrix, H. (1988). *Getting the love you want: A guide for couples.* New York: Henry Holt.

Henry, J. P. (1986). Neuroendocrine patterns of emotional response. In R. Plutchick & H. Kellerman (Eds.), *Emotion: Theory, research, and experience. Vol. 3: Biological foundations of emotion.* New York: Academic Press.

Henry, K., & Holmes, J. G. (1998). Childhood revisited: The intimate relationships of individuals from divorced and conflict-ridden families. In J. A. Simpson, W. S. Rholes, et al. (Eds.), *Attachment theory and close relationships.* New York: Guilford.

Hepworth, J., Ryder, R. G., & Dreyer, A. S. (1984). The effects of parental loss on the formation of intimate relationships. *Journal of Marital and Family Therapy, 10*(1), 73–82.

Herdt, G. (1996). Issues in the cross-cultural study of homosexuality. In R. P. Cabaj & T. S. Stein (Eds.), *Textbook of homosexuality and mental health* (pp. 65–82). Washington, DC: American Psychiatric Press.

Hershberger, S. L. (1997). A twin registry study of male and female sexual orientation. *Journal of Sex Research, 34*(2), 212–222.

Herz, R. S., & Cahill, E. D. (1997). Differential use of sensory information in sexual behavior as a function of gender. *Human Nature, 8*(3), 275–286.

Hess, B., & Ferree, M. (1987). *Analyzing gender.* Beverly Hills, CA: Sage.

Hess, E. H., & Petrovich, S. B. (1987). Pupillary behavior in communication. In A. W. Siegman, S. Feldstein, et al. (Eds.), *Nonverbal behavior and communication (2nd ed.)* (pp. 327–349). Hillsdale, NJ: Lawrence Erlbaum.

Hess, L. H. (1965). Attitude and pupil size. *Scientific American, 212,* 46–54.

Hetherington, E. M. (1972). Effects of father absence on personality development in adolescent daughters. *Developmental Psychology, 7,* 313–326.

Hetherington, E. M. (1987). Family relations six years after divorce. In K. Pasley & M. Ihinger-Tallman (Eds.), *Remarriage and stepparenting: Current research and theory.* New York: Guilford.

Hetherington, E. M., Cox, M., & Cox, R. (1985). Long-term effects of divorce and remarriage on the adjustment of children. *Journal of the American Academy of Child Psychiatry, 24*(5), 518–530.

Hiedeman, B., Suhomlinova, O., & O'Rand, A. (1998). Economic independence, economic status and empty nest in midlife marital disruption. *Journal of Marriage and the Family, 60,* 219–231.

Hill, C. T., Rubin, Z., & Peplau, L. A. (1976). Breakups before marriage: The end of 103 affairs. *Journal of Social Issues, 32*(1), 147–168.

Hilton, J. M., & Haldeman, V. A. (1991). Gender differences in the performance of household tasks by adults and children in single-parent and two-parent, two-earner families. *Journal of Family Issues, 12*(1), 114–130.

Hingst, A. G., Hyman, B. M., & Salmon, J. L. (1983). Male children of divorce grown up: Parental bonding, relationship satisfaction, commitment and sex role identification. *Australian Journal of Sex, Marriage & Family, 6*(1), 15–32.

Hite, S. (1976). *The Hite report.* New York: Macmillan.

Hite, S. (1981). *The Hite report on male sexuality.* New York: Knopf.

Hite, S. (1987). *Women and love: A cultural revolution in progress.* New York: Knopf.

Hobart, C. (1990). Conflict in remarriages. *Journal of Divorce and Remarriage, 15,* 69–86.

Hodapp, V., Bongard, S., & Heiligtag, U. (1992). Active coping, expression of anger, and cardiovascular reactivity. *Personality and Individual Differences, 13*(10) 1069–1076.

Hoffman, S. D., & Duncan, G. J. (1988). What are the economic consequences of divorce? *Demography, 25,* 641–645.

Hoffman, L. W., & Manis, J. D. (1978). Influences of children on marital interaction and parental satisfactions and dissatisfactions. In R. M. Lerner & G. B. Spanier (Eds.), *Child influences on marital and family interaction.* New York: Academic Press.

Hokanson, J. E. (1970). Psychophysiological evaluation of the catharsis hypotheses. In E. I. Megargee & J. E. Hokanson (Eds.), *The dynamic of aggression.* New York: Harper & Row.

Holahan, C. K. (1984). Marital attitudes over 40 years: A longitudinal and cohort analysis. *Journal of Gerontology, 39,* 49–57.

Holmes, J. G., & Rempel, J. K. (1989). Trust in close relationships. In C. Hendrick (Ed.), *Review of personality and social psychology, Vol. 10. Close relationships* (pp. 187–220). Newbury Park, CA: Sage.

Holmstrom, P. (1972). The two-career family. Cambridge, MA: Schenkman.

Holt, P. A., & Stone, G. L. (1988). Needs, coping strategies, and coping outcomes associated with long-distance relationships. *Journal of College Student Development, 29,* 136–141.

Holtzworth-Munroe, A., & Jacobson, N. (1985). Causal attributions of married couples. When do they search for causes? What do they conclude when they do? *Journal of Personality and Social Psychology, 48,* 1398–1412.

Hood, T. (1983). Becoming a two-job family. New York: Praeger.

Hoon, P. W., Wineze, J. P., & Hoon, E. F. (1977). A test of reciprocal inhibition: Are anxiety and sexual arousal in women mutually inhibitory? *Journal of Abnormal Psychology, 86,* 65–74.

Hope, D. A., & Heimberg, R. G. (1990). Dating anxiety. In H. Leitenberg (Ed.), *Handbook of social and evaluation anxiety* (pp. 217–246). New York: Plenum Press.

Hopper, R., Knapp, M., & Scott, L. (1981). Couples personal idioms: Exploring intimate talk. *Journal of Communication, 31,* 23–33.

Houts, R. M., Robins, E., & Huston, T. L. (1996). Compatibility and the development of premarital relationships. *Journal of Marriage and the Family, 58*(1), 7–20.

Howard, J. A., Blumstein, P., & Schwartz, P. (1986). Sex, power, and influence tactics in intimate relationships. *Journal of Personality and Social Psychology, 51*(1), 102–109.

Howell, S. H., Portes, P. R., & Brown, J. H. (1997). Gender and age differences in child adjustment to parental separation. *Journal of Divorce and Remarriage, 27*(3–4), 141–158.

Hrdy, S. B. (1986). Empathy, polyandry and the myth of the coy female. In R. Blair (Ed.), *Feminist approaches to science.* New York: Pergamon.

Hsu, B., Kling, A., Kessler, C., Knapke, K, et al. (1994). Gender differences in sexual fantasy and behavior in a college population: A ten-year replication. *Journal of Sex and Marital Therapy, 20*(2), 103–118.

Hudson, P., & O'Hanlon, W. (1991). *Rewriting love stories.* New York: W. W. Norton.

Hupka, R. B., & Ryan, J. B. (1990). The cultural contribution to jealousy: Cross-cultural aggression in sexual jealousy situations. *Human Relations Area Files, 24,* 51–71.

Huston, T., McHale, S., & Crouter, A. (1986). When the honeymoon is over: Changes in the marriage relationship over the first year. In R. Gilmour & S. Duck (Eds.), *The emerging field of close relationships.* Hillsdale, NJ: Lawrence Erlbaum.

Huston, T. L. (1983). Power. In H. Kelley, E. Berscheid, A. Christensen, J. Harvey, T. Huston, G. Levinger, F. McClintock, L. Peplau, & D. Peterson (Eds.), *Close relationships.* New York: WH Freeman.

Hyde, J. S., & Linn, M. C. (1988). Gender differences in verbal ability: A meta-analysis. *Psychological Bulletin, 104,* 53–69.

Hyde, J. S. (1981). How large are cognitive gender differences? A meta-analysis using w2 and d. *American Psychologist, 36,* 892–901.

I ching, or book of changes. The Richard Wilhelm translation. (1950). (C. F. Baynes, Trans.). Princeton, NJ: Princeton University Press.

Ickes, W. (1993, June). *Empathic accuracy in close relationships.* Invited lecture at conference of International Network on Personal Relationships, Milwaukee, WI.

Ihinger-Tallman, M., & Pasley, K. (1987). *Remarriage.* Newbury Park, CA: Sage.

Insel, T. R. (1997). A neurobiological basis of social attachment. *American Journal of Psychiatry, 154*(6), 726–735.

Insel, T. R. (1992). Oxytocin—a neuropeptide for affiliation: Evidence from behavioral, receptor autoradiographic, and comparative studies. *Psychoneuroendocrinology, 17*(1), 3–35.

Irons, W. (1979). Investment and primary social dyads. In N. A. Chagnon & W. Irons (Eds.), *Evolutionary biology and human social behavior: An anthropological perspective.* North Scituate, MA: Duxbury Press.

Izard, C. E. (1992). Basic emotions, relations among emotions, and emotion-cognition relations. *Psychological Review, 99*(3), 561–565.

Jackson, D. D. (1965). Family rules: Marital quid pro quo. *Archives of General Psychiatry, 12,* 564–589.

Jacobs, J. R. (1989). *Factors facilitating romantic attraction and their relation to styles of loving, relationship satisfaction and complementarity theory.* (Doctoral dissertation, City University of New York).

Jacobs, L. E., Berscheid, E., & Walster, E. (1971). Self-esteem and attraction. *Journal of Personality and Social Psychology, 17,* 84–91.

Jacobson, N. S. (1996, July). *Are marriage and family disappearing?* Panel presentation at International Network for Personal Relationships, Seattle, WA.

Jacobson, N. S., & Addis, M. E. (1993). Research on couples and couple therapy. What do we know? Where are we going? *Journal of Consulting and Clinical Psychology, 61,* 85–93.

James, D., & Drakich, J. (1993). Understanding gender differences in amount of talk: A critical review of research. In D. Tannen (Ed.), *Gender and conversational interaction* (pp. 281–312). New York: Oxford University Press.

James, P. S. (1991). Effects of a communication training component added to an emotionally focused couples therapy. *Journal of Marital and Family Therapy, 17,* 263–294.

James, T. W., & Kimura, D. (1997). Sex differences in remembering the locations of objects in an array: Location-shifts versus location-exchanges. *Evolution and Human Behavior, 18,* 155–163.

Jankowiak, W. R., & Fischer, E. F. (1992). A cross-cultural perspective on romantic love. *Ethnology, 31*(2), 149–155.

Janus, S. S., & Janus, C. L. (1992). *The Janus report on sexual behavior.* New York: John Wiley & Sons.

Jaremko, M. E. (1982). Differences in daters: Effects of sex, dating frequency, and dating frequency of partner. *Behavioral Assessment, 4*(3), 307–316.

Jedlicka, D. (1980). A test of the psychoanalytic theory of mate selction. *The Journal of Social Psychology, 112,* 295–299.

Johnson, D. R., & Booth, A. (1998). Marital quality: A product of the dyadic environment or individual factors? *Social Forces, 76*(3), 883–904.

Johnson, E. M., & Huston, T. L. (1998). The perils of love, or why wives adapt to husbands during the transition to parenthood. *Journal of Marriage and the Family, 60,* 195–204.

Johnson, M. E., Brems, C., & Alford-Keating, P. (1997). Personality correlates of homophobia. *Journal of Homosexuality, 34*(1), 57–69.

Johnson, P., & Nelson, M. D. (1998). Parental divorce, family functioning, and college student development: An intergenerational perspective. *Journal of College Student Development, 39*(4), 355–363.

Johnson, P. A. (1983). *Two types of dating relationships: Long distance and close couples.* Doctoral dissertation, University of Minnesota.

Johnston, V., & Oliver-Rodriguez, J. C. (1997). Facial beauty and the late positive component of event-related potentials. *Journal of Sex Research, 34*(2), 188–198.

Jones, E. E., & Nisbett, R. E. (1972). *The actor and the observer: Divergent perceptions of the causes of behavior.* Morristown, NJ: General Learning Press.

Jones, J. C., & Barlow, D. H. (1990). Self-reported frequency of sexual urges, fantasies, and masturbatory fantasies in heterosexual males and females. *Archives of Sexual Behavior, 19*(3), 269–279.

Jordan, J. V. (Ed.). (1997). *Women's growth in diversity. More writings from the Stone Center.* New York: Guilford.

Jordan, J. V., Kaplan, A. G., Miller, J. B., Stiver, I. P., & Surrey, J. L. (1991). *Women's growth in connection.* New York: Guilford Press.

Jordan, K. M. (1995). Coming out and relationship quality for lesbian women. (Doctoral dissertation, University of Maryland, 1995). Dissertation Abstracts International, 56-05B, 2941.

Jorday, K. M., Vaughan, J. S., & Woodworth, K. J. (1997). I will survive: Lesbian, gay, and bisexual youths' experience of high school. *Journal of Gay & Lesbian Social Services, 7*(4), 17–33.

Jorgenson, S. R., & Gaudy, T. C. (1980). Self disclosure and satisfaction in marriage: The relation examined. *Family Relations 29,* 281–287.

Josselson, R. (1987). *Finding herself: Pathways to identity development in women.* San Francisco: Jossey-Bass.

Jourard, S. M. (1971). *Self disclosure: An experimental analysis of the transparent self.* New York: John Wiley & Sons.

Jung, C. G. (1964). Approaching the unconscious. In C. G. Jung (Ed.), *Man and his symbols*. New York: Dell.

Jung, C. G. (1925/1971). Marriage as a psychological relationship. (R. C. F. Hull, Trans.). In J. Campbell (Ed.), *The portable Jung*. New York: Viking Press.

Jung, C. G. (1928/1989). The love problem of a student. (R. C. F. Hull, Trans.). In J. Beebe (Ed.), *Aspects of the masculine*. Princeton, NJ: Princeton University Press.

Jung, C. G. (1946/1954). The psychology of the transference. In *The Collected Works of C. G. Jung, Vol. 16* (R. C. F. Hull, Trans.). Princeton, NJ: Princeton University Press.

Juran, S. (1989). Sexual behavior changes as a result of concern about AIDS: Gays, straights, males, and females. *Journal of Psychology and Human Sexuality, 2,* 61–77.

Kaczmarek, M. G., & Backlund, B. A. (1991). Disenfranchised grief: The loss of an adolescent romantic relationship. *Adolescence, 26*(102), 253–259.

Kagan, J., Reznick, J. S., & Snidman, N. (1988). Biological bases of childhood shyness. *Science, 240,* 167–171.

Kahn, M. (1970). Nonverbal communication and marital satifaction. *Family Process, 9,* 449–456.

Kakar, S. (1981). *The inner world: A psycho-analytic study of childhood and society in India*. Delhi, India: Oxford University Press.

Kalb, M. (1987). The effects of biography on the divorce adjustment process. *Sexual and Marital Therapy, 2*(1) 53–64.

Kalter, N. (1987). Long-term effects of divorce on children: A developmental vulnerability model. *American Journal of Orthopsychiatry, 57*(4), 587–600.

Kalter, N. (1989/1991). Effects of divorce on boys versus girls. In O. Pocs (Ed.), *Marriage and family 91/92* (pp. 179–182). Guilford, CT: Dushkin.

Kalter, N. (1990). *Growing up with divorce: Helping your child avoid immediate and later emotional problems*. New York: Free.

Kantor, D., & Lehr, W. (1975). *Inside the family: Toward a theory of family process*. San Francisco, CA: Jossey-Bass.

Kaplan, H. S., Lancaster, J. B., & Anderson, K. G. (1998). Human parental investment and fertility: The life histories of men in Albuquerque. In A. Booth & A. C. Crouter (Eds.), *Men in families. When do they get involved? What difference does it make?* (pp. 55–110). Mahwah, NJ: Lawrence Erlbaum.

Kaslow, F. W. (1984). Divorce: An evolutionary process of change in the family system. *Journal of Divorce, 7*(3), 21–39.

Kast, V. (1987). *Das Paar: Mythos und Wirklichkeit* [The couple: Myth and reality]. In P. M. Pflueger (Ed.), *Das Paar - Mythos und Wirklichkeit: Neue Werte in Liebe und Sexualitaet*. Olten, Germany: Walter-Verlag.

Katz, L. F., & Gottman, J. M. (1995). Marital interaction and child outcomes: A longitudinal study of mediating and moderating processes. In D. Cicchetti & S. L. Toth (Eds.), *Rochester symposium on developmental psychopathology. Vol 6: Emotion, cognition, and representation* (pp. 301–342). Rochester, NY: University of Rochester Press.

Katz, L. F., & Gottman, J. M. (1997). Buffering children from marital conflict and dissolution. *Journal of Clinical Child Psychology, 26*(2), 157–171.

Kaufman, G. (1996). *The psychology of shame. Theory and treatment of shame-based syndromes* (2nd ed.). New York: Springer.

Kaufman, G., & Raphael, L. (1996). *Coming out of shame: Transforming gay and lesbian lives*. New York: Doubleday.

Kaufman, P. A., Harrison, E., & Hyde, M. L. (1984). Distancing for intimacy in lesbian relationships. *American Journal of Psychiatry, 141,* 530–533.

Keelan, J. P. R., Dion, K. L., & Dion, K. K. (1994). Attachment style and heterosexual relationships among young adults: A short-term panel study. *Journal of Social and Personal Relationships, 11*(2), 201–214.

Keith, P. & Schafer, R. (1991). *Relationships and well-being over the life stages.* New York: Praeger Publishers.

Keller, H. (1997). Evolutionary approaches. In J. W. Berry, Y. H. Poortinga, & J. Pandey (Eds.), *Handbook of cross-cultural psychology, Vol 1. Theory and method* (pp. 215–256). Boston: Allyn and Bacon.

Kelley, H. H. (1979). *Personal relationships: Their structures and processes.* Hillsdale, NJ: Erlbaum.

Kelly, C., Huston, T. L., & Cate, R. M. (1985). Premarital relationship correlates of the erosion of satisfaction in marriage. *Journal of Social and Personal Relationships, 2,* 167–178.

Kelly, E. L., & Conley, J. J. (1987). Personality and compatibility: A prospective analysis of marital stability and marital satisfaction. *Journal of Personality and Social Psychology, 52*(1), 27–40.

Kelly, V. C., Jr. (1996). Affect and the redefinition of intimacy. In D. L. Nathanson (Ed.), *Knowing feeling: Affect, script, and psychotherapy* (pp. 55–104). New York: W. W. Norton.

Keltner, D., Young, R. C., & Buswell, B. N. (1997). Appeasement in human emotion, social practice, and personality. *Aggressive Behavior, 23,* 359–374.

Kenny, D. A., & Acitelli, L. K. (1994). Similarity in couples. *Journal of Family Psychology, 8*(4),417–431.

Kenrick, D. T., Sadalla, E. K., Groth, G., & Trost, M. R. (1990). Evolution, traits, and the stages of human courtship: Qualifying the parental investment model. *Journal of Personality, 58*(1), 97–116.

Kenrick, D. T., & Trost, M. R. (1987). A biosocial theory of heterosexual relationships. In K. Kelley (Ed.), *Females, males, and sexuality: Theories and research.* Albany: State University of New York Press.

Kerns, K. A. (1994). A longitudinal examination of links between mother-child attachment and children's friendships in early childhood. *Journal of Social and Personal Relationships, 11*(3), 379–381.

Keverne, E. B., Martensz, N. D., & Tuite, B. (1989). Beta-endorphin concentrations in cerebrospinal fluid of monkeys are influenced by grooming relationships. *Psychoneuroendocrinology, 14*(1–2), 155–161.

Kiecolt, K. J., & Acock, A. C. (1988). The long-term effects of family structure on gender-role attitudes. *Journal of Marriage and the Family, 50,* 709–717.

Kimura, D. (1992). Sex differences in the brain. *Scientific American (September),* 119–125.

King, C. E., & Christensen, A. (1983). The relationship events scale: A Guttman scaling of progress in courtship. *Journal of Marriage and the Family, 45*(3), 671–678.

Kingma, D. R. (1987). *Coming apart: Why relationships end and how to live through the ending of yours.* New York: Ballantine Books.

Kinnaird, K. L, & Gerrard, M. (1986). Premarital sexual behavior and attitudes toward marriage and divorce among young women as a function of their mothers' marital status. *Journal of Marriage and the Family, 48*(4), 757–765.

Kinsey, A. C., Pomeroy, W. B., Martin, C. E., & Gebhard, P. H. (1953). *Sexual behavior in the human female.* Philadelphia: W. B. Saunders.

Kinsey, A. C., Pomeroy, W. B., & Martin, C. E. (1948). *Sexual behavior in the human male*. Philadelphia: W. B. Saunders.

Kirkpatrick, L. A., & Davis, K. (1994). Attachment style, gender and relationship stability: A longitudinal analysis. *Journal of Personality and Social Psychology, 66*, 502–512.

Kirkpatrick, L. A., & Hazan, C. (1994). Attachment styles and close relationships: A four-year prospective study. *Personal Relationships, 1*(2), 123–142.

Kirkpatrick, M. (1991). Lesbian couples in therapy. *Psychiatric Annals, 21*, 491–496.

Kissman, K. (1992). Single parenting: Interventions in the transitional stages. *Contemporary Family Therapy, 14*(4), 323–333.

Kitson, G. C., Babri, K. B., & Roach, M. J. (1989). Adjustment to widowhood and divorce: A review. *Journal of Family Issues, 10*, 5–32.

Kitson, G. C., & Holmes, W. M. (1992). *Portrait of divorce: Adjustment to marital breakdown*. New York: Guilford Press.

Klagburn, F. (1992). *Married people*. New York: Doubleday.

Klein, F. (1978). *The bisexual option*. New York: Arbot House.

Kleinke, C. L. (1977). Assignment of responsibility for marital conflict to husbands and wives: Sex stereotypes or a double standard. *Psychological Reports, 41*, 219–222.

Kleinke, C. L., Meeker, F. B., & Staneski, R. A. (1986). Preference for opening lines: Comparing ratings by men and women. *Sex Roles, 15*, 585–600.

Klinetob, N. A, & Smith, D. A. (1996). Demand-withdraw communication in marital interaction: Tests of interspousal-contingency and gender role hypothesis. *Journal of Marriage and the Family, 58*(4), 945–957.

Klinger, R. L. (1996). Lesbian couples. Men. In R. P. Cabaj & T. S. Stein (Eds.), *Textbook of homosexuality and mental health* (pp. 339–351). Washington, DC: American Psychiatric Press.

Klinger, R. L., & Stein, T. S. (1996). Impact of violence, childhood sexual abuse, and domestic violence and abuse on lesbians, bisexuals, and gay men. In R. P. Cabaj & T. S. Stein (Eds.), *Textbook of homosexuality and mental health* (pp. 801–817). Washington, DC: American Psychiatric Press.

Klutky, N. (1990). *Geschlechtsunterschiede in der gedaechtnisleistung fuer gerueche, tonfolgen und farben* [Gender differences in the memory of smells, sounds, and colors]. *Zeitschrift fuer experimentelle und angewandte Psychologie, 37*(3), 437–446.

Knapp, M. L. (1978). *Social intercourse: From greeting to goodbye*. Newton, MA: Allyn & Bacon.

Knapp, M. L. (1984). *Interpersonal communication and human relationships*. Boston: Allyn & Bacon.

Knox, D., & Wilson, K. (1981). Dating behaviors of university students. *Family Relations, 30*, 255–258.

Knox, D., & Wilson, K. (1983). Dating problems of university students. *College Student Journal, 17*, 225–228.

Knudson-Martin, C., & Mahoney, A. R. (1996). Gender dilemmas and myth in the construction of marital bargains: Issues for marital therapy. *Family Process, 35*, 137–153.

Knudson-Martin, C., & Mahoney, A. R. (1998). Language and processes in the construction of equality in new marriages. *Family Relations, 47*, 81–91.

Komarovsky, M. (1962). *Blue collar marriage* (1st ed.). New York: Random House.

Komarovsky, M. (1976). *Dilemmas of masculinity*. New York: W. W. Norton.

Koren, P., Carlton, K., & Shaw, D. (1980). Marital conflict: Relations among behaviors, outcomes and distress. *Journal of Consulting and Clinical Psychology, 48*, 460–468.

Koss, M. P. (1988). Hidden rape. Sexual aggression and victimization in a national sample of students in higher education. In A. W. Burgess (Ed.), *Sexual assault. Vol. II* (pp. 3–25).

Koss, M. P., Dinero, T. E., Seibel, C. A., & Cox, S. L. (1988). Stranger and acquaintance rape. Are there differences in the victim's experience? *Psychology of Women Quarterly, 12*, 1–24.

Kovacs, L. (1992). Today's marriage: The six stages [60 minute video]. Sacramento, CA: Center for Marriage and Family Therapy.

Kramer, C. (1977). Perceptions of female and male speech. *Language in Speech, 20*, 151–161.

Krantzler, M. (1987). *Learning to love again.* New York: HarperCollins.

Krause, N. (1993). Early parental loss and personal control in later life. *Journals of Gerontology, 48*, 117–125.

Kressel, K., Lopez-Morillas, M., Weinglass, J., & Deutsch, M. (1978). Professional intervention in divorce: A summary of the views of lawyers, psychotherapists, and clergy. *Journal of Divorce, 2*, 119–115.

Krokoff, L. (1987). Recruiting representative samples for marital interaction research. *Journal of Social and Personal Relationships, 4*, 317–328.

Krugman, S. (1995). Male development and the transformation of shame. In R. F. Levant & W. S. Pollack (Eds.), *A new psychology of men.* New York: HarperCollins.

Kübler-Ross, E. (1969). *On death and dying.* New York: MacMillan.

Kulka, R. A., & Weingarten, H. (1979). The long-term effects of parental divorce in childhood on adult adjustment. *Journal of Social Issues, 35*(4), 50–78.

Kunkel, L. E., & Temple, L. L. (1992). Attitudes toward AIDS and homosexuals: Gender, marital status, and religion. *Journal of Applied Social Psychology, 22*(13), 1030–1040.

Kurdek, L. A. (1988a). Perceived social support in gays and lesbians in cohabitating relationships. *Journal of Personality and Social Psychology, 54*, 504–509.

Kurdek, L. A. (1988b). Cognitive mediators of children's adjustment to divorce. In S. A. Wolchik & P. Karoly (Eds.), *Children of divorce: Empirical perspectives on adjustment.* New York: Gardner.

Kurdek, L. A. (1991). The dissolution of gay and lesbian couples. *Journal of Social and Personal Relationships, 8*, 265–278.

Kurdek, L.A. (1994). Conflict resolution styles in gay, lesbian, and heteroseuxal couples. *Journal of Marriage and the Family, 56*, 705–722.

Kurdek, L. A. (1995). Lesbian and gay couples. In A. R. D'Augelli & C. J. Patterson (Eds), *Lesbian and gay identities over the lifespan: Psychological perspectives.* New York: Oxford University Press.

Kurdek, L. A. (1997). Relation between neuroticism and dimensions of relationship commitment: Evidence from gay, lesbian, and heterosexual couples. *Journal of Family Psychology, 11*, 109–124.

Kurdek, L. A. (1998a). Relationship outcomes and their predictors: Longitudinal evidence from heterosexual married, gay cohabiting, and lesbian cohabiting couples. *Journal of Marriage and the Family, 60*, 553–568.

Kurdek, L. A. (1998b). Developmental changes in marital satisfaction: A 6-year prospective longitudinal study of newlywed couples. In T. N. Bradbury (Ed.),

The developmental course of marital dysfunction (pp. 180–204). New York: Cambridge University Press.

Kurdek, L. A., & Schmitt, J. P. (1986a). Early development of relationship quality in heterosexual married, heterosexual cohabiting, gay, and lesbian couples. *Developmental Psychology, 22,* 305–309.

Kurdek, L. A., & Schmitt, J. P. (1986b). Relationship quality of gay men in closed or open relationships. *Journal of Homosexuality, 12*(2) 85–99.

Kurdek, L. A., & Schmitt, J. P. (1986c). Relationship quality of partners in heterosexual married, heterosexual cohabitating, and gay and lesbian relationships. *Journal of Personality and Social Psychology, 51,* 711–720.

Kurdek, L. A., & Schmitt, J. P. (1986d). Interaction of sex role self-concept with relationship quality and relationship beliefs in married, heterosexual cohabiting, gay, and lesbian couples. *Journal of Personality and Social Psychology, 51,* 365–370.

Kurdek, L. A., & Sinclair, R. J. (1988). Adjustment of young adolescents in two-parent nuclear, stepfather, and mother-custody families. *Journal of Consulting and Clinical Psychology, 56,* 91–96.

Lackovic-Grgin, K., Dekovic, M., & Opacic, G. (1994). Pubertal status, interaction with significant others, and self-esteem of adolescent girls. *Adolescence, 29,* 691–700.

Lakoff, R. (1973). Language and women's place. *Language in Society, 2,* 45–80.

Lang-Takac, E., & Osterweil, Z. (1992) Separateness and connectedness: Differences between the sexes. *Sex Roles, 27*(5–6), 277–289.

Lansky, M. R. (1987). Shame and domestic violence. In D. L. Nathanson (Ed.), *The many faces of shame.* New York: Guilford Press.

Lansky, M. R. (1997). Envy as process. In M. R. Lansky & A. P. Morrison (Eds.), *The widening scope of shame* (pp. 327–338). Hillsdale, NJ: The Analytic Press.

LaPrelle, J., Hoyle, R. H., Insko, C. A., & Bernthal, P. (1990). Interpersonal attraction and descriptions of the traits of others: Ideal similarity, self similarity and liking. *Journal of Research in Personality, 24,* 216–240.

Larson, J., Hammond, C., & Harper, J. (1998). Perceived equity and intimacy in marriage. *Journal of Marital and Family Therapy, 24*(4), 487–506.

Laumann, E. O., Gagnon, J. H., Michael, R. T., & Michaels, S. (1994). *The social organization of sexuality: Sexual practices in the United States.* Chicago: University of Chicago Press.

Lawson, D., Gaushell, H., & Karst, R. (1993). The age onset of personal authority in the family system. *Journal of Marital and Family Therapy, 19,* 287–292.

Lazarus, R. S. (1991). *Emotion and adaptation.* New York: Oxford University Press.

LeDoux, J. E. (1992). Brain systems and emotion memory. In K. T. Strongman (Ed.), *International review of studies on emotion, Vol. 2* (pp. 23–29). Chichester, UK: Wiley.

LeDoux, J. E. (1989). Cognitive-emotional interactions in the brain. *Cognition and Emotion, 3*(4), 267–289.

LeDoux, J. E. (1993). Cognition versus emotion, again—this time in the brain: A response to Parrott and Schulkin. *Cognition and Emotion, 7*(1), 61–64.

Lee, J. A. (1973). *Colours of love: An exploration of the ways of loving.* Toronto: New Press.

Lee, J. A. (1988). Love-styles. In R. J. Sternberg & M. L. Barnes (Eds.), *The psychology of love* (pp. 38–67). New Haven, CT: Yale University Press.

Lee, J. A., (1998). Ideologies of lovestyle and sexstyle. In V. C. De Munck (Ed.), *Romantic love and sexual behavior: Perspectives from the social sciences* (pp. 33–76). Westport, CT: Praeger.

Lee, L. (1984). Sequences in separation: A framework for investigating endings of the personal (romantic) relationship. *Journal of Social and Personal Relationships, 1,* 49–73.

Lee, M. (1995). Trajectory of influences of parental divorce on children's heterosexual relationships. *Journal of Divorce and Remarriage, 22*(3/4), 55–76.

Lee, M. Y. (1997). Post-divorce interparental conflict, children's contact with both parents, children's emotional processes, and children's behavioral adjustment. *Journal of Divorce and Remarriage, 27* (3–4), 61–82.

Lee, V. E., & Bryk, A. S. (1986). Effects of single-sex secondary schools on student achievement and attitudes. *Journal of Educational Psychology, 78*(5), 381–395.

Lerner, H. G. (1989). *The dance of anger; A woman's guide to changing the patterns of intimate relationships.* New York: Harper & Row.

LeVay, S. (1993). *The sexual brain.* Cambridge, MA: M.I.T. Press.

Levenson, H., & Harris, C. N. (1980). Love and the search for identity. In K. S. Pope & Associates, *On love and loving: Psychological perspectives on the nature and experience of romantic love* (pp. 244–265). San Francisco: Jossey-Bass.

Levenson, R. (1984). Intimacy, autonomy, and gender: Developmental differences and their reflection in adult relationships. *Journal of the American Academy of Psychoanalysis, 12*(4), 529–544.

Levenson, R. W., & Gottman, J. M. (1985). Physiological and affective predictors of change in relationship satisfaction. *Journal of Personality and Social Psychology, 49,* 85–94.

Levi-Strauss, C. (1969). *The elementary structures of kinship.* Boston: Beacon Press.

Levitz-Jones, E. M., & Orlofsky, J. L. (1985). Separation-individuation and intimacy capacity in college women. *Journal of Personality and Social Psychology, 49*(1), 156–169.

Levine, H. (1997). A further exploration of the lesbian identity development process and its measurement. *Journal of Homosexuality, 34*(2), 67–78.

Levine-MacCombie, J., & Koss, M. P. (1986). Acquaintance rape: Effective avoidance strategies. *Psychology of Women Quarterly, 10,* 311–320.

Levinger, G., & Senn, D. (1967). Disclosure of feelings in marriage. *Merrill-Palmer Quarterly, 13,* 237–249.

Levinson, R. A., Jaccard, J., & Beamer, L. (1995). Older adolescents' engagement in casual sex: Impact of risk perception and psychosocial motivations. *Journal of Youth and Adolescence, 24*(3), 349–364.

Levy, J., & Munroe, R. (1938). *The happy family.* New York: Alfred A. Knopf.

Lewis, H. B. (1987). The role of shame in depression over the life span. In H. B. Lewis (Ed.), *The role of shame in symptom formation* (pp. 29–49).

Lewis, J. A. (1986). Family structure and stress. *Family Process, 25,* 235–247.

Lewis, R. A. (1978). Emotional intimacy among men. *Journal of Social Issues, 34*(1), 108–121.

Liebowitz, M. R. (1983). *The chemistry of love.* Boston: Little, Brown & Company.

Lindenbaum, J. P. (1985). The shattering of an illusion: The problem of competition in lesbian relationships. *Feminist Studies, 11*(1), 85–103.

Lindholm, C. (1998). The future of love. In V. C. DeMunck (Ed.), *Romantic love and sexual behavior: Perspectives from the social sciences* (pp. 17–32). Westport, CT: Praeger.

Linton, R. (1936). *The study of man.* New York: Appleton-Centry.

Lisak, D., & Ivan, C. (1995). Deficits in intimacy and empathy in sexually aggressive men. *Journal of Interpersonal Violence, 10*(3), 296–308.

Lloyd, S. A. (1987). Conflict in premarital relationships: Differential perceptions of males and females. *Family Relations, 36,* 290–294.

Lloyd, S. A. (1990). A behavioral self-report technique for assessing conflict in close relationships. *Journal of Social and Personal Relationships, 7,* 265–272.

Lloyd, S. A., & Cate, R. M. (1985). The developmental course of conflict in dissolution of premarital relationships. *Journal of Social and Personal Relationships, 2,* 179–194.

Lloyd, S. A., & Emery, B. C. (1993, June). *Physically aggressive conflict in romantic relationships.* Paper presented at the Conference of the International Network on Personal Relationships, Milwaukee, WI.

Lloyd, S. A., Cate, R. M., & Henton, J. M. (1984). Predicting premarital relationship stability: A methodological refinement. *Journal of Marriage and the Family, 46,* 71–76.

Loftus, E. F., Mahzarin, R. B., Schooler, J. W., & Foster, R. A. (1987). Who remembers what? Gender differences in memory. *Michigan Quarterly Review, 26*(1) 64–85.

Long, B. H. (1987). Perceptions of parental discord and parental separations in the United States: Effects on daughters' attitudes toward marriage and courtship progress. *The Journal of Social Psychology, 127*(6), 573–582.

Long, B. H. (1989, November). Heterosexual involvement of unmarried undergraduate females in relation to self-evaluations. *Journal of Youth and Adolescence, 18*(5), 489–500.

Lorber, J., & Farrell, S. (1991). *The social construction of gender.* Newbury Park, CA: Sage.

Loyer-Carlson, V. L. (1989). *Causal attributions and the dissolution of casual-dating relationships.* (Doctoral dissertation, Oregon State University, 1989.)

Lumsden, C. J., & Wilson, E. O. (1981). *Genes, mind, and culture: The coevolutionary process.* Cambridge, MA: Harvard University Press.

Lykken, D. T., & Tellegen, A. (1993). Is human mating adventitious or the result of lawful choice? A twin study of mate selection. *Journal of Personality and Social Psychology, 65*(1), 56–68.

Lyons-Ruth, K. (1991). Rapprochement or approchement: Mahler's theory reconsidered from the vantage point of recent research on early attachment relationships. *Psychoanalytic Psychology, 8*(1), 1–23.

Mack, R. W., & Snyder, R. C. (1957). The analysis of social conflict: Toward an overview and synthesis. *Journal of Conflict Resolution, 1,* 212–248.

Madanes, C. (1997). Shame: How to bring a sense of right and wrong into the family. In J. K. Zeig (Ed.), *The evolution of psychotherapy: The third conference* (pp. 257–267). New York: Brunner/Mazel.

Mahler, M. S., Pine, F., & Bergman, A. (1975). *The psychological birth of the human infant.* London: Hutchinson & Co.

Mahler, M. S. (1979a). On the first three subphases of the separation-individuation process. In *The selected papers of Margaret S. Mahler, M.D. Vol. 2.* New York: Jason Aronson.

Main, M., Kaplan, N., & Cassidy, J. (1985). Security in infancy, childhood, and adulthood: A move to the level of representation. *Monographs of the Society for Reseach in Child Development, 50*(1–2), 67–104.

Malatesta-Magai, C., Jonas, R., Shepard, B., & Culver, L. C. (1992). Type A behavior pattern and emotional expression in younger and older adults. *Psychology and Aging, 7*(4), 551–561.

Malone, T. P., & Malone, P. T. (1987). *The art of intimacy.* New York: Prentice Hall.

Mandell, D. (1995). Fathers who don't pay child support: Hearing their voices. *Journal of Divorce & Remarriage, 23*(1–2), 85–116.

Mandler, G. (1997). *Human nature explored.* New York: Oxford University Press.

Manning, J. T., Scott, D., Whitehouse, G. H., & Leinster, S. J. (1997). Breast asymmetry and phenotypic quality in women. *Evolution and Human Behavior, 18,* 223–236.

Manning, J. T., Scott, D., Whitehouse, G. H., Leinster, S. J., & Walton, J. M. (1996). Asymmetry and the menstrual cycle in women. *Ethology and Sociobiology, 17,* 129–143.

Manodori, C. (1998). This powerful opening of the heart: How ritual affirms lesbian identity. *Journal of Homosexuality, 36*(2), 41–58.

Margolin, G., & Wampold, B. (1981). Sequential analysis of conflict and accord in distressed and nondistressed marital partners. *Journal of Consulting and Clinical Psychology, 49,* 554–567.

Markman, H. J., Renick, M. J., Floyd, F. J., Stanley, S. M., & Clements, M. (1993). Preventing marital distress through communication and conflict management: A 4- and 5-year followup. *Journal of Consulting and Clinical Psychology, 61,* 70–77.

Marmor, J. (1996). Nongay therapists and gay men and lesbians: A personal reflection. In R. P. Cabaj & T. S. Stein (Eds.), *Textbook of homosexuality and mental health* (pp. 539–545). Washington, DC: American Psychiatric Press.

Maroldo, G. K. (1982). Shyness and love on a college campus. *Perceptual and Motor Skills, 55*(3), 819–824.

Martin, J. I., & Knox, J. (1997). Self-esteem instability and its implications for HIV prevention among gay men. *Health and Social Work, 22*(4), 264–273.

Martin, M. W. (1985). Satisfaction with intimate exchange: Gender-role differences and the impact of equity, equality, and rewards. *Sex Roles, 12,* 597–605.

Marx, B. P., & Gross, A. M. (1995). An analysis of two contextual variables. *Behavior Modification, 19*(4), 451–463.

Masheter, C. (1989). Postdivorce relationships between exspouses: A literature review. *Journal of Divorce & Remarriage, 14*(1), 97–122.

Masheter, C. (1997a). Former spouses who are friends: Three case studies. *Journal of Social and Personal Relationships, 14*(2), 207–222.

Masheter, C. (1997b). Healthy and unhealthy friendship and hostility between former spouses. *Journal of Marriage and the Family, 59*(2), 463–477.

Matthews, L. S., Wickrama, K. A., & Conger, R. D. (1996). Predicting marital instability from spouse and observer reports of marital interaction. *Journal of Marriage and the Family, 58,* 641–655.

Mattison, A. M., & McWhirter, D. P. (1987). Male couples: The beginning years. *Journal of Social Work and Human Sexuality, 5*(2), 67–68.

Mattison, T. R. (1995). Is homosexuality genetic? A critical review and some suggestions. *Journal of Homosexuality, 28*(1–2), 115–145.

May, R. (1969). *Love and will.* New York: W. W. Norton.

Mazur, A., Susman, E. J., & Edelbruck, S. (1997). Sex difference in testosterone response in a video game contest. *Evolution and Human Behavior, 18,* 317–326.

McAdams, D. P. (1988). Personal needs and personal relationships. In S. W. Duck (Ed.), *Handbook of personal relationships: Theory, research, and interventions.* New York: John Wiley & Sons.

McAdams, D. P. (1985). *Power, intimacy, and the life story: Personological inquiries into identity.* Homewood, IL: Dorsey Press.

McBride, P. A., Anderson, G. M., Herzig, M. E., Snow, M. E., Thompson, S. M., Khair, V. D., Shapiro, T., & Cohen, D. J. (1998). Effects of diagnosis, race, and puberty on platelet serotonin levels in autism and mental retardation. *Journal of the American Academy of Child and Adolescent Psychiatry, 37*(7), 767–776.

McBurney, D. H., Gaulin, S. J. C., Devineni, T., & Adams, C. (1997). Superior spatial memory of women: Stronger evidence for the gathering hypothesis. *Evolution and Human Behavior, 18*, 165–174.

McCall, G., & Simmons, J. (1978). *Identities and interactions: An examination of human associations in everyday life* (rev. ed.). New York: Free.

McClanahan, K. K., Gold, J. A., Lenney, E., Ryckman, R. M., & Kulberg, G. E. (1990). Infatuation and attraction to a dissimilar other: Why is love blind? *Journal of Social Psychology, 130*(4), 433–445.

McClelland, D. C. (1987). *Human motivation.* Cambridge, UK: Cambridge University Press.

McClelland, D. C., Davis, W. N., Kalin, R., & Wanner, E. (1972). *The drinking man.* New York: The Free Press.

McClelland, D. C., Maddocks, J. A., & McAdams, D. P. (1985). The need for power, brain norepinephrine turnover, and memory. *Motivation and Emotion, 9*(1), 1–10.

McCollaum, B., & Lester, D. (1997). Sexual aggression and attitudes toward women and mothers. *Journal of Social Psychology, 137*(4), 538–539.

McConaghy, N. (1967). Penile volume changes to moving pictures of male and female nudes in heterosexual and homosexual males. *Behavior Research and Therapy, 5*, 43–48.

McGuinness, D. (1985). Sensory biases in cognitive development. In R. L. Hall, P. Draper, M. E. Hamilton, D. McGuinness, C. M. Otten, & E. A. Roth (Eds.), *Male–female differences: A bio-cultural perspective.* New York: Praeger.

McGuire, K. A. (1987). *Adult children of divorce: Curative factors of support group therapy.* (Psy. D. research paper, Biola University.

McGuire, T. T. (1995). Is homosexuality genetic? A critical review and some suggestions. *Journal of Homosexuality, 28*(1–2), 115–145.

McHale, S., & Huston, T. (1985). The effect of the transition to parenthood on the marriage relationship: A longitudinal study. *Journal of Family Issues, 6*, 409–434.

McWhirter, D. P., & Mattison, A. M. (1984). *The male couple. How relationships develop.* Englewood Cliffs, NJ: Prentice-Hall.

Meer, J. (1987, April). Homosexuality: An effeminate beginning? *Psychology Today, 66.*

Messing, R. (1989). *Couples' stories of meeting and attraction: A technique for identifying the marital contract.* (Doctoral dissertation, Wright Institute, Berkeley, CA, 1989).

Metts, S., Cupach, W. R., & Bejlovec, R. A. (1989). 'I love you too much to ever start liking you': Redefining romantic relationships. *Journal of Social and Personal Relationships, 6*(3), 259–274.

Metts, S., & Cupach, W. R. (1993, June). *Negotiating cross-sex friendships.* Paper presented at the conference of the International Network on Personal Relationships, Milwaukee, WI.

Meyer, D. R., & Bartfeld, J. (1996). Compliance with child support orders in divorce cases. *Journal of Marriage & the Family, 58*(1), 201–212.

Michaels, S. (1996). The prevalence of homosexuality in the United States. In R. P. Cabaj & T. S. Stein (Eds.), *Textbook of homosexuality and mental health* (pp. 43–64). Washington, DC: American Psychiatric Press.

Michelson, L. (1985). Flooding. In *Dictionary of behavioral therapy techniques*, (pp. 126–131). Elmsford, NY: Pergamon Press.

Milardo, R. M., Johnson, M. P., & Huston, T. L. (1983). Developing close relationships: Changing patterns of interaction between pair members and social networks. *Journal of Personality and Social Pyschology, 44*(5), 964–976.

Milkman, H. B., & Sunderwirth, S. G. (1987). *Craving for ecstasy: The consciousness and chemistry of escape*. Lexington, MA: Heath.

Miller, J. (1976). *Toward a new psychology of women.* Boston: Beacon.

Miller, S., Nunnally, E. W., & Wackman, D. (1975). *Alive and aware: Improving communication in relationships*. Minneapolis, MN: Interpersonal Communications Programs, Incorporated.

Miller, S., Miller, P., Nunnally, E., & Wackman, D. (1991). *Talking and listening together: The Minnesota Couples Communication Program.* Littleton, CO: Interpersonal Communications Programs, Incorporated.

Miller, R., & Simpson, J. A. (1991, May). *The "grass may be greener" elsewhere, but happy gardeners are less likely to notice: Relationship satisfaction and attention to alternatives.* Paper presented at the conference of the International Network on Personal Relationships, Normal/Bloomington, IL.

Mills, P. J., Schneider, R. H., & Dimsdale, J. E. (1989). Anger assessment and reactivity to stress. *Journal of Psychosomatic Research, 33*(3), 379–382.

Mirowsky, J., & Ross, C. E. (1995). Sex differences in distress: Real or artifact? *American Sociological Review, 60,* 449–468.

Mitchell, B.A., & Gee, E. M. (1996). "Boomerang kids" and midlife parental marital satisfaction. *Family Relations, 45,* 442–448.

Mokros, H. B. (1995). Suicide and shame. *American Behavioral Scientist, 38*(8), 1091–1103.

Money, J. (1980). *Love and lovesickness*. Baltimore, MD: Johns Hopkins University Press.

Monroe, M., Baker, R. C., & Roll, S. (1997). The relationship of homophobia to intimacy in heterosexual men. *Journal of Homosexuality, 33*(2), 23–37.

Montgomery, B. M. (1984). Communication in intimate relationships: A research challenge. *Communication Quarterly, 32,* 318–325.

Monti-Bloch, L., Jennings-White, C., & Berliner, D. L. (1998). The human vomeronasal system: A review. *Olfaction and taste XII, Vol. 855. The annals of the New York Academy of Sciences* (pp. 171–389). New York: New York Academy of Sciences.

Monti-Bloch, L., & Grosser, B. I. (1991). Effect of putative pheromones on the electrical activity of the human vomeronasal organ and olfactory epithelium. *Journal of Steroid Biochemistry and Molecular Biology, 39*(4B), 573–582.

Monti-Bloch, L., Jennings-White, C., Dolberg, D. S., & Berliner, D. L. (1994). The human vomeronasal system. Proceedings of the International Conference on Hormones, Brain, and Behavior. *Psychoneuroendocrinology, 19*(5–7), 673–686.

Moore, M. M. (1985). Nonverbal courtship patterns in women: Context and consequences. *Ethnology and Sociobiology, 6*(4), 237–247.

Moran, D. T., Jafek, B. W., & Rowley, J. C., III. (1991). The vomeronasal (Jacobson's) organ in man: Ultrastructure and frequency of occurrence. *Journal of Steroid Biochemistry and Molecular Biology, 39*(4B), 545–552.

Morin, S. F., & Garfinkel, E. M. (1978). Male homophobia. *Journal of Social Issues, 34*(1), 29–47.

Morrison, A. P., & Stolorow, R. D. (1997). Shame, narcissism, and intersubjectivity.

In M. R. Lansky & A. P. Morrison (Eds.), *The widening scope of shame* (pp. 63–87). Hillsdale, NJ: The Analytic Press.

Morrow, G. D., Clark, E. M., & Brock, K. F. (1995). Individual and partner love styles: Implications for the quality of romantic involvements. *Journal of Social and Personal Relationships, 12*(3).

Morrow, G. D., & O'Sullivan, C. (1998). Romantic ideals as comparison levels: Implications for satisfaction and commitment in romantic involvements. In V. C. De Munck (Ed.), *Romantic love and sexual behavior: Perspectives from the social sciences* (pp. 171–199). Westport, CT: Praeger.

Moss, M. S., & Moss, S. Z. (1996). Remarriage of widowed persons: A triadic relationship. In D. Klass, P. R. Silerman, et al. (Eds.), *Continuing bonds: New understandings of grief*. Washington, DC: Taylor & Francis.

Motley, M. T., & Reeder H. M. (1995). Unwanted escalation of sexual intimacy: Male and female perceptions of connotations and relational consequences of resistance messages. *Communication Monographs, 62*(4), 355–382.

Mowatt, M. H. (1987). *Divorce counseling: A practical guide*. Lexington, MA: D. C. Heath.

Muehlenhard, C. L., & Hollabaugh, L. C. (1988). Do women sometimes say no when they mean yes? The prevalence and correlates of women's token resistance to sex. *Journal of Personality and Social Psychology, 54*, 872–879.

Muehlenhard, C. L., Koralewski, M. A., Andrews, S. L., & Burdick, C. A. (1986). Verbal and nonverbal cues that convey interest in dating: Two studies. *Behavior Therapy, 17*, 404–419.

Muehlenhard, C. L., & Linton, M. A. (1987). Date rape and sexual aggression in dating situations: Incidence and risk factors. *Journal of Counseling Psychology, 34*(2), 186–196.

Muehlenhard, C. L., & McCoy, M. L. (1991). Double standard/double bind. The sexual double standard and women's communication about sex. *Psychology of Women Quarterly, 15*, 447–461.

Mueller, C. W., & Pope, H. (1977). Marital instability: A study of its transmission between generations. *Journal of Marriage and the Family, 39*, 83–93.

Mueller, D. P., & Cooper, P. W. (1986). Children of single parent families: How they fare as young adults. *Family Relations, 35*, 169–176.

Murdock, G. P., & White, D. R. (1969). Standard cross-cultural sample. *Ethnology, 8*, 329–369.

Murray, S. L., & Holmes, J. G. (1998). A leap of faith? Positive illusions in romantic relationships. *Personality and Social Psychology Bulletin, 23*(6), 586–604.

Murstein, B. I. (1986). *Paths to marriage*. Beverly Hills, CA: Sage.

Mutovkina, L. G., & Lapin, I. P. (1990). Attenuation of effects of phenylethylamine on social and individual behaviour in mice by ethanol pretreatment. *Alcohol & Alcoholism, 25*(4), 417–420.

Nathanson, D. L. (1987). A timetable of shame. In D. L. Nathanson (Ed.), *The many faces of shame*. New York: Guilford.

Nathanson, D. L. (1992) *Shame and pride: Affect, sex, and the birth of the self*. New York: W. W. Norton.

Nathanson, D. L., & Pfrommer, J. M. (1993). Affect theory and psychopharmacology. *Psychiatric Annals, 23*(10), 584–593.

National Gay and Lesbian Task Force Policy Institute. (1992). Anti-gay/lesbian violence, victimization and defamation in 1992. New York: Author.

National Institute of Mental Health Task Force on Homosexuality. (1972). Final

Report and Background Papers. Washington, DC: U. S. Government Printing Office.

Navran, L. (1967). Communication and adjustment in marriage. *Family Process, 6*, 173–184.

Neil, J. R., & Kniskern, D. P. (1982). *Selected writings of Carl Whitaker: The growth of a therapist.* New York: Guilford.

Nelson, E., Allison, J., & Sundre, D. (1992). Relationships between divorce and college students' development of identity and intimacy. *Journal of Divorce & Remarriage, 18*(3–4), 121–135.

Nelson, E. S., & Krieger, M. A. (1997). Changes in attitudes toward homosexuality in college students: Implementation of a gay men and lesbian peer panel. *Journal of Homosexuality, 33*(2), 63–81.

Nelson, C., & Vaillant, P. M. (1993). Personality dynamics of adolescent boys where the father was absent. *Perceptual and Motor Skills, 76*, 435–443.

Neumarker, K. J., & Bartsch, A. J. (1998). Anorexia nervosa und "Anorexia athleticau." *Wiener Medizinische Wochenschrift, 148*(10), 245–250.

Newman, H. M., & Langer, E. J. (1981). Post-divorce adaptation and attribution of responsibility. *Sex Roles, 7*, 223–232.

Nichols, M. (1982). The treatment of inhibited sexual desire (ISD) in lesbian couples. *Women and Therapy, 1*, 49–66.

Noller, P. (1980). Misunderstandings in marital communication: A study of couples' nonverbal communication. *Journal of Personality and Social Psychology, 39*, 1135–1148.

Noller, P. (1993). Gender and emotional communication in marriage: Different cultures or differential social power? *Journal of Language and Social Psychology, 12*, 132–152.

Noller, P., & Gallois C. (1988). Understanding and misunderstanding in marriage: Sex and marital adjustment differences in structured and free interaction. In P. Noller & M. A. Fitzpatrick (Eds.), *Perspectives on marital interaction* (pp. 53–77). Clevedon, England: Multilingual Matters.

Noller, P. & Fitzpatrick, M. A. (1988). *Perspectives on marital interaction.* Clevedon, England: Multilingual Matters.

Noller, P. & Fitpatrick, M. A. (1990). Marital communication. *Journal of Marriage and the Family, 52*, 832–843.

Noller, P., & Ruzzene, M. (1991). Communication in marriage: The influence of affect and cognition. In G. J. O. Fletcher & F. D. Fincham (Eds.), *Cognition in close relationships* (pp. 203–233). Hillsdale, NJ: Lawrence Erlbaum.

Normen, R. H., & Olson, D. H. (1983). Interaction patterns of premarital couples: Typological assessment over time. *American Journal of Family Therapy, 11*, 25–37.

Norton, A. J., & Moorman, J. E. (1987). Current trends in marriage and divorce among American women. *Journal of Marriage and the Family, 40*, 3–14.

Notarius, C. E., & Johnson, J. S. (1982). Emotional expression in husbands and wives. *Journal of Marriage and the Family, 44*, 483–489.

Novak, W. (1983). *The great American man shortage and other roadblocks to romance.* New York: Rawson.

Nugent, M., & Constantine, L. (1988). Marital paradigms: Compatibility, treatment and outcome in marital therapy, *Journal of Marital and Family Therapy, 14*, 351–369.

Nurius, P. S., Norris, J., Dimeff, L. A., & Graham, T. L. (1996). Expectations regarding acquaintance sexual aggression among sorority and fraternity members. *Sex Roles, 35*(7–8), 427–444.

O'Brien, E. J. (1991). Sex differences in components of self-esteem. *Psychological Reports, 68,* 241–242.

O'Sullivan, P. B., Gurien, R. A., & Wiemann, J. M. (1993, June). *Interpersonal communication media use in long-distance relationships.* Paper presented at the conference of the International Network on Personal Relationships, Milwaukee, WI.

Oden, T. C. (1974). *The twelve kinds of intimacy.* Unpublished manuscript.

Oderberg, N. (1986). College students from divorced families: The impact of post-divorce life on long-term psychological adjustment. *Conciliation Courts Review, 24*(1), 103–110.

Oggins, J. , Veroff, J., & Leber, D. (1993). Perceptions of marital interaction among black and white newlyweds. *Journal of Personality and Social Psychlgy, 65,* 495–511.

Olesker, W. (1990). Sex differences during the early separation-individuation process. *Journal of the American Psychoanalytic Association, 38*(2), 325–346.

Oliver, M. B., & Hyde, J. S. (1993). Gender differences in sexuality: A meta-analysis. *Psychological Bulletin, 114*(1), 29–51.

Olson, D., Russell, C., & Sprenkle, D. (1983). Circumplex model of marital and family systems: VI. Theoretical update. *Family Process, 22,* 69–83.

Olson, D. H., McCubbin, H., Barnes, H., Larsen, A., Maxen, M., & Wilson, M. (1983). *Families: What makes them work.* Beverly Hills: Sage.

Oppenheimer, K. (1987). The impact of daily stress on women's adjustment to marital separation. *Journal of Family Practice, 24* (5), 507-511.

Ornstein, R., & Carstensen, L. (1991). *Psychology: The study of human experience* (3rd ed.). New York: Harcourt Brace Jovanovich.

Ornstein, R., Herron, J., Johnstone, J., & Swencionis, C. (1979). Differential right hemisphere involvement in two reading tasks. *Psychophysiology, 16*(4), 398–401.

Orvis, B. R., Kelley, H. H., & Butler, D. (1976). Attributional conflict in young couples. In J. H. Harvey, W. J. Ickes, & R. E. Kidd (Eds.), *New directions in attribution research (Vol. 1).* Hillsdale, NJ: Erlbaum.

Osbon, D. K. (1991). *Reflections on the art of living: A Joseph Campbell companion.* New York: HarperCollins.

Ovid, (Ca 1B.C.˜8A.D./1988). *Art of love.* New York: Riverrun Press.

Panksepp, J., Nelson, E., & Mekkedal, M. (1997). Brain systems for the mediation of social separation-distress and social-reward. Evolutionary antecedents and neuropeptide intermediaries. In C. S. Carter, I. I. Lederhandler, & B. Kirkpatrick (Eds.), *The integrative neurobiology of affiliation. Annals of the New York Academy of Sciences, Vol. 807* (pp. 78–100). New York: New York Academy of Sciences.

Panksepp, J., Herman, B. H., Vilberg, T., Bishop, T., & DeEskinazi, F. G. (1980). Endogenous opioids and social behavior. *Neuroscience and Biobehavioral Reviews, 4,* 473–487.

Papousek, H., & Papousek, M. (1975). Cognitive aspects of preverbal social interaction between human infants and adults. In C. F. Symposium (Ed.), *Parent-infant interaction.* New York: Association of Scientific Publications.

Papp, P. (1988). The process of change. New York: Guilford.

Parker, S. T. (1987). A sexual selection model for hominid evolution. *Human Evolution, 2*(3), 235–253.

Parker, S. T. (1998). A social selection model for the evolution and adaptive significance of self-conscious emotions. In M. Ferrari & R. J. Sternberg (Eds.), *Self-awareness. Its nature and development,* (pp. 108-134). New York: Guilford Press.

Parks, M. R., & Adelman, M. B. (1983). Communication networks and the development of romantic relationships: An expansion of uncertainty reduction theory. *Human Communication Research, 10*(1), 55–79.

Parsons, T. & Bales, R. F. (1955). *Family, socialization & interaction process.* Glencoe, IL: The Free Press.

Pascal, B. (1670/1966). *Pensees* (A. J. Krailsheimer, Trans.) (Sec. 4, no. 277). New York: Viking Press.

Pasley, K. (1988). Family boundary ambiguity: Perceptions of adult stepfamily family members. In K. Pasley & M. Ihinger-Tallman (Eds.), *Remarriage and stepparenting: Current research and theory.* New York: Guilford Press.

Patterson, G. S. (1986). Performance models for antisocial boys. *American Psychologist, 41,* 432–444.

Patterson, G., & Stouthamer-Loeber, M. (1984). The correlation of family management practices and delinquency. *Child Development, 55,* 1299–1307.

Paul, J. P. (1984). The bisexual identity: An idea without social recognition. *Journal of Homosexuality, 9,* 45–63.

Paul, L., & Hirsch, L. R. (1996). Human male mating strategies: II. Moral codes of "quality" and "quantity" strategists. *Ethology and Sociobiology, 17,* 71–86.

Pearce, W. B., & Sharp, S. M. (1973). Self-disclosing communication. *Journal of Communication, 23,* 409–425.

Pearlin, L., & Johnson, J. (1977). Marital status, life strains and depression. *American Sociological Review, 42,* 704–715.

Peck, F. S. (1984). *The road less traveled.* New York: Simon & Schuster.

Peck, J. S. (1989). The impact of divorce on children at various stages of the family life cycle. *Journal of Divorce, 12,* 81-106.

Peele, S. (1975). *Love and addiction.* New York: New American Library.

Penn, C. D., Hernandez, S. L., & Bermudez, J. M. (1997). Using a cross-cultural perspective to understand infidelity in couples therapy. *The American Journal of Family Therapy, 25*(2), 169–185.

Peplau, L. (1983). Roles and gender. In H. Kelle, E. Berscheid, A. Christensen, J., Harvey, T. Huston, G. Levinger, F. McClintock, L. Peplau, & D. Peterson, *Close Relationships.* New York: W. H. Freeman.

Peplau, L. A., & Gordon, S. L. (1983). The intimate relationships of lesbians and gay men. In E. R. Allgeier & N. B. McCormick (Eds.), *Gender roles and sexual behavior: The changing boundaries* (pp. 226–244). Palo Alto, CA: Mayfield.

Peplau, L., & Gordon, S. (1985). Women and men in love: Gender differences in close heterosexual relationships. In V. O'Leary, R. Unger, & B. Walston (Eds.), *Women, gender and social psychology* (pp. 257–291). Hillsdale, NJ: Lawrence Erlbaum.

Peplau, L. A., Viniegas, & Campbell, S. M. (1996). Gay and lesbian relationships. In R. C. Savin-Williams & K. M. Cohen (Eds.), *The lives of lesbians, gays, and bisexuals: Children to adults* (pp. 250–273). Fort Worth, TX: Harcourt Brace.

Perlman, D. (1998, October). *Current trends in the study of close relationships.* Paper presented at the meeting of the VII Mexican Congress of Social Psychology, Toluca, Mexico.

Perper, T. (1985). *Sex signals: The biology of love.* Philadelphia: Institute for Scientific Information Press.

Perper, T., & Weis, D. L. (1987). Proceptive and rejective strategies of U. S. and Canadian college women. *Journal of Sex Research, 23*(4), 455–480.

Person, E. S. (1986a). Male sexuality and power. *Psychoanalytic Inquiry, 6,* 3–25.

Person, E. S. (1986b). The omni-available woman and lesbian sex: Two fantasy themes and their relationship to the male developmental experience. In G. I. Fogel, F. M. Lane, & R. S. Liebert (Eds.), *The psychology of men: New psychoanalytic perspectives.* New York: Basic Books.

Person, E. S. (1988). *Dreams of love and fateful encounters: The power of romantic passion.* New York: W. W. Norton.

Peterson, C., Rosenbaum, A. C., & Conn, M. K. (1985). Depressive mood reactions to breaking up: Testing the learned helplessness model of depression. *Journal of Social and Clinical Psychology, 3*(2), 161–169.

Peterson, D. R. (1979). Assessing interpersonal relationships by means of interaction record. *Behavioral Assessment, l,* 221–226.

Peterson, D. R. (1983). Conflict. In H. Kelley, & Associates (Eds.), *Close relationships* (pp. 360–396). New York: W. H. Freeman.

Petronio, S., & Endres, T. (1987). Dating Issues: How single mothers and single fathers differ with full time children in the household. *Journal of Divorce, 9*(4), 79–87.

Phillips, K. (1990, October). Why can't a man be more like a woman . . . and vice versa? *Omni,* 44–47.

Philpot, C., & Borum, J. (1992). *Look before you leap: Premarital couples group program.* Unpublished manuscript. Melbourne, FL: Florida Technological University.

Pierce, C. A. (1996). Body height and romantic attraction: A meta-analytic test of the male-taller norm. *Social Behavior and Personality, 24*(2) 143–149.

Pillard, R. C. (1990). The Kinsey Scale: Is it familial? In D. P. McWhirter, S. A. Sanders, & J. M. Reinisch (Eds.), *Homosexuality/heterosexuality: Concepts of sexual orientation* (pp. 88–100). New York: Oxford University Press.

Pillard, R. C., & Weinrich, J. D. (1986). Evidence of familial nature of male homosexuality. *Archives of General Psychiatry, 43,* 808–813.

Pistole, M. C. (1989). Attachment in adult romantic relationships: Style of conflict resolution and relationship satisfaction. *Journal of Social and Personal Relationships, 6,* 505–510.

Pittman, F. (1989). *Private lies: Infidelity and the betrayal of intimacy.* New York: W. W. Norton.

Pittman, F. S. (1991). The secret passions of men. *Journal of Marital and Family Therapy, 17*(1), 17–23.

Pittman, J. F., & Blanchard, D. (1996). The effects of work history and timing of marriage on the division of household labor: A life-course perspective. *Journal of Marriage and the Family, 58,* 78–90.

Planalp, S., & Honeycutt, J. M. (1985). Events that increase uncertainty in personal relationships. *Human Communication Research, 11,* 593–604.

Planalp, S., Rutherford, D. K., & Honeycutt, J. M. (1988). Events that increase uncertainty in personal relationships: II. Replication and extension. *Human Communication Research, 14,* 516–547.

Pleck, J. (1976). The male sex role: Definitions, problems and sources of change. *Journal of Social Issues, 32*(3), 155–164.

Pleck, J. (1985). Working wives/working husbands. Beverly Hills, CA: Sage.

Pleck, J. (1987). American fathering in historical perspective. In M. S. Kimmel

(Ed.), *Changing men: New directions in research on men and masculinity* (pp. 83–97). Beverly Hills, CA: Sage.

Pliner, P., Chaiken, S., & Flett, G. L. (1990). Gender differences in concern with body weight and physical appearance over the life span. *Personality and Social Psychology Bulletin, 16*(2), 263–273.

Porges, S. W. (1997). Emotion: An evolutionary byproduct of the neural regulation of the autonomic nervous system. In C. S. Carter, I. I. Lederhendler, & B. Kirkpatrick (Eds.), *The integrative neurobiology of affiliation. Annals of the New York Academy of Sciences, 80* (pp. 62–77). New York: New York Academy of Sciences.

Potuchek, J. L. (1995, June). *Gender boundaries and the persistence of gender inequality.* Paper presented at the conference of the International Network on Personal Relationships, Williamsburg, Virginia.

Prager, K. J. (1991). Intimacy, status and couple conflict resolution. *Journal of Social and Personal Relationships, 8*(4), 505–526.

Price, S. J., & McKenry, P. C. (1988). *Divorce.* Newbury Park, CA: Sage.

Prisbell, M. (1987). Factors affecting college students' perception of satisfaction in and frequency of dating, *Psychological Reports, 60*(2), 659–664.

Prochaska, J. O. (1977). *Restriction of range on date and mate selection in college students.* Unpublished manuscript. Providence, RI: University of Rhode Island.

Pruett, B. M. (1989). Male and female communicators style differences: A meta analysis. In C. M. Lont & S. A. Friedley (Eds.), *Beyond boundaries: Sex and gender diversity in communication* (pp. 107–120). Fairfax, VA: George Mason University Press.

Pruitt, D. G., & Carnevale, P. J. D. (1980). The development of integrative agreements in social conflict. In V. J. Derlega & J. Grzelak (Eds.), *Living with other people.* New York: Academic.

Putnam, H. (1987). *The many faces of realism.* Leslie, IL: Opencourt.

Rainville, R. E., & Gallagher, J. G. (1990). Vulnerability and heterosexual attraction. *Sex Roles, 23,* 25–31.

Ramafedi, G., French, S., Story, M., Resnick, M. P., & Blum, R. (1998). The relationship between suicide risk and sexual orientation: Results of a population-based study. *American Journal of Public Health, 88*(1), 57–60.

Rank, M. R., & Davis, L. E. (1996). Perceived happiness outside of marriage among Black and White spouses. *Family Relations: Journal of Applied Family & Child Studies, 45*(4), 435–441.

Rankin-Esquer, L., Burnett, C., Baucom, D., & Epstein, N. (1997). Autonomy and relatedness in marital functioning. *Journal of Marital and Family Therapy, 23*(2), 175–190.

Rapaport, K., & Burkhart, B. R. (1984). Personality and attitudinal characteristics of sexually coercive college males. *Journal of Abnormal Psychology, 93*(2), 216–221.

Rapoport, R., & Rapoport, R. (1976). *Dual career familly re-examined.* New York: Harper Colophon.

Raush, H. L., Barry, W. A., Hertel, R. K., & Swain, M.A. (1974). *Communication, conflict and marriage.* San Francisco: Jossey- Bass.

Rauter, T., & Gibson, R. (1995). *The impact of sexual encounters with friends of the opposite sex. The perspective of Uncertainty Reduction Theory.* Unpublished manuscript.

Raven, B. H., Centers, R., & Rodrigues, A. (1975). The bases of conjugal power. In

R. E. Cromwell & D. H. Olson (Eds.), *Power in families.* New York: Halstead.

Ravich, R. A. (1972). The marriage/divorce paradox. In C. J. Sager & H. S. Kaplan (Eds.), *Progress in group and family therapy* (pp. 531–536). New York: Brunner/Mazel.

Ravich, R. A. (1985). Dyadic interaction patterns. In L. L. Andreozzi (Ed.), *Integrating research and clinical practice* (pp. 80–89). Rockville, MD: Aspen.

Reece, R., & Segrist, A. E. (1981). The association of selected "masculine" sex-role variables with length of relationship in gay male couples. *Journal of Homosexuality, 7,* 33–48.

Reiss, D. (1981). *The family's construction of reality.* Cambridge, MA: Harvard University Press.

Remafedi, G., French, S., Story, M., Resnick, M. D., & Blum, R. (1998). The relationship between suicide risk and sexual orientation: Results of a population-based study. *American Journal of Public Health, 88*(1), 57–60.

Rempel, J. K., Holmes, J. H., & Zanna, M. P. (1985). Trust in close relationships. *Journal of Personality and Social Psychology, 49,* 95–112.

Retzinger, S. M. (1991). *Violent emotions: Shame and rage in marital quarrels.* Newbury Park, CA: Sage.

Rhodes, E. (1977). A developmental approach to the life cycle of the family. *Social Casework, 58,* 301–311.

Rey, A. M., & Gibson, P. R. (1997). Beyond high school: Heterosexuals' self-reported anti-gay/lesbian behaviors and attitudes. *Journal of Gay & Lesbian Social Services, 7*(4), 65–84.

Rholes, W. S., Simpson, J. A., & Grich-Stevens, J. (1998). Attachment orientations, social support, and conflict resolution in close relationships. In J. A. Simpson, W. S. Rholes, et al. (Eds.), *Attachment theory and close relationships* (pp. 166–188). New York: Guilford Press.

Ricciutti, A. (1992). *Child-mother attachment: A twin study.* Unpublished Ph. D. dissertation, University of Virginia, Charlottesville.

Rice, J. K., & Rice, D. G. (1986). *Living through divorce: A developmental approach to divorce therapy.* New York: Guilford Press.

Riesman, D., Denny, R., & Glazer, N. (1950). *The lonely crowd: A study of the changing American character.* New Haven, CT: Yale University Press.

Riessman, C. K. (1990). *Divorce talk: Women and men make sense of personal relationships.* New Brunswick, NJ: Rutgers University Press.

Rindfleisch, A., Burroughs, J. E., & Denton, F. (1997). Family structure, materialism, and compulsive consumption. *Journal of Consumer Research, 23*(4), 312–325.

Riordan, C. A., & Tedeschi, T. J. (1983). Attraction in aversive environments: Some evidence for classical conditioning and negative reinforcement. *Journal of Personality and Social Psychology, 44,* 683–692.

Risman, B. J., & Johnson-Sumerford, D. (1998). Doing it fairly: A study of postgender marriages. *Journal of Marriage and the Family, 60,* 23–40.

Risman, B. J., & Park, K. (1988). Just the two of us: Parent-child relationships in single-parent homes. *Journal of Marriage and the Family, 50,* 1049–1052.

Ritter-Schaumburg, H. (1986). *Novalis und seine erste braut: Sie war die seele meines lebens.* [Novalis and his first fiancee: She was the soul of my life.] Stuttgart, Germany: Urachhaus.

Rivlin, B. V. (1985). Manipulative techniques of children in the transitional family. Conciliation Courts Review, 23(1), 21–26.

Robbins, C. J. (1986). Sex role perceptions and social anxiety in opposite-sex and same-sex situations. *Sex Roles, 14*, 383–395.

Roberts, L., & Krokoff, L. (1990). A time-series analysis of withdrawal, hostility, and displeasure in satisfied and dissatisfied marriages. *Journal of Marriage and the Family, 52*, 95–105.

Roberts, T. W., & Price, S. J. (1989). Adjustment in remarriage: Communication, cohesion, marital and parental roles. *Journal of Divorce, 13*(1), 17–43.

Roche, J. P. (1986). Premarital sex: Attitudes and behavior by dating stage. *Adolescence, 21*(81), 107–121.

Rodgers, B. (1994). Pathways between parental divorce and adult depression. *Journal of Child Psychology and Psychiatry and Allied Disciplines, 35*(7), 1289–1308.

Rodgers, R. H., & Conrad, L. M. (1986). Courtship for remarriage: Influences on family reorganization after divorce. *Journal of Marriage and the Family, 48*, 767–775.

Rodman, H. (1972). Marital power and the theory of resources in cultural context. *Journal of Comparative Family Studies, 3*, 50–69.

Roese, N. J., Olson, J. M., Borenstein, M. N., Martin, A., et al. (1992). Same-sex touching behavior: The moderating role of homophobic attitudes. *Journal of Nonverbal Behavior, 16*(4), 249–259.

Rogers, C. R. (1972). *Becoming partners: Marriage and its alternatives.* New York: Dell.

Rogers, K. M. (1966). *The troublesome helpmate, a history of misogyny in literature.* Seattle: University of Washington Press.

Rogers, S. J., & White, L. K. (1998). Satisfaction with parenting: the role of marital happiness, family structure, and parent's gender. *Journal of Marriage and the Family, 60*, 293–308.

Roscoe, B., Kennedy, D., & Pope, T. (1987). Adolescents' views of intimacy: Distinguishing intimate from nonintimate relationships. *Adolescence, 22*(87), 511–516.

Rose, S., & Frieze, I. (1989). Young singles' scripts for the first date. *Gender and Society, 3*(2), 258–268.

Rosen, E. (1987). *Bitter choices: Blue-collar women in and out of work.* Chicago: University of Chicago Press.

Ross, M., & Sicoly, F. (1979). Egocentric biases in availability and attribution. *Journal of Personality and Social Psychology, 37*, 322–326.

Rossiter, A. B. (1991). Initiator status and separation adjustment. *Journal of Divorce and Remarriage, 15*(1–2) 141–155.

Roth, S. (1985). Psychotherapy with lesbian couples: Individual issues, female socialization, and the social context. *Journal of Marital and Family Therapy, 11*, 273–286.

Rubin, L. (1983). *Intimate strangers.* New York: Harper & Row.

Rubin, Z., Peplau, L. A., & Hill, C. T. (1981). Loving and leaving: Sex differences in romantic attachments. *Sex Roles, 7*, 821–835.

Rusbult, C. E. (1983). A longitudinal test of the investment model: The development (and deterioration) of satisfaction and commitment in heterosexual involvements. *Journal of Personality and Social Psychology, 45*(1), 101–117.

Rusbult, C. E. (1987). Responses to dissatisfaction in close relationships: The exit-voice-loyalty-neglect model. In D. Perlman & S. W. Duck (Eds.), *Intimate relationships: Development, dynamics and deterioration.* Newbury Park, CA: Sage.

Rusbult, C. E., Johnson, D. J., & Morrow, G. D. (1986). Impact of couple patterns of problem solving on distress and nondistress in dating relationships. *Journal of Personality and Social Psychology, 50*(4), 744–753.

Rusbult, C. E., Verette, J., Whitney, G. A., Slovik, L. F., & Lipkus, I. (1991). Accommodation processes in close relationships: Theory and preliminary empirical evidence. *Journal of Personality and Social Psychology, 60*(1), 53–78.

Sabelli, H. C., & Javaid, J. I. (1995). Phenylethylamine modulation of affect: Therapeutic and diagnostic implications. *The Journal of Neuropsychiatry and Clinical Neurosciences,* (7), 6–14.

Sabelli, H. C., Carlson-Sabelli, L., & Javaid, J. I. (1990). The thermodynamics of bipolarity: A bifurcation model of bipolar illness and bipolar character and its psychotherapeutic applications. *Psychiatry, 53,* 346–368.

Sacher, J. A., & Fine, M. A. (1996). Predicting relationship status and satisfaction after six months among dating couples. *Journal of Marriage and the Family, 58,* 21–32.

Sack, W. H., Mason, R., & Higgins, J. E. (1985). The single-parent family and abusive child punishment. *American Journal of Orthopsychiatry, 55*(2), 252–259.

Sager, C. (1976). *Marriage contracts and couple therapy.* New York: Brunner/Mazel.

Sadker, M., & Sadker, D. (1992). *Failing at fairness: How America's schools shortchange girls.* New York: Scribners.

Sadker, M., Sadker, D., Fox, L., & Salata, M. (1993/1994). *Gender equity in the classroom: The unfinished agenda.*

Safilios-Rothschild, C. (1967). A comparison of power structure and marital satisfaction in urban Greek and French families. *Journal of Marriage and the Family, 29,* 345–351.

Sagrestano, L. M. (1992). The use of power and influence in a gendered world. *Psychology of Women Quarterly, 16,* 439–447.

Salovey, P., & Rothman, A. J. (1991). Envy and jealousy: Self and society. In P. Salovey (Ed.), *The psychology of jealousy and envy.* New York: Guilford Press.

Salovey, P., & Rodin, J. (1989). Envy and jealousy in close relationships. In C. Hendrick (Ed.), *Review of personality and social psychology. Vol. 10: Close relationships* (pp. 221–246). Newbury Park, CA: Sage.

Saluter, A. (1988). *Studies in marriage and the family: Singleness in America.* Current Population Reports, Series P-23, No. 162, Washington, DC: U.S. Government Printing Office.

Sanders, C. M. (1992). *Surviving grief . . . and learning to live again.* New York: John Wiley & Sons.

Sanik, M. M., & Mauldin, T. (1986). Single versus two parent families: A comparison of mothers' time. *Family Relations, 35,* 53–56.

Sansom, D., & Farnill, D. (1997). Stress following marriage breakdown: Does social support play a role? *Journal of Divorce & Remarriage, 26*(3–4), 39–49.

Santrock, J. W., & Sitterle, K. A. (1988). Parent-child relationships in stepmother families. In K. Pasley & M. Ihinger-Tallman (Eds.), *Remarriage and stepparenting: Current research and theory.* New York: Guilford Press.

Satir, V., & Baldwin, M. (1983). *Step by step: A guide to creating change for families.* Palo Alto, CA: Science and Behavior Books.

Satir, V. (1972). *Peoplemaking.* Palo Alto, CA: Science and Behavior Books.

Savin-Williams, R. C. (1990). *Gay and lesbian youth: Expressions of identity.* New York: Hemisphere.

Scanzoni, J. (1982a). A historical perspective on husband-wife bargaining power and marital dissolution. In G. Levinger & O. C. Moles (Eds.), *Divorce and separation: Context, causes, and consequences* (pp. 20–36). New York: Basic Books.

Scanzoni, J. (1982b). *Sexual bargaining: Power politics in the American marriage* (2nd ed.). Chicago: University of Chicago Press.

Scanzoni, L., & Scanzoni, J. (1976). *Men, women and change: A sociology of marriage and the family*. New York: McGraw Hill.

Schaap, C. (1992, July). Styles of conflict resolution in marital relationships. Paper presented at conference of the International Society for the Study of Personal Relationships, Orono, ME.

Schachtel, E. G. (1961). On alienated concepts of identity. *The American Journal of Psychoanalysis*, November.

Schachter, J., & O'Leary, K. D. (1985). Affective intent and impact in marital communication. *American Journal of Family Therapy, 13*, 17–23.

Schafer, R. (1986). Men who struggle against sentimentality. In G. I. Fogel, F. M. Lane, & R. S. Liebert (Eds.), *The psychology of men: New psychoanalytic perspectives*. New York: Basic Books.

Scheff, T. J., & Retzinger, S. M. (1991). *Emotions and violence: Shame and rage in destructive conflicts*. Lexington, MA: D. C. Heath.

Schewe, P. A., & O'Donohue, W. (1996). Rape prevention with high-risk males: Short-term outcome of two interventions. *Archives of Sexual Behavior, 25*(5), 455–471.

Schlegel, A., & Barry, H., III. (1980). The evolutionary significance of adolescent initiation ceremonies. *American Ethnologist, 7*, 696–715.

Schmidt, G., & Sigusch, V. (1973). Women's sexual arousal. In J. Zubin & J. Money (Eds.), *Contemporary sexual behavior: Critical issues in the 1970's*.

Schmitt, A., & Sofer, J. (Eds.). (1992). *Sexuality and eroticism among males in Moslem societies*. New York: Harrington Park Press/Haworth Press.

Schnarch, D. M. (1991). *Constructing the sexual crucible: An integration of sexual and marital therapy*. New York: W.W. Norton.

Schuldberg, D., & Guisinger, S. (1990). Divorced fathers describe their former wives: Devaluation and contrast. *Journal of Divorce and Remarriage, 14*(3–4) 61-76.

Schwalbe, M. L., & Staples, C. L. (1991). Gender differences in sources of self-esteem. *Social Psychology Quarterly, 54*(2), 158–168.

Schwartz, J. C., & Shaver, P. (1987). Emotions and emotion knowledge in interpersonal relations. In *Advances in personal relationships, Vol. 1* (pp. 197–241). New York: JAI Press.

Schwartz, P. (1991, June). Paper presented at the conference of the International Network on Personal Relationships, Normal/Bloomington, IL.

Schwartz, P., (1994). *Peer marriage*. New York: Free.

Schwartz, P., & Blumstein, P. (1976, November). Bisexuals: Where love speaks louder than labels. *Ms.*, 80–81.

Schwebel, A. I., Dunn, R. L., Moss, B. F., & Renner, M. A. (1992). Factors associated with relationship stability in geographically separated couples. *Journal of College Student Development, 33*(3), 222–230.

Seal, D. W., & Palmer-Seal, D. A. (1996). Barriers to condom use and safer sex talk among college dating couples. *Journal of Community and Applied Social Psychology, 6*, 15–33.

Seligman, M. E. P. (1975). *Helplessness: On depression, development, and death*. San Francisco: P. Freeman.

Sergios, P. & Cody, J. (1986). Importance of physical attractiveness and social assertiveness skills in male homosexual dating behavior and partner selection. *Journal of Homosexuality, 12*(2), 71–84.

Sethi, S., & Nolen-Hoeksema, S. (1997). Gender differences in internal and external focusing among adolescents. *Sex Roles, 37*(9–10), 687–700.

Shapiro, A., & Swensen, C. (1969). Patterns of self-disclosure among married couples. *Journal of Counseling Psychology, 16*, 179–180.

Sharpsteen, D. J., & Kirkpatrick, L. A. (1997). Romantic jealousy and adult romantic attachment. *Journal of Personality & Social Psychology, 72*(3), 627–640.

Shaver, P., Hazan, C., & Bradshaw, D. (1988). Love as attachment: The integration of three behavioral systems. In R. J.

Shaw, L. (1993, January). Examining bisexuality and feminism: Review of Closer to home. *The Lavender Network*, 48–49.

Shaywitz, B. A., Shaywitz, S. E., & Pugh, K. R. (1995). Sex differences in the functional organization of the brain for language. *Nature, 373*, 607–609.

Shepher, J. (1983). *Incest: A biosocial view.* New York: Academic Press.

Shepher, J. A., & Reisman, J. (1985). Pornography: A sociobiological attempt at understanding. *Ethology and Sociobiology, 6*, 103–114.

Shepperd, J. A., & Strathman, A. J. (1989). Attractiveness and height: The role of stature in dating preference, frequency of dating, and perceptions of attractiveness. *Personality and Social Psychology Bulletin, 15*(4), 617–627.

Sherrod, D., & Nardi, P. M. (1998). Homophobia in the courtroom: An assessment of biases against gay men and lesbians in a multiethnic sample of potential jurors. In G. M. Herek (Ed.), *Stigma and sexual orientation: Understanding prejudice against lesbians, gay men, and bisexuals* (pp. 24–38). Thousand Oaks, CA: Sage.

Sherwin, R., & Corbett, S. (1985). Campus sexual norms and dating relationships: A trend analysis. *Journal of Sex Research, 21*(3), 258–274.

Shively, M. G., & De Cecco, J. P. (1978). Sexual orientation survey of students on the San Francisco State University campus. *Journal of Homosexuality, 4*, 29–39.

Shortt, J. W., Bush, L. K., Roth-McCabe, J. L., Gottman, J. M., & Katz, L. F. (1994). Children's physiological responses while producing facial expressions of emotions. *Merrill-Palmer Quarterly, 40*(1), 40–59.

Shulman, D. G. (1987). Female subordination and male vulnerability: An integration of psychological and anthropological data. *Journal of Social Behavior and Personality, 2*(1) 49–61.

Sidel, R. (1986). *Women and children last.* New York: Viking.

Silberstein, L. R., Striegel-Moore, R. H., & Rodin, J. (1987). Feeling fat: A woman's shame. In H. B. Lewis (Ed.), *The role of shame in symptom formation* (pp. 89–107). Hillsdale, NJ: Lawrence Erblbaum.

Silver, R. (1992). Environmental factors influencing hormone secretion. In J. Beckler, M. Breedlove, & D. Crews (Eds.), *Behavioral endocrinology* (pp. 401–422). New York: Behavioral Science Press.

Silverman, I., & Eals, M. (1992). Sex differences in spatial abilities: Evolutionary theory and data. In J. Barkow, L. Cosmides, & J. Tooby (Eds.), *The adapted mind: Evolutionary psychology and the generation of culture* (pp. 487–503). New York: Oxford University Press.

Simenauer, J. & Carroll, D. (1982). *Singles: The new Americans.* New York: Simon and Schuster.

Simon, J. (1990). The single parent: Power and the integrity of parenting. *The American Journal of Psychoanalysis, 50,* 187–199.

Simpson, J. A. (1987). The dissolution of romantic relationships: Factors involved in relationship stability and emotional distress. *Journal of Personality and Social Psychology, 53*(4), 683–692.

Singer, I. (1984). *The nature of love: Vol. 2. Courtly and romantic.* Chicago: University of Chicago Press.

Slater, E. J., & Calhoun, K. S. (1988). Familial conflict and marital dissolution: Effects on the social functioning of college students. *Journal of Social and Clinical Psychology, 6*(1), 118–126.

Slater, S. (1995). *The lesbian life cycle.* New York: Free.

Slater, S. & Mencher, J. (1991). The lesbian family life cycle: A contextual approach. *American Journal of Orthopsychiatry, 61*(2), 372–382.

Smith, K. (1971). Homophobia: A tentative personality profile. *Psychological Reports, 29,* 1091–1094.

Smith, R. B., & Brown, R. A. (1997). The impact of social support on gay male couples. *Journal of Homosexuality, 33*(2), 39–61.

Smith, R. B., Goslen, M. A., Byrd, A. J., & Reece, L. (1990). Self- other orientation and sex-role orientation of men and women who remarry. *Journal of Divorce and Remarriage, 14*(3/4) 3–32.

Smith, R. L. (1984). Human sperm competition. In R. L. Smith (Ed.), *Sperm competition and the evolution of animal mating systems* (pp. 601–659). New York: Academic Press.

Smoll, F. L., & Schutz, R. W. (1990). Quantifying gender differences in physical performance: A developmental perspective. *Developmental Psychology, 36,* 360–369.

Snell, W. E., Hawkins, R. C., & Belk, S. S. (1988). Stereotypes about male sexuality and the use of social influence strategies in intimate relationships. *Journal of Social and Clinical Psychology, 7*(1), 42–48.

Snyder, M., Berscheid, E., & Glick, P. (1985). Focusing on the exterior and the interior: Two investigations of the initiation of personal relationships. *Journal of Personality and Social Psychology, 48,* 1427–1439.

Snyder, M., & Simpson, J. A. (1984). Self monitoring and dating relationships. *Journal of Personality and Social Psychology, 47*(6), 1281–1291.

Snyder, M., Simpson, J. A., & Gangestad, S. (1986). Personality and sexual relations. *Journal of Personality and Social Psychology, 51*(1), 181–190.

Solomon, F. F. (1989). *Narcissism and intimacy. Love and marriage in an age of confusion.* New York: W. W. Norton.

Spanier, G. B., & Castro, R. F. (1979). Adjustment to separation and divorce: A qualitative analysis. In G. Levinger & O. C. Moles (Eds.), *Divorce and separation: Context, causes, and consequences* (pp. 211–227). New York: Basic Books.

Spanier, G. B., & Thompson, L. (1984). *Parting: The aftermath of separation and divorce.* Beverly Hills, CA: Sage.

Speed, A., & Gangestad, S. W. (1997). Romantic popularity and mate preferences: A peer-nomination study. *Personality and Social Psychology Bulletin, 23*(9), 928–936.

Sprague, H. E., & Kinney, J. H. (1997). The effects of interparental divorce and conflict on college students' romantic relationships. *Journal of Divorce & Remarriage, 27*(1–2), 85–104.

Sprague, J., & Quadagno, D. (1989). Gender and sexual motivation: An exploration of two assumptions. *Journal of Psychology and Human Sexuality, 2,* 57–76.

Sprecher, S. (1989). The importance to males and females of physical attractiveness, earning potential, and expressiveness in initial attraction. *Sex Roles, 21,* 591–607.

Sprecher, S. (1994). Two sides to the breakup of dating relationships. *Personal Relationships, 1,* 199–222.

Sprecher, S., Cate, R. & Levin, L. (1998). Parental divorce and young adults' beliefs about love. *Journal of Divorce & Remarriage, 28* (3–4), 107–120.

Sprecher, S., & Duck, S. (1994). Sweet talk: The importance of perceived communication for romantic and friendship attraction experienced during a get-acquainted date. *Personality and Social Psychology Bulletin, 20*(4), 391–400.

Sprecher, S., & McKinney, K. (1987). Barriers in the initiation of intimate heterosexual relationships and strategies for intervention. *Journal of Social Work & Human Sexuality, 5*(2), 97–110.

Spring, J. A. (1996). *After the affair: Healing the pain and rebuilding trust when a partner has been unfaithful.* New York: HarperCollins.

Stagner, R. (1967). *The dimensions of human conflict.* Detroit, MI: Wayne State University Press.

Stafford, L., & Canary, D. J. (1991). Maintenance strategies and romantic relationship type, gender and relational characteristics. *Journal of Social and Personal Relationships, 8,* 217–242.

Stafford, L., & Reske, J. R. (1990). Idealization and communication in long-distance premarital relationships. *Family Relations, 39*(3), 274–279.

Staines, G., & Libby, P. (1986). Men and women in role relationships. In R. D. Ashmore & F. K. DelBoca (Eds.), The social psychology of female-male relations: A critical analysis of central concepts (pp. 211–258). New York: Academic.

Stake, J., & Lauer, M. L. (1987). The consequences of being overweight: A controlled study of gender differences. *Sex Roles, 17,* 31–47.

Stanley, S., Markman, H. J., St. Peters, M., & Leber, B. D. (1995). Strengthening marriages and preventing divorce: New directions in prevention research. *Family Relations, 44,* 392–401.

Stapelton, J., & Bright, R. (1976). *Equal marriage.* New York: Harper & Row.

Steefel, N. M. (1992). A divorce transition model. *Psychological Reports, 70,* 155–160.

Stein, R. M. (1983). Coupling–uncoupling: Bindung und Freiheit: Gedanken ueber die Entwicklung des Ehe-Archetyps. *Analytische Psychologie, 14,* 1–14.

Stein, T. S. (1996). The essentialist/social constructionist debate about homosexuality and its relevance for psychotherapy. In R. P. Cabaj & T. S. Stein (Eds.), *Textbook of homosexuality and mental health* (pp. 83–100). Washington, DC: American Psychiatric Press.

Steinberg, L. (1987). Single parents, stepparents, and the susceptibility of adolescents to antisocial peer pressure. *Child Development, 58,* 269–275.

Steinberg, L., & Silverberg, S. (1986). The vicissitudes of autonomy in early adolescence. *Child Development, 57,* 841–851.

Stensaas, L. J., Lavker, R. M., Monti-Bloch, L., Grosser, B. I., & Berliner, D. L. (1991). Ultrastructure of the human vomeronasal organ. *Journal of Steroid Biochemistry and Molecular Biology 39*(4B), 553–560.

Stephen, T. (1987). Attribution and adjustment to relationship termination. *Journal of Social and Personal Relationships, 4,* 47–61.

Stephen, T. (1986). Communication and interdependence in geographically separated relationships. *Human Communication Research, 13*(2), 191–210.

Stephen, T. (1984). Symbolic interdependence and post-break-up distress: A re-formulation of the attachment construct. *Journal of Divorce, 8*(1), 1–16.

Stern, D. N. (1985). *The interpersonal world of the infant: A view from psychoanalysis and developmental psychology.* New York: Basic Books.

Sternberg, R. J. (1987). *The triangle of love: Intimacy, passion, commitment.* New York: Basic Books.

Sternberg, R. J. (1988). Triangulating love. In R. J. Sternberg, & M. L. Barnes (Eds.), *The Psychology of Love* (pp. 119–138). New Haven, CT: Yale University Press.

Sternberg, R. J. (1996). Love stories. *Personal Relationships, 3*, (1), 59-79.

Stets, J. E. (1990). Verbal and physical aggression in marriage. *Journal of Marriage and the Family, 52*, 501–514.

Stets, J. E. (1992). Interactive processes in dating aggression: A national study. *Journal of Marriage and the Family, 54*, 165–177.

Stets, J. E., & Pirog-Good, M. A. (1989a). Patterns of physical and sexual abuse for men and women in dating relationships: A descriptive analysis. *Journal of Family Violence, 4*(1), 63–76.

Stets, J. E., & Pirog-Good, M. A. (1989b). Sexual aggression and control in dating relationships. *Journal of Applied Social Psychology, 19*, 1392–1412.

Stevens, A. (1982). *Archetypes: A natural history of the self.* New York: William Morrow.

Stewart, A. J., & Chester, N. L. (1982). Sex differences in human social motives: Achievement, affiliation, and power. In A. J. Stewart (Ed.), *Motivation and Society.* San Francisco: Jossey-Bass.

Stewart, A. J., Copeland, A. P., Chester, N. L., Malley, J. E., & Barenbaum, N. B. (1997). *Separating together: How divorce transforms families.* New York: Guilford Press.

Stewart, A. J., & Rubin, Z. (1976). The power motive in the dating couple. *Journal of Personality and Social Psychology, 34*(2) 305–309.

Stokes, J. P., Damon, W., & McKirnan, D. J. (1997). Predictors of movement toward homosexuality: A longitudinal study of bisexual men. *Journal of Sex Research, 34*(3), 304–312.

Stoller, R. J. (1987). Pornography: Daydreams to cure humiliation. In D. L. Nathanson (Ed.), *The many faces of shame.* New York: Guilford Press.

Storms, M. D. (1980). Theories of sexual orientation. *Journal of Personality and Social Psychology, 38*(5), 783–792.

Straus, M. B. (1988). Divorced mothers. In B. Birns & D. F. Hay (Eds.), *The different faces of motherhood.* New York: Plenum.

Strodbeck, F. L. (1974). Husband-wife interaction over revealed differences. In P. Brickman (Ed.), *Social conflict.* Lexington, MA: D.C. Heath.

Straus & Gelles, (1986). Societal change and change in family violence from 1975 to 1985 as revealed by two national surveys. *Journal of Marriage and the Family, 48*(3), 465–479.

Stuart, R. B. (1980). *Helping couples change: A social learning approach to marital therapy.* New York: Guilford.

Sumpter, S. (January, 1993). The myths of bisexuality. *The Lavender Network, 19.*

Summers, P., Forehand, R., & Armistead, L. (1998). Parental divorce during early adolescence in Caucasian families: The role of family process variables in predicting the long-term consequences for early adult psychosocial adjustment. *Journal of Consulting and Clinical Psychology, 66*(2), 327–336.

Sunnafrank, M. (1984). A communication-based perspective on attitude similarity and interpersonal attraction in early acquaintance. *Communication Monographs, 51,* 372–380.

Surra, C. A. (1985a). Courtship types: Variations in interdependence between partners and social networks. *Journal of Personality and Social Psychology, 49*(2), 357–375.

Surra, C. A. (1985b). Reasons for changes in commitment: Variations by courtship type. *Journal of Social and Personal Relationships, 4,* 17–33.

Surra, C. A., Arrizi, P., & Sasmussen, L. S. (1988). The association between reasons for commitment and the development and outcome of marital relationships. *Journal of Social and Personal Relationships, 5,* 47–63.

Surra, C. A., Batchelder, M. L., & Hughes, D. K. (1992, July). *His and her relationship: Partners' agreement on attributions about commitment.* Paper presented at conference of the International Society for the Study of Personal Relationships, Orono, ME.

Surra, C. A., & Bohman, T. (1991). The development of close relationships: A cognitive perspective. In G. Fletcher & F. D. Fincham (Eds.), *Cognition in close relationships* (pp. 281–305). Hillsdale, NJ: Lawrence Erlbaum.

Swartzberg, L., Shmukler, D., & Chalmers, B. (1983). Emotional adjustment and self-concept of children from divorced and nondivorced unhappy homes. *The Journal of Social Psychology, 121,* 305–312.

Swenson, D. (1997). A model of the remarried family. *Journal of Divorce & Remarriage, 27*(1–2), 150–185.

Symons, D. (1979). *The evolution of human sexuality.* New York: Oxford University Press.

Symons, D. (1987). If we're all Darwinians, what's the fuss about? In C. Crawford, M. Smith, & D. Krebs (Eds.), *Sociobiology and psychology: Ideas, issues and applications.* Hillsdale, NJ: Lawrence Erlbaum.

Symons, D. & Ellis, B. (1989). Human male-female differences in sexual desire. In A. E. Rasa, C. Vogel, & E. Voland (Eds.), *The sociobiology of sexual and reproductive strategies.* London: Chapman and Hall.

Szinovacz, M. (1984). Changing roles and interactions. In B. Hess & M. Sussman (Eds.), *Women and the family: Two decades of change* (pp. 164–201). New York: Haworth.

Takami, S., Getchell, M. L., Chen, Y., Monti-Block, L., Berliner, D. L., Stensaas, L. J., & Getchell, T. V. (1993). *Vomeronasal epithelial cells of the adult human express neuron-specific molecules.* Neuroreport,

Talmadge, L., & Dabbs, J., Jr. (1990) Intimacy, conversational patterns, and concommitant cognitive/emotional processes in couples. *Journal of Social and Clinical Psychology, 9*(4), 473–488.

Tan, U. (1996). Correlations between nonverbal intelligence and peripheral nerve conduction velocity in right-handed subjects: Sex-related differences. *International Journal of Psychophysiology, 22*(1–2), 123–128.

Tangney, J. P., & Fischer, K. W. (Eds.). (1995). *Self-conscious emotions. The psychology of shame, guilt, embarrassment, and pride.* New York: Guilford Press.

Tangney, J. P., Miller, R. S., & Flicker, L. (1996). Are shame, guilt, and embarrassment distinct emotions? *Journal of Personality and Social Psychology, 70*(6), 1256–1269.

Tangney, J. P., Wagner, P. E., Hill-Barlow, D., Marshall, D. E., & Gramzow, R. (1996). Relation of shame and guilt to constructive versus destructive responses to anger across the lifespan. *Journal of Personality and Social Psychology, 70*(4), 797–809.

Tannen, D. (1990). *You just don't understand: Women and men in conversation.* New York: Ballantine Books.

Tavris, C., & Wade, C. (1984). *The longest war: Sex differences in perspective.* San Diego, CA: Harcourt Brace Jovanovich.

Tavris, C. (1989). *Anger: The misunderstood emotion.* New York: Simon & Schuster.

Taywaditep, K. J., & Stokes, J. P. (1998). Male bisexualities: A cluster analysis of men with bisexual experience. *Journal of Psychology & Human Sexuality, 10*(1), 15–41.

Teisman, M. W., & Mosher, D. L. (1978). Jealous conflict in dating couples. *Psychological Reports, 42,* 1211–1216.

Tennov, D. (1979). *Love and limerence: The experience of being in love.* New York: Stein & Day.

Tennov, D. (1997). Love madness. In V. C. DeMunck (Ed), *Romantic love and sexual behavior: Perspectives from the social sciences* (pp. 77–88). Westport, CT: Praeger.

Thabes, V. (1997). Survey analysis of women's long-term postdivorce adjustment. *Journal of Divorce & Remarriage, 27*(3–4), 163–175.

Thibaut, J. W., & Kelley, H. H. (1959). *The social psychology of groups.* New York: Wiley.

Thiessen, D., & Ross, M. (1990). The use of a sociobiological questionnaire for the assessment of sexual dimorphism. *Behavior Genetics, 20*(2), 297–305.

Thomas, H. E. (1995). Experiencing a shame response as a precursor to violence. *Bulletin of the American Academy of Psychiatry and the Law, 23*(4), 587–593.

Thompson, L., & Walker, A. (1989). Gender in families: Women and men in marriage, work, and parenthood. *Journal of Marriage and the Family, 51,* 845–871.

Tienda, M., & Angel, R. (1982). Headship and household composition among blacks, hispanics, and other whites. *Social Forces, 61,* 509–531.

Tolhuizen, J. H. (1989). Communication strategies for intensifying dating relationships: Identification, use and structure. *Journal of Social and Personal Relationships, 6*(4), 413–434.

Tomkins, S. S. (1962). *Affect, imagery, consciousness. Vol. 1: The positive affects.* New York: Springer.

Tomkins, S. S. (1980). Affect as amplification: Some modifications in theory. In R. Plutchick & H. Kellerman (Eds.), *Emotion: Theory, research, and experience. Vol. 1: Theories of emotion* (pp. 141–164). New York: Academic Press.

Tomkins, S. S. (1982). Affect theory. In P. Ekman (Ed.), *Emotion in the human face, second edition,* (pp. 353–395). Cambridge, UK: Cambridge University Press.

Tomkins, S. S. (1987). Shame. In D. L. Nathanson (Ed.), *The many faces of shame.* New York: Guilford Press.

Tomkins, S. S. (1991). *Affect, imagery, consciousness. Vol. 3: The negative affects: Anger and Fear.* New York: Springer.

Tomkins, S. S. (1994). Script theory, edited. In E. V. Demos (Ed.), *Exploring affect: The selected writings of Silvan S. Tomkins* (pp 312–388). New York: Cambridge University Press.

Tooby, J., & Cosmides, L. (1990). The past explains the present: Emotional adaptations and the structure of ancestral environments. *Ethology and Sociobiology, 11,* 375–424.

Tourney, G. (1980). Hormones and homosexuality. In J. Marmor (Ed.), *Homosexual behavior: A modern reappraisal.* New York: Basic Books.

Tousignant, M., & Hanigan, D. (1993). Crisis support among suicidal students following a loss event. *Journal of Community Psychology, 21*(2), 83–96.

Townsend, J. M., & Levy, G. D. (1990). Effects of potential partners' physical attractiveness and socioeconomic status on sexuality and partner selection. *Archives of Sexual Behavior, 19*(2) 149–164.

Townsend, J. M., & Wasserman, T. (1998). Sexual attractiveness: Sex differences in assessment and criteria. *Evolution and Human Behavior, 19*(3), 171–191.

Trivers, R. (1985). *Social evolution.* Menlo Park, CA: Benjamin/Cummings.

Trost, M. R., & Alberts, J. K. (1998). An evolutionary view on understanding sex effects in communicating attraction. In D. J. Canary & K Dindia (Eds.), *Sex differences and similarities in communication. Critical essays and empirical investigations of sex and gender in interaction* (pp. 233–255). Mahwah, NJ: Lawrence Erlbaum.

Troyer, D. J. (1993). The impact of parental divorce on heterosexual functioning: Testing the modeling hypothesis. (Doctoral dissertation, Arizona State University.)

Truman, D. B., Tokar, D. B., & Fischer, A. R. (1996). Dimensions of masculinity: Relations to date rape supportive attitudes and sexual aggression in dating situations. *Journal of Counseling and Development, 74*(6), 555–562.

Tschann, J. M. (1988). Self-disclosure in adult friendship: Gender and marital status differences. *Journal of Social and Personal Relationships, 5,* 65–81.

Tsuda, A., Tanaka, M., Ida, H., Shirao, I., Gondoh, Y., Oguchi, M., & Yoshida, M. (1988). Expression of aggression attenuates stress-induced increases in rat brain noradrenaline turnover. *Brain Research, 474,* 174–180.

Tulku, T. (1978). *Kum Nye relaxation. Part 2: Movement exercises.* Berkeley, CA: Dharma Publishing.

Turgeon, L. , Julien, D., & Dion, E. (1998).Temporal linkages between wives' pursuit and husbands' withdrawal during conflict. *Family Process, 37,* 323–334.

Turner, J. H. (1978). *The structure of sociological theory* (rev. ed.). Homewood, IL: Dorsey.

Turner, R. H. (1962). Role-taking: Process versus conformity. In A. R. Rose (Ed.), *Human behavior and social processes: An interactionist approach.* Boston: Houghton Mifflin.

Turner, R. H. (1970). *Family interaction.* New York: Wiley.

Ulbrich, P. M. (1988). The determinants of depression in two-income marriage. *Journal of Marriage and the Family, 50,* 121–131.

USA Today. (1994, March). Keeping in touch when out of touch. (p. 10).

U.S. Bureau of the Census. (1989). *Current Population Reports, Series* P-20, No. 450. Washington, DC: U.S. Government Printing Office.

U.S. National Center for Health Statistics. (1994). *Annual summary of births, marriages, divorces, and deaths, United States, 1993* (Vol. 44, no. 13). Washington, DC: U.S. Government Printing Office.

Uvnas-Moberg, K. (1997). Physiological and endocrine effects of social contact. In C. S. Carter, I. I. Lederhandler, & B. Kirkpatrick (Eds.), *The integrative neurobiology of affiliation. Annals of the New York Academy of Sciences, Vol. 807* (pp. 146–163). New York: New York Academy of Sciences.

Vaillant, C. O., & Vaillant G. E. (1993). Is the U-Curve of marital satisfaction an illusion? A 40-year study. *Journal of Marriage and the Family, 55,* 230–239.

Van Tassel Hamilton, G. (1936). Defensive homosexuality: Homosexuality as a defense against incest. *Encyclopedia Sexualis.* New York: Dingwell-Rock.

Van den Berghe, P. L., & Frost, P. (1986). Skin color preference, sexual dimorphism and sexual selection: A case of gene culture co-evolution? *Ethnic and Racial Studies, 9*(1), 87–113.

Van Horn, K. R., Arnone, A., Nesbitt, K., Desilets, L., Sears, T., Giffin, M., & Brudi, R. (1997). Physical distance and interpersonal characteristics in college students' romantic relationships. *Personal Relationships, 4*(1), 25–34.

Van Wyk, P. H., & Geist, C. S. (1995). Biology of bisexuality: Critique and observations. *Journal of Homosexuality, 28*(3/4), 357–373.

Vaughan, D. (1986). *Uncoupling: How relationships come apart*. New York: Random House.

Velle, W. (1987). Sex differences in sensory functions. *Perspectives in Biology and Medicine, 30*(4), 490–522.

Vemer, E. N. (1989). A quantitative review of marital satisfaction in remarriage. Dissertation Abstract International, 49(7-A), 1981–1982.

Veroff, J. (1982). Assertive motivations: Achievement versus power. In A. J. Stewart (Ed.), *Motivation and society*. San Francisco: Jossey-Bass.

Veroff, J., Sutherland, L., Chadra, L., & Ortega, R. (1993). Predicting marital quality with narrative assessments of marital experience. *Journal of Marriage and the Family, 55*, 326–337.

Visher, E. B., & Visher, J. S. (1979). *Stepfamilies: A guide to working with stepparents and stepchildren*. New York: Brunner/Mazel.

Visher, E. B., & Visher, J. S. (1990). Dynamics of successful stepfamilies. *Journal of Divorce & Remarriage, 14*(1), 3–12.

Waldenfoger, J. (1997). The effect of children on women's wages. *American Sociological Review, 62*, 209–217.

Waller, W. W., & Hill, R. (1951). *The family, a dynamic interpretation*. New York: Dryden Press.

Wallerstein, J. S. (1985). Children of divorce: Preliminary report of a ten-year follow-up of older children and adolescents. *Journal of the American Academy of Child Psychiatry, 24*(5), 545–553.

Wallerstein, J. S., & Kelly, J. B. (1998). The long-term impact of divorce on children: A first report form a 25-year study. *Family and Conciliation Courts Review, 36*(3), 368–383.

Wallerstein, J. S. (1989/1991). Children after divorce: Wounds that don't heal. In O. Pocs (Ed.), *Marriage and family 91/92* (pp. 170–175). Guilford, CT: Dushkin.

Wallerstein, J. S., & Blakeslee, S. (1989). *Second chances: Men, women, and children a decade after divorce*. New York: Ticknor & Fields.

Wallerstein, J. S., & Blakeslee, S. (1995). *The good marriage: How and why love lasts*. Boston: Houghton Mifflin.

Wallerstein, J. S., Corbin, S. B., & Lewis, J. M. (1988). Children of divorce: A 10-year study. In E. M. Hetherington & J. D. Arasteh (Eds.), *Impact of divorce, single parenting and stepparenting on children* (pp. 197–214). Hillsdale, NJ: Lawrence Erlbaum

Walterstein, J. S., & Kelly, J. B. (1980). *Surviving the breakup: How children and parents cope with divorce*. New York: Basic Books.

Walsh, A. (1991a). Self-esteem and sexual behavior: Exploring gender differences. *Sex Roles, 25*(7/8), 441–450.

Walsh, A. (1991b). *The science of love: Understanding love & its effects on mind & body*. Buffalo, NY: Prometheus.

Walsh, A., & Balazs, G. (1990). Love, sex, and self-esteem. *Free Inquiry in Creative Sociology, 18*, 37–41.

Walsh, F. (1989). Reconsidering gender in the marital quid pro quo. In M. McGoldrick, C. Anderson, & F. Walsh (Eds.) *Women in Families: A framework for family therapy* (pp. 267–285). New York: W. W. Norton.

Walster, E. (1965). The effect of self-esteem on romantic liking. *Journal of Experimental Social Psychology, 1*, 184–197.

Walster, E., Berscheid, E., & Walster, G. W. (1973). New directions in equity. *Journal of Personality and Social Psychology 25*, 151–176.

Walters-Champman, S. F., & Price, S. J. (1995). The effects of guilt on divorce adjustment. *Journal of Divorce & Remarriage, 22*(3–4), 163–177.

Warner, R. (1986). Alternative strategies for measuring household division of labor: A comparison. *Journal of Family Issues, 7*, 179–195.

Watzlawick, P., Bavelas, J,. & Jackson, D. (1967) *Pragmatics of human communication.* New York: W. W. Norton.

Webster, P. S., Orbuch, T. L., & House, J. S. (1995). Effects of childhood family background on adult marital quality and perceived stability. *American Journal of Sociology, 101*(2), 404–432.

Wedekind, D., Seebeck, T., Bettens, F., & Paepke, A. J. (1995). MHC-dependent mate preference in humans. *Proceedings of the Royal Society of London, B 260*, 245–249.

Weinberg, L. (1991). Infant development and the sense of self: Stern vs. Mahler. *Clinical Social Work Journal, 19*(1), 9–22.

Weinberg, G., & Williams, C. J. (1974). *Male homosexuals: Their problems and adaptations.* New York: Oxford University Press.

Weiner, M. F. (1980). Healthy and pathological love—psychodynamic views. In K. S. Pope & Associates (Eds.), *On love and loving: Psychological perspectives on the nature and experience of romantic love,* (pp. 114–132). San Francisco: Jossey-Bass.

Weisfeld, G. E. (1997). Discrete emotions theory with specific reference to pride and shame. In N. L. Segal, G. E. Weisfeld, & C. C. Weisfeld (Eds.), *United psychology and biology: Integrative perspectives on human development* (pp. 419–443). Washington, DC: American Psychological Association.

Weiss, R. S. (1975). *Marital separation.* New York: Basic Books.

Weiss, R. S. (1979a). The emotional impact of marital separation. In G. Levinger & O. C. Moles (Eds.), *Divorce and separation: Context, causes, and consequences* (pp. 201–210). New York: Basic Books.

Weiss, R. S. (1979b). *Going it alone: The family life and social situation of the single parent.* New York: Basic Books.

Weiss, R. S. (1988). Loss and recovery. *Journal of Social Issues, 44*(3), 37–52.

Weitzman, L. (1985). *The divorce revolution.* New York: Free.

Werner, E. E. (1993). Children of the garden island. In M. Gauvain & M. Cole (Eds.), *Readings in the development of children.* New York: W. H. Freeman.

West, C., & Zimmerman, D. (1991). Doing gender. In J. Lorber & S. Farrell (Eds.), *The social construction of gender* (pp. 13–37). Newbury Park, CA: Sage.

Westoff, A. L. (1977). *The second time around: Remarriage in America.* New York: Viking Press.

Wetzel, C. G., & Insko, C. A. (1982). The similarity-attractions relationship: Is there an ideal one? *Journal of Experimental Social Psychology, 18,* 253–276.

Whitaker, C. A. (1976). A family is a four-dimensional relationship. In P. J. Guerin (Ed.), *Family therapy.* New York: Gardner.

Whitaker, C. A., Greenberg, A., & Greenberg, M. (1981). In G. P. Sholevaar (Ed.), *The handbook of marriage and marital therapy.* New York: Spectrum Publications.

White, B. (1989). Gender differences in marital communication patterns. *Family Process, 28,* 89–106.

White, G. L., Fishbein, S., & Rutstein, J. (1981). Passionate love and misattribution of arousal. *Journal of Personality and Social Psychology, 41,* 56–62.

White, G. L., & Helbick, T. R. M. (1988). Understanding and treating jealousy. In R. A. Brown & J. R. Field (Eds.), *Treatment of sexual problems in individual and couples therapy* (pp. 245–265). New York: PMA Publishing.

White, G. L., & Mullen, P. E. (1989). *Jealousy: Theory, research, and clinical strategies.* New York: Guilford Press.

White, J., & Humphrey, J. (1992, August). *Predictors of repeated victimization.* Paper presented at the conference of the American Psychological Association, Washington, DC.

White, L. (1992). The effect of parental divorce and remarriage on parental support for adult children. *Journal of Family Issues, 13*(2), 234–250.

White, L. K., Booth, A., & Edwards, J. N.(1986). Children and marital happiness: Why the negative correlation? *Journal of Family Issues, 7,* 131–147.

White, M. B., & Tyson-Rawson, K. J. (1995). Assessing the dynamics of gender in couples and families. *Family Relations, 44,* 253–260.

Wiederman, M. W. (1997). Extramarital sex: Prevalence and correlates in a national survey. *The Journal of Sex Research, 34*(2), 167–174.

Wilcoxon, S. A., & Hovestadt, A. J. (1983). Perceived health and similarity of family of origin experiences as predictors of dyadic adjustment for married couples. *Journal of Marital and Family Therapy, 9,* 431–434.

Williams, G. P., & Kleinke, C. L. (1993). Effects of mutual gaze and touch on attraction, mood, and cardiovascular reactivity. *Journal of Research in Personality, 27*(2), 170–183.

Williamson, D. (1981). Personal authority via termination of the intergenerational hierarchical boundary: A new "stage" in the family life cycle. *Journal of Marital and Family Therapy, 7,* 441–452.

Williamson, D. S., Bray, J. S., & Malone, P. E. (1982). *Personal Authority in the Family System Questionnaire.* Houston: Houston Family Institute.

Wills, T. A., Weiss, R. L., & Patterson, G. R. (1974). A behavioral analysis of the determinants of marital satisfaction. *Journal of Consulting and Clinical Psychology, 42,* 802–811.

Wilson, B. J., & Gottman, J. M. (1996). Attention—The shuttle between emotion and cognition: Risk, resiliency, and physiological bases. In E. M. Hetherington & E. A. Blechman (Eds.), *Stress, coping and resiliency in children and families. Family research consortium: Advances in family research* (pp. 185–228). Mahwah, NJ: Lawrence Erlbaum.

Wilson, E. O. (1978). *On human nature.* Cambridge, MA: Harvard University Press.

Wilson, E. O. (1998). The biological basis of morality. *The Atlantic Monthly, 4,* 53–70.

Wilson, G. (1982). *The Coolidge effect: An evolutionary account of human sexuality.* New York: William Morrow & Company.

Wilson, K., Faison, R., & Britton, G. M. (1983). Cultural aspects of male sex aggression. *Deviant Behavior, 4,* 241–255.

Wilson, M., & Daly, M. (1992). The man who mistook his wife for a chattel. In J. H. Barkow, L. Cosmides, & J. Tooby (Eds.), *The adapted mind: Evolutionary psychology and the generation of culture.* New York: Oxford University Press.

Winkler, I., & Doherty, W. J. (1983). Communication style and marital satisfaction in Israeli and American couples. *Family Process, 22,* 221–228.

Winslow, J. T., Hastings, N., Carter, C. S., Harbaugh, C. R., & Insel, T. R. (1993, October 7). A role for central vasopressin in pair bonding in monogamous prairie voles. *Nature, 365,* 5445–5548.

Winter, D. G. (1973). *The power motive.* New York: Free.

Winter, D. G. (1988). The power motive in women and men. *Journal of Personality and Social Psychology, 54*(3), 510–519.

Winter, D. G., Stewart, A. J., & McClelland, D. C. (1977). Husband's motives and wife's career level. *Journal of Personality and Social Psychology, 35*(3), 159–166.

Wojtkiewicz, R. A., McLanahan, S., & Garfinkel, I. (1990). The growth of families headed by women: 1950–1980. *Demography, 27,* 19–30.

Wood, F. B., Flowers, D. L., & Naylor, C. E. (1991). Cerebral laterality in functional neuroimaging, In F. L. Kitterle (Ed.), *Cerebral laterality: Theory and research.* Hillsdale, NJ: Lawrence Erlbaum.

Wright, R. A., & Contrada, R. J. (1986). Dating selectivity and interpersonal attractiveness: Toward a better understanding of the "elusive phenomenon." *Journal of Social and Personal Relationships, 3,* 131–148.

Wu, S., & Shaver, P. R. (1992, July). *Conceptions of love in the United States and the People's Republic of China.* Paper presented at the conference of the International Society for the Study of Personal Relationships, Orono, ME.

Yang, J. (1994). Intrathecal administration of oxytocin induces analgesia in low back pain involving the endogenous opiate peptide system. *Spine, 19*(8), 867–871.

Yarab, P. E., Semsibaugh, C. C., & Allgeier, E. R. (1998). "More than just sex" Gender differences in the incidence of self-defined unfaithful behavior in heterosexual dating relationships. *Journal of Psychology and Human Sexuality, 10*(2), 45–57.

Yelsma, P. (1996). Affective orientations of perpetrators, victims, and functional spouses. *Journal of Interpersonal Violence, 11*(2), 141–161.

Yogev, S. (1981). Do professional women have egalitarian marriage relationships? *Journal of Marriage and the Family, 43,* 865–871.

Young, M., & Willmott, P. (1973). *The symmetrical family.* New York: Random.

Zaslow, M. J. (1989). Sex differences in children's response to parental divorce: 2. Samples, variables, ages, and sources. *American Journal of Orthopsychiatry, 59*(1), 118–141.

Zavella, P. (1987). *Women's work and Chicano families.* Ithaca, NY: Cornell University Press.

Zelkowitz, P. (1987). Social support and aggressive behavior in young children. *Family Relations, 36*(2) 129–134.

Zilbergeld, B. (1978). *Male sexuality: A guide to sexual fulfillment.* Boston: Little, Brown & Company.

Zimmerman, J. L., & Dickerson, V. C. (1994). Using a narrative metaphor: Implications for theory and clinical practices. *Family Process, 33,* 233–245.

Zvonkovic, A. M., Greaves, K. M., Schmiege, C. J., & Hall, L. D. (1996). The marital construction of gender through work and family decisions: A qualitative analysis. *Journal of Marriage and the Family, 58,* 91–100.

Appendix
Breaking up
with dignity and recovery
from the loss of a love

The long journey back to singlehood from being coupled has occupied counselors and self-help literature for decades. We offer specific guidelines for this journey for three reasons. First, few of us experience this transition often enough to get good at it. Second, the way we experience this loss and transition can influence the way we view ourselves: as resilient or helpless, as worthy or not worthy of love. It can lead us to view our emotions as crazy or sane, and our future relationships as safe or as unsafe or unworthy places to invest our emotions. Finally, dealing with lingering feelings for our former loves challenges us to arrange any contacts between us in a way that supports the well-being of both people making the influence of our past a positive force in our lives.

Respect the pain

We cannot prepare for the variety and intensity of emotional reactions we feel during and after a breakup. We are shocked at the differences and mismatches between what one partner and the other feels, no matter who initiates the breakup. These feelings are most difficult when we haven't had practice dealing with separation and loss. When we are unable or unwilling to ride these emotional waves of sadness, fright, helplessness, guilt, shame, rage, etc., we are likely to escape them and then act them out without being aware of where our behavior is coming from. We can oscillate between depression (no interest in life) and escapism (intoxicants, adventures, etc.). We may also keep doing things for revenge or keep "plugging people in" to bury our pain, as this student admits:

TABLE A.1. Seven steps in recovering from a love

1. Respect the pain and deal with it.
2. Gain understanding of what happened.
3. Recollect parts of yourself experienced in the relationship.
4. Embrace singlehood and change your life.
5. Be conscious of healing and transition relationships.
6. Recognize and release residual attachments to past loves.
7. Completion. Acknowledge the value of your partner and the relationship and then close the chapter.

I don't even remember feeling any emotions after a breakup. I just went on with my business. I get drunk quite often. This makes me feel a lot better. The one thing I do is get drunk, then pick up girls to prove to myself I can do without the previous one.

At first, we may be unable to feel our emotions (shock and denial of grief). We may be hyperanxious or hyperactive, unable to sleep unless totally exhausted, with our minds racing, often trying to get the lost person back. Or we may slow down and be barely able to get out of bed. Our normal defenses may just "lock up tight" to stem the emotional tide of emotions. This desperate struggle between defences and emotions can make our characteristic psychological abnormalities get so extreme that we feel and act quite crazy ("exaggeration principle," Chapter 11).

In the movies, men facing sudden grief often go on a destructive rampage, as if this is the most "manly" way to achieve emotional release. Releasing our emotions when they are struck inside often relieves some of our "craziness" and allows us to sleep. We may dream of our emotions like this:

I'm running from a tidal wave that looms high above me as I run up the beach. I'm sure I won't get away from it. Everything is happening in slow motion.

Though grief may feel as scary as a tidal wave, and rage as scary as a wildfire, the intensity does pass. Our emotions are designed to pass through like waves and then our natural buoyancy brings us up for air. We are built to experience and survive emotional pain; tears contain endorphins to soothe us. Table A.2 explains some physical and psychological exercises for releasing emotions.

Partner's pain

As important as it is to respect and deal with our own pain, it is equally important to **respect our partner's pain, but not to try to take it away**. Both parts of this statement need careful explanation. When we terminate a relationship or "demote" our partner to a lower position in our lives, we are

TABLE A.2. Physical ways to release pent-up emotions

1. Sit and take deep breaths, expanding both your chest and your stomach. Think about your breakup, your partner, and your losses. It is impossible to hold back powerful emotions without restricting our breathing. Be sure to make a sound every time you breathe out, a humming sound that fits with how you feel at that moment. Making sound may feel embarrassing at first, but it will soon connect with your emotions inside. You may feel out of control when your emotions first emerge: it is just like a "gusher" that erupts when underground fluids under pressure finally break through the earth's surface. You may be sobbing, shaking, or raging uncontrollably, but you are not crazy. Symptoms of a nervous breakdown occur when we have spent too long blocking this sort of emotional release. If you are afraid of these feeling, have someone watch over you. If you feel hyperventilated, dizzy, and scared of exploding, but still can't get any sound or feeling out, stop. Use exercise 2 or 3, or seek help.

2. This Tibetan yoga exercise accentuates the bodily barriers to emotions in order to break through them. Sit with your back straight and eyes closed. Restrict your breathing by gradually tightening and depressing your chest. Hold your forearms horizontally in front of your chest, gradually tensing all muscles against each other and clenching fists tightly so that they almost touch each other and your chest. Then clench your teeth, jaw, and neck, making sure all other muscles down to your diaphragm are locked up, and breathe very shallowly in your abdomen. Focus on your emotions inside your chest and imagine that you are trying to press them back into your back wall. Hold this for 30 seconds, or until a little after you have made your torso-to-jaw tension as painful as you can. Then take two quick breaths into your abdomen and suddenly throw off all the tension as if exploding. Throw your arms out straight in front of you and push all the air in your lungs out with a loud sound of "HA!" Letting your arms come down to your lap, breathe easily and focus silently on your emotions for a minute or two. Begin tensing again. Repeat the sequence until your emotions begin to flow out, then breathe life through them.

3. If anger seems to be the main thing trapped inside you, combine deep breathing, sound, and beating on a pillow, couch, or bed. Take in a full breath while arching up tall with your hands over your head, as if for a vertical swing of an axe. Clench both fists and interlock your fingers into a double fist or grasp a tennis racket in both hands. As you exhale, swing your whole upper body down as a unit so your fists or racket hit the cushion squarely. Make a loud sound each time you exhale and hit and express any words that come to mind when thinking of any person you can imagine, including your ex-partner. Be sure you can get violent with your blows with no possibility of injury. Do not be frightened if you go into an uncontrolled fury, or if rage and tears tumble over each other. Remember that the positive goal of your rage is to destroy your *love relationship*, not to harm your ex-partner. While momentary murderous impulses can be safely expressed through this exercise, it is important to separate them from actions. We can release such hostile impulses in a ritualized way, so that they will *not* linger to poison our thoughts or lead us toward revenge.

Sources: #1, Reichian therapy; #2, Adapted in yoga training (Tulku, 1978); #3, Gestalt therapy.

causing pain, no matter how cleverly or humanely we try to handle it. We are not responsible for the ways our partner expresses emotions, but we are responsible for choosing to take actions or to not take expected actions, which make some sort of reactions to loss almost inevitable. Responsibility implies guilt. Often, we try to avoid or criticize, invalidating our partner's feelings in order to dodge guilt—our own withdraw and attack on other shame responses. Or we treat our ex-partner so nicely that she can't feel justified in staying mad at us.

If we keep ex-partners liking us, they may keep their "love-fires" lit and undermine the anger that helps them turn away from us and heal. We need to respect our partner's need for anger and hurt, even when we don't like what that could do to our self-image or reputation. Though some immediately post-breakup friendships may be comfortable (see Chapter 3), this coed found out that it didn't work for her:

> *During my recovery period, Joe contacted me several times. Each time he did it was like starting all over for me. His phone calls, letters, and surprise visits just seemed to stir up the pain all over again. He kept insisting that I was his best friend and that he didn't want to lose our friendship too. I finally told him that if he ever hoped to have a friendship with me, he would have to give me time to get over what we once had. It really felt good to me to finally have control over my life again.*

We make contribute to both our own and our partner's *dignity* with two attitudes: **1) No matter how unusually or outrageously our partner's feelings come out, there is some truth and value in them; 2) We are responsible for our actions in the breakup, so we can acknowledge our guilt.** Guilt is no more popular than any other shame emotion. Just as many habitual criminals are either unwilling or unable to recognize their guilt, many "habitual heartbreakers" have found ways to short-circuit their awareness of guilt for their actions. Feeling "bad" about the pain that our breakups cause motivates us to make our post-relationship dealings more humane and our next romantic involvement more thoughtful. It takes courage (literally "heart-stuff') to feel and express our responsibility for actions that lead to pain for others. But, like many other emotions, guilt turns out to be less devastating than we expected once we stop maneuvering to avoid it.

It is a precious experience to exchange painful emotions with our ex-partner after a breakup, and it can further both partners' healing. But if consoling each other becomes a regular pattern, it will hold back our separation process. And it can become part of a dangerous cycle:

> When Kevin and Sylvia broke up, everybody in their department knew about it, because Kevin was a graduate assistant and Sylvia was a grader. They also ran into each other every day and seemed to end up in intense emotional discussions after the workday was over. Kevin wanted to get back together, while Sylvia was trying to get him to accept being just friends. When Sylvia went out with Carl two weeks after the breakup, her encounters with Kevin got more tense. A week later Kevin met Carl and Sylvia at a wedding, and the two men got into fight. After Sylvia and Carl returned to her apartment that night, Kevin banged on the door. Then he got a gun from his car and broke in. Carl tried to defend himself, and Kevin shot him dead. Then he walked right up to Sylvia, who was cowering in her closet, and put a bullet through his own head.

Every year, there are hundreds of suicides among college students. In 1991, there were 30,810 suicides in the United States, of which 4,751 were of people from 15 to 24 years old. Statistics on specific motivations are not kept, but studies indicate that relationship problems with lovers, family, or friends are the primary precipitating factor among young adults (Clark, 1992).

Looking at the above situation with 20-20 hindsight, it appears that the ex-partners spent too much time together. After listening to him once or twice, Sylvia needed to **build a fireproof wall** between them so that his feelings would no longer affect her and her actions would not trigger him. She needed to refuse his approaches and insist that he talk to someone else (that's what legal restraining orders are for). Kevin needed to stop pursuing her and express himself to other sympathetic people. Those like Kevin, who won't talk to anyone else, are at the greatest risk of suicide. Carl needed to "smell the smoke" and steer clear until Sylvia was not tangling with Kevin every day. Their friends could have been recruited to act as a buffer between them and as confidants for each one separately.

The campus was devastated by the deaths, but other students still didn't understand how much separation and recovery are needed before long-term lovers like Kevin and Sylvia could "hang out as friends." We have described many aspects of the extended grief processes from a break-up in Chapter 3 and 5. Here are some tips for coping with feelings.

This student testifies to the value of talking out his feelings with someone else:

> I spent many hours at night before sleep thinking about what had happened. However, I failed to really talk it out with a friend. It seemed to me that most people would just say, "Hey, don't worry about it man, it's just a girl." At my lowest point, I had a very long conversation with a female friend of mine. I never thought that maybe my first love wasn't ready for a commitment. I was so sure that I was ready that I never took the time to ask her what she wanted. My friend pointed this out to me, and I felt a little better.

Suicide

When we are out of control, fantasies, dreams, and fears of death, as well as suicidal and homicidal thoughts, are quite common. Some parts of ourselves are indeed dying, as we can discover by doing task 3 in Table A.3. We may feel unbearable shame and grief that someone we want so much will not come to us, so we want to eliminate our shameful self through death (Mokros, 1995). We may also direct attacks or other rage at our partner. If we take steps to eliminate our relationship, instead of our partner or ourselves, our emotions can motivate us to heal. Table A.4 is a "first aid kit" for thoughts of suicide and for others who want to help them.

TABLE A.3. Coping with the loss of a love

1. Feeling loss requires both time alone dwelling on thoughts and feeling, and expressing oneself to trusted others. Give yourself permission to seek both solitude and confidants when you feel like it. But if one of these is impossible for you, ask for help with it.
2. List the telephone numbers of three kinds of support: public assistance talk lines such as suicide prevention, parent support, etc.; mental health professionals; and mentors, pastors, and friends. Ask friends what hours it would be OK to call and write those hours down. You may never need to call any of these numbers, but you are more in charge when you have them.
3. Make a list of your losses, both large and small. Besides your partner's presence, they may include dialogue; emotional support; activities; families and friendships; possessions; a dwelling place; your hopes, dreams, and goals; and parts of your identity, social connections, and possibilities. Each time you find yourself depressed, you may discover another one of your losses. Making them explicit helps you to be more focused and careful about coping with them.
4. Take a few minutes to be still and feel your sensations and emotions. Noticing your feelings makes you aware that they change, which furthers your process of change.
5. Rest when you feel like resting. At first, your mind may race and keep you awake as it tries to recover the lost relationship. This is an instinctual emergency stress reaction that will exhaust you and deplete your immune system. You will need unusual amounts of rest for your body to recover.
6. Stick to some parts of your regular schedule. Maintain the essential elements of your everyday life, such as work, study, and reduced exercise.
7. Don't make any important decisions for the first month, such as moving or changing jobs, plans, and goals. But if present commitments bring you in close contact with your ex-partner, make adjustments to aid in separation.
8. Do things that make you feel good, both alone and with others. List what comforted you as a child and what comforts you now. Include treat and "sick-day" foods; leisure pleasures; reading and entertainment; physical treats such as bathing, swimming, exercise, and massage; and aesthetic treats such as music, painting, or natural settings.
9. Talk to people who have been through something similar. Write down what you would tell a close friend in a similar situation and what a good relative or friend would say and do for you. Then consider how you could use this advice.
10. Ask yourself how long it is likely to be before you are back to feeling more or less normal. Would it be 6 months or a year? It doesn't matter how long you decide on, but only that *you are willing to project that you will recover. You will recover.*

Adapted from Surviving, Healing, & Growing by Colgrove, Bloomfield, & McWilliams (1991b), Surviving Grief by Sanders (1992), and other clinicians' strategies.

Gain understanding of what happened

If we recognize what went well and poorly in our past relationship, we can try to change for the future. There are three aspects to examine: 1) Find out what you yourself did, thought, and felt that fostered and hindered the relationship. Your own observations of yourself are only one part; you also need to seek input from your ex-partner and friends. 2) Examine your **ex-partner's** actions, thoughts, and feelings. It almost always takes two to tangle, even if one is merely too "saintly" to object to the other's "sins." 3) Study the interaction between partners, that systemic dance you two created together. Did you do the pursuer-distancer, reasonable-emotional, or

TABLE A.4. First aid kit for those considering suicide: Do's and Don't's

1. A. ***Don't drink or take drugs.*** Distorted thoughts and feelings can lead to very poor decisions.
   B. ***Do talk about your situation.*** Call a hotline, pastor, mental health professional, or friend. Friends and professionals can make sure someone talks you through your state of mind.
   C. You can protect yourself by calling 911. The police can take you to a hospital where you will get protection, good rest, and a chance to discuss what you are going through.
2. You may have an uncontrollable emergency reaction, with both panic and rage, and be unable to relax or sleep. You may feel unbearable shame from having your love rejected, and want to eliminate yourself so that you will not have to bear the pain anymore. You need a temporary end to your hyperaroused state, not a permanent end. Call your doctor for help. Antidepressants and tranquilizers may relieve your emotional state. Be sure your doctor knows you are suicidal, so you don't get something you can use to kill yourself
3. Before you snuff out your connection with the entire world, consider the following thoughts:
   A. If you could be selective about snuffing out your world, what would you want to eliminate? What parts might you keep? Who and what would you miss, if you could never see them again?
   B. Are there any people who would be very upset or suffer deprivation if you died? How long might these other people's suffering last? Does your present suffering justify triggering such suffering for them?
   C. Is there anyone who you would *like* to upset? Perhaps it might serve someone right if he or she felt guilty, abandoned, or robbed by your death. You can write a letter about what they deserve to feel. But don't send it until you have thought it over in a different state of mind. And don't use it as a suicide note.
   D. Imagine that you died and then were reincarnated into another situation. Specifically, how would your new life be different? Then list every idea you can think of, fanciful or feasible, that could help shift your present situation to be more like the new life you imagined. You can begin building a new life as soon as you stop spending your energy on death. Many of your fantasized changes may not be achievable, but dying is the most costly and most unreliable method of achieving any future you can envision.
4. Suicide is a spiritual crisis, so reconnect with your spiritual beliefs and resources.
   A. Pray or take other steps to get spiritual guidance. Talk to religious people you respect.
   B. Perhaps you want to die because someone you love has died. Consider whether that person would want you to die or to do something more with your life.
   C. Is anybody else suffering too? Helping somebody else can help you gain perspective on your own life.

Sources: Colgrove et al., 1991b; the authors and other mental health professionals.

overfunctioner-underfunctioner dances? Repetitive interaction patterns are often too subtle to be singled out as reasons for breaking up. But they may have led to the more obvious "crimes" that stick in our memories.

It is an act of compassion to write or tell our ex-partners why we cannot continue with them. Rejectees normally try to relieve their helplessness by understanding as much as they can about what led to their loss.

> *After our break-up, I had a strong feeling to know what went wrong that caused her to not want to be with me anymore. I felt then and still feel today*

that if I had that knowledge, I could have learned from it and then moved on with my life a lot sooner.

We often don't want to tell a lover our own truth about why we are leaving because we don't want to hurt them "any more than necessary." Or perhaps we cannot justify it to ourselves, since it is based on uncomfortable feelings rather than "solid" facts. A careful explanation of what bothered us and what was not working, as well as admitting how we ourselves helped make the relationship untenable, may hurt both of us more at first. But it will help in the long run. We can sort out what was specific to the dance of this partnership and what has been a persistent aspect of our character and way in life. And we can recognize what we may be able to change, such as coping strategies and behavior, and what we cannot change, such as our size, shape, and core values. One coed finally heard an unpleasant truth.

*About a year later he told me he needed to get something off of his chest. It wasn't just [his] summer romance he felt bad about. The bottom line was that he didn't feel attracted to me, and that made him feel really awful. It wasn't until now, **when I had lost some weight**, that he could tell me. It really made me mad. But I'm sure going to keep my weight down if I can.*

Our explanations of past relationships contribute to our identities as intimate partners, so we need to construct them conscientiously. Daphne Kingma (1987) suggests that we can also seek to understand each relationship as a *contribution to our development as a person*. What was going on in your life when the relationship began? What were each of you trying to accomplish when you met? What were you doing in relation to the outside world and in other emotional relationships, including family, friends, and other romantic partners? Were you establishing or changing life directions? Were you struggling to move closer or further away from a parent, friend, or past lover? If you compare yourself at the beginning of your relationship with yourself now, what have you gained and lost in yourself? What skills, abilities, knowledge, and attitudes have you developed? What parts of your new development did you provide for yourself, and what came from your partner or as a result of your interaction? How have you sparked or helped with your partner's development?

Kingma further suggests that some breakups are "graduations" from a personal development course, rather than failures or mistakes. Some examples are: "I outgrew my need for a parent;" "I got a sense of my attractiveness, generosity, or power;" "I finally got mad, vulnerable, or in love and was able to express it to a partner;" and "We finished building careers." Along with such awareness of our own growth may come a new appreciation of our partner's role, without any desire to restart the partnership.

Images and symbols that come spontaneously to mind can help to combine thinking and feeling in order to "graduate from" our relationships. One may encounter an ex-partners in dreams and fantasies. Dialoguing with the characters in these appearances supports the healing process that our minds have begun (Kast, 1987).

Recollect parts of yourself experienced in a relationship

There are many aspects of ourselves that blossom in intimacy, including some abilities we never knew we had that our partner has loved into existence. When a relationship ends, it feels as if our relationship-self is suddenly in limbo, like a phantom-limb. We lose touch with the characteristics of ourselves as partners. If we explicitly acknowledge what all these facets are, we can begin recollecting them into our "single-self." One way to do this is "re-owning projections," a Gestalt Therapy exercise:

1a. Think of all the aspects you admired or were attracted to in your partner. List them by saying (or writing) "You are ____" (e.g. "so easygoing," "very smart").
1b. Say "I am ____" followed by the same words you used in 1a. Consider how each of your statements may apply to yourself, in addition to your partner. Be specific about where and how you manifest some of the features you have seen in your mate.
2a. Make a second list of your own "couple-self" qualities by finishing this sentence: "With you I was ____."
2b. Now note where and how you could manifest these features you saw in yourself and note what could stop you.

Embrace singlehood and change your life

In Chapter 10, we suggested that individual development could be likened to the growth and branching-out process of a tree or bush. A parable about transplanting a rose bush can help us understand some effects that can occur in any major change:

> When a gardener transplants a rose bush, it will go into root shock. Its life energy will retreat from its limbs and thinner roots back into its central core. If most limbs are not trimmed off, they will become brittle

and may splinter and further deplete the plant's energy. The good gardener trims the limbs very far back to help the plant survive its loss. When the roots have taken hold in the new soil, brand new limbs will sprout, and they will take some new directions and new forms more fitting to their new growing conditions. Thus a new expression of the rose's nature grows out of the revitalized core.

When people make a drastic change in location, work, or love relationships, they should treat themselves the way the good gardener treats the rose. They should cut back on some of their activities, especially those that seem lifeless unless stimulated by alcohol or drugs. A period of relative hibernation prepares us for the next growth stage. Withdrawing from a couple allows us to grow new friends and activities, and to live with the old ones in new ways. Thus our new branches reflect our new identity as a single person.

One key issue after a breakup is how much energy goes into the "phantom limb" of being a romantic partner. Some people replace this partner role with a close companionship, others with a parent-child relationship. Still others practically live in their phantom-limb, feeling empty and depressed until a new prospect comes along with whom they can "be themselves" again.

Many young women have lived with an series of dating relationships ever since high school, so they haven't had a chance to learn how to live without one. They get pressure from other women to "have a boyfriend." They are frightened of "being alone" because they have no experience with it. Spending six months without a romantic partner offers a chance to devote more energy to oneself and to discover how to be balanced and happy on one's own. Table A.5 summarizes some key features of self-care.

Men often rely on alcohol as more than the pillars of self-care because they must be "tough" and convey the implicit gender-statement that **"What I do is not motherly or comfortable in any way identifiable as feminine."** So male apartments may be meagerly furnished, with more booze than nourishing food in the refrigerator. Weight-lifting and contact sports may be preferred to walking, baths, or massages for physical care. Self-reliance is such an important pillar of male identity that many men bolster their self-esteem by denying any dependency on others, ignoring the pillars of self-care, and adamantly "going it alone" (Goldberg, 1987). While this "I can handle it" attitude does provide symbolic identity support, it leaves men blind and vulnerable to their needs for feeding, companionship, affection, and emotional support. Awareness of the pillars of self-care can help men to care for themselves in less heroic, and more realistic and supportive, ways.

We see the effects of affection hunger on divorcees in this excerpt from a newspaper column by Ruthe Stein titled "Why Men Still Can't Be Trusted:"

TABLE A.5. The pillars of self care, or being your own mother/friend

1. **Feed yourself well**. Cook meals that make you feel cared for, rather than just refueled. Instead of watching TV, take some mealtimes to pay attention to good food, a cozy table, candlelight, dinner music, and rituals such as prayers or conversation with a guest.

2. **Emotional support.** Give some friends the kind of understanding and support you gave your partner and ask the same from them. People with larger, more conflict-free support networks cope better with stress, loneliness, and romantic loss (Tousignant & Hanigan, 1993).

3. **Support yourself.** Take time each day to remember and contemplate your thoughts and feelings, such as by writing in a journal. Give yourself appreciation and supportive attention for your experiences each day, as if you were someone you loved through thick and thin.

4. **Make your dwelling comfortable.** Let your dwelling and decorations give you symbolic support for your self-concept (through pictures, objects, etc.), as well as material comfort and restoration from the stress of the world.

5. **Affection.** Exchanging affection need not be connected to sex. Increase the affection shared with friends by giving it and asking for it. Pets and stuffed animals are easy. Exchange back rubs or pay for a massage. Children, the elderly, and the disabled can also provide affectionate contact.

6. **Self-fulfillment.** Both active and passive self-fulfillment anchor a mature form of object constancy; the awareness that **I myself am a good source of fulfillment.** Active self-fulfillment includes hobbies, reading, solo activities, or artistic pursuits. Through practice, learn to **like** new things you do alone. Video and music offer passive entertainment, but a special, secure fulfillment can be achieved through prayer, meditation, self-hypnosis, or fantasy. All these induce mental states of relaxation and contentment. Thus they show us that we ourselves, or the spiritual source we connect with, are the source of our own fulfillment. This is healing if we have always relied on companionship, work, activities, entertainment, or alcohol to keep from ever feeling empty. By focusing on empty consciousness, meditation shows that emptiness can be bliss.

7. **Expand the list.** What did your family members do that made you feel good? Find what has been fulfilling for you in the past and list the things you have done for others that have made them feel good. Think of ways to translate each item so you could do it or have it done for you now. If your plans require another participant, list which people could be candidates for the role.

8. **Implementation.** You don't have to do everything at once. You have the rest of your life to develop your self-fulfillment. Experiment with a few aspects each week and practice until they become new habits. Join a divorce adjustment group or ask a friend to join in developing self-fulfillment. You can plan your individual projects together, encourage each other, and learn through your personal successes and setbacks. Personal growth isn't always hard work, and doing it with buddy or group support can build good friendships.

---

*I got a hysterical phone call from my girlfriend . . . She had run into this man at a party, and "He came over as soon as he saw me. We were talking— about work and what we had been up to—when suddenly he moved closer and put his hand on **my hip as if we had just spent the night together.***

*"I should have excused myself and walked away. But I liked the **way his hand felt.** I was sure he was signaling me he was interested, and I wanted him to know I was too. We stood that way for maybe 10 minutes. Before we parted, he whispered he would call soon.*

*"I haven't heard a word from him. I feel like I've been defrauded. **His gesture was so intimate.** How could he not have meant anything by it?"*

This encounter is fueled by attraction and affection. Its intimacy is confusing since neither participant knows enough about the other's personality or intentions for a relationship.

Relating needs

Embracing singlehood involves spreading our needs out among several friends and relatives, so we don't unconsciously expect to meet them with each "dating/mating prospect" that comes our way. A pond-skipper can walk on water because it has eight legs to take advantage of the surface tension. If it only had one leg, it would quickly sink. Many ex-lovers also sink when they pour too many needs into one person, whether family member, friend, or new date. It may seem strange to be rational about your emotional and relational needs, but if you are prone to get in too deep too fast, you can clarify your needs by writing them out. Start with this generic set of pair relationship needs (Drigotas & Rusbult, 1992):

1. companionship
2. emotional involvement
3. security
4. self-esteem
5. intimate self-sharing
6. sex and/or affection

Make each of these needs more personal and specific, such as 1) "go to parties and baseball games with me" and 5) "respond supportively when I talk about my day." Add additional, specific things you like to do with another person's company. Now you are ready to cultivate your social network. Throughout history we have lived in clans, tribes, and villages, where almost everybody was a pond-skipper!

New identity

We don't need to be consistent or reliable, so we can try on and discard new activities and projects as rapidly as new clothes. We may plunge ourselves into our career or hobbies to avert an "identity crisis." But we *do* have the opportunity to ask ourselves a basic existential question: "Since I'm no longer living with or **for** anybody else, what do I really want to do?"

Don't expect to be comfortable and secure during these new beginnings. "April is the cruelest month" said T. S. Eliot (1922/1968), because new sprouts are easily burned and broken. Sometimes another wintry depression or confusing encounter with our family or ex can nip our sprouts in the bud. Making our way through life is like riding a bicycle, but more difficult; we alternate between keeping our balance and falling over. Each time we lose our balance physically, psychologically, socially, economically, or spiritually, we have to learn something new in order to resume our ride. Falling off hurts and is embarrassing, but coping with internal and external assaults on our psychological balance helps us build our humility and wisdom.

Be conscious about healing and transition relationship

We noted in Chapter 3 that rebounds can can help us heal. Besides the humiliation of prior failure, they can soothe specific wounds or afford new chances to deal with issues that were unsatisfactory in prior relationships (see *leapfrogging* in Chapter 3). But they start to feel "sticky" when our initial attraction and their "loneliness quenching" function fade. We start to feel guilty about "using" our partner and want to back out unobtrusively and perhaps to redefine our partner as a platonic friend.

> *The main reason [my first relationship] ended was that I moved to go to college. The night I left Sandy's house was the saddest moment of my life. On the drive I was unusually quiet but didn't hurt as much as I thought I would. I was too preoccupied and anxious about school to think about much else. At school I immediately met Patty and started to date. We got intimate quickly and were very open. About a month and a half later I began to feel very guilty. After sex I couldn't be very intimate because of the guilt I had inside. I knew I wronged Sandy and felt like breaking up with Patty. Patty and I broke up a week later.*
>
> *But nothing was better. I saw Patty at school the next day and got very sad and teary-eyed. We couldn't stay broken up. I wonder whether I felt I was breaking up with Sandy or Patty at that time.*

Here are a few postulates about grieving and rebounds:

1. Every relationship can aid in healing the past. There is no way to avoid using our partners for our own recovery and growth except by not having any partners.
2. Not every long-term relationship leaves a lot of grief or requires a lot of recovery time.
3. When there is little noticeable grief and recovery (less than one month) after a medium- to long-term relationship, it may be that we weren't fully passionate or attached to our partner. Our passion may have been unavailable because of our own history, or we may have chosen our partner as a healer for something that happened before.
4. Sometimes a long period of relationship decay or hurtful fighting can make our initial separation a **relief.** But subtler grief reactions may still come up later.

Advice on rebounds

Don't use rebounds to obliterate your grief and loneliness. It is hard to convince yourself of the value of "feeling bad," withdrawing, and missing your ex-partner and the relationship when most peers reward the person who "feels better" and finds a replacement more quickly. Yet some people decide not to date at all, or to not date frequently or seriously, for 3 or 6 months as a way to insure they will confront and benefit from the recovery process. Wise friends and mentors can help us balance extraverted ways of coping, such as working and dating, with introverted focus on ourselves in order to absorb our feelings, learn our lessons.

> *After I did most of my recovering from my break-up, I learned many things. The most important was that I can depend on myself to make it through even the toughest times. I didn't have to settle for less in a relationship just because I was afraid of having to go through a break-up.*

A duty to warn?

Should we inform our partners of our psychological state when we are in recovery after a break-up? Should we point out issues that still burn in our minds from before? Until our feelings of loss have abated, we usually don't want to risk losing our "healer" and plunging back into our emotional depths again. We can, however, relieve our growing guilt by expressing our respect for our healer's generosity in responding to our desires. She or he will feel less "used" or "codependent" for caring for us if we honor the sacrifice and give gratefulness when we cannot give romantic passion. Almost everybody has some relationship wounds from the past, so perhaps we can benefit our healer as well. Healing connections can become fuller relationships. Openly acknowledging our wounds and the healer's effect on our emotions may lead to the end of our healing rebound, but that ending makes room for a new and different love to be born, perhaps even between the same two people.

Advice for healers

If we join in our partner's breakup experience early, we may ride the spinning end of a yo-yo. When our partner feels lonely or angry at the ex, we go in. When the ex wants him/her back, we go out. When our partner is hurting, we are the savior. When she withdraws, we are helpless. What can we do?

We can always take a long vacation and hope our prospective partner gets over their break-up without us. That means holding back on being a damsel or knight in distress, which is not easy to do when a heart is so open to our love. If we get involved anyway, does that mean we will never get equal power and passion in return?

It is in our own interest to teach our rebounding partner about breaking up. We can assert with him or her that we want all future contacts with the ex-partner to be aimed at extinguishing love's flame, rather than supporting it on low. We should not start believing we are a weaker, more codependent, less popular, or less valuable person—although our natural shame response may suggest these feelings just because we have less power in this relationship at this time. We can experience a whole spectrum of feelings, including uncontrollable ones that we would usually avoid, and thus learn more about ourselves. We can stop fearing that we're just asking to get dumped, and realize that we're also practicing *opening ourselves up and loving unselfishly, so we can be better at it* from now on. Love is not just about winning and losing or making sure we have our power, but also about surrender and sacrifice, letting go of control, and healing whoever needs to be healed. And finally, when we have had enough of an unbalanced relationship, we can back off and insist on better reciprocity or no relationship. But even if we never do that, most healing processes dwindle away in time, so our partner's former motivation for wanting us will pass. Then both partners can make choices without the yo-yo in between them.

If we find ourselves playing the healer in a whole string of relationships, then we may want to look for what we are getting and avoiding with those choices. If this is not all we want, more self-examination is in order.

Transition relationships

Even after the healing phases have passed, we may continue to form romantic relationships in which **our *commitment to ourselves is stronger than to the partnership.*** When "push comes to shove" in a relationship, we will get out rather than compromise. Such relationships are particularly good for testing our ability to be our own person in relation to another. From our commitment to autonomy, we can experiment with issues we had trouble with in past relationships. Choices and strategies don't have to work out, and we don't have an overriding concern to keep our partner feeling good about being with us. Prioritizing ourselves over partnership gives us the power of "whoever's hand is closest to the door to leave" and our partner will often give in.

> *Every time he'd get real set on what he wanted from me, I'd say "there's the door." If he didn't go out then, things would just get worse until he did. When he came back, it was always on my terms. I got to like not ever having to back down if I didn't want to. But I didn't like him being a push-over.*

We should recognize this unequal power condition for what it is so what we don't get hooked on always having this much control. Realizing that transition relationships are unequal in emotional energy investments can help us respect ourselves and our partners more, despite differences in the ways we act and feel.

Zigging and zagging through our love-lives

We may follow some normal patterns of romantic commitment and recovery, of peaks and valleys of emotional investment in love partners, over which we may have quite a bit less control than we think. From extensive work with divorce groups, Weiss (1975) concluded that it takes about 3 years to recover from a marriage, but this has not been verified by research. People in recovery from a committed love (and sometimes from raising children) may go zigging into low investment healing and transition relationships for years, while many of their partners are zagging out of recovery and into deeper romantic commitment. The less-invested relater can evoke greater passion and commitment by catalyzing the pursuer-distancer dance. One person is ready for independent, uncommitted self-exploration, experimentation, and erotic fun ("zigging") and the other is ready for the mating dance to lead into a committed partnership with a future ("zagging").

This tendency for mismatches between "committed" and "transitional" romantic involvements can lead to a chain reaction. On student glimpsed such a chain in his history:

> After **Diana,** I swore to myself that I wouldn't get involved in another relationship. But, soon after, I went through more than a couple of relationships. When I was ready to move on to the next woman, I could do so without any feelings of attachment for the last. It wasn't a very fair game to play.
>
> The only transition relationship I had was with Frances (the girl who told me that she loved me and scared me off). I had the power over her because if anything didn't go the way I wanted I could just back out of it. I felt good about myself because I was in control of my life again, but I felt guilty for misleading her.
>
> I have never thought about it until now, but I was probably a transition partner for **Diana.** She was ending her seven year relationship when we met, which was probably a lot to get over. I'm not sure how that makes me feel, but it all stands to reason. I feel relieved in a way.

Do our serial relationship lives have to be like a perpetual soap opera? Not if we understand which direction we are headed in ourselves and pick up clues to a prospective partner's likely direction as well. Both of our directions may be unconscious and difficult to discover. We may have to resist our emotions and get out when we discover a commitment mismatch, so we can be more intact and available for a better match in the future. We can also focus on personal growth in the hope that we will become more ready unconsciously for what we consciously want. However, chaos theory suggests, and future research may reveal that commitment patterns are not as orderly as the zig-zag theory projects.

Recognize and release residual attachments to past loves

Specific attachments to aspects of our former partner, as well as to the whole person, can last for years after a breakup. From size and shape to a body part, personality trait, or shared activity, anything can serve as a cue for the attachment we once had. Sometimes people declare "natural pro-clivities" without realizing what residual attachments they may be based on.

> He: I always date blondes. I'm just not attracted to anyone else.
> She: I want a man to be tall and dark. I want to look up to him.

Other residual attachments may prompt avoidance of "the way I got burned" and may appear as defensive "rules of engagement":

1. *If you want to be happy for the rest of your life, never make a pretty woman your wife.*
2. *Never get involved with anyone who is less than 2 years out of a long-term marriage.*

But there are far more subtle aspects of ex-partners to which we can remain attached, such as a sense of humor, ways of moving, or tone of voice. These qualities rarely show up on our list of desirable aspects in a new partner, but they can affect our process of rebonding without fully coming into awareness.

Comparisons are obvious clues to residual attachment. But so is feel-ing **numb** or **confused** when our new partner is buoyantly playful or gets the same haircut as our former love. Or we may get **irritated** or unthink-ingly reject a new partner who is too warm or kind. Numbness and confu-sion may be the beginning shock of a grief reaction. Irritation and rejection may be defences against experiencing deeper feelings that have not sur-faced since our previous love. Any time we have these reactions or say that something about a new partner "leaves me cold," we could pause and ask how that something relates to comparable aspects of a former love. Here is a example of physical attachment.

> A man in my men's group was explaining how the thrill of his new girlfriend had worn off after six months, but he was still happy with her, especially compared to his exwife. He said she was very pretty, too, but, well, her legs were quite nice, but they didn't really turn him on. What was wrong with them? Not anything, really. They just . . .
> So I asked him what he used to think about his wife's legs. Hymns of praise started to pour out! He stopped himself. "I can't stand her as a person, but her legs were perfection in flesh. Am I crazy or what?" I told him he

*missed his exwife's legs. I suggested he think some more her about legs and say goodbye to them when he went to bed that night. At the next meeting I asked him what he thought of his new girlfriend's legs, and he smiled broadly. "They're **her** legs, and I love her. They're great!"*

Developing intimacy with a new partner is like digging into successive strata in a mine and encountering different veins of precious experience at each level. Each time we touch a precious association to our past, we may feel confused, irritable, stuck, repulsed, or just automatically numb ourselves with alcohol. These reactions can occur when we hold hands, kiss, talk romantically, share hopes or secrets, or at any other time. We may inwardly recoil, acutely aware of the "strangeness" or even "wrongness" of our present partner for this intimate action. Later, alone, we can reminisce and feel how much we loved and now miss the person with whom we used to share that kind of moment. *Bringing that grief into consciousness is frequently enough to release the attachment and free us up to engage in similar intimacy with our new love.* Some of what we once loved can never be replaced. But being aware of what we miss allows us to choose to let go of it, rather than being driven to dissatisfaction by something we can't understand.

Grief therapy

When you can't stop thinking about your past love, you can do implosive grief therapy. Immerse yourself in reliving and talking about your loss over a few days or weeks, always looking for more feelings and connections that may come up. (This is prescribed grief in some cultures.) Continue until the flood of emotions is down to a trickle. Or use "flooding" (Michelson, 1985) to wear out and desensitize your emotional responses. Instead of trying *not* to think about your ex-partner, find out how long you usually spend reminiscing and do it *much more than you want to.* If you are stuck on a picture, stare at it, think all your usual thoughts, and continue after you want to shift your attention to something else. This can create an aversion to dwelling on your ex.

Completion: Acknowledge the value of your partner and the relationship and close the chapter

It is likely that we will remember every long-term romantic partner for the rest of our lives. It seems to be the exception, rather than the rule, that ex-lovers will become life-long friends who actually spend significant time together. (Some divorced parents do this, however.) The majority of former partners drift apart and exist for each other primarily as internalized figures.

Since our romantic partnerships have often been as intimate as any family relationships, it is in our own interest to carry our images of them in our minds as mutually supportive, respectful, and caring. We may carry our family, mentors, long-lasting friends, and deeply connected lovers with us as an "internal choir" of supporters and detractors, while we wish to keep the detractors and their sour notes to a minimum.

During the break-up, we often need to create a negative portrait of our partner's characters. This helps dissolve our attachment and restore our self-esteem. But it is helpful later to revise our history with a former love through occasional post-breakup encounters until we reach a sense of mutual respect and support. A positive reevaluation can do a lot to relieve old emotional burdens:

> *I called my old live-in boyfriend from three years ago to tell him I now enjoy the woods the way he always wanted me to and to thank him for trying so hard. He told me he was grateful for all the fights we had, because he got to get mad at me, and he never could do that with anybody before. It didn't seem like much of an honor to me, but he said it had helped him stand up to women ever since. Afterwards, it did seem nice to have my fiery temper respected for a change. That's one way of lighting a guy's lights I hadn't given myself credit for.*

Another way of feeling lovable after a breakup is to allow our ex-partner to carry a torch for us, while we go merrily on our way. The tactics for fueling an ex-partner's torch are subtle, from virtuous concern for the other's welfare to glowing praise or wistful hints to friends. Many leave the door to rekindling the relationship open a crack because it offers a symbolic security for future disappointments. But when we want to put all our romantic and erotic energy into one partner, it helps to do what we can to put previous love fires out all the way. Therefore, we suggest three goals for post-breakup communication:

1. Spell out the value of the partner and the relationship.
2. Shift the feelings of both parties towards mutual respect and caring.
3. Make it clear that the relationship is over and support both people to move on in their romantic lives.

These goals do not fit everyone. Many people remain loyal after their spouse's death, so they are not interested in "moving on." Both they and their children do not want to replace a revered memory with a new person. They may take on a new "friend" or mate, but not as a "one and only." In addition, some of the experiences one has had in a relationship may have been so abusive or horrible that one does not want to ever forgive, respect, or care for one's ex-partner. Forgiveness is a healing force for both people, but not if it means denying our hurt and anger. For that reason, we may need to wait a long time after our breakup, easily one to five years, before we are ready to embrace all of these goals with both mind and heart.

How would you feel if your ex-partner truly "moved on" and loved someone else fully? You need to consider your reservations before you are ready to let go. Perhaps you won't believe you are capable of an equal love until you have felt it with someone new. Many people are unable or unwilling to commit wholeheartedly to one partner because they don't want to cut off imaginary or real access to past loves.

There is a distinct difference between keeping a past lover alive in our imagination as an caring, respectful supporter and nurturing the glory of old romantic stories or anticipating possible future liaisons. One reason for waiting a long time before communicating our positive personal evaluation and warm wishes toward our ex-partner is to make sure that we don't fuel a flickering romantic torch or keep the door to reconnection open a crack. For our freedom to be mutual, we must support our ex-partner in getting free of us as well as vice versa. Helping our partner get past the attachment supports getting past it ourselves.

Post-breakup communication

To move post-breakup attitudes toward mutual respect and letting go, there are four levels of communication that can be used: 1) face to face; 2) vocal (telephone); 3) written (letter, e-mail); 4) internal (prayer, fantasy, personal journal, dreams).

The most intense is face to face. This can have great impact because our visual image of the ex-partner may be revised by connecting it to our message. However, a personal meeting can also foster desires to "see you one more time again," which may keep post-breakup fires alive. In contrast, a telephone conversation is less intense, but still offers the opportunity for mutual and spontaneous exchange. Writing a letter has the advantage of allowing us to choose every word carefully and not be interrupted in midstream. We can also practice formulating our intentions in successive drafts of the letter until we "get it right" for ourselves and for the expectations we have about our partner's response.

Communicating our feelings and intentions internally can occur through prayer, journal-keeping, writing letters we don't send, or talking it

over with a confidant. Although this level would seem to do little to make forgiveness, respect, caring, and letting go a *mutual* experience, it is central to our own well-being. The stability and authenticity of our own feelings and intentions is the best guarantee of success. Once we are at peace with our own intentions, any communication with our expartner, and to others about our partner, will be clearer and more effective. When direct contact is impossible (as in death), unhealthy (if the person is dangerous), or psychologically overwhelming, writing or internal reflection and expression are the only roads open. The goal is a mind-set of mutual respect and altruistic love, perhaps as a *spiritual secure base of symbolic support* for each other's diverging lives. This goal supports you, even if your expartner can't achieve it.

Conclusion

We are partially formed by our history of relationships. This begins with our family in childhood and continues with the impact of each love and its aftermath. We cannot expect to "keep our balance" and be consistently "upbeat" emotionally all the time for a lifetime if we allow passion, intimacy, and commitment to play major roles. But embracing the whole spectrum of love, with its gains and losses, leads us to many of life's most precious experiences and insights.

Index

gays and lesbians, 269–273
resolution stage, 112–116
Passion, 39–40, 42, 329–330
deepening relationships, 55
Passive aggression, 476
Pearson, P. T., 353–355, 357
Peplau, L. A., 3, 65, 112, 215, 219–224, 231, 237, 266, 270, 272–273, 275–276, 333
Peterson, D. R., 486–499
Phaedrus (Plato), 278, 331
Plausible deniability, 15
Possessiveness, 58–59
Post-separation adjustment, 155–160
child support, 160
dating, 165–168
emotional recovery, 161–162
gains, 164–165
gender differences, 158–160
long-term attachment, 162–164
remarriage, 170–171
staying single, 168–170
trajectories, 156–157
turning points, 157
Power
and attraction, 16–19
changes, 64–65
gays and lesbians, 263
gender issues, 216–226, 296–297
in termination stage, 82
issues in marriage, 110–111, 219–224
motivation, 224–226
romantic love, 45–46
tactics, 219
types, 217–219
women and divorce, 140
Premarital relationships
casual dating, 19–28
decay of, 72–78
deepening, 46–70
initiating, 6–19
in-love stage, 39–46
terminating, 78–89
Prior conditions stage, 487–489
Priorities, 58–59
Promiscuity, 291–296
Prophet, The (Gibran), 115–116
Psychic divorce, 152
Pursuer-distancer dance, 52–55, 75–76, 467, 504

Questing-experimental stage, 166–167

Random paradigm, 384–394
Rapid Couples Interaction Scoring System, 123–124
Rapport talk, 208
Reasonable-emotional dance, 435–436, 467
Rebounding, 89–90
Relationship development, 39–71
deepening, 46–71
gay and lesbian, 241–281
romantic love, 39–46
Relationship histories, 90–96
imprinting, 93
leapfrogging, 94–96
Religion and homophobia, 251–253
Remarriage, 170–171
effects on children, 182–187
stepfather relationships, 183–186
stepmother relationships, 186–187
Remembered pain stage, 166
Report talk, 208
Resolution stage, 112–116
Retzinger, S. M., 469–470
Romantic love, 39–46
anger, power, and control, 45–46
biochemistry of, 313–319
commitment, 40
intimacy, 40
origins, 325–327
passion, 39–40
psychosocial properties, 41

Salovey, P., 457, 460–461
Scanzoni, J., 140, 220–222, 487, 491
Scanzoni, L., 220–222
Scheff, T. J., 469–470
Schwartz, P., 104, 214, 223, 230, 252, 260, 263, 265, 269, 272–273, 275, 298, 385, 388, 506
Selective-distancing stage, 167–168
Self-disclosure, 417–423
guidelines, 423
practicing, 420–423
Self-esteem, 16–19
Separation, 496–497
deepening relationships, 54–70
termination stage, 86–87
young lovers, 43–44
Separation/individuation, 347–349
in adolescence, 352–354
Sex
changing customs, 24–25